Renaissance to Goya

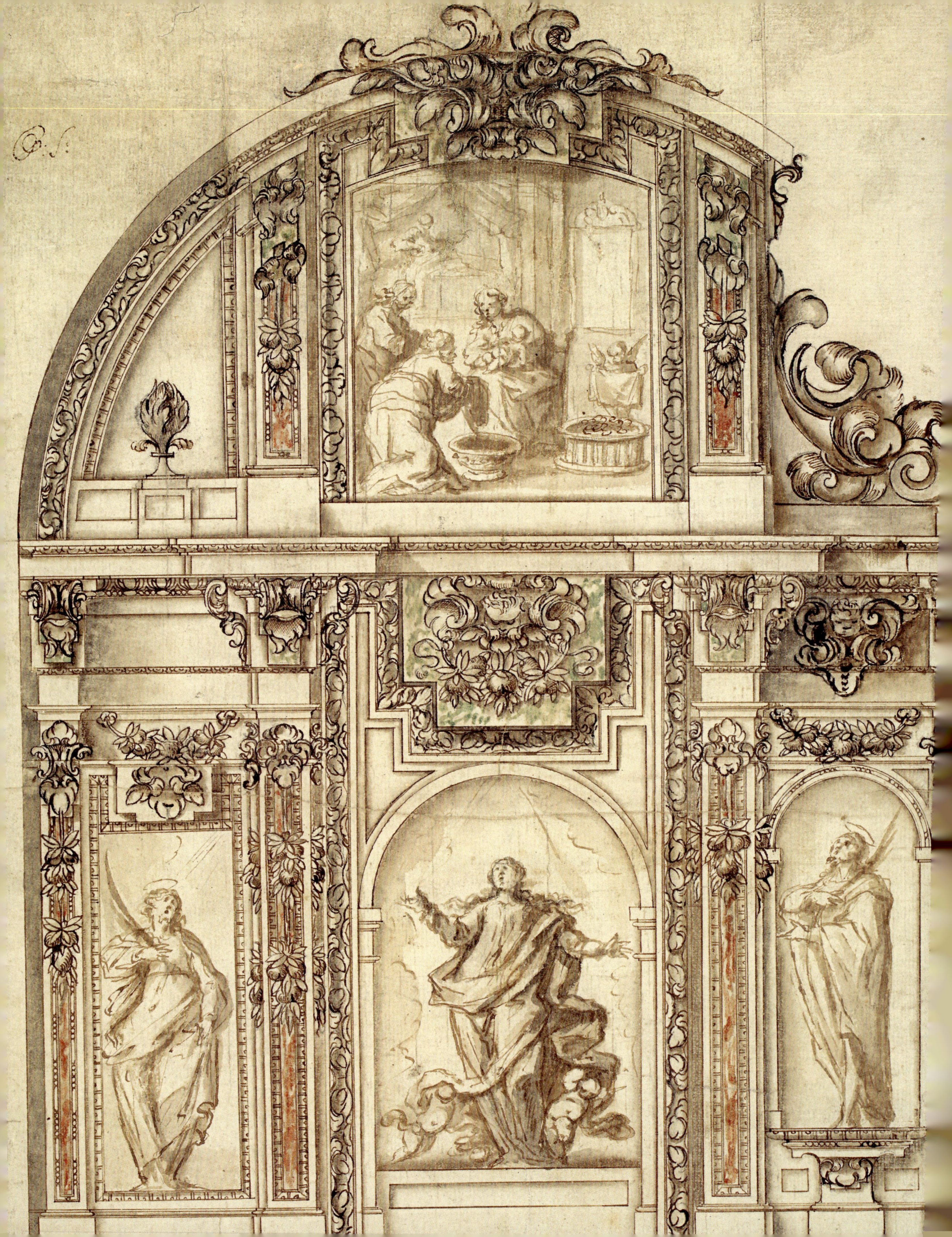

Renaissance to Goya

PRINTS AND DRAWINGS FROM SPAIN

Mark P. McDonald

THE BRITISH MUSEUM PRESS

The Trustees of the British Museum gratefully acknowledge the generous assistance from the Centro de Estudios Europa Hispánica towards the publication of this book.

Published to accompany the exhibition *Renaissance to Goya: Prints and drawings from Spain* at the British Museum from 20 September 2012 to 6 January 2013.

This exhibition has been made possible by the provision of insurance through the Government Indemnity Scheme. The British Museum would like to thank the Department for Culture, Media and Sport, and Arts Council England for providing and arranging this indemnity.

Research supported by the Arts and Humanities Research Council.

Arts & Humanities
Research Council

First published in 2012 by The British Museum Press
A division of The British Museum Company Ltd
38 Russell Square, London WC1B 3QQ

britishmuseum.org.uk/publishing

A catalogue reference for this book is available from the British Library.

ISBN (hardback) 978-0-7141-2680-7
ISBN (paperback) 978-0-7141-2677-7

Designed by Andrew Shoolbred
Printed in China by C&C Offset Printing Co., Ltd.

Papers used by The British Museum Press are recyclable products and the manufacturing processes are expected to conform to the environmental regulations of the country of origin.

The majority of the works illustrated in this book are from the collection of the British Museum. Museum reference numbers are included in the image captions. Further information about the Museum and its collection can be found at britishmuseum.org.

Frontispiece: Sebastián de Herrera Barnuevo,
Design for an Altar in a Chapel, c.1650–60. See fig. 38, page 106.

Contents

Publication sponsor's foreword 6

Director's foreword 7

Introduction 8

1 Prints and drawings in Spain: attitudes and evidence 14

2 Drawings and prints before 1500 and early collecting in Spain 44

3 Importing graphic practices: Castile 1550–1600 56

4 Madrid as artistic capital 1600–1700 80

5 Andalusia 1500–1700 122

6 Valencia 1500–1700 and Ribera in Naples 162

7 The eighteenth-century reinvention of the graphic arts 188

8 Francisco de Goya (1746–1828) 234

Appendix 274
Paper and papermaking in Spain
Clara de la Peña Mc Tigue

Notes 282

Bibliography 297

List of exhibits 307

Acknowledgements 313

Illustration acknowledgements 314

Index 316

Publication sponsor's foreword

It is generally still assumed that drawing was uncommon among Spanish artists, and that the few who cared to undertake such preparations for their works were exceptions in a national school known for its bravura, a quality opposed to the studiousness of draughtsmanship. Fortunately this exhibition and other recent displays of Spanish drawings outside Spain prove wrong the idea of a nation of improvisers. The growing international attention to this subject shows that the long-standing attitude regarding the dearth of drawings is at last being challenged and revised.

Our views on the use and function of drawing in Spain are rapidly changing as systematic research continues. Catalogues raisonnés provide new evidence to refute the attitude of an uncultivated art among the Spaniards, while more studies and exhibitions of Spanish drawings from American and European museums allow scholars to further Angulo and Pérez Sánchez's courageous yet incomplete enterprise, *A Corpus of Spanish Drawings*. Hopefully the scholarly advances will soon spread to the art market, where dealers and auction houses still shy away from a school that was for many years an unchartered territory compared to its European counterparts. Now that more experts take a stand on what is, or what is not, a work by a specific artist, museum curators and private collectors might begin to feel less threatened by the previous uncertainties of attribution.

The Centro de Estudios Europa Hispánica (CEEH) promotes research on the Spanish Golden Age and collaborates with other organizations producing high-standard scholarship on her arts and culture in their international context. Among other programmes, CEEH and its sister entity in the United States, the Center for Spain in America (CSA), jointly encourage the study of collections of Spanish drawings around the world and foster public access to them through special exhibitions. Indeed, it is a great honour to be associated with the British Museum not only in the first exhibition of its splendid holdings of Spanish prints and drawings, but also in the publication of this monograph, the first to present in the English language a coherent history of the origins, form and function of the graphic arts in Spain. We are very grateful to Mark McDonald for this undertaking and the scrupulous zeal of his research, which has led to many new and exciting discoveries. The publication will surely become a reference tool for students and scholars while promoting further interest in Spanish works on paper.

José Luis Colomer
Director, Centro de Estudios Europa Hispánica (CEEH), Madrid

Director's foreword

The British Museum's Old Master prints and drawings are such a celebrated part of its collection that it comes as something of a surprise that the present exhibition is the first large-scale evaluation of its Spanish holdings. Admittedly a handful of them count among the Museum's most celebrated images, such as Francisco de Zurbarán's haunting study of a hooded monk's head or Goya's mesmeric portrait of the Duke of Wellington. Yet a sense of how they relate to a wider narrative has until now been missing.

Despite the fact that drawing was a key preparatory stage in the creation of pictures, Spanish prints and drawings from the Golden Age onwards have long been overshadowed by the dazzling brushwork and theatrical bravura of Spanish paintings. The poor survival rate of drawings by some of the most renowned Spanish artists, most notably Diego Velázquez, was often in the past used to downgrade the significance of the graphic arts in Spain, a claim discounted by the quality and diversity of the works in this exhibition. A more likely explanation is that an appreciation of drawings was rare outside artistic circles until much later, so that counterparts of seventeenth-century collectors such as the 2nd Earl of Arundel in England, or the Dutch merchant Nicolaes Anthonius Flinck, are not found in Spain.

The uneven survival makes recounting the history of Spanish drawing and printmaking particularly challenging. This scarcity adds greater significance to the exhibition because it presents a number of new discoveries about the Museum's drawings. In addition, these works are used as a springboard for a broader account of how drawing and printmaking took root and flourished in the different regions of Spain, a history that has never been addressed before with such completeness and depth.

Renaissance to Goya: Prints and drawings from Spain celebrates the unique contribution that Spanish artists brought to working on paper, one that inevitably developed out of the cultural links it enjoyed with other countries, most notably Italy, where for centuries the Spanish crown ruled Naples. These ties nourished the artistic traditions of both countries, with major Italian artists such as Luca Giordano and the Tiepolo family coming to Spain, while Spanish painters travelled in the other direction to combine study with employment, in the case of Velázquez for a year or two in Rome while Ribera settled permanently in Naples.

Spanish art was greatly enriched by such contacts. But it was never overwhelmed by foreign influences, nor did it lose its pungent national character, as can be seen from the unflinching naturalism of Ribera's depiction in red chalk of the aged body of a bound saint in his signed and dated drawing. The present exhibition traces how that artistic character was forged as much on paper as on canvas, and fittingly it follows one dedicated to another great Spanish artist, Picasso. For the latter, like his fellow exile Goya, whom he revered, continued all his life to draw inspiration from the artistic tradition of Spain, despite his self-imposed absence from his homeland.

Neil MacGregor
Director, British Museum, London

Introduction

The subject of Spanish prints and drawings is little known outside Spain. It is generally assumed these were marginal arts practised by a few well-known artists such as José de Ribera (1591–1652), Bartolomé Esteban Murillo (1617–82) and Francisco de Goya (1746–1828). The aim of this study is to present an overview of the rich history of the graphic arts in Spain from around the end of the fourteenth century through to and including Goya. Examples of prints and drawings from the fifteenth until the mid-sixteenth century are few. Those that survive reflect the style and techniques of foreign artists working in Spain, a subject that is vital for clarifying origins that become much clearer in the later period, when the evidence is more abundant. From the second half of the sixteenth century, drawing became an integral part of artistic practice, and a survey of Spanish drawings shows that they were made and used as elsewhere in Europe. Printmaking developed at a slower pace and it was not until the eighteenth century that it caught up with the rest of Europe.

As it is not feasible to discuss every Spanish draughtsman or printmaker over a 400-year period, this study concentrates on the most significant of them, where possible using examples from the British Museum. Two broad principles guide the selection of works both in this book and in the exhibition it accompanies. The first is to show the variety in form and function of prints and drawings made in Spain, and the second is to dispel the myth that drawing was a fringe activity and printmaking even more so. On the whole, this study concentrates on securely attributed examples by the artists involved, thereby avoiding the prickly issues of connoisseurship.

The study is divided into eight chapters, with an appendix analysing the history and types of paper used by artists in Spain. The first chapter provides an overview of the historiography of prints and drawings in Spain, how they have been regarded and, in order to demonstrate simply what was made, a summary of their principal types and characteristics. The second chapter looks at the earliest prints and drawings and the chapters that follow are arranged by major Spanish cities, mainly for convenience but also to emphasize regional differences. Most of the discussion relates to Madrid because it was the most vibrant artistic centre from the late sixteenth century and had enormous influence throughout Spain. With regard to Madrid, prints and drawings are discussed separately, whereas in the chapters on the regional centres (Seville and Valencia) they are integrated because the evidence is less compelling. The last chapter is devoted to Goya, because his prodigious activity as a draughtsman and printmaker redefined the role of prints and drawings in Spanish art. While a list of the works in the exhibition is given on p. 307, more complete entries and biographical information about the artists can be found on the

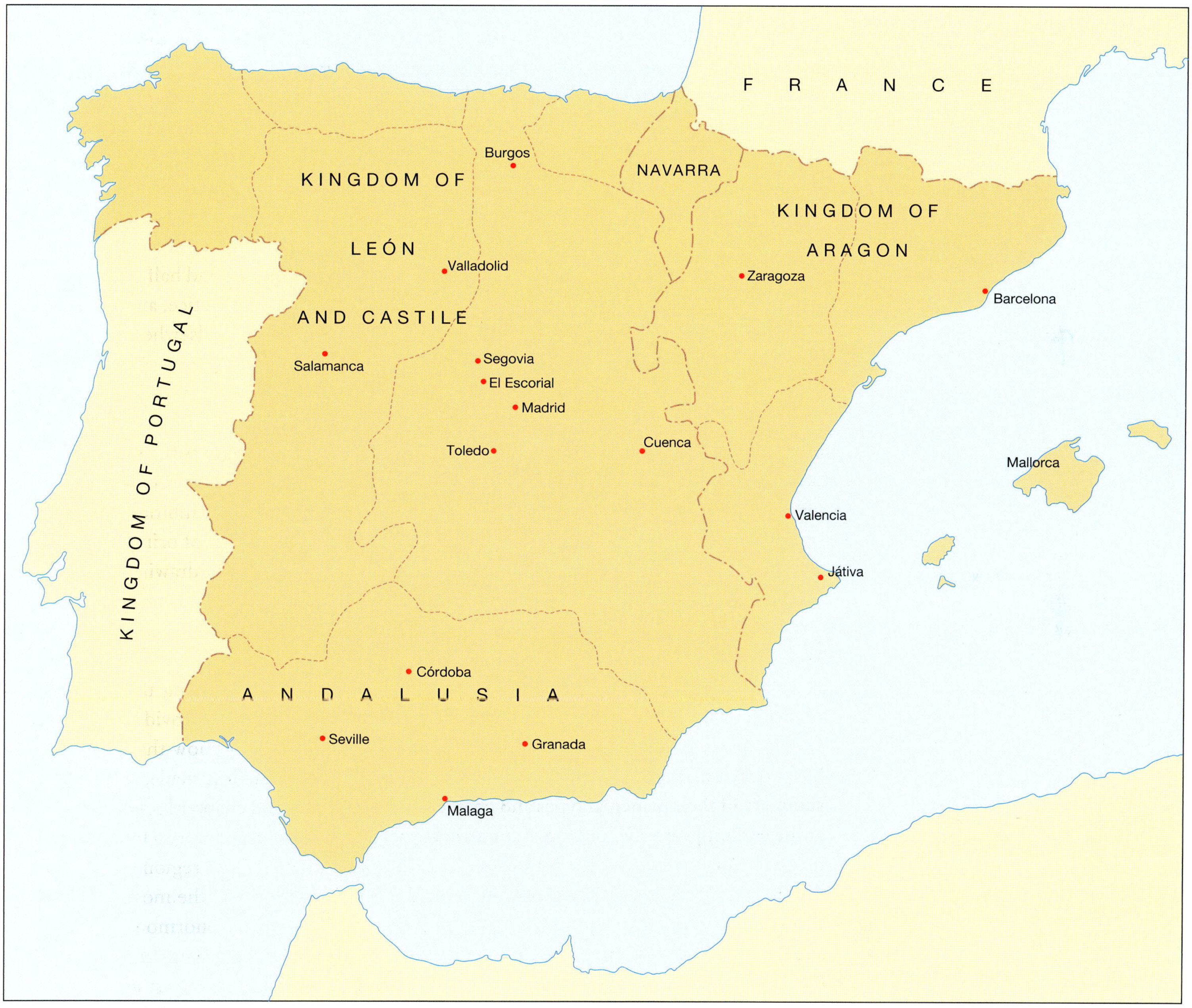

Spain in the sixteenth and seventeenth centuries

British Museum's online database (britishmuseum.org/research), which is being augmented as our knowledge increases.

Most printmakers in Spain made prints for books, a subject to which many excellent studies have been devoted. Here, book illustration is discussed briefly in relation to the fifteenth century, as the first evidence for printmaking in Spain, but thereafter only when it relates to broader issues of printmaking.

Historical note

With our understanding of modern Europe, especially after the creation of the European Union, it is easy to assume that the Spain of today echoes her historical past. However, from the fourteenth to eighteenth centuries, far from having a single identity, Spain was a linguistically diverse and disunited collection of regions, cultures and traditions, with autonomous institutions and laws often in conflict. It was not until the early eighteenth century that Spain became a recognizable, coherent political unit. With this in mind, 'Spain' is used in these pages to describe the kingdoms in the Iberian Peninsular excluding Portugal (see map, p. 9).

The history of Spain is often told from the perspective of her relationship with the wider world, for example the colonization of parts of South America from the late fifteenth century, the many wars in which she was involved (especially during the seventeenth century), her annexation of parts of Europe, and her role in international politics. As a result, Spain's relationship to the rest of the world is well understood but her internal history less so. The same may be said of her art historical status: foreign artists of standing who went to Spain, such as Italians Federico Zuccaro (*c.*1542–1609), Luca Giordano (1634–1705) and Giambattista Tiepolo (1696–1770) are well known, but patterns and relationships of artistic interchange, patronage and influence inside Spain are not as widely understood. The present study is concerned with the history of prints and drawings intimately tied to patronage, mainly from the Church and the monarchy.

The marriage in 1469 of Isabel of Castile (1451–1504) to Ferdinand (1452–1516), Prince of Aragon and King of Sicily, initiated an alliance of kingdoms that provided the basis for modern-day Spain. Their initial action was to expel the Moors and unite five kingdoms into one dominated by Castile. The kingdom of Granada was freed from the Moors' control in January 1492, and thus gave the monarchs the confidence to implement further radical changes in all other areas of their administration. The reforms to the government were sweeping and left no institution untouched. By 1500 Spain's political and cultural framework and character had completely changed and, as a result, the country became increasingly dominant as a European power.

Charles V (d.1558), the son of Joanna the Mad (1479–1555, daughter of Isabel and Ferdinand) and Philip the Handsome (1478–1506, the first Habsburg king of Castile), was born in Ghent in 1500. He was the ruler of the Holy Roman Empire from 1519 and of the Spanish Empire from 1516 until 1556, when he abdicated in favour of his younger brother Ferdinand I and his son Philip II. Charles's first trip to Spain was in 1517, when his position as sovereign was conditional on him learning Castilian. It is significant that when Charles moved to Spain he was a complete foreigner, and as such his world-view and policies were based on his experiences outside Spain.

Philip II (1527–98) was Charles's only son to reach adulthood. Like his father, he spent his early years in the Netherlands but decided to settle permanently in Spain where he was the first monarch to style himself King of Spain (King of Castile and Aragon). Under his rule Spain reached the height of her influence and power, fuelled largely by the influx of precious metals from the mines in South America. On Philip's death in 1598, sovereignty passed to his son, Philip III (1578–1621), who ruled until his death. His reign has generally been overshadowed by that of his father and his son, Philip IV (1605–65), whose long rule of forty-four years is regarded as much more significant. Philip IV's reign was marked by economic decline, due in part to dwindling income from foreign investments and the demands of constant engagement in European warfare.

On Philip's death in 1665, Charles II (1661–1700) succeeded him as the last Hapsburg king of Spain. He was the only surviving male heir from his father's two marriages and his life was marked by illness and disability. Charles inherited a vast empire burdened by economic crises and uncertainties. Since he produced no male heir, the line of the Spanish Hapsburgs ended on his death. He named his great-nephew, Philip, Duke of Anjou (1683–1746), as his successor, the first member of the House of Bourbon to rule Spain. The possibility of the Spanish Empire passing into French control prompted the marshalling of forces, and in 1701 the War of the Spanish Succession began. After eleven years the Duke of Anjou was confirmed as King of Spain (as Philip V) but he was removed from the French line of succession in order to avert a union of the two kingdoms. The House of Bourbon has intermittently occupied the Spanish throne ever since. Philip V ruled until January 1724, when he abdicated in favour of his son, Louis I; however, he resumed the throne in August the same year, Louis having died just six months after his ascension, and he remained there until his own death in 1746.

Ferdinand VI (1713–59), the fourth son of Philip V and the third ruler of the Spanish Bourbon dynasty, was King of Spain from 1746 until his death. The throne then passed to his eldest son, Charles III (1716–88). As Duke of Parma Charles had conquered the kingdoms of Naples and of Sicily in 1734 and was crowned their King in July the following year. His second son, Charles IV (1748–1819), became King of Spain in 1788 and ruled until his abdication on 19 March 1808. The eldest surviving son of Charles IV and María Luisa of Parma, Ferdinand VII, was King of Spain twice, for three months in 1808 and again in 1813–33. In early May 1808 Charles relinquished Ferdinand's right to the Spanish throne in favour of Napoleon Bonaparte, who appointed his brother, Joseph, as the new monarch. Ferdinand was detained in France until he returned to Spain in 1813.

The effects of monarchy and geography

From the time of Isabel and Ferdinand, Spain's development was shaped by the many different policies of its rulers, driven by internal and external forces. A key feature of Isabel's peripatetic court was her patronage of artists and her love of culture. Her example established a fashion soon followed by noble Spanish families; later, Hapsburg rulers also emulated her example.[1] Philip II and Philip IV in particular were committed art patrons and collectors, and also initiated important architectural programmes.

The court had an enormous impact not only on defining artistic taste in Spain, but also on the movement of artists. The fact that until the late sixteenth century the monarchy was largely peripatetic created a pattern of patronage very different to the fixed courts elsewhere in Europe. But the court was not the only source of patronage. The cities of Valencia, Barcelona and Toledo, for example, had flourished as artistic centres for centuries, benefiting from the support of trade, the Church and wealthy private patrons. In the case of Madrid, patronage grew from the early years of the seventeenth century, allowing artists to set up studios, workshops and centres of teaching that had an effect on all the main Spanish cities. This stability was important to the artistic development of Madrid during the early modern period because it promoted local artistic style while consolidating the city's dominance.

Because Spain was surrounded on three sides by ocean and separated in the north-east by the Pyrenees, it did not have the same pressures as landlocked countries to deal with bordering neighbours. Although in this sense isolated, Spain engaged with the wider world and established many economic, political, artistic and social connections. These international links were vital in fostering the artistic cross-pollination that is such a feature of Spanish art. Isabel of Castile greatly favoured Flemish artists, as did Charles V, who also employed those from German speaking lands as well as the Venetian painter Titian (*c.*1488–1576). Philip II was mainly interested in Italian art, although he also employed Flemish artists such as Antonis Mor (*c.*1517–77). Philip III continued his father's taste, but employed Spanish-born artists such as Juan Pantoja de la Cruz (1553–1608). By the early seventeenth century the court and nobility patronized both local and foreign artists. Philip IV cultivated Spanish artists, most notably Diego Velázquez (1599–1660), and by the time Charles II ascended the throne Madrid attracted artists not only from within Spain, but across Europe. The Bourbon kings greatly favoured French and Italian artists, to the detriment of the Spaniards, but in the second half of the eighteenth century a resurgence of native talent came to dominate.

Cities and towns within Spain from the fifteenth to the eighteenth centuries developed very differently as a result of contrasting internal needs and external influences. This has as much to do with their historical character – for example, Granada being the seat of Al-Andalus (the region referred to as Moorish Iberia) – as it does with their development during the early modern period. From the early years of the sixteenth century Seville became the springboard for the New World. Her wealth was dependant on sending materials from her port and receiving shipments mainly of precious metals. It is reasonable to describe Seville as existing on the periphery of Europe and looking outwards, rather than responding only to wider Europe. On the east coast of Spain, Valencia for many centuries controlled a thriving commercial trade in the Mediterranean and had strong cultural ties with Italy. Barcelona, under the crown of Aragon, also had strong links with Italy and in the late fifteenth century controlled the kingdom of Naples and Sicily. In the north of Spain, along one of the most important routes of Christian pilgrimage, the Camino de Santiago, churches and monuments were built for the pilgrims. Burgos, for example, had long received artists and architects from the Low Countries to complete ambitious commissions, such as the Carthusian monastery of Miraflores nearby (1401–84). Artists from the same region also worked in Toledo and Seville. For example, the Flemish Pieter Dancart (d.1487) created the spectacular retable (framed altarpiece) in Seville Cathedral in the second half of the fifteenth century. Madrid only developed from the late sixteenth century, after which it became a magnet for foreign artists as well as, increasingly, those born in Spain.

Spanish cities evolved as independent and distinctive artistic centres where individual artists could rise to great prominence. The style of Spanish artists, even from the same period, was often remarkably different. There could be no greater contrast, for example, than that between the roughly contemporaneous work of Francisco de Zurbarán (1598–1664), Bartolomé Esteban Murillo and Diego Velázquez, despite their common training in Seville. The size and geographic diversity of Spain, the different sources of patronage and the many artistic influences have meant that the story of her art from the Renaissance and early modern period has many anomalies. For example, Fernando Yáñez de la Almedina (*c.*1465/70–1536), El Greco (1541–1614), Velázquez, Murillo, Luis Paret y Alcázar (1746–99) and Goya developed such highly individualized styles that it is hard to fit them into established artistic traditions within Spain. They had few followers, apart from those who slavishly imitated their style, in the cases of Murillo and Zurbarán exporting a successful formula through paintings sent to the New World.

It is therefore unhelpful to view the history of art of Spain as a linear narrative rather than as one that considers the evolution of individual style and practice. This is not to say that common artistic threads cannot be identified throughout Spain: the broad stylistic characteristics of seventeenth-century painting can, for example, be identified in the work of many artists, despite the differing form of expression. Furthermore, the internationalism that developed mainly in Madrid during the eighteenth century ironed out many regional differences. Accepting that stories are rarely seamless makes it easier to account for the erratic and episodic history of artistic practices in Spain.

Over the past few decades, the regional character in Spain has again been highlighted. The country's heritage is now celebrated as much for its many distinctive elements as for its contribution to a collective 'Spanishness'. The manifestation of identity through political, religious, cultural, economic and social pursuits has provided many points of comparison. This trend reinforces the imperative in the present volume to discriminate between the artistic forces evolving across Spain from the early fifteenth century in order to assess their effect on prints and drawings – and not, by virtue of the shared nature of their media, to regard them as having the same origins, intentions and function across the entire peninsular.[2]

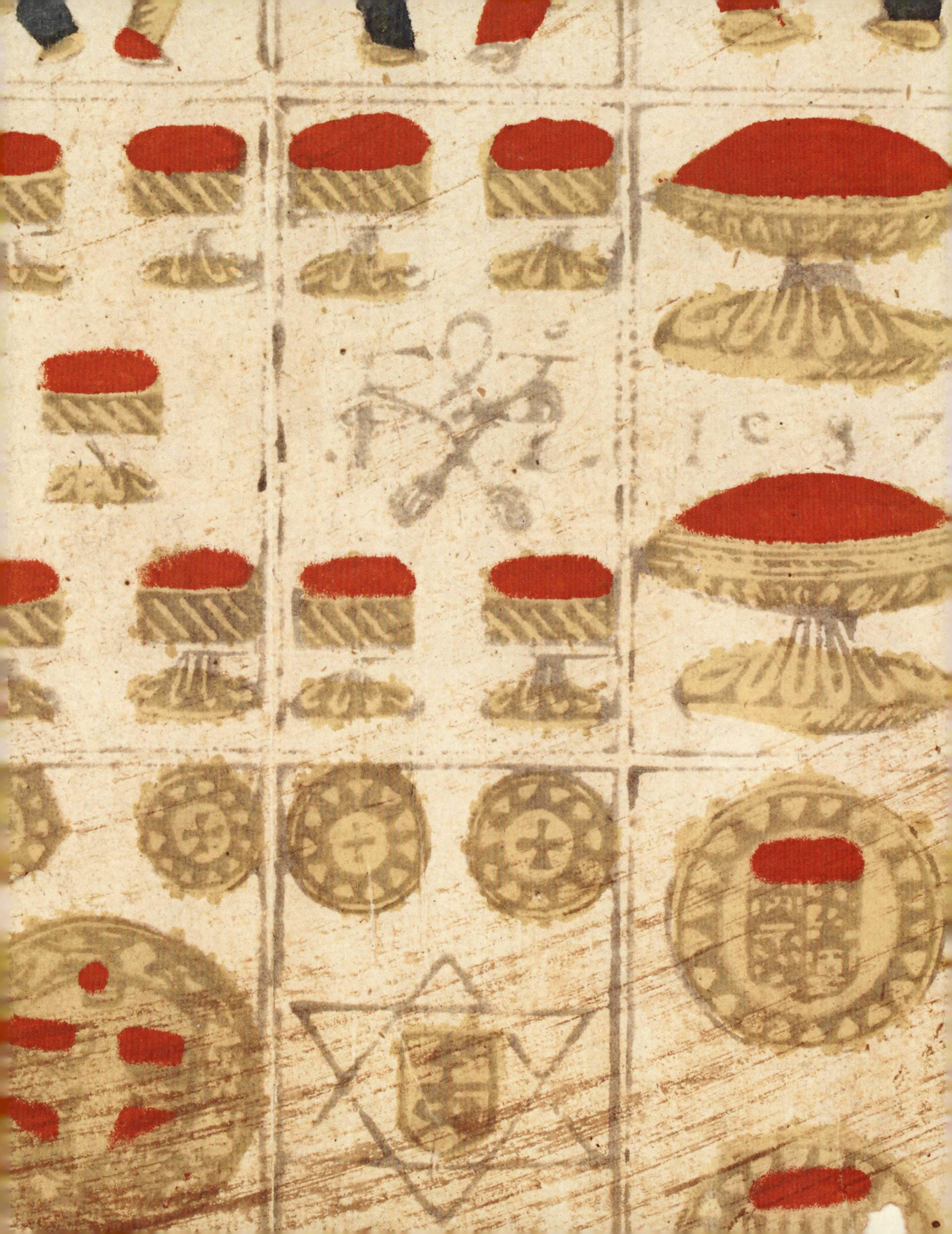

CHAPTER 1

Prints and drawings in Spain: attitudes and evidence

In accounts of art in Spain during the Renaissance and early modern period it has often been suggested that Spanish artists did not draw and that print production was insignificant. These attitudes should broadly be understood not so much as the result of an unwillingness to engage with such prints and drawings as a reflection of the difficulties of identifying them as Spanish and understanding the background to their creation. Various theories have been put forward to explain the supposed absence of a significant tradition of prints and drawings in Spain. The underlying evidence needs to be examined in order for these assumptions to be challenged.

Research into other arts in Spain – painting, sculpture and architecture – reveals a visual culture remarkable for its variety and richness. In the case of prints and drawings, however, relatively little scholarship exists and only in cases of the best-known artists have works been looked at together. The reasons for this are complex but rooted in the nineteenth-century *desmortización* (confiscation of Church possessions) and subsequent dispersal of collections of Spanish art; the inaccessibility of surviving collections in Spain, especially during the Franco era; the problem of identifying works, many of which languish in boxes marked 'anonymous' and, even if identifiable, with no explanation of the rationale of the attribution. Scholars of Spanish prints and drawings have historically focused their attention largely on much-needed collection catalogues and on defining the work of individual artists.[1] Only in recent decades has attention begun to turn to their broader artistic and cultural significance.[2]

Drawings

Spanish drawings are scarce compared with those of other schools, but it cannot be assumed from this that Spanish artists did not draw. Modern attitudes can be traced to the nineteenth century. In 1880 the French art historian Philippe de Chennevières wrote that Spanish drawings had never been abundant in collections, noting the few in foreign hands including those bought from the Madrazo family in Spain by John Charles Robinson and passed to the British Museum. Chennevières observed that when he made enquiries about Spanish drawings in Madrid and Seville in 1870, 'no one had anything to say'.[3]

The paucity of Spanish drawings gave rise to theories about artistic practice in Spain based on Romantic ideas of artistic temperament. These were augmented by the study of psychology during the twentieth century. In Erwin Gradmann's introduction to his 1946 study of Spanish drawings he

Detail of fig. 21, see p. 39

links the drawing practices of Spanish artists to their national character:

> The student must in fact be capable of a profound sympathy with the special characteristics of Spanish people, in order to do justice to their mode of artistic expression. What strikes the Northerner as particularly difficult to understand, is that combination of a keen sense of reality with burning religious feeling, which distinguishes the art of Spain so sharply from that of other peoples.

Marshalling his evidence, Gradmann continues:

> … the Spaniard is always more readily recognizable by his choice of subject, than by the peculiarities of his draughtsmanship.… Italian feeling for form is as foreign to the Spaniard as it is to the German, and in this respect there exists between the two Latin peoples a contrast, which applies not only to the period of the Renaissance, but remains constantly latent in their work. All that the beauty of perfect form means to the Italian, is sought by the Spaniard in the visible representation of the Spiritual.[4]

Gradmann regards Murillo as lacking the requisite 'self-tormenting spirit' and his striving for beauty 'a very un-Spanish characteristic'. He believes Goya's deafness to be fundamental to the nightmare visions of his interior life.

Around the same time José Gómez Sicre expounded a different theory for the scarcity of Spanish drawings. For him, 'a better explanation [can be found] in the very core of the Spanish spirit, in the lusty realism of the painting of Spain, alien to such profound intellectual executions as drawings'.[5] He contrasts the classic idealism of Italian artists in the sixteenth century and Flemish artists' search for 'inner profundities' with the work of Spanish artists, for whom reality was more a question of emotion than description. Gómez Sicre was not a drawings specialist and his brief study was essentially a personal reflection on a subject that interested him.[6]

The views voiced by Gradmann and Gómez Sicre were not restricted to those with a passing interest in Spanish drawings, but also by scholars in the field. In 1964 Francisco Sánchez Cantón, Director of the Prado and noted scholar of Spanish art, wrote that 'the Spanish artistic temperament was and is undoubtedly given more to the magic of colour than to the discipline of drawing, so that artists frequently drew on canvas with brush and paint without previous attempts on paper or, when they did render drawings, discarded them after use'.[7] His comment is all the more surprising considering that the principal biographers of Spanish artists, who by that time were very well known – Antonio Palomino (1655–1726), Marcos Antonio de Orellana (1731–1813) and Juan Agustín Ceán Bermúdez (1749–1829) – described in great detail Spanish artists' regular dedication to drawing. Such attitudes were countermanded by Antonio Rodriguez-Moñino, who in 1954 published a brief article, transparently entitled 'On the supposed non-existence of Spanish Old Master drawings', which immediately transformed the state of the debate.[8] Rodriguez-Moñino's article is concerned with material evidence and does not rely on national character to explain artistic production. He simply demonstrates that he has encountered many Spanish drawings and makes occasional reference to those mentioned in artists' inventories.

There are however, few surviving drawings by some of the best-known sixteenth- and seventeenth-century Spanish artists and this has been used as evidence for generalized lack of interest in the activity by artists from the Iberian Peninsular. This dismissal is contradicted by the inventory made on El Greco's death in 1614, which records 150 drawings by his hand (see Chapter 3). Only a handful of these survive today. There is evidence that Diego Velázquez prepared initial designs directly on the canvas but this alone cannot explain the lack of drawings securely attributed to him (see Chapter 4). The extent to which these and other prominent artists made drawings will probably never be known, but it seems fair to suggest that the culture of collecting works on paper was not sufficiently established during their lifetimes for their drawings to be systematically preserved. This is a difficult argument to take further, suggesting as it does that the necessary consequence of a presumed body of work entails its absence. However, a comparison of drawings made throughout Spain with those made in other European countries shows a much higher incidence of damaged sheets among the former, clearly indicating a lack of regard for their preservation. It is even more instructive to look at biographical accounts, documentary evidence (which is substantial) and historical context. This parallel evidence reveals a far greater level of activity than is suggested by the extant body of drawings alone.

From the early twentieth century publications of Spanish drawings have concentrated on highlights.[9] August Mayer's two-volume *Die Handzeichnungen spanischen Meister* (1915, Spanish edition 1920), Sánchez Cantón's five-volume *Dibujos Españoles* (1930) and Angulo's *Cuarenta dibujos españoles* (1966) represent this sort of publication, on the one hand invaluable for their illustrations and bringing to light significant works, but with little discussion of the context in which the drawings were made. Attitudes to artistic practice change with each generation, and scholarship of the past fifty years has introduced a keener critical sense to the study of Spanish drawings. The myth of the Spanish artist 'half Don Juan and half Don Quixote', hostile to the discipline of drawing, has been overturned.[10] Exhibitions, such as those at the Hamburg Kunsthalle in 1966 and the Uffizi in 1972, have introduced Spanish drawings from museum collections to new audiences.[11] Angulo Iñiguez and Pérez Sánchez's four-volume *Corpus of Spanish Drawings* (1975–88) brought together all known sheets of artists working in Spain, arranged by region. This remains the key resource, providing the means of identifying different hands and schools. In recent years there has been an increase in monographs on individual artists, contributing to a much better knowledge of drawing in Spain.

Prints

The situation regarding prints in Spain during the Renaissance and early modern period is rather different. Discussion on this subject has not provoked a reaction comparable to the strident responses of Gradmann and Gómez Sicre cited above. It is generally true that print studies are simpler, probably because issues of connoisseurship are rarely involved. That prints are produced mechanically and in multiples means that, unlike drawings, they are not seen as unique objects, expressive of the maker's soul.

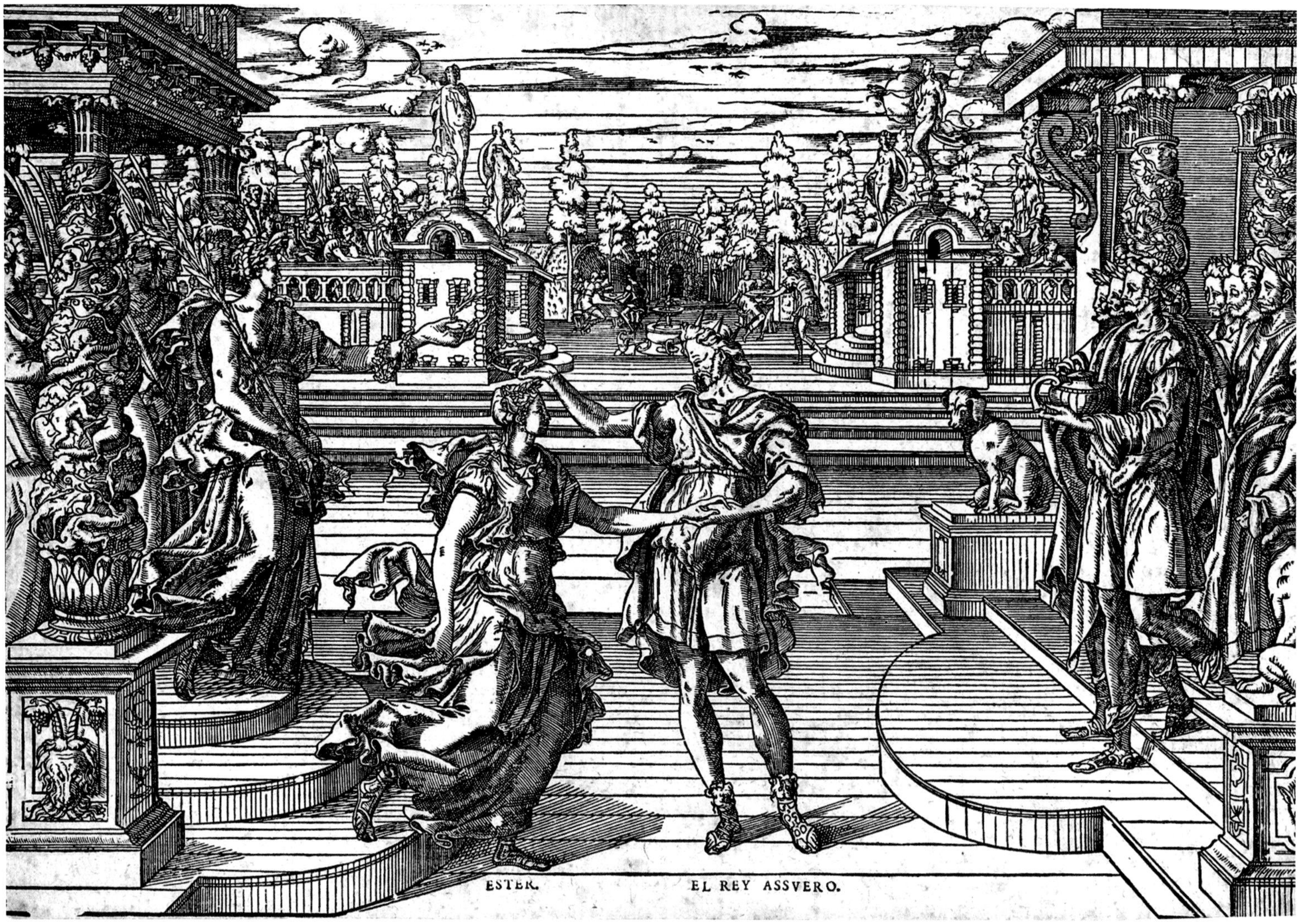

1
Denis de Mathonière
The Crowning of Esther, *c.*1580
Woodcut, 262 x 366 mm
Kunstsammlungen der Veste Coburg
XIII,7,89

It was not until the second half of the eighteenth century that a significant single-sheet print industry developed in Spain. The fact that the Spanish were perfectly capable printmakers, as demonstrated by their high-quality book illustrations, raises the question of why a single-sheet tradition began so late. The answer lies partly in the massive influx of prints from other parts of Europe from the mid-sixteenth century that hindered the development of a local print industry. The effect of this should not be underestimated, and many examples may be used to illustrate this point. In 1580, for example, the Lombard painter Pietro Paolo de Montalbergo and the Aretine merchant Francesco Testa, both resident in Barcelona, organized the sale and distribution in Madrid via Seville of around three thousand engravings printed in Rome, amongst them 176 by Cornelis Cort (1533–78).[12] The six large woodcuts produced by Denis de Mathonière (*c.*1545–*c.*1596) in Paris around the same time depicting the Old Testament story of Esther were originally published with the protagonists' names in French, a title in the upper margin and a description of the scene below. For the southern European market the French text was replaced with Spanish (fig. 1).[13] A pair of large early seventeenth-century etchings published in Italy, the *Ages of Man* and *Woman*, attributed

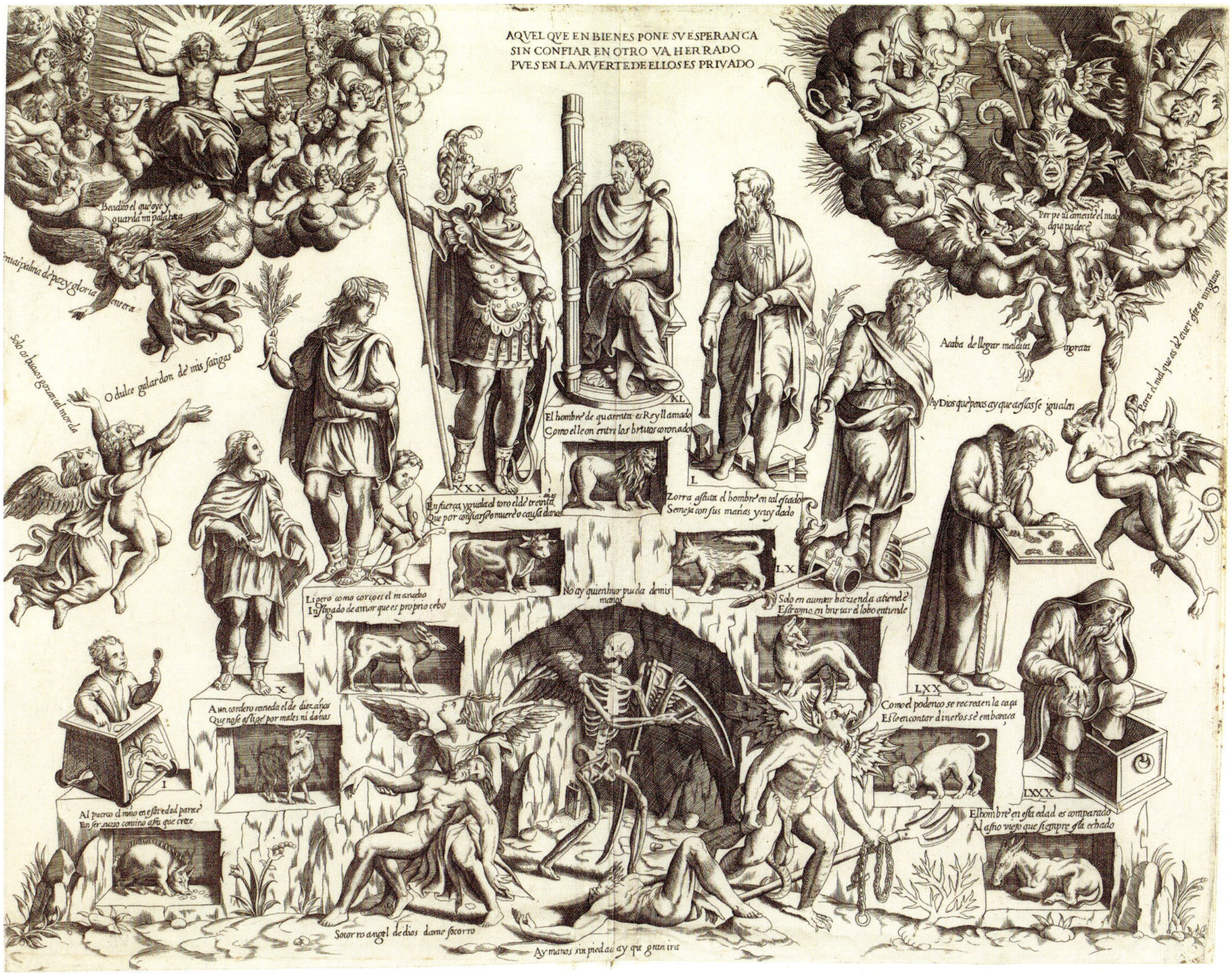

2
Attributed to Nicolò Nelli after Cristofano Bertelli
The Ages of Man, 1560–80
Engraving, 400 x 500 mm
British Museum, London
1871,0812.788

to Nicolò Nelli (active 1552–79) after Cristofano Bertelli (active *c.*1526–80), have a Spanish text indicating their audience (fig. 2).[14]

European printmaking in the sixteenth century was big business, producing vast numbers of prints on every conceivable subject.[15] The success of production and marketing operations in Paris, Rome and Antwerp is demonstrated by the collections of prints accumulated in Spain, such as at the Escorial.[16] With so much printed material being imported there was little incentive in Spain itself for a printmaking industry to develop. Sometimes foreign artists who received commissions from Spanish patrons had reproductive prints made of their paintings. Giovanni Lanfranco (*c.*1582–1647), for example, was commissioned by the Viceroy of Naples, the Conde de Monterrey, in 1634 to paint scenes from ancient Roman history for the Buen Retiro palace in Madrid.[17] He then published a large etching of his *Triumph of a Roman Emperor*, probably in Naples around 1640 (fig. 3). It was only when prints were required for a specific purpose that a printing industry began to develop in Spain. In 1789, for example, a state-sponsored project was begun to promote the Spanish Old Masters through high-quality reproductive engravings (see Chapter 7).

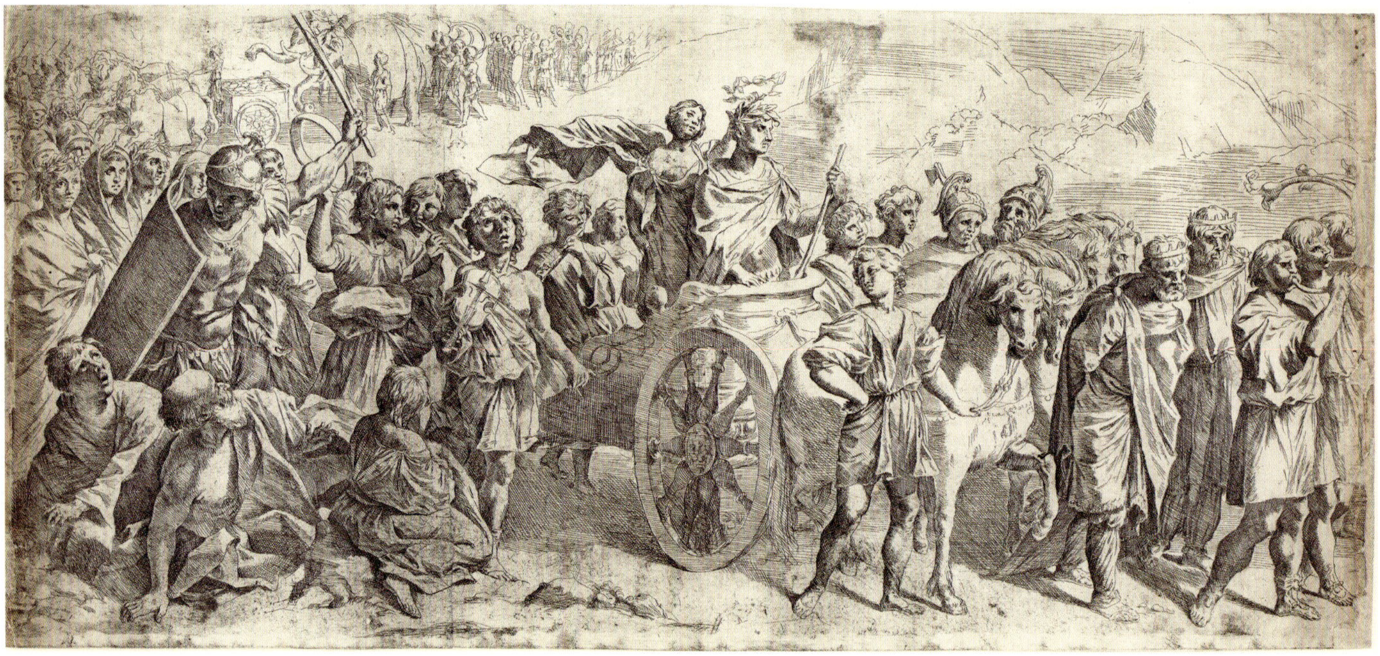

3
Giovanni Lanfranco
Triumph of a Roman Emperor, c.1640
Etching, 295 x 621 mm
British Museum, London
W,8.75

The issue of censorship in relation to printed images in Spain was also highly influential. The far-reaching powers of the Office of the Inquisition enabled it to inspect the premises of those selling prints and to examine incoming shipments from abroad. In some cases the inappropriate representation of a saint in a print made in Spain resulted in litigation.[18] The constraints surrounding the licensing of printed images thus added a further layer of complexity to their production in Spain.

The Renaissance model

'The reflected light of the Italian Renaissance shines with pure radiance in the drawings of the Spanish artists of the early sixteenth century'. With this observation Elizabeth du Gué Trapier began her long essay 'Notes on Spanish Drawings'.[19] A number of sixteenth- and seventeenth-century Spanish artists studied in Italy before returning home, and there is clear evidence of the influence of Italian art in Spain. But this is a complex issue, and Spanish art of this period should not simply be seen through the lens of the Italian Renaissance, a specific, well-ordered system of artistic representation. While such influence may be unmistakable, this form of direct comparison cannot accommodate the significant differences between the two countries.[20] Artistic centres in Spain continued to maintain their own traditions, and the process by which Spanish artists absorbed foreign influence and the nature of that influence on their art is a complex one.[21] Direct comparisons between Spanish and Italian art of this period tend to present the former in a negative light – see, for example, Trapier's assessment: 'If, as Berenson says, light and shade are murderers of pure drawing, then many of the Spanish sketches are cold and lifeless. Often as finished as the paintings for which they were the first inspiration, they fail by their over-statement of detail to stir the imagination.'[22]

Evoking the Renaissance model is understandable: it is a well-rehearsed narrative predicated on a belief in coherent artistic development culminating in the work of great artists. The mechanisms of studio practice, the status of the artist and the types and functions of prints and drawings made in Renaissance Italy are well understood and supported by a wealth of scholarship. However, the social, political, historical and geographic factors specific to the Iberian Peninsular produced results that require a different investigative approach: while for many Spanish artists their time spent in Italy was important for their development, their subsequent work does not by definition hark back to the Italian model.

The development of drawing and printmaking was very different in Spain from other parts of Europe, and began much later, long after academies and networks of artistic activity became established elsewhere. Cultural centres such as courts flourished across Europe during the Renaissance, attracting scholars, writers and artists from far and wide, with artistic homogeneity shaped by local patronage, often with a dominant figure disseminating and controlling his individual style through his disciples. Such centres did not evolve in Spain until the mid-sixteenth century, however. Until then Spain was a country that imported artists rather than exporting them, preventing the development of a distinctly Spanish style. It took time for the influence of foreign artists to transform into a local idiom, and it was not until the late sixteenth century that it becomes possible to identify styles that are particular to Spain.

The significance of prints and drawings in Spain

A letter dated 15 May 1610 from an Italian painter, Pedro Antonio Torri, to his friend in Rome, Bartolommeo Crescenzio (later copied by Jusepe Martínez in the *Discursos practicables del noblísimo arte de la pintura*, *c.* 1673), addresses the status of the artist in Spain. Torri's discussion of prints and drawings provides an indication of how they were perceived:

> the great desire to see the court made me leave this noble city [Seville] and I went to Madrid where I tried to meet with our fellow artists, who greeted me with great hospitality and courtesy. And what most surprised me was to see how little Spaniards esteemed their own native painters.... Sympathising with this miserable state, I spoke with an excellent painter Eugenio Cajés who responded as follows: Dear sir, there are many reasons for it, and the first is the little confidence we have in ourselves, and in particular in this profession of drawing and to those who know little of the profession, it seems as if we were not apt in it. Because there are so few intelligent people among the masses, [our talent] never comes to be known. The second cause is that all the gentlemen who go abroad from Spain attempt to bring back great quantities of pictures from foreign provinces, but they take nothing with them when they leave which, if it were done, would make the value of our talents known. The third reason is that all nations except ours are inclined to make prints so that the whole world can see the subtlety of their designs, important works as well as small works, and as we know, in our Rome and Italy the same subject is engraved three and even four times, thus acquiring great fame and esteem and this includes any ancient stones. The opposite can be said about Spain,

which would surpass many other nations, even if only a minimum part of the admirable works that the country possesses in painting, sculpture and architecture were engraved.[23]

Nothing similar appears in Martínez's treatise, but the letter reinforces earlier remarks about the low regard for artists made by commentators such as Francisco de Holanda (1517–84), painter at the Portuguese court in 1548: 'we Spaniards still despise art, and indeed it is fashionable to hold it in low esteem'.[24] Whereas his comments refer to art in general, they recognize the basis for ongoing prejudice. The disabling effect of the influx of foreign prints to Spain was reinforced by the low regard for Spanish arts that the Madrid painter Eugenio Cajés identified as having hindered the development of reproductive printmaking there. Cajés' comments on drawing are more complex, and hinge on the Spanish artists' lack of confidence exacerbated by the reactions of others. By the time Torri's letter was written, drawing was established in Madrid but the work of local artists might have appeared amateurish compared with drawings by foreign artists, such as Raphael, Michelangelo or the Italian artists working at the monastery of the Escorial (see Chapter 3), whose work was highly praised by writers on Spanish art, Francisco Pacheco and Vicente Carducho. During the early decades of the seventeenth century art in Castile was dominated by the Italian artists who had arrived several decades earlier; the most talented Spanish draughtsmen were yet to emerge. As the century progressed, drawing became widespread culminating in the structured syllabus of the Academy of Madrid in the eighteenth century. But a general sense of dissatisfaction stemming from the promotion of foreign artists runs well into the eighteenth century. After meeting Martínez in 1625, the Spanish-born artist José de Ribera, who worked in Italy, describes his homeland as 'a merciful mother to foreigners but a most cruel stepmother to her own'.[25]

The attempts by artists to establish academies in Spain provides further insight into to how prints and drawings were used and regarded. This is a somewhat different issue from Cajés' description of their low aesthetic status and more concerned with their practical value. Every theoretical tract and treatise written in Spain from the sixteenth century onwards refers to the important role of drawing, and most discuss the significance of prints.[26] In 1624 the painters of Madrid drew up a statement entreating the government of Castile to establish an academy.[27] The author of this statement, Vicente Carducho, gave high priority to *disegno*, revealing his knowledge of Italian art theory and practice. Instruction was to begin with compulsory life drawing, and the programme required studio aids including books, models, paintings, geometric instruments, drawings and prints.[28] Schools with academic aspirations began to be established in Spain during the remaining years of the seventeenth century. Francisco Herrera the Younger and Bartolomé Esteban Murillo established an academy in Seville in 1660 where its main purpose was the 'exercise of drawing',[29] and another was established a little later in Valencia. In Madrid, it was not until 1744 that the Academy of San Fernando was founded (see Chapter 7). Spanish academies promoted drawing as the basis of artistic training, while prints were used for instruction – as evidenced by the many extant Spanish drawings and paintings based on foreign engravings.[30] For example, *The Circumcision of Christ* by Eugenio Cajés (fig. 4) is an early example of this phenomenon where the central figures derived from a print by Hendrick Goltzius (fig. 5).[31]

Information regarding academic aspirations filtered through treatises, confirming the importance of drawing in the workshop and the significance of prints in artistic education. Vicente Carducho's *Diálogos de la Pintura* (1633),[32] Francisco Pacheco's *El Arte de la Pintura* (1649) and Antonio Palomino's *Museo pictórico y escala óptica* (1715–24) are the principal sources of information. Pacheco's treatise provides abundant evidence of his attitude towards the role of drawing, which he regarded as the substance of painting, 'the soul and life without which it would be dead, without grace or beauty or movement', identifying Michelangelo and Raphael as supreme draughtsmen.[33] Antonio Palomino similarly promotes drawing as fundamental to training.[34] His recommendation for a structured approach, first copying less ambitious figures in prints by Van Dyck, amongst others, before moving on to Michelangelo, Annibale Carracci, and Lanfranco, reflects how embedded in artistic practice prints had become by the early eighteenth century.[35] Significantly, in the treatises only non-Spanish and mainly Italian artists are accorded the highest status, which should be seen in light of the prejudice against Spanish artists discussed above.

Artists' inventories in Spain that do not record at least some works on paper are rare.[36] The 1638 inventory of Vicente Carducho's possessions records 700 prints and drawings kept in portfolios and albums according to subject or engraver.[37] At the time of his death the court painter Juan van der Hamen y León (1596–1631) owned around 1000 prints and drawings, amongst them works by Dürer, Jacques Callot and Lucas van Leyden.[38] The 1621 inventory of El Greco's books records 'Antonio Labaco', which no doubt refers to the Italian architect Labacco's *Libro … appartenente a l'Architettura nel qual si figurano alcune notabili antiquità di Roma*, first published in Rome in 1552, along with 'Un escurial estampado', Pedro Perret's engravings of the Escorial (see Chapter 3).[39] The Madrid painter Francisco de Solís (1620–84) assembled an important collection of Italian and Spanish drawings.[40] A number of artists in Seville are also known to have formed collections.[41] For example, Palomino refers to Jerónimo de Bobadilla (*c.*1620/30–1709) as having a very important collection of drawings by eminent artists.[42] It is significant that during the seventeenth century, when these collections were being formed by private individuals, there were no royal collectors of drawings in Spain; this is surprising given the interest in the graphic arts shown by Philip II a century earlier.

Beyond recording the existence of prints and drawings, artists' inventories generally do not give details of their arrangement, which might shed light on how they were regarded. A distinction should be made between artists gathering prints and drawings as iconographic and compositional source material or for teaching purposes, and collectors motivated by aesthetic concerns. This is not to suggest that the two are mutually exclusive. The now-dispersed print collection formed by Ferdinand Columbus (1488–1539; see Chapter 2) in Seville was the earliest and most remarkable of them all. Benito Arias Montano (1527–98) was responsible for assembling a print collection for Philip II during the second half of the sixteenth century, and this survives at the Escorial. During the seventeenth century the nobility began to collect drawings, for example Manuel de Acevedo y Zuñiga, 6th Conde de Monterrey (1586–1653), and Gaspar de Haro y Guzmán, 7th Marqués del

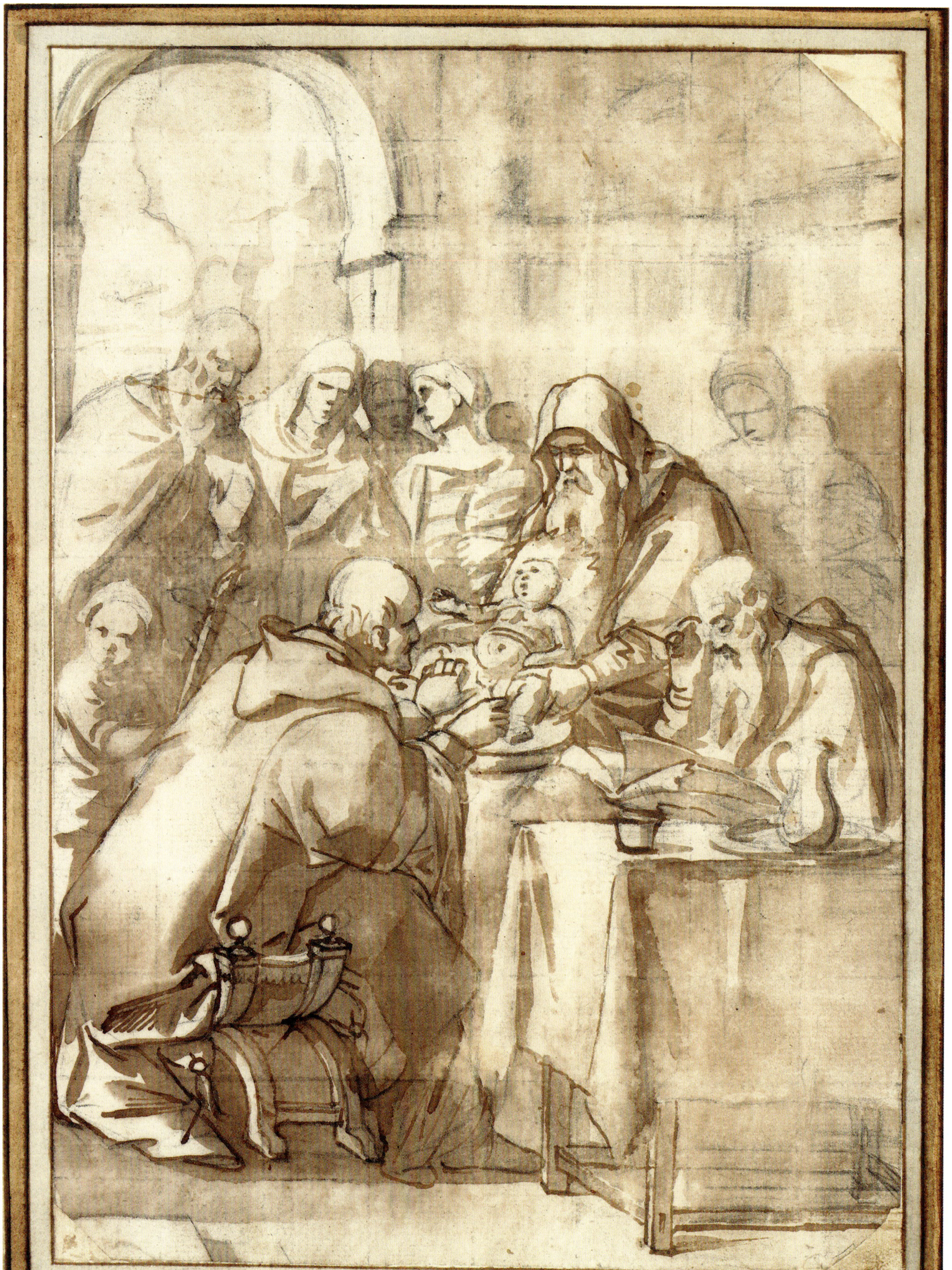

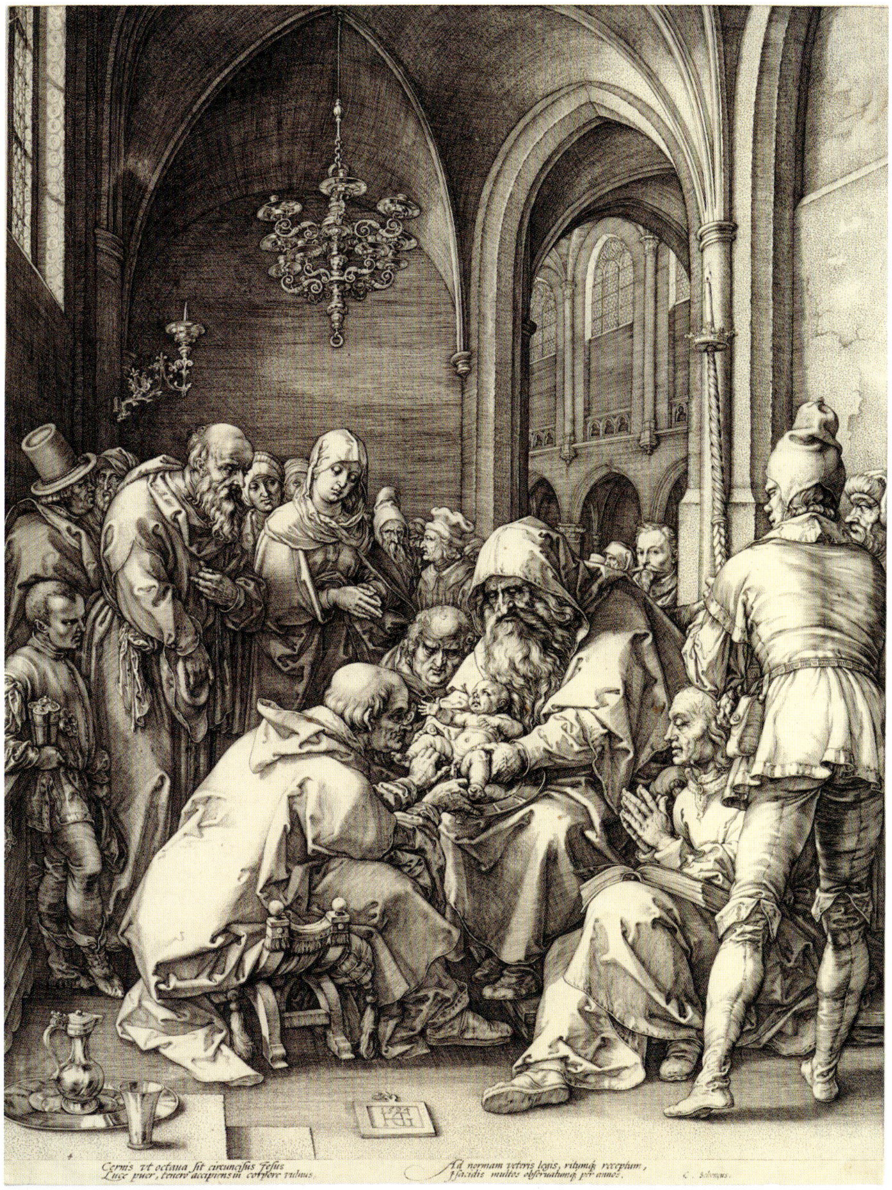

4
Eugenio Cajés
The Circumcision of Christ, c.1600–15
Pen and brown ink and brown wash over black chalk, squared for transfer, 251 x 172 mm
British Museum, London
1938,1210.4

5
Hendrick Goltzius
The Circumcision of Christ, 1594
Engraving, 475 x 355 mm
British Museum, London
F,3.129

Carpio (1629–87), whose collection of Italian drawings was outstanding.[43] Carducho refers to the sort of aristocratic collector he witnessed at gatherings in Madrid where they bought and sold drawings.[44] The Marqués del Carpio is known to have framed a large number of his drawings for display on his walls, both in Madrid and after he moved to Italy in 1677.[45] More evidence about collecting prints and drawings survives from the eighteenth century. The art historian Juan Augustín Ceán Bermúdez, for example, himself a devoted collector, describes earlier collections in Spain, mainly of painting but also prints and drawings, assembled by artists and the nobility.[46]

Types of prints and drawings

Prints and drawings made in Spain may be usefully viewed in groups according to their type and function, although the categories outlined here embrace a rich variety of examples: for instance, there are many types of architectural drawing. A general characteristic of Spanish drawings is that they were mainly

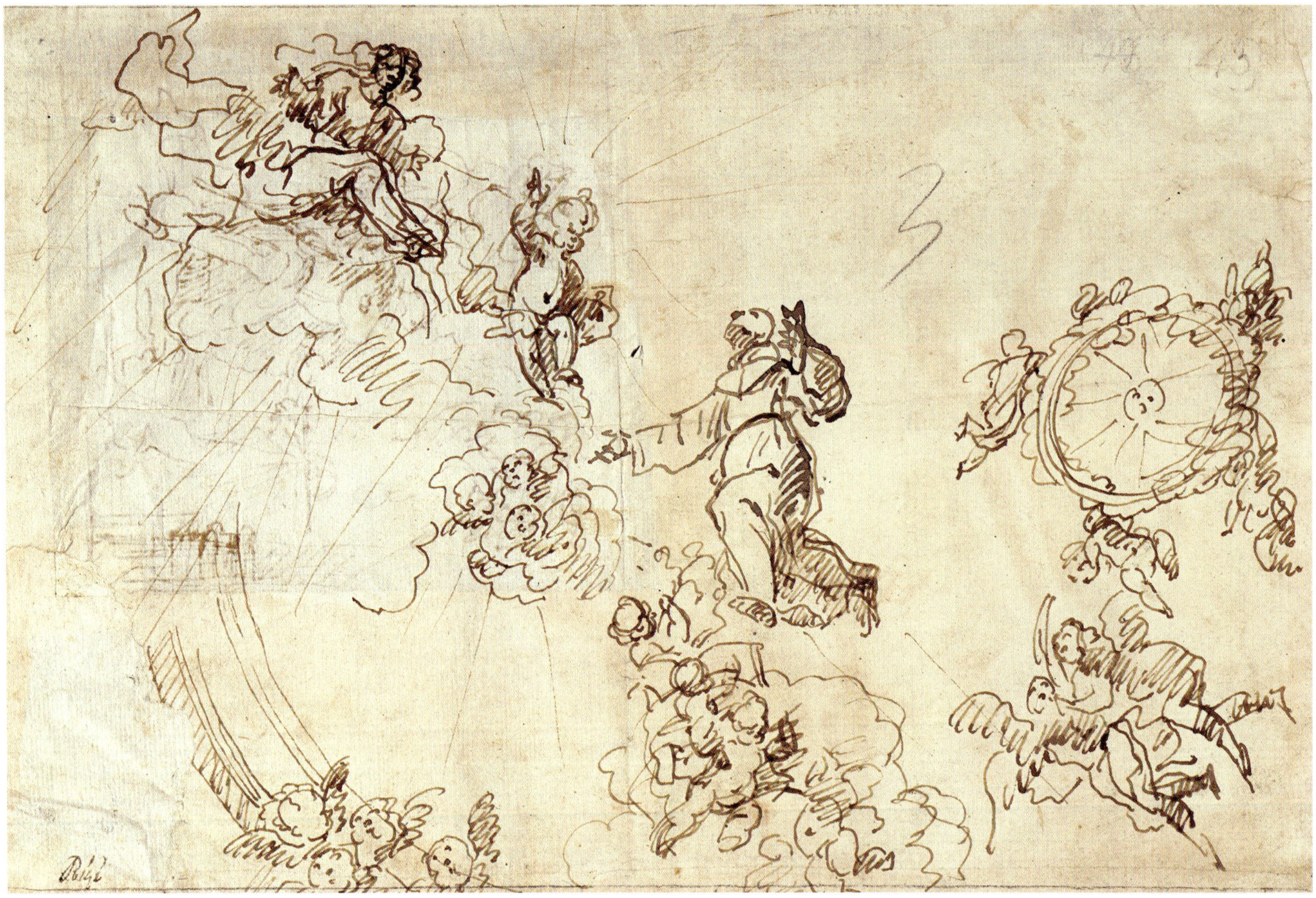

6
Francisco Rizi
Saint Anthony of Padua in Glory, c.1668
Pen and brown ink, 185 x 275 mm
Museo del Prado, Madrid
D.3814

preparatory for other works of art. There is very little evidence until the eighteenth century of drawing as a formal end in itself (a feature of the Italian and French traditions), of drawings being made as models to be copied by students, or for collectors. Until the eighteenth century there are also very few landscape drawings or studies of the nude.

Drawings

Preparatory drawings for paintings can broadly be divided into three groups: preliminary design ideas, more detailed studies, and complete compositional drawings. Few drawings in the first category made before the eighteenth century survive, no doubt because they were not regarded as worthy of preservation. Many Spanish drawings are small and unfinished, but this does not necessarily imply that they are first thoughts. Clearer evidence comes from artists whose draughtsmanship is sufficiently varied to allow the different function of their drawings to be gauged. Francisco Rizi is one such artist. His quick pen-and-ink study from around 1668 for the fresco in the cupola of San Antonio de los Portugeses (now San Antonio de los Alemanes) in Madrid describes the main figures, their position in relation to each other and the edge of the cupola (fig. 6 and see p. 98). Studies of details for compositions are more common, such as Vicente Carducho's squared drawing of Christ on the cross, which is in the background of his painting the *Virgin Appearing to Father Juan Fort* (figs 7–8). Eugenio Cajés' study of *Saint Ildephonsus at the Tomb of Saint*

Leocardia is a finished study for his painting (figs 6–7, p. 86). Like the Carducho drawing, it is squared so that each section could be transferred to the canvas.

Cartoons are full-scale drawings made to transfer a design to another surface.[47] These are different from squared drawings because the size of the sheet corresponds to the final composition. Cartoons were not normally intended to be preserved and most were destroyed in the process of transfer, so very few survive. How they were used can often be determined from evidence on the surface of the painting or fresco, such as incised lines, pinpricks or other marks. There is evidence for the use of cartoons in late sixteenth-century Spain in surviving drawings by artists working at the monastery of the Escorial (see Chapter 3). An example is Gaspar Becerra's half-figure of a male, a fragment of a highly finished cartoon for a now destroyed fresco at the palace of the Alcázar in Madrid (fig. 22, p. 72).[48] Cartoons were used in a variety of ways at the Escorial: an unusual survival is a large group of carefully pricked drawings by different artists for embroidered liturgical vestments. One of the drawings from the group is *Christ Distributing Bread to His Disciples after his Resurrection* (fig. 25, p. 74).

7
Vicente Carducho
The Virgin Appearing to Father Juan Fort (detail showing *Christ Appearing to Father Juan Fort*), 1626–32
Oil on canvas, 3450 x 3190 mm (whole painting)
Museo del Prado, Madrid
P.5577

8
Vicente Carducho
Christ Appearing to Father Juan Fort, 1626–32
Black chalk, squared for transfer, 387 x 194 mm
British Museum, London
1920,1116.21

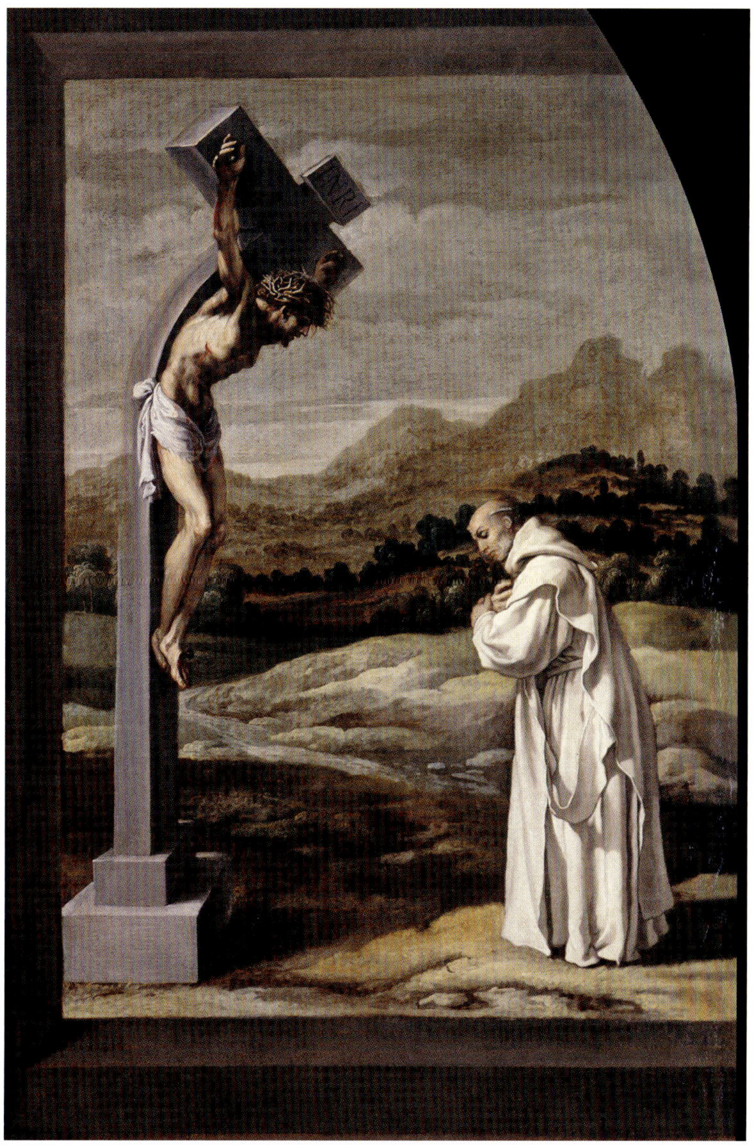

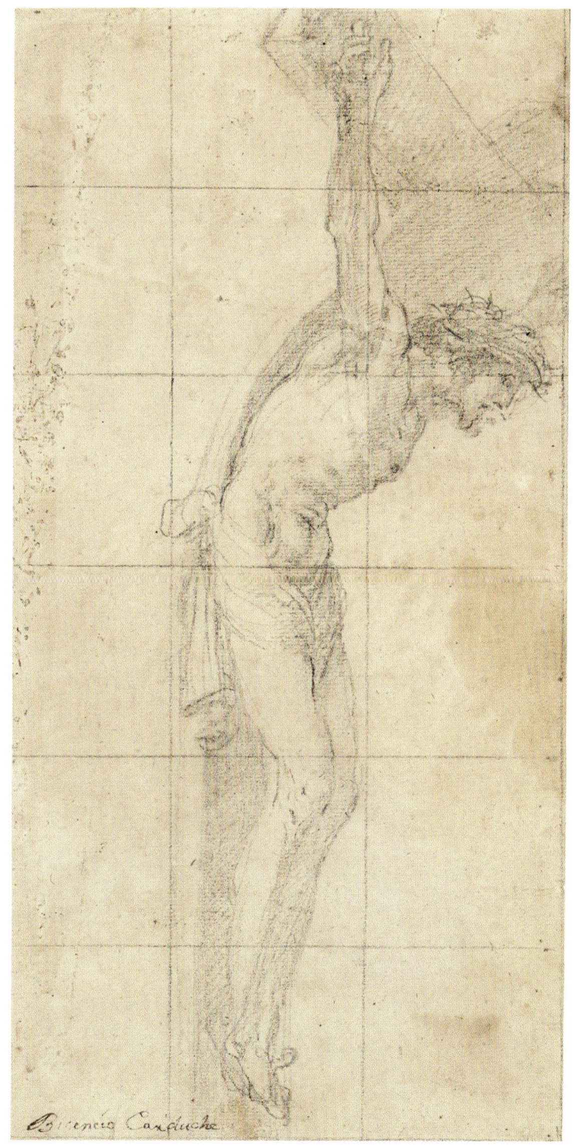

Many different types of architectural drawing were made in Spain, where they were traditionally preserved. Philip II, for example, devoted a room at the Alcázar in Madrid to his collection.[49] Architectural drawings include plans, sections, elevations, interior and exterior details, *retablos* (altarpieces), permanent and temporary structures.[50] This category of drawings has the highest survival rate because in addition to being working drawings, many were kept as contractual records: a spectacular example of this is Juan Guas' drawing of the main chapel of San Juan de los Reyes in Toledo (fig. 4, p. 49), made around 1477.

Architectural drawings often had more than one function. Juan Gómez de Mora's 1614 drawing for the high altar in the church of the monastery of Guadalupe carries a long inscription describing how the work was to be executed, in addition to providing a design recording details of the decoration (fig. 5, p. 85). During the seventeenth century a distinctive type of architectural drawing was developed to provide the patron with alternative designs on a single sheet. For example, Sebastián de Herrera Barnuevo's design for an altarpiece (fig. 38, p. 106) shows the upper left pediment completed to form an arch, with the alternative, a sculpted scroll decoration, on the right. This sheet also shows the proposed carved elements and paintings. Ventura Rodríguez's 1753 drawing of an interior section for a new church of San Bernardo in Madrid is signed, dated and has a title running across the top (fig. 9).[51] The precision of the scaled section, the detail of its interior decoration (sculpture

9
Ventura Rodríguez
Interior Section of a New Temple Devoted to San Bernardo in Madrid, 1753
Pen and ink and grey wash over black chalk,
443 x 638 mm
Biblioteca Nacional, Madrid
DIB/14/6/13

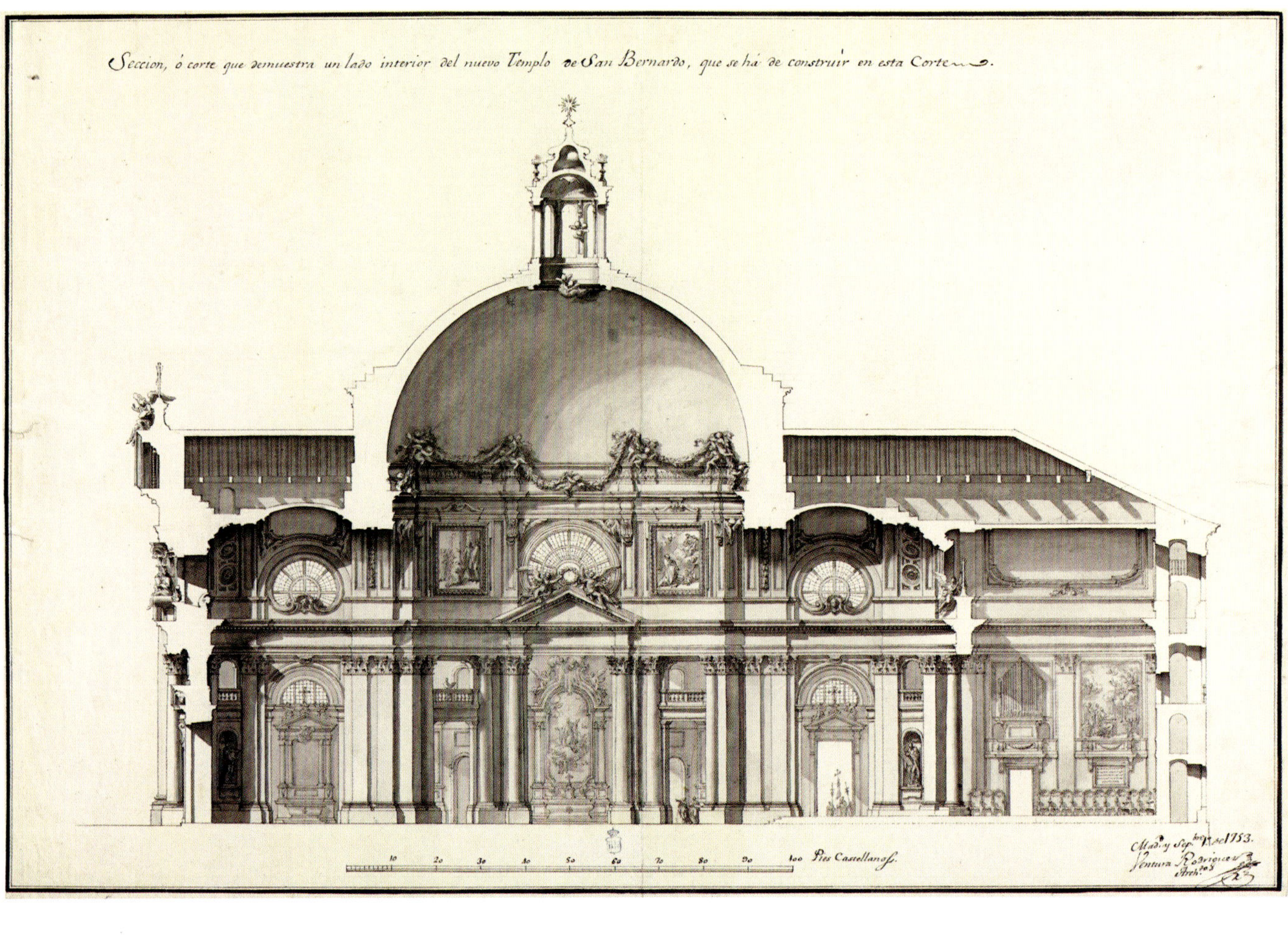

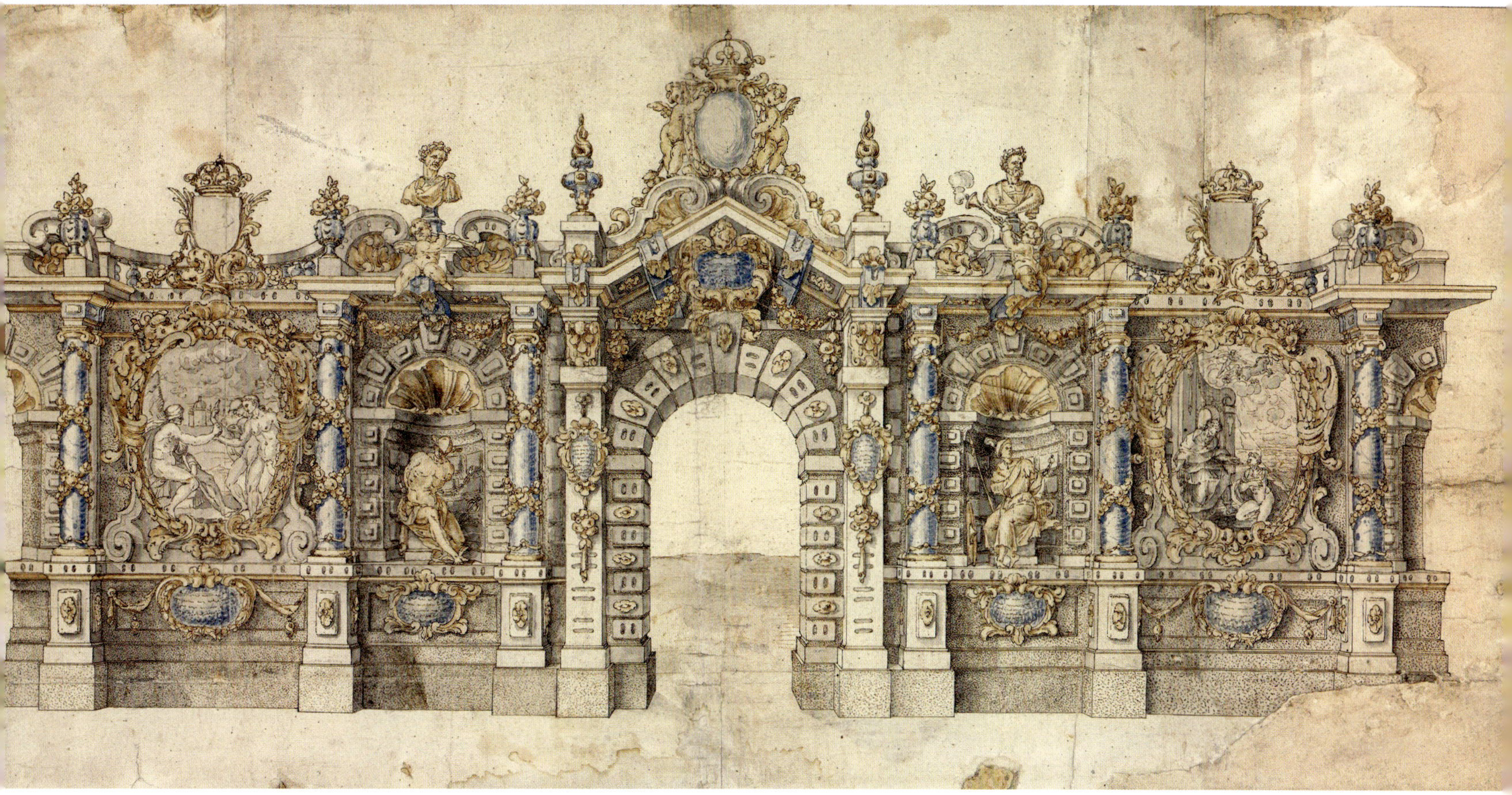

10
Anonymous
An Ephemeral Structure for a Royal Entry, *c.*1700–30
Pen with brown and black ink with blue, brown and grey wash, 435 x 852 mm
Biblioteca Nacional, Madrid
DIB/18/1/8449

and paintings) and the double-ruled black border suggest that as an architectural presentation drawing it was made to be preserved, although the project was never realized.

A major source of employment for artists and architects in Spain during the seventeenth and eighteenth centuries was designing and decorating ephemeral structures for exequies (funeral ceremonies), coronations and royal entries.[52] Whereas prints showing these structures are relatively abundant, preparatory drawings for them are far rarer. An anonymous eighteenth-century drawing of an ephemeral arch for a royal entry, possibly of Philip V, shows how ambitious the structures could be – large enough for the procession to pass through, and with rich decoration and complex iconography (fig. 10).[53] Matías de Torres' drawing of *Saint Isidore Praying* is for the central painting of a similar arch erected on the Puerta del Sol in Madrid, for the entry of María Luisa de Orleans on 13 January 1680 (figs 51–3, p. 113).

Ornament drawings are often discussed alongside architectural drawing, and their range is illustrated here by two examples. A sixteenth-century pen-and-ink sheet of arabesques, serpents and putti now in the Museo del Prado (fig. 11) depicts decoration similar to that commonly found on tiles and sometimes on decorated choir stalls in Spain,[54] while the design for an overmantel by Francisco Herrera the Younger (fig. 45, p. 110) of around 1670–80 presents the decorative elements of the design.

Contractual drawings are finished designs normally signed by the patron and the artist, along with any other parties involved in a commission,

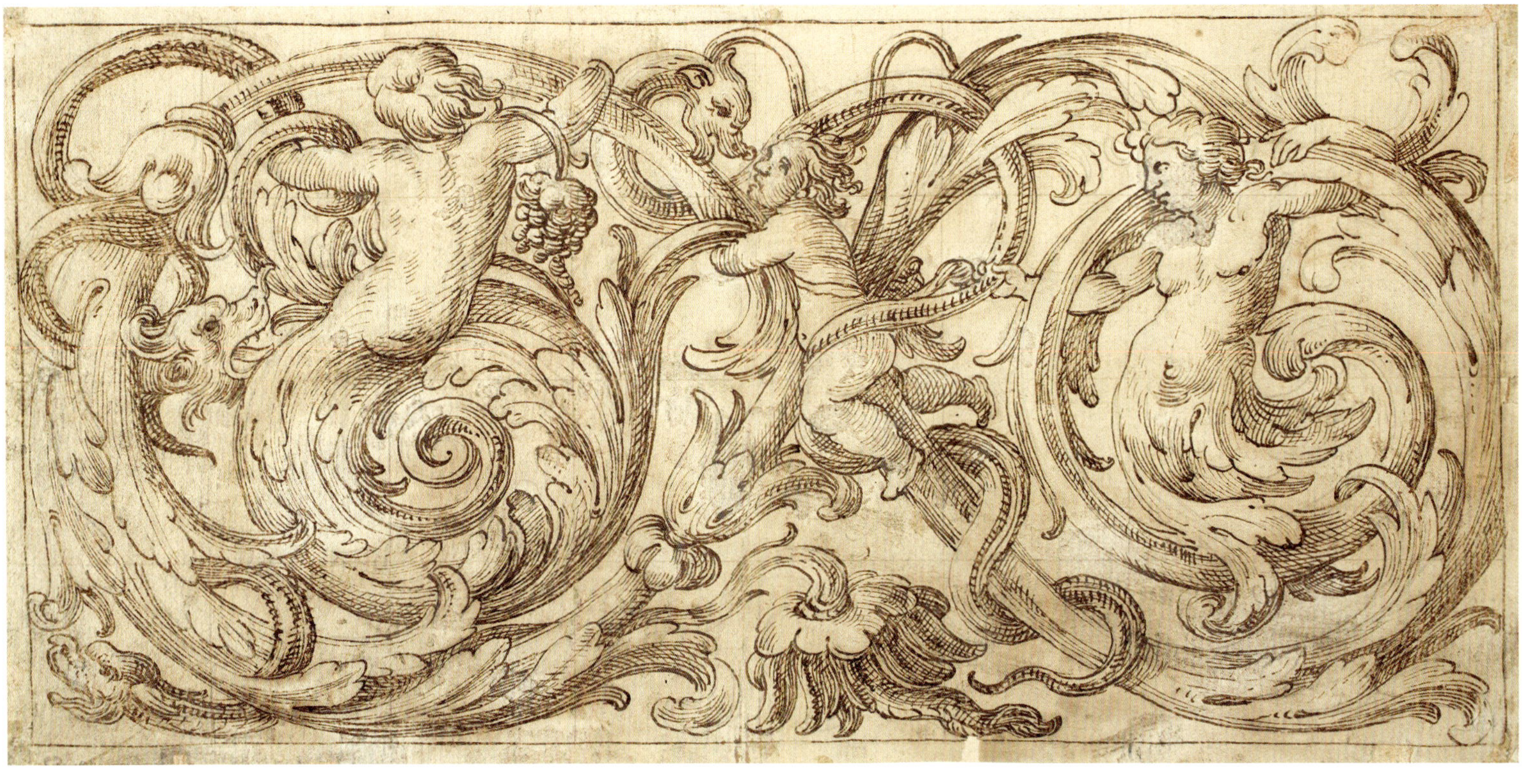

11
Anonymous
Arabesques, Serpents and Putti, *c.*1550–1600
Pen and brown ink over black chalk, 180 x 350 mm
Museo del Prado, Madrid
F.D.105

12
Attributed to Fabrizio Castello
The Escorial under Construction, *c.*1576
Pen and grey ink and grey wash over black chalk, 508 x 775 mm
Marquis of Salisbury, Hatfield House

13
Attributed to Diego Velázquez
The 1632 Auto de Fé in the Plaza Mayor, Madrid, 1632
Pen and brown ink with brown wash over black chalk, partly incised, 297 x 542 mm
British Museum, London
1850,0713.5

giving the drawing the force of a legal document. Once a design was accepted the drawing was often destroyed during the process of making the commissioned piece, being used by the artists as they worked.[55] Early examples of surviving contractual drawings in Spain are related to the main altarpiece for the church of San Esteban in Burgos by Gil de Silóe and Diego de la Cruz, dated 1494.[56] The only known seventeenth-century contractual drawings from Spain to have survived are the two from the workshop of Pedro de Mena from around 1673–4, for statues of Queen Isabel and King Ferdinand in the main chapel transept arch of Granada Cathedral (fig. 31, p. 145).

The technique of printmaking required preliminary drawings in order to transfer the design to the matrix from which the print was made, but again the drawing was often destroyed in the process. Surviving examples include Francisco Rizi's title-page drawing for the book commemorating the official entry into Madrid of Mariana of Austria, on 15 November 1649, for her marriage to Philip IV, engraved by Pedro de Villafranca (figs 24–5, p. 97).[57] By the eighteenth century attitudes toward the preservation of drawings had changed. Goya, for example, used a transfer process that did not result in his drawings being destroyed (see Chapter 8). New techniques such as lithography did not require incising the sheet, so preparatory drawings had a greater chance of survival – as with Goya's ink-wash drawing of the *Inferno* for his lithograph from around 1818–19 (figs 46–7, pp. 266–7).

Only in exceptional cases were drawings (as opposed to prints and paintings, for example) made to record specific events. A drawing of about 1576, sometimes attributed to Fabrizio Castello, shows the Escorial under construction (fig. 12).[58] This shows the machinery for moving the building materials, such as the crane with double wheels in the centre, and records

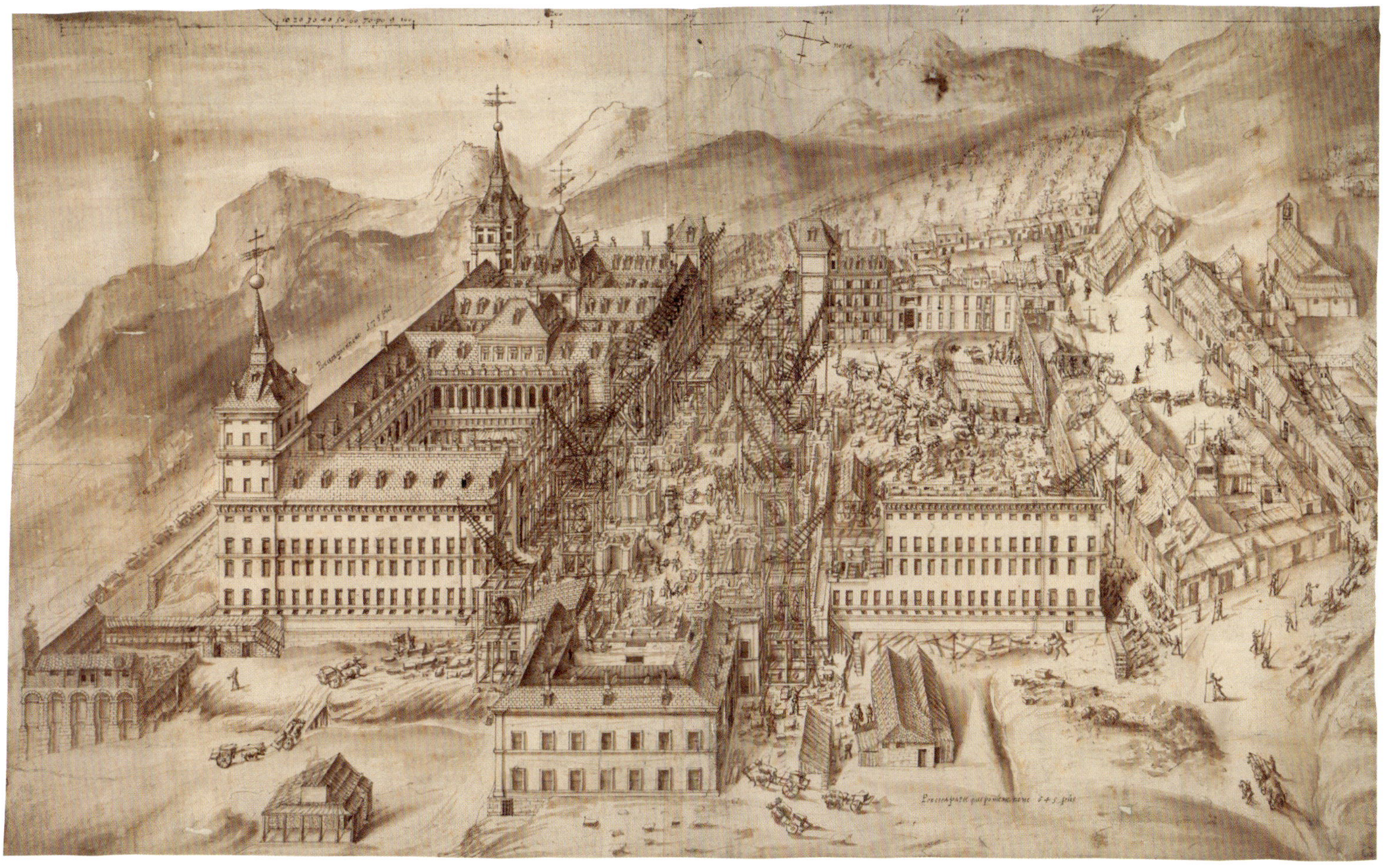

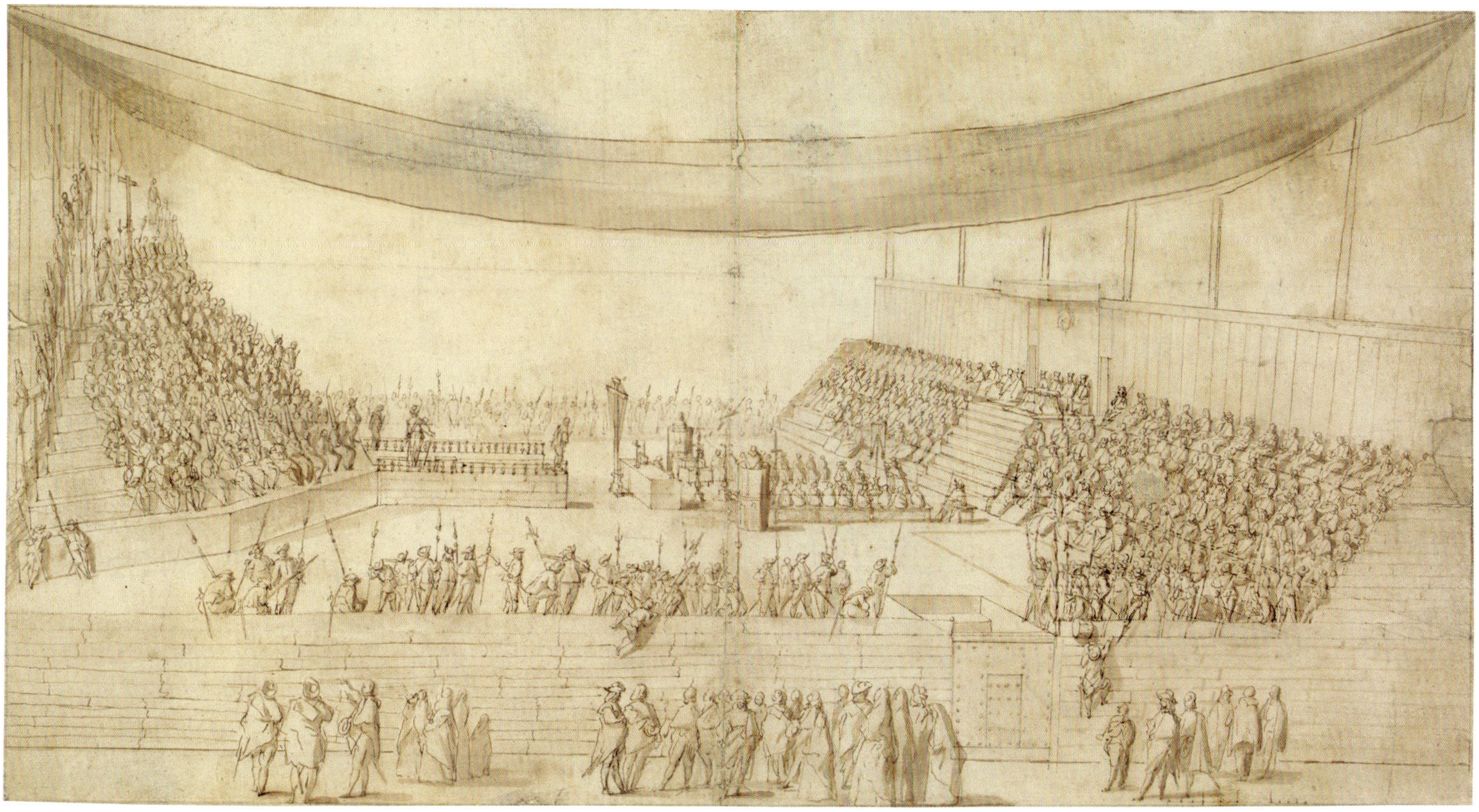

the transporting of blocks of stone and many other activities, providing a snapshot of a stage in building the monastery. Another remarkable survival is a pen-and-ink drawing of an *auto de fé* (a ritual of public penance of condemned heretics) that took place in the Plaza Mayor, Madrid, on 4 July 1632 (fig. 13). Its primary purpose is to record the event in detail, although the scale in the lower right and the carefully drawn and incised perspective lines suggest that it was probably intended as a study for a painting or possibly a print.

Drawing as an independent exercise only became widespread in Spain during the eighteenth century, as part of academic training. An earlier exception is José de Ribera, who made a number of independent drawings such as *A Saint (Albert?) Tied to a Tree* (fig. 32, p. 186). The drawing is not related to a painting and its extraordinary degree of finish, the signature and date, demonstrate that it was considered a work in its own right, even if it was also intended to provide the basis for a print. The study of the nude was fundamental to academic training, in order to gain an understanding of the human body. Juan Antonio Conchillos y Falcó's study of a partly kneeling male nude (fig. 20, p. 178) is one of a large group he made at the end of the seventeenth century (see Chapter 6). Artistic training in the eighteenth century featured highly finished drawings such as Francisco Bayeu's *Head of a Woman* (fig. 22, p. 206). Landscape drawing also developed in Spain during the eighteenth century, although it never became as popular as in other parts of Europe. The *View of Toledo* (fig. 4, p. 194) of about 1750–60 is a striking example, with human activity in the foreground set against a recognizable backdrop.

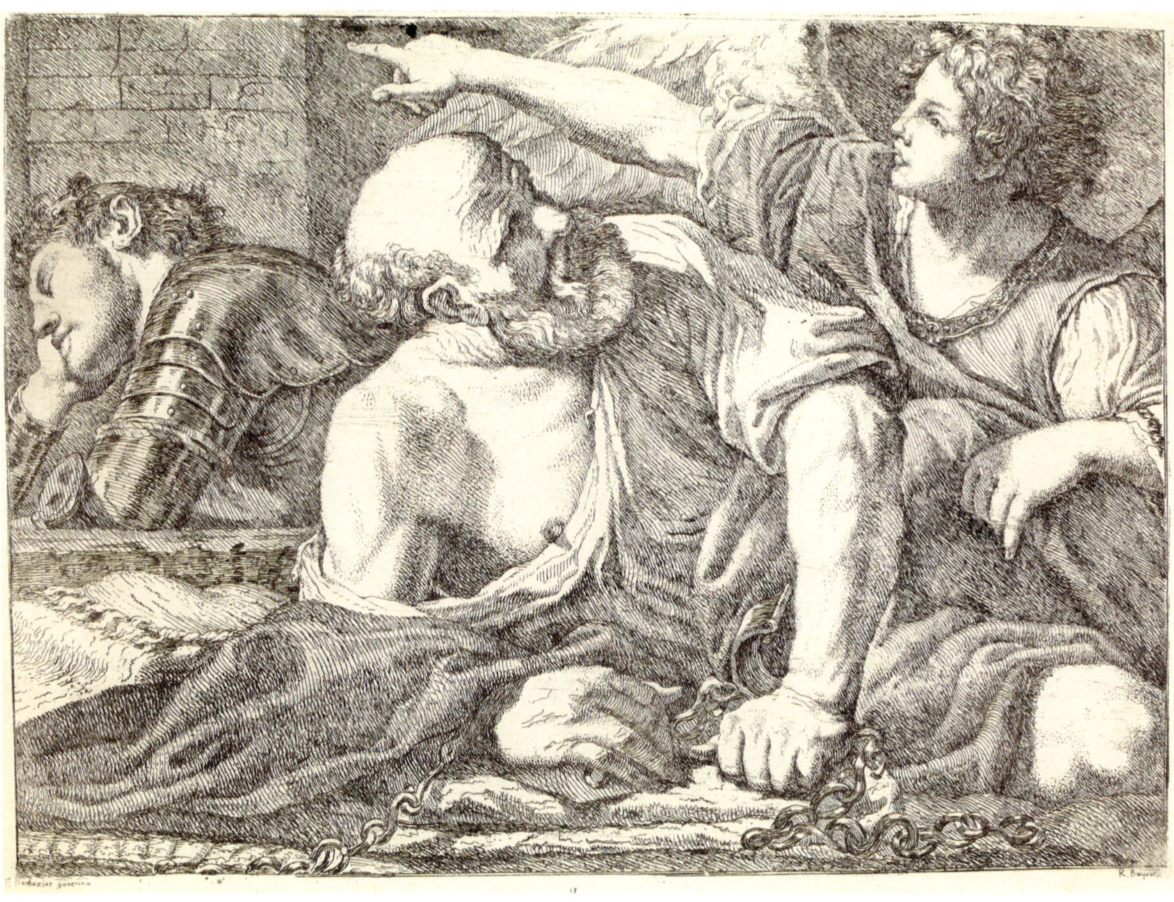

14
Ramón Bayeu y Subías after Guercino
The Liberation of Saint Peter, *c.*1770–93
Etching, 191 x 257 mm
British Museum, London
1929,1021.5

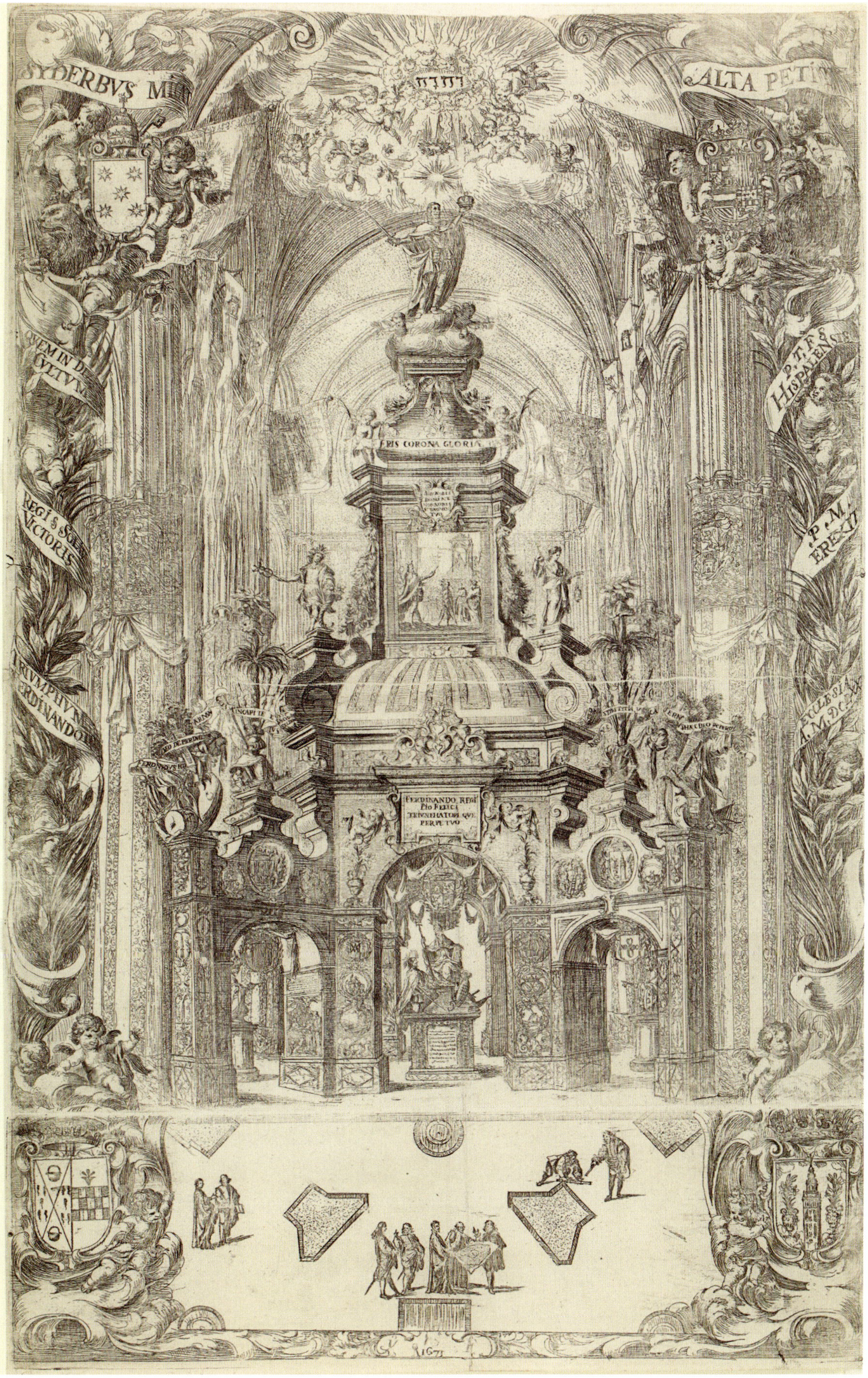

15
Juan de Valdés Leal

An Ephemeral Structure in Seville Cathedral, from two plates, 1671

Etching, 542 x 342 mm
British Museum, London
1868,1114.399

16
Anonymous

Virgin of the Pillar, c.1550–1600

Engraving, 205 x 110 mm
British Museum, London
1914,0904.1*

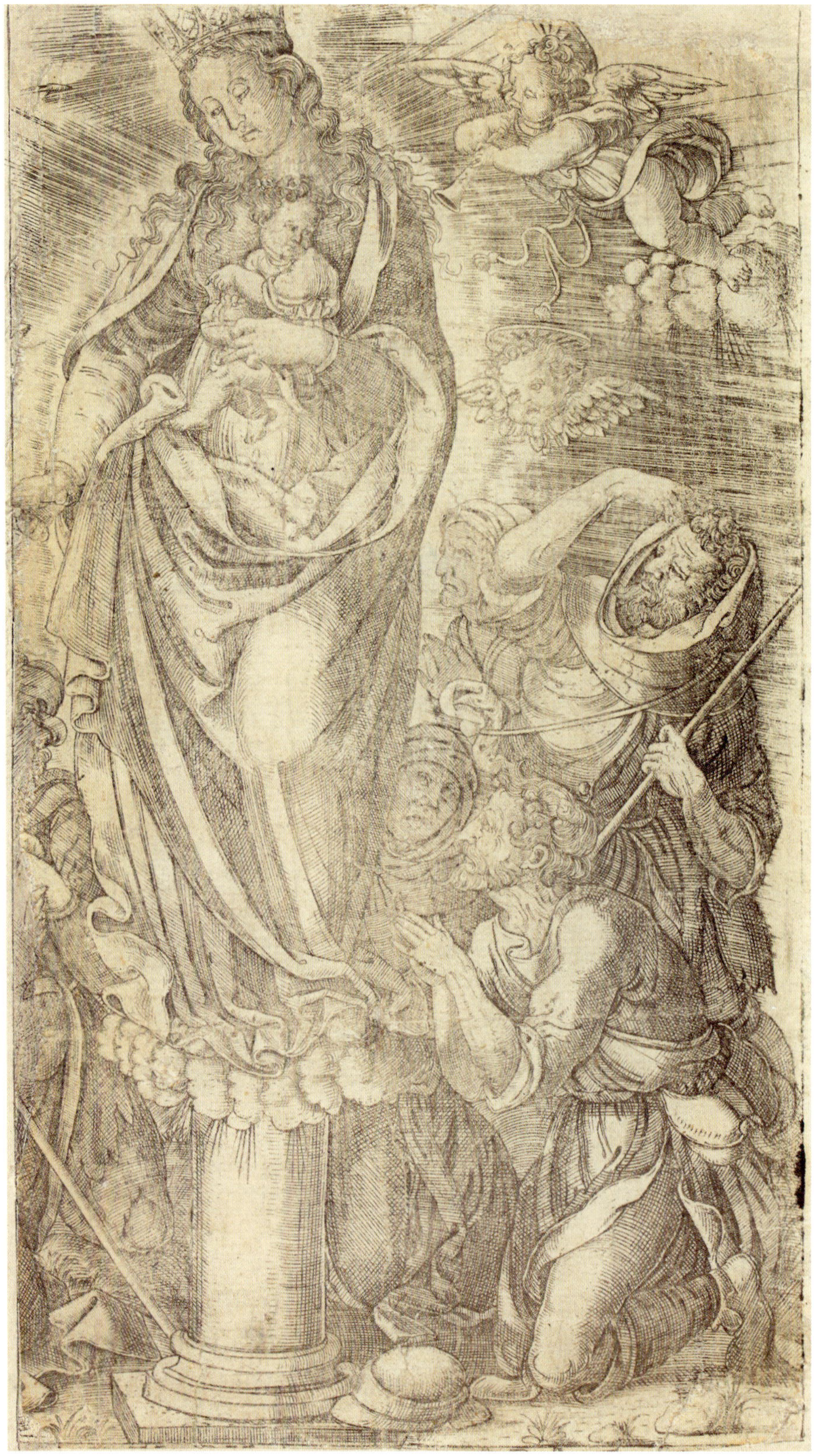

Prints

Prints reproducing a work of art usually bear the designer's name.[59] These were uncommon in Spain before the second half of the eighteenth century, although an early exception is Diego de Astor's 1606 etching after El Greco's *Saint Francis and Brother Leo Meditating on Death* (fig. 32, p. 79). During the seventeenth century a type of print developed in Madrid where part of the composition was original and part of it reproduced. For example, Pedro de Villafranca's engraved portrait of Philip IV reproducing Velázquez's painting is embedded within an elaborate design devised by Villafranca (fig. 58, p. 117). Reproductive prints produced in Spain during the eighteenth century fall into two categories: copper-plate engravings and etchings. The former faithfully follow the model, and are exemplified here by Fernando Selma's engraved *Saint Ildephonsus Receiving the Chasuble from the Virgin* (1789–1800) after Murillo (fig. 41, p. 218). The expressive quality of the technique of etchings, on the other hand, was used to interpret the painted original, as in Ramón Bayeu's *Liberation of Saint Peter* after Guercino (fig. 14).[60]

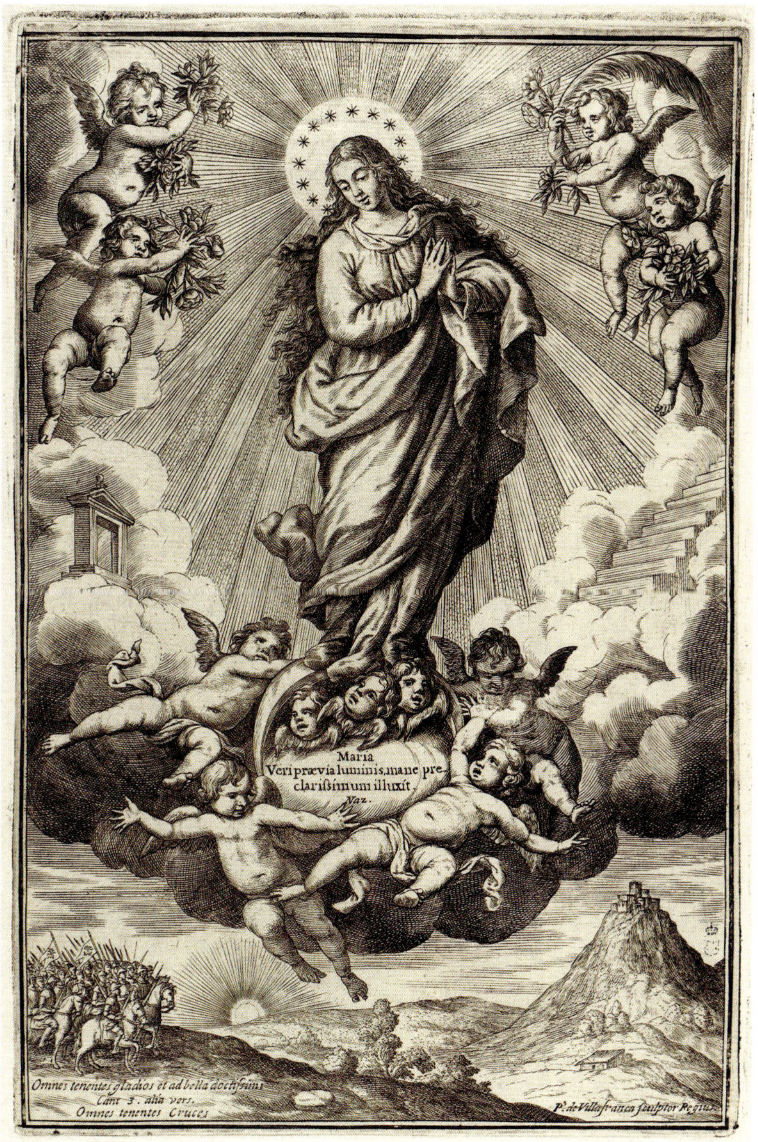

17
Pedro de Villafranca
Virgin of the Immaculate Conception, 1670s
Engraving, 268 x 171 mm
Biblioteca Nacional, Madrid
12893

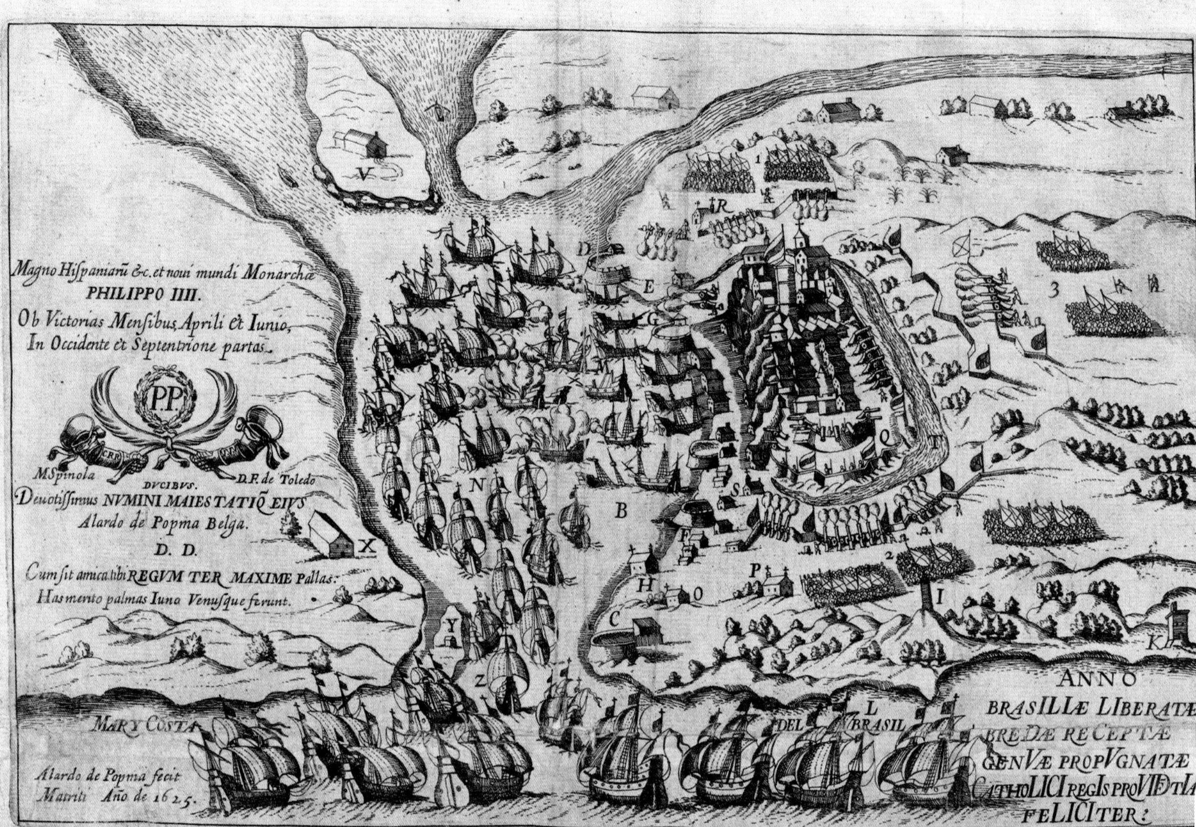

DESCRIPCION DE LA BAIA DE TODOS LOS SANTOS y ciudad de Sansaluador en la costa del Brasil; en que se fortificaron los Olandeses: aora restaurada por don Fadrique de Toledo, Capitan General por el Rey nuestro señor don Felipe IIII en veinte y nueue de Abril de mil y seiscientos y veinte y cinco.

A La ciudad de Sansaluador.
B La Baia de Todos los Santos.
C Fuerte de San Antonio.
D Fuerte de Tapaiqua.
E Santa Maria de Esperança.
F Fuerte de San Alberto.
G Fuerte de aguas dos meninos.
H Santa Maria de la Ayuda.
I Bexia, ò centinela.
K Torre de Garcia Dauila.
L La costa de Atapoan.
M Nauios de los Olandeses.
N Armada del Rey de España.
O Ermita de San Antonio.
P Santa Maria de Mirabella.
Q Fuerte de San Benito.
R Conuento de nuestra Señora del Carmen.
S Ermita de San Pedro.
T Foso de agua que va a salir al fuerte de los meninos.
V Isla y casa de la melaza.
X Sitio donde los Vizcainos hazen el azeyte de Vallenas.
Y Isla Taparique.
Z Entrada de la Baia, que tiene de ancho dos leguas y media.
1 Quartel de don Fadrique, que està en el Carmen.
2 Quartel del Marques de Cropani.
3 Quartel de don Iuan de Orellana, que està a las palmas.

C. R. R. *Cunctando Restituit Rem.* P. P. *Patri Patriæ.* V. V. V. *Venit, Vidit, Vicit.*

LO Capitulado ha sido tan en fauor de las armas de su Magestad, como en ello se verà; saliendo los Olandeses con tanta afrenta. Hallaronse mil y nouecientos y nouenta tan luzidos y valientes soldados, que es voz, no tienen los Olandeses en los Estados tal gente; y la nuestra se marauillò de verla tal. Las vanderas que se han ganado son diez y seis, sin el estandarte que tenian en la Iglesia mayor. Demas desto todas las vanderas de los nauios, y estandarte de la Capitana. La artilleria que se ha hallado en la ciudad parece son ciento y sesenta y nueue pieças, algunas dellas muy buenas de bronze, tan gruessas como las nuestras: y otras de hierro De todo esto tendra su Magestad particular relacion en acabando de ajustarse: y assi mismo de los nauios, municiones, bastimentos, y demas armas. Los muertos de nuestra parte sobre la plaça, han sido ciento y veinte y quatro, y los heridos ciento y quarenta y quatro. Los nauios que se han tomado en el puerto, son veinte y vno. Fuera de la artilleria que estaua en la ciudad, se han tomado otras cincuenta y seis pieças, que auian quedado en los nauios. Los muertos son, don Pedro Osorio, Maesse de Campo, el Capitan don Francisco Manuel del habito de San Iuan, el Capitan don Alonso de Gana. el Morgado de Oliueyre, don Fernando de Meneses del habito de Calatraua, Layudante Frego, el Capitan don Diego de Santisteuan, el ingeniero mayor, Iuan de Ouiedo, del habito de Montesa, don Iuan de Torreblanca Alferez, don Ioseph Manrique, don Lucas de Figuerea, don Diego de Espinosa, Capitan de Infanteria. Los heridos, don Enrique Dalagon, Capitan don Diego Ramirez, Capitan don Diego de Guzman, Capitan don Pedro Medrano, don Diego de Mallea. Vinieron con el auiso don Pedro de Porres y Toledo, y don Enrique Dalagon y Pimentel, Capitanes, y sobrinos del General.

Vendese en la calle de Toledo, en casa de Alardo de Popma, en frente del estudio de la Compañia de Iesus.

18
Alardo de Popma
The Recapture of the City of Salvador da Bahia (Brazil), 1625
Engraving and etching, 207 x 303 mm
Biblioteca Nacional, Madrid
14804

Book illustration reached a high level of sophistication during the seventeenth century in Spain, with ambitious and inventive compositions reflecting the ability of those who designed and engraved them. Many books included illustrations that were larger than the page, such as Juan Schorquens' engraving of Philip II disembarking in Lisbon (fig. 56, p. 116). To recoup the costs involved in making large prints, they were also sold as single sheets. However, this strategy depended entirely on the nature of the print: a title-page engraving would have little relevance beyond its specific context, but prints of a popular subject or an event could expect a wider audience. For example, Juan de Valdés Leal's 1671 etching of the structure erected for the canonization of Ferdinand III in the cathedral of Seville and published in the *Fiesta de la S. Iglesia metropolitana y patriarcal de Sevilla* was also sold as a single sheet (fig. 15 and see p. 160). We know from surviving documentation that it was very expensive to publish a 1780 edition of *Don Quijote*; as a consequence, all the engravings were also sold as loose impressions (fig. 42, p. 219).

Prints not primarily made to reproduce works of art, including, for example, broadsides, are described here as independent or autonomous prints. These were initially made to meet a specific need, such as representing a local saint, but this did not preclude them from being adapted for another context. Some of the earliest prints made in Spain were loose-leaf devotional images, such as the *Virgin of the Pillar* (fig. 16), to meet the demand for images of the Virgin's miraculous appearance to Saint James the Apostle on the banks of the Ebro River.[61] Pedro de Villafranca's *Virgin of the Immaculate Conception*

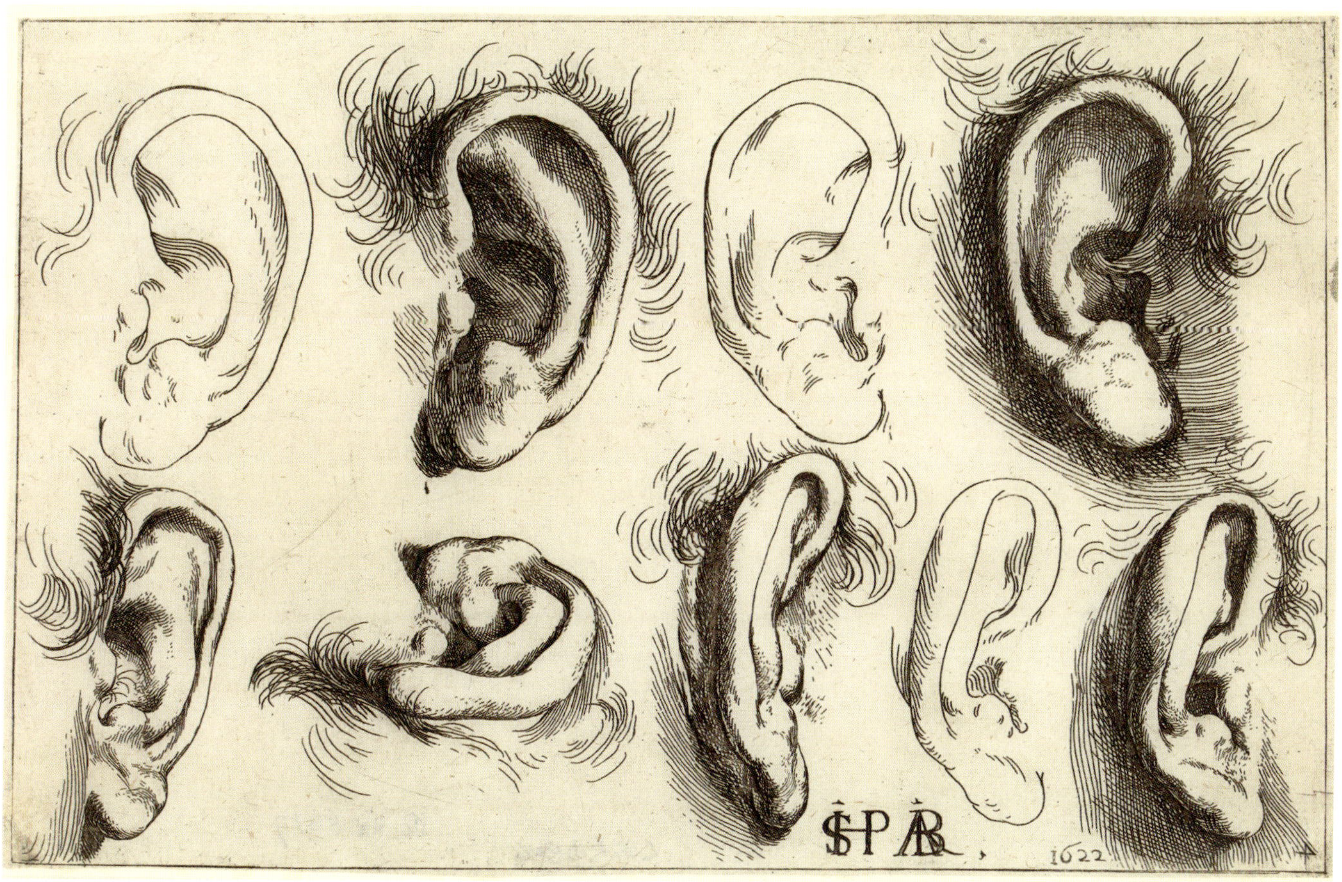

19
José de Ribera
Studies of Ears, 1622
Etching, 140 x 216 mm
British Museum, London
1874,0808.749

20
José García Hidalgo
Studies of the Female Nude, 1693
Etching, 159 x 115 mm
British Museum, London
1854,1020.8

21
Anonymous
Uncut Sheet of Twenty-four Playing Cards, 1587
Woodcut, hand coloured using stencils, additions in pen and ink, 235 x 353 mm
British Museum, London
1896,0501.1346

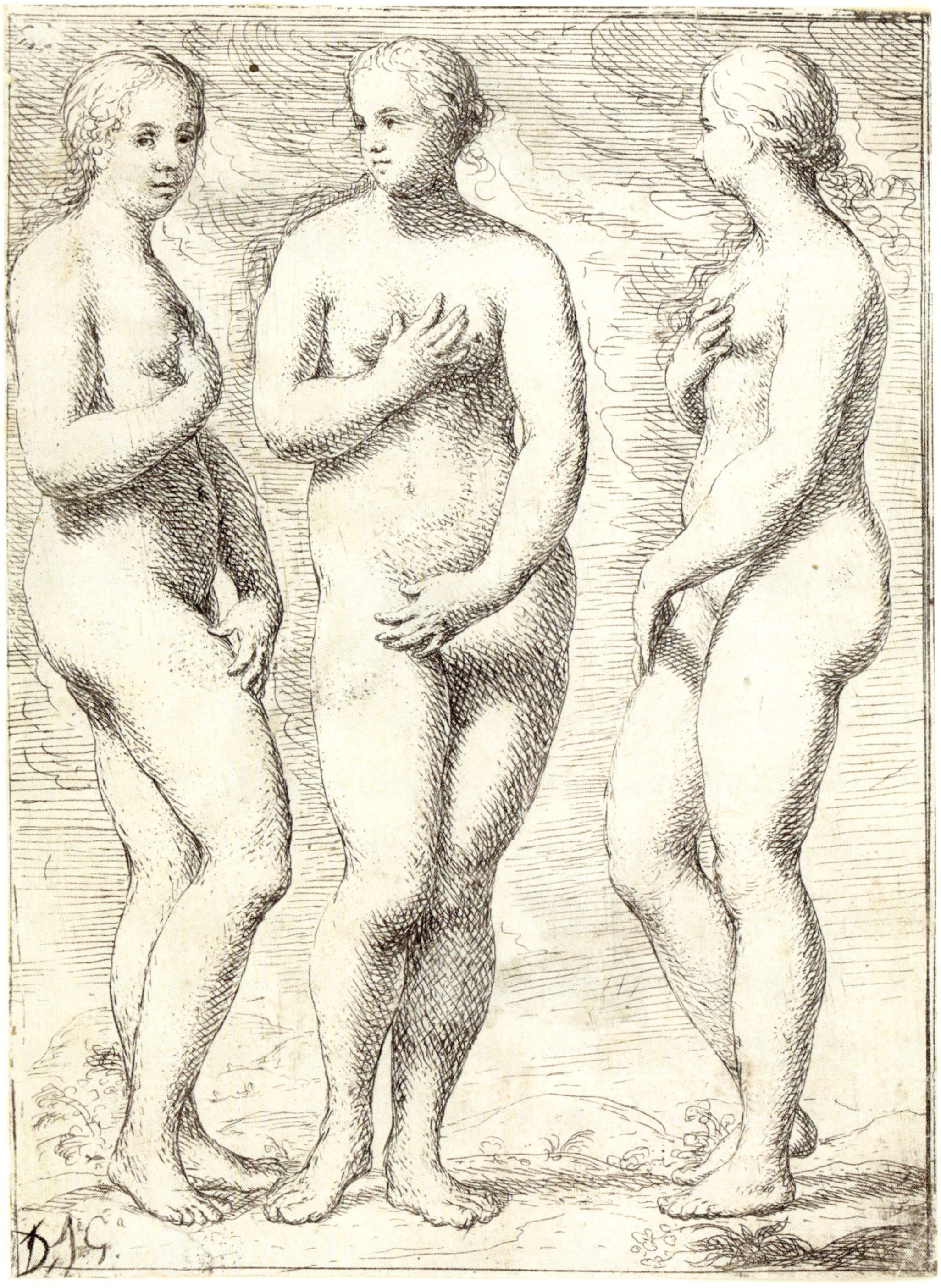

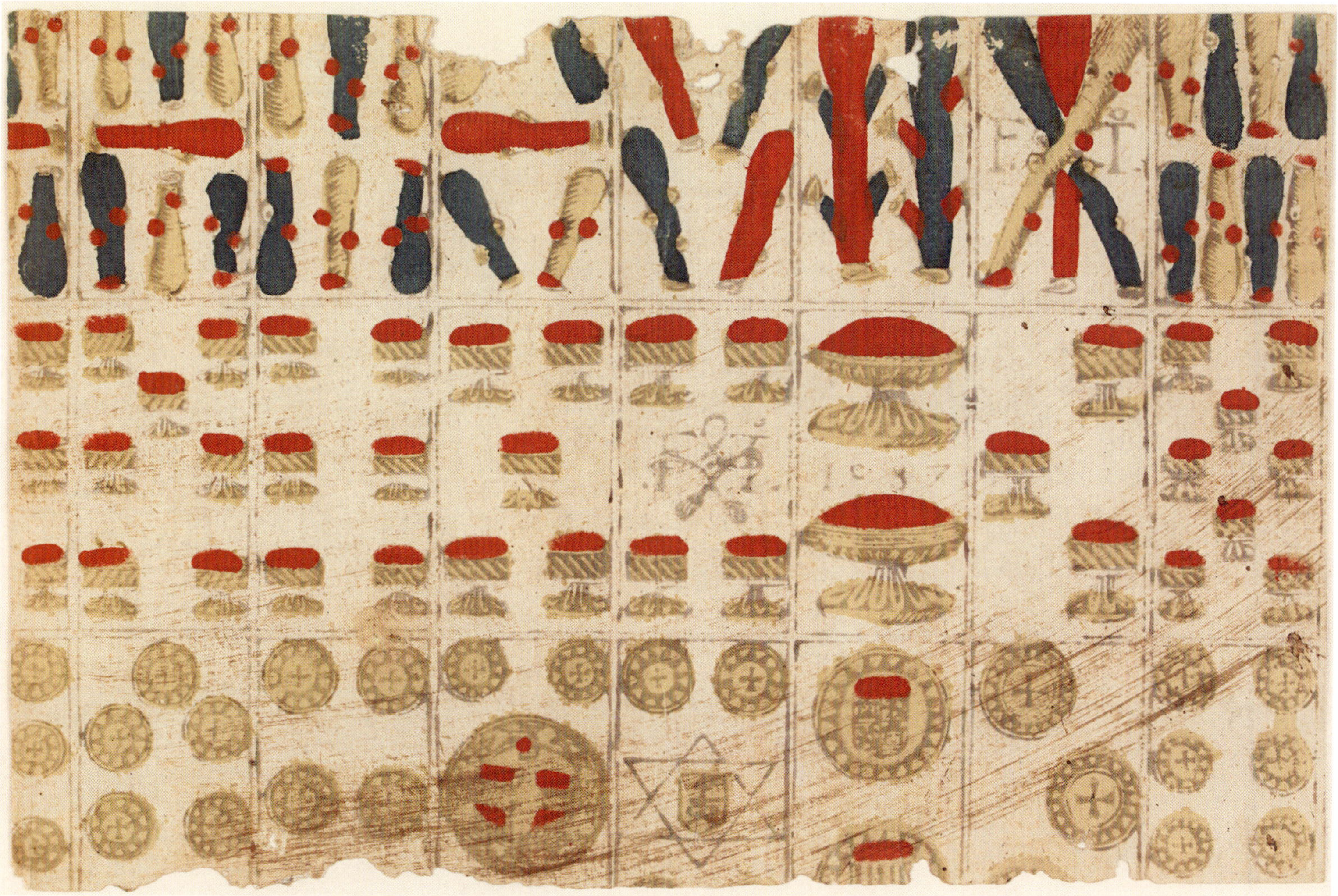

from the 1670s appears originally to have been a devotional print, but in the eighteenth century it was included in Ignatius Joseph de Ortega et Cotes' *Bullarium Ordinis Militæ de Calatrava*... (fig. 17).[62] Broadsides tended mainly to depict contemporary events such as battles, royal entries and marriages; those showing battles and sieges survive in few impressions because their relevance diminished once the event had passed. A rare exception is Alardo de Popma's 1625 engraving of the recapture of Salvador da Bahia on the coast of Brazil by a combined Spanish-Portuguese force (fig. 18). The main elements of the siege are described in the letterpress text section at the bottom of the print. Events such as the entry of a royal figure into a city or a coronation belong to a slightly different category because interest in the main protaganist tended to be more enduring.

In the first half of the eighteenth century prints began to appear in series. Subjects relating to costume and pastimes were particularly suited to this treatment, where their many variations could be explored. The *Colección de trajes de España* (*Collection of Spanish Costume*) engraved by Juan de la Cruz Cano from 1777 (figs 44–5, p. 221) depicts dress from throughout Spain and her territories, while Antonio Carnicero's bullfight series illustrates a popular pastime (fig. 48–9, p. 223). These are examples of highly collectable popular

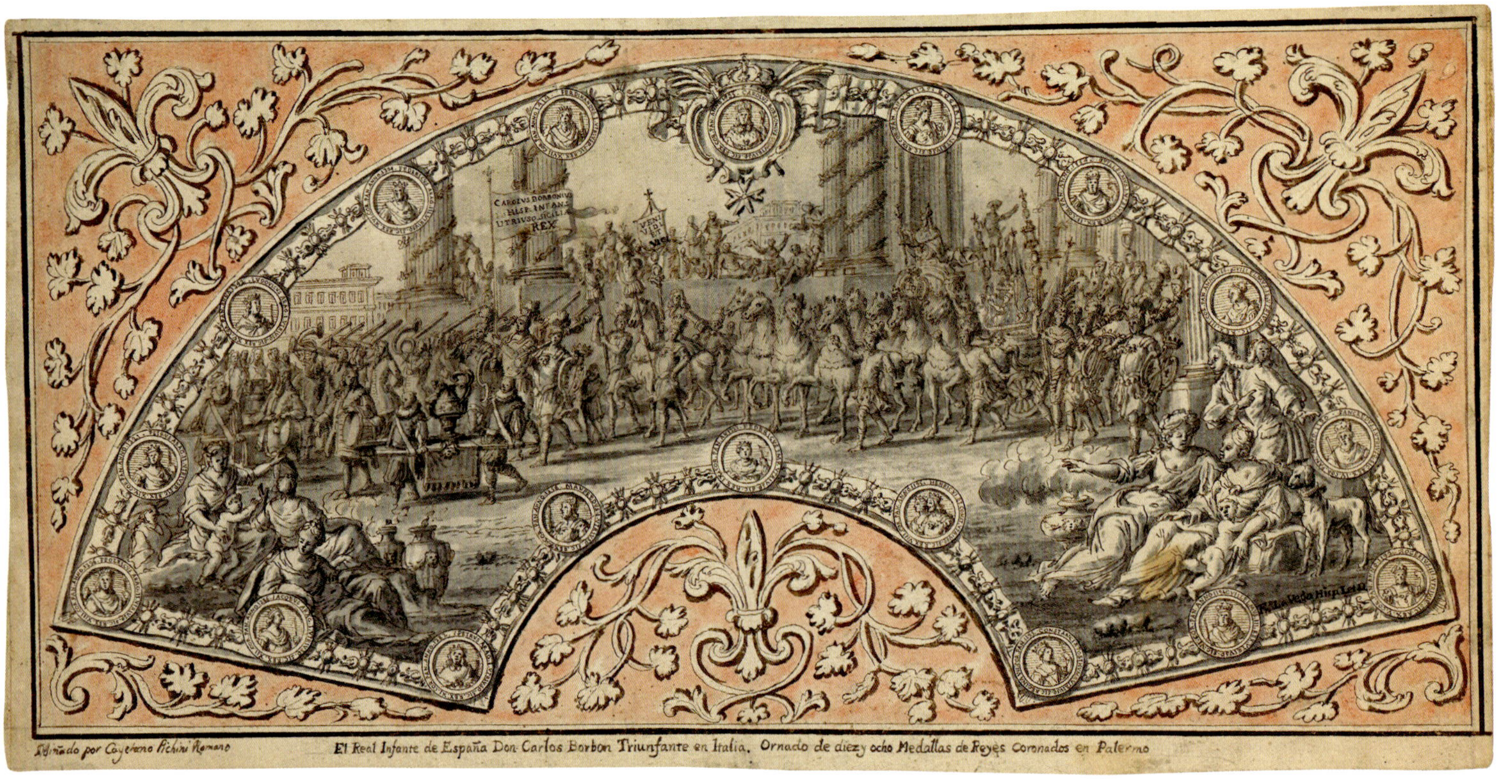

22
Francisco la Vega
Design for a Fan showing the Triumphal Procession of Charles VII entering Naples, after 1734
Pen and brown ink, with pink, brown and grey washes over black chalk, 275 x 533 mm
British Museum, London
1891,0713.606

prints, but many less accomplished images were also made in Spain.[63] The best-known print series are by Goya, who transformed the possibilities of exploring subjects through sequences, for example, *Los Caprichos* (figs 12–16, pp. 242–3) and the *Disasters of War* (figs 22–7, pp. 248–50).

Prints made as teaching aids for art students are known as pattern prints, and these were used to learn the fundamentals of drawing according to a prescribed formula through step-by-step practice. José de Ribera's pattern prints made around 1622 are the best-known examples (fig. 19).[64] The techniques used for drawing individual features were then transferred to complete figures using, for example José García Hidalgo's *Studies of the Female Nude* published in the *Principios para estudiar el Nobilísimo y Real arte de la Pintura* in 1693 (fig. 20 and fig. 65, p. 121).

A wide range of printed and occasionally drawn ephemera survives, which does not always fit conventional categories of works on paper. These objects were generally made for mass consumption and were not intended for preservation or collection. Printed ephemera include playing cards, fans, games and images relating to events such as the miraculous apparition or intercession of a saint. They might also be incorporated into or printed on a non-paper support such as fabric, or pasted to a panel to become part of a more permanent devotional object. An uncut sheet of twenty-four playing cards made in Toledo in 1587 has probably survived intact because of a printing problem suggested by the ink smears across its surface (fig. 21 and detail p. 14).[65] Prints cut and mounted on the durable support of fan leaves survive in considerable numbers, but less common are drawings made for the fans. The drawing by Francisco La Vega (fig. 22) depicting the triumphal procession of Charles VII of Naples (future King Charles III of Spain) in 1734 on his election to the crown of the two Sicilies, one of a series commemorating the reign of the Bourbon Charles, is a rare survivor.[66]

The practice of incorporating religious prints into a fabric support to create devotional objects was widespread in Spain: see, for example, the engraved *Virgin of Trapa* (monastery of Santa María de la Trapa de Santa Susana, Aragon) sewn into an embroidered cloth.[67] Impressions of Mariano Brandi's print after Mariano Salvador Maella's *San Felipe Neri before the Virgin and the Holy Trinity* were printed on silk, its sides folded and stitched to form a border suggesting that it might have been a wall hanging.[68]

The context of prints in Spain

Portús and Vega's work on religious prints and their many uses demonstrates the complexity of the topic. Documentary and literary evidence reveals that many prints were destroyed by the very devotional practices for which they were made. Their physical properties also made them easy to pin to walls, and this seems to have frequently occurred. Francisco Ribalta's painting of *The Musical Appearing to Saint Francis* of *c.*1620 (fig. 23) includes a print of a crucifixion flanked by the Virgin and John the Baptist in the upper right. In the domestic context prints were also fixed to walls, as is shown in Luis Paret's *A Family Saying the Rosary* of *c.*1784 (fig. 24) that depicts several printed religious images and a calendar. Pedro de Acosta's 1741 *trompe l'oeil* of prints pinned to

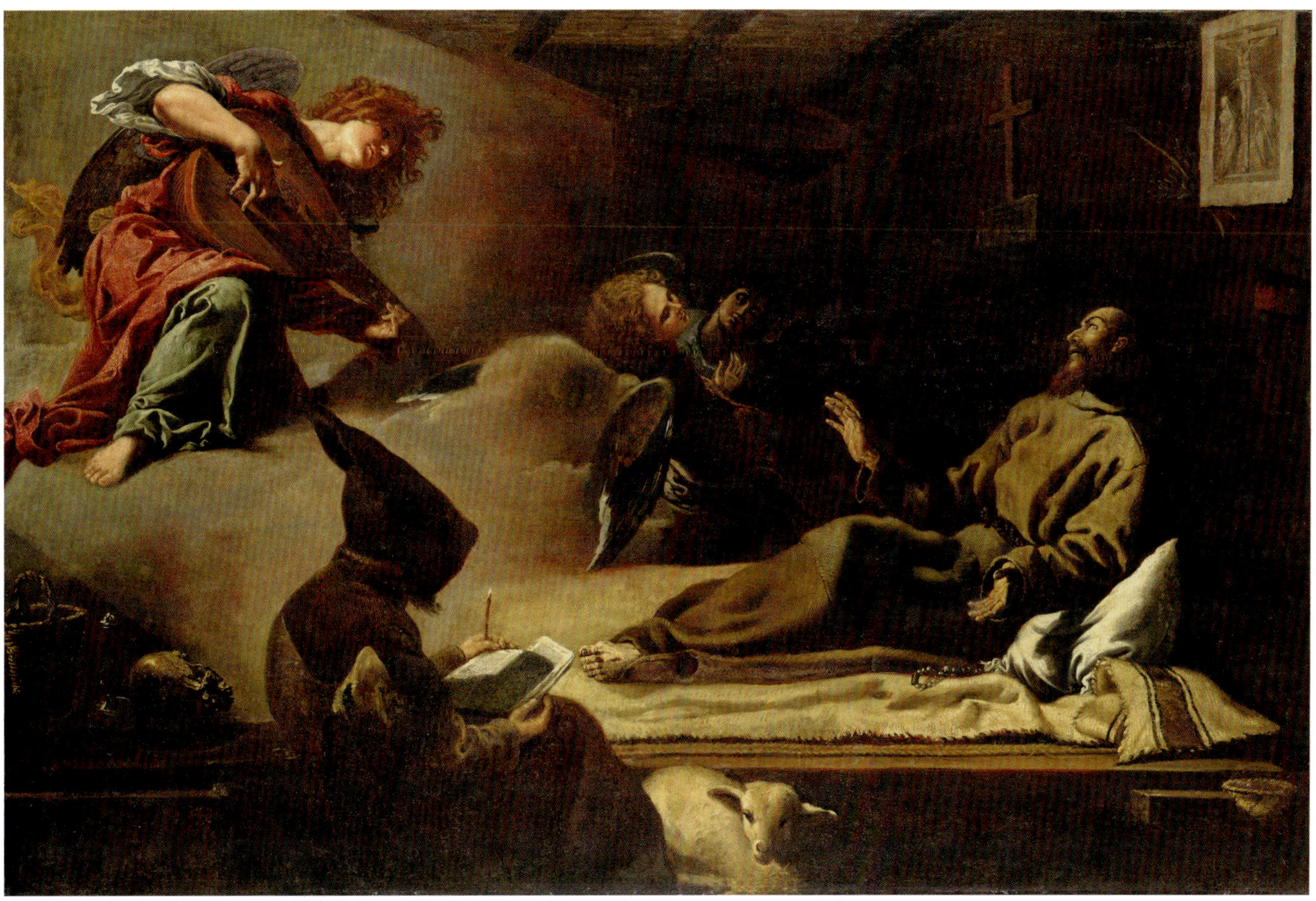

23
Francisco Ribalta
The Musical Appearing to Saint Francis, *c.*1620
Oil on canvas, 1069 x 1592 mm
Wadsworth Atheneum Museum of Art
1957.254

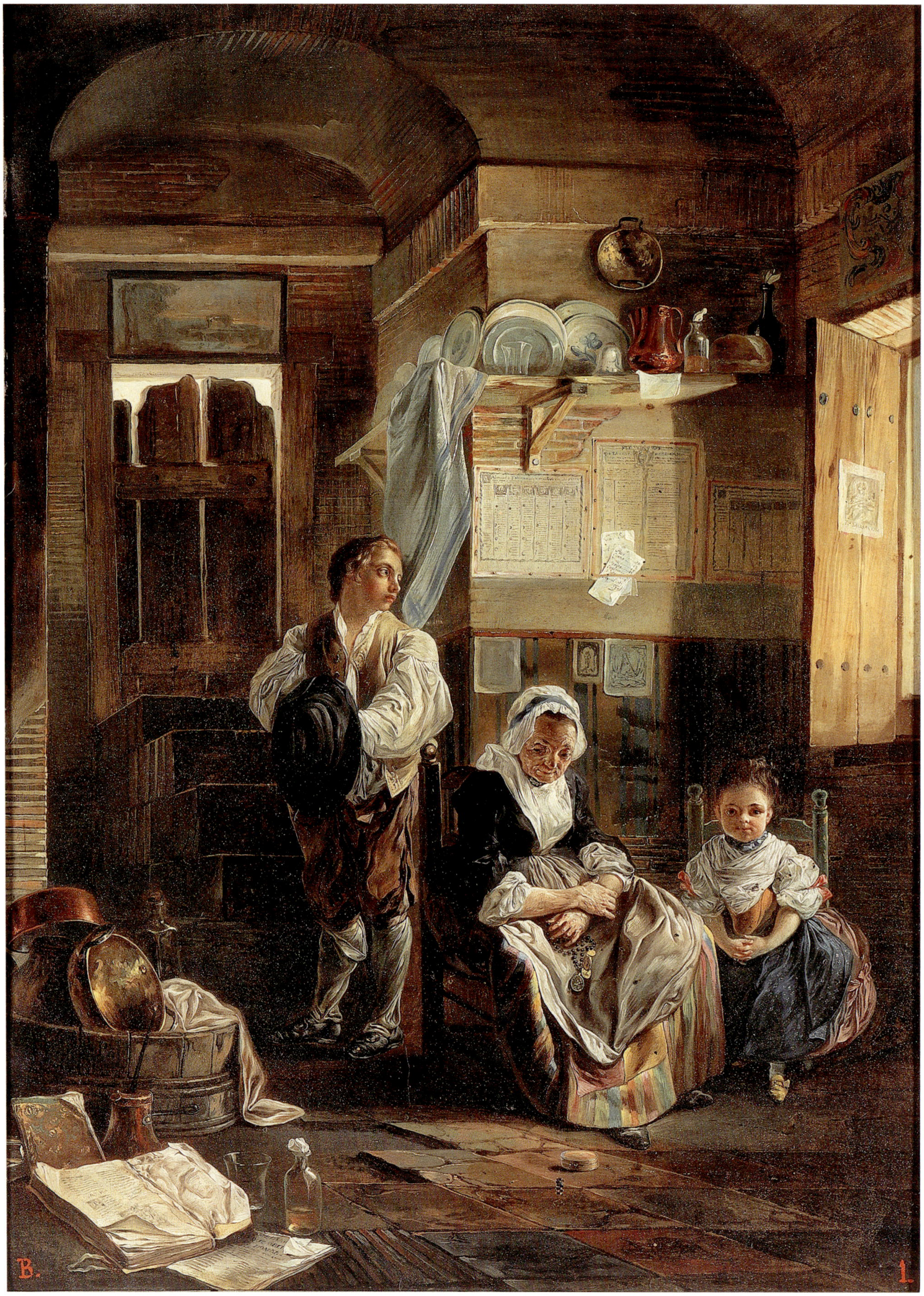
B.
1.

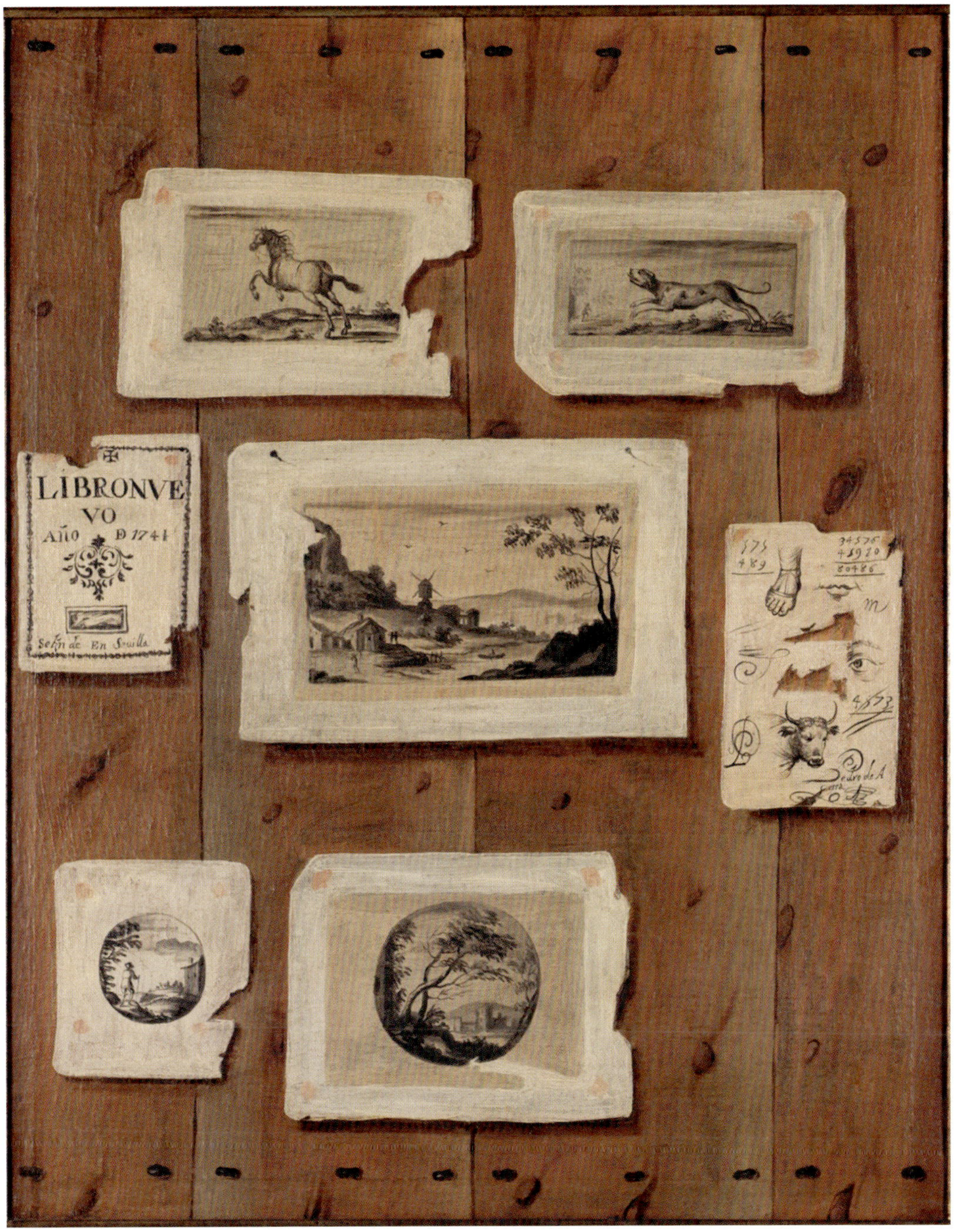

24
Luis Paret y Alcázar
A Family Saying the Rosary, c.1784
Oil on copper, 570 x 400 mm
Palacio Real, Madrid
10010067

25
Pedro de Acosta
Trompe l'oeil of Prints pinned to a Wall, 1741
Oil on canvas, 1020 x 790 mm
Museo de Bellas Artes, Seville
CE0911P

a wall (fig. 25), intended to demonstrate his skill as a painter, clearly shows how they suffered as a result. In all three paintings the materiality of the print is emphasized, even when it cannot be easily read: the edges of the paper curl and several show signs of damage, a potent reminder of their fragile state and potentially short life. Thus today we are forced to rely upon those prints that do survive, together with occasional images showing prints being put to use, in order to piece together the full story.

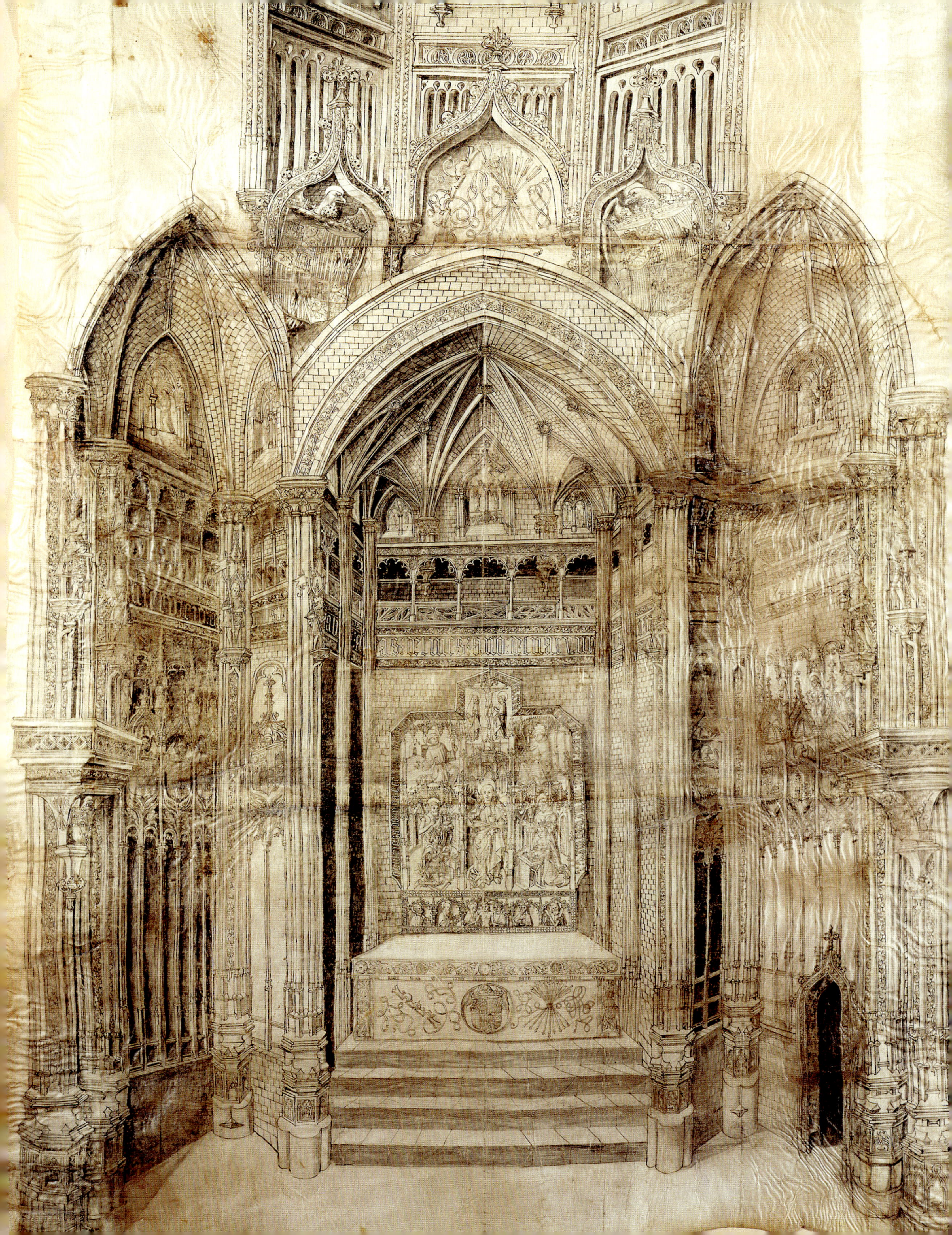

CHAPTER 2

Drawings and prints before 1500 and early collecting in Spain

Drawings

The evidence for drawing in Spain before the middle of the sixteenth century is scarce. Few sheets dating from before 1500 have been identified, and they are so different in appearance and purpose that any attempt to find unifying characteristics requires careful qualification. Moreover, a fundamental problem with identifying these early drawings is that there is little in their character to identify them as Spanish, except the knowledge that they were made in the Iberian Peninsular at a time when it comprised different kingdoms. They are not indicative of a national or local style but of an emerging artistic practice that became much more distinctive later in the sixteenth century.[1] The sheets that date from before 1500 broadly reflect Franco-Flemish and Italian traditions of design; Italian influences dominated after 1500.[2]

The origins of autonomous drawings have been much debated, and sometimes images in manuscripts of the tenth to fifteenth centuries have been regarded as early evidence of drawing in Spain.[3] Although drawing in different forms occurred well before the Renaissance, a distinction must be made between underdrawing serving a directly preparatory function (as in a manuscript illustration, a mural or a panel painting) and drawing in the more creative, independent sense that it is used here.[4] This discussion focuses on drawings having a degree of independent validation as a particular artistic process often associated with an identified artist. The Italian concept of *disegno*, with its dual meaning of design and drawing, is a helpful indicator of independent intention, recognizing as it does the specific elements of intellectual idea and artistic practice.[5] Definitions are invariably challenged by exceptions, and there is no moment when past practices were abandoned and modern drawing in a creative sense was suddenly born. The point at which drawings were recognized as independent objects to be valued, preserved and collected seems however to have been later in Spain than in Italy.

While it is difficult to gauge the extent of drawing in fifteenth-century Spain, from the surviving evidence it seems to have been widespread. They were mainly executed on the durable surface of parchment, intended as independent objects, their intentions different from drawings on paper. The use of pen, ink and paper (a relatively fragile and less expensive material) indicates a significant shift in artistic practice with regard to drawing. Sets of bound drawings were sometimes produced to provide a pictorial archive for artists, and these were usually drawn on parchment to increase their longevity.[6] Unusually, a set of twenty-one pen-and-ink drawings on paper made around 1395–1400 in a Valencia workshop were bound into a model book.[7] These have been associated with at least two artists, the Master of the Retable of San Jorge del

Detail of fig. 4, see p. 49

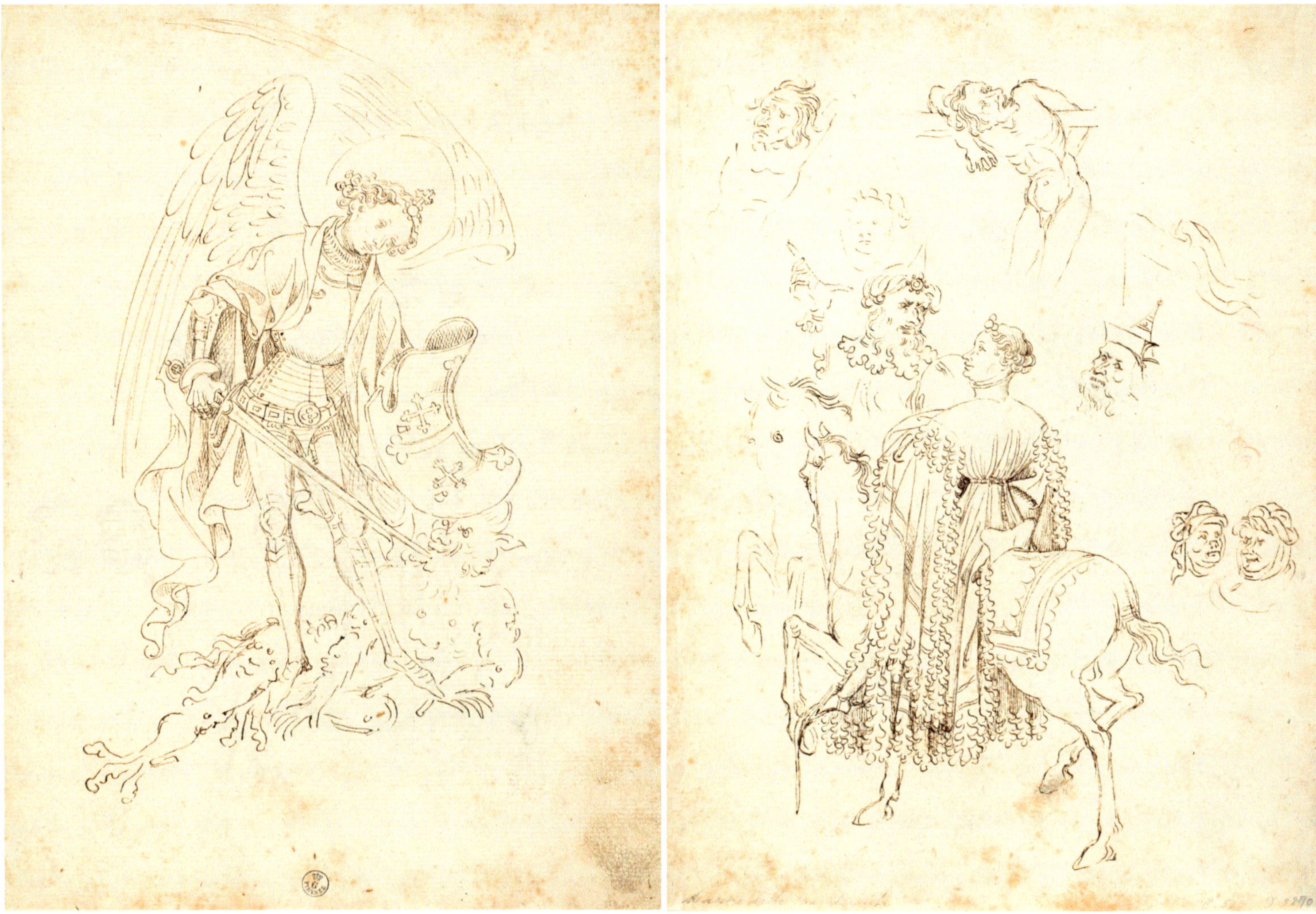

1
Master of the Retable of San Jorge del Centenar / Gherardo Starnina

Archangel Michael (recto); *Various Figures* (verso), *c.*1390–1400

Pen and brown ink, 295 x 211 mm
Gabinetto Disegni e Stampe degli Uffizi, Florence
2270 F

Centenar (Marçal Sax?), documented in Valencia between 1390–1410, and the Florentine Gherardo Starnina, who worked in Valencia and possibly took the model book with him when he returned to Florence in 1404.[8] A drawing of the *Archangel Michael* from this model book (fig. 1, left) shows the figure in simple outline, with some cross-hatching. On the verso are a number of studies of figures that might be put to use in compositions, including heads and a man on a cross (fig. 1, right). The Uffizi model book is most valuable for what it tells us about the dissemination in Valencia of artistic practices normally associated with the north and Italy (particularly Florence) and demonstrates the role of drawing in the workshop.[9]

Other drawings are yet to be discovered, as archival documents often refer to works on paper, mainly in generic terms: 'papers' or 'models on parchment'.[10] The 1418 will of the unknown Valencian painter Bartomeu Salset, for example, refers to 'many papers with drawn images' that were apparently 'of little value'.[11] Similarly, the will of the Mallorcan Rafael Monells (1468) describes a large number of drawings regarded as of no value.[12] The 1428 post-mortem inventory of goods owned by the Valencia painter Joan Vicent records a chest of drawings and other large sheets that might well be model sheets.[13] These brief notices are telling in that they reveal the existence of drawings in Spain during the fifteenth century and demonstrate that they were not considered worthy of preservation as artworks in their own right.[14]

The reliquary with *The Veronica of the Virgin* of about 1398 (fig. 2), attributed to the Valencian silversmith Bartomeu Coscollà, reflects the changes in artistic practice taking place at that time.[15] The Virgin's head is executed in tempera on a sheet of parchment measuring 260 x 225 mm, and the outlines are drawn in ink. Similar heads painted on panel from Catalonia also survive, suggesting that these types of design have a common origin. The artist achieved a striking directness and simplicity in the image on parchment using monochrome tempera, with depth of tone indicated by shading, in a style very different from carefully executed and detailed images often executed on parchment. Over a century later, in 1522, an inventory of silver objects in the Sacristy of Barcelona Cathedral describes a head of Christ, presumably similar to the Veronica, 'drawn on white paper' within an elaborate silver frame set with precious stones.[16]

French architect Maestro Carlí's design for the façade of Barcelona Cathedral of about 1408 was drawn on eight sheets of parchment that when glued together measured 2600 x 1400 mm.[17] Although damage has rendered it almost illegible today, and hence not illustrated here, this key work is one of the earliest large-scale architectural drawings produced in Spain, demonstrating a technique imported by a foreign artist. It was not a preparatory study but a record of a design, a type of drawing that had a long tradition elsewhere in medieval Europe.[18] A number of similar fifteenth-century pen-and-ink designs on paper for altarpieces were attached to contractual documents, such as the large (300 x 220 mm) drawing made in 1461 of the altarpiece in the church of San Juan Bautista de Pompién (Huesca).[19] Whereas most only show the contours of such structures, several, such as the design for the altarpiece in the parish church of Mallén (Zaragoza) of 1506, include carved decorative details with individual figures identified, demonstrating an interest in the combination of elements of the piece.[20]

The use of parchment continued in the fifteenth century. A drawing on parchment by the Florentine-born brothers Dello and Sansone Delli of *Christ at the Column* (fig. 3) of around 1440–60 is unique for its combination of Italian and Franco-Flemish (Northern) styles that defined painting in Spain during the first half of the fifteenth century.[21] The Italian elements include the delicate features of Christ, the receding architecture of the interior and the landscape panorama in the background. The Franco-Flemish characteristics include the angular draperies of the kneeling figures and the banderoles containing prayers in Gothic script. Executed in pen and brown and black carbon ink,

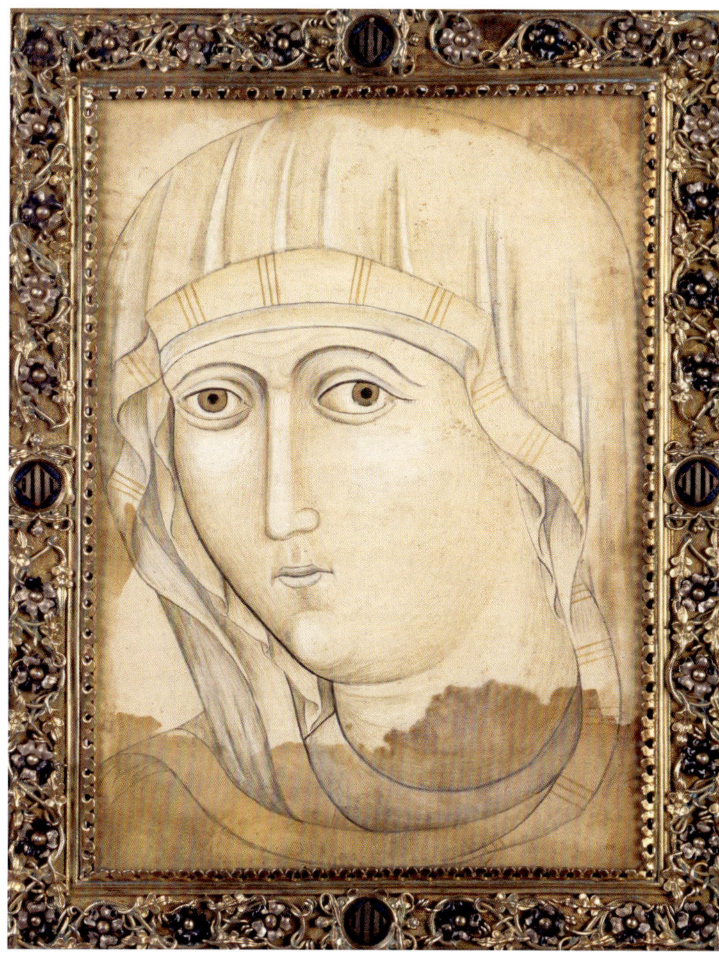

2
Attributed to Bartomeu Coscollà
The Veronica of the Virgin, *c.*1398
Tempera on parchment, 260 x 225 mm
Valencia Cathedral

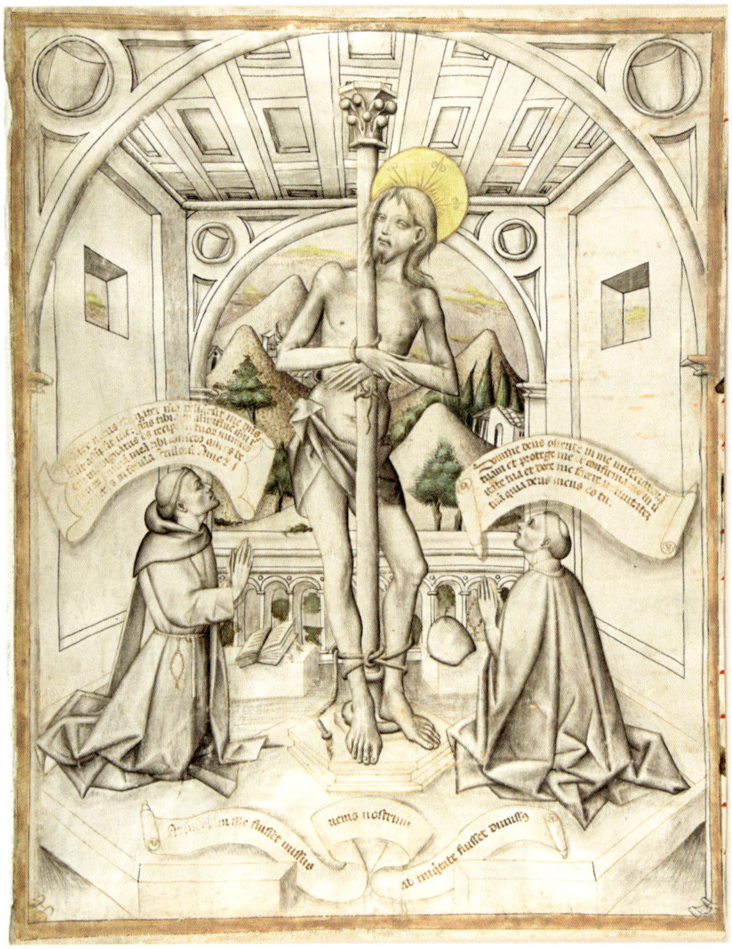

3
Dello and Sansone Delli
Christ at the Column, *c.*1440–60
Pen and brown ink and black carbon ink, brush with grey wash, watercolour and gouache on parchment, 403 x 304 mm
Metropolitan Museum of Art, New York
2004.137

brush with grey wash, watercolour and gouache, the drawing seems to have begun as a preparatory study but was later reworked as an autonomous devotional scene. A less finished drawing might not have been preserved.

A drawing made after 1477 by Juan Guas (*c.*1430–96), a French-born architect who worked and died in Spain, depicts the main chapel of San Juan de los Reyes in Toledo (fig. 4, and detail p. 44), founded by Queen Isabel and King Ferdinand to commemorate their triumph over the Portuguese at Toro in 1476.[22] It is drawn in pen and ink on nine glued sheets of parchment measuring a total of 1880 x 910 mm. The design reflects hybrid architectural styles: the delicacy of Flemish decoration on the large vertical surfaces, and the Mudéjar repetition of motifs (originating with Muslim craftsmen working in Christian territory). The carefully detailed altarpiece, with all the figures rendered recognizable, was not executed as shown here. The drawing has been described as a contractual work, with changes to the design made later,[23] although it is more likely to have been an independent project, a significant work of art separate from its legal role of recording the commission. Its conception is not so different from the Barcelona Cathedral façade, but it reflects a more modern approach to drawing. The sections of greatest importance, the lower part of the chapel and the altar, are rendered in painstaking detail, while other less significant sections, such as the decorative finials in the uppermost section, are less finished, resembling freehand sketches (fig. 5). The use of wash to fill gives the composition a sense of depth. Thus the media of pen, ink and wash were variously used to achieve different effects.

Drawings by Egas Cueman (active 1452–95), a Flemish artist from Brussels working in Spain during the second half of the fifteenth century, demonstrate another function of drawing.[24] Three sheets, one a rejected design of *c.*1478 for the tomb for Alonso de Velasco in Guadalupe, another depicting an angel with a banderole, and the last a detail for a rib vault, were drawn on paper rather than parchment. The drawings carry signatures with elaborate flourishes in the upper corners, presumably because they were related to contracts. Elsewhere, a number of heads and objects drawn in charcoal and black chalk by the Catalan painter Bernat Martorell (active 1427–52) and his workshop can be seen on the back of an altarpiece in the church of San Pedro, Púbol (Girona) commissioned in 1437.[25] The sketch of the head and bust of a woman seem to be preparatory for the figure of the Magdalene on the recto of the predella. Remarkably fresh and spontaneous, the heads are probably drawn from life and relate to the model-book tradition.

The practice of preparatory underdrawing for painting has in recent years become much better understood.[26] Since it is covered in the process of painting, underdrawing functions differently from the independent study, which offers the artist an opportunity to explore ideas before finalizing the composition. The frequent use of underdrawing in fifteenth-century Europe – including Spain – suggests a preparatory process that did not rely on preliminary drawn studies. In the case of Fernando Gallego (active 1468–1507), who worked in Salamanca, the extensive and careful black brush underdrawing detectable in his paintings suggests that this was his only preliminary preparation, and may also indicate why there are no surviving studies for fifteenth-century Spanish panel paintings.[27]

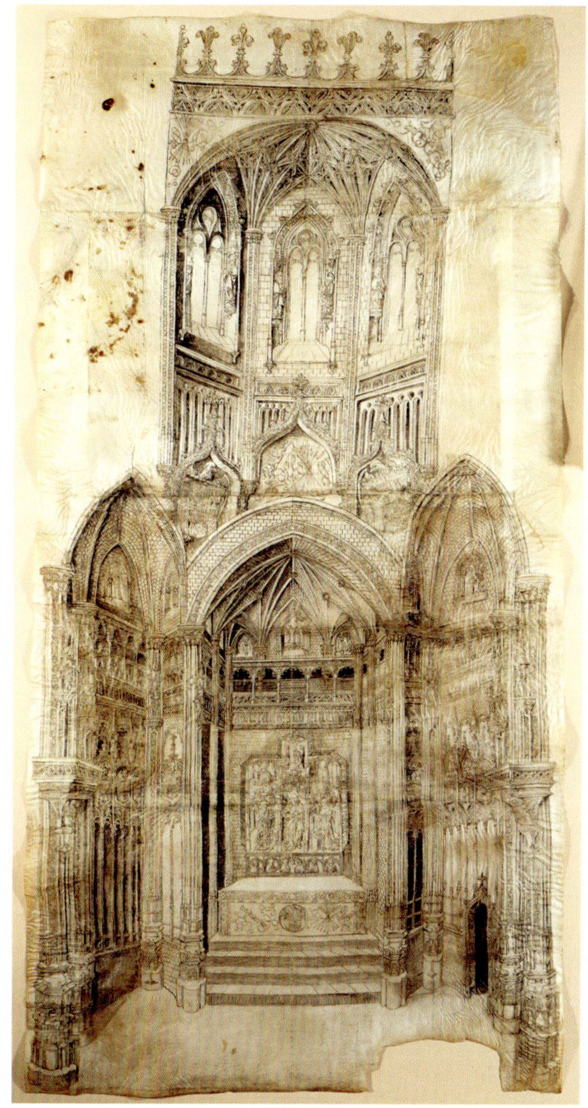

Another factor that undoubtedly had an impact on the development of drawing in late fifteenth-century Spain was the widespread availability of prints, recorded in inventories of shipments from Flanders bound for Spain.[28] The seven panels from the Ciudad Rodrigo altarpiece of the 1480s, painted by Fernando Gallego and Master Bartolomé, for example, borrow from prints by Martin Schongauer and Master IAM of Zwolle.[29] The panel of *The Transfiguration* (fig. 6) contains figures copied from Schongauer's *Saint John the Evangelist on Patmos* (fig. 7): infrared reflectography (fig. 8) reveals that the underdrawing of the altarpiece panels is precise and linear, with areas of cross-hatching closely following the engraving, thus reducing the need for separate preparatory drawings on paper.[30] For other panels of this altarpiece entire prints have been adapted.[31] We cannot rely solely on the evidence of infrared reflectography, however. Cennino Cennini recommends in his *Libro dell'arte* that charcoal be used for the preliminary layer of underdrawing, to be reworked with aqueous medium and the charcoal then brushed away with a feather to leave no trace – invisible even under infrared light.[32]

Most of these examples of drawing as an emerging independent practice were labour-intensive and costly, requiring a commitment in time and expense that far exceeded the freer drawing techniques on paper that developed in the sixteenth century.[33] Documents suggest that far greater numbers of drawings for a wide variety of purposes were made but have not survived. The Delli drawing owes its survival to

4
Juan Guas
The Main Chapel of San Juan de los Reyes, Toledo, c.1477
Brush, pen and black ink on parchment, 1880 x 910 mm
Museo del Prado, Madrid
D.5526

5
Detail of fig. 4
The decorative finials in the uppermost section

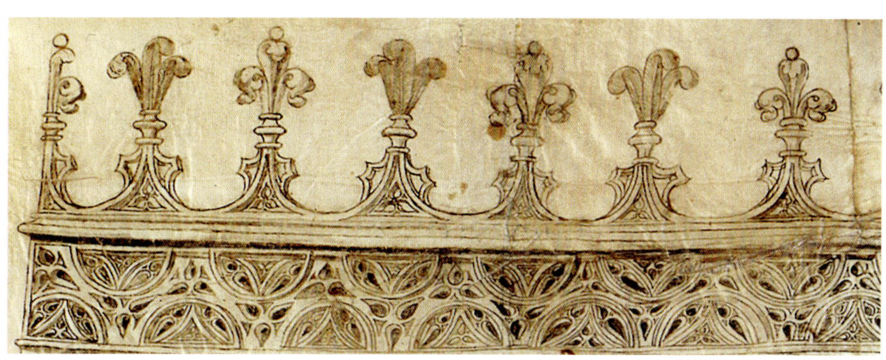

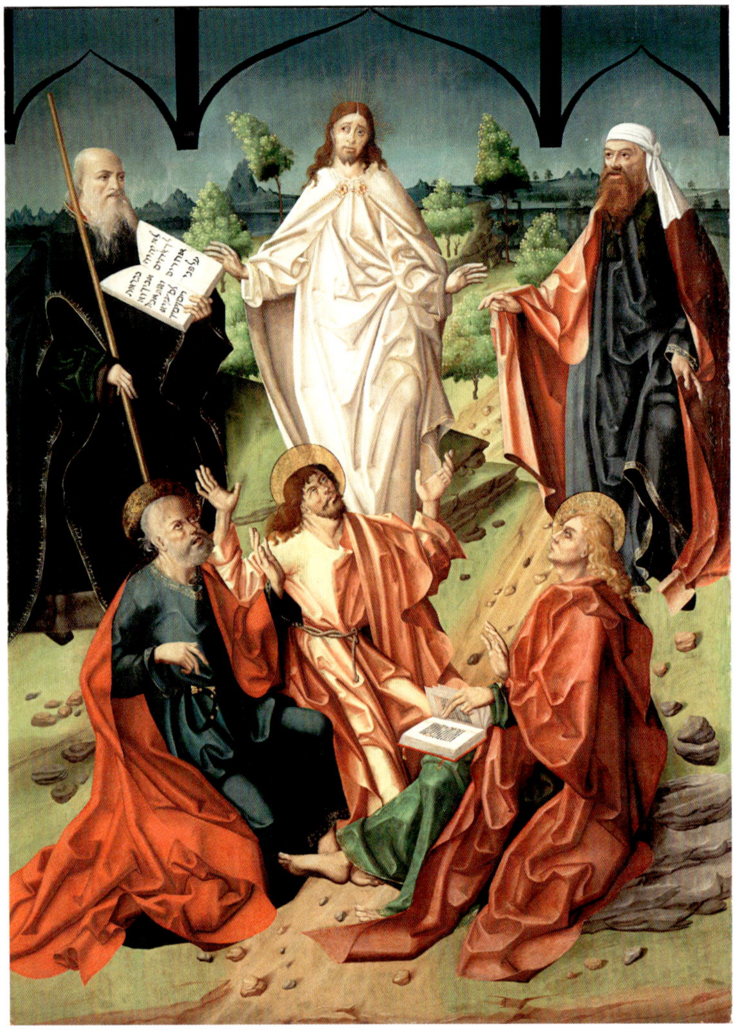

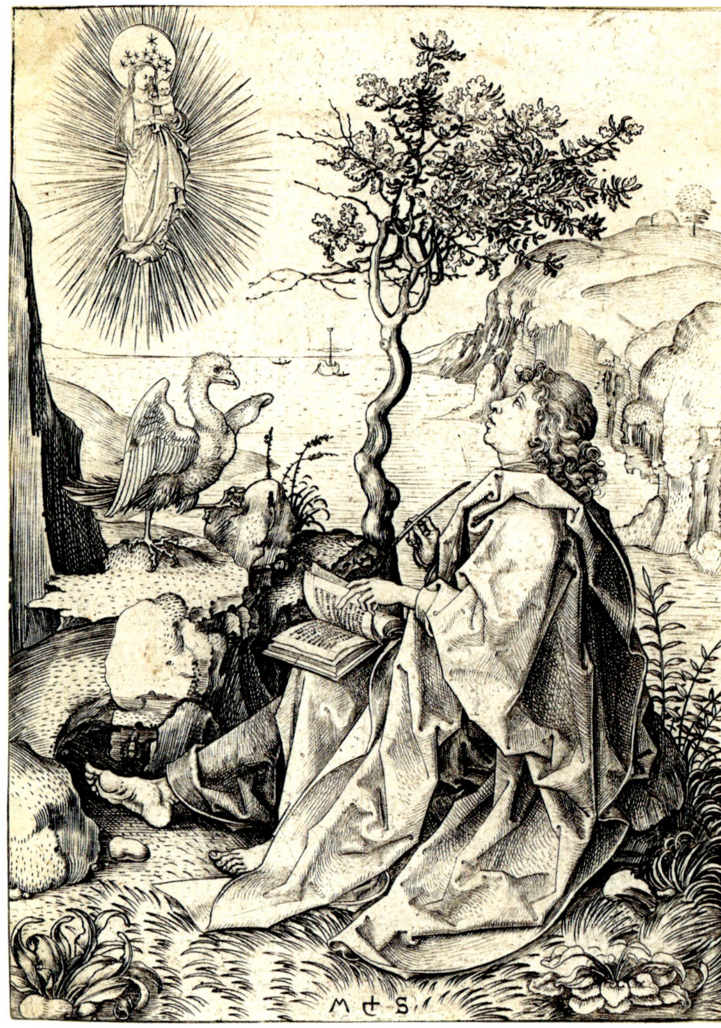

6
Master Bartolomé
The Transfiguration, c.1480–88
Oil on panel, 1540 x 1100 mm
Collection of the University of Arizona Museum of Art and Archive of Visual Arts, Tuscon
1961.013.041

7
Martin Schongauer
Saint John the Evangelist on Patmos, 1469–74
Engraving, 160 x 113 mm
British Museum, London
1845,0809.269

having been pasted into a choir book, while the Barcelona and Guas drawings show clear signs of prolonged folding, suggesting that they, too, were carefully stored away in order to preserve them.

1500 is a convenient year to conclude this discussion of early drawing in Spain, and turn briefly to its closely related disciplines of printmaking and the art of the book. The dawn of the new century brought noticeable changes in drawing practices. These are reflected in the increasing number and variety of drawings that survive, discussed by region of origin in later chapters of the present volume.

Prints

The cultural reforms introduced by Isabel of Castile extended to her direct intervention in trade regulations, such as the abolition of duties on books in 1480. This had an enormously positive effect on the printing industry,[34] since the origins of printmaking in Spain lie mainly in book illustration.[35]

Printmaking first made its appearance in the Iberian Peninsular when printing houses were established in Valencia and Segovia around 1470 and shortly after in Barcelona, Zaragoza and Zamora.[36] During the course of the next two decades, all the major towns acquired printing presses. With few exceptions, from about 1480 to the third quarter of the sixteenth century Spanish prints were mainly woodcut book illustrations. The earliest wood engravers and printers in Spain were foreigners, and they were responsible for most of the Spanish *incunabula* (books printed before 1501). Among the most important were Arnao Guillén de Brocar (active 1489–1523), a Frenchman who worked mainly in Alcalá de Henares and Logroño;[37] Jorge Coci (active around the end of the fifteenth century), a German who worked in Zaragoza;[38] and Coci's fellow countrymen the Crombergers, in Seville.[39] The contribution made by immigrants to printmaking in the Peninsular and their influence on the development of local industries has long been recognized. It was their expertise that gave the initial impetus for more ambitious printmaking.

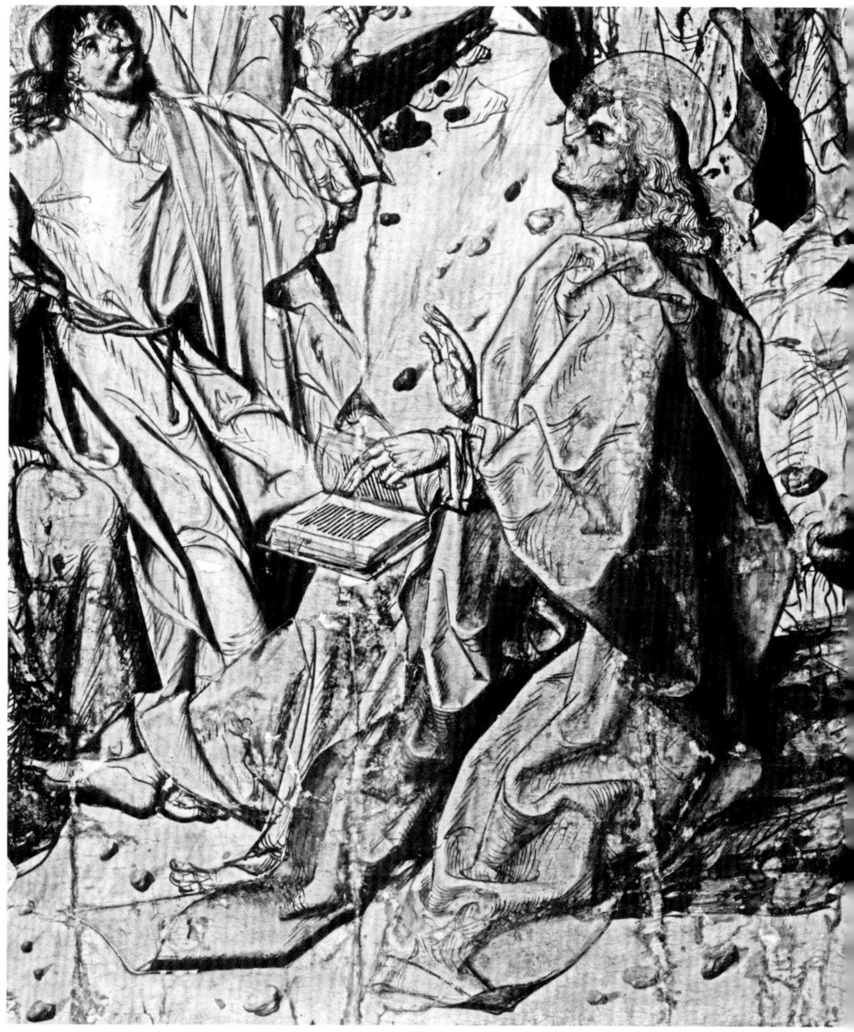

8
Infrared reflectogram mosaic of fig. 6

In the early woodcuts by immigrant engravers stylistic characteristics from their countries of origin are evident.[40] Some printers, such as Jorge Coci, are known to have sent to their homelands for pre-cut blocks that were then printed in Spain.[41] Prints cut by Spanish engravers took on foreign characteristics, such as the illustrations to the *Cárcel de amor*, cut by Diego de San Pedro and printed by Juan Rosenbach in Barcelona in 1493, which indicate a familiarity with Italian Renaissance styles, especially in the dress of the figures.[42] In other prints foreign influence is more generalized. A splendid example of this is *King Juan II on Horseback* (fig. 9) from Fernán Pérez de Guzmán's *Cronica del serenissimo rey don Juan Segundo* (1517), a print is made from several blocks with the lettering in red ink.[43]

During the first half of the sixteenth century the main centres of book production in Spain were Salamanca, Valladolid, Zaragoza and Seville.[44] These large towns all contained teaching institutions and therefore a cultivated and professional class who bought books. One of the best-known books published in Spain in many editions was the *Flos Sanctorum* (*Lives of the Saints*), an early edition of which was published by Coci in Zaragoza in 1521. The elaborately ornamented border of the title page and the illustrations that appear in many editions mark a significant advance in woodcut design and set a new standard – the highly decorated border was to become a characteristic of Spanish printing. It was not until the last quarter of the century that printmaking of any note made an appearance in Madrid, when in 1566 Pierre Cosin and Alonso Gómez established the first press there.[45]

Several examples survive of early Spanish metalcut printing, in which an impression is made using a metal plate. These mark an important stage in the history of printmaking in Spain demonstrating the development of prints other than for book illustration.[46] An anonymous metalcut (fig. 10) from about 1454 depicts Death in the lower left shooting down people from all walks of life, a common fifteenth-century theme.[47] An engraving of similar date portrays Prince Carlos Viana (fig. 11).[48] Its large size (platemark 295 x 220 mm) immediately sets it apart from anything else to have survived from Spain during the fifteenth century and calls into question its function. As suggested by the lettering along the bottom, it is a type of commemorative or honorific print dedicated to a living person. The coats of arms in the upper corners (the Two Sicilies at left and Barcelona at right) are partly coloured. Given the unornamented sections of the sheet (such as the canopy coffering and the background), it is possible that the print was intended for hand colouring to serve a more elevated purpose, perhaps similar to a panel painting.[49]

Of the surviving single-leaf prints, few are signed, an exception being two signed by the Dominican monk Francisco Doménech, who worked in Barcelona and Valencia in the second half of the fifteenth century. *The Virgin*

9
Anonymous
King Juan II on Horseback, 1517
Woodcut printed in red and black, 270 x 189 mm
British Library, London
G.6283

10
Anonymous
Death Shooting Down the Human Race, c.1454
Metalcut, 220 x 118 mm
Biblioteca Nacional, Madrid
42639

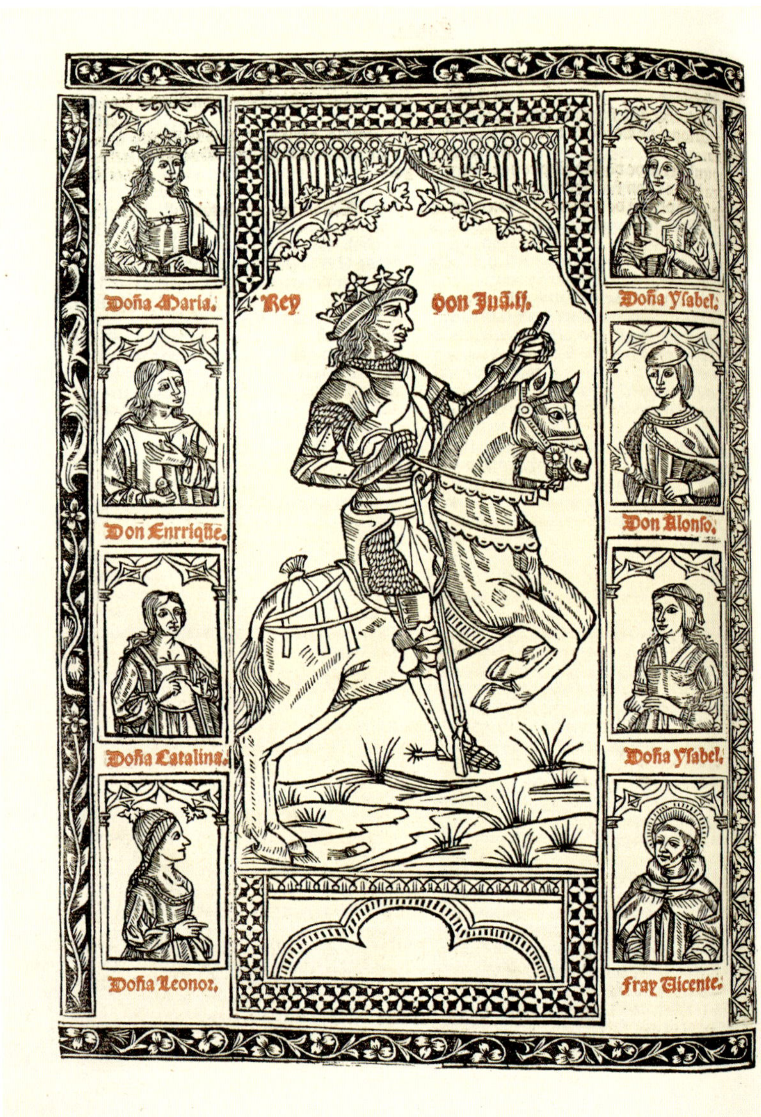

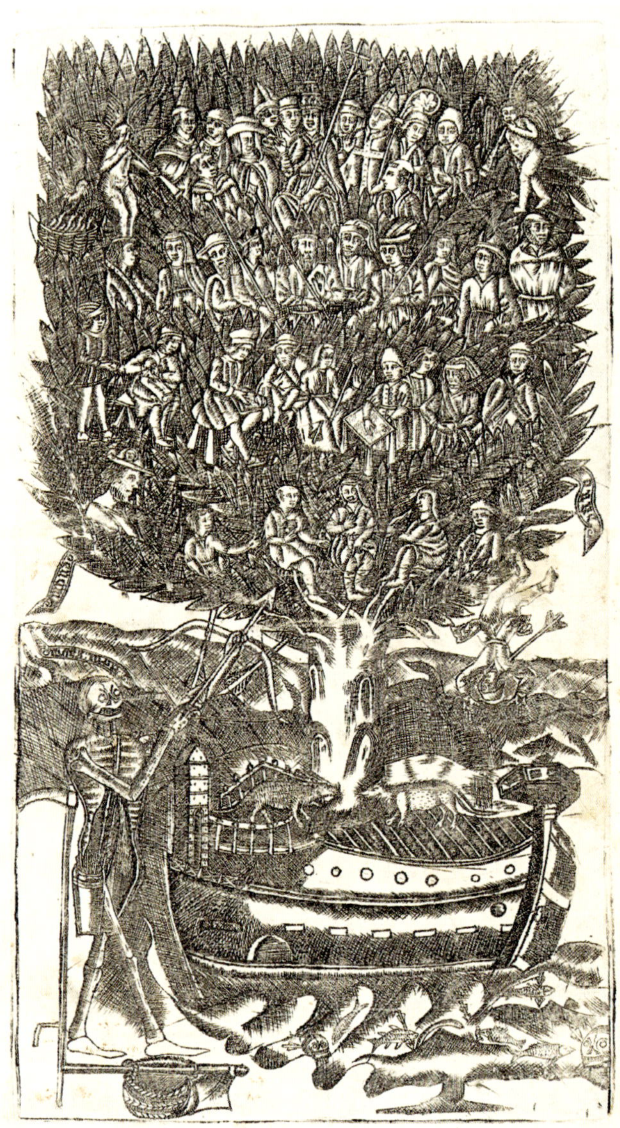

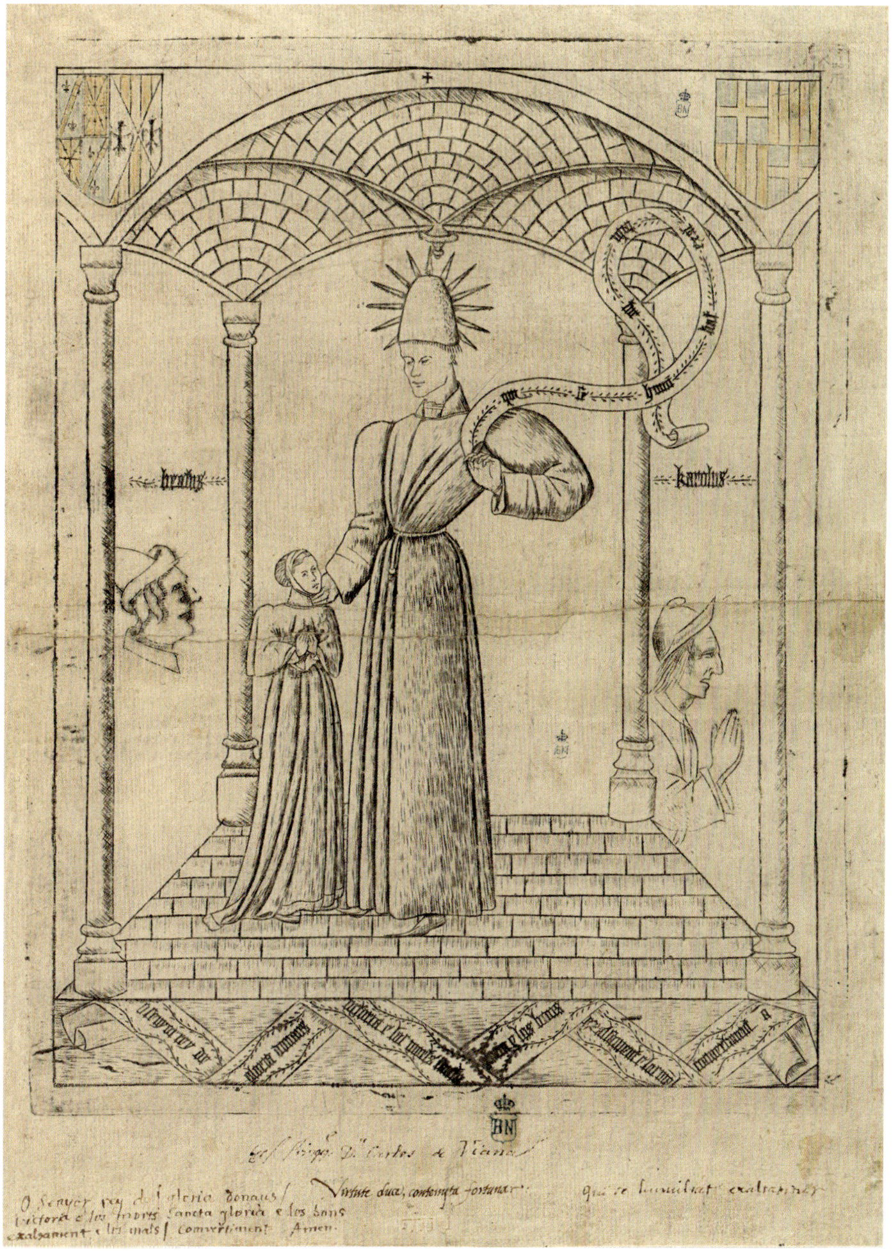

11
Anonymous
Prince Carlos Viana, *c.*1461
Engraving with hand colouring, 295 x 220 mm
Biblioteca Nacional, Madrid
42365

of the Rosary (fig. 12), for example, is signed 'fº Domenec (A d S) 1488'.[50] A slightly abbreviated form of his signature with the same date occurs on the print of Saint Anthony Abbot.[51] These prints reveal a range of functions and subject matter reflecting the versatility and new possibilities of printmaking.

By the middle of the sixteenth century book production in Spain was a highly developed and organized industry employing large numbers of designers and cutters. In other parts of Europe, single-sheet copper-plate prints had become the main focus of printmaking, having developed alongside book illustration. Single-sheet printing had major commercial and artistic advantages and, although it did not develop independently in Spain until much later, there is clear evidence of its importance as a source for artists and collectors in Spain at this date (see Chapter 1).

12
Francisco Doménech
The Virgin of the Rosary, 1488
Metalcut, 415 x 325 mm
Biblioteca Nacional, Madrid
42364

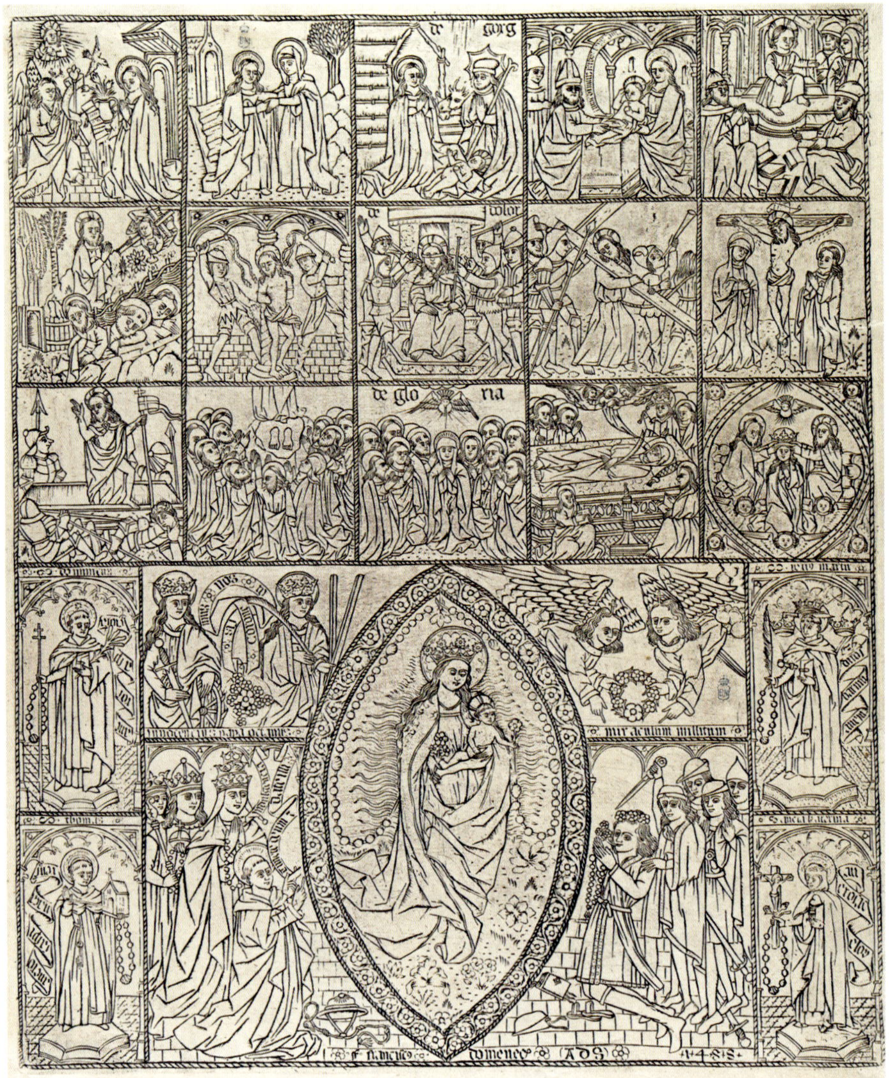

Early collecting of prints and drawings in Spain

It is clear from evidence of growing collections in Spain in the early sixteenth century that prints and drawings were highly regarded. The print collection of Ferdinand Columbus (1488–1539), illegitimate son of Christopher Columbus, is known through an inventory in the Columbus Archive and Library in Seville.[52] The inventory describes in careful detail 3,200 prints (engravings, woodcuts and maps) bought by Ferdinand during his travels around Europe, mainly on diplomatic missions for the Spanish Hapsburgs. The prints are arranged and described in the inventory according to the size of the sheet, its subject and the number of figures in an image.[53] This is the only known surviving inventory of a print collection from the first half of the century, and it has recently been used to identify and publish prints by many of the major European printmakers, including Albrecht Dürer, Lucas Cranach, Lucas van Leyden, Urs Graf, Marcantonio Raimondi and Giovanni Battista Palumba. Around half of the prints described in the inventory no longer appear to survive in any impression. Only two prints listed, of the Virgin of Monserrat accompanied by motets in Castilian, were possibly made in Spain, which suggests the absence of a single-sheet print industry.[54]

The inclusion of prints and drawings in Spanish collections was more widespread than previously thought. Another collector and member of the court of Charles V, Mencía de Mendoza, Marquesa de Zenete (1508–54), was an indefatigable collector of tapestries, jewellery, medals, paintings, books and objects from the New World.[55] Her inventories reveal a significant number of prints and drawings but these were integrated into her broader collections rather than forming a separate category. After she married Hendrik III of Nassau, in 1524 Mencía moved from Spain to the Netherlands, where printmaking was thriving. Albrecht Dürer had spent time in the Low Countries in 1520–1, promoting and selling his prints, which were by then very well known.[56] Artists' names are rarely recorded in Mencía's inventories, but descriptions of the subjects of the works in her collection give an indication of their remarkable range, from what we now regard as artists' prints to ephemeral objects made from paper, including printed maps, genealogies, portraits, a small paper altar and drawings of fabric designs.[57] The drawings seem to have had a utilitarian function, recording, for example, designs and plans to be consulted, rather than reflecting the activity or interests of a specialist collector like Ferdinand Columbus. One entry describes a master drawing or model for a cage, probably an elaborate birdcage, for the garden of her palace in Breda erected around 1536.[58] Mencía was closely involved with the design, drawn by an artist referred to only as 'Felipus'. It is likely that the prints in her collection, on the other hand, were by known printmakers. For example, the description '… pintura del gran turco en papel', no doubt Süleyman the Magnificent, possibly refers to the woodcut of him attributed to Erhard Schön after Georg Pencz (after 1530), of which coloured impressions still survive.[59] Another entry describes a print from five sheets of Our Lady of Monserrat, a large print probably glued together. We will never know more about the entries that describe, for example, 'another chest with many drawings', but we are here reminded of references to drawings in artists' inventories mentioned earlier.[60]

It is not known how many prints Mencía owned, but they were probably collected for what they represented. Like Columbus, she collected books, many of them illustrated. Titles in her collection include Albrecht Dürer's *Institutionum Geometricarum*, which refers to the *Four Books on Human Proportion* published in Nuremberg in 1528; the edition of Ptolemy's *Geographia* published by Francesco Berlinghieri in Florence in 1482 under the title 'Geographia de Francisco Verlinguero florentino'; and Bordone's *Isolaria* (*Book of Islands*) published in Venice in 1528 as *Benedetto Bordone de le isole del mondo en Italia*. These last two were lavishly illustrated with engravings, and Mencía could hardly have failed to be impressed by them.

In the fifteenth and early sixteenth centuries prints and drawings had not evolved into separate artistic categories in Spain: they are referred to in contemporary documents as 'images', without details of medium. Emerging technologies are characterized by experimentation and the examples discussed above testify to the recognition of the benefits of paper and parchment. This was matched by increasing artistic ambition in the sixteenth century, which made both prints and drawings a more recognizable feature of the artistic landscape in their own right.

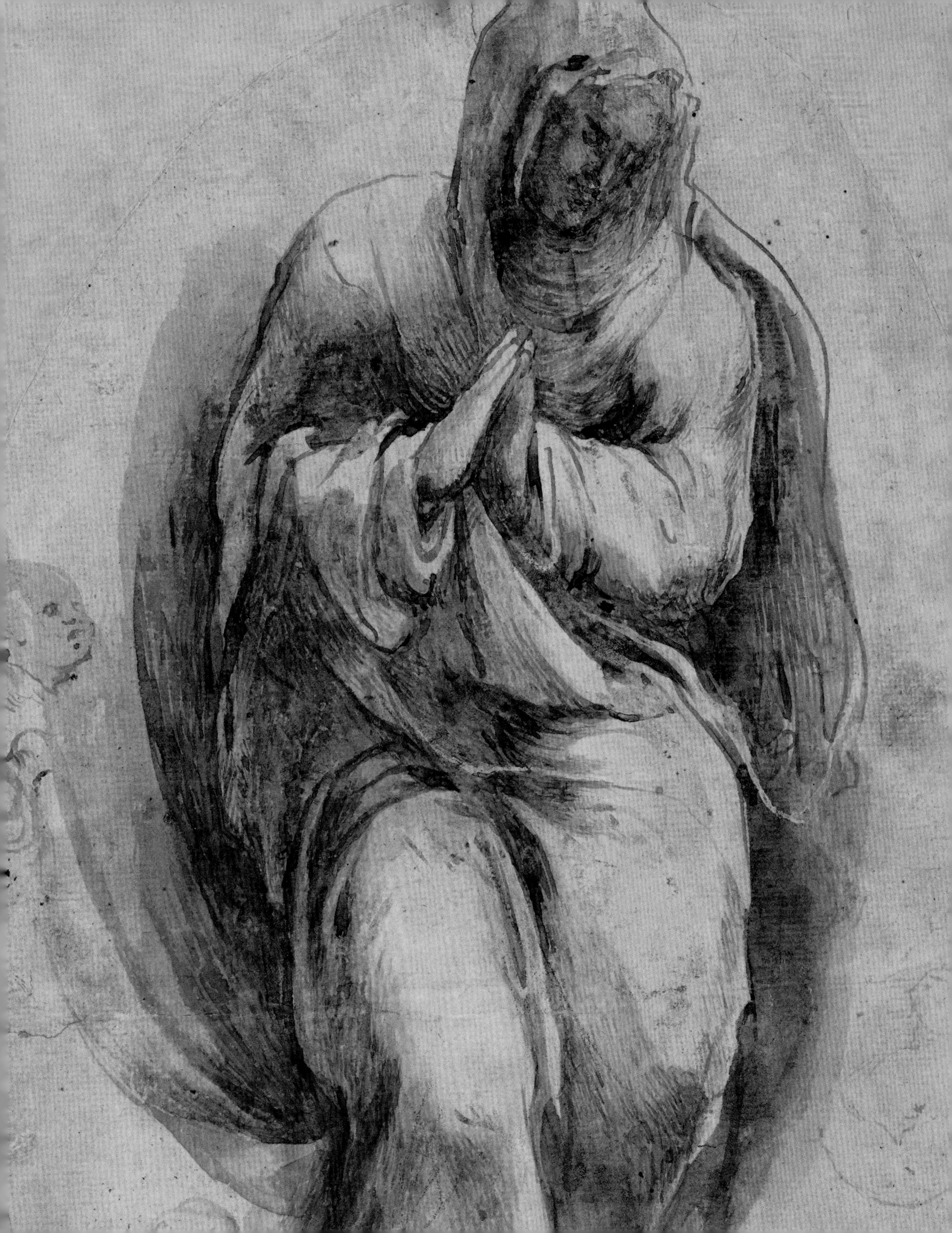

CHAPTER 3

Importing graphic practices: Castile 1550–1600

In October 1555 Charles made Philip ruler of the Netherlands, and in January 1556 King of Spain. Four years later, in 1561, Philip II installed the first permanent court at Madrid. This established the town as a centre of political power and the base from which the Spanish monarchy governed its empire. By the end of the century Madrid had undergone a dramatic transformation thanks to a tremendous increase in population and size.[1] It became a magnet for different trades, professional groups and administrative offices. The effect that Philip II had on the development of culture in Madrid has long been recognized. His patronage of foreign and Spanish-born artists to decorate his residences and his dedication to collecting signalled a new era in Spain.[2]

Before returning to Spain in August 1559, Philip had spent five years extensively touring Europe to familiarize himself with the territories under his rule. His visits during this period to palaces, noble residences and monasteries laid the foundation for his lifelong interest in architecture, and helped him crystallize plans to build a significant monument. The monastery-palace of the Escorial, 50 km north-west of Madrid, was to be the greatest architectural achievement of Philip's reign and has played a central role in Spain's history since it was built. Begun in 1563, the Escorial was the designated burial chamber of the Hapsburg dynasty. The need to find a suitable burial place for Charles V, whose body lay at the Hieronymite monastery at Yuste in Estremadura, was uppermost in Philip's mind during the planning stages of the project. It was to become not only the symbolic bastion of Catholicism, but also a lasting monument to Philip's name and the repository for his vast collections of art, relics and natural objects, and his library. The personal significance of the monastery for Philip is also revealed by its dedication to Saint Lawrence in recognition of the Spanish victory over the French at the battle of St Quentin, on the saint's feast day of 10 August 1557, at which the king was present.[3]

The principal designer of the monastery, Juan Bautista de Toledo (*c.*1515–67), had been called to Madrid from Naples and appointed Royal Architect in 1559 to renovate Philip's existing residences.[4] In August 1563 he was made master of the Escorial fabric. In the same year Juan de Herrera was appointed a draughtsman in his office; he became chief in 1579.[5] The extensive surviving documentation reveals that Philip worked closely with Juan Bautista from the initial stages of planning and monitored the project throughout the twenty-one years it took to build.[6] The most important record is that of the historian and librarian Fray José de Sigüenza, whose *La fundación del monasterio de El Escorial* (1605) provides a detailed account of the monastery's construction and decoration, and often includes a critique of the works of art. The

Detail of fig. 14, see p. 67

construction of the Escorial required a workforce of almost a thousand men, including engineers, architects and artists from across Europe.

The time Philip had spent outside Spain during his youth and the influence of his father, Charles V, and his aunt, Mary of Hungary, shaped his taste for art from abroad. He had seen the work of some of the best Flemish and Italian artists and was eager to augment his collections with similar pieces. His favourite artist, Titian, provided him with paintings until the artist's death in 1576.[7] Works by Titian and other Venetian artists including Veronese, Bassano, Tintoretto, and Sebastiano del Piombo, as well as those of Northern artists such as Albrecht Dürer and Joachim Patinir, formed the basis of his collection.[8] Philip also employed artists to work at the Escorial, some of them Spanish by birth, others Italian and Flemish. The Flemish portraitist Antonis Mor returned to Spain with Philip in 1559, and proceeded to set the standard for court portraiture. He trained the Spaniard Alonso Sánchez Coello, who continued his manner after Mor returned to the north.[9] Philip's choice of Italian artists was guided by their facility as fresco painters. The renowned Italian painters Federico Zuccaro, Pellegrino Tibaldi and Luca Cambiaso executed most of the major fresco programmes at the Escorial.[10] These practitioners from overseas had significant impact on printmaking and drawing in Spain through the artistic practices they introduced.

Drawing at the Escorial

The Italian artists brought in to decorate the Escorial and Spanish royal residences in the second half of the sixteenth century were active draughtsmen, and drawing played an important part in their training and their working methods. Their drawings for these Spanish projects had a lasting impact on those working alongside them, and on future generations of artists.

The Italian drawing tradition of *disegno* enabled artists to express their thoughts on paper,[11] to experiment and explore aspects of design as a preparatory stage in the process of creating a work of art. This practice, born in fifteenth-century Italy and subsequently developed in the academies, was carried out by sculptors, painters and architects alike and transcended the divisions between their different disciplines. It was not until some time later that drawing became widespread in Spain (see Chapter 1).

The Italian artists Francesco da Urbino (*c.*1545–82) and Giovanni Battista Castello ('il Bergamasco', *c.*1509–69) were among the earliest to arrive in Spain, in 1567.[12] Castello, who was appointed Philip II's court architect and painter, was in charge of a large workshop of artists and craftsmen at the Escorial, and from there he organized the pictorial and decorative programmes of the monastery and other royal residences. These projects required drawings for the planning, recording and dissemination of the designs. Philip insisted from the outset on drawn designs for the Escorial because they allowed him to oversee its construction, control expenses and ensure that no changes were made after he had given his approval.[13] No architectural drawings by Castello survive and figurative studies by him are few, but a double-sided sheet depicting *Mars and Apollo* (fig. 1), thought to be from his time in Spain, clearly shows the influence of Perino del Vaga, who came to Genoa after training in Raphael's Roman studio.[14] More is known of Francesco da Urbino, who assisted Castello in decorating the Alcázar in Madrid. After Castello died in

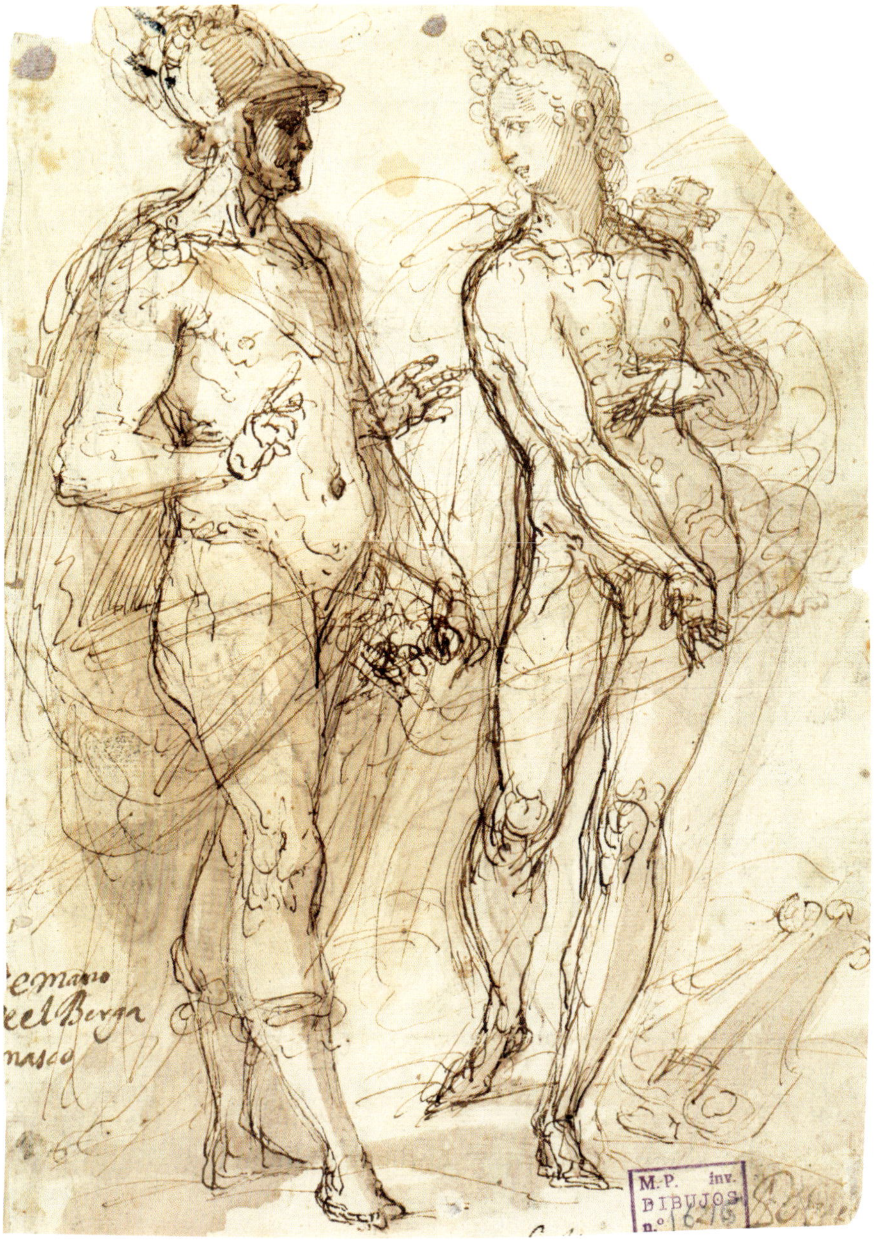

1
Giovanni Battista Castello
Mars and Apollo, c.1566/7–9
Pen and brown ink and brown wash, 255 x 173 mm
Museo del Prado, Madrid
D.1856 (recto)

1569, Urbino worked with the latter's brother before going to the Escorial in 1575; he remained here until his death in 1582.[15]

More than twenty studies by Urbino and his assistants survive for his fresco *The Judgement of Solomon* (fig. 2) painted in the Prior's Cell at the Escorial around 1581, along with others showing individual figures of prophets and biblical figures for the lunettes.[16] The drawings provide the most valuable information we have for the complex process of fresco decoration in Spain. *The Executioners with the Living Child* (fig. 3), drawn in chalk and wash on blue prepared paper, is a highly finished scaled presentation cartoon made to demonstrate the artist's composition and drawing skills, and was not intended to be used for the transfer of the design.[17] Other drawings, or 'substitute cartoons', probably by an assistant, were traced from Urbino's drawing to record the main outlines of the figures (fig. 4).[18] These sheets have been squared in red chalk, the outlines pricked for transfer: the remains of charcoal

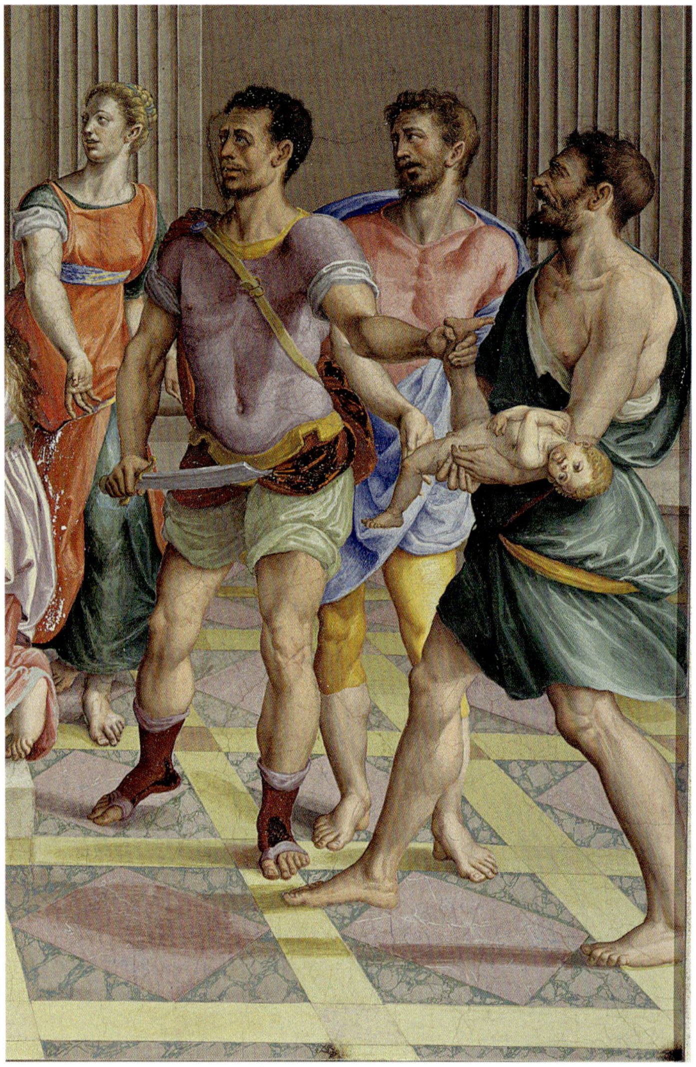

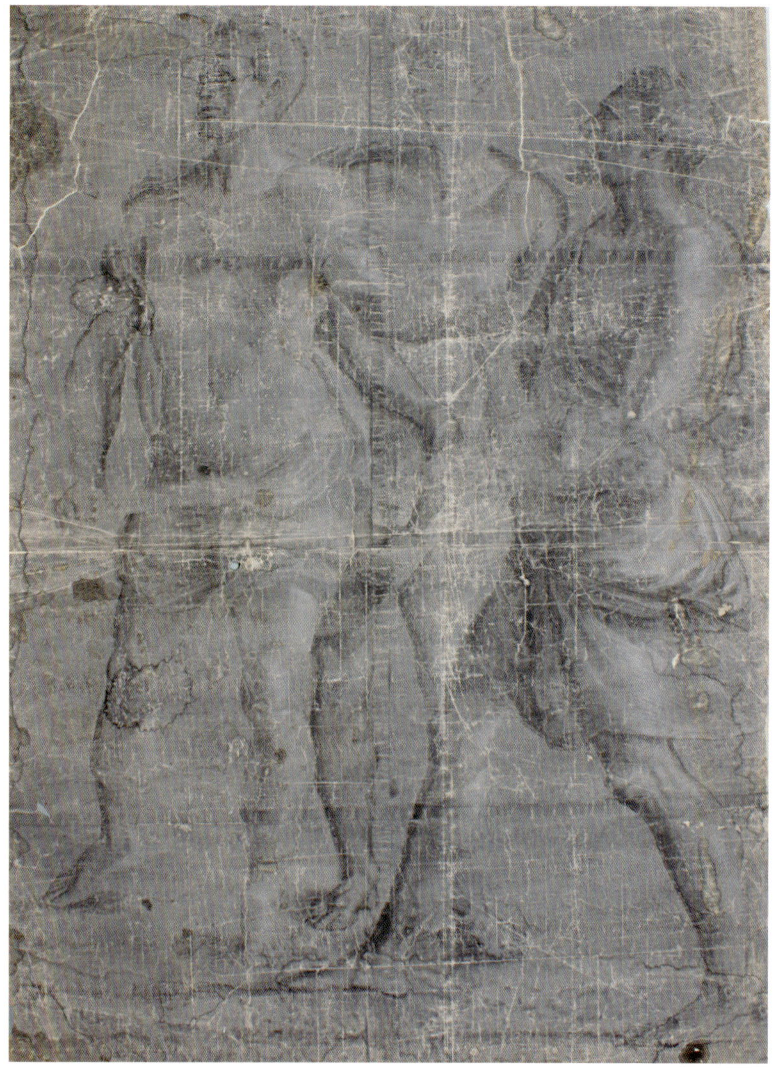

2
Francesco da Urbino
The Judgement of Solomon (detail), c.1581
Fresco
Real Monasterio de San Lorenzo de El Escorial

3
Francesco da Urbino
The Executioners with the Living Child (presentation cartoon), c.1581
Black chalk and wash with white highlights on prepared paper, 1590 x 1250 mm
Real Monasterio de San Lorenzo de El Escorial
D-34

dusted through the lines is visible on the verso.[19] Other fragments of the same composition (not joined) are also squared and pricked and were used to transfer the design to the wall (fig. 5).[20] A pen-and-ink study of a prophet for another part of the same fresco represents an early stage of Urbino's design, where he was resolving how the figure would relate to the corner of the architecture as seen from below (fig. 6).[21]

The Genoese artist Luca Cambiaso (1527–85) was brought to Spain at the end of 1583 specifically to paint frescos, but when he arrived he began by painting four large altarpieces for the Escorial basilica.[22] The drawings for the commission show his unmistakable geometric style (fig. 7). Other drawings he prepared for his fresco of the *Gloria* in the vault are executed in the same manner. After Cambiaso's death, the cosmopolitan painter and architect Pellegrino Tibaldi (1527–96) was appointed Architect to his Majesty in 1586.[23] It was difficult to convince Tibaldi to come to Spain but his fresco decoration in the *Sagrario* behind the main altar in the basilica was Philip's favourite work among all the Italian decorations.[24] Tibaldi prepared drawings for all of his work at the Escorial. His *Christ Presented to the People* (fig. 8) is a highly finished squared drawing for the fresco in the cloister painted

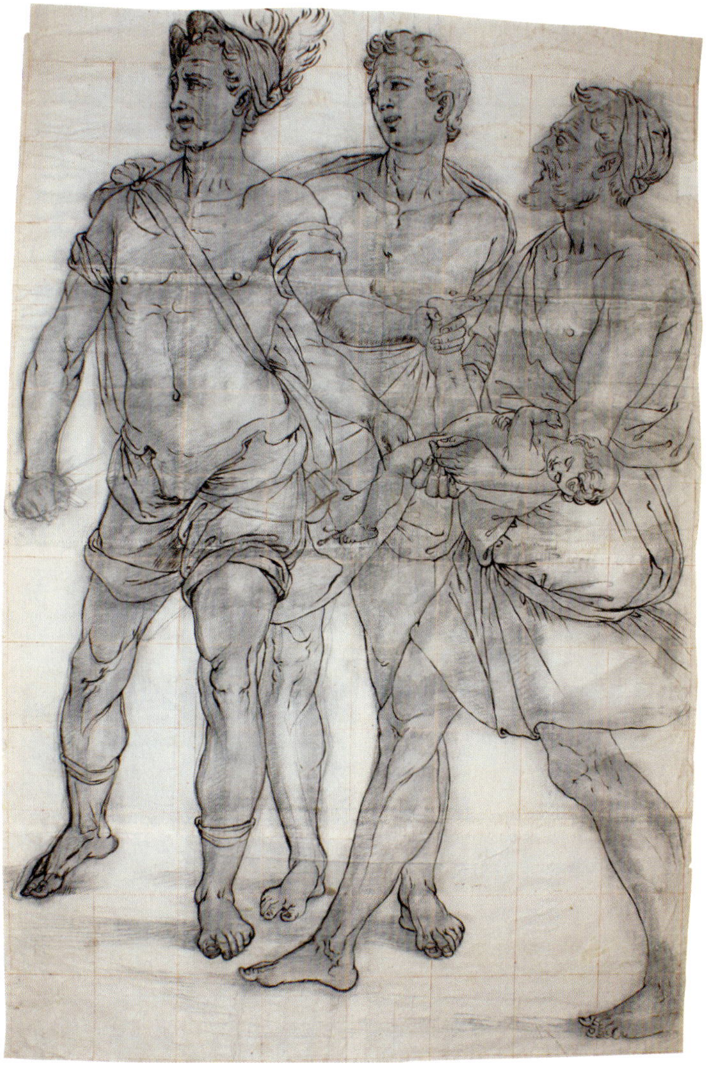

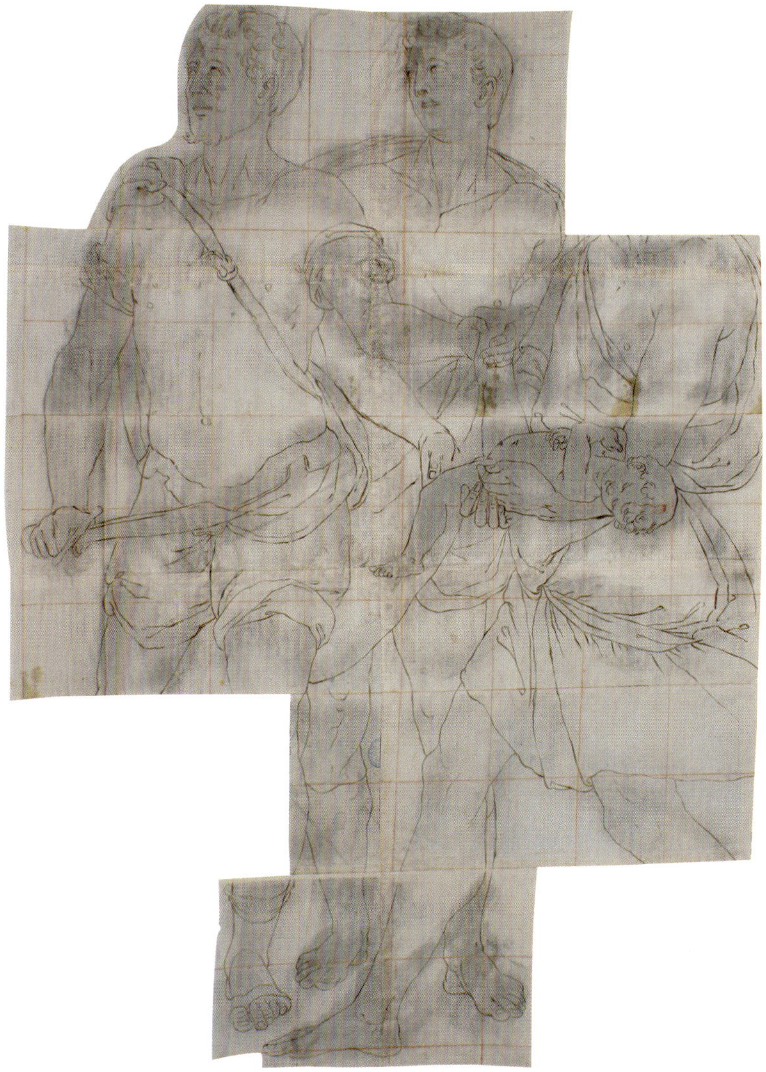

between 1587 and 1590. It is more a model for the fresco than a working drawing, conveying exactly how the details were to appear.[25] Tibaldi's study for the decoration of the Library of the Escorial (fig. 9) is a very different type of working drawing.[26] It does not correspond with any particular section of the decoration but is made up of various elements that appear in the bays. The extensive annotations, by Tibaldi in Italian and by the architect Juan de Herrera in Spanish, detail how the space and dividing elements, such as pilasters, should be decorated. The drawing is of considerable interest because it gives a clear indication of the complicated process by which a decorative scheme of this kind was brought to completion.

The most renowned Italian artist employed by Philip II was Federico Zuccaro (*c.*1542–1609). He arrived from Rome in December 1585 and worked at the Escorial for three years, where he painted the high altarpiece of the basilica, the reliquary altars on both sides and the frescoes in the cloister. Zuccaro's work did not please Philip, mainly, it seems, because the iconography did not agree with his sense of decorum.[27] Several of Zuccaro's drawings for his Escorial projects survive.[28] *The Pentecost* (fig. 10) is a large finished study for the painted composition on the upper story of the high altar, but with some

4
After Francesco da Urbino
The Executioners with the Living Child (subsitute cartoon), *c.*1581
Brown ink and brush for figures, rubbed with charcoal, squared for transfer, pricked, 1590 x 1250 mm
Real Monasterio de San Lorenzo de El Escorial
D-30

5
After Francesco da Urbino
The Executioners with the Living Child (transfer cartoon), *c.*1581
Brown ink and brush for figures, rubbed with charcoal, squared for transfer, pricked, 1430 x 1010 mm
Real Monasterio de San Lorenzo de El Escorial
D-29

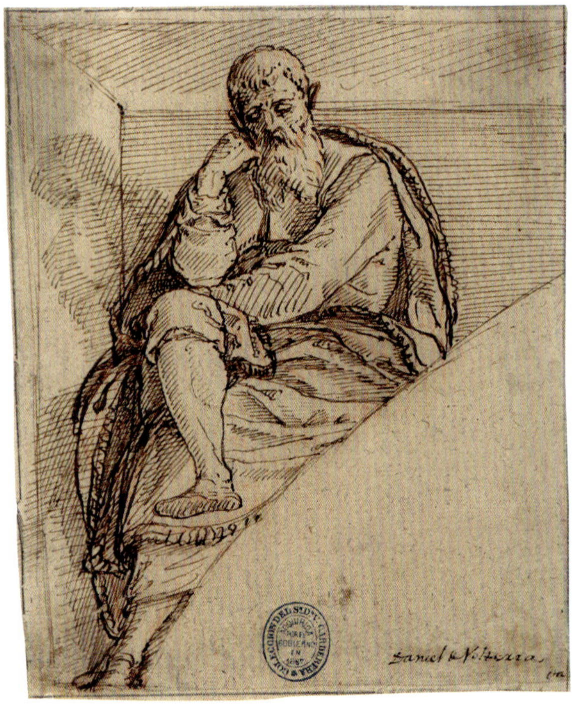

6
Francesco da Urbino
Study of a Prophet, c.1581
Pen and brown ink with touches of red chalk, 185 x 145 mm
Biblioteca Nacional, Madrid
DIB/15/13/15

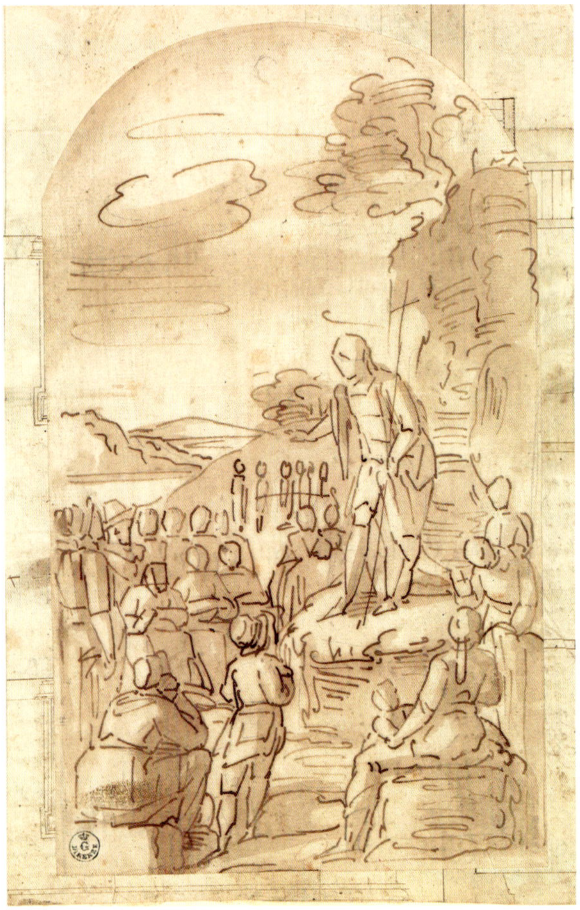

7
Luca Cambiaso
Saint John the Baptist Preaching, 1583–4
Pen and brown ink and brown wash over black chalk, 370 x 235 mm
Gabinetto Disegni e Stampe degli Uffizi, Florence
13756 F

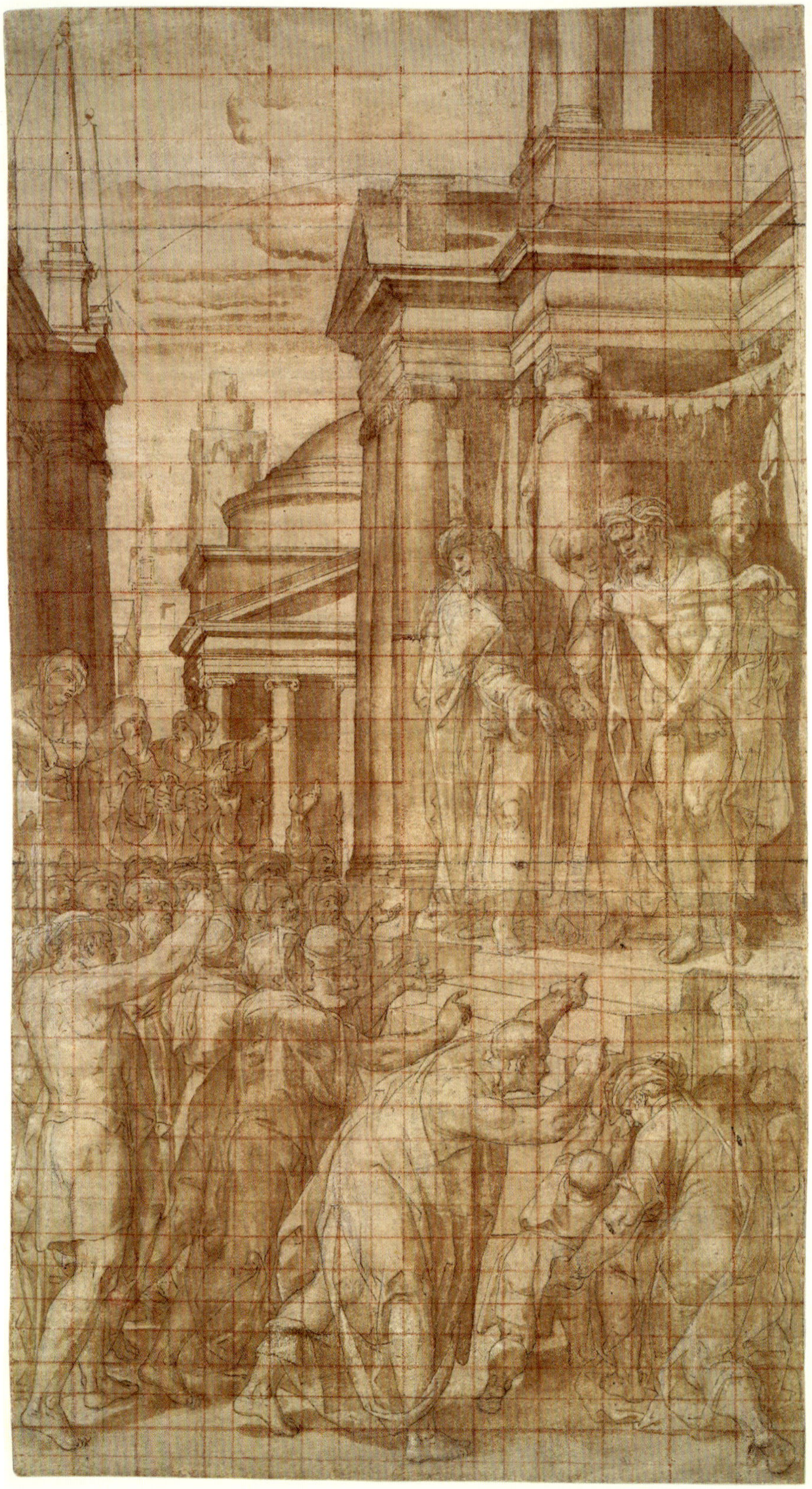

8
Pellegrino Tibaldi
Christ Presented to the People, 1587–90
Pen and brown ink and brown wash over black chalk, heightened with white, squared for transfer, 548 x 293 mm
British Museum, London
1946,0713.608

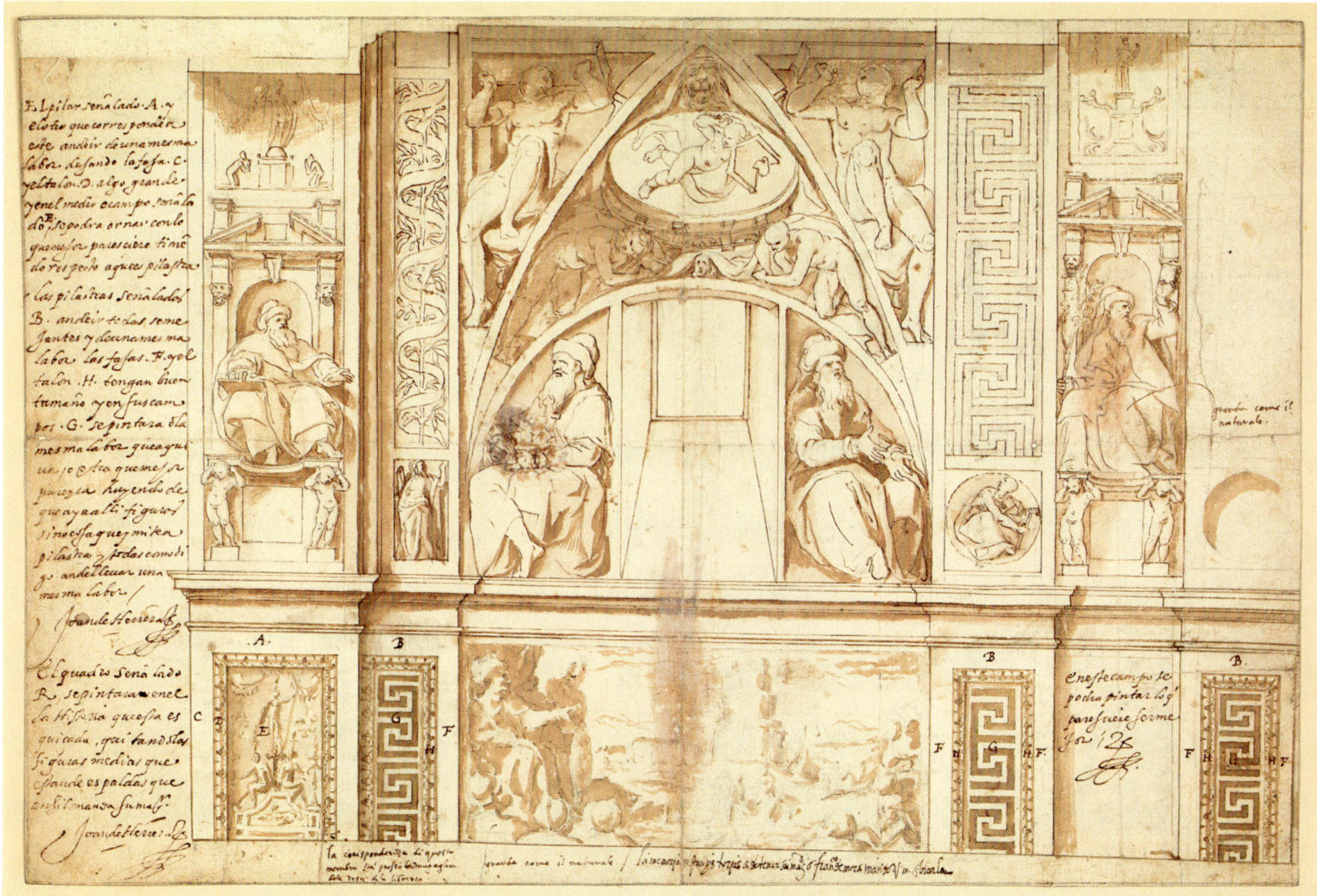

differences.[29] Executed in pen and ink with grey wash and white highlights on blue paper and squared for transfer, this drawing embodies the elements that Zuccaro introduced to Spain which had such influence on his contemporaries. The figure outlines are rapidly drawn and their form built through additional pen strokes. The wash creates shadow and depth and the white highlights give substance. The faces and expressions of the Apostles are rendered using quick pen annotations.

9
Pellegrino Tibaldi
Study for the Decoration of the Escorial Library, 1588–92
Pen and brown ink with brown wash over black chalk, 332 x 485 mm
British Museum, London
1846,0509.176

Zuccaro's Roman mannerist style greatly influenced Bartolomé Carducho (1560–1608), his assistant in Florence and Rome who accompanied him to the Escorial. A number of drawings have been attributed to Bartolomé, but few can be tied to specific works.[30] They are executed in a variety of techniques and there is sometimes confusion between his work and that of his son Vicente (see figs 2–3, p. 83).[31] Bartolomé's drawing of *Saint Lawrence Baptizing the Prisoners* (fig. 11) is a preliminary study for his painting, one of a series in the Escorial on the life of the saint painted in 1598, the year in which he was appointed Painter to the King.[32] The study is executed in brown wash on blue paper, with thick white highlights over a preliminary drawing in black chalk providing some of the detail, such as the pattern on Saint Lawrence's mantle. Bartolomé uses the colour of the paper in a similar way to Zuccaro, as an effective means of defining light and dark within the composition; this is also very close to drawings by other artists working at the Escorial, Miguel Barosso and Diego López de Escuriaz (fig. 25).

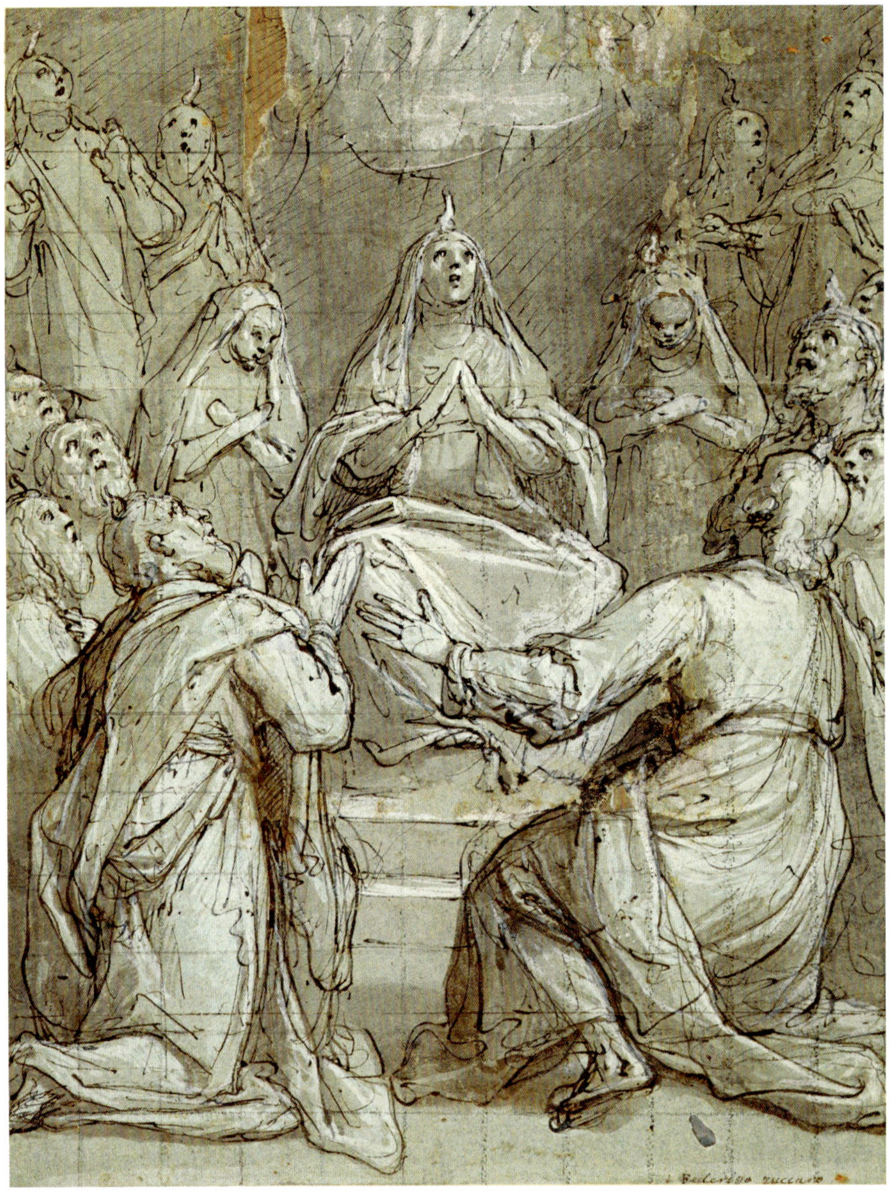

10
Federico Zuccaro
The Pentecost, 1586–8
Pen and brown ink with grey wash and white highlights on blue paper, squared for transfer, 355 x 260 mm
Royal Library, Windsor Castle
RL 06015

El Greco (Domenicos Thetokopoulos, 1541–1614) stands apart from the Italians who worked in Spain but was very much part of their tradition. Trained in Crete, he moved to Venice around 1567 where he seems to have worked on his own, although he was strongly influenced by Titian and Tintoretto. Arriving in Spain in 1576, El Greco settled in Toledo where he remained for the rest of his life. In 1580 he was commissioned to paint the *Martyrdom of Saint Maurice* for an altar at the Escorial, but two years later it was rejected by Philip II on the grounds of its inappropriate iconography and also perhaps its style, and he received no further commissions from the king. El Greco was profoundly interested in drawing, and in Spain he continued what he had learned in Italy.[33] The annotations he made in his copy of Vitruvius' *Ten Books on Architecture* recommend that students attain proficiency in drawing through constant practice, for it was fundamental to good painting, more so than measurement or proportion.[34] Later in his annotations El Greco quotes Michelangelo who, when asked what was the most important part of painting,

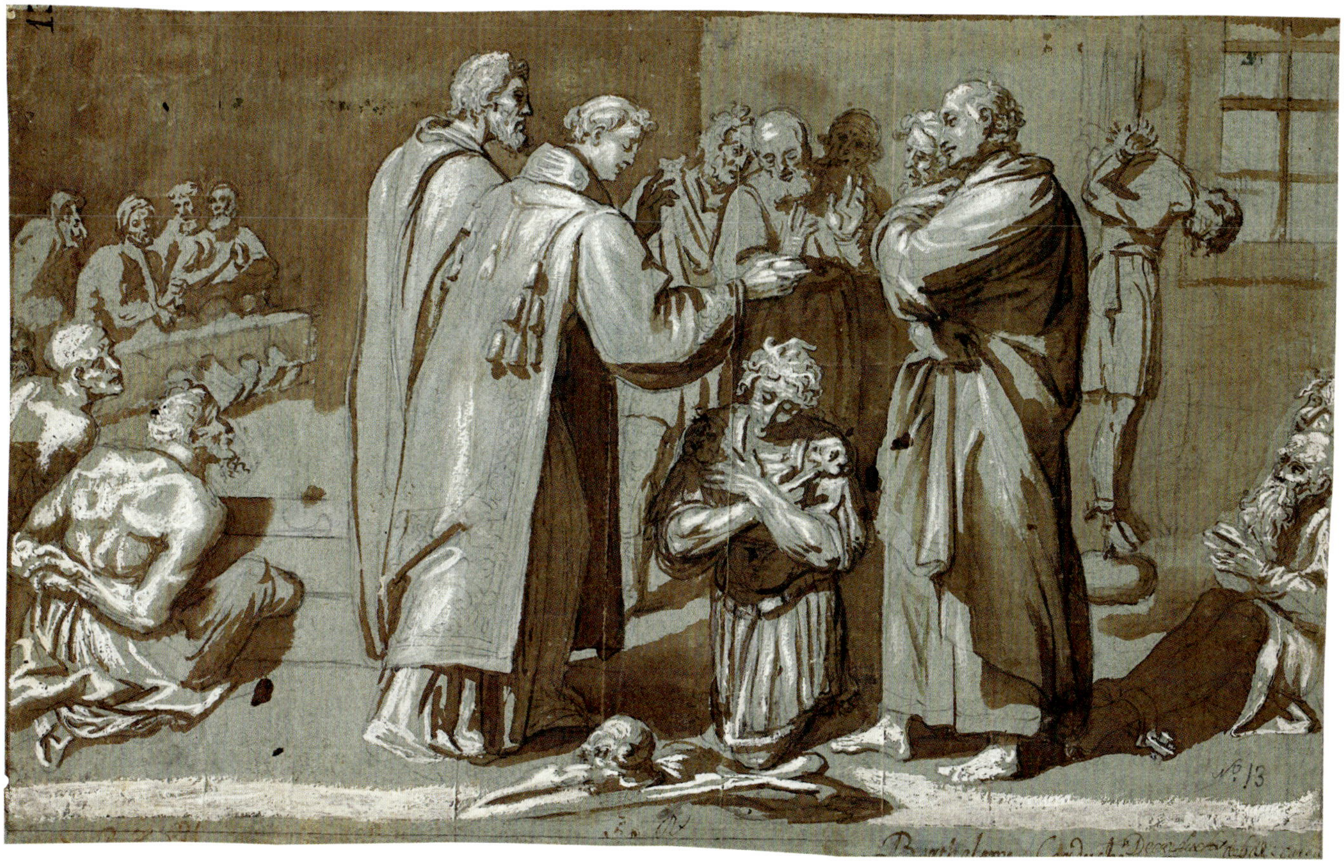

11
Bartolomé Carducho
Saint Lawrence Baptizing the Prisoners, c.1598
Brown wash and white heightening over black chalk on prepared paper,
220 x 345 mm
Museo del Prado, Madrid
D.8

responded that it was constant drawing.[35] Only a very small group of sheets accepted to be by El Greco's hand survive, but there can be little doubt that he made preparatory drawings for his works.[36] An inventory made after his death in 1614 records around 150 drawings probably by him, as well as thirty architectural elevations.[37]

El Greco's earliest known drawing is a variation on Michelangelo's sculpture of *Day* on one of the Medici tombs in the church of San Lorenzo, Florence, possibly made when he was in the city around 1570 (fig. 12).[38] Although not drawn in Spain, it reflects El Greco's early attitude to drawing and something of his reaction to art in Italy: the mix of charcoal, black and white chalk on blue prepared paper was a combination sometimes used by Tintoretto for his figure studies.[39] The drawing has been interpreted as Michelangelesque form corrected by Venetian *colore*, where distinct traditions are combined on the same sheet.[40] This drawing is unique among El Greco's work: the few surviving sheets from his career in Spain are very different, being working studies for painted compositions. These show the influence of drawing practices he picked up during six or so years in Rome. His *Saint John the Evangelist* of around 1577 (fig. 13) is a preparatory study for his painting on the high altar of the church of Santo Domingo el Antiguo in Toledo.[41] El Greco used the flat side of the chalk to indicate the folds in the fabric and the shadow around the saint's feet, as well as simulating the flickering effects of light and dark in the painting. There was also originally a contract or demonstration drawing for the altar commission, and this, together with the present piece and drawings of two other single figures, were part of the artist's

12
El Greco

Variation on Michelangelo's Sculpture of Day, c.1570

Black chalk with white heightening (pen and brown ink and blue wash added by Giorgio Vasari), 598 x 345 mm
Staatliche Graphische Sammlung München
13756

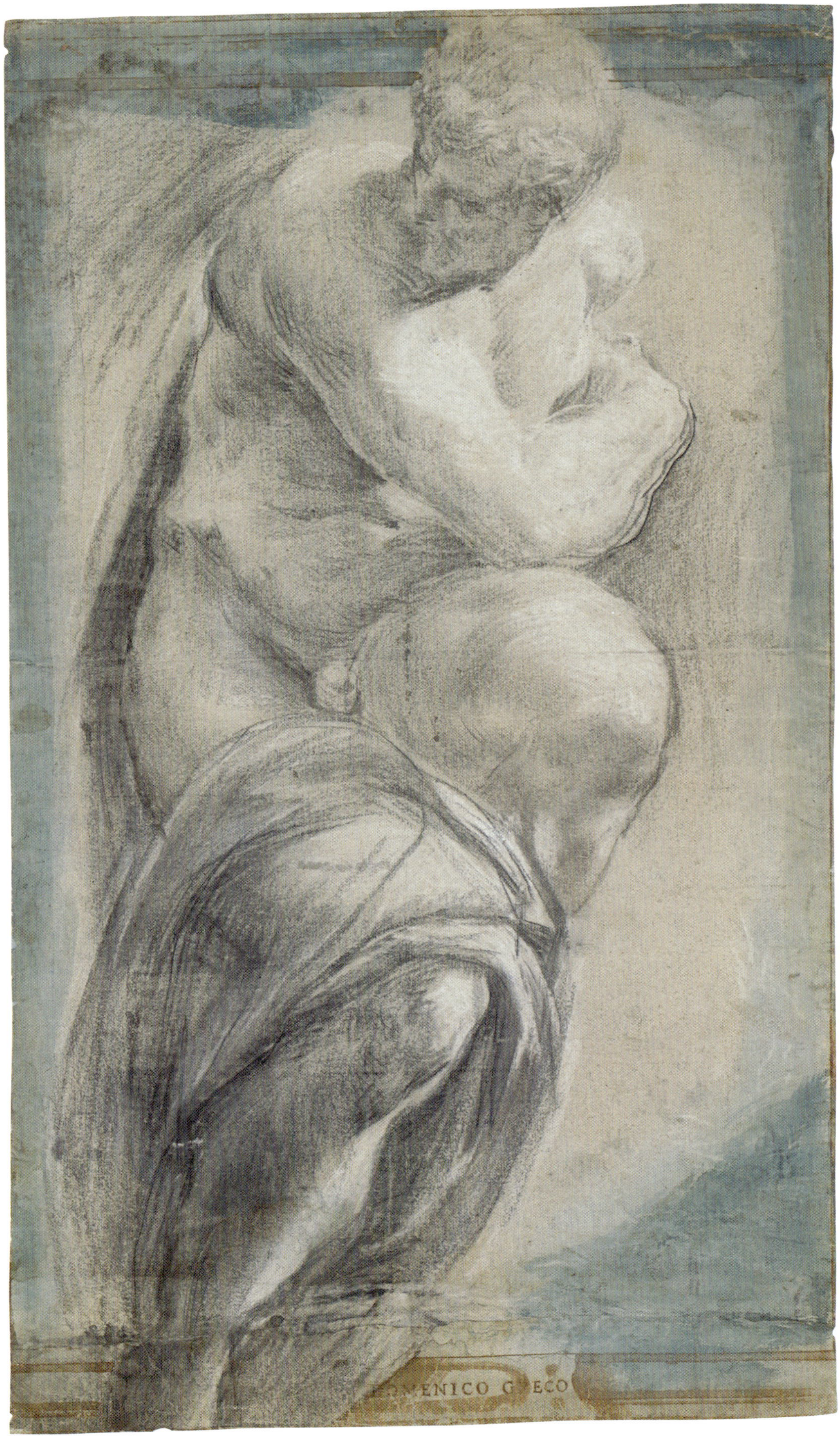

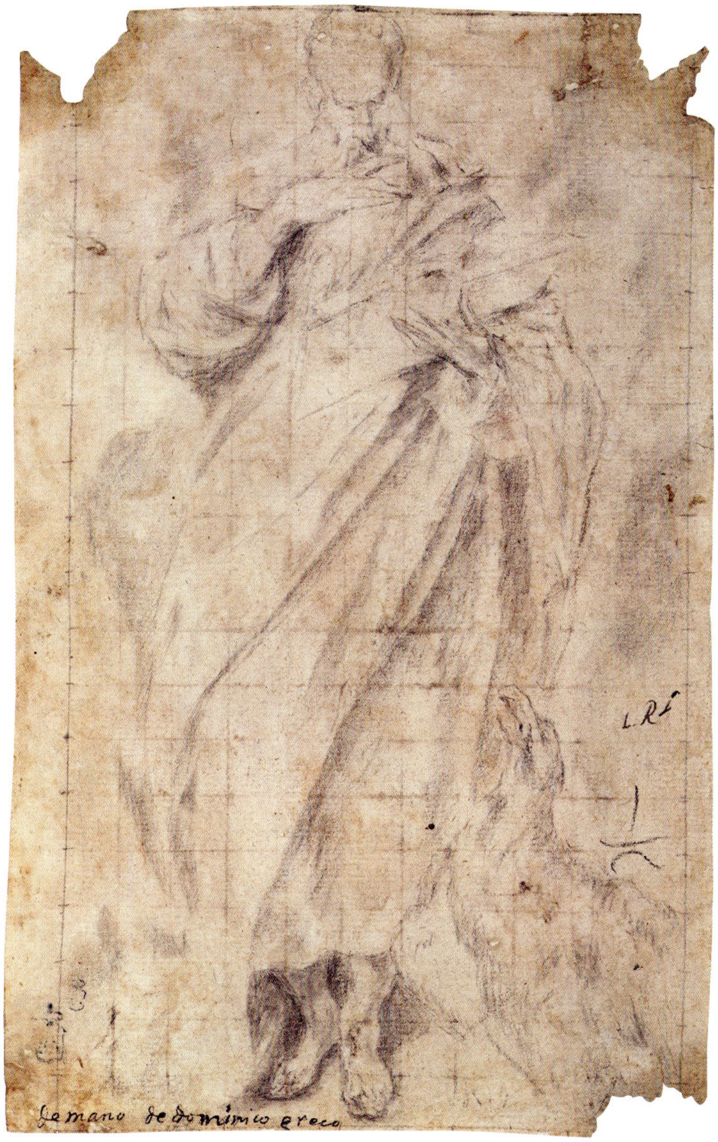

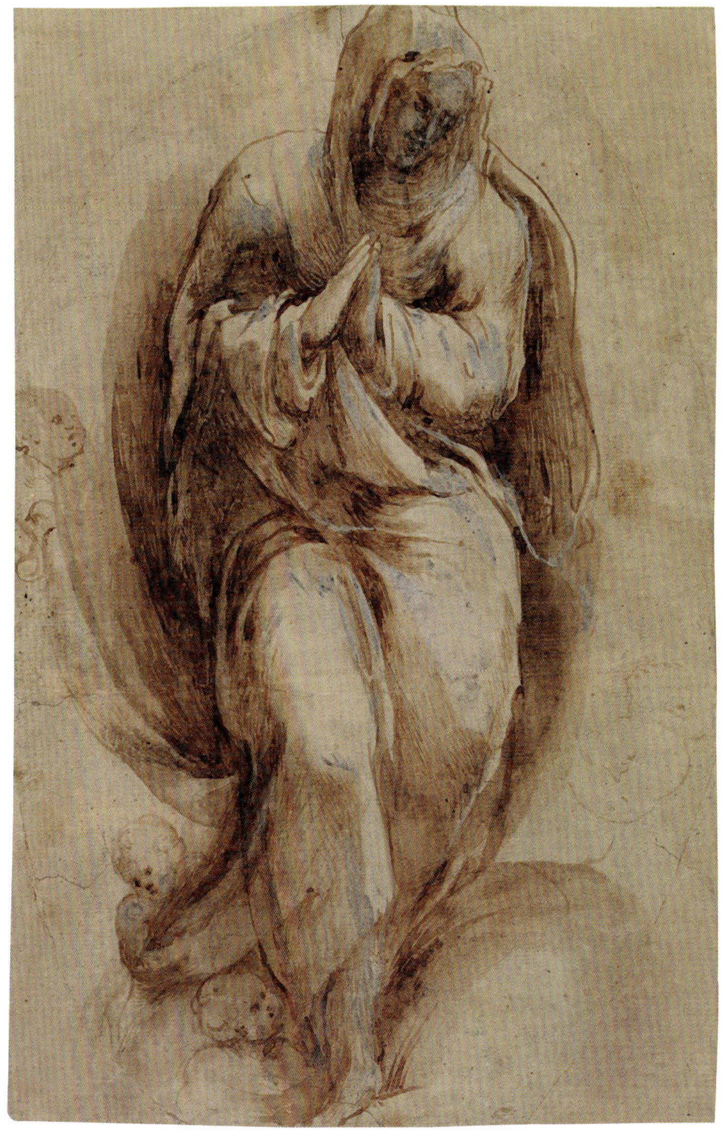

thorough preparatory drawing process.[42] There is some disagreement over the authenticity of the other drawings attributed to El Greco, which however do not form a sufficiently distinctive body of work to allow useful discussion.[43]

13
El Greco
Saint John the Evangelist, *c.*1577
Black chalk, 225 x 155 mm
Biblioteca Nacional, Madrid
DIB/16/39/12

14
Alonso Berruguete
Assumption of the Virgin, 1555–61
Brush drawing in brown ink and wash with pen and brown ink, heightened with white, over black chalk, 313 x 193 mm
British Museum, London
1895,0915.866

Spanish artists

A number of Spanish artists also introduced new approaches to drawing in Castile having spent time abroad.[44] At the beginning of the sixteenth century Alonso Berruguete (*c.*1489–1561) worked in Rome and Florence, where he apparently copied Masaccio's frescoes in the Brancacci Chapel.[45] Giorgio Vasari notes that Berruguete greatly admired Michelangelo and copied his *Battle of Cascina* cartoon.[46] These copies have not survived, but Berruguete's interest in Michelangelo is amply demonstrated by a red chalk drawing of the prophet Daniel on the ceiling of the Sistine Chapel, as well as his pen-and-ink drawings.[47] Berruguete was back in Spain (Valladolid and Salamanca) around 1516, and two years later he was appointed painter to Charles V. His drawing of the *Assumption of the Virgin* of around 1555–61 (fig. 14 and detail p. 56)

15
Attributed to Alonso Berruguete

The Entombment of Christ, *c.*1530–50

Engraving, 150 x 167 mm
British Museum, London
1860,0414.16

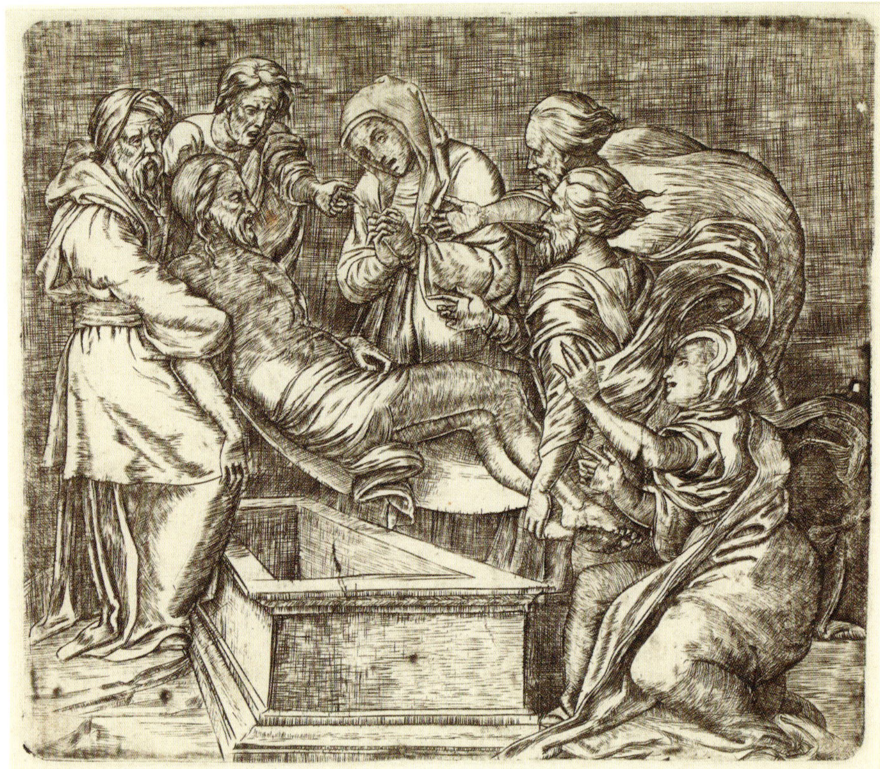

16
Alonso Berruguete

The Entombment of Christ, *c.*1530–40

Oil on Panel, 900 x 1000 mm
Church of San Pedro, Fuentes de Nava (Palencia)

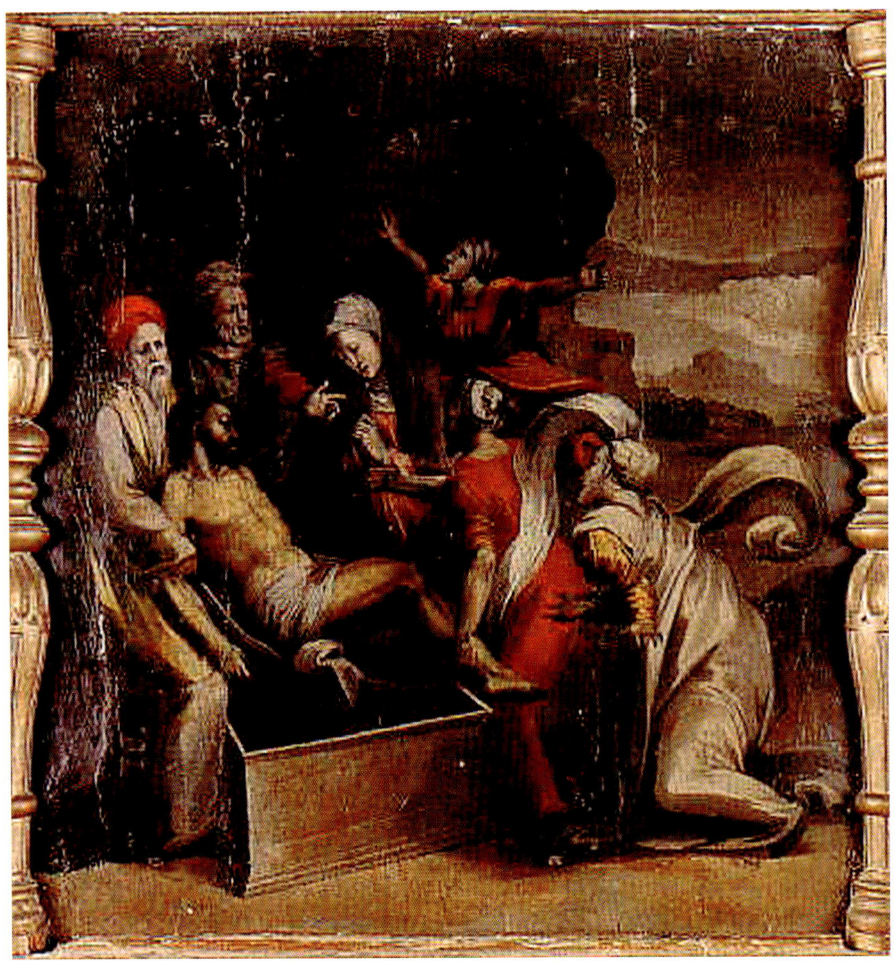

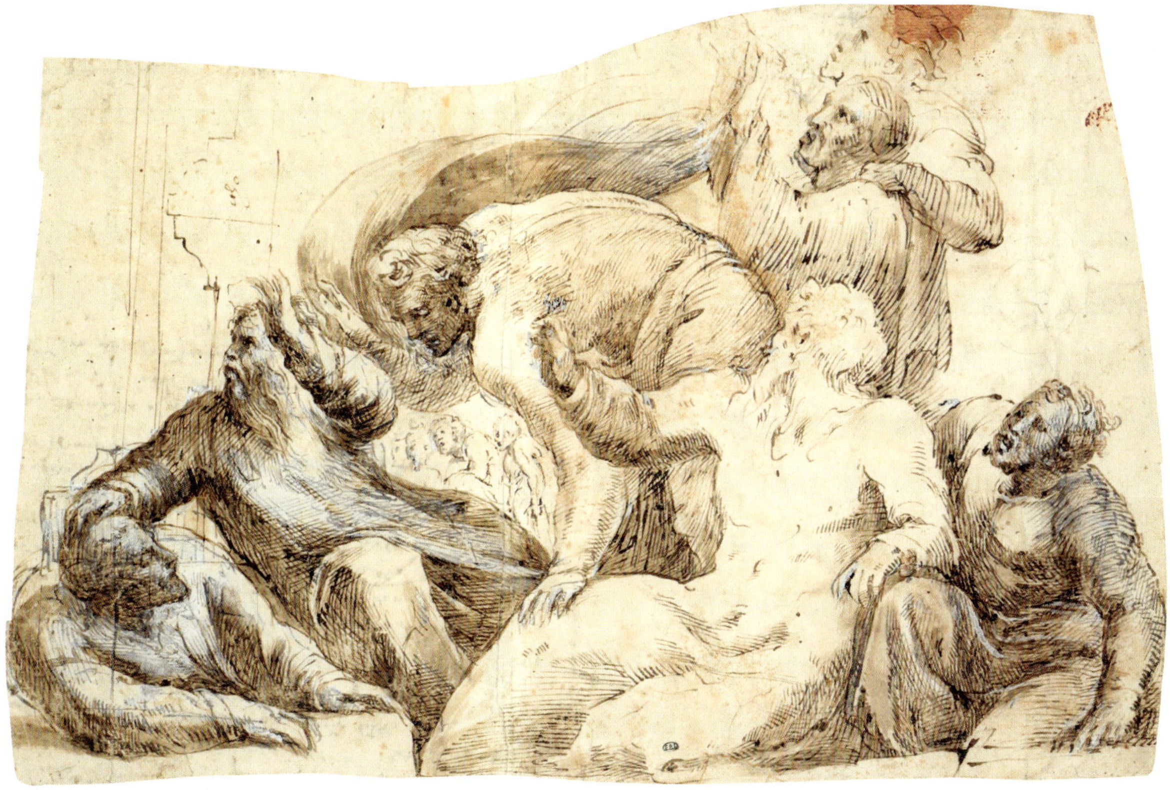

demonstrates his mature style of draughtsmanship. A large number of drawings have been associated with Berruguete, several of which form a pattern book, demonstrating how important drawing was in the preparation of paintings and sculpture.[48] He employed assistants to help with commissions; their style, mostly in pen and ink, closely resembled his own.[49]

An engraving attributed to Berruguete, *The Entombment of Christ* of around 1530–50 (fig. 15), is stylistically very close to his draughtsmanship. This is the only print thought to be by Berruguete, and one of the earliest engravings made in Spain. It reproduces – with some differences – Berruguete's painting of *The Entombment of Christ* (fig. 16) in the Church of San Pedro in Fuentes de Nava (Palencia), dated to around 1530–40. The print's idiosyncratic details mark it out as Berruguete's work. The old man at the right with the voluminous garments is a model used for the sculpted Prophet Elijah in the choir of Toledo Cathedral (1539–43) and for a figure in *The Ascension of Christ* in the church of San Salvador in Úbeda (1554). The swirling draperies of the three figures on the right of the print also occur in Berruguete's fragment of an architectural drawing of seven figures (fig. 17). Several drawings recognized by Lizzie Boubli as from Berruguete's circle in Spain are in fact copied after Italian prints.[50] His workshop has been described as along the lines of a 'commercial company' where he directed its many activities, including planning, iconography and execution of projects in collaboration with other artists.[51]

Juan Fernández de Navarrete, 'El Mudo' (*c.*1538–79), trained at the Hieronymite monastery of La Estrella in Logroño and was one of a number of Spanish artists who worked alongside the Italians at the Escorial.[52] Before arriving there around 1566, Navarrete is thought to have visited Italy. Sigüenza writes of his trip to Rome, Florence, Venice, Milan and Naples and that he

17
Alonso Berruguete
Fragment of an Architectural Drawing Showing Seven Figures, c.1540–50
Pen and brown and wash, white highlights, over black chalk, 262 x 385 mm
Ecole nationale supérieure des Beaux-Artes, Paris
473

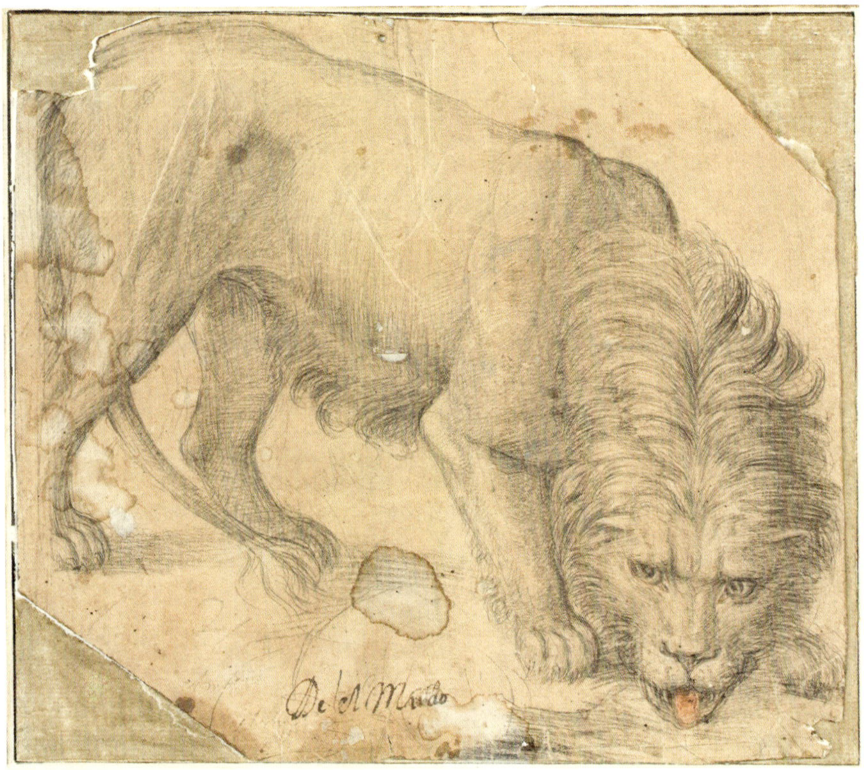

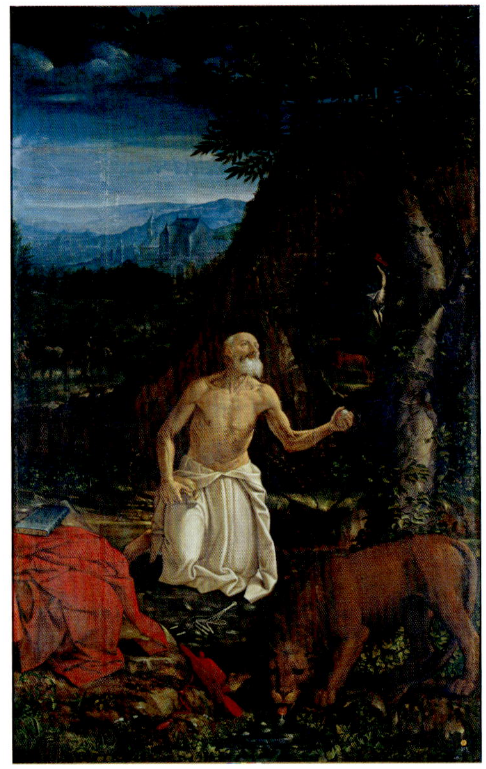

18
Juan Fernández de Navarrete
A Lion Drinking, c.1569
Black and red chalk,
233 x 256 mm
Museo del Prado, Madrid
D.3408

19
Juan Fernández de Navarrete
Saint Jerome in the Desert,
1569
Oil on canvas,
3470 x 2130 mm
Real Monasterio de San
Lorenzo de El Escorial

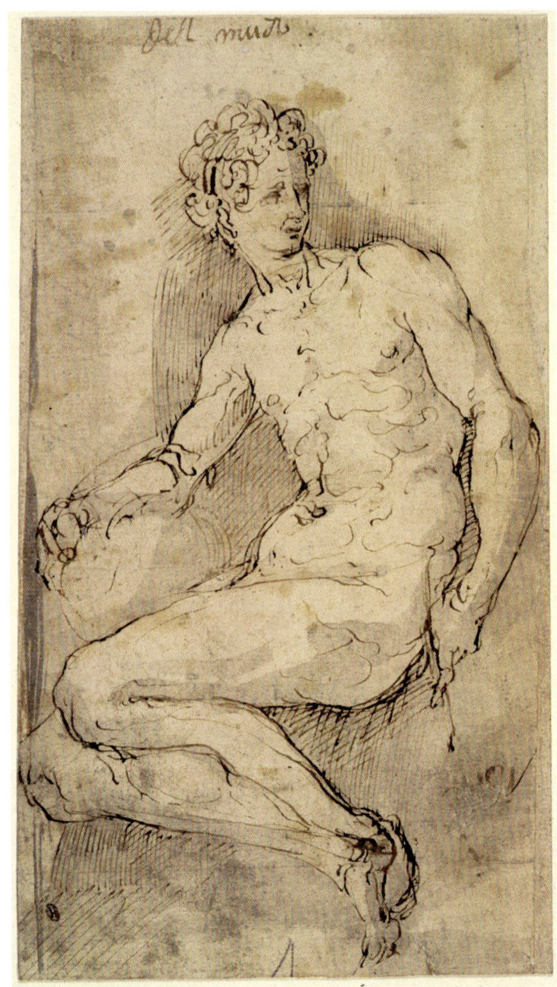

20
Attributed to
Juan Fernández de Navarrete
A Seated Male Nude,
c.1560–79
Pen and brown ink and grey
wash, 223 x 122 mm
British Museum, London
1895,0915.867

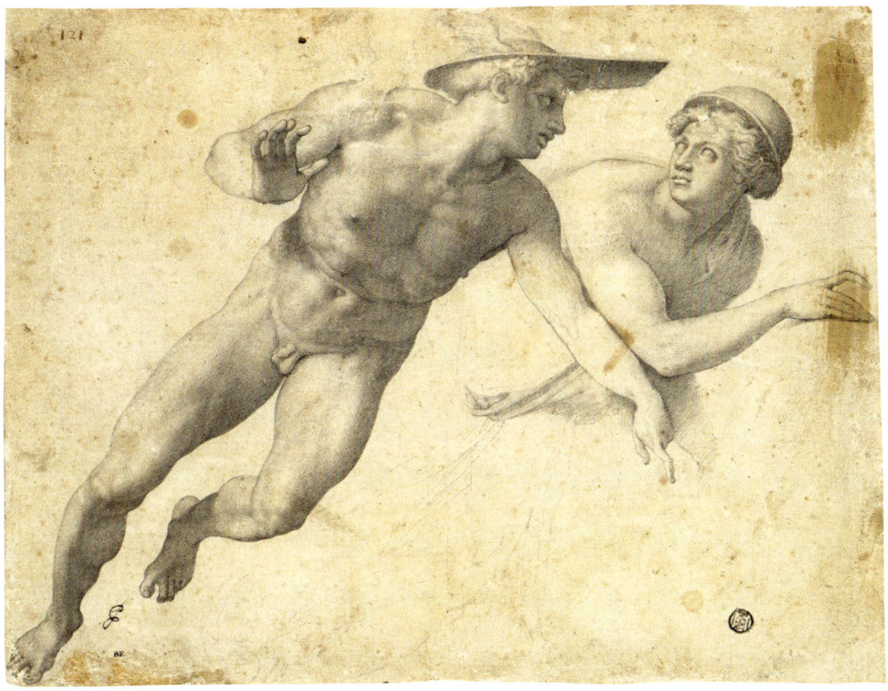

21
Gaspar Becerra
Mercury and Minerva, *c.*1562–3
Black chalk and traces of red chalk, 282 x 369 mm
Musée du Louvre, Paris
2763

worked in Titian's house along with other 'valiant men of the time'.[53] At the Escorial, Navarrete was Philip II's favourite painter of religious subjects. Drawings associated with him are scarce and their attributions rest mainly on their inscriptions; since they lack stylistic coherence, little can be said about them.[54] Navarrete's chalk study of a lion drinking (fig. 18) is a detail from his painting of *Saint Jerome in the Desert* executed in 1569 (fig. 19). Whether this is preparatory for the painting or a record made of a detail after it was completed cannot be determined.[55] A pen-and-ink study of a seated male nude (fig. 20) is inscribed in a contemporary hand 'del Mudo'; if the identification is correct, its Roman style suggests that it dates from his time in Italy.[56]

Gaspar Becerra's (*c.*1520–68) lifelong commitment to drawing distinguishes him from his Spanish contemporaries, with the exception of Berruguete. Becerra received his early training in Baeza (Jaén) before moving to Rome, where his name appears among those at the Academia de San Luca in 1544.[57] He remained in Italy until 1557, working in the studios of Giorgio Vasari and Daniele da Volterra, and contributed, for example, to the decoration of the churches of Santissima Trinità dei Monti and San Giacomo degli Spagnoli.[58] For his (unfinished) fresco of the *Descent into Limbo* in the Assunta Chapel at San Giacomo he made a large (437 x 233 mm) finished black chalk drawing of Christ.[59] This is Becerra's earliest known sheet and shows the unmistakable influence of Michelangelo, whose drawings he might well have seen through his association with Volterra.[60] Two other large and carefully executed drawings, possibly pre-dating his drawing of Christ, show sections of the Sistine Chapel fresco.[61] In Rome, Becerra also designed the frontispiece for Juan de Valverde's *Historia de la composición del Cuerpo Humano* (1556) demonstrating the range of his graphic work – entirely to be expected of an artist working in a centre of book and print publishing.[62]

In 1557 Becerra returned to Spain (Burgos), where his first documented work was the altarpiece in the Cathedral of Astorga (1558–63); later he also worked in Valladolid.[63] In late 1562 he entered the service of Philip II, where he was employed to decorate the Alcázar in Madrid and the nearby hunting lodge of El Pardo.[64] Becerra's drawing of *Mercury and Minerva* (fig. 21) shows part of the ceiling decoration of the Torre de la Reina (Queen's Chamber) in El Pardo.[65] This highly finished sheet was probably a presentation drawing. Becerra used a fine-quality laid paper that allowed him to manipulate the chalk to achieve subtle effects: the firm outline of Mercury's body, for example, and the parallel lines on his legs and left arm contrast with the rubbed chalk to articulate the flesh of the torso. This particular technique closely resembles that of the Italian artist Giulio Clovio, who befriended Becerra in Rome. Francisco Pacheco anecdotally relates a conversation between Becerra and Philip II that reveals his own estimation of Becerra's drawings and the artist's dedication and pride in his practice. Becerra showed the king drawings for the El Pardo fresco: 'He drew a celebrated flying Mercury after a good model of his, and he showed it to His Catholic Majesty Philip II, who replied: "Is this all you have made?", which caused him great sadness'.[66]

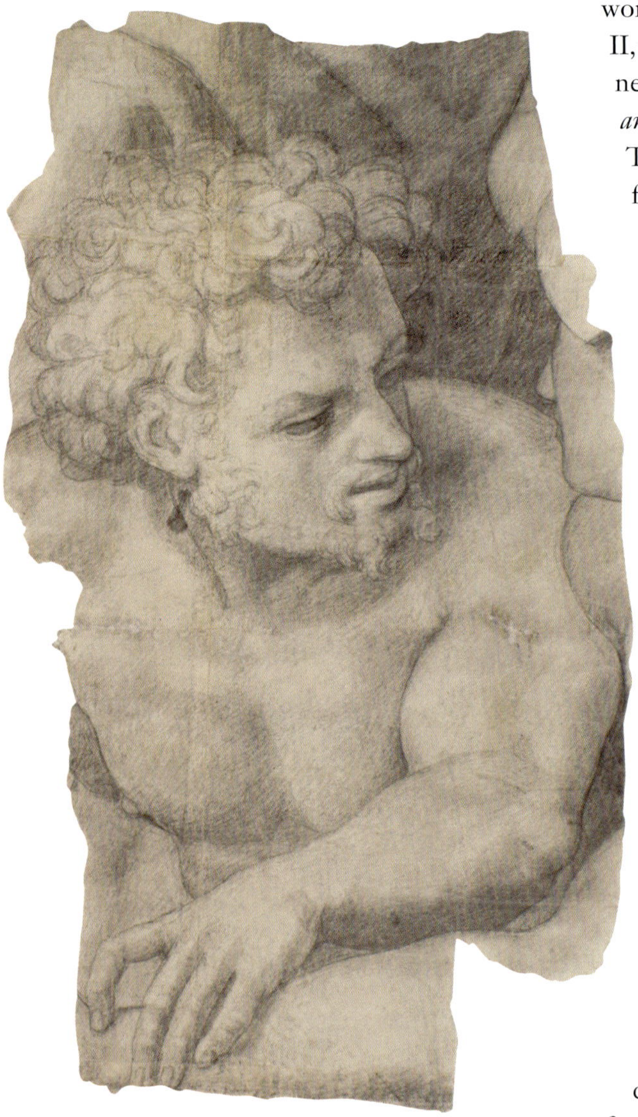

22
Gaspar Becerra
Half Male Figure and a Female Profile, *c.*1562–8
Black chalk, 550 x 332 mm (maximum)
Real Monasterio de San Lorenzo de El Escorial
D-12

Fragments of Becerra's highly finished cartoons survive, of which the male figure (fig. 22) is a striking example.[67] He learned to use cartoons in Italy and, like Urbino, continued to do so in Spain. Philip II was not Becerra's only patron: commissions also came from religious orders, such as that for the high altar for the church of the Descalzas Reales in Madrid, recorded in a pen, ink and wash drawing dated 1563 (fig. 23).[68] Across the middle of the drawing are two superimposed pieces of paper showing continuous architectural detail, beneath which are female allegorical figures representing Fortitude on the right and Religion on the left (fig. 24). This type of architectural drawing, providing alternatives for the patron, became common in Spain in the following century. The tabernacle in the lower centre has also been pasted down; this presumably also offered an alternative design. Becerra ran a sculpture workshop in Madrid, but no drawings from this have survived – although the drawings he brought back with him from Italy are referred to in the last will and testament of his widow, Paula Velázquez.[69] Becerra was much admired in Italy and in Spain. In *Dei veri precetti della pittura* (1587) Giovan Battista Armenini praised his talents and in the *Diálogos de la pintura* (1633) Vicente Carducho singled out his drawings, observing that they were 'so soundly based on art and science, and so perfect in every way that they made me feel sorry about the present time, for there is scarcely anyone who wishes to look at them, let alone imitate them'.[70]

An unusual survival is a group of drawings in three albums made from 1587–9 onwards for embroidered liturgical vestments at the Escorial. Two albums contain drawings with pricked and unpricked outlines, and a third album mainly substitute cartoons rubbed with pouncing dust that are traced copies of the primary drawing.[71] The drawings are by a group of artists no doubt working in the same workshop; some have been attributed to Miguel

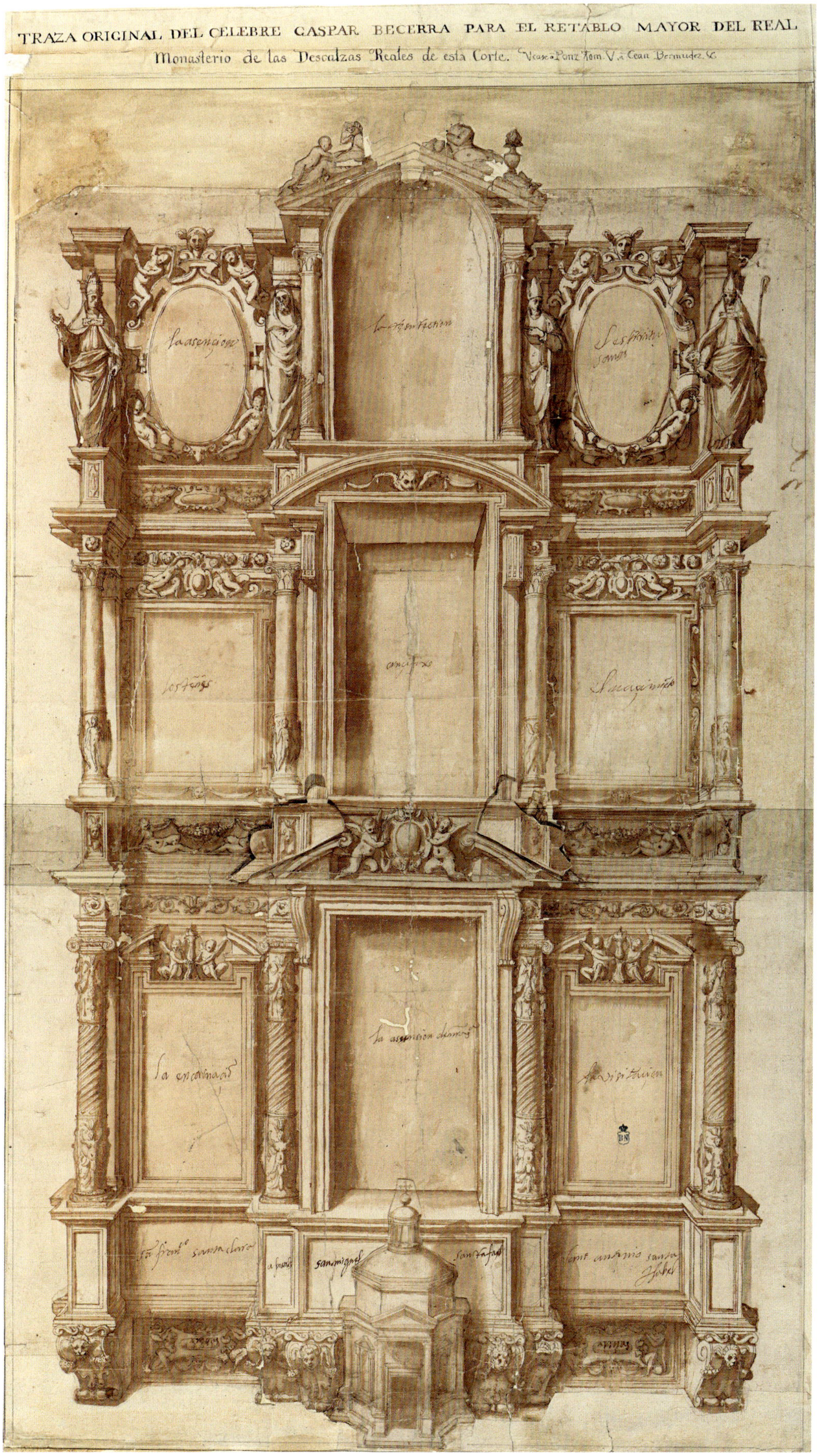

23
Gaspar Becerra
The High Altar in the Church of the Descalzas Reales, Madrid, 1563
Pen and brown ink and wash over black chalk,
870 x 500 mm
Biblioteca Nacional, Madrid
DIB/16/34/1

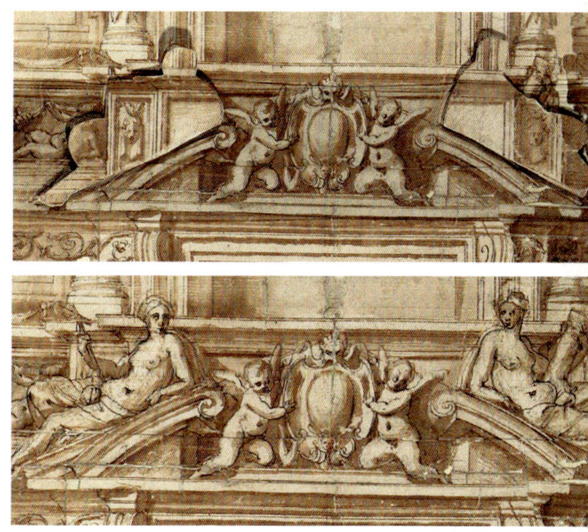

24
Detail of fig. 23
Middle section showing alternative design solutions

25
Miguel Barosso / Diego López de Escuriaz
Christ Distributing Bread to his Disciples after his Resurrection, 1587–9
Pen and brown ink, brown wash, white heightening over black chalk, pricked for transfer, 170 x 270 mm
British Museum, London
2011,7109.1

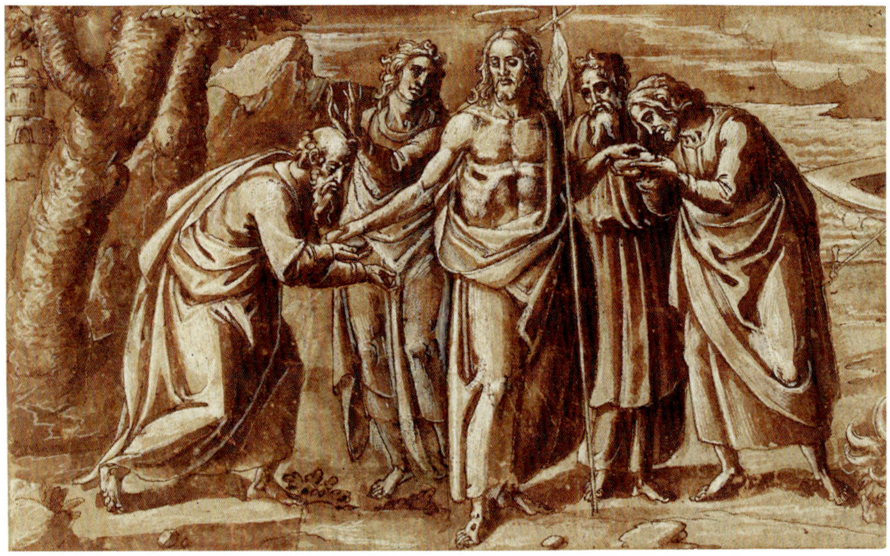

26
Detail of fig. 25
Showing the precision and regularity of the pricking for transfer

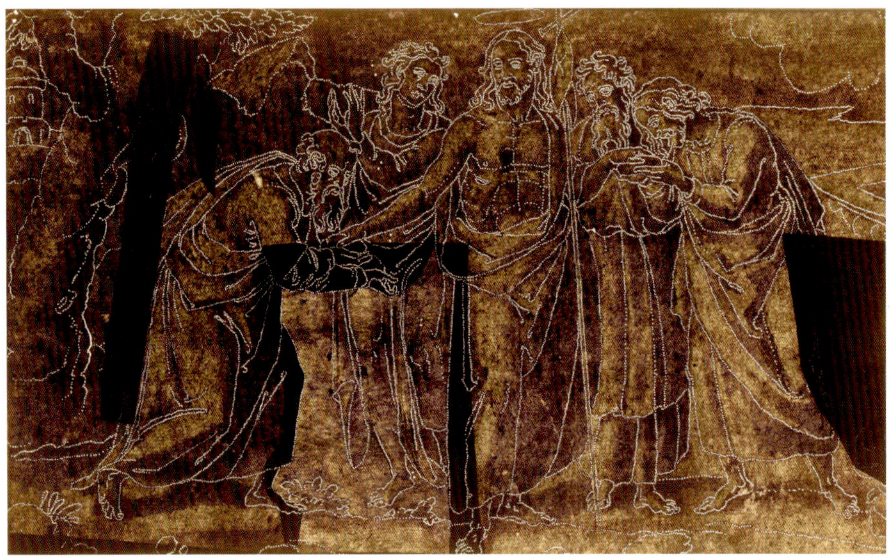

Barroso (*c.*1538–90), a student of Gaspar Becerra, and others to Diego López de Escuriaz, about whom nothing is known.[72] Drawings from the group have been dispersed, including *Christ Distributing Bread to his Disciples after his Resurrection* now in the British Museum (fig. 25).[73] Like most of the drawings in the group, this is executed in a carefully worked mixed technique: pen and brown ink, brush and brown wash, and white heightening over light black underdrawing on blue paper. The precision and regularity of the pricking is remarkable (fig. 26), demonstrating the importance of transferring an accurate copy of the image for the embroidery while preserving the original sheet.

Often on the basis of old inscriptions, little-known artists who worked in Castile during the second half of the sixteenth century have had drawings attributed to them. For example, two very different sheets in the British Museum have been attributed to Blas de Prado (*c.*1546–99), who worked in Toledo and Madrid: a head of a woman (probably the Virgin) and a prelate being presented with a devotional image of the Virgin.[74] Evidence for drawings by other artists is even more shadowy. Palomino writes that Teodosio Mingot (active *c.*1551–1619), who was in Italy before being called back to Spain to work with Becerra, was a great draughtsman and anatomist, 'as is demonstrated by several of his drawings, which I have seen and own'.[75] Only one drawing with his name inscribed in a seventeenth-century hand is known, a red and black chalk *Deposition of Christ* that confirms the qualities identified by Palomino.[76]

Not all of the Italian drawing practices introduced to Spain had a lasting impact. Because there was not much demand for large-scale fresco decoration after the later sixteenth century, cartoons seem to have died out fairly quickly. Carducho's comment about Becerra quoted above is revealing, for not only does it indicate that his drawings were available to those who were interested, but that his style did not sit well with artists in the first decades of the seventeenth century. He may have been regarded as somewhat old fashioned, whereas others, such as Federico Zuccaro, Tibaldi and Cambiaso, represented a more modern approach to drawing, embodying freedom and expressiveness.

The artists whose drawings were most up to date were those who came to Spain from Italy as children or were the first generation born there. Eugenio Cajés was born in Madrid in 1574 and trained with his father, Patricio Cajés, who arrived from Florence in 1567.[77] Vicente Carducho arrived in Spain in 1585, around the age of nine, with his older brother Bartolomé.[78] Romulo (Romolo) Cincinnato's sons Diego de Romulo and Francisco were born in Spain and trained with their father, who had worked in Italy from 1567.

The introduction of copper-plate engraving to Spain

Philip II's interest in prints and his awareness of their efficacy for disseminating images and information had a major impact on the development of engraving in Spain. His travels throughout Europe exposed him to the highly organized printmaking industry there. He had a particular interest in maps, reflecting his enthusiasm for new printing technologies while also fulfilling a practical need for information about his empire. In 1558 he commissioned the Flemish cartographer Jacob van Deventer to make town plans of the Netherlands to be engraved.[79] Ten years later Abraham Ortelius dedicated to Philip his *Theatrum orbis terrarum*, which contained many beautifully engraved maps published in Antwerp by Christophe Plantin. Printmakers also vied for Philip's attention. In 1571 Cornelis Cort dedicated an engraving (fig. 27) to him, which was related to two versions of Titian's painting of the *Martyrdom of Saint Lawrence*, one of which had been sent to the Escorial in 1567.[80] The print is a remarkable demonstration of Cort's mastery as a printmaker, conveying all the subtlety of Titian's manner. Through prints dedicated to

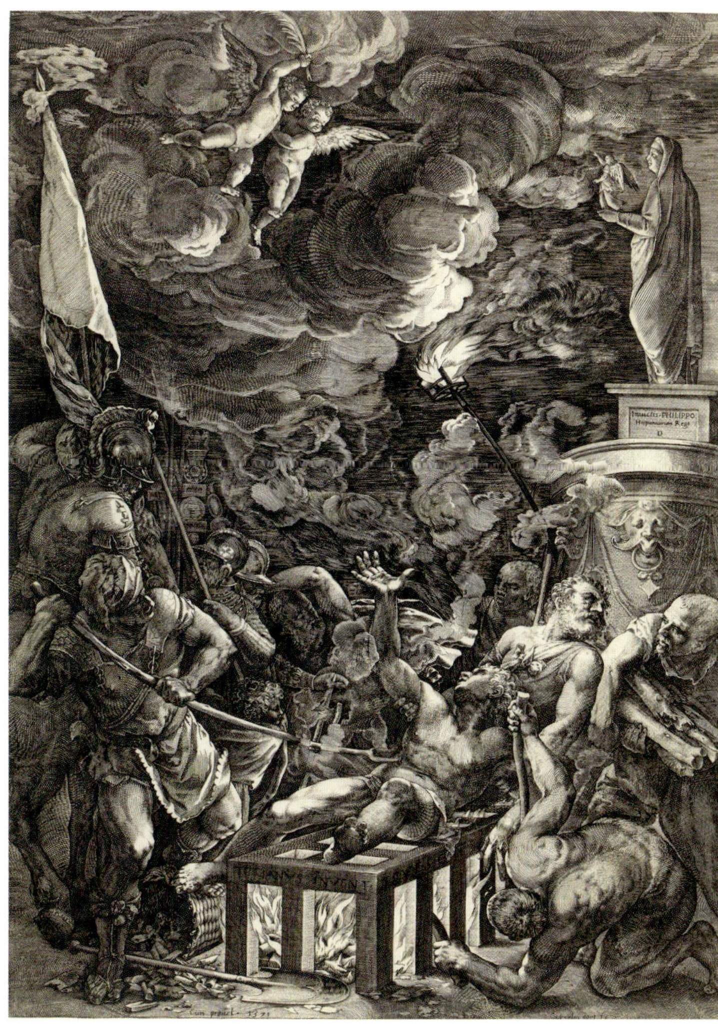

27
Cornelis Cort after Titian
The Martyrdom of Saint Lawrence, 1571
Engraving, 485 x 340 mm
British Museum, London
X,1.68

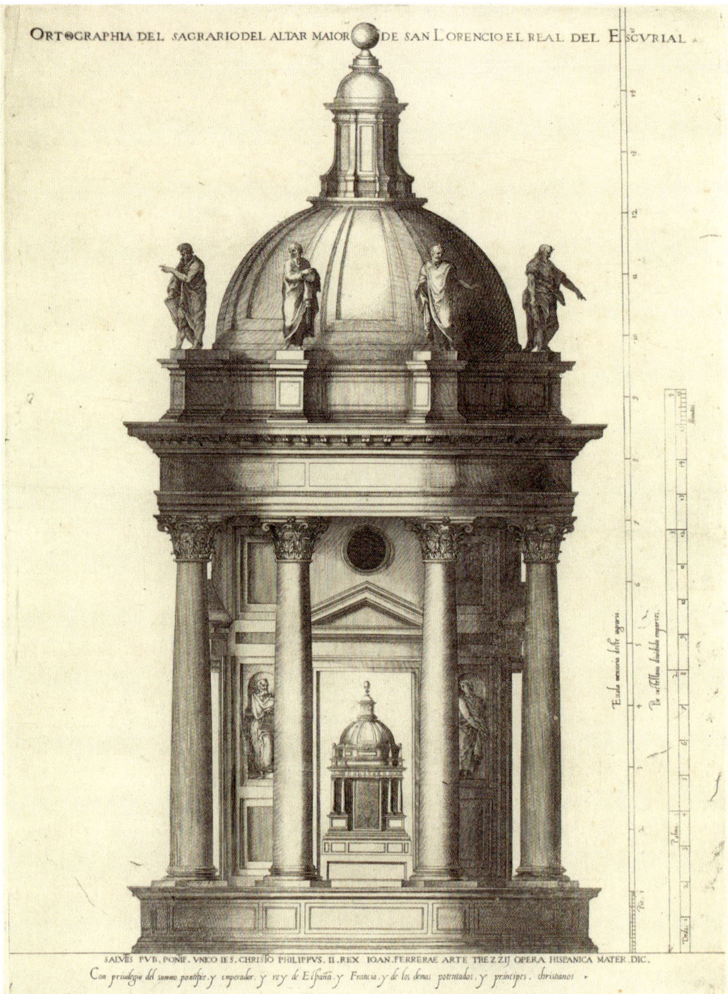

28
Pedro Perret
The Tabernacle of the Holy Sacrament in the Church of San Lorenzo el Real de El Escorial, 1583
Engraving, 480 x 344 mm
British Museum, London
1937,0915.240

him, as well his own commissions, Philip was well aware of their significance.[81]

The humanist scholar Benito Arias Montano (1527–98) worked as an agent for Philip II in Antwerp between 1568 and 1575. There he bought many books for the Escorial library and supervised production of the Polyglot Bible, the *biblia regia*, first suggested by the publisher Christophe Plantin and later sponsored by Philip.[82] Montano acted as a mediator between the king and the publisher, advising on questions of theological interpretation while also providing commentaries for the Bible. He was appointed librarian at the Escorial in 1576.[83] Montano was also responsible for assembling the collection of around seven thousand prints that formed part of Philip's library and today survives in thirty-six albums.[84] He knew personally many of printmakers in Antwerp whose work entered the Escorial, including Philip Galle, with whom he collaborated on several publishing projects, where Montano provided dedicatory inscriptions, legends or verse on prints.[85] Alongside Philip's books and print collection were his albums of drawings on parchment and paper. Among the most important is the so-called *Codex Escurialensis*, an album of drawings possibly from the studio of Domenico Ghirlandaio (by 1509) that entered the library in 1576.[86] Natural history drawings formed part of the collections, for example, the *Historia Plantarum Novae Hispaniae …*, which Philip had bound in blue leather embellished in gold and silver, a remarkable sixteen-volume work by his chief medical officer of the Indies, Francisco Hernández.[87]

The arrival of printmakers to Spain from the late sixteenth century was a response to the development of Madrid as a centre of publishing where they could reasonably expect to find work.[88] But unlike the painters or architects, whose reputation and skill were their passport, printmakers required presses, making it costly to establish themselves.[89] The Flemish-born Pedro Perret (1555–*c.*1625), who had worked in France and Rome, was the most important engraver, arriving in Madrid in 1583.[90] He was invited by Philip's site architect Juan de Herrera to produce a set of engravings illustrating the Escorial; these introduced large-scale copper-plate engraving to Spain.[91] The twelve engravings on eleven plates after drawings by Herrera and his assistants are among the most striking printed architectural reproductions of the sixteenth century. The idea of making the prints originated with the king, who recognized that they were a highly effective medium for disseminating information.[92] He wanted to broadcast the Escorial, his great project, as widely as possible.[93] However, the publication of the prints was a private business venture for Herrera, who secured the necessary privileges[94] and published them in 1589, six years after their conception,[95] accompanied by an explanatory booklet, the

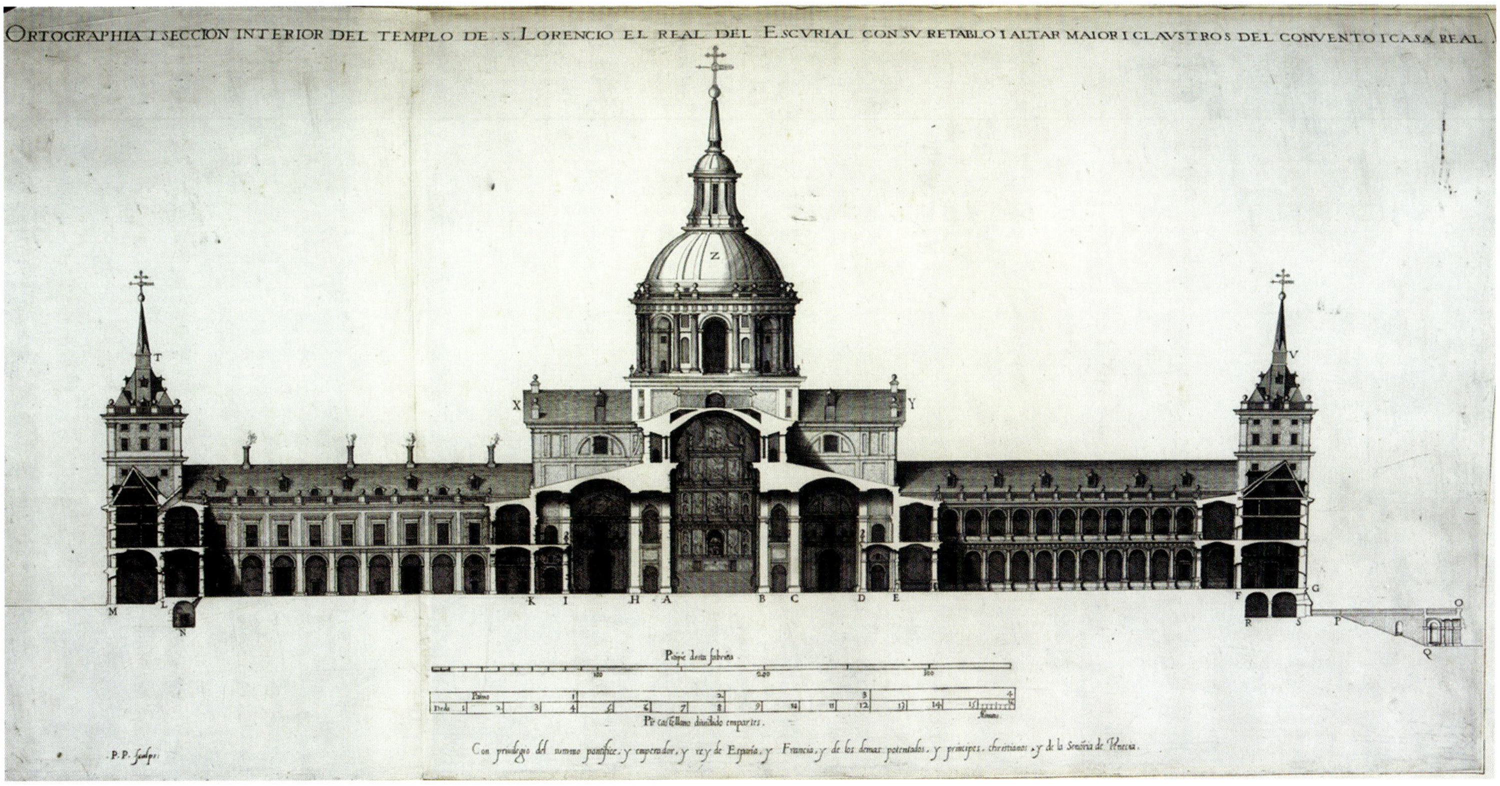

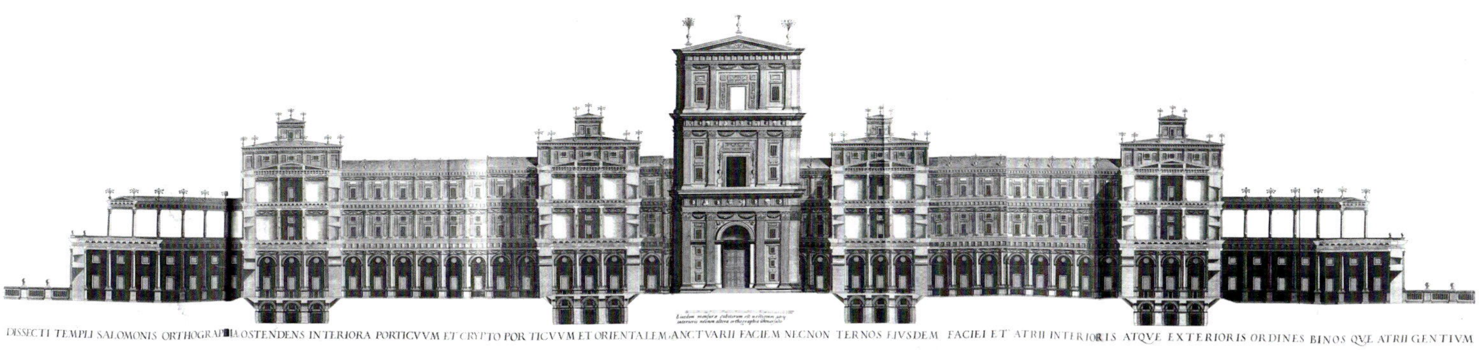

Summario y breve declaración de los diseños y estampas de la fábrica de San Lorenzo del Escorial. There were no sufficiently skilled Spaniards in Madrid to print the engravings, so two resident Italian printers, Francesco Testa and Gerónimo Gaeta, were contracted for the task.[96] The engravings consist of plans, elevations (fig. 28), sections of the monastery (fig. 29) and a bird's-eye view. In their own genre the prints themselves were as ambitious an undertaking as building the Escorial itself, and comprised the most technically complete and accomplished architectural publication of the sixteenth century.[97]

The Escorial prints provided the model for a set of fifteen engravings of measured plans, elevations and sections of the reconstructed Temple of Solomon based on Ezekiel's vision, after drawings by Juan Bautista Villalpando and published in the second volume of *De postrema Ezechielis prophetae* (Rome 1604).[98] The engravings were by printmakers working mainly in Rome.[99] Plate XV, the cross-section of the reconstructed temple (fig. 30), demonstrates the

29
Pedro Perret
Section through Middle of the Basilica on North-South Axis Revealing the Interior, 1583–9
Engraving, 870 x 720 mm
British Library, London
Maps 3.tab.34 (fol. 83)

30
Cherubino Alberti (?) after Juan Bautista Villalpando
Cross-section of the Reconstructed Temple of Solomon, 1604
Engraving, 330 x 1385 mm (plate mark, max.)
Warburg Institute, London
GMB.775 Large

31
Pedro Perret after Otto van Veen
Allegory of Philip II, c.1594
Engraving, 457 x 364 mm
Bibliothèque Nationale de France, Paris
Cc.92, f.t.2

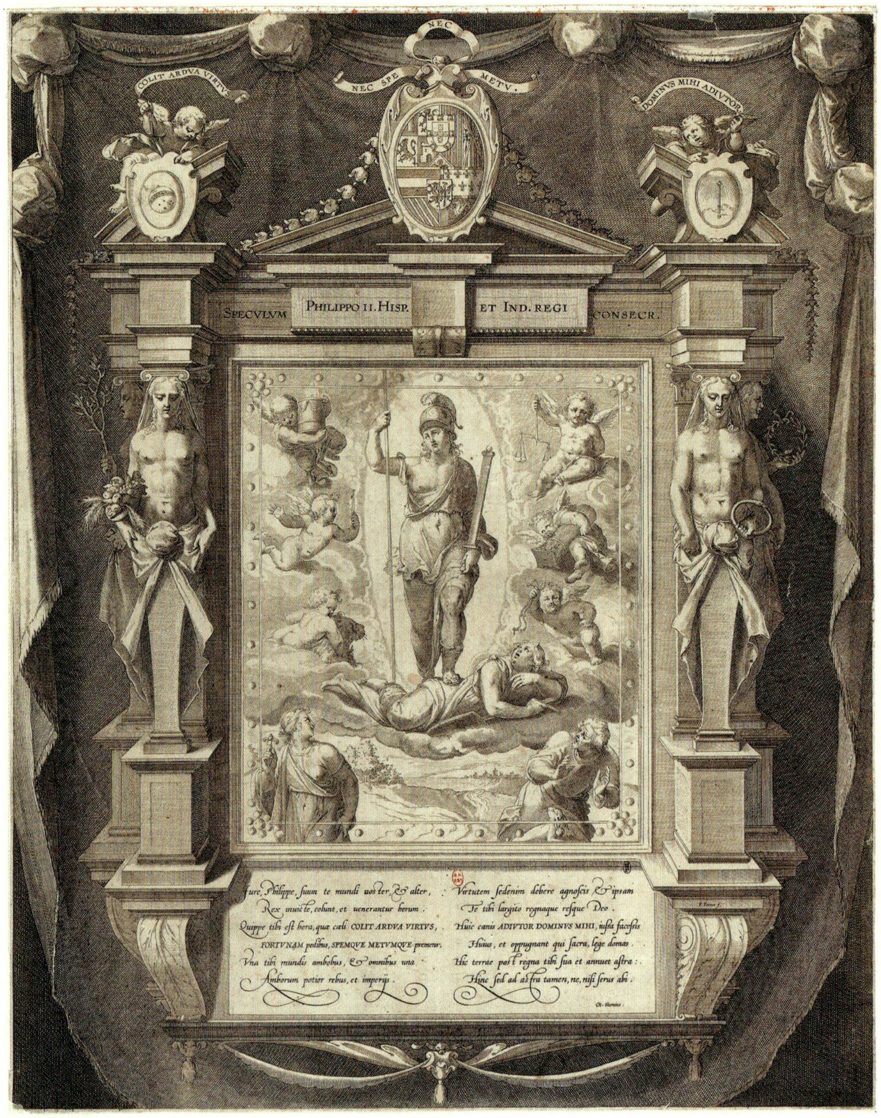

connection between the two projects.[100] Villalpando studied with Herrera at the Escorial, probably before 1580. The publication was dedicated to Philip II, who sponsored it in its early stages and financed the engraving of the plates, reflecting his continued interest in printed architectural material.[101]

During Perret's long reign as the most accomplished printmaker in Madrid he engraved title pages and portraits, an example of which is the *Allegory of Philip II* (fig. 31) after Otto van Veen from around 1594.[102] In the centre stands Virtue with Fortune at his feet surrounded by allegorical figures, including Piety, Religion, Fortitude and Prudence, representing qualities attributed to the king, who is named on the lintel above and referred to in the verse below.[103] Perret also engraved *Minerva Protecting Youth* after van Veen and dedicated it to Juan de Herrera.[104] These examples are significant because they demonstrate that prints made in Spain served the same purposes as those made elsewhere in Europe. In recognition of his professional accomplishments, Perret was appointed Servant to the King (*criado del rey*) in 1589, and Printmaker to the Privy Chamber (*tallador de cámara*) in 1595.[105]

Perret signalled a new era in Spanish printmaking, but his work does not seem to have inspired other artists to strive for similar results. This is because few Spanish publishing houses could produce high-quality engravings, a point reinforced by the fact that the prints after Villalpando were engraved and printed in Rome. The privileges conceded by Philip II to Northern publishing houses also had an adverse effect on the establishment of presses in Madrid during the second half of the sixteenth century.[106] Despite the competition, between the years 1566 and 1600 as many as sixteen publishing houses were established in Madrid.[107] The most important press, the Imprenta Real, was established around 1590. A Florentine, Giovanni Giunti (Juan de Junta) first settled in Salamanca in 1513 where he established a dynasty of publishers. Philip II invited his descendant Julio Giunti to move from Salamanca to Madrid, probably in 1593, where he began operations a year later.[108] Julio's nephew Tomás de Junti was granted to the title of Printer to the King (*impresor del rey*) in 1594, the first such title given to a printer in Spain, which granted him the right to print the official documents, pamphlets and books approved by the monarch.[109]

The prints made by Perret's contemporaries were much more modest and the majority continued to be made for books. Working in Toledo, Pedro Angel (active 1588–1617), for example, based his illustrations for the *Flos Sanctorum* on works of Raphael, Federico Zuccaro, Pieter van der Borcht, amongst others.[110] His contemporary Diego de Astor (*c.*1584–*c.*1650) was one of the first makers of reproductive prints in Spain, and his 1606 print after El Greco's *Saint Francis and Brother Leo Meditating on Death* (fig. 32) was probably supervised by the painter himself.[111] A native of Flanders, Astor would have been familiar with reproductive prints in his home country before he moved, in the early years of the seventeenth century, to Toledo, where he seems to have worked in El Greco's studio.[112] His technique is noteworthy: the variety and density of lines and modulated hatching with areas of the paper left untouched simulate the dramatic light and dark effects of El Greco's painting.

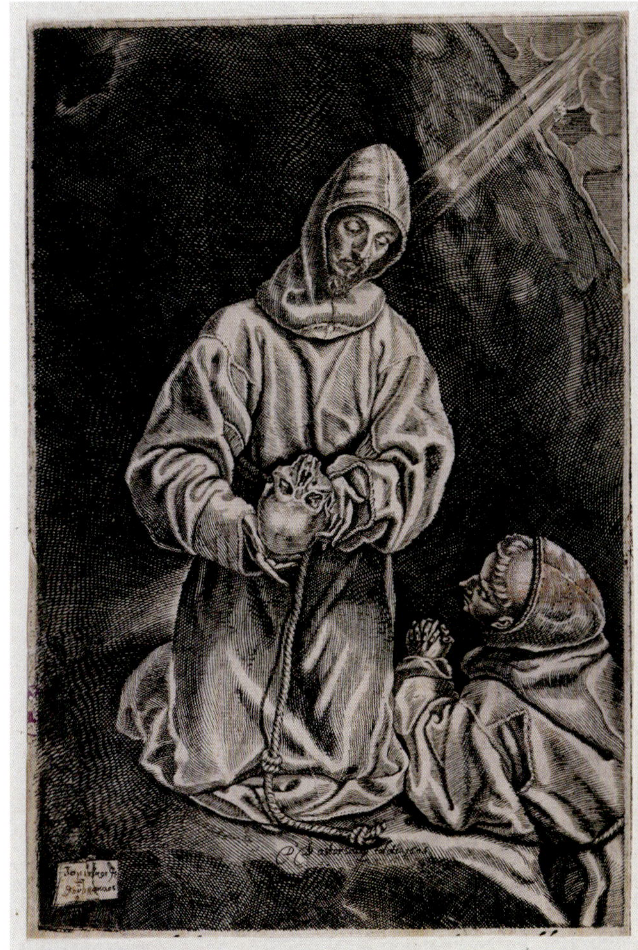

32
Diego de Astor after El Greco
Saint Francis and Brother Leo Meditating on Death, 1606
Engraving and etching, 228 x 147 mm
Biblioteca Nacional, Madrid 42372

Many of the Italian painters who worked in Castile also trained as printmakers. These include Luca Cambiaso (in Spain 1583–5), Vicenzo Campi (in Spain 1583–8) and Pellegrino Tibaldi (in Spain 1586–96), although none is known to have made prints in Spain. The only Italian painter-printmaker to work as an engraver was Patricio Cajés (Cascese), who arrived in Madrid with Romulo Cincinnato in 1567. He worked at the royal hunting lodges El Pardo (fig. 4, p. 84) and Valsaín and, from around 1571, at the Escorial.[113] In 1593, on the advice of Juan de Herrera, he published a translation of Vignola's *Regola delli cinque ordini*,[114] for which, according to Ceán Bermúdez, he engraved the title page and the architectural plates.[115] Cajés is not known to have engraved any other prints before he died in Madrid in 1612.

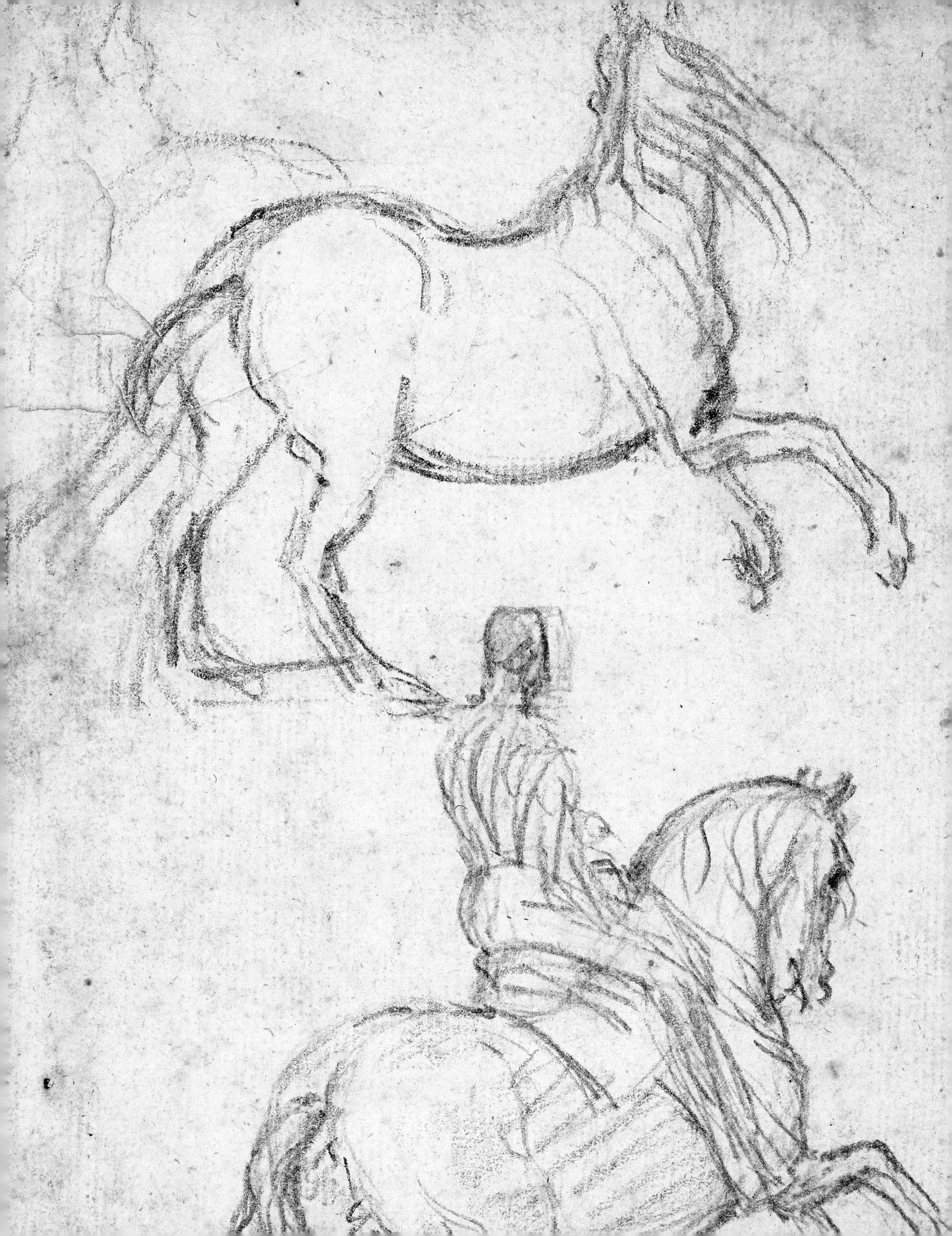

CHAPTER 4

Madrid as artistic capital 1600–1700

The main developments in the evolution of prints and drawings in Spain in and around Madrid during the second half of the sixteenth century can be summarized as changes in techniques and practices in an environment receptive to innovation. The urban development that followed the court settling in Madrid shaped artistic ambitions. Whereas the court was the main body responsible for nourishing the artistic economy, religious communities and a wealthy middle class became economically powerful clients.

Philip II died in September 1598, after a reign of almost fifty years, during which he became one of the most powerful collectors and patrons of the arts in the world. He was succeeded by his son, Philip III, whose political achievements and status as a collector and patron are overshadowed by those of his father and his own son, Philip IV, who succeeded him, in 1621. But Philip III achieved considerable success as a patron, as did members of his circle, most notably his de facto prime minister, the Duke of Lerma (Francisco Gómez de Sandoval).[1] Philip left the duke to assume the public role of patron of the arts, and he became the driving force behind much of the artistic activity at court.[2] The duke was devoted to building his collection and patronized artists such as El Greco, Peter Paul Rubens and others.

With regard to prints and drawings, after the wheels of change had been set in motion by Philip II, it is difficult to discern whether his son had any impact on their development. By the time Philip III ascended the throne the drawing styles of the emerging generation of artists, including Vicente Carducho and Eugenio Cajés, had largely been shaped by contact with the Italians at the Escorial. The decorations of the palace and monastery continued to be a major influence on Spanish art. Similarly, the types of prints and their uses introduced during the reign of Philip II continued largely unchanged. A subtle difference emerging at the turn of the century was the increasing number of prints relating to Spain's relations with wider Europe, and to political events such as the conquest of Malacca in Indonesia in 1605, or the expulsion of the moors from Spain in 1609–14.[3] Printing became more developed during the early seventeenth century because it could quickly disseminate news about contemporary events. As in the late sixteenth century, many of the prints that relate to Philip III's reign were made outside Spain. Notable exceptions are the engravings by Juan Schorquens on the subject of the king's voyage to Portugal in 1622, which were made in Madrid (fig. 56, p. 116).

In the first two years of his reign Philip III reverted to the practice of his forebears of having an itinerant court that rarely settled in one place for more than a fortnight. In 1601 he decided to relocate the entire court from Madrid to Valladolid, where it remained until 1606. The people of Madrid mourned

Detail of fig. 14, see p. 90

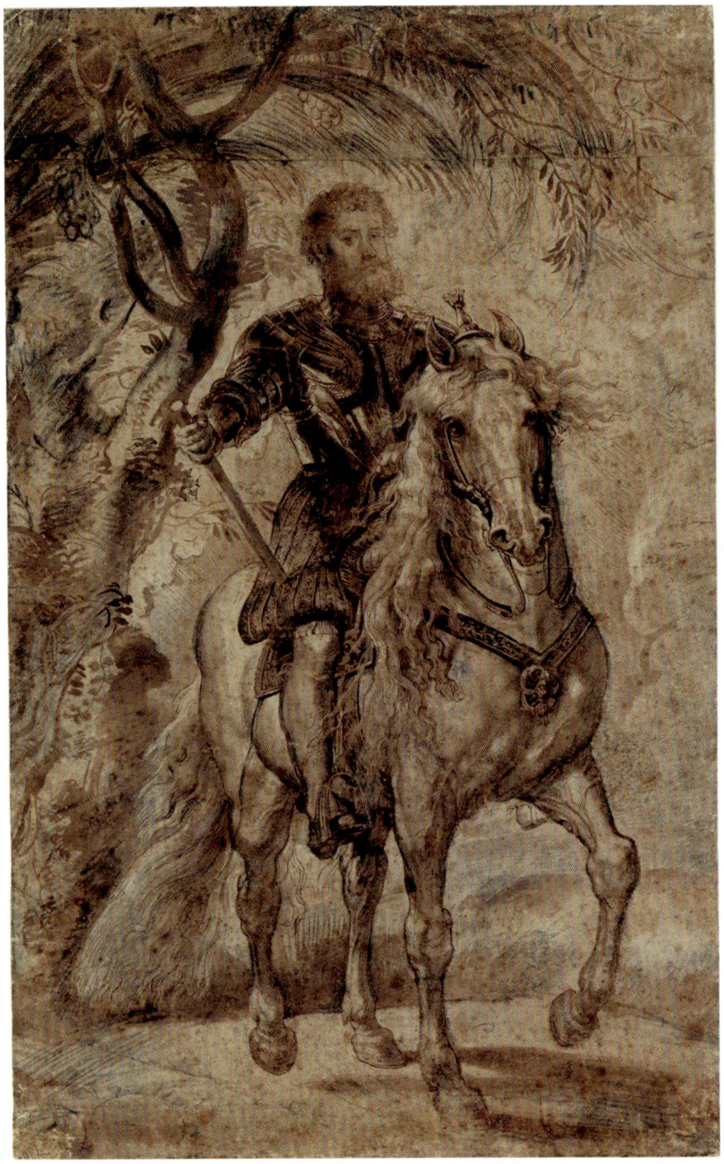

1
Peter Paul Rubens
The Duke of Lerma on Horseback, 1603
Pen and brown ink and brown wash with touches of white wash over black chalk, 673 x 410 mm
Staatliche Graphische Sammlung, Munich
1983.84

the decision: in the words of one commentator, 'deprived of the court, the town has suffered the greatest calamity that any locality has ever experienced, because everyone of every category found some way of making a living'.[4] One effect of the move was the dispersal of artists and publishers, which temporarily slowed Madrid's development as a cultural hub.

The most active artists whose careers span the reign of three monarchs are Eugenio Cajés (1574–1634) and Vicente Carducho (*c.*1576–1638). Their drawings illustrate the continuity of artistic practice that originated at the Escorial and had a great impact on artists who trained and worked with them during the first half of the seventeenth century. The evidence of wider drawing activity in Spain at this time is fragmentary but nevertheless significant.

No drawings by significant artists working in Castile, such as Luis Tristán (*c.*1590–1624) or Juan Bautista Maino (1581–1649), are known to have survived. However, Maino was appointed drawing master to the Infante Felipe (later Philip IV), which suggests that he had some expertise in drawing.[5] A letter sent in 1616 by the poet and playwright Lope de Vega to his patron, the Duke of Sessia, describes a drawing of a ceiling design that Maino had prepared for Vega's residence.[6] This sort of shadowy reference to drawing occurs throughout the documentation concerning artists. Only one tiny sketch of a Roman emperor securely attributed to Juan Pantoja de la Cruz (1553–1608) has survived,[7] yet it is known that he sent a drawing of a statue of Philip III on horseback to Giambologna in Florence in 1606.[8] Maino and Pantoja typify the sort of problems that make it hard for scholars to assess the role of drawing in early modern Spain. As a result of the changing locations of patronage, artists, especially those attached to the court, had to travel considerable distances in order to work on commissions. Their preparatory prints and drawings would perhaps have had a greater chance of survival in a stable environment such as an established workshop.

The Flemish-born artist Peter Paul Rubens (1577–1640) was one of the most prolific and committed draughtsmen of the seventeenth century, copying the work of other artists, retouching drawings and making preparatory studies for most of his painted compositions and prints.[9] Rubens arrived at the court in Valladolid on 13 May 1603 as part of a diplomatic mission on behalf of his patron, Vincenzo Gonzaga, Duke of Mantua, and he remained there for more than eight months. Shortly after he arrived, Rubens began working on an equestrian portrait of the Duke of Lerma, for which two preparatory drawings survive.[10] It is thought that he gave the drawing now in Munich (fig. 1) to the duke before he returned to Mantua.[11] We know nothing of how other artists responded to the drawing or the painting,[12] but the duke was apparently extremely pleased with it; no doubt the approbation of such a powerful patron had an impact on artists at the court, especially given that they were eager to gain his favour.[13] Rubens' painting epitomized a flamboyant and confident style not seen before in Spain, and his preparatory drawings are entirely different from those produced, for example, at the Escorial. While the effect of one or two sheets should not be over-emphasized, Rubens' dedication to drawing and his position in the court doubtless ensured his influence.

Vicente Carducho, Eugenio Cajés and the role of drawing

Vicente Carducho, just a year older than Rubens, moved with his brother Bartolomé from the Escorial to Valladolid and Lerma in 1600 to work for the court.[14] Vicente succeeded his brother as court painter in 1609, and his friend and lifelong collaborator Eugenio Cajés was appointed Painter to the King in 1612.[15] The two artists had returned to Madrid in 1606 as part of a team to redecorate El Pardo, the royal residence that had been damaged by fire two years earlier.[16]

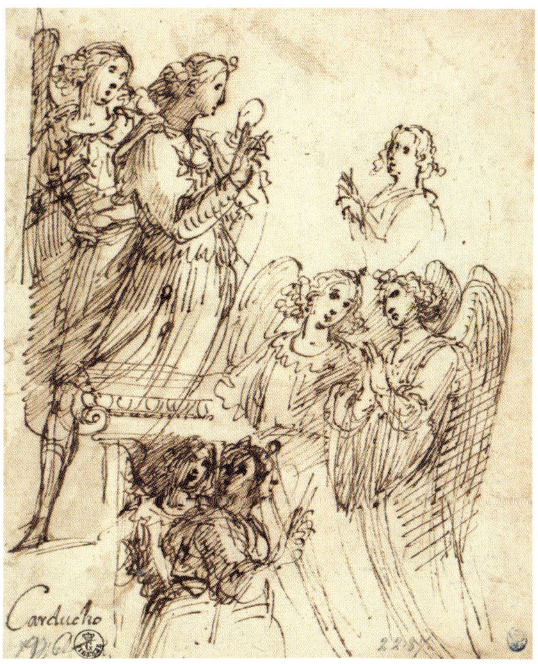

2
Vicente Carducho
A Group of Angels, c.1607–9
Pen and brown ink, 186 x 150 mm
Gabinetto Disegni e Stampe degli Uffizi, Florence
S 2287

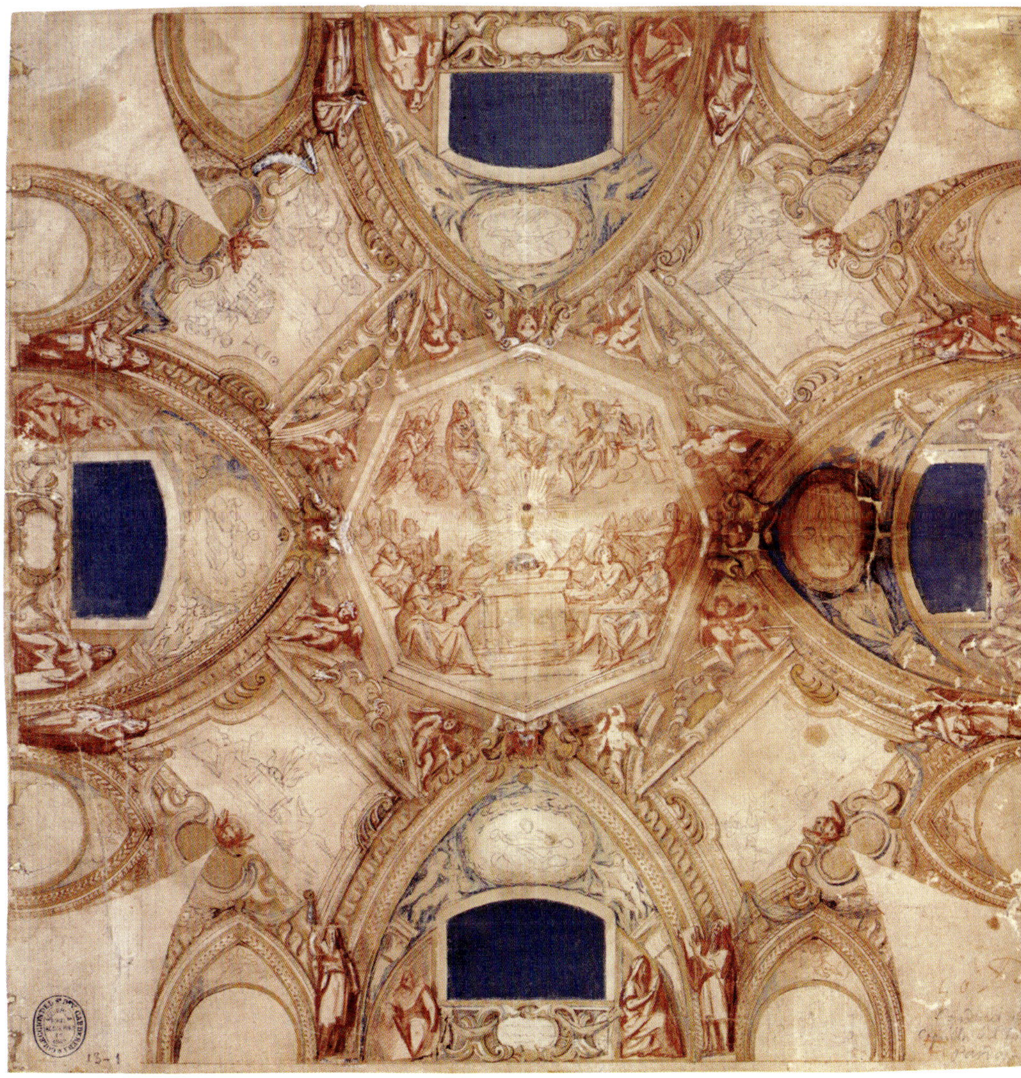

3
Vicente Carducho
Triumph of the Eucharist, c.1607–9
Pen and brown ink over black chalk, red and blue wash, blue bodycolour, gold, touches of lead white, 363 x 360 mm
Biblioteca Nacional, Madrid
DIB/13/1/73

4
Patricio Cajés
The Sons of Jacob Presenting him with Joseph's Tunic, *c*.1607–12
Pen and brown ink, black chalk, pink and brown wash over incised lines, 241 x 295 mm
Biblioteca Nacional, Madrid
DIB/13/10/3

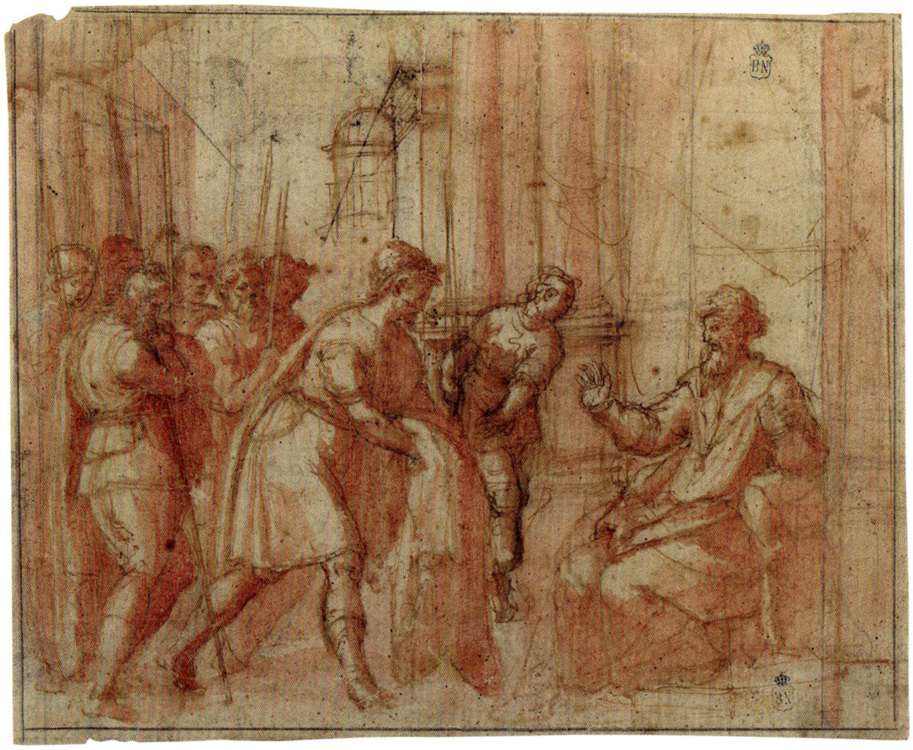

Between 1607 and 1609 Carducho produced a number of drawings for a ceiling design in the chapel of El Pardo.[17] One of these shows several sketches of an angel in pen and ink (fig. 2), one of them holding the Host. A finished study of the entire ceiling, with the *Triumph of the Eucharist* in the centre (fig. 3), was probably submitted for approval. The studies reflect Carducho's approach to drawing, his technique corresponding closely to its purpose. His drawings should also be seen in context of other artists working alongside him, as they reflect the continuation of earlier practices. For example, the Italian-born Patricio Cajés (*c.*1540–1612) was amongst the older artists working at El Pardo. His pen-and-wash drawing for the Queen's Gallery fresco, *The Sons of Jacob Presenting him with Joseph's Tunic* (fig. 4) is incised using a blind stylus to guide the design, a tried and tested Italian drawing technique.[18] Patricio made extensive use of wash, which greatly influenced his son Eugenio, for whom it became the medium he used most often and to greatest effect.

Vicente Carducho and Eugenio Cajés collaborated on commissions throughout their careers. An imposing drawing for the high altar of the church for the monastery of Guadalupe (Cáceres) by the architect Juan Gómez de Mora (1586–1648) shows a four-storey structure with sculptures of saints standing in niches, a painted crucifixion in the uppermost section flanked by the Virgin and Saint John the Baptist, coats of arms and allegorical figures (fig. 5).[19] Reinforcing a point made earlier, that artists based in Madrid often had to undertake work in distant places, the sheet is especially valuable for what it reveals about the practical use of drawings and the process of designing an altar in the early seventeenth century. The inscription along the bottom, signed and dated by Mora 20 December 1614, describes the pictorial programme, the arrangement of the figures and the type of stone to be used, and lists those involved in its execution.[20] The altar structure was designed by

5
Juan Gómez de Mora
The High Altar of the Church of the Monastery of Guadalupe, 1614
Pen and brown ink, brush and red ink, washes in brown and red over incised lines, 635 x 346 mm
Biblioteca Nacional, Madrid
DIB/16/34/2

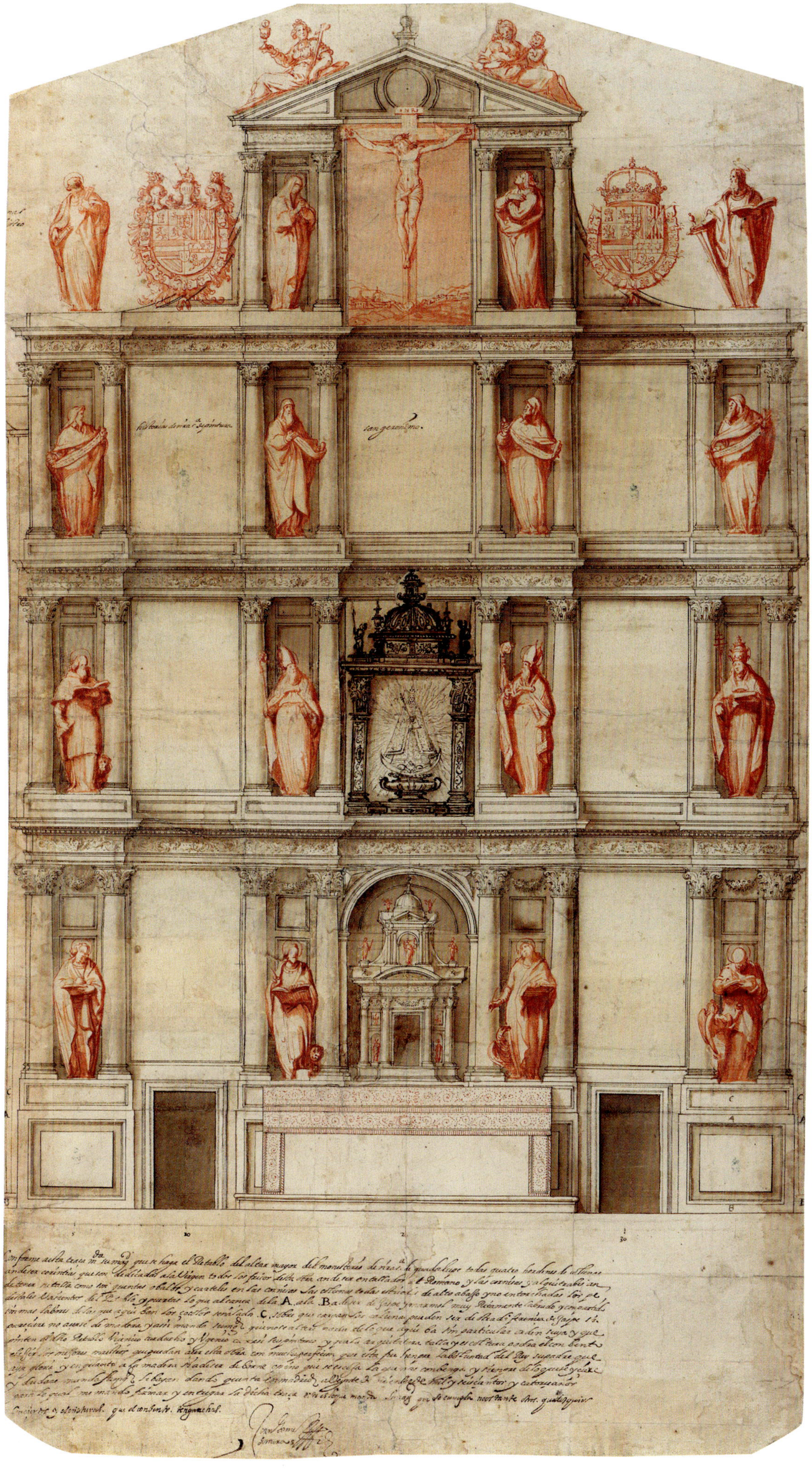

Mora, while Carducho and Eugenio Cajés executed the paintings. Cajés also probably drew the delicate figures on the sheet: the application of the wash, the facial features and the figure types are typical of his hand.

A little later Carducho and Cajés worked on the fresco decoration for the chapel of the sacristy in Toledo Cathedral. Cajés painted four works illustrating the story of Saints Ildephonsus and Leocardia (fig. 6).[21] A comparison between his drawing for *Saint Ildephonsus at the Tomb of Saint Leocardia* (fig. 7) and Carducho's *Adoration of the Magi* (fig. 8), made a couple of years later and closely related to a version of the painting on the altar of the parish church at Algete (another commission shared with Cajés; fig. 9), reveals their similar

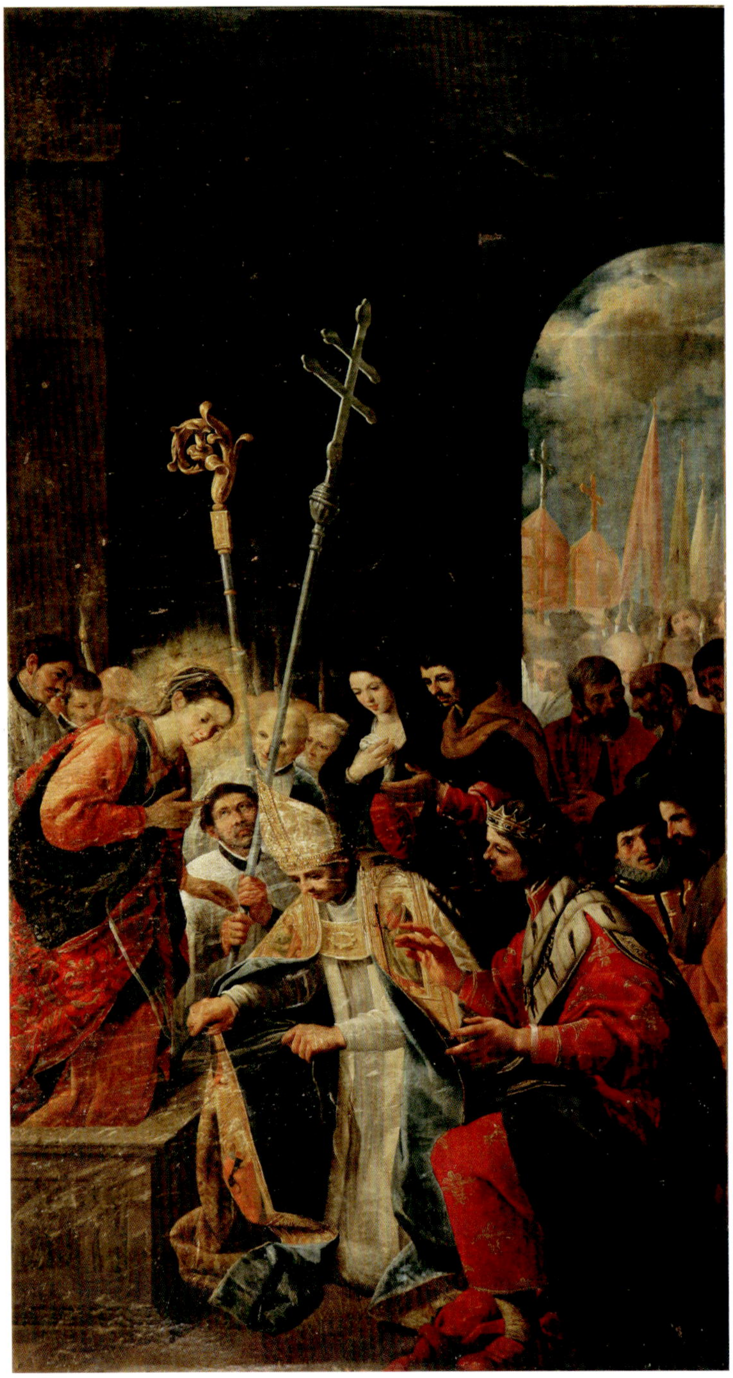

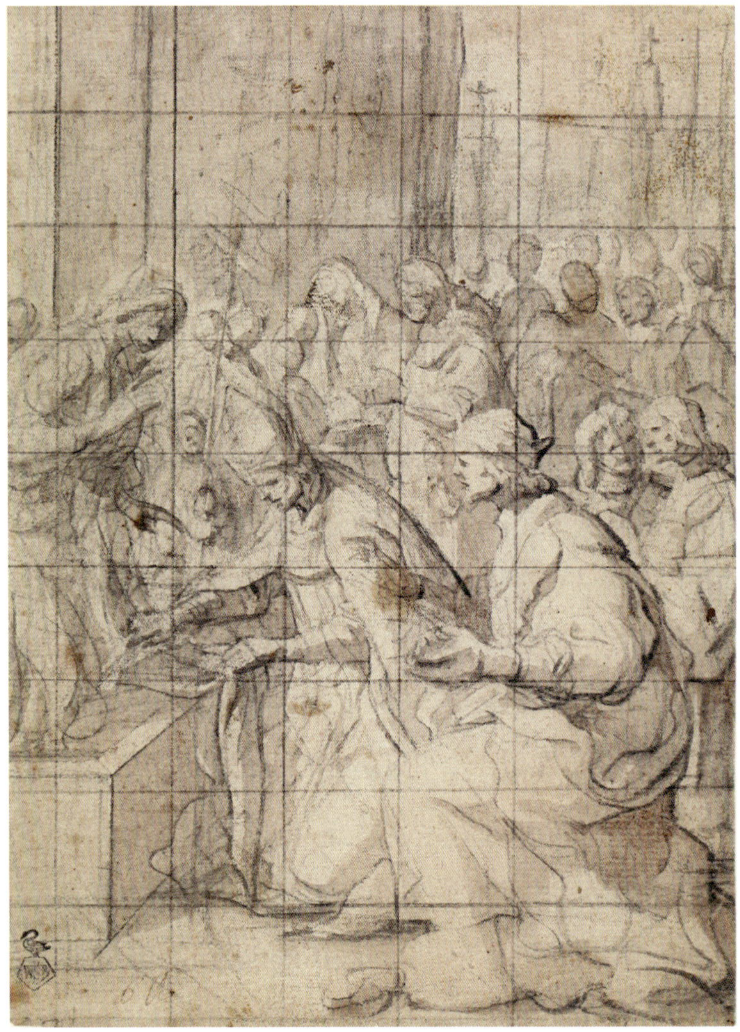

6
Eugenio Cajés
Saint Ildephonsus at the Tomb of Saint Leocardia, c.1615
Oil on canvas
Toledo Cathedral

7
Eugenio Cajés
Saint Ildephonsus at the Tomb of Saint Leocardia, c.1615
Black chalk and brown wash, squared for transfer,
228 x 160 mm
British Museum, London
1973,0721.1

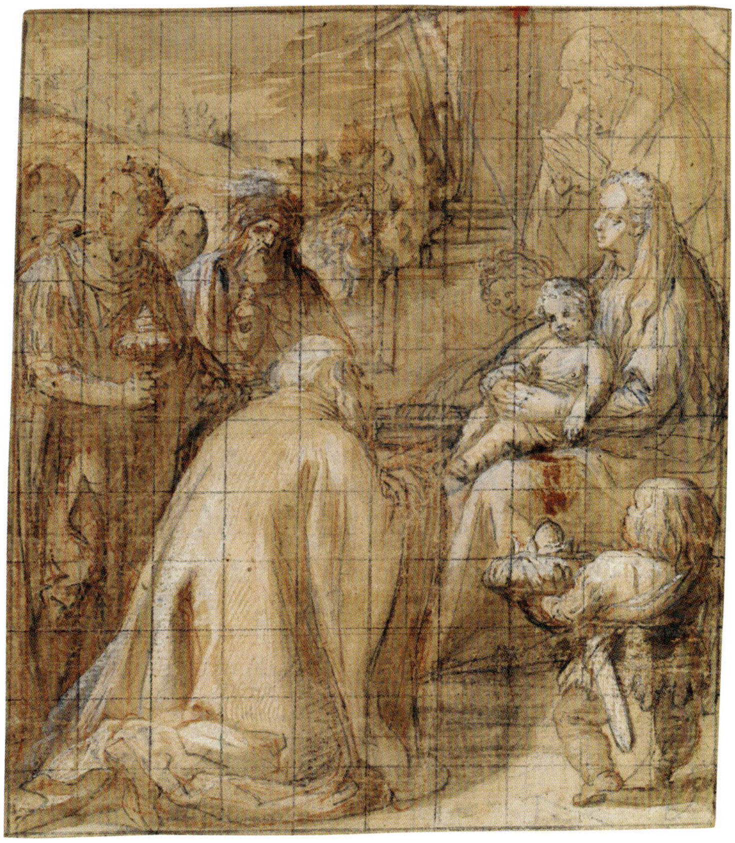

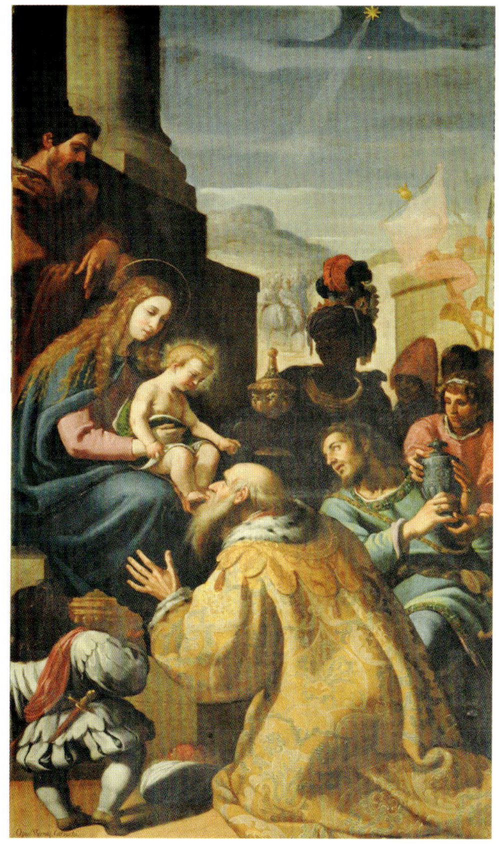

approach. Both compositions are small, carefully planned and squared for transfer, but their drawing techniques reflect their individual styles, Cajés' flickering effects of light and dark and Carducho's solid forms.

Cajés' *Study of Christ for the Flagellation* (fig. 10) echoes earlier drawing traditions. The use of the edge of the chalk to outline Christ's body and the soft modelling of his flesh by working the chalk with his fingers produces a highly finished appearance reminiscent of the work of Becerra or Urbino, discussed in Chapter 3. Of the two, Carducho was the more ambitious draughtsman, experimenting in different media and sometimes on unusually large sheets. In 1626 he received the most important commission of his career, for fifty-six paintings for the Carthusian monastery of El Paular, near Segovia.[22] For each painting (fig. 11) he made preliminary drawings and studies of individual figures, details (see figs 7–8, p. 27) and oil sketches. *Saint Bruno praying in La Torre-Calabria* (fig. 12) is one of the finished sheets from the group showing an entire composition.

Carducho and Cajés were dedicated to improving the professional status of painters through implementing academic training based on their knowledge and experiences gained at the Escorial.[23] Between 1603 and 1606 a group of painters including Cajés sought royal approval to create 'a school where the art of drawing is scientifically taught to all who want to learn it'.[24] The petition, which had much in common with that of the Academy of Saint Luke in Rome, was unsuccessful, but the artists' need for recognition did not diminish. In 1624, having gained the support of the Count-Duke of Olivares, Carducho presented to Philip IV a plan for a proposed Academy.[25] This laid

8
Vicente Carducho
Adoration of the Magi, c.1616–22
Red and black chalk, with brown wash, heightened with white, squared for transfer,
195 x 166 mm
British Museum, London
1946,0713.1024

9
Vicente Carducho
Adoration of the Magi, 1619
Oil on canvas, 2500 x 1300 mm
Church of the Assumption of Our Lady, Algete

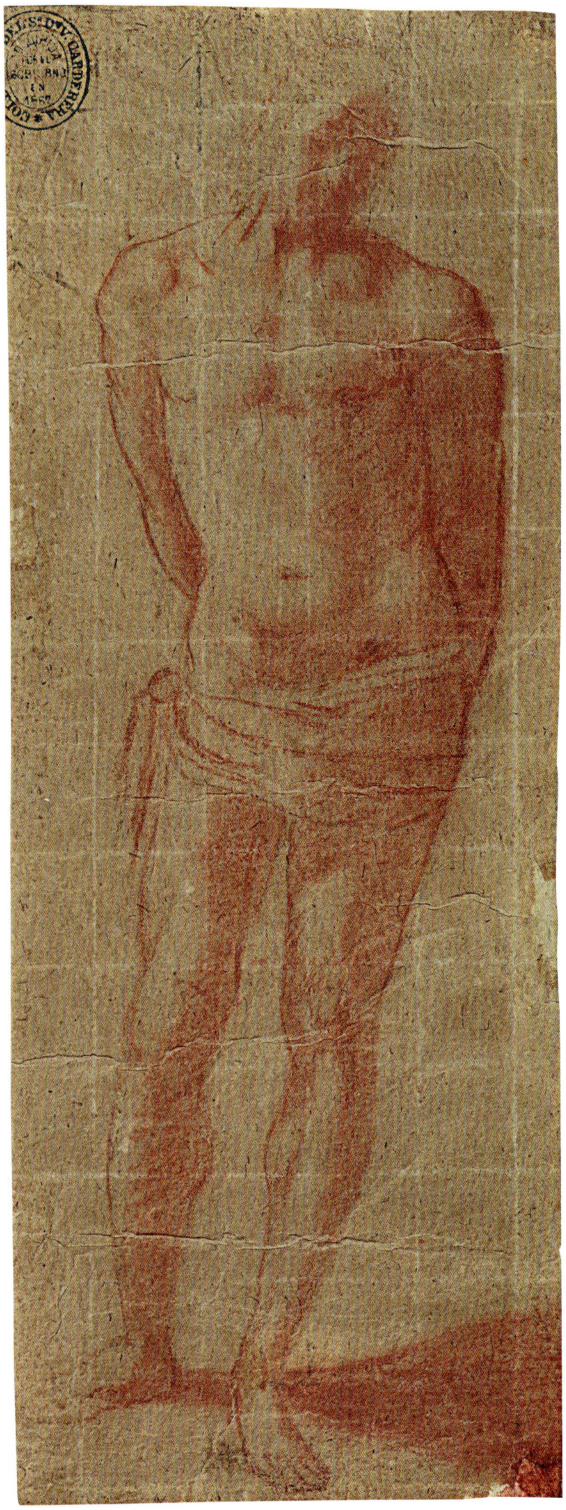

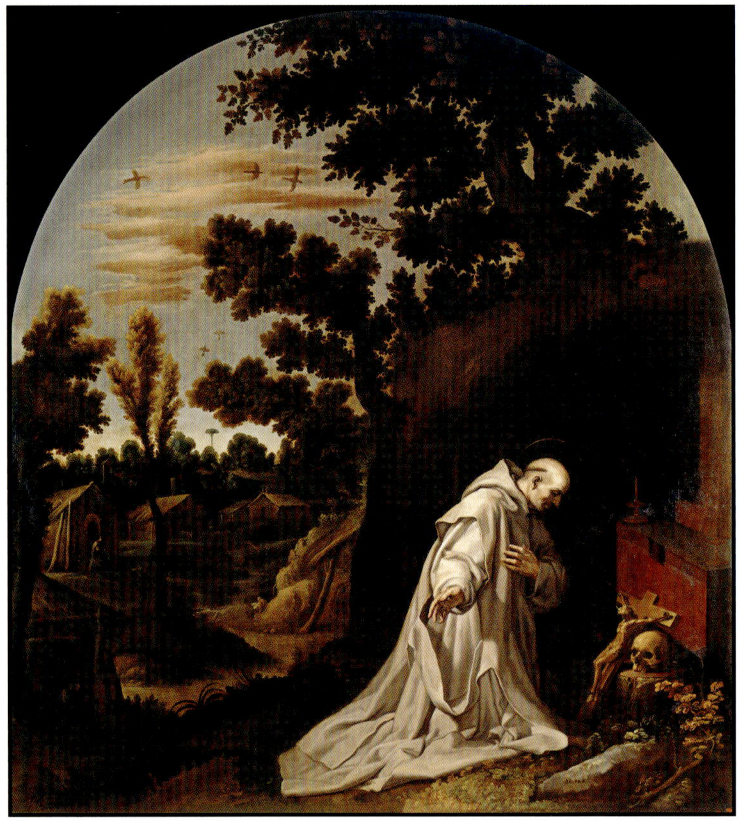

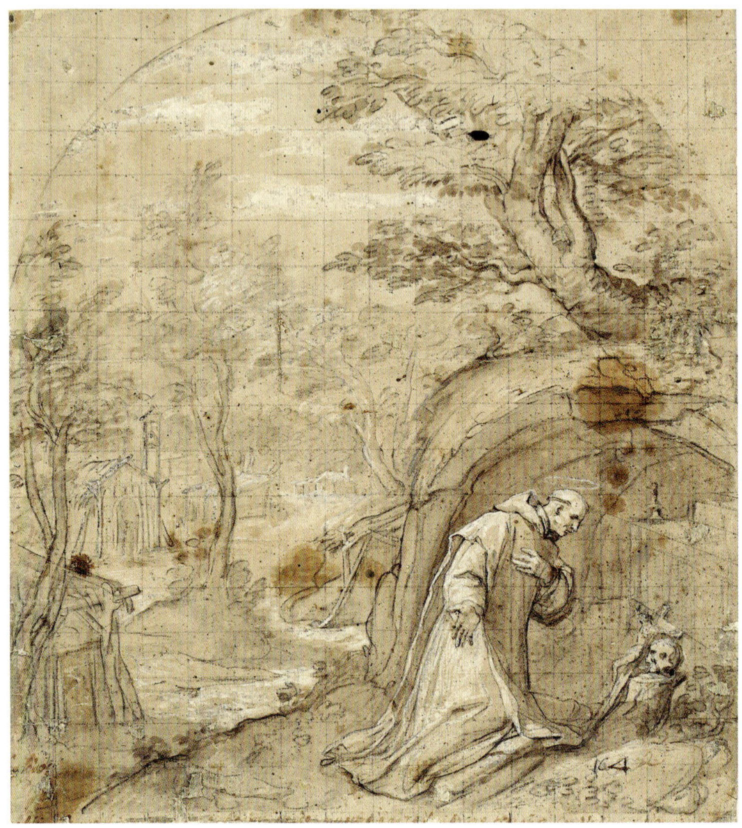

10
Eugenio Cajés
Study of Christ for the Flagellation, *c.*1600–20
Red chalk, squared for transfer
268 x 98 mm
Biblioteca Nacional, Madrid
DIB/16/39/5

out a carefully devised programme based on Italian principles that promoted the scientific basis of artistic instruction within an organized and professional context.[26] Carducho's instructional methods promoted the principles of good design, giving highest priority to *disegno*. Once again, the plan was unsuccessful.[27]

The most enduring testimony to Carducho's academic commitment was his *Diálogos de la pintura*, a treatise published in 1633 comprising eight dialogues in which the Master, a spokesperson for Carducho's own views, discusses with his disciple the virtues and practice of painting.[28] The *Diálogos* represent painting as a liberal art in which the importance of a solid grounding in the principles of artistic practice is made abundantly clear. Although Carducho's and Cajés' attempts to establish an academy did not bear fruit, they passed to their pupils the academic rigour of drawing from life and studying past masters.[29] Cajés' drawing after Goltzius (fig. 4, p. 24) shows the process of selective copying. The absence of an academy in Madrid largely explains the erratic evidence for drawing there, since there was no formal structure for their preservation. However, the large number of sheets by Carducho and Cajés that do survive must have provided examples for apprentices in their workshops, many of whom became the best artists of the next generation.

11
Vicente Carducho
Saint Bruno Praying in la Torre-Calabria, 1626–32
Oil on canvas,
3450 x 3150 mm
Museo del Prado, Madrid
P.5405

12
Vincente Carducho
Saint Bruno Praying in La Torre-Calabria, 1626–32
Pen and black ink, chalk and brown wash, heightened with white, squared for transfer,
326 x 285 mm
British Museum, London
1875,0710.2621

Drawing during the reign of Philip IV

When Philip IV came to the throne in 1621 the artistic patronage of his forebears provided a powerful model. His main interest lay in painting rather than architecture or sculpture, and his activities as a collector developed in a new direction.[30] Although he inherited the substantial collections formed by Philip II, the strongest influence on his interest in painting was Rubens, who returned to Madrid on a diplomatic mission for a second time in late 1628. Rubens' earliest activity as a draughtsman in Spain is discussed above. On his return to Madrid he was given lodging in the Alcázar, where the king paid him daily visits.[31] The drawing of *Philip IV in Outdoor Dress* (fig. 13) from around 1628–9 shows his continued work here, where his sophistication, knowledge of art and creative brilliance had a tremendous impact.[32] He also painted copies after works by Titian in the royal collection and later, in 1636, he received a major commission for sixty-three paintings based on Ovid's *Metamorphosis* for the Torre de la Parada.[33]

Madrid's urban expansion was a magnet for artists from regional centres seeking work. Their mobility is an important point to keep in mind because it helps to explain the different artistic styles that converged in the capital. The story of the rapid ascendancy of Diego Velázquez (1599–1660) in the court of Philip IV has been told many times.[34] After training in Seville with Francisco Pacheco, Velázquez came first to Madrid in 1622 and was appointed Royal Painter on his return the following year. At that time there were five royal painters, of whom Carducho and Cajés were prolific draughtsmen.[35] Thus Velázquez entered an environment where drawing was commonplace; he probably also shared a studio with Rubens in the Alcázar.[36] But the extent of his own drawing practice is very uncertain. Only a handful of sheets, executed in different techniques, appear to be autograph, and attributions often rest on typological similarities with figures in his paintings.[37] It is hard, however, to believe that Velázquez did not draw. Pacheco wrote that in his youth Velázquez

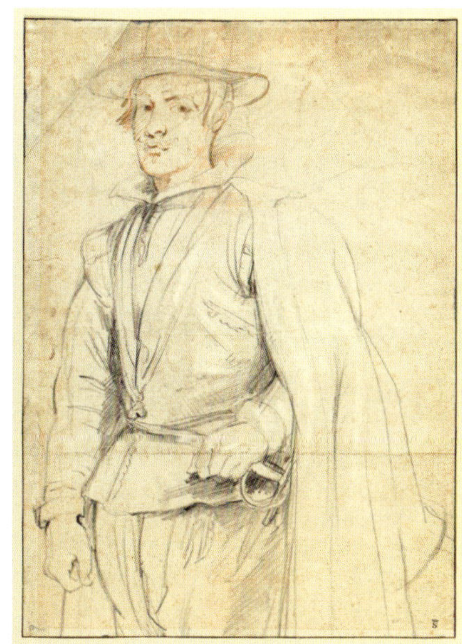

13
Peter Paul Rubens
Philip IV in Outdoor Dress, c.1628–9
Black and red chalk, pen, brush with brown ink and wash with white heighening,
383 x 265 mm
Musée Bonnat, Bayonne
1439

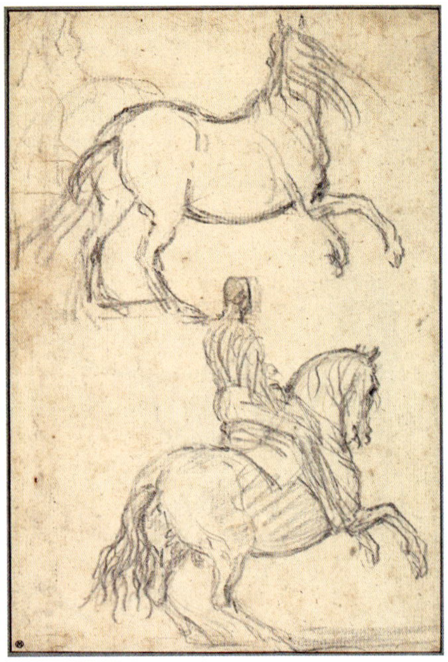

14
Diego Velázquez
Studies of Rearing Horse and Horseman, c.1625–35
Black chalk, 247 x 164 mm
British Museum, London
1850,1014.101

sketched expressions of a peasant boy in charcoal with white highlights on blue paper, which would have been a strange thing to fabricate were it not true.[38] According to Pacheco and Palomino, when Velázquez was in Rome during his first trip to Italy in 1629–31 he made drawings in the Vatican galleries and Venice, none of which seems to have survived.[39] A set of studies of a rearing horse and horseman believed to be by Velázquez (fig. 14 and detail p. 80) is typologically similar to the figures in several of his paintings.

Velázquez's arrival in Madrid is thought to have been part of Olivares' plan to distance the king from his predecessor's entourage, including Carducho and Cajés.[40] In 1627 a famous competition was held to select a painting of Philip III expelling the Moriscos from Spain, as part of the decoration for a room in the Alcázar dedicated to extolling the virtues of the Spanish Habsburgs as defenders of the faith. This pitted Velázquez against Carducho, Cajés and another Italian painter, Angelo Nardi.[41] The only surviving record of the competition is Carducho's large drawing – which, strangely, does not include Philip.[42] Velázquez was the victor, both consolidating his position and causing tension among the royal painters.[43] His success casts important light on court taste at this time. Velázquez represented an entirely new, realistic approach to painting. In Carducho's Sixth Dialogue (1633) the Master refers to an unnamed artist: 'I know another, so audacious, so favoured in painting, that we may say of him that he was born a Painter, whom brushes and colours obey, working more out of natural frenzy than on the basis of study.'[44] This has been interpreted as a veiled reference to Velázquez.[45] If intended as such, Carducho would seem to be referring to Velázquez's lack of preparatory drawings. Elsewhere he attacks Caravaggio for his naturalistic manner of painting, believing that it lacks the required preparation.[46] Again, he is referring to drawing.

It is perhaps most prudent to conclude that drawing did not play a conventional role in Velázquez's artistic practice. The fact that so few sheets can be attributed to him might reflect his distancing from the conservative practices of the older generation of artists. However, there are no signs of underdrawing on his paintings and it is difficult to see how his complex multi-figure compositions could have been achieved without the use of preliminary studies, perhaps discarded after use. This would suggest that he regarded finished drawings as largely unnecessary, which seems plausible given all that survive are quick sketches, nothing like the carefully planned drawings of his contemporaries.

The expansion of Madrid provided continued opportunities for architects and artists. The palace of the Buen Retiro in the spacious gardens on the eastern outskirts of the city was built for Philip IV during the 1630s.[47] Its decoration included more than eight hundred paintings, many by leading European artists of the day. The series commissioned by Olivares for the Hall of Realms, to celebrate the glory of Philip IV's regime, involved all the prominent artists working in Madrid: Carducho, Cajés, Maino, Velázquez, Francisco de Zurbarán and, from the younger generation, José Leonardo, Félix Castelo and Antonio Pereda.[48] Preparatory drawings for several of the paintings survive and provide an excellent indicator of drawing in Madrid at the time.

Carducho's sheet *The Duke of Feria at the Siege of Rheinfelden* (figs 15–16) is the most spectacular of these preparatory drawings, revealing his complete confidence as a draughtsman.[49] José (Jusepe) Leonardo (1601–52)

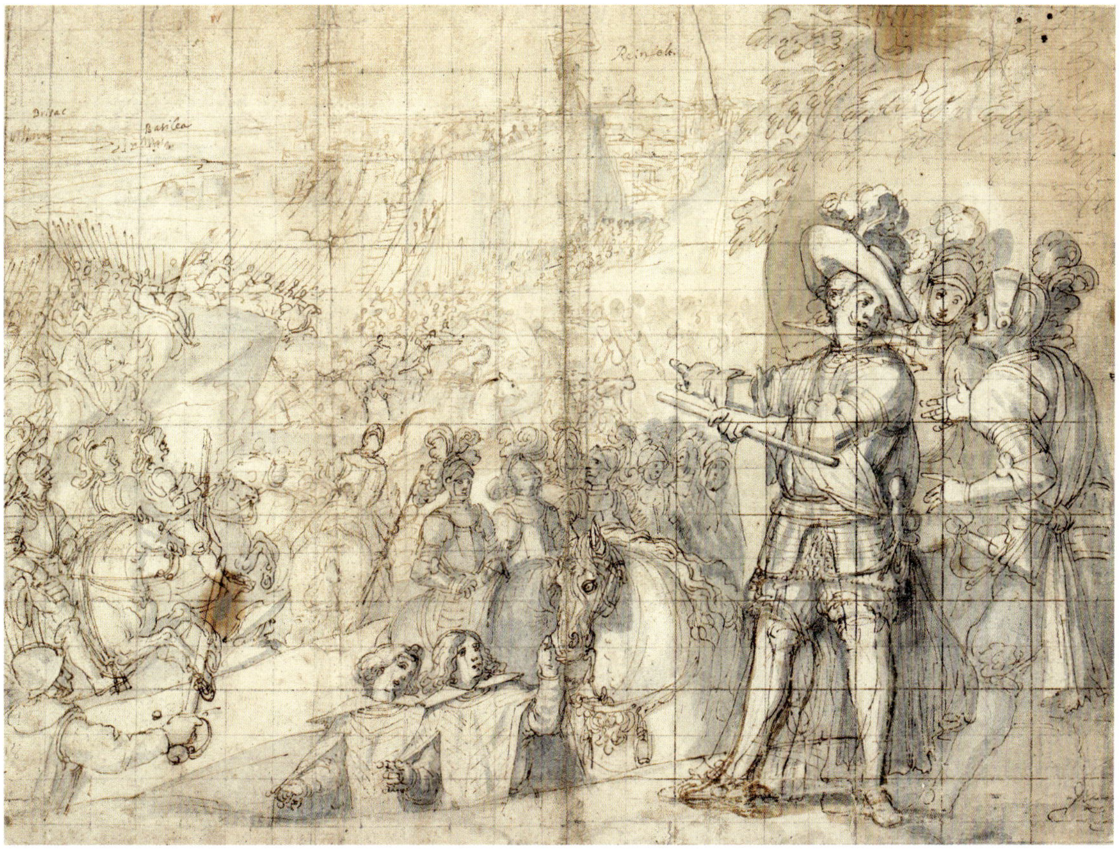

15
Vincente Carducho

The Duke of Feria at the Siege of Rheinfelden, 1634

Pen and brown ink, blue and brown wash over black chalk, squared for transfer,
318 x 415 mm
British Museum, London
1850,0713.9

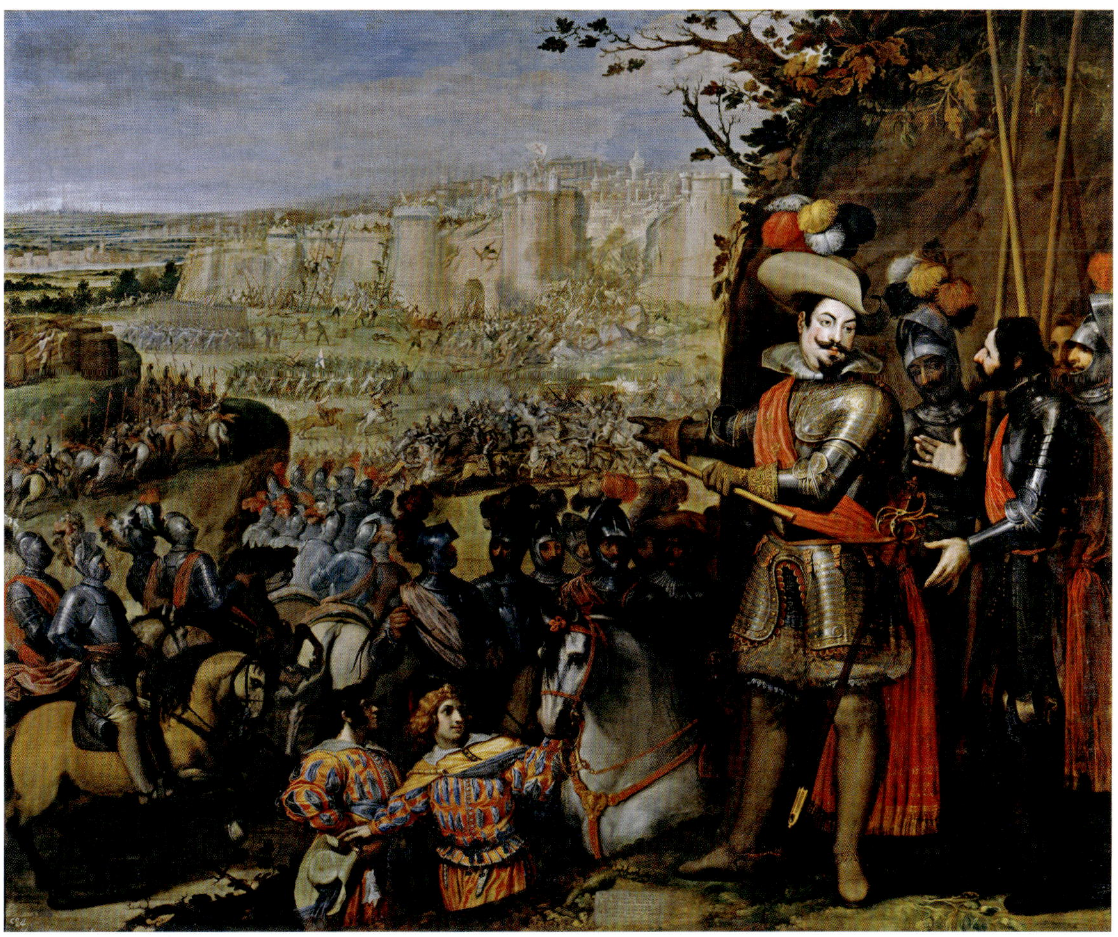

16
Vicente Carducho

The Duke of Feria at the Siege of Rheinfelden, 1634

Oil on canvas,
2970 x 3570 mm
Museo del Prado, Madrid
P.637

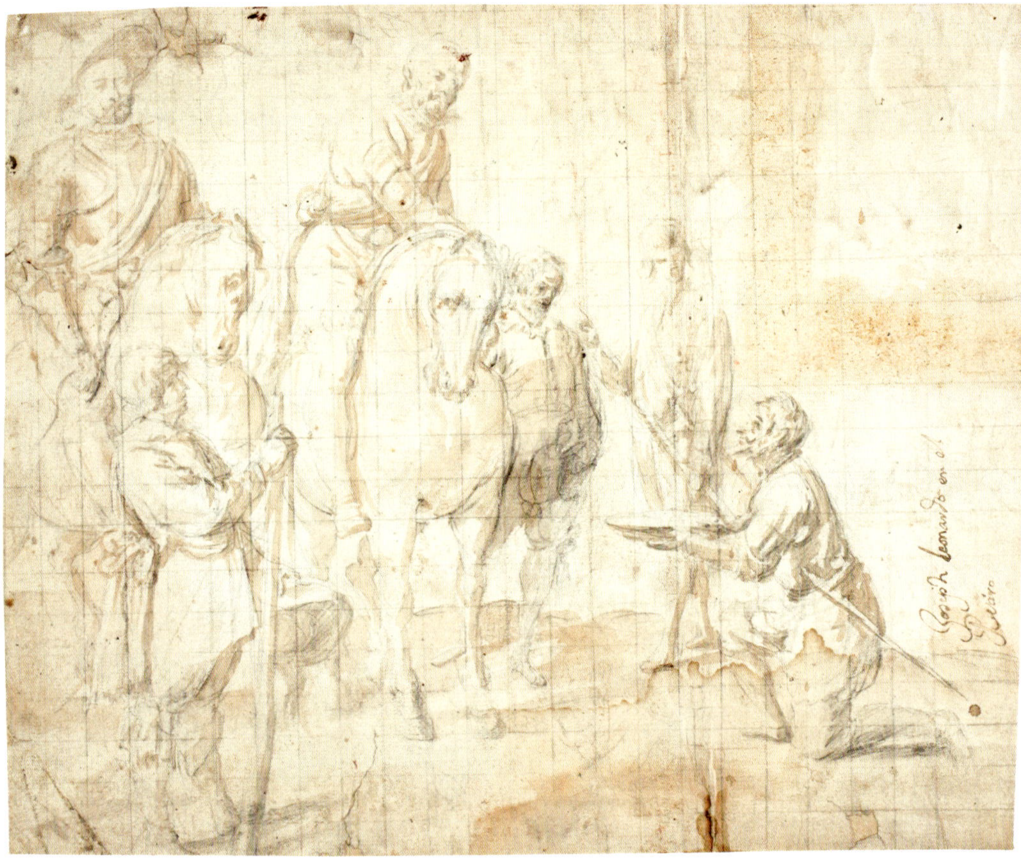

17
José Leonardo

The Surrender of Jülich, c.1634–5

Brush and brown ink over black chalk, squared for transfer, 260 x 307 mm
Museo del Prado, Madrid
D.3891

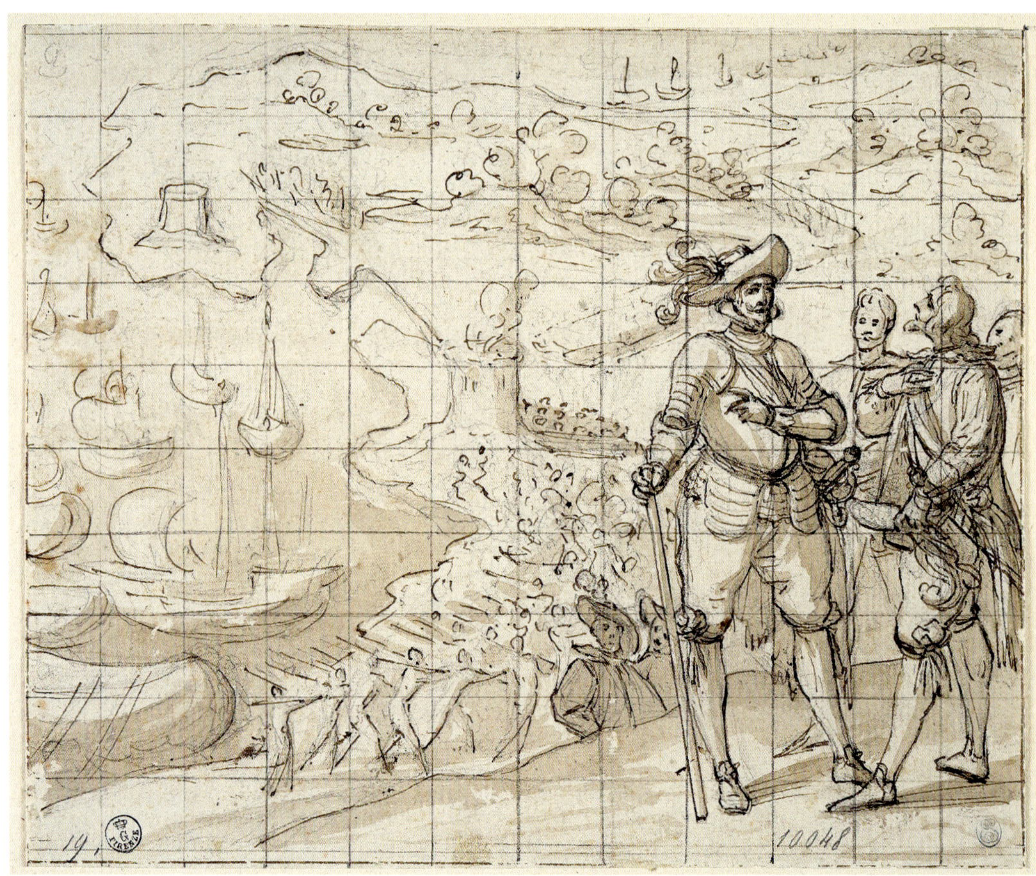

18
Félix Castelo

Recapture of the Island of San Cristobal by Don Fadrique de Toledo, c.1634–5

Pen and brown ink and wash over black chalk, squared for transfer, 190 x 225 mm
Gabinetto Disegni e Stampe degli Uffizi, Florence
S.10048

painted two works for the Hall of Realms, *The Surrender of Jülich* and *The Relief of Breisach*.[50] The preparatory drawing for *Jülich* survives (fig. 17).[51] Leonardo trained in Madrid with Pedro de las Cuevas but he is regarded as a follower of Eugenio Cajés, whose influence is unmistakable in this sheet.[52] The wash creating form over black chalk and the flickering effects of light recall Cajés drawing of *Saint Ildephonsus* discussed above (p. 87). Also for the Hall of Realms, Félix Castelo (1595–1651), probably a student of Carducho, painted the *Recapture of the Island of San Cristobal*.[53] His preparatory drawing in pen, ink and wash (fig. 18) was once thought to be by Antonio Tempesta.[54] Castelo's drawing owes much to Carducho's study of Rheinfelden in its use of more than one media, the composition, its carefully drawn figures at the right and the cursory details in the background.

The outstanding painting for the Hall of Realms is Velázquez's *Surrender of Breda* (or *The Lances*). A sheet depicting three figures, two showing the commander of the Spanish forces, Ambrosio Spinola, has been identified as preparatory for the painting (fig. 19). If this is indeed by Velázquez, it reinforces the observations regarding his drawing practice made above: it has nothing of the finish of studies by the other artists and seems marginal by comparison.[55]

Cajés died in 1634 and Carducho four years later, ending their dominance particularly of ecclesiastic commissions, and a new generation of artists in Madrid began to emerge. The most prominent were Antonio de Pereda y Salgado (1611–78) and Francisco Rizi (1614–85). Palomino reports that Pereda,

19
Diego Velázquez
Studies for the 'Surrender of Breda' (recto and verso), *c.*1634–5
Black chalk, 262 x 168 mm
Biblioteca Nacional, Madrid
DIB/16/40/20

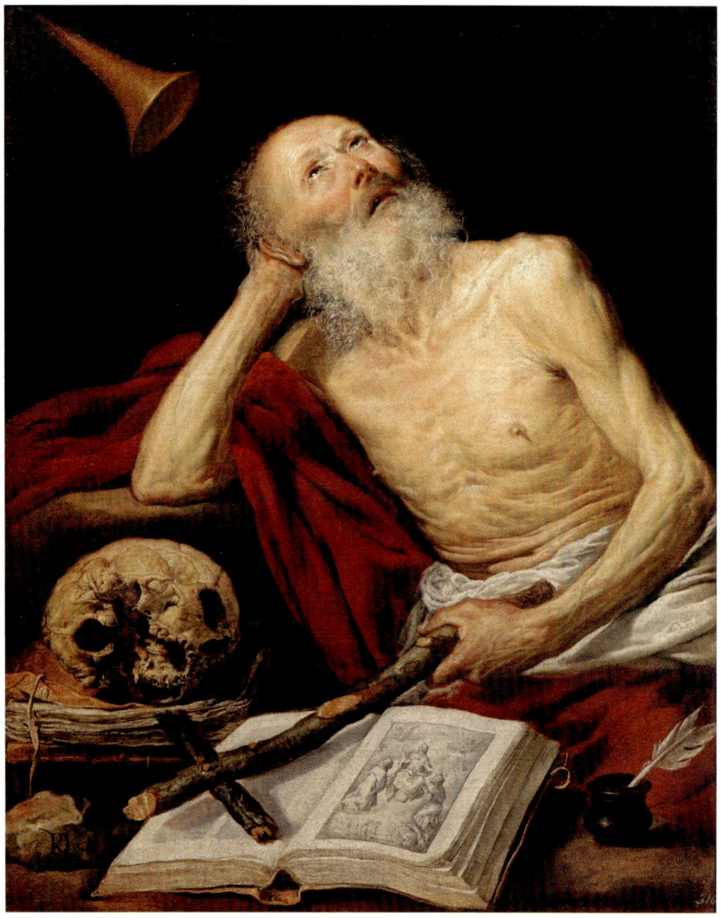

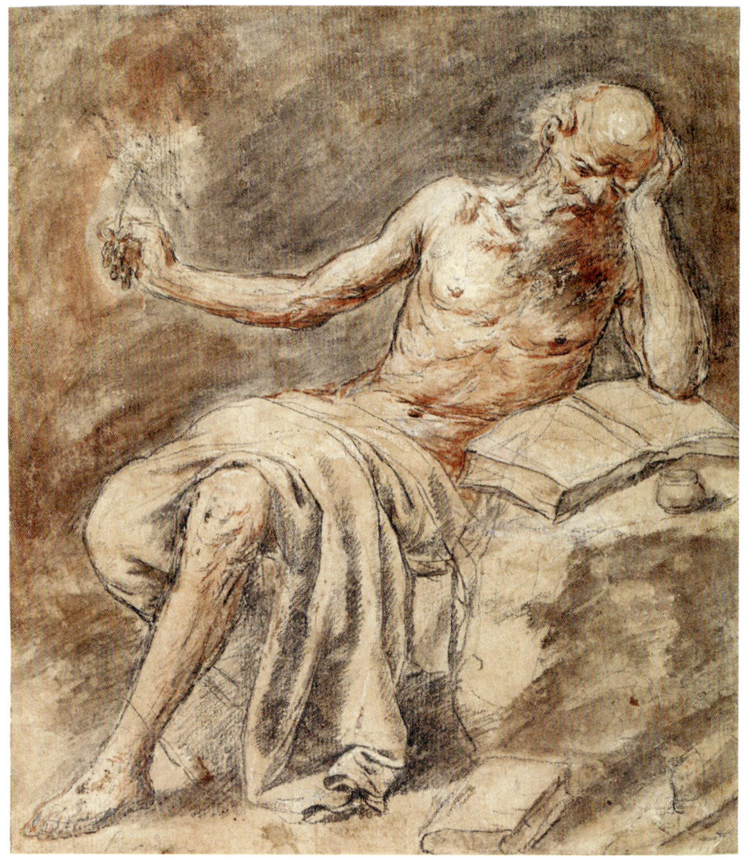

20
Antonio Pereda y Salgado
Saint Jerome, c.1643–4
Oil on canvas, 1043 x 840 mm
Museo del Prado, Madrid
P.1046

21
Antonio Pereda y Salgado
Saint Jerome in the Desert, c.1640–5
Red, black and white chalk with brown and grey wash, 255 x 215 mm
British Museum, London
1895,0915.883

a native of Valladolid, moved to Madrid (probably a little after 1622) where he learned the rudiments of painting with Pedro de las Cuevas.[56] He then studied under the protection of the Italian Giovanni Battista Crescenzi, Marques de la Torre, who involved him in the decoration of the Hall of Realms in the Buen Retiro.[57] Pereda's drawings combine the Tuscan tonal heritage of the Escorial artists with Flemish and Venetian design.[58] Related to his painting from around 1643–4 (fig. 20), *Saint Jerome in the Desert* (fig. 21) is executed in a rich combination of red and black chalk with brown and grey wash heightened with white, a complex mix hitherto unseen in Madrid. The composition recalls Ribera's models of the 1620s, which Pereda probably knew through his prints.[59] Pereda seems most interested in exploring colouristic effects in his drawings. For several of his sheets he used a luminous red wash with highlights on buff paper, creating nuanced tonalities of which the outstanding example is *Saint Ildephonsus Receiving the Chasuble from the Virgin Mary* (fig. 22).

Drawing in Madrid from around 1650

The year 1650 is often taken as a convenient point to begin assessing the development of painting that gave rise to a distinctive school of Madrid.[60] The work of Francisco Rizi, Juan Carreño de Miranda, Francisco Camilo, Francisco de Herrera the Younger and other, lesser-known artists from the second half of the century, is characterized by dynamic settings, a brighter palette and painterly brushwork, distinguishing them from the more laboured work of earlier decades. Drawing techniques became more varied, with mixed media and larger sheets of better-quality paper. The uses of drawing now included theatre design, architectural projects and planning decorations for triumphal entries, and these new developments were encouraged by a number of factors. An important catalyst was Rubens, whose work inspired many. The dissemination of prints after the work of European masters increased the body of knowledge from which artists could draw. The art market in Madrid had also greatly expanded, giving artists access to a wider variety of material. Together these factors had much greater influence than Velázquez who, although he was the pre-eminent court painter, had limited impact on his contemporaries.

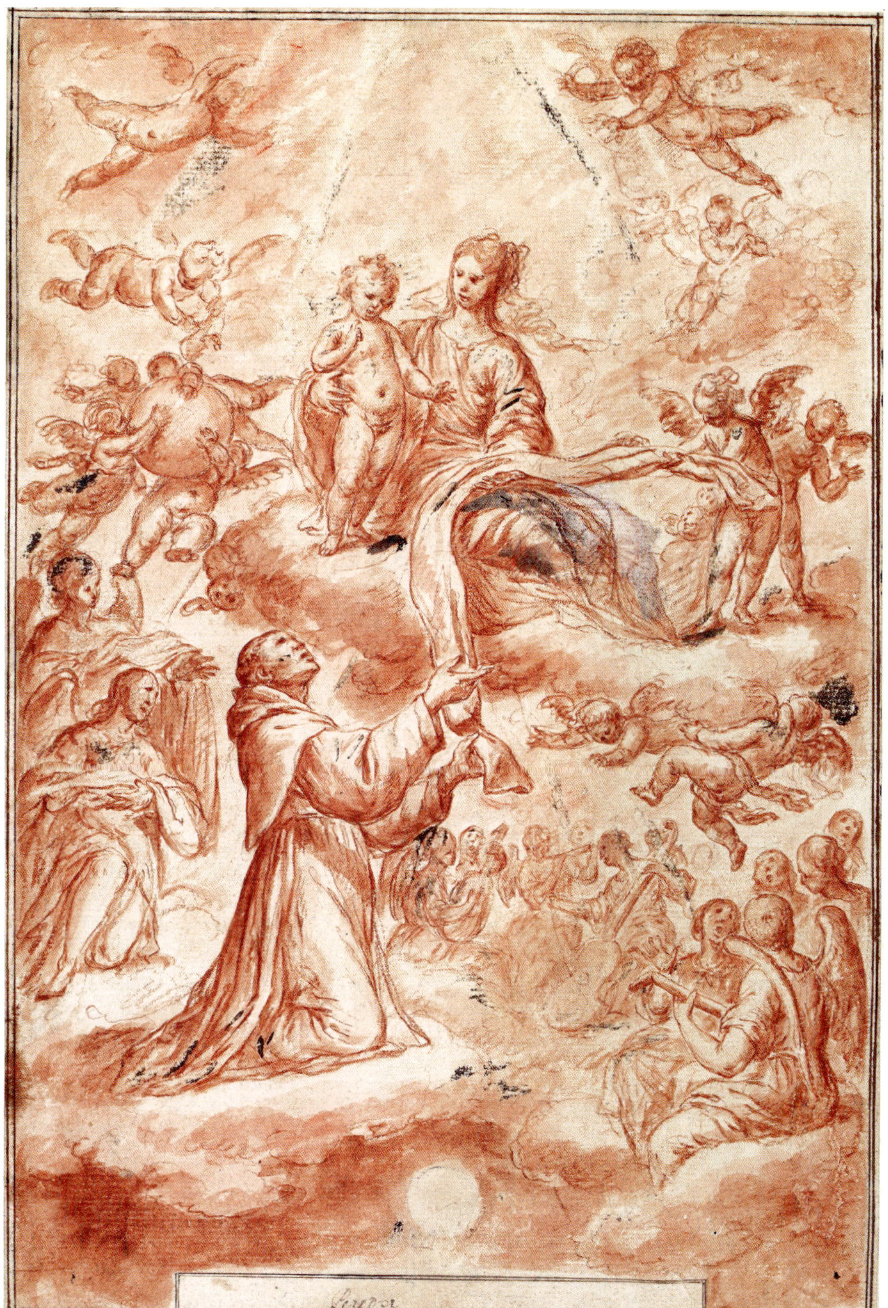

22
Antonio Pereda y Salgado
Saint Ildephonsus Receiving the Chasuble from the Virgin Mary, c.1640–60
Red chalk with red wash and white heightening,
320 x 210 mm
British Museum, London
1846,0509.181

By mid-century Philip IV and the nobility were collecting on an unprecedented scale, the renovation of royal residences continued, and ecclesiastic communities needed works to decorate their foundations. Artists from abroad continued to arrive in Madrid, though in much smaller numbers than during the previous century, and they did not dominate artistic production. On his second trip to Italy in 1650, Velázquez invited to Madrid two Bolognese fresco painters, Angelo Michele Colonna (1604–87) and Agostino Mitelli (1609–60).[61] They were supposed to return with Velázquez in May 1651, but they did not arrive in the end until 1658, when they began decorating rooms in the Álcazar and remained there until 1662.[62] Through their fresco work Colonna and Mitelli introduced illusionistic architectural perspective later taken up by their assistants, Juan Carreño de Miranda (1614–85) and the aforementioned Francisco Rizi.[63] Several drawings have been attributed to Colonna and Mitelli for their projects in Spain, but they are hard to verify because almost nothing of their painted work survives.[64] Two sheets, once joined, form two halves of a ceiling decoration attributed to Mitelli, Colonna or a Spanish follower (fig. 23).[65] Each part is drawn in perspective in pen and ink with a mix of washes and white heightening, mostly applied to projecting features. Most of the squaring lines were incised first with a blind stylus; at the intersection of the lines are pinholes indicating the use of a device to measure out the quadrants. One of the sheets has colour notes indicating that the flowers were to be blue and yellow. These drawings, with their added strips of paper and many marks, demonstrate how important and useful drawing was in the process of realizing a work of art.

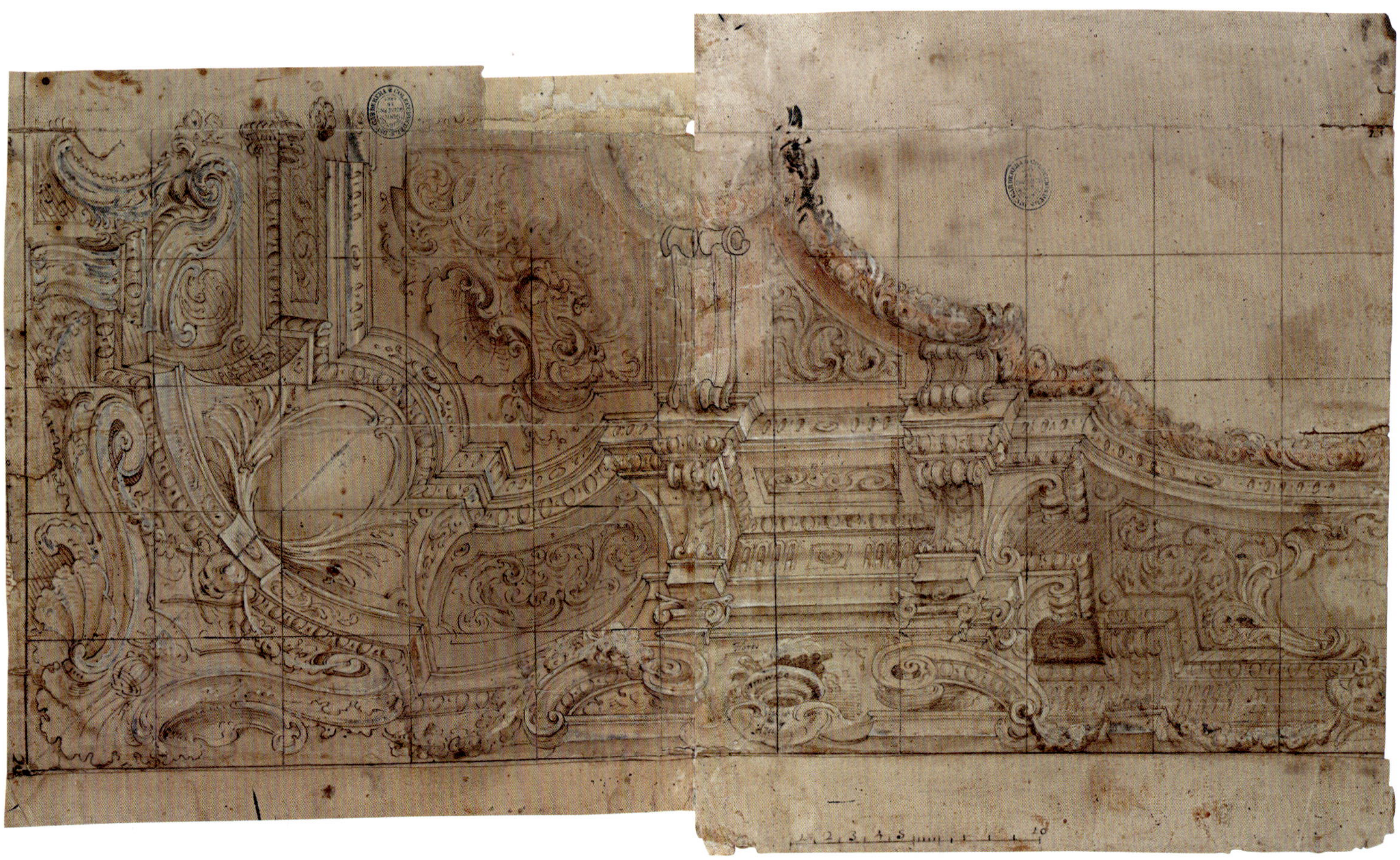

23
Anonymous
Design for a Ceiling Decoration, c.1660–70
Pen with brown and black ink, brown and blue wash, with white heightening over black chalk, squared for transfer, 294 x 268 mm (sheet) and 334 x 272 mm (sheet)
Biblioteca Nacional, Madrid
DIB/14/47/4 and DIB/14/47/5

Francisco Rizi was the son of a minor Italian painter, Antonio Ricci, who arrived at the Escorial in 1585 as part of Federico Zuccaro's entourage. Although Francisco was trained in Carducho's studio, his work reflects the artistic changes that took place in Madrid from the mid-1640s.[66] In his biography of Claudio Coello, Antonio Palomino writes that Coello's master, Francisco Rizi, 'was in the habit of making a sketch or quick notation of whatever work he had in hand – be it for a composition or for a perspective view – on any little piece of paper and then would tear it up and throw it away'. Coello would then collect and carefully reassemble the pieces to study them.[67] Palomino's observations about Rizi's commitment to drawing can be verified through his surviving sheets – and might also reflect a growing awareness of the importance of preserving drawings.

Throughout his long career Rizi was involved in theatre design and ephemeral decorations.[68] Palomino reports on this aspect of Rizi's work, noting that he was for many years in charge of the stage sets and comedies at the Buen Retiro, where the royal theatre (Coliseo) was inaugurated in 1640.[69] During this time he made many designs for the movable sets and left 'countless drawings'.[70] One of his earliest known sheets,[71] made when he was working regularly for the court, is the drawing for the title-page of a book commemorating Mariana of Austria's official entry into Madrid on 15 November 1649 for her marriage to Philip IV (fig. 24); this was subsequently engraved by Pedro de Villafranca (fig. 25).[72] The celebrations were organized by Lorenzo Ramírez de Prado, Knight of the Order of Santiago and Adviser to the King, whose name appears on the engraved title-page as the author of the design. Because it was intended for engraving, Rizi's drawing is concise with clear outlines, with a sense of movement in the figures that reflects the dynamism of his paintings.[73]

The types of decorative detail that occur in Rizi's drawings for theatrical projects can also be found in his religious works. His *Virgin Appearing to a Trinitarian Monk* (fig. 26) of about 1650 is framed by an illusionistic proscenium arch; he uses the same device to indicate dramatic perspective in his painting of *The Virgin and Child Adored by Saints Philip and Francis* (fig. 27) for the chapel of the Capuchin church of El Pardo. Professionally the

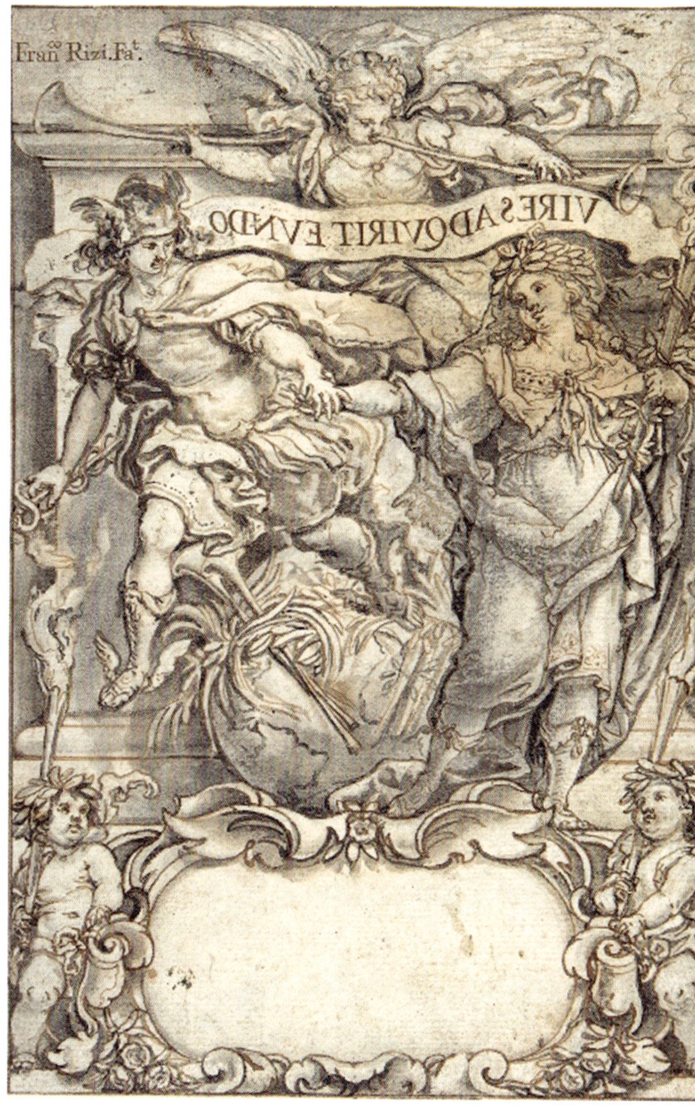

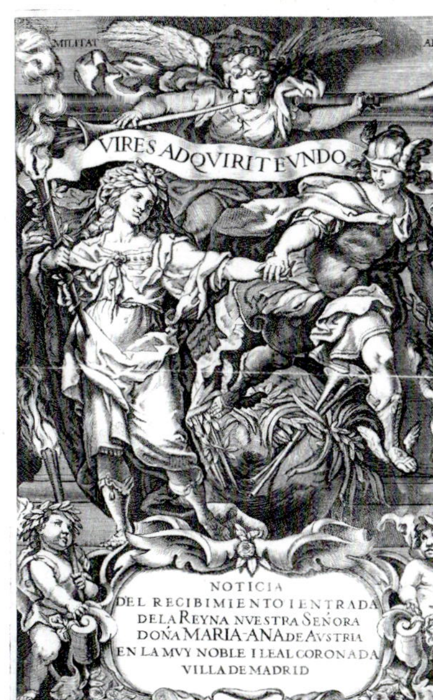

24
Francisco Rizi
Title-page Design for the Book Commemorating the Entry into Madrid of Mariana of Austria, 1649
Pen and brown and black ink with grey wash over black chalk, 275 x 181 mm
Metropolitan Museum of Art, New York
1975.131.226

25
Pedro de Villafranca
Title-page for the Book Commemorating the Entry into Madrid of Mariana of Austria, 1650
Engraving, 275 x 178 mm
Biblioteca Nacional, Madrid
2-61823

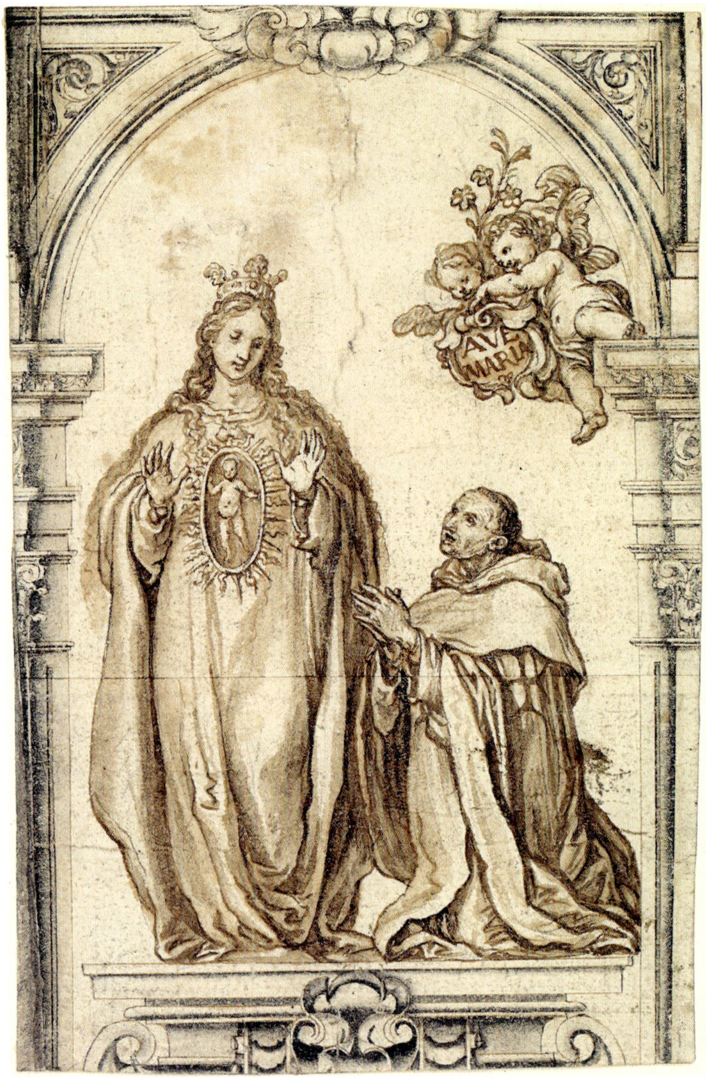

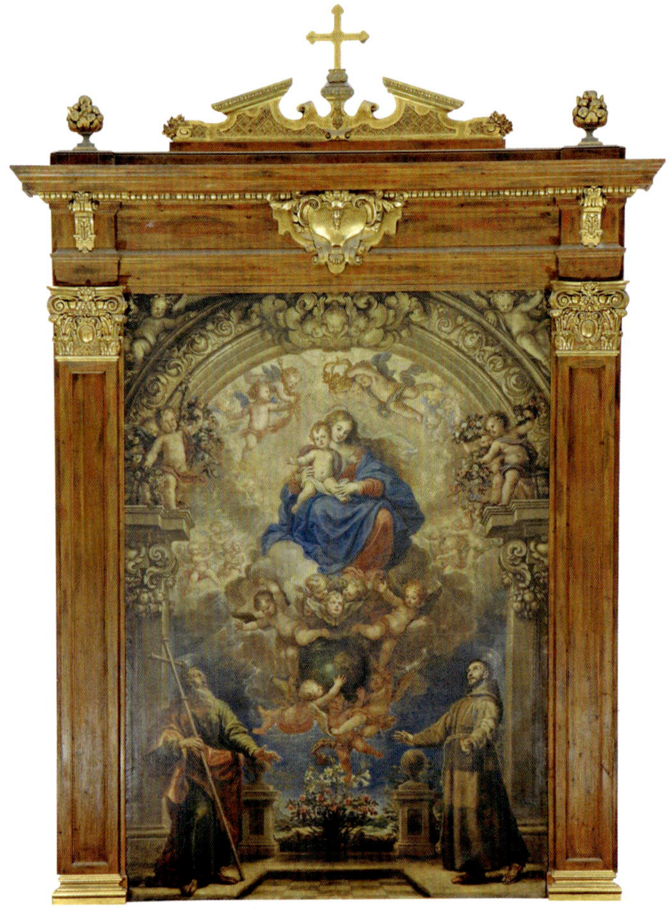

26
Francisco Rizi
The Virgin Appearing to a Trinitarian Monk, c.1650
Pen and brown ink, brown and grey wash over black chalk partly incised, 196 x 125 mm
British Museum, London
1895,0915.878

27
Francisco Rizi
The Virgin and Child Adored by Saints Philip and Francis, 1650
Oil on canvas
El Pardo, Madrid

1650s was an important decade for Rizi: he received commissions for paintings in the cathedrals of Toledo and Plasencia, and in 1656 he was appointed Painter to the King.[74] In 1659, under Velázquez's supervision, Rizi and Carreño assisted the Italian painters working on the fresco decorations depicting the myth of Pandora for the Hall of Mirrors in the Alcázar.[75] Although the frescos were destroyed in the 1734 fire, Rizi's drawing of *Jupiter Delivering the Vase to Pandora* (fig. 28), the third of the five episodes, provides a record of the central scene.[76] The carefully drawn figures in brown ink filled with grey wash, together with the raised stucco cartouche on top of the band of the foliage frame, suggest that this was the definitive design for this part of fresco.[77]

Rizi modified his drawing style to meet different needs, demonstrating his consummate draughtsmanship. His pen-and-ink study of *Saint Anthony of Padua in Glory* (fig. 6, p. 26) of around 1668, for the cupola fresco of San Antonio de los Portugueses (today San Antonio de los Alemanes) in Madrid, shows him quickly working out the relative positioning of the figures.[78] In a very different moment, his study of the dwarf 'Lusillo' is the only surviving drawing related to his painting of the *auto de fé* held in the Plaza Mayor in Madrid on

30 June 1680 (figs 29–30). Loosely executed in chalk, it was probably intended as an independent portrait of this well-known figure in the court.[79]

The earliest known work, from the 1640s, by Juan Carreño de Miranda, like that of his collaborator Francisco Rizi, was tied to the earlier generation of artists.[80] Palomino records that Carreño studied drawing with Pedro de las Cuevas and painting with Bartolomé Román.[81] Throughout the 1650s he painted works for churches in Madrid, and he increasingly came under the influence of Rubens and Van Dyck.[82] Carreño worked mainly in chalk. A drawing of two Apostles from around 1660 demonstrates his facility in this medium and is one of a number of works on fairly coarse tan paper, where he uses its texture to catch and model the coloured chalk in different ways (fig. 31).[83] In contrast to Rizi, who was concerned mainly with controlling the drawing medium, Carreño was conscious of the relationship between medium and paper. In *Christ Baptized* (fig. 32) of about 1682 he carefully modulates the chalk, pausing to strengthen outlines. The pose of Christ relates to two painted versions of the subject, but Carreño probably regarded the sheet a work of art in its own right. The few known pen, ink and wash drawings by Carreño are characterized by their nervous intensity; this seems to have been his preferred this technique for complex scenes.[84]

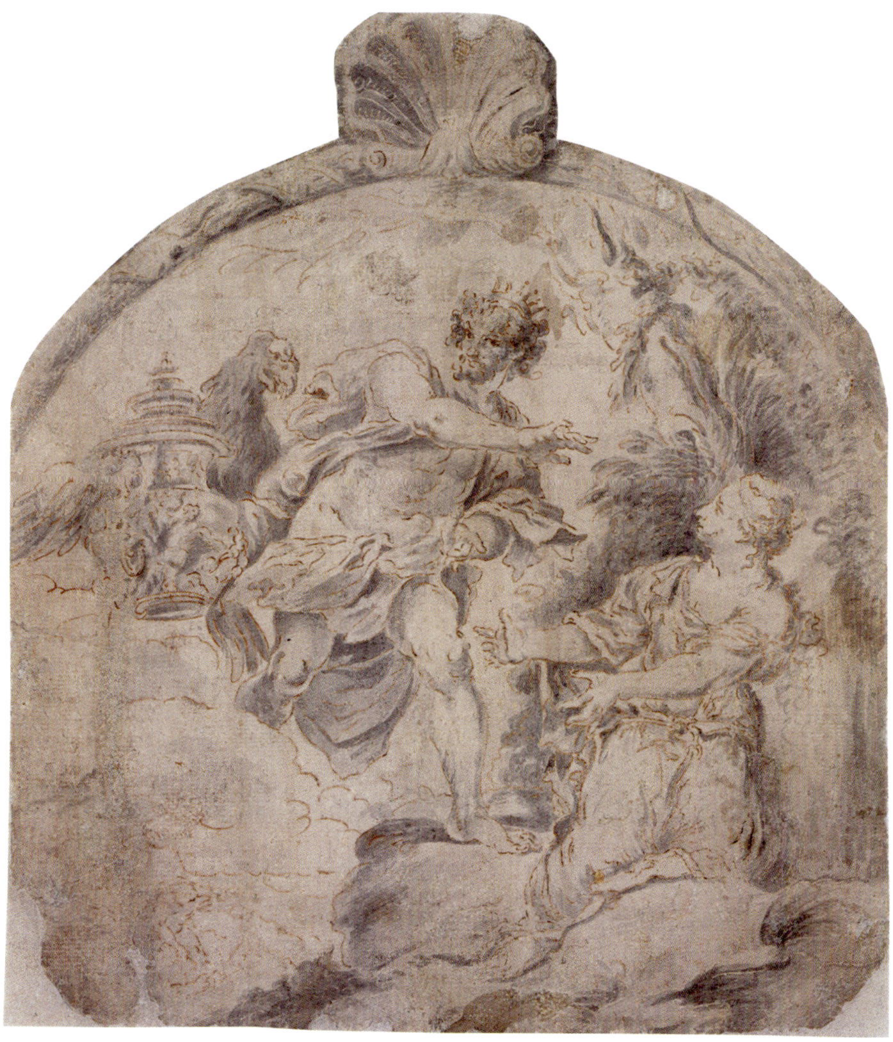

28
Francisco Rizi
Jupiter Delivering the Vase to Pandora, c.1659
Pen and brown ink and grey wash, 336 x 285 mm
Museo de Bellas Artes, Valencia
935AE

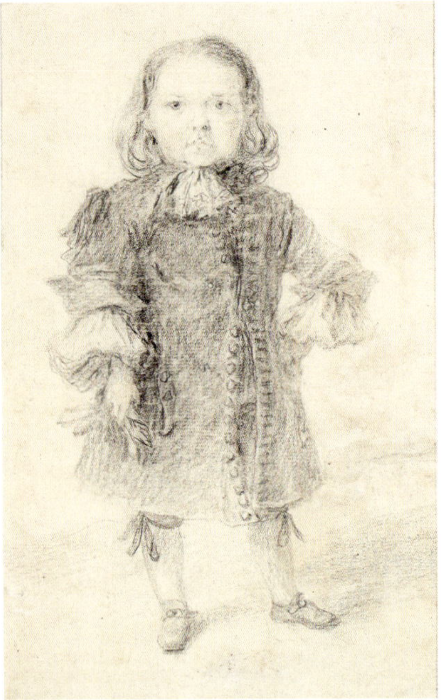

29
Francisco Rizi
The Dwarf 'Lusillo', c.1680–3
Black chalk with touches of red chalk, 268 x 161 mm
British Museum, London
1850,0713.6

30 (below and detail, right)
Francisco Rizi
The 1680 Auto de Fé in the Plaza Mayor, Madrid, 1683
Oil on canvas,
2770 x 4380 mm
Museo del Prado, Madrid
P.1126

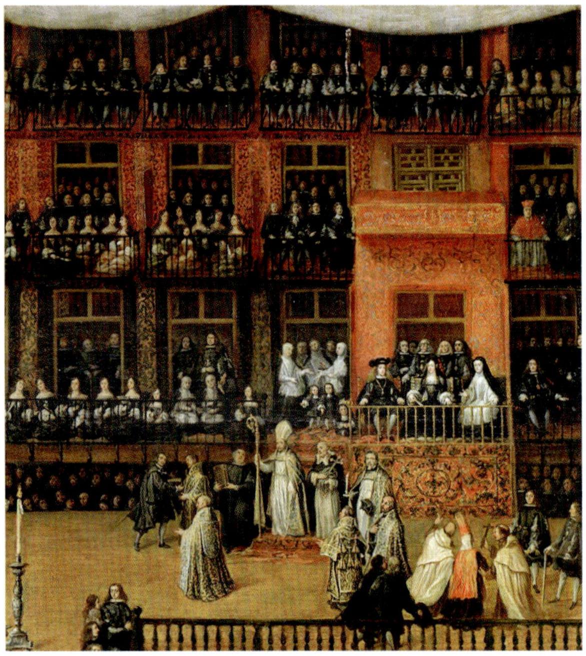

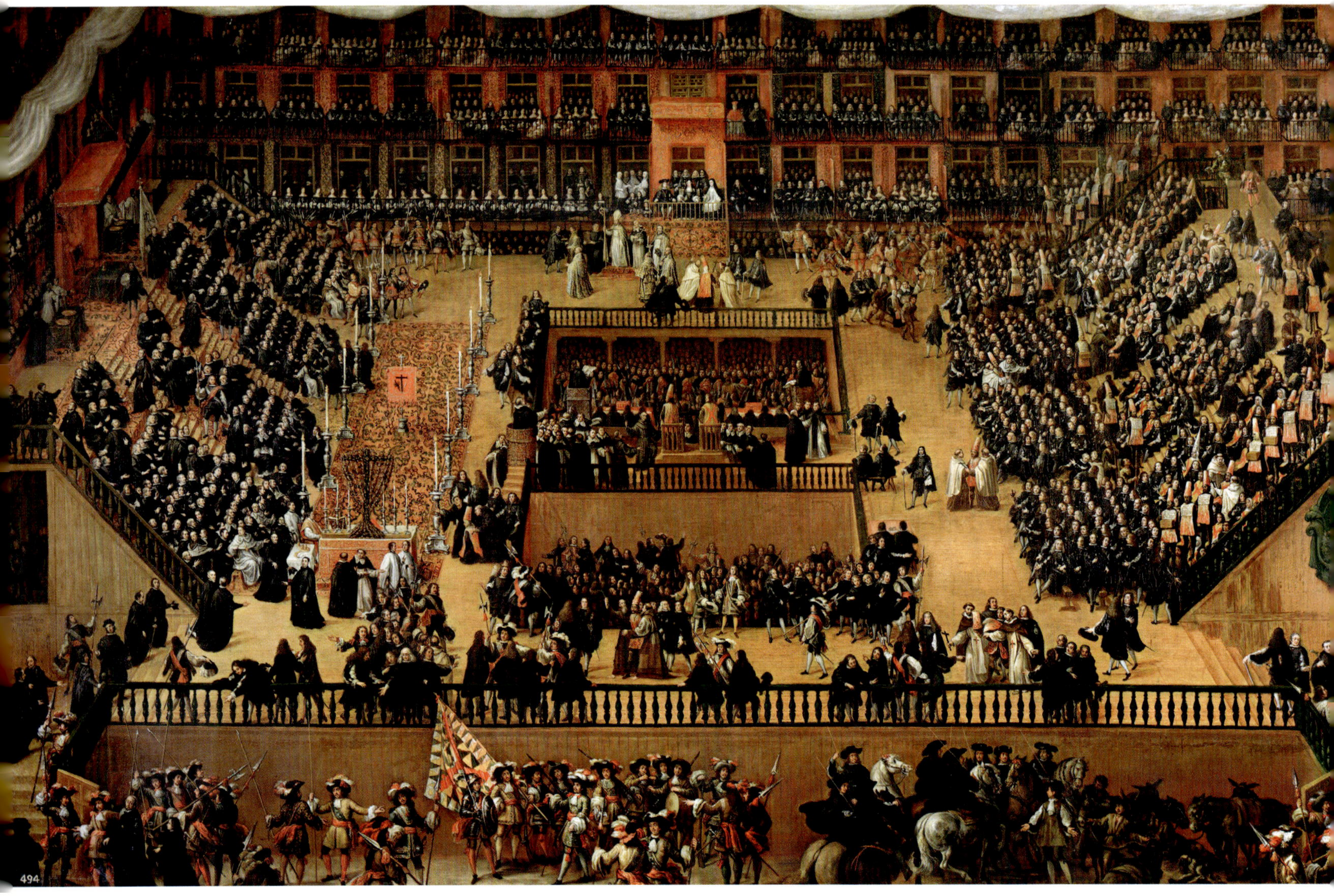

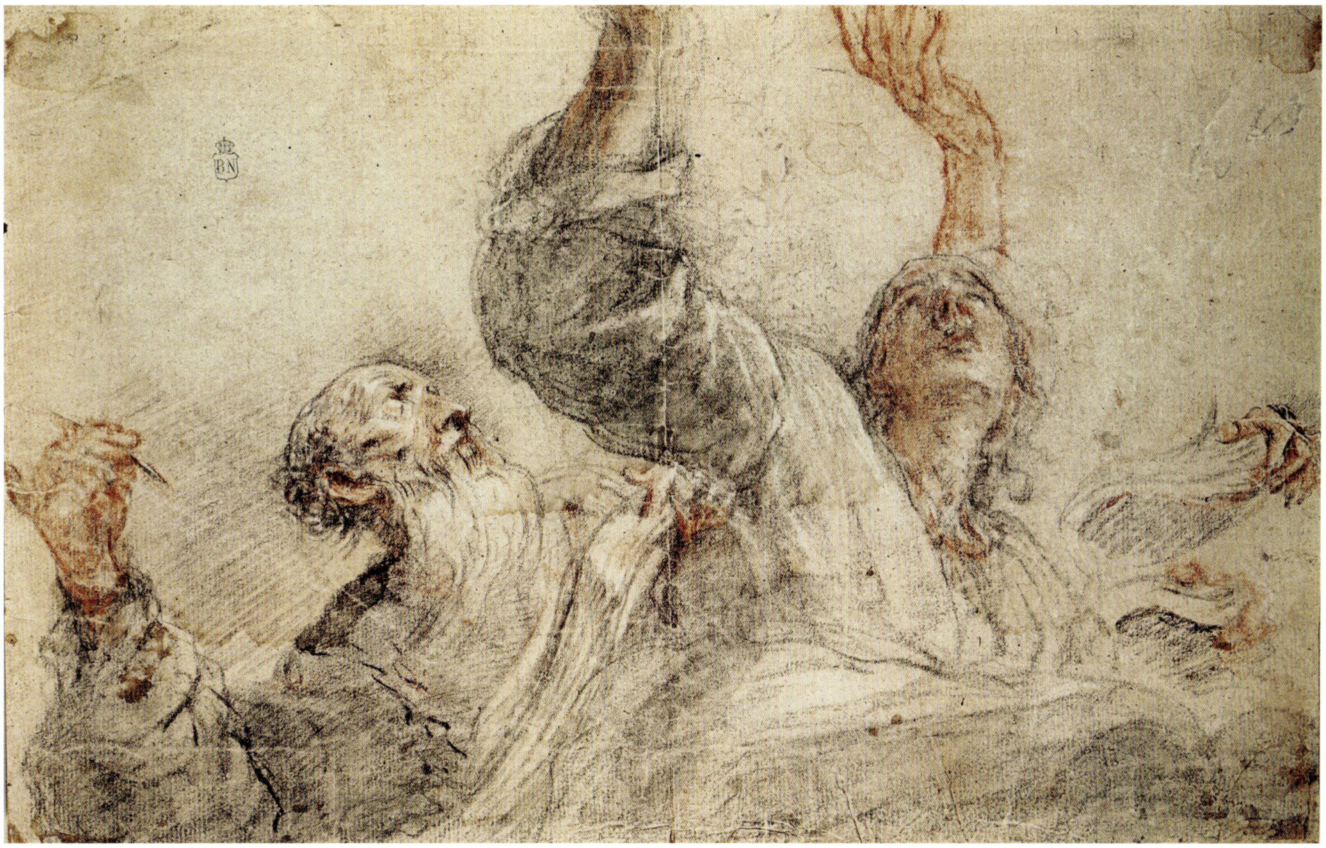

31
Juan Carreño de Miranda
Two Apostles, *c.*1660
Red and black chalk with white heightening, 258 x 395 mm
Biblioteca Nacional, Madrid
DIB/13/2/90

Born a year after Carreño, Francisco Camilo (1615–73), the son of a Florentine artist, enjoyed a highly successful career in Madrid, mainly as a painter of religious works.[85] Palomino writes of Camilo's tender, fresh, and sweet colouring and his inclination to sacred subjects.[86] In addition to his paintings, a large number of drawings survive; these are generally highly finished and often executed in several media. In *The Rest of the Holy Family on the Flight into Egypt* (fig. 33), Camilo's refined use of brush and ink complements the intimacy of the subject: its composition is very close to his now-lost *Holy Family*,[87] but the drawing might have been an independent work to record the painting and provide a basis for other compositions.[88] A survey of Camilo's drawings suggests they played a sophisticated role in his work. Some are squared for transfer and relate to surviving compositions,[89] whereas others, such as *Saint Charles Borromeo Interceding for the Pestilent* (fig. 34), show no marks of transfer, only faint scale marks along the bottom.[90] This was probably made as an independent version of the subject he painted for Salamanca Cathedral: the composition and arrangement of the figures is the same, but there are differences relating mainly to its iconography. A faithful copy made by an artist in Camilo's workshop suggests that drawings had other uses beyond their role in the preparatory process, such as forming a library of reference images.[91] These would have served a very practical use for artists like Camilo, who worked for clients outside Madrid, in Segovia, Salamanca and Toledo, where knowledge of his compositions could only have been conveyed through drawings.[92]

Evidence of specific drawing processes in seventeenth-century Spain is limited. However, Camilo's drawing of *Saint Felix of Cantalice* (fig. 35) shows

32
Juan Carreño de Miranda
Christ Baptized, c.1682
Charcoal, red and white chalk,
350 x 197 mm
The J. Paul Getty Museum,
Los Angeles
2003.24

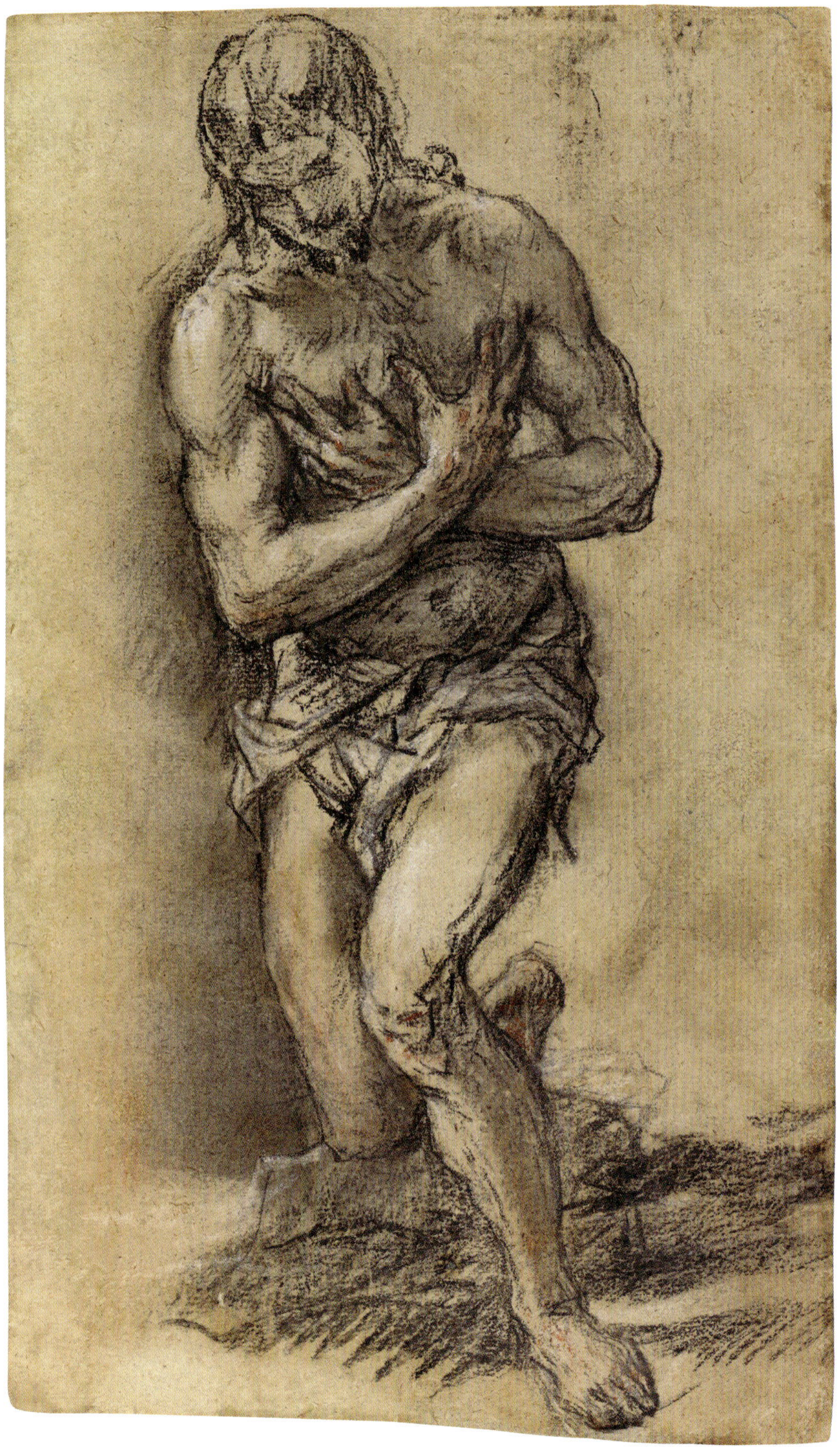

his practical corrective technique of superimposing small flaps of paper over the saint's head and the Christ Child's leg in order to make improvements (fig. 36). Thus the left leg of the Christ Child is extended to create a more harmonious composition, and the angle of the saint's head – more significantly – is altered so that he looks directly at the Christ Child rather than towards the viewer. As a result of these changes, the Christ Child becomes the focus of the composition in its final form.[93]

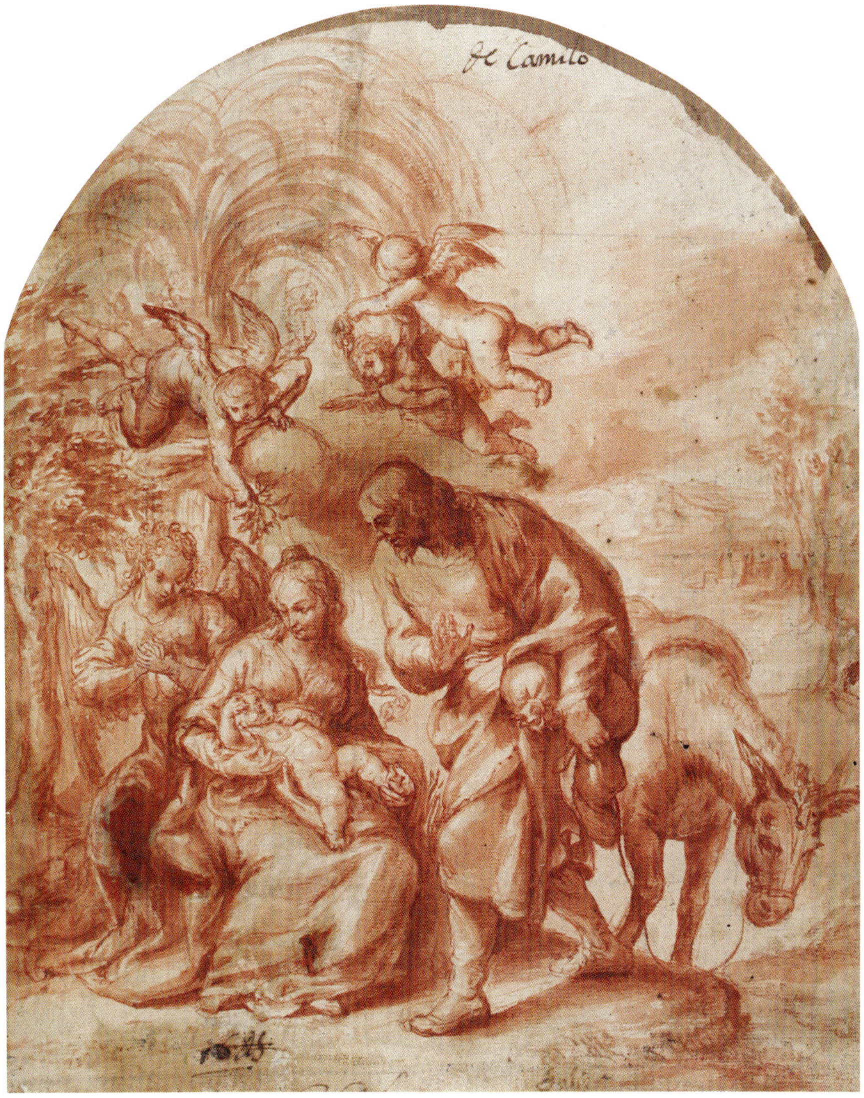

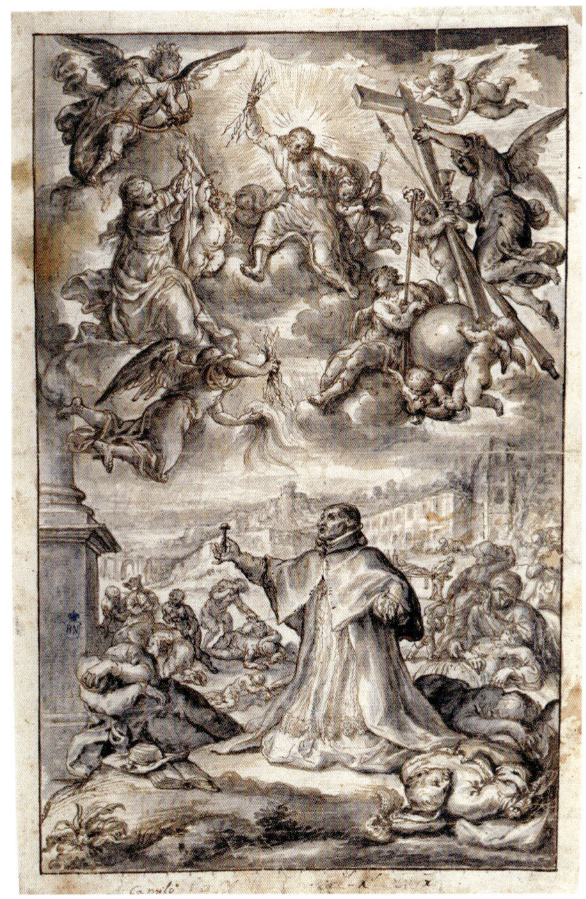

One of the most distinctive and prolific draughtsmen working in Madrid during second half of the seventeenth century was Sebastían de Herrera Barnuevo (1619–71), who became Alonso Cano's principal assistant after Cano arrived in the capital from Seville in 1638.[94] Like Cano (see Chapter 5), Herrera Barnuevo was a painter, sculptor and architect, and he prepared designs for all three on paper.[95] His various court appointments are an indication of his artistic prowess: he became Chamberlain in 1649, Chief Architect of Royal Works in 1662 and Painter to the Privy Chamber in 1667.[96] Herrera's earliest drawings, relating to Mariana of Austria's entry into Madrid in 1649, have not survived, but his work preparing designs for similar events continued to occupy him throughout his life.[97] In 1666, towards the end of his career, he designed the decorations for the church of La Encarnación in Madrid for Philip IV's exequies, as well as the title page for a commemorative publication, the *Descripción de las honras*, engraved by Pedro de Villafranca.[98]

Herrera's *Assumption of the Virgin* (fig. 37) of *c.*1650–8, which is in a remarkable state of preservation, is characteristic of his precise style, with the figures drawn in clear, strong outline with wash to provide their form. Once

33
Francisco Camilo
The Rest of the Holy Family on the Flight into Egypt, *c.*1650–70
Brush with red-brown ink and red wash over red chalk, 266 x 206 mm
British Museum, London
1875,0710.2620

34
Francisco Camilo
Saint Charles Borromeo Interceding for the Pestilent, *c.*1660
Pen and brush with brown ink, grey wash, over black chalk, 404 x 258 mm (sheet)
Biblioteca Nacional, Madrid
DIB/13/2/119

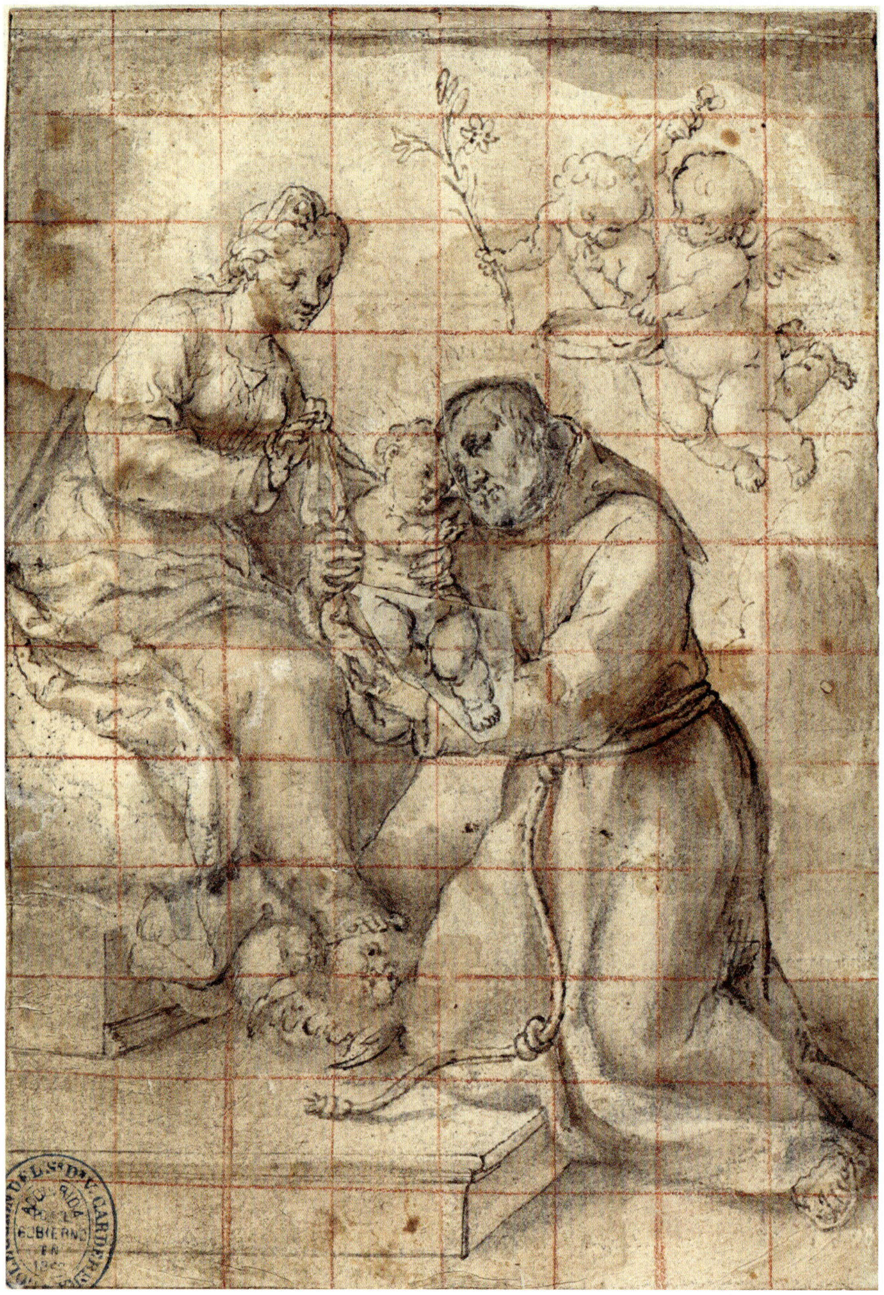

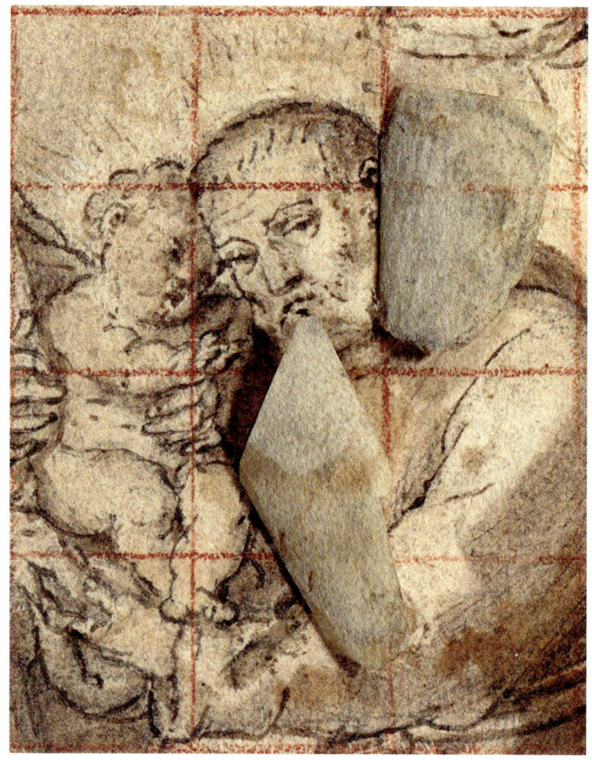

35
Francisco Camilo
Saint Felix of Cantalice, before 1657
Pen and brown ink, black chalk, washes in two tones of brown, 182 x 123 mm
Biblioteca Nacional, Madrid
DIB/13/2/120

36
Detail of fig. 35

thought to be by Cano, this drawing makes clear Herrera's debt to him.[99] The drawing also demonstrates artistic exchange in Madrid: it provided the model for a painting by José Antolínez (1635–75) of the *Assumption of the Virgin* in the church of San Nicolás de Toledo, signed and dated 1658.[100] Antolínez was something of a specialist in paintings of the Immaculate Conception, but how he came to use Herrera Barnuevo's drawing for this painting is not known. Both artists produced a type of religious art that was in high demand in the second half of the seventeenth century. Antolínez, who was fifteen years younger than Herrera Barnuevo, may even have worked in his studio.

Little of Herrera Barnuevo's architectural work survives, but his magnificent drawing for an altar demonstrates his ability in this area (fig. 38 and frontispiece).[101] It is no longer possible to identify a specific commission

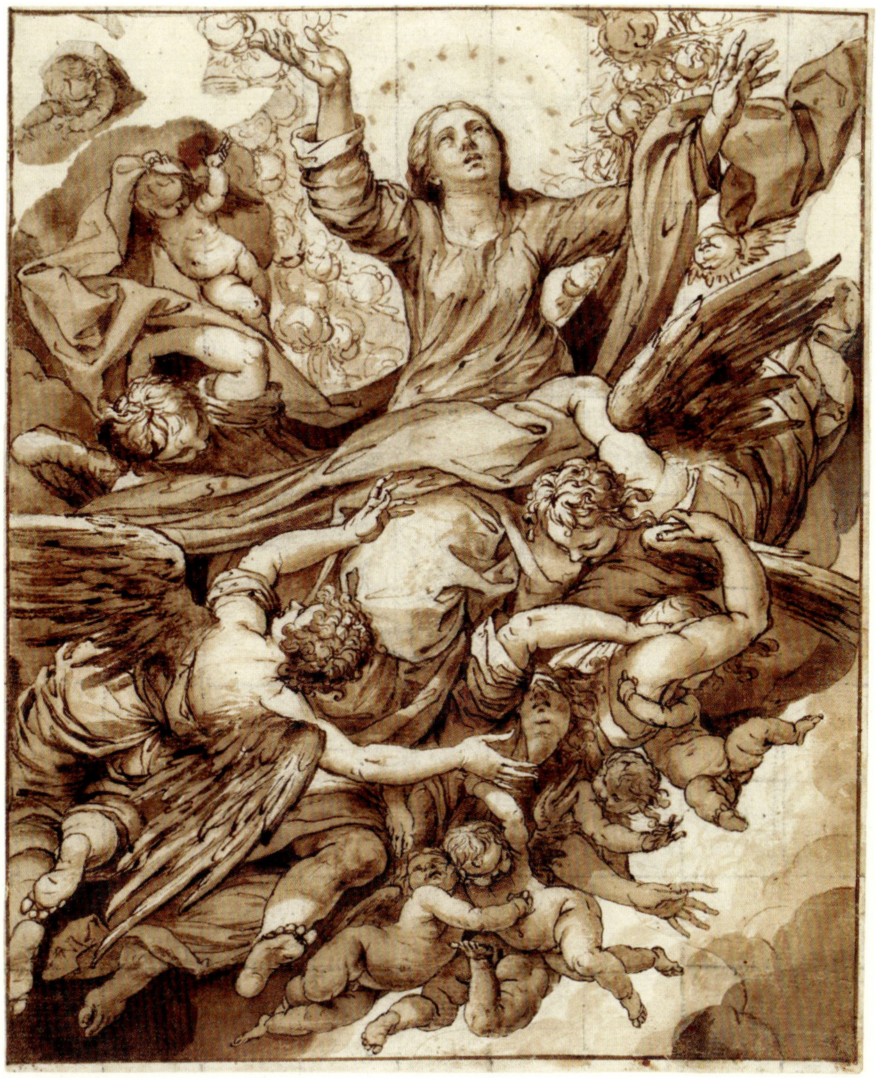

37
Sebastián de Herrera Barnuevo
The Assumption of the Virgin, c.1650–8
Pen and brown ink and brown wash over black chalk, squared for transfer, 250 x 198 mm
British Museum, London
1895,0915.876

for this, but its iconography suggests that it was for an altar dedicated to the Virgin. Palomino describes Herrera Barnuevo's 'designs for the retable and decorations of the chapel of Nuestra Señora del Buen Consejo ... also the designs for the retable and sculptures of [the altar of] Our Lady of the Seven Sorrows, which is in the church of the College of Santo Tomás in this court ...'.[102] Herrera's drawing relates to work for which he was competing during the 1650s, and its structure is broadly similar to the altarpiece in the church of San Isidro, Madrid (1650–5; fig. 39), one of a handful of his works to have survived. Alternative designs are presented on either side of the drawing; the figures and painted scenes are the work of another artist, reflecting the division of labour seen also in the drawing by Gómez de Mora (fig. 5). Herrera Barnuevo was an accomplished figurative draughtsman, but his bold pen style would have competed with the architectural design; the softer wash figures are much more complementary here.[103] His design for a cupola decoration (fig. 40) shows the influence of the illusionistic fresco techniques introduced to Spain by Mitelli and Colonna discussed earlier (p. 96), while at the same time incorporating motifs visible in his ceiling fresco in the church of San

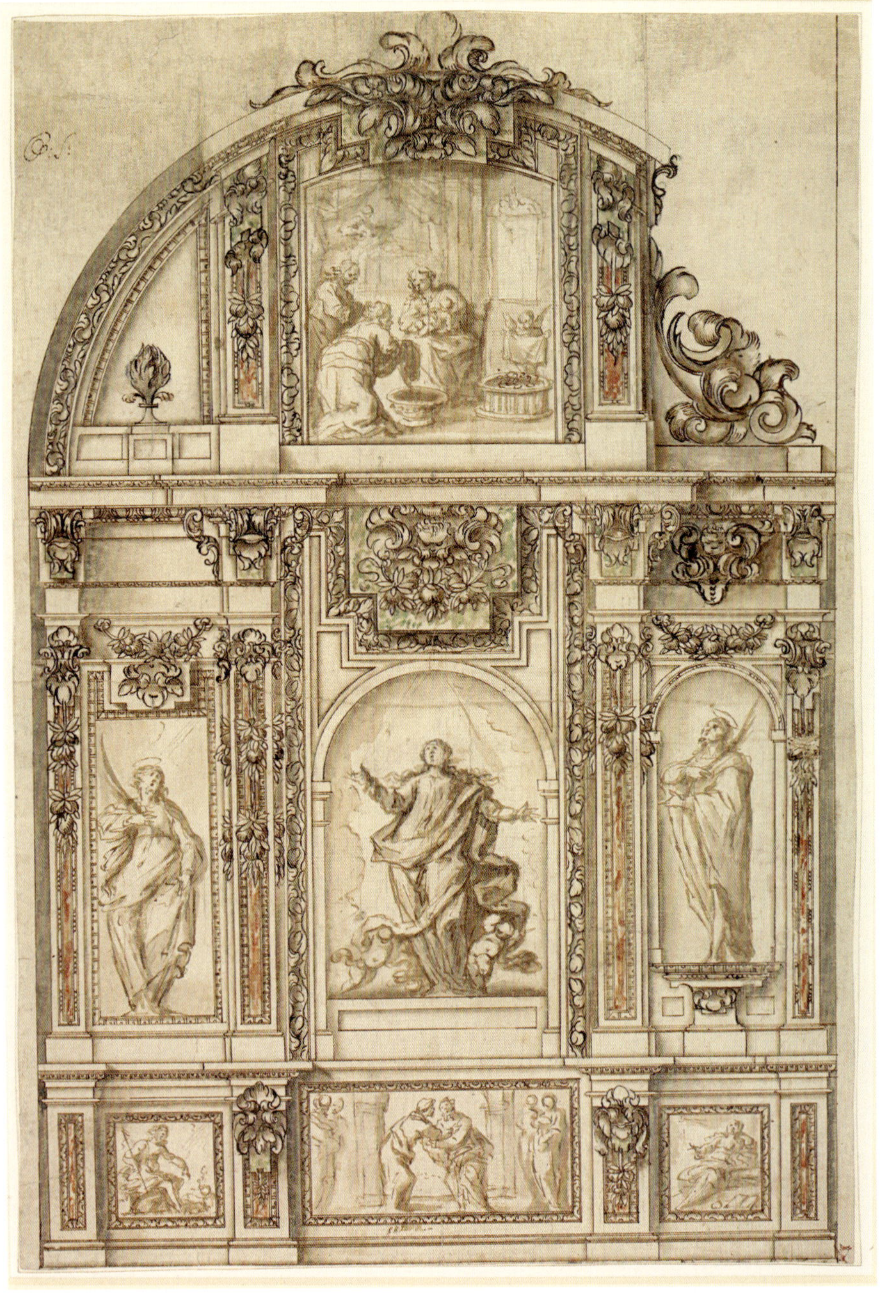

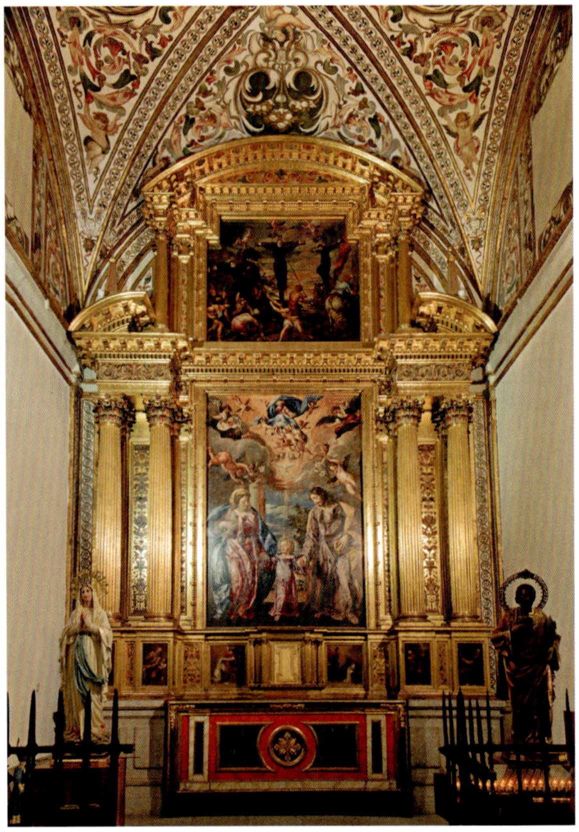

38
Sebastián de Herrera Barnuevo
Design for an Altarpiece in a Chapel, c.1650–60
Pen and brush, brown and black ink over black chalk, brown, grey, red and green wash, 517 x 345 mm
British Museum, London
1993,0724.2

39
Sebastían de Herrera Barnuevo
The High Altar of the Church of San Isidro, Madrid, 1650–5
Church of San Isidro, Madrid

Isidro.[104] Only half of the sheet is worked, suggesting that he was testing ideas before he later abandoned the project.

Madrid's cosmopolitanism attracted artists from regional centres. Francisco de Herrera the Younger (1627–85) from Seville, described by Palomino as boastful and affected, while also gallant, talented and handsome, spent significant parts of his career from around 1650 in Madrid, where he produced his most important works.[105] Drawings from his years in Seville are hard to identify, but a *Baptism of Christ* (fig. 41) is a likely candidate on account of the brown ink and pronounced linework that connects it to the technique of his father and teacher, Francisco de Herrera the Elder (see Chapter 5).[106] The drawing combines robust penwork with the delicate physiognomy of his later drawings. In 1653 Herrera the Younger received a commission for an altar for

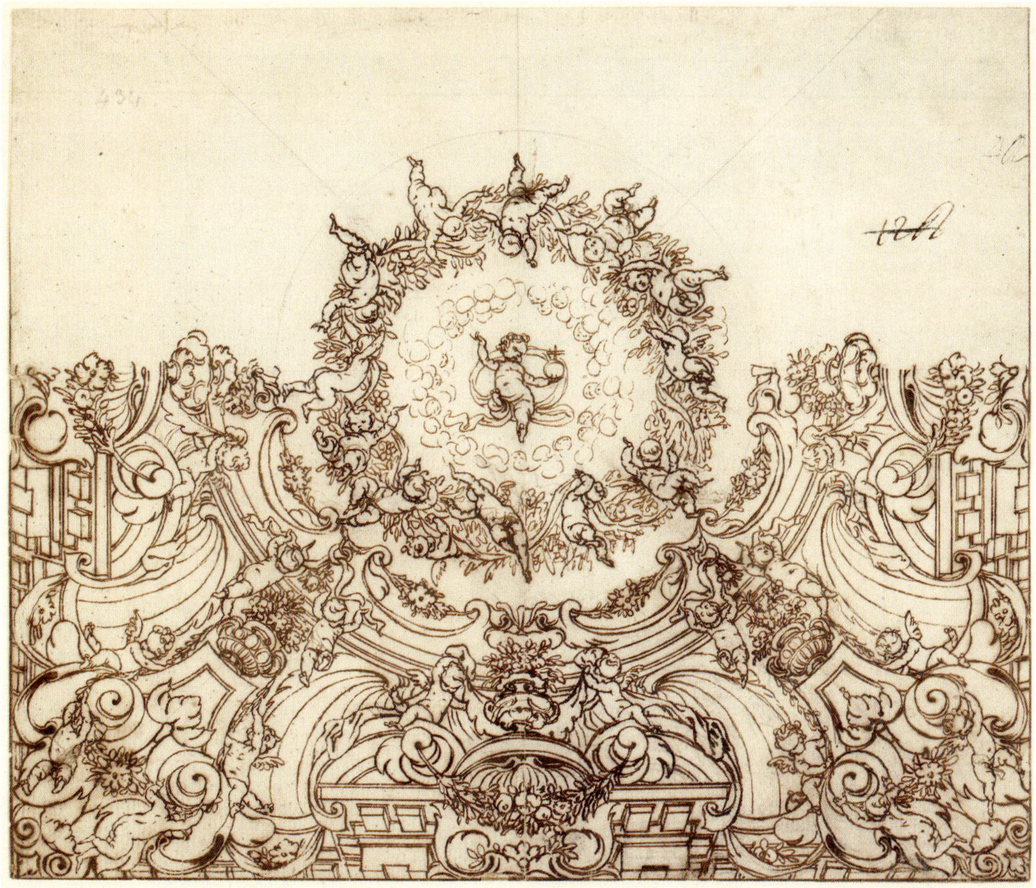

40
Sebastián de Herrera Barnuevo

Design for a Cupola Decoration, c.1660–70

Pen and brown ink over black chalk, 228 x 263 mm
British Museum, London
1895,0915.882

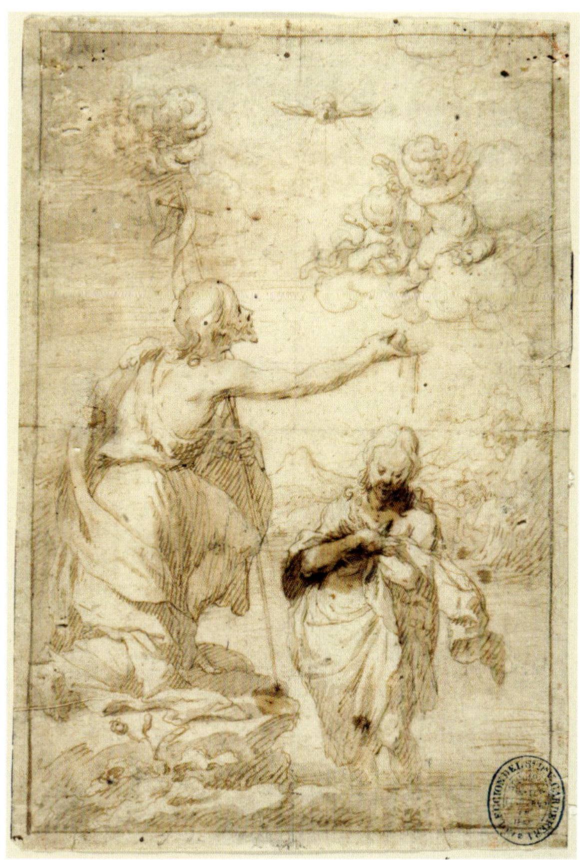

41
Francisco de Herrera the Younger

The Baptism of Christ, before 1654

Pen and brown ink and brown wash, 196 x 129 mm
Biblioteca Nacional, Madrid
DIB/15/4/2

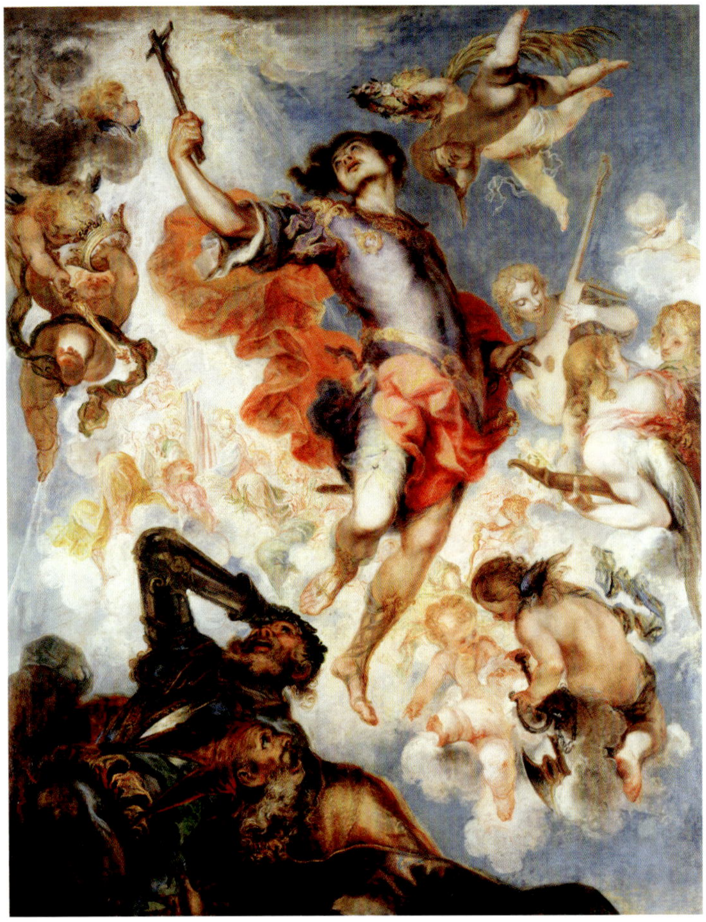

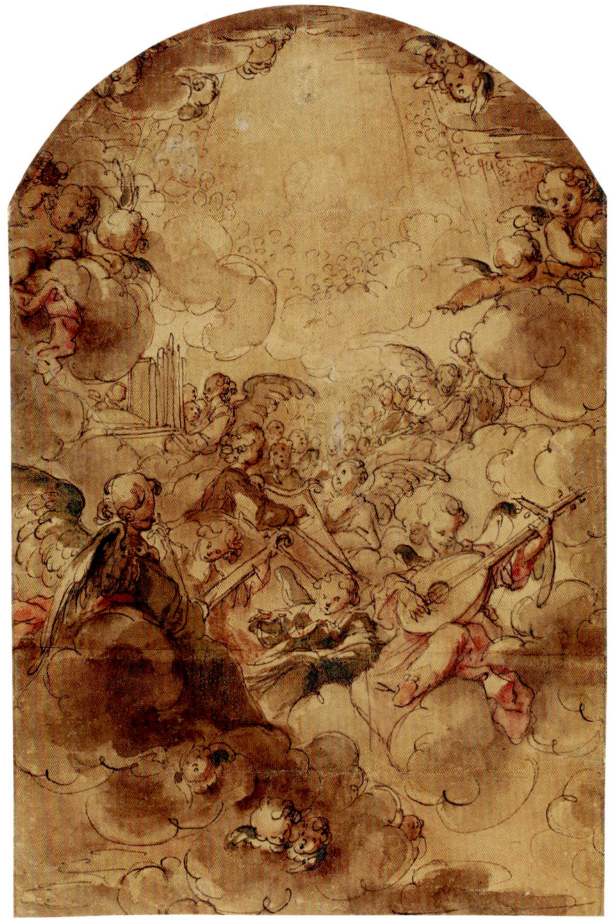

42
Francisco de Herrera the Younger
The Triumph of Saint Hermenegild, 1654
Oil on canvas, 3260 x 2280 mm
Museo del Prado, Madrid
P.833

43
Francisco de Herrera the Younger
Angels in the Clouds Playing Musical Instruments, c.1650–6
Pen and brown ink and brown wash, touched with watercolour, 296 x 189 mm
British Museum, London
1846,0509.184

the Carmelites of San Hermenegild in Madrid; the following year he executed the only work to survive from the commission, the exuberant *Triumph of Saint Hermenegild* (fig. 42). His drawings from the same period are conceived in a similar spirit: for example, the *Angels in the Clouds Playing Musical Instruments* (fig. 43) shows the figures set in a vortex of spiralling movement. The angel playing the organ in the drawing appears in the centre left background of the *Triumph*, while those in the upper left and right recall those in Herrera's *Baptism of Christ* (fig. 41).[107] The dynamic manner of his drawing and his coloured washes are unlike anything else produced in Madrid at this time, and was possibly inspired by what he encountered in Rome around 1649.[108]

Herrera the Younger returned to Seville in 1655 and may have been back in Madrid by 1660, the decade in which began to work for the court. Several of his chalk drawings have been recognized, most from late in his career, after 1670, when he worked in Madrid and Seville (see Chapter 5). Like many of his contemporaries, such as Francisco Rizi, Herrera also worked as a theatre designer. His *Vision of Elisha* (fig. 44) may be a study for a stage set or painting, its arched top indicating the physical space it was intended to occupy.[109] He made a group of five watercolour drawings for the stage set (possibly also designed by him) for the play (*zarzuela*) *Los celos hacen estrellas*, written by Juan Vélez de Guevara to celebrate the Queen Mother Mariana's birthday and performed at the theatre of the Álcazar in Madrid on 22 December 1672.[110] Watercolour was not a medium often used by itself by artists in Spain during the seventeenth century, but Herrera was attracted to its qualities, no doubt because of its capacity to convey rich colouristic effects. A pair of watercolour drawings for an overmantel made around the same time as *Los celos* show Herrera's mastery of the medium (fig. 45). Given the decorative nature of the drawings with their playful putti, they might have been designed for a stage set rather than a permanent structure. During the 1670s Herrera became increasingly occupied with architectural design, resulting in his appointment as Royal Architect in 1677.[111]

Rizi, Carreño and Herrera the Younger all died in 1685, bringing to an abrupt end their dominance of the art world in Madrid. Of the next generation, Claudio Coello (1642–93) was the most talented. He trained in Rizi's workshop, where he learned drawing and possibly stage design. Relative to most artists working in Madrid during the second half of the century, a good

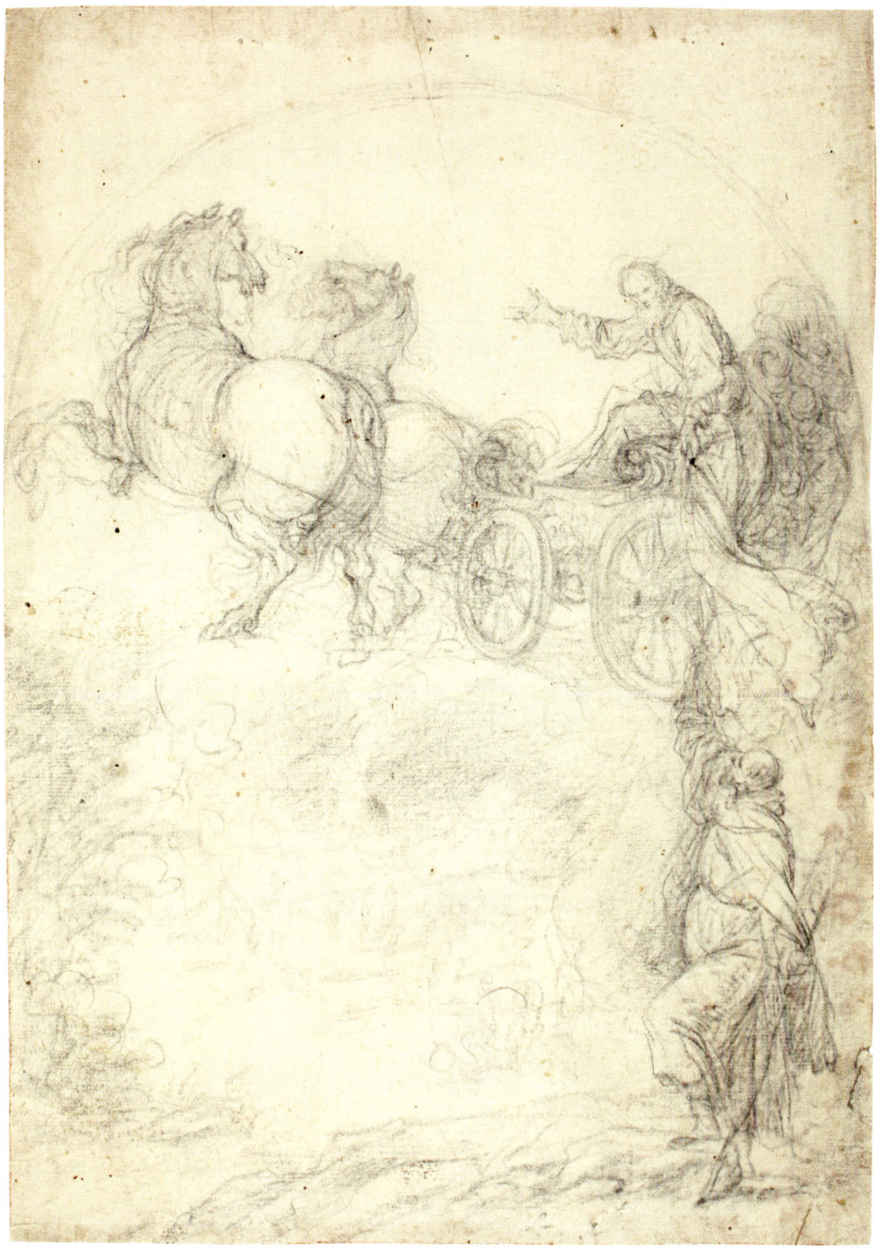

44
Francisco de Herrera the Younger
The Vision of Elisha, *c.*1665–80
Black chalk, 305 x 210 mm
Museo del Prado, Madrid
F.D.1202

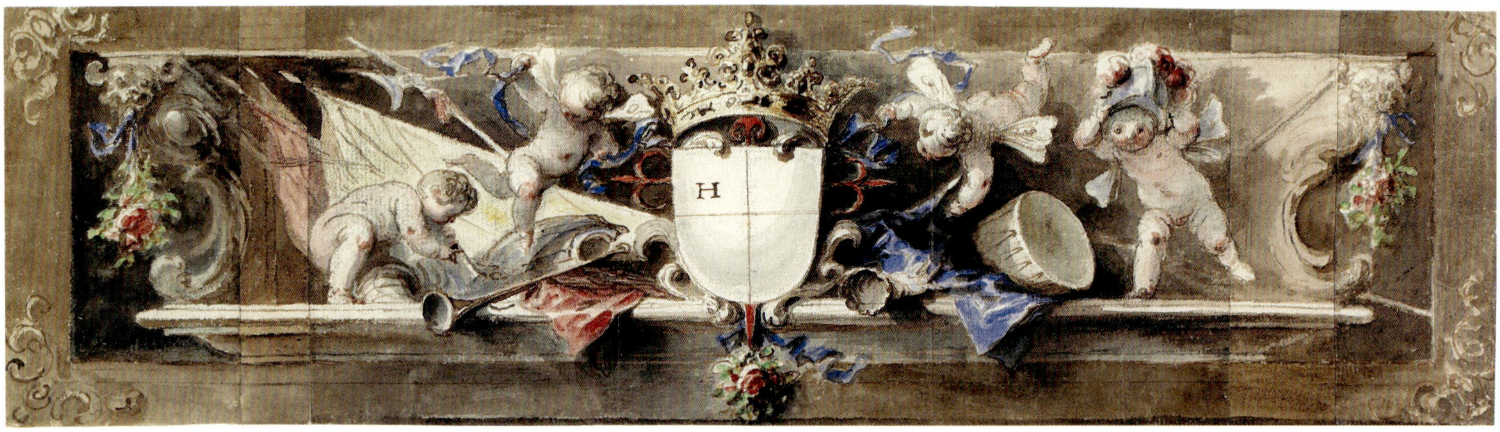

45
Francisco de Herrera the Younger
Design for an Overmantel, c.1670–80
Watercolour, with pen, brown and black ink over black chalk, on several conjoined sheets, 136 x 479 mm
British Museum, London
1914,0901.2

46
Attributed to Francisco Ignacio Ruiz de la Iglesia
The Virgin Bestowing the Rosary on Saint Dominic Guzmán, c.1690
Pen and grey ink and brown wash over black chalk, 267 x 203 mm
British Museum, London
1850,0713.1

number of drawings by Coello survive, and like those of his teacher, their technique is varied, making it difficult to determine a stylistic progression in his work.[112] Coello worked in pen and ink, coloured washes and chalk, a range to be expected from an artist who had been exposed to the many types of drawing in Madrid. His earliest-known sheets are from the mid-1660s.[113] Most surviving drawings by Coello, however, date from after 1680, presumably when his reputation was secure and his sheets more assiduously preserved. Several for the decorations of the entry into Madrid of María Luisa de Orleans on 13 January 1680 are known.[114] Coello also made prints based on his own drawings, for example the title page for the *Theologia Mistica* (1683), where the lettering 'deli et sculp' identifies his role as designer and printmaker.[115] By the early 1680s Coello had begun work on the most important commission of his career, the painting of the *Sagrada Forma* now in the sacristy of the church of the Escorial, showing King Charles II and his family adoring the Eucharist. For the individual figures, for example the Hieronymite monk standing behind the officiating priest Francisco de los Santos, Coello prepared chalk portrait studies that had no precedent in Spain. He seems to have drawn them directly from the models, giving them remarkable realism and individual character (fig. 47).[116]

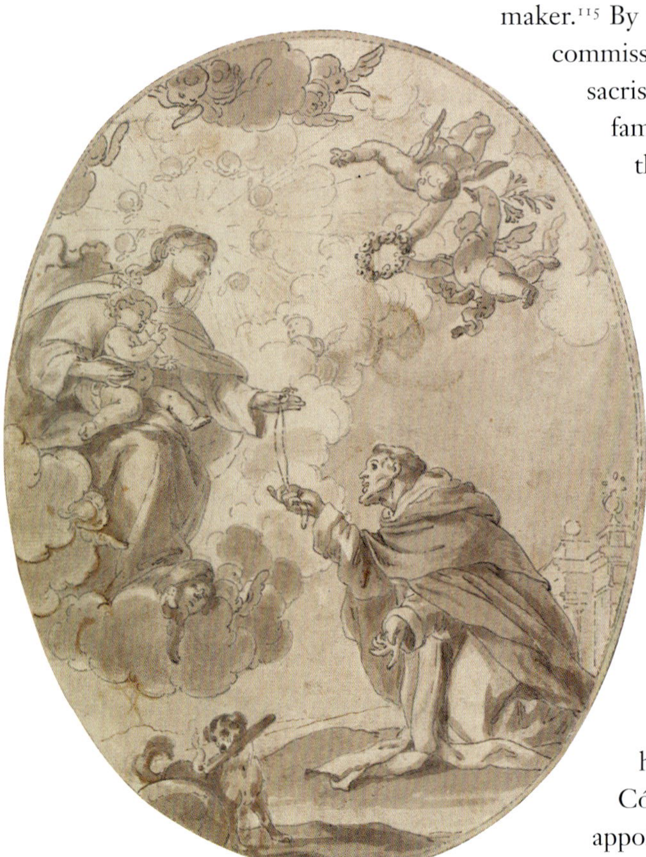

A drawing traditionally thought to be by Coello, the *Virgin Bestowing the Rosary on Saint Dominic Guzmán*, has recently been attributed to Francisco Ignacio Ruiz de la Iglesia (1649–1703) and dated to around the same time he was appointed Painter to the King, the end of 1689 (fig. 46).[117] It is a study for a composition that has not survived, but foreshortened figures and the low horizon line suggests the work was intended to be positioned high up on a wall or ceiling.

Coello's student Acisclo Antonio Palomino y Velasco (1655–1726) is best known for his biographical lives of Spanish artists, *El parnaso español pintoresco laureado*, the third volume of his *Museo pictórico y escala óptica* (1724). Born in Bujalance near Córdoba, Palomino was in Madrid by 1678 and ten years later was appointed Royal Painter. Throughout the *Museo pictórico* Palomino makes frequent reference to the drawing practices of artists, so it is no surprise that he, too, was a dedicated draughtsman in a variety of media.[118] The catafalque design for the exequies of María Luisa de Orleans in about 1689 (fig. 48), drawn in black and brown ink, is very close to Coello's style.[119] There is no record of Palomino having been involved in its design – the commission went to José Benito de Churriguera (see Chapter 7) – so this drawing might have been intended for a print to illustrate a report he wrote on the funeral. Palomino's highly finished study of *Ahimelec Giving to David the Sword of Goliath* (fig. 49) corresponds closely to his painting in the sacristy of the Carthusian monastery of Granada (fig. 50) of about 1711, where only the position of the sword held by Ahimelec has been altered.[120] It is likely that this drawing was made as a final design to show his patron, Prior Francisco de Bustamente who commissioned Palomino to create a number of paintings for the sacristy.[121]

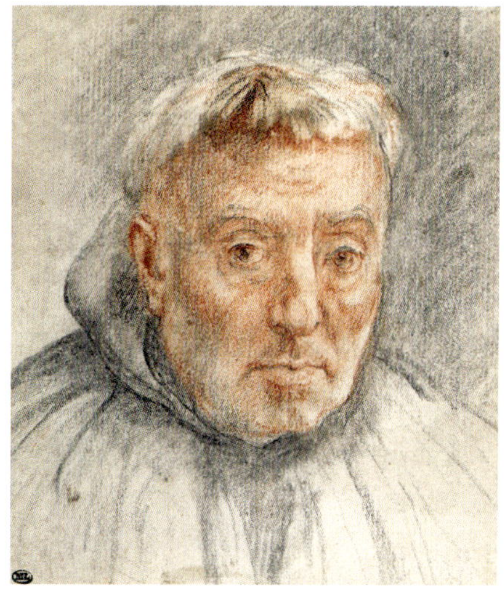

47
Claudio Coello
A Hieronymite Monk, c.1685
Red and black chalk,
159 x 129 mm
Musée du Louvre, Paris
18419 bis

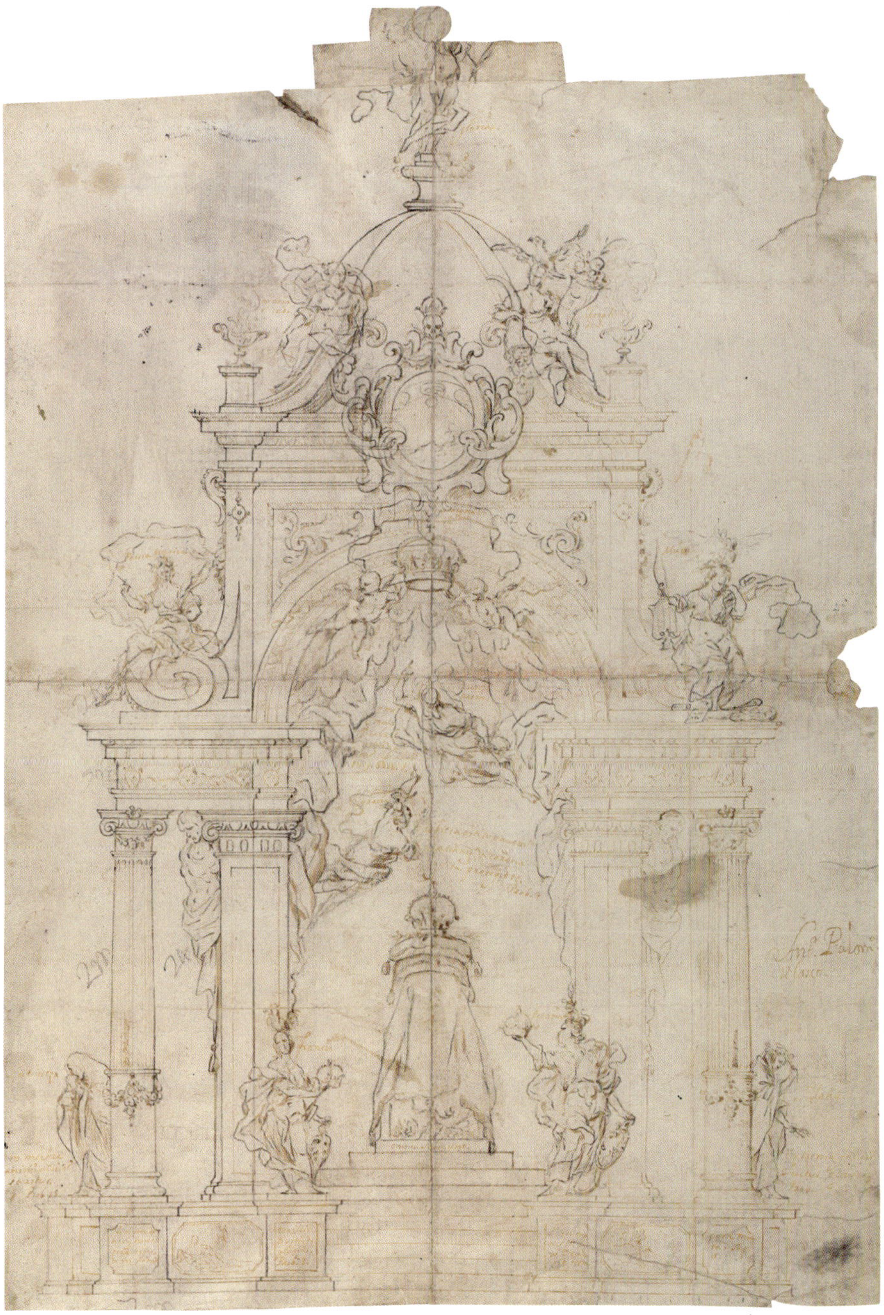

48
Antonio Palomino
Design for the Catafalque for the Exequies of María Luisa de Orleans, c.1689
Pen and black and brown ink, brown wash and black chalk,
510 x 337 mm
Biblioteca Nacional, Madrid
DIB/13/2/112.

49
Antonio Palomino
Ahimelec Giving to David the Sword of Goliath, c.1711
Pen and brown ink and grey wash, 135 x 154 mm
British Museum, London
1846,0509.170

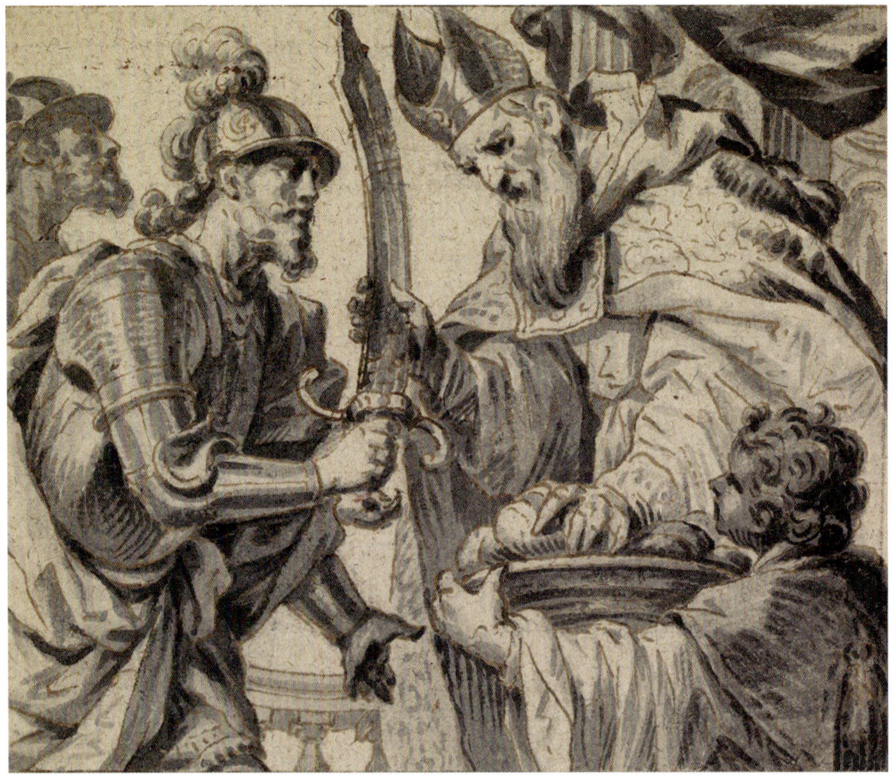

50
Antonio Palomino
Ahimelec Giving to David the Sword of Goliath, c.1711
Oil on canvas
Sacristy of the Carthusian Monastery, Granada

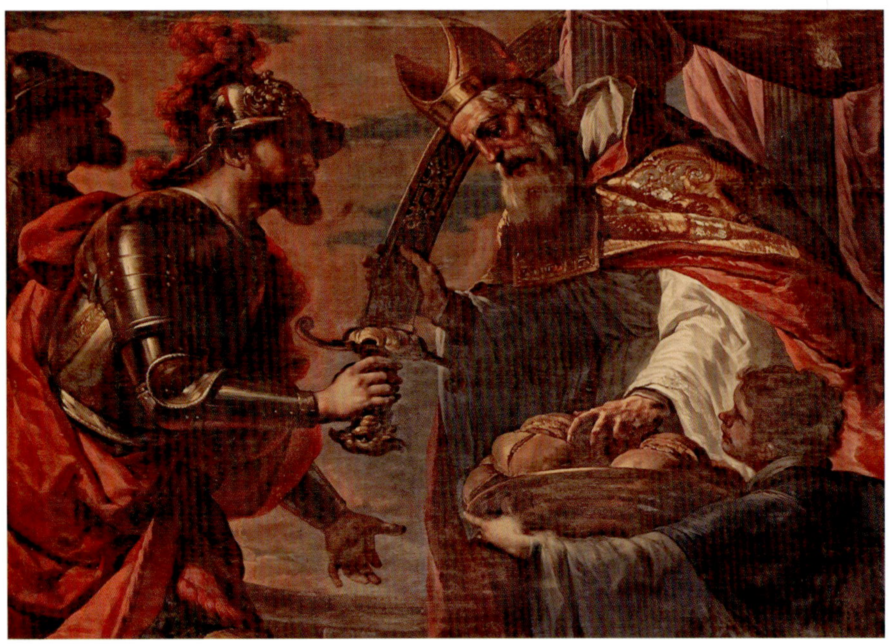

Lesser-known artists, many of whom worked alongside the court painters and architects were often active draughtsmen. Matías de Torres (1635–1711), whose artistic personality has in recent years become clearer, worked with Claudio Coello on the decorations for the entry into Madrid of María Luisa de Orleans in 1680.[122] Torres' drawing of *Saint Isidore Praying* (fig. 51), once thought to be by Coello, is a study for the arch erected on the Puerta del Sol, along the processional route.[123] The painting is reproduced on the central façade of the arch in the spectacular etching, also by Torres (figs 52–3).

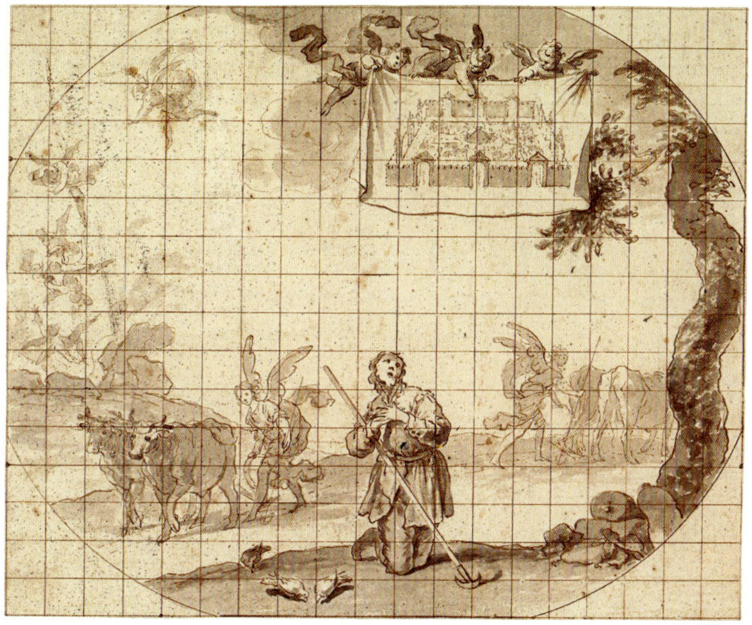

51
Matías de Torres
Saint Isidore Praying, *c.*1680
Pen and brown ink, grey-brown wash, squared for transfer, 217 x 257 mm
British Museum, London
1846,0509.166

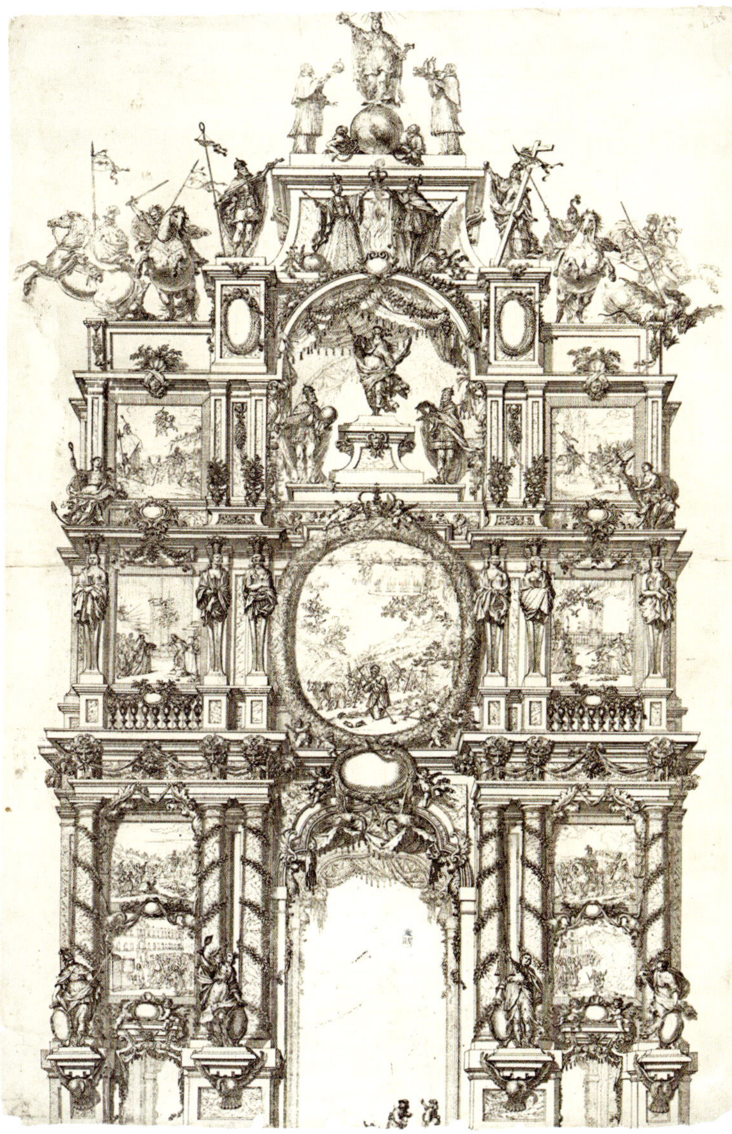

52
Matías de Torres
Triumphal Arch on the Puerta del Sol, Madrid, 1680
Etching and engraving, 748 x 485 mm
Biblioteca Nacional, Madrid
70861

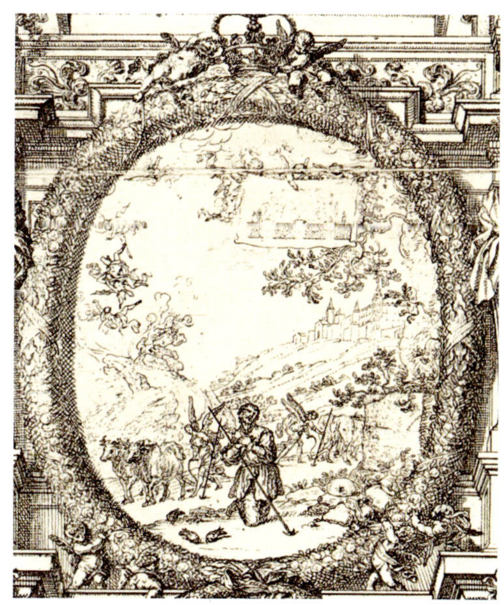

53
Detail of fig. 52

54
José de Cieza
Saint Francis de Paul before the King of Naples, c.1691
Pen and brown ink and brown wash, over black chalk,
210 x 207 mm
British Museum, London
1846,0509.169

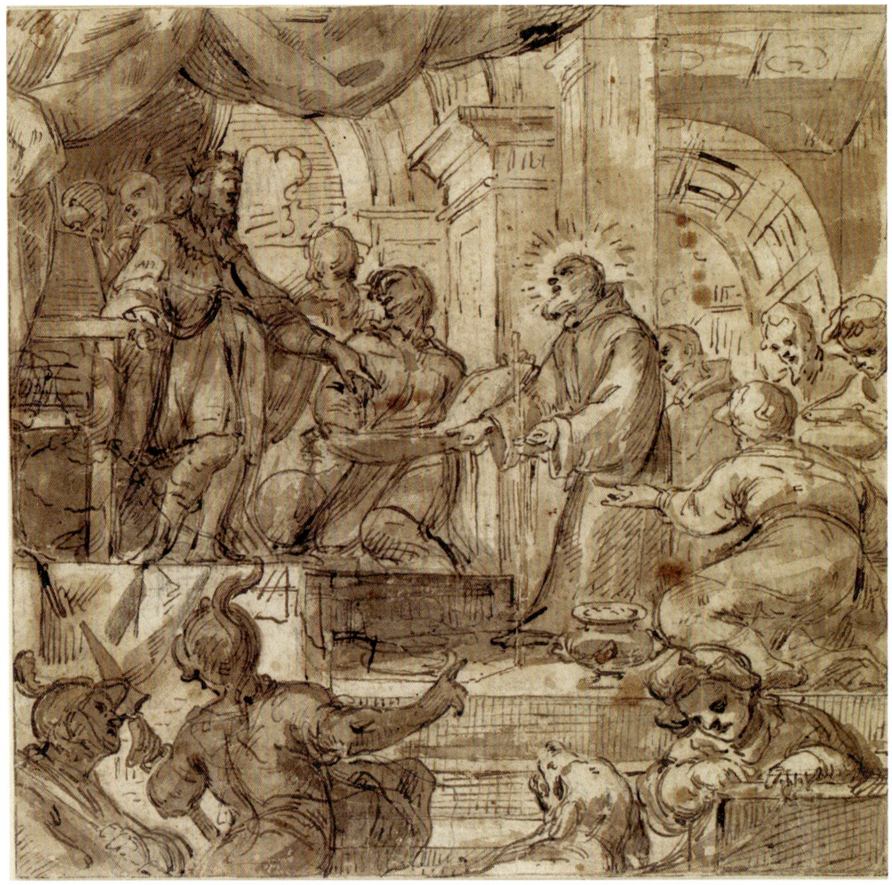

Ceán Bermúdez reports that José de Cieza (1652–92) moved from Granada to Madrid, where he worked on theatre decorations for the Buen Retiro, in 1686, and two years later he was appointed Painter to the King.[124] Only one drawing from his hand is known, *Saint Francis de Paul before the King of Naples* (fig. 54). Executed in pen, ink and wash, it was a preparatory study for his now destroyed painting for the church of San Francisco de Paula in Madrid that was signed and dated 1691, described by Palomino as 'in which the glorious saint made the King of Naples see that the money that he showed him was the blood of the poor'.[125] Other draughtsmen in Madrid include José García Hidalgo (1645–1717), who worked in Coello's circle and is known through one drawing, a black pen and grey wash preparatory study for his painting *Saint Augustine Wounded by Christ*.[126] Mateo Cerezo (1637–66) and Juan Antonio de Frías y Escalante (1633–69), who worked with Juan Carreño and Francisco Rizi respectively, were also active draughtsmen.[127] But few of their drawings have been identified, and it is not yet possible to form a coherent picture of their artistic personalities. It is likely that once the work of these minor artists becomes better known, many anonymous drawings will find an author.

In 1692 Luca Giordano (1634–1705) arrived in Spain from Naples to work on frescos at the Escorial.[128] Over a hundred years had elapsed since the first Italians had arrived to decorate the monastery. In the intervening period, the drawing practices they introduced had been completely absorbed by successive generations of Spanish artists working in Madrid. In

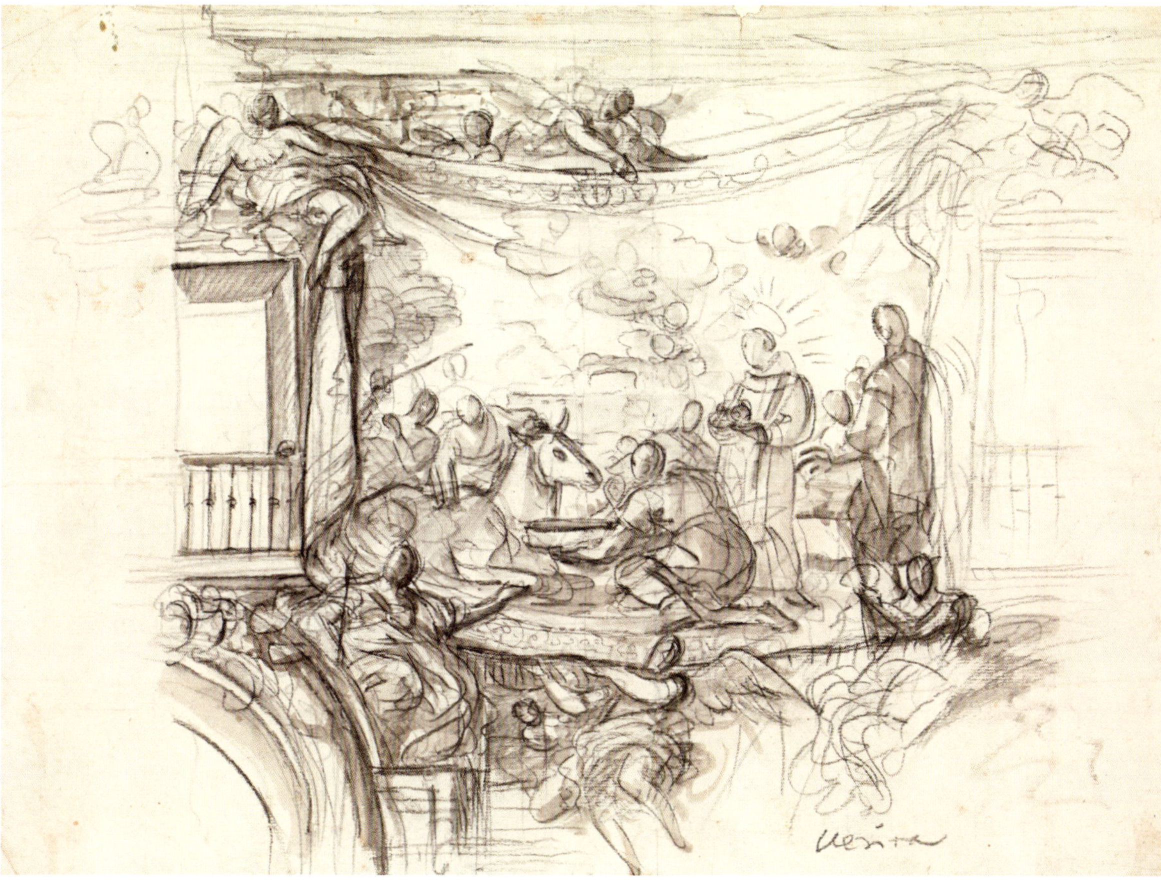

55
Luca Giordano
Miracle of Saint Anthony of Padua, 1698–1700
Black chalk, grey-brown wash, 300 x 382 mm
British Museum, London
1950,1111.6

Spain Giordano prepared drawings for his frescos, such as his *Miracle of Saint Anthony of Padua* of 1698–1700 (fig. 55) in the church of San Antonio de los Alemanes, Madrid.[129] Giordano's hand is distinctive but as a preparatory study this drawing is no different from those made by Spanish artists in the second half of the seventeenth century, demonstrating a practice corresponding to that in other parts of Europe.

But the workshop environment in Spain seems generally to have been detrimental to the preservation of drawings, many of which are in poor condition. A survey of the major collections shows that many drawings have stains or other invasive marks, are torn, folded and often joined together. There are signs of considerable use, sometimes with little regard for the original design. On the verso of a charcoal study of Saint Francis by Juan Carreño in the Biblioteca Nacional, Madrid, for example, is a decorative motif that has been completely pricked for transfer, irrespective of the drawing on the recto.[130]

Printmaking in Madrid

Many of the artists discussed above were involved in printmaking, but this was generally a very minor part of their activity. Following the establishment of printing houses in Madrid during the late sixteenth century, the demand for printed material was met by an influx of images, mainly from the Netherlands and France. The development of a local industry was uneven and did not take hold until the third decade of the seventeenth century, for reasons discussed earlier: the move of the court of Philip III to Valladolid, the influx of printed

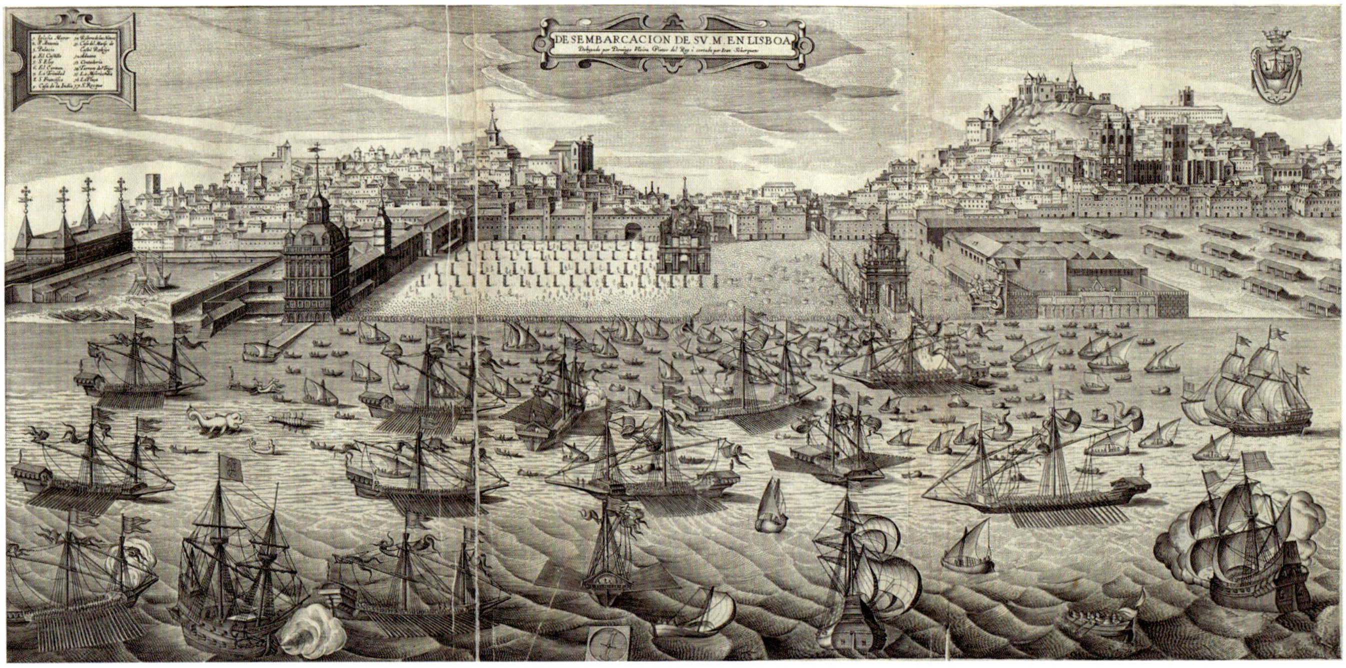

56
Juan Schorquens after Domingo de Vieira
Philip II Disembarking in Lisbon, 1622
Engraving, 322 x 640 mm (combined dimensions of three plates)
Biblioteca Nacional, Madrid
ER 4071

57
Pedro de Villafranca
Isabel de Borbón, 1645
Engraving, 323 x 213 mm
Biblioteca Nacional, Madrid
R-3035

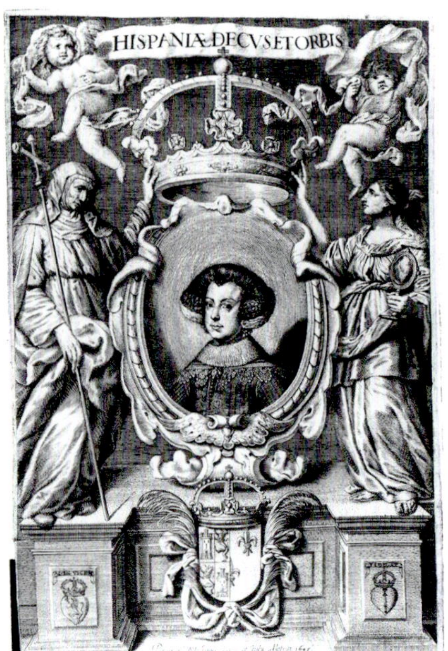

materials from other parts of Europe, and Pedro Perret's stranglehold on engraving until his death in about 1625.

From the second decade of the seventeenth century, foreign engravers began to arrive in Madrid. From the Netherlands came Juan Schorquens, Alardo de Popma, Cornelio Boel, Juan de Noort, Herman Panneels, and from France, Juan de Courbes and Roberto Cordier.[131] The types of prints they introduced to the capital are represented by several extant examples. One of the most successful printmakers from outside Spain – if not the most accomplished – was Juan de Courbes (1592–1641), who arrived in Madrid in 1620.[132] His earliest prints were engravings for Melchor Prieto's *Psalmodia Eucharistica* (Madrid 1622), which also contained prints by Popma and Schorquens.[133] Active in Madrid between 1618 and 1630, Schorquens is best known for the engravings he made for Juan Bautista Lavaña's *Viage de la Cathólica Real Magestad del Rei D. Felipe III N.S. al reino de Portugal* of 1622.[134] The large view (fig. 56) showing Philip III disembarking in Lisbon, designed by Domingo de Vieira and printed from three plates, far exceeded the size of the book.[135] This is similar to the single sheet prints made elsewhere in Europe, although its use as book illustration was unprecedented in Spain at this date.

Printmakers from abroad continued to dominate in Madrid until the middle of the seventeenth century. The first native artist to challenge their hegemony was Pedro de Villafranca y Malagón (*c.*1615–84), who became the most important printmaker in Spain in the seventeenth century.[136] From the time of Perret's appointment as Engraver to the Privy Chamber in 1595, no other royal dispensations for printmakers were granted until Villafranca was made Engraver of Royal Works in 1654 (*tallador de las obras reales*). His appointment is especially significant because he was the first native artist to be invested with such a title, indicating the status of the printmaker to the king in Philip IV's court. Ceán Bermúdez singles out Villafranca's apprenticeship in painting but not in printmaking, saying only that once he had progressed in drawing he moved onto engraving, and that he was outstanding in that field.[137] Why was Villafranca made Royal Engraver? The most obvious answer is that amongst his contemporaries he had no peer. At the time of his appointment Villafranca was producing engravings of a quality not seen since the death of Perret some thirty years earlier.

The main function of the Engraver to the King was to produce portraits of the monarch and the royal family. Philip IV was aware of the importance of promoting his image but, unlike his predecessors, he rejected those that flattered him or diverged from accurate representation. Velázquez best reflected this style of portraiture, his portraits of the king being characterized by austerity and clarity.[138] The influence Velázquez had over Villafranca was profound, and the latter's facility for assimilating aspects of Velázquez's

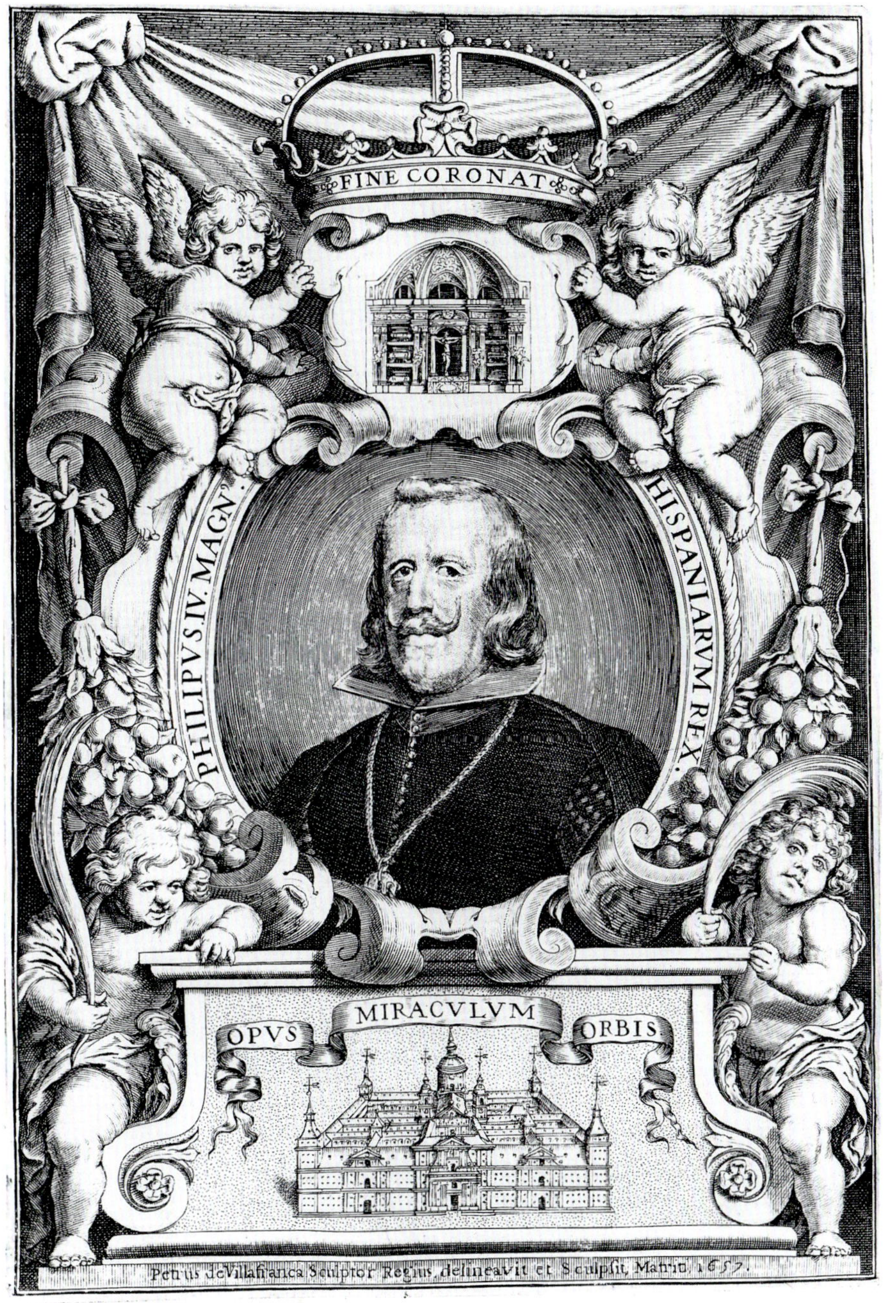

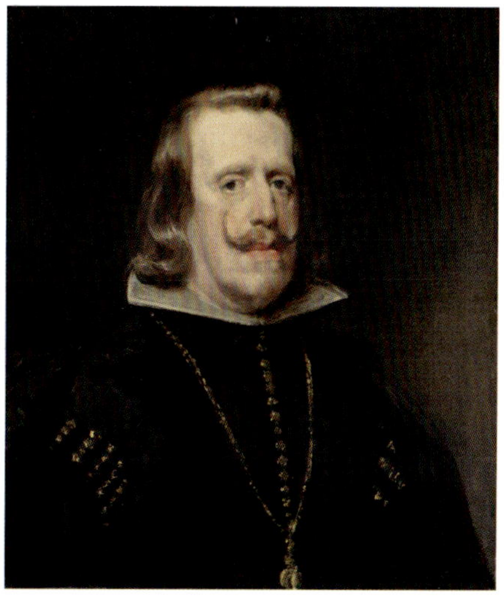

58
Pedro de Villafranca
Philip IV in the *Descripción breve del monasterio de S. Lorenzo el Real del Escorial ...*, 1657
Engraving, 277 x 185 mm
British Library, London
787.I.2

59
Diego Velázquez
Philip IV, *c.*1655
Oil on canvas, 641 x 537 mm
National Gallery, London
NG745

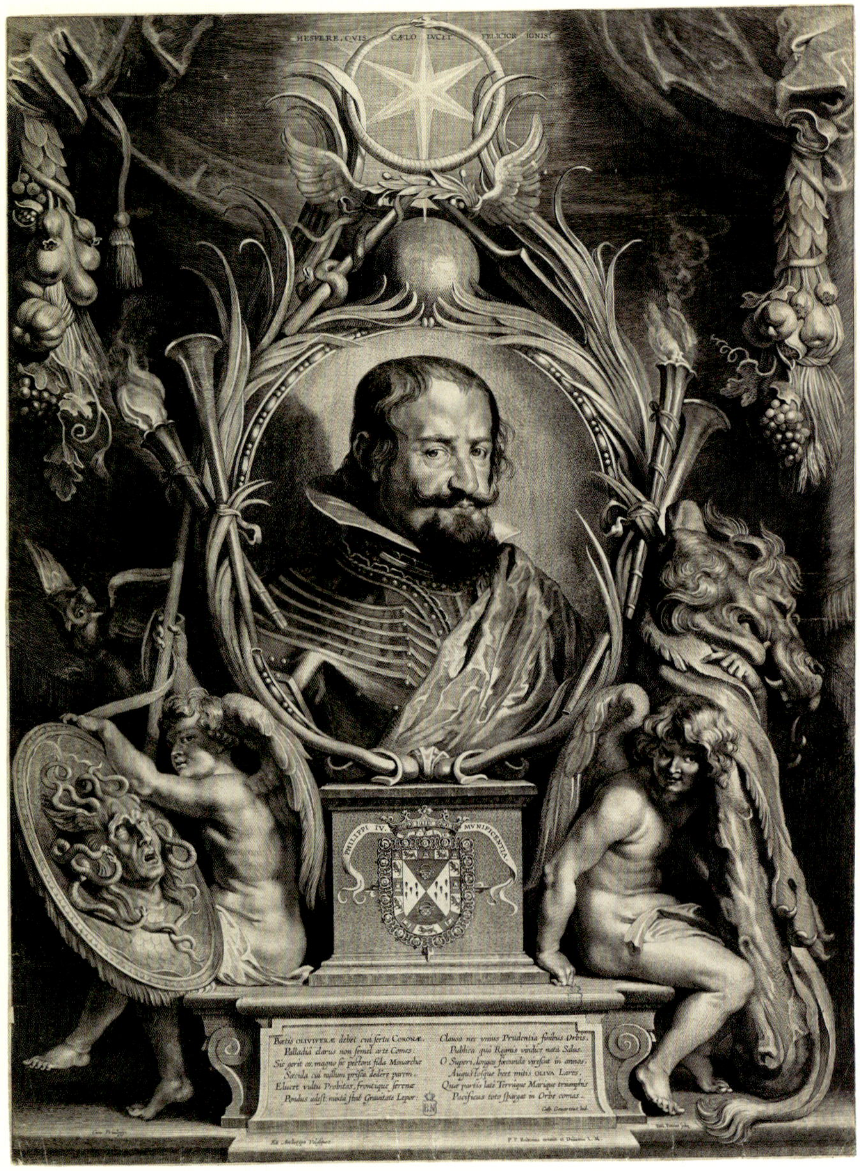

60
Paulus Pontius and Peter Paul Rubens after Diego Velázquez
The Count Duke of Olivares, 1626
Engraving and etching, 612 x 441 mm
Biblioteca Nacional, Madrid
IH/4219/5 G/2

manner would have secured his appointment and success in the court.[139] The 1645 portrait of Isabel de Borbón (fig. 57), engraved for the commemorative publication of her funeral rites, is testament to his ability to assimilate Velázquez's style.[140] After Villafranca was appointed Royal Engraver, he made a number of portrait engravings of Philip IV after Velázquez. His 1657 engraving (fig. 58) was probably copied from Velázquez's portrait of Philip IV of about 1655, now in the National Gallery, in London (fig. 59).[141]

Rubens' commitment to printmaking was highly influential. The 1626 allegorical portrait of Olivares (fig. 60) – hitherto the most impressive portrait print of a Spanish subject – is an unambiguous demonstration of the aggrandizing power of the printed image.[142] Pontius engraved the plate after Velázquez's portrait of the duke; the allegorical surround was designed by Rubens. Printed allegories relating to Olivares from this period abound (fig. 20, p. 137).[143] Rubens' title-page designs had the greatest influence in Madrid, but this was more a gradual dissemination of his principles than the

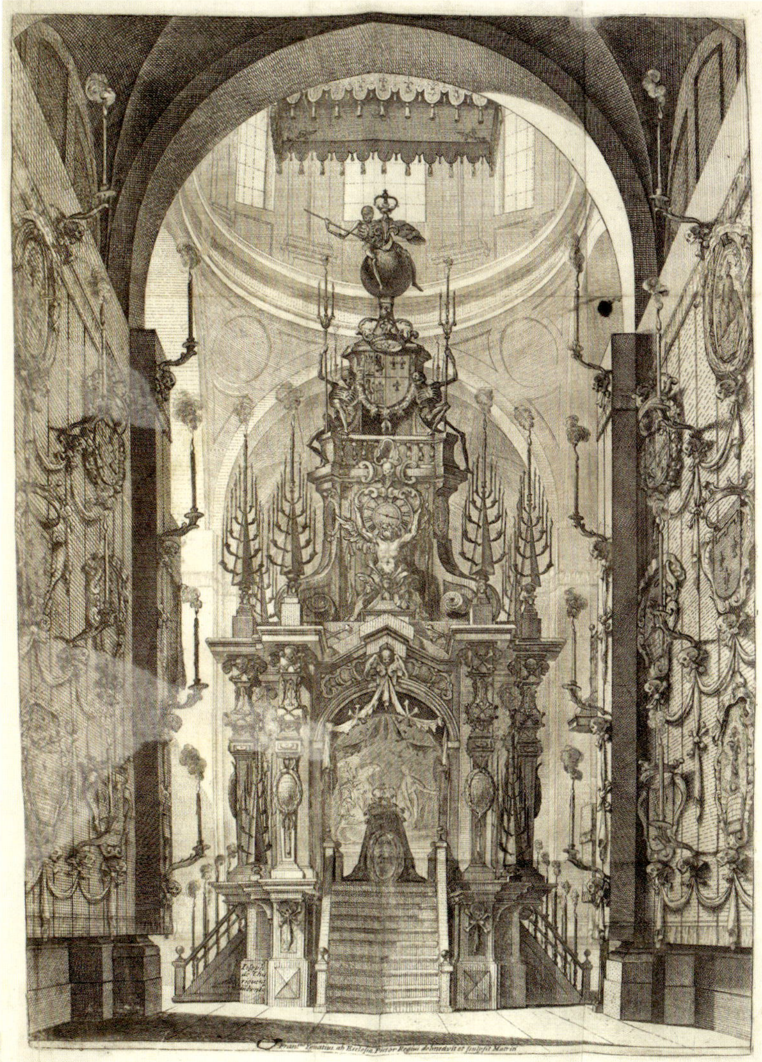

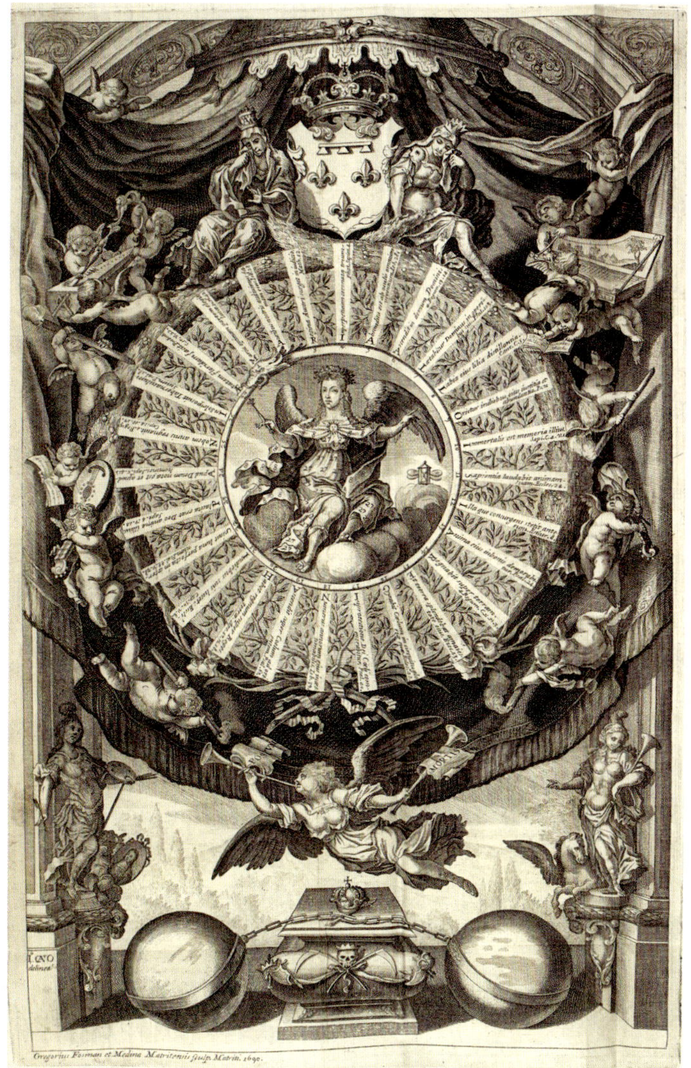

61
Francisco Ignatio
Catalfalque Raised for the Exequies of María Luisa de Orleans, 1690
Etching and engraving, 522 x 364 mm (plate mark)
British Library, London 595.m.5.

62
Gregorio Fosman
Allegory of the Death of María Luisa de Orleans, 1690
Etching and engraving, 485 x 310 mm (plate mark)
British Library, London 595.m.5.

impact of a single publication.[144] Herman Panneels – who according to Ceán Bermúdez worked in Rubens' studio – and Juan de Courbes absorbed his innovations.[145] Villafranca's title page for volume four of the *Commentaria theologica in primam partem* (1665) is a close copy in reverse of the title page of the *Opera* by Blosius, designed by Rubens and engraved by Cornelis Galle, published in 1632.[146]

Royal entries and funeral exequies provided abundant work for printmakers, mainly for commemorative publications. Matías de Torres' print of the arch erected for the entry into Madrid of María Luisa de Orleans was published in such a description (p. 112).[147] Her death was commemorated in other publications, mostly without illustration. An exception is Juan de Vera Tassis y Villarroel's *Noticias historiales de la enfermedad y muerte y exequias de … Doña María Luisa de Orleans* (Francisco Sanz, Madrid 1690), which contained a number of prints including two large engravings: a view of the catafalque designed by José Benito de Churrigera, drawn and engraved by Francisco Ignatio (Ygnatius), and a large allegory of her death, drawn by Juan Cano and engraved by Gregorio Fosman (figs 61–2). There is strong evidence that this sort of print was sold in single sheets, no doubt to recoup some of the financial

63
Pedro Rodríguez
View of a Harbour with Boats, c.1642
Etching and engraving, 153 x 216 mm
Biblioteca Nacional, Madrid
12973

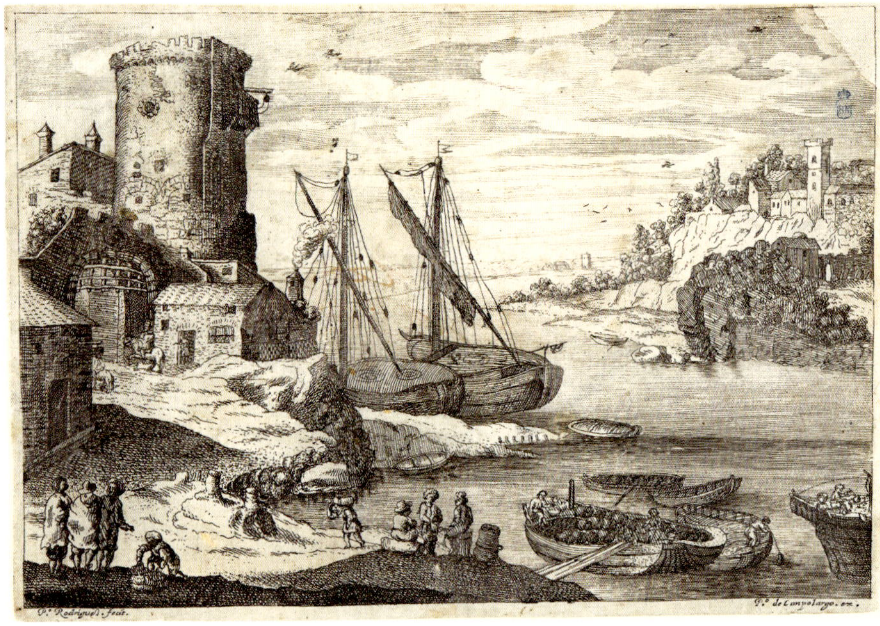

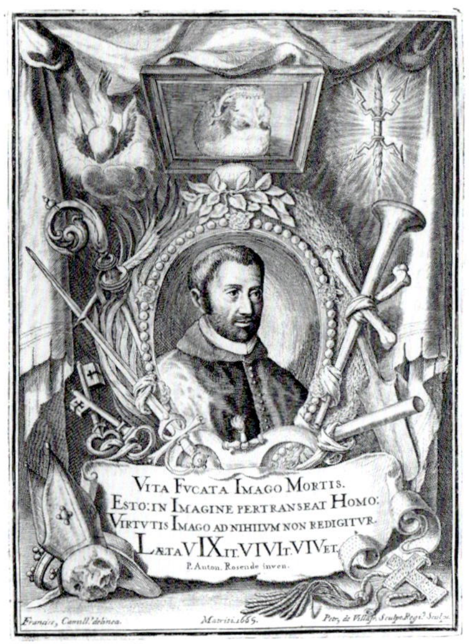

64
Pedro de Villafranca
Juan de Palafox y Mendoza, 1665
Engraving, 234 x 166 mm
Biblioteca Nacional, Madrid
3-70075

outlay. As such, these prints straddle the boundary between book illustration and stand-alone works. Fosman and Ignatio's prints reflect the very high quality of engraving achieved in Madrid during the second half of the seventeenth century, although printmakers with this level of skill were rare.

Etching was the preferred medium of artists who occasionally made prints because it allowed them greater expressive freedom. Writing in the late sixteenth and early seventeenth centuries, the theoreticians and practising artists Pablo de Céspedes and Francisco Pacheco saw etching as a manifestation of drawing (see Chapter 5).[148] Artists' etchings from Spain are not common, a situation that continued until the late eighteenth century. The first artists' etchings in Madrid, Vicente Carducho's *Penitent Saint Jerome* and *Cain and Abel* of about 1620–38, seem to have been printed in very few impressions.[149] Of the many artists who worked in his studio, several were printmakers, including Francisco Fernández, Francisco López and Pedro de Obregón. Carducho designed the illustrations for his *Diálogos de la pintura* that were etched by Fernández and López.[150] One of the earliest reproductive prints made in Madrid was Villafranca's 1638 *Portrait of Saint Domingo de Soriano* after Carducho's painting.[151] Diego de Obregón (active 1658–99) later made an etching of the same subject after Alonso Cano.[152] Both are rudimentary attempts at reproduction. Two engravings by Pedro Rodríguez (active 1636–8), one after Ribera's *Martyrdom of Saint Bartholomew* (fig. 25, p. 182) and the other after Rubens' *Saint Lawrence*, are of much higher quality.[153] These are no different from the prints made in other European cities, but it is significant that they reproduce other prints. *Saint Lawrence* was dedicated by another printmaker, Cornelio de Beer, to the collector and politician Lorenzo Ramírez de Prado. Nothing is known about Rodríguez except that he later moved to Seville, where he made a series of landscape prints which stand out in the history of printmaking in seventeenth-century Spain (fig. 63).

In the second half of the seventeenth century many artists who were primarily painters or architects became involved in printmaking, either providing designs for prints or cutting the plates themselves. Francisco Camilo is identified as the intermediary draughtsman for the 1665 engraved portrait of Juan de Palafox y Mendoza in the book commemorating his life and virtues (fig. 64).[154] The print was designed by the author of the book, Antonio González de Rosende, and engraved by Villafranca, demonstrating the number of individuals involved in producing such an image. In addition to the title pages designed and engraved by Claudio Coello discussed above, Ceán Bermúdez refers to three etchings of a Crucifixion and portraits of Charles II and his wife, none of which appears to have survived.[155] Ceán Bermúdez also mentions an etching by Juan Carreño of *Saint Anthony of Padua*, of which no impression is known; another, the *Martyrdom of Saint Lawrence*, has been tentatively attributed to him.[156]

Carreño's student José García Hidalgo, a painter who worked in Madrid during the late seventeenth century, was a committed printmaker. His treatise, *Principios para estudiar el Nobilísimo y Real arte de la Pintura* (Madrid 1693), contains 152 etchings for the instruction of students.[157] The first print depicts a drawing academy which, although modified for legibility, probably fairly accurately represents how such a studio was arranged. The students draw a model on a pedestal; the teacher, at the left, points to the model while looking at a student's work; in the left background, students copy a statue of Hercules. The many other prints illustrate heads, hands, eyes, studies of geometry, perspective and complete figures, some of the most arresting of which show the human body foreshortened (fig. 65). Prints from García Hidalgo's treatise exist in numerous single impressions that were probably printed especially for use in the studio.[158]

By the end of the seventeenth century, drawing was as much an established part of artistic life in Madrid as it was in other European capitals. This was less true of printmaking, because of the inadequate systems for training apprentices and the absence of a local reproductive print industry. The greatest change that took place in Madrid in the eighteenth century was the establishment of an industry that made printmaking competitive on the European stage.

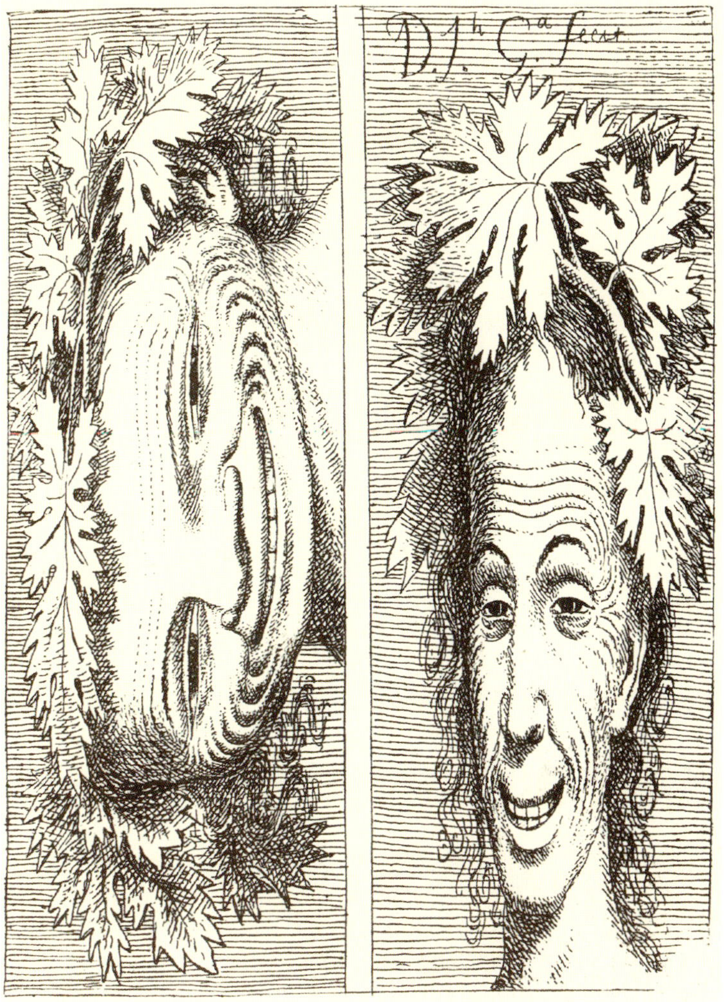

65
José García Hidalgo
Anamorphosis of a Face, 1693
Etching, 200 x 142 mm
Private collection

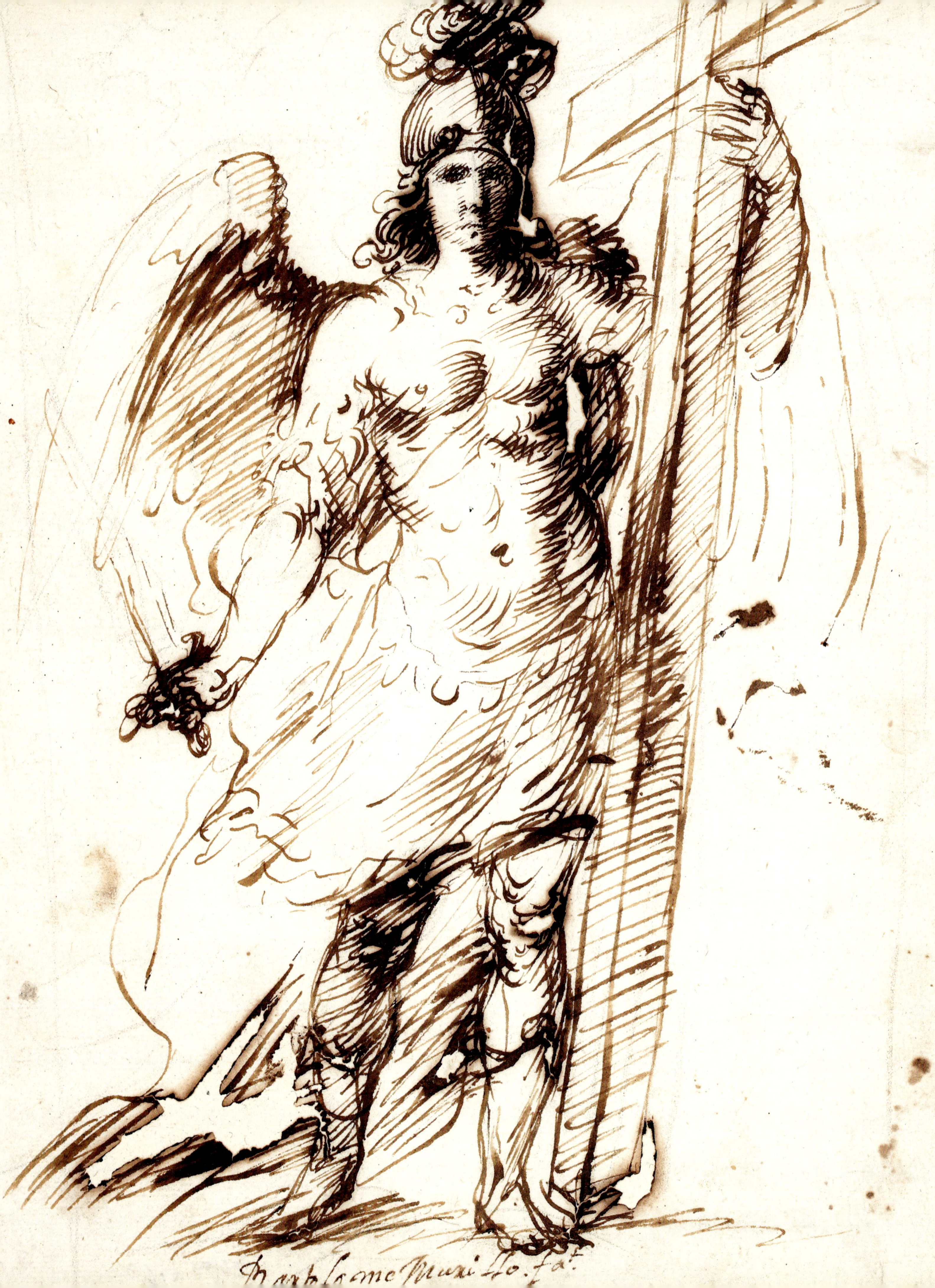
Bartolome Murillo. fat.

CHAPTER 5

Andalusia 1500–1700

The majority of prints and drawings by artists working in Andalusia during the sixteenth and seventeenth centuries are not well known. Significantly, regional centres such as Seville had no court to act as a focus for artistic practice, to provide impetus for printmaking or to encourage the preservation of drawings. In regional centres commissions came mainly from church and private patrons. Artists who trained in Seville and went on to have successful careers in Madrid include Diego Velázquez, Francisco Herrera the Younger and Alonso Cano (see Chapter 4). While the mobility of these and other artists complicates the question of regional style, dominating figures such as Francisco Pacheco in Seville and Antonio del Castillo in Córdoba strongly influenced those who worked with them.

Drawing in Andalusia during the sixteenth century

During the early years of the sixteenth century, after the discovery of the New World, Seville became the largest city in Spain and the commercial centre of the Spanish Empire. Her years of greatest prosperity were between 1592 and 1622; at the turn of the seventeenth century growth reached a peak, with a population of over 150,000.[1] The vitality of Seville's commerce meant that more individuals were now able to commission and buy works of art, although the highly cultivated urban elite was mainly interested in the classical past rather than in patronizing local artists, several of them forming important collections of mostly Italian art.[2] During the sixteenth century Seville was an urban conurbation predominately responding to its role as a commercial hub[3] and it is difficult to form a clear picture of workshop practice during these years: it was not until the seventeenth century that the city became a centre of artistic production.[4]

The dominant style of painting in sixteenth-century Seville blended Italian and Flemish elements into a form of Spanish mannerism that later turned to naturalism.[5] The most significant Spanish artists to work in Andalusia, Luis de Vargas (*c.*1505/6–67) and Pablo de Céspedes (*c.*1540–1608), like their Castilian counterparts, travelled to Italy where they were exposed to the vibrancy and sophistication of Italian art.[6] Vargas, who was born in Seville, is thought to have spent two periods in Rome, in 1527–34 and around 1555–61. Here he was greatly influenced by Francesco Salviati and collaborated with Perino del Vaga on fresco projects.[7] He also made a copy in red chalk of the figure of the Christ Child from Perino's 1534 *Nativity*,[8] one of a group of similar drawings produced while he was in Italy.[9] His delicate study for the *Virgin and Child* (fig. 1), also in this group, clearly shows Italian influence.[10]

Detail of fig. 36, see p. 149

1
Luis de Vargas
The Virgin and Child, *c.*1530–4
Red chalk, wash and white hightening over traces of black chalk, 136 x 84 mm
Gabinetto Disegni e Stampe degli Uffizi, Florence
S 2474

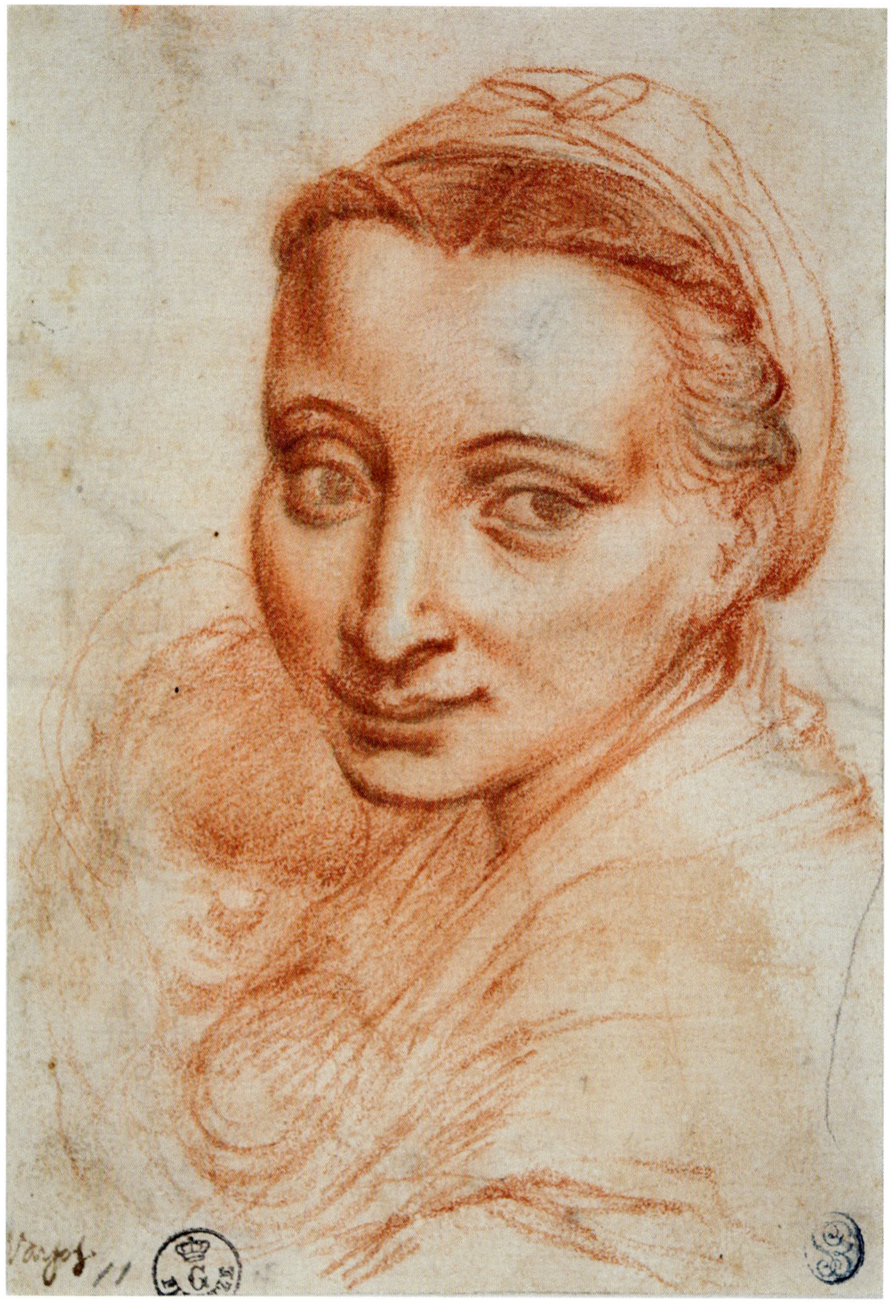

The principal source of information on Vargas is Francisco Pacheco, who describes him as a great draughtsman and the father of painting in Seville.[11] Vargas is credited with being the first local painter to use the fresco technique for which he became famous.[12] His unrecorded drawing of *The Execution of Jephthah's Daughter* (fig. 2), although damaged, is his most impressive surviving sheet and reinforces his debt to Italian models. Squared for transfer, it does not relate to a surviving work but its slightly elevated perspective suggests that it was intended for a fresco. While it is stylistically similar to several of Vargas' other drawings, it relates most strongly to his 1561 painting of the *Allegory of the Immaculate Conception* (fig. 3), probably inspired by Giorgio Vasari's painting in the church of Santissimi Apostoli, Florence, of 1541.[13] The group of Church Fathers at the left of the painting, for example,

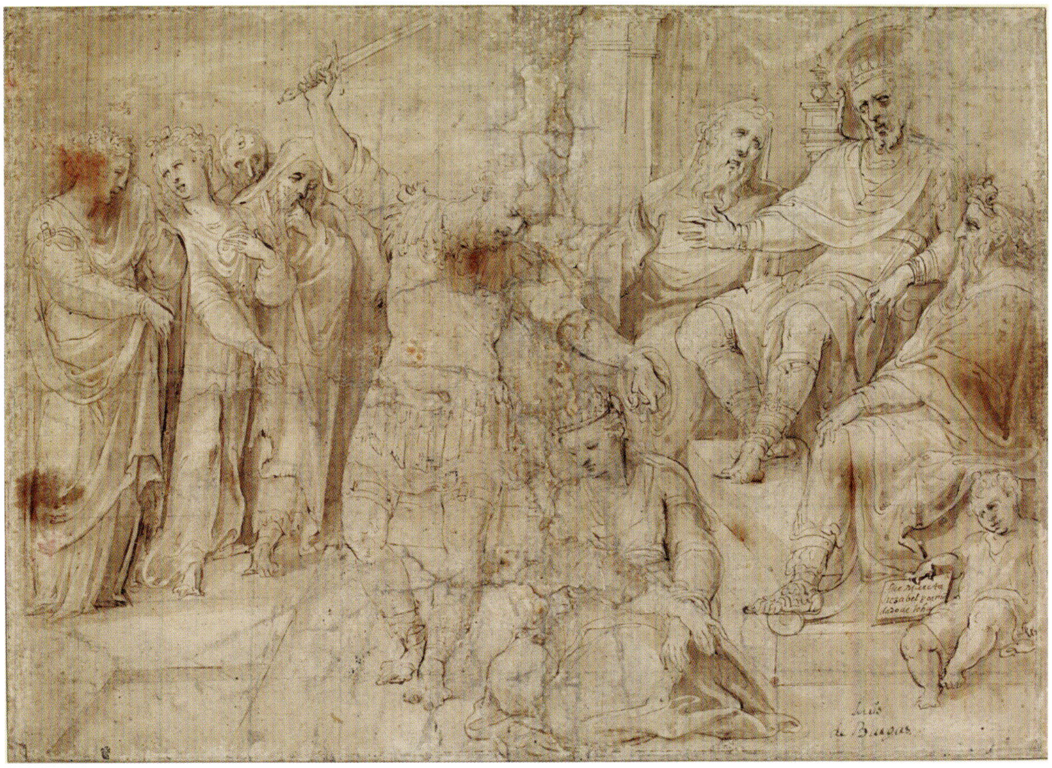

2
Luis de Vargas
The Execution of Jephthah's Daughter, 1550–68
Pen and brown ink, brown wash over black chalk, squared for transfer, 280 x 382 mm
British Museum, London
Nn,7.52.2

is very similar to those in the right of the drawing, with their elongated heads and beards. The baby in the lower centre of the painting echoes the small child holding the plaque in the drawing, especially in the position of his legs and his slightly turned head.

Pablo de Céspedes was educated at the University of Alcalá de Henares before moving to Córdoba. He also occasionally worked in Seville; his first recorded visit was in 1585, when he met Francisco Pacheco. He spent a number of years in Rome, probably between about 1559 and 1577 and again in 1583–5.[14] His earliest-known surviving Roman work is the fresco decoration of the Orsini chapel in Trinitá dei Monte; he is also said to have decorated the façades of houses in the manner of Polidoro da Caravaggio.[15] Like Gaspar Becerra (see Chapter 3), Céspedes learnt to draw in Italy. Ceán Bermúdez describes life-size cartoons, red and black chalk drawings and others in wash that he seems to have known first hand, to judge from his accounts.[16] The surviving sheets attributed to Céspedes, mostly on the basis of later inscriptions, are too few to allow us to form a clear view of his style.[17] A highly finished red chalk study of Saint Bartholomew on which his name has been inscribed in a later hand shows a technique and figure type similar to those by artists in Rome in the middle of the sixteenth century.[18] In his *Arte de la pintura* Pacheco refers to the drawings of both Vargas and Céspedes as deriving from the style of Raphael.[19] He also mentions having seen cartoons 'very dexterously drawn with charcoal' by Céspedes, which may have resembled those by Gaspar Becerra (fig. 22, p. 72).[20]

In his *Poema de la pintura*, a theory of art in poetic stanzas not published in his lifetime, Céspedes discusses the importance of colour and design, describing Michelangelo's *Last Judgement* as the model to emulate. Another

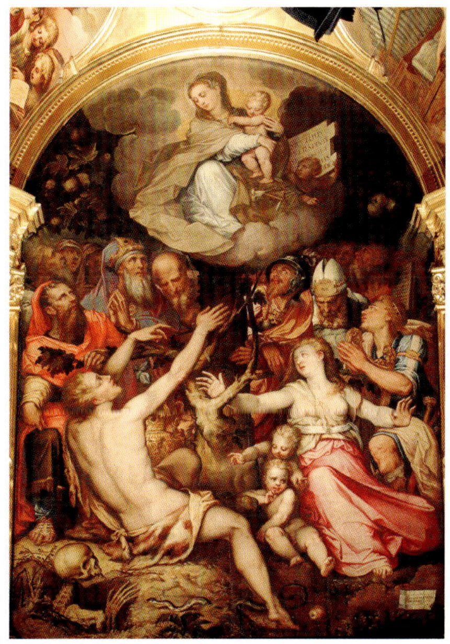

3
Luis de Vargas
Allegory of the Immaculate Conception, 1561
Oil on canvas
Seville Cathedral

of his theoretical tracts, the *Discurso de la comparación de la Antigua y moderna pintura y escultura*, was contained in a long letter to fellow humanist Pedro de Valencia written in 1604. Here Céspedes asks 'how could the sculptor make a worthy thing if he were not assisted first by drawing, which is the principal and greatest part of painting'.[21] Given his years in Rome and his contact with artists who were devoted draughtsmen, such as the Zuccaro brothers, and the recognition in his writings of the central role of drawing, Céspedes was no doubt much more active as a draughtsman than extant evidence suggests.[22]

Seville's immense commercial importance attracted artists from throughout Spain and further afield. Peter Kempeneer (1503–*c.*1587), known in Spain as Pedro de Campaña, originally from Brussels, spent time in Italy where he was involved in decorating one of the triumphal arches for the coronation of Charles V in Bologna in 1530. He arrived in Seville in 1537, where he remained until 1562.[23] A number of sheets by his hand show his drawing style to reflect his Northern origins much more than his contact with Italy.[24] A clear example is his study of *Saint George and the Dragon* (fig. 4) of about 1550–6, which corresponds to his painted altarpiece for the church of Santa Ana, Seville.[25] The figures are drawn in pen, ink and wash with highlights (now oxidized) on blue prepared paper.[26] The degree of finish is typical of many sixteenth-century drawings; in this case it may also have provided a record of his painting, with minor differences.

4
Pedro de Campaña
Saint George and the Dragon, *c.*1550–6
Pen and brown ink and brown wash with white highlights, 270 x 233 mm
Museo de la Casa de la Moneda, Madrid
14

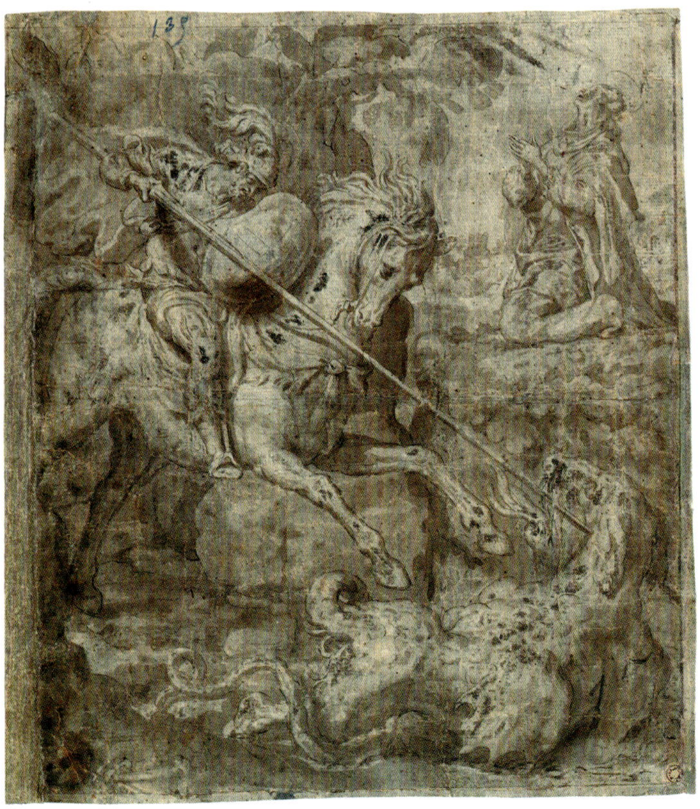

Pedro Machuca (*c.*1490–1550), from Toledo, spent time in Italy before settling permanently in Granada in 1520; in 1527 he was appointed head of the construction of the palace of Charles V at the Alhambra. He was known in Rome as 'Pietro Spagnolo', and it is believed he worked in Raphael's workshop as a fresco painter, participating in decorations of the Vatican Loggia, the Ponzetti Chapel in Santa Maria della Pace and elsewhere.[27] A number of drawings have been identified that are thought to be from his time in Italy.[28] Among the few secure attributions is the drawing of *The Descent from the Cross* (fig. 5), which is closely related to his painting of the same subject (fig. 6) made after his return to Spain.[29] The drawing was probably made towards the end of his time in Italy or just after he arrived in Spain, and is striking for its combination of pen and ink, wash and touches of highlight creating an effect similar to grisaille. It is pendant to *Christ Being Prepared for Burial*, executed in the same technique, but not to the same degree of finish.[30] Whereas other paintings from Machuca's long career in Spain are known, no other drawings have been securely identified.

The sheets by Vargas, Campaña and Machuca illustrate very different approaches and reflect Italian and Northern drawing practices. While Vargas' *Execution of Jephthah's Daughter* is a working sheet, the drawings by Campaña and Machuca are finished records of their work, which may explain why they have survived. That the

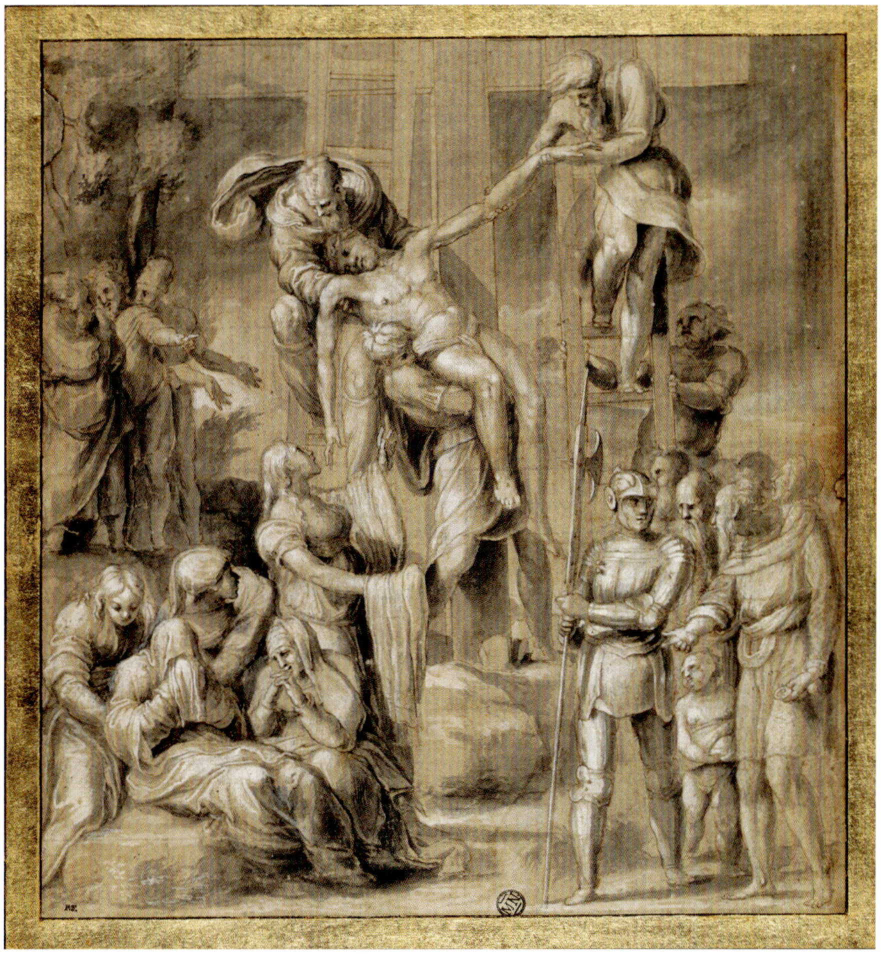

5
Pedro Machuca
The Descent from the Cross, *c.*1520
Pen and brown ink, grey wash over black chalk, white heightening with later retouching, traces of squaring, 315 x 284 mm
Musée du Louvre, Paris
6303

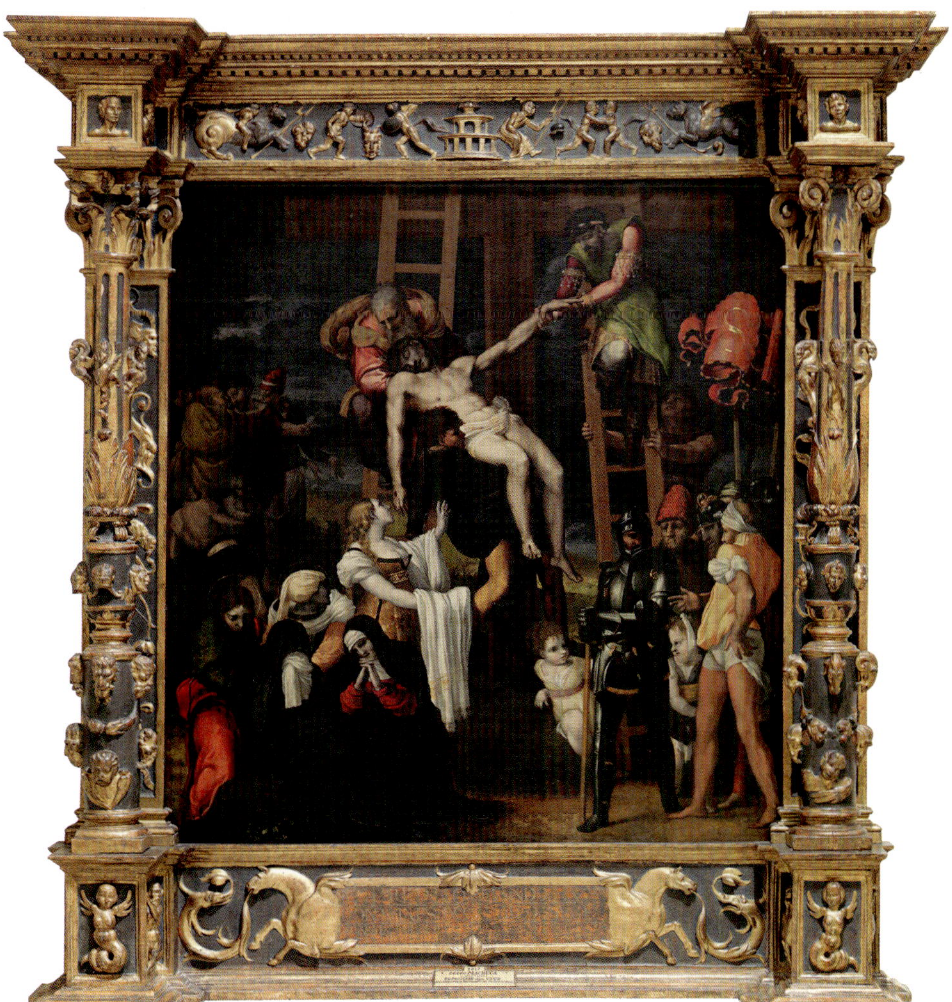

6
Pedro Machuca
The Descent from the Cross, 1547
Oil on panel, 1410 x 1280 mm
Museo del Prado, Madrid
P.3017

drawings do not exactly match the painted compositions suggest that they may be regarded as stand-alone pieces: they might have served several purposes, to demonstrate artistic ability, to provide a record of a composition and as source material for other artists. Copies of Machuca's drawings strongly suggest this to be the case.[31] The work of these artists had a pronounced impact on the next generation, most visibly on Francisco Pacheco, in whose oeuvre it is possible to detect the emergence of a manner of drawing that might be regarded as distinctly Sevillian.

Francisco Pacheco and his contemporaries

Francisco Pacheco (1564–1644) is remembered for his contribution to the intellectual life of Seville and the artists who trained and worked in his studio, among them Alonso Cano and his son-in-law Diego Veláquez. In 1599 Pacheco assumed leadership of an informal academy in Seville that had been founded in the 1560s and led by the humanist Juan de Mal Lara. The academy was modelled on Italian Neoplatonic Renaissance academies where scholars met to discuss subjects of mutual interest.[32] As such it was not a place for the formal instruction of artists, although they were among its members.

Pacheco commemorated many of his Sevillian acquaintances, including poets, theologians and artists, in his *Libro de descripción de verdaderos retratos y memorables varones* (1599), a book of portraits probably began in the second half of the 1580s.[33] These are among his best works and reveal his considerable ability as a portraitist. Each sitter has a short biography and a eulogy that sometimes refers to when the portrait was made (fig. 7).[34] For example, Pacheco records that when Pablo de Céspedes was his guest in Seville he drew his portrait and composed a sonnet to him.[35] As confirmed by his comments on the role of portraiture in his *Arte de la pintura*, their most important quality was veracity, achieved using red and black chalk and grey wash. Pacheco's choice of material is significant for what it reveals about the relationship between technique and function: chalk allowed for the sensitive modelling of flesh tones in a way that would not have been possible with pen and ink, for example.

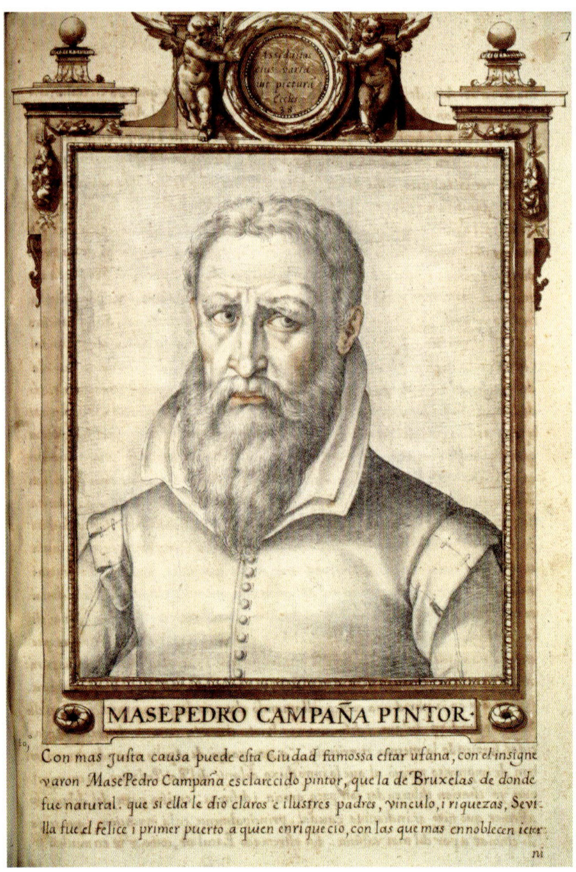

7
Francisco Pacheco
Pedro de Campaña, c.1585–98
Pen and brown ink and wash, red and black chalk, 185 x 150 mm
Museo Lázaro Galdiano, Madrid
15654

Pacheco's views on art expressed in the *Arte de la pintura*, composed over a forty-year period from about 1600 and published posthumously in 1649, reflect the intellectual atmosphere and aspirations of the academy in Seville. Together with Carducho's *Diálogos de la pintura* discussed in Chapter 4, Pacheco's *Arte de la pintura* provides the basis for our understanding of the role of drawing in Spain during the early modern period. It comprises three books, of which the first two discuss painting as a liberal art while the third is devoted to artistic practice; the lengthy appendix focuses on religious iconography.[36] Pacheco refers constantly to the authority of Italian artists, greatly praising the drawings of the 'Divine' Michelangelo, for example, especially his figure studies. Of his own experience, he observes that 'driven by some hidden instinct, I have always tried to imitate [Raphael] from an early age. For I was moved by his beautiful inventions and by an

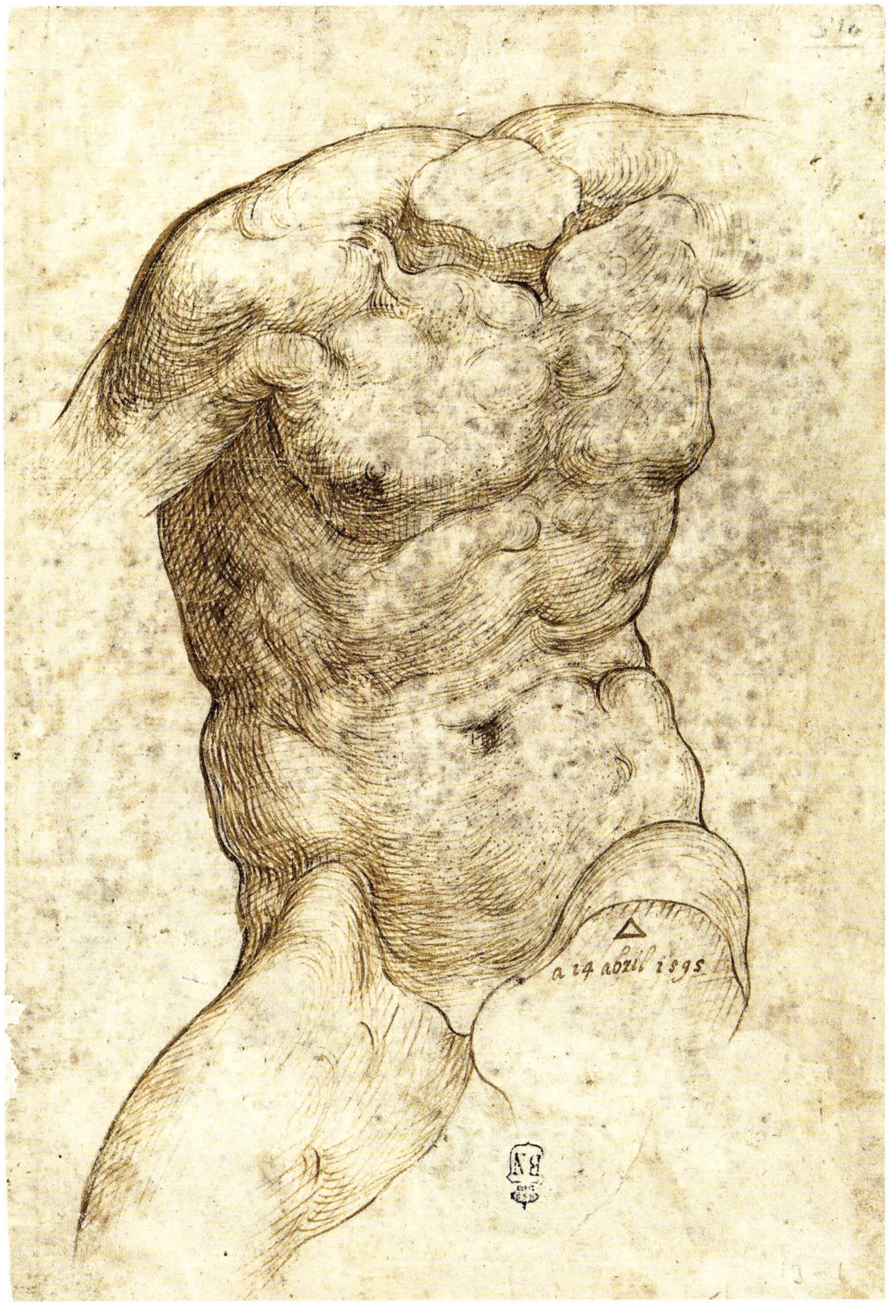

8
Francisco Pacheco
Torso, 1595
Pen with brown and black ink, 261 x 175 mm
Biblioteca Nacional, Madrid
DIB/13/1/65/1

original drawing from his school in his own hand that came into my possession which I preserved for many years. It was drawn with marvellous dexterity and beauty.'[37]

In the first chapter of Book Three, 'how to make sketches, drawings cartoons, and the various ways to use them', Pacheco provides valuable discussion of the drawing techniques of Italian masters and their Spanish followers.[38] He describes the tried and trusted practice of making several rough sketches of movements, expressions and actions, the best of which were then worked up into final compositions.[39] He recommends that students copy drawings by their master as well as prints, drawing simple outlines at first, then working up features into finished compositions.[40] Elsewhere, he advises drawing from antique statuary in order to understand anatomy.[41] His pen-and-ink drawing

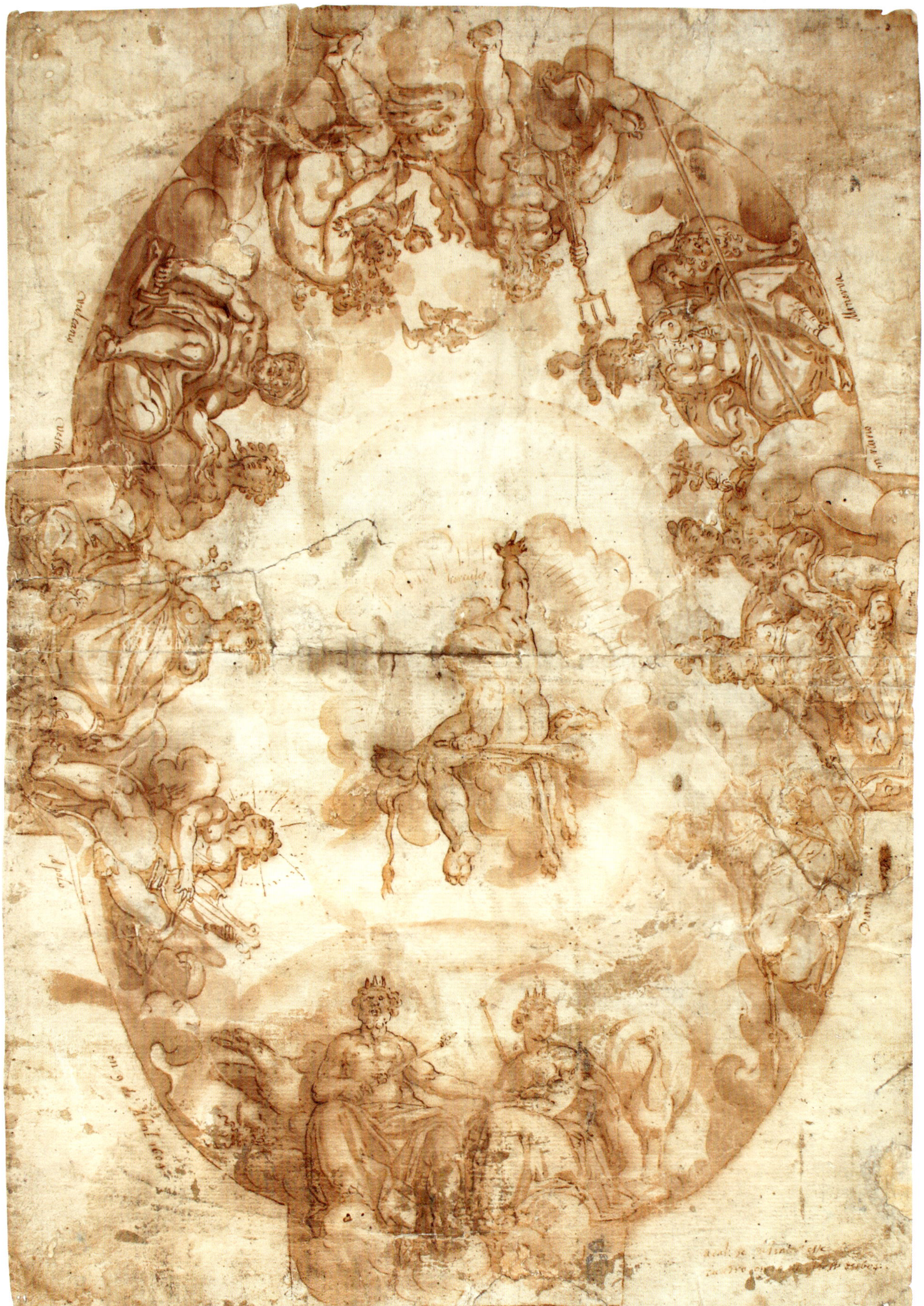

of a torso (fig. 8), inscribed in his own hand '14 April 1595', is just the sort of sheet he suggests as a model for students.[42] This sheet was part of a sketchbook, and was attached to a drawing by another hand of Venus and Adonis within a cartouche.[43] Pacheco's ambition to understand form and composition through drawing is reflected in the large number of his surviving sheets, which present the most complete evidence we have for art in Seville at this period.[44]

One of the most prominent members of the Seville academy was the 3rd Duke of Alcalá, Fernando Enríquez de Ribera, for whose palace, the Casa de Pilatos, Pacheco painted a mythological ceiling in 1603.[45] Pacheco made a number of preparatory drawings for this work, including *The Apotheosis of Hercules* (fig. 9) for the central panel.[46] This sheet is dated '9 April 1604' and in the bottom right records 'this painting was finished on 19 August 1604', both inscriptions in the artist's own hand.[47] The drawing is a finished record

9
Francisco Pacheco
The Apotheosis of Hercules, 1604
Pen with brown ink and brown wash, 390 x 270 mm
Museo de la Real Academia de Bellas Artes de San Fernando
D/2200

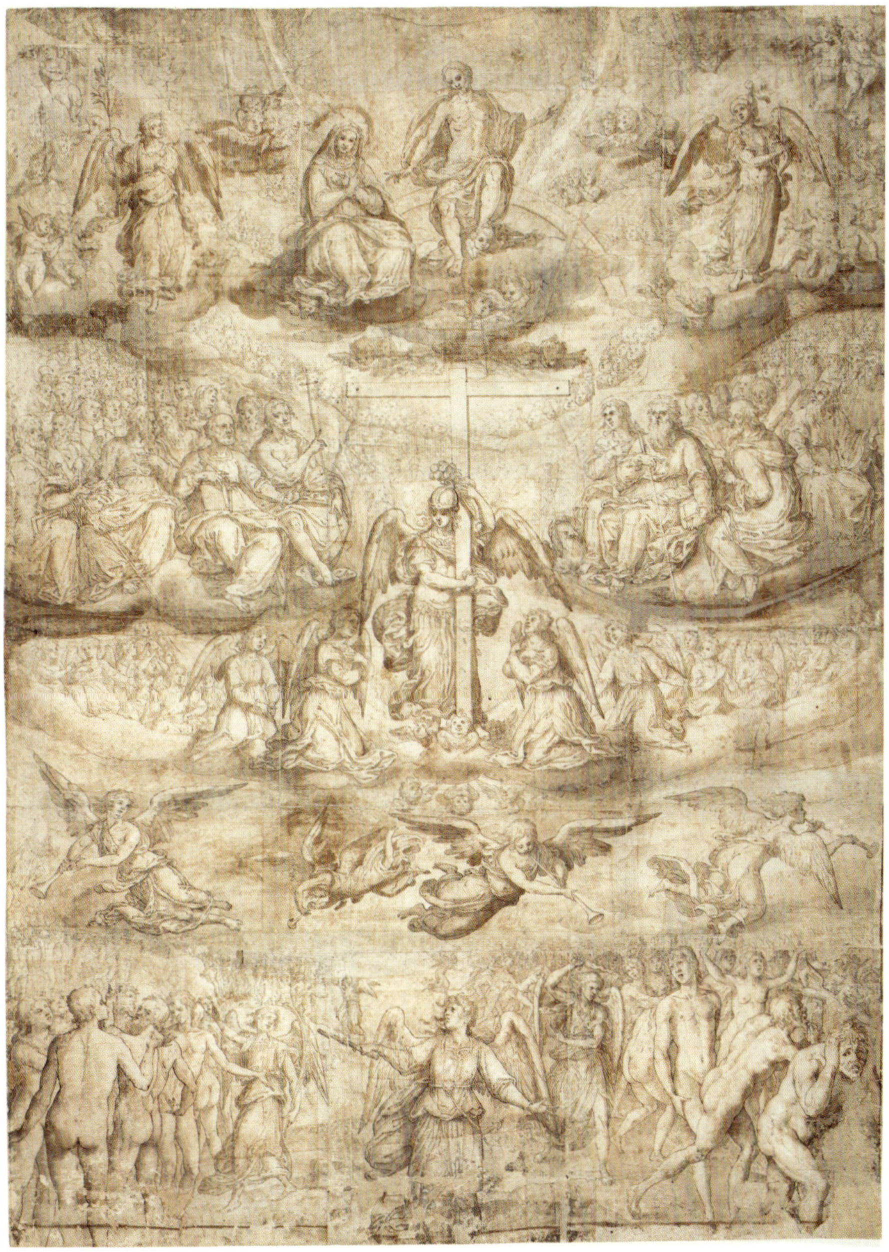

10
Francisco Pacheco
The Last Judgement, c.1610–14
Pen and brown ink with brown wash over black chalk, 553 x 387 mm
Museo del Prado, Madrid
D.8557

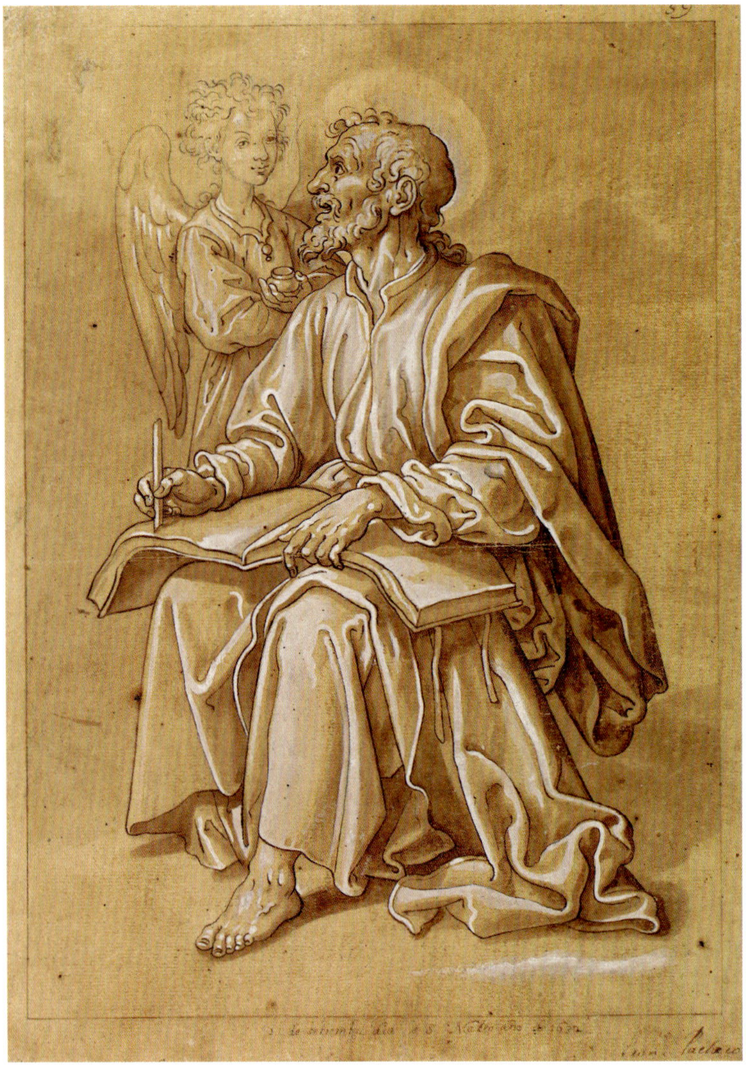

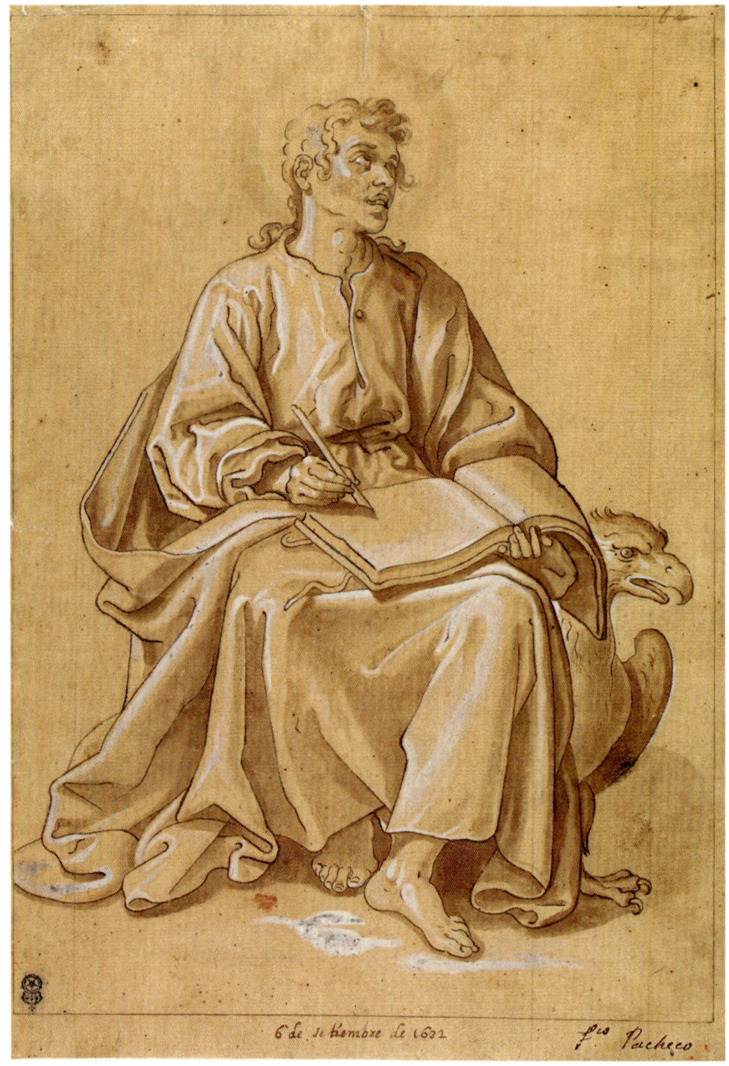

11
Francisco Pacheco
Saint Matthew and the Angel, 1632
Pen and dark brown ink, brown wash, heightened with white over black chalk on prepared paper, 342 x 236 mm
British Museum, London
1977,0507.11

12
Francisco Pacheco
Saint John the Evangelist, 1632
Pen and dark brown ink, brown wash, heightened with white, over black chalk, squared on prepared paper, 330 x 223 mm
British Museum, London
1928,0714.1

of the final design to show his patron. Pacheco prepared a very different sort of drawing for his 1614 painting of *The Last Judgement* (fig. 10) for the convent church of Santa Isabel in Seville.[48] The drawing comprises about twenty pieces of paper assembled to create a type of graphic collage. It seems that this method allowed Pacheco to carefully plan each section of the composition in separate groups. In the *Arte de la pintura* he refers both to the painting and to this drawing, acknowledging his debt to the Sistine Chapel frescos, and citing several of Michelangelo's figures that he knew through prints.[49] Although very different in their function and, in many respects, their execution, *The Apotheosis of Hercules* and *The Last Judgement* demonstrate Pacheco's approach to drawing and its role in his own practice.

Pacheco's painstaking attention to technical matters demonstrated in the *Arte de la pintura* is also manifest in his drawings. He made copies of his own drawings, probably to provide material for other artists. For example, his *Saint Lucy* and *Saint Agnes* exist in two drawn versions, with and without a detailed egg-and-dart border, dated 1612 and 1614 respectively.[50] *Saint Agnes* replicates his painting of around 1610.[51] The annotations on many of his drawings demonstrate what can broadly be regarded Pacheco's interest in documentation and process. *Saint Matthew and the Angel* (fig. 11) and *Saint John the Evangelist* (fig. 12), for example, are both inscribed with the day, month and year, 1632. Dating sheets in this way confers a degree of authority and finality, marking them for preservation; there would be little point dating a drawing if it was intended to be discarded. Furthermore, none of these sheets is a rough sketch of the type Pacheco mentions in the *Arte de la pintura* as the starting-point for drawing. His programmatic approach suggests that he intended some of his sheets to form a corpus or a visual iconography, to be compiled into books or albums.[52] *Saint John the Evangelist* and *Saint Matthew and the Angel* also show how little his drawing technique changed throughout his life. His pen-and-wash drawings have a undeniable clarity inherited by artists who worked in his studio: Alonso Cano for example, carried it to a much more sophisticated level.

Drawings by Pacheco's contemporaries in Seville are rare, suggesting that his dedication to drawing, driven by his academic aspirations, was unusual – or alternatively, that the early works of his pupils were discarded. Juan de Roelas (*c.*1558/68–1625) was kept busy fulfilling commissions rather than engaging with the theoretical aspects of art, an approach that, as we have seen, encouraged prolific drawing. A delicate pen-and-wash study of *The Infant Christ* (fig. 13) has been attributed to him: this was a subject he painted on a number of occasions and he included the figure in group compositions.[53] His name appears on the recto, while an inscription on the verso indicates a Sevillian provenance. No other drawings by Roelas have been firmly identified, but his broader engagement in graphic art is demonstrated by the survival of two

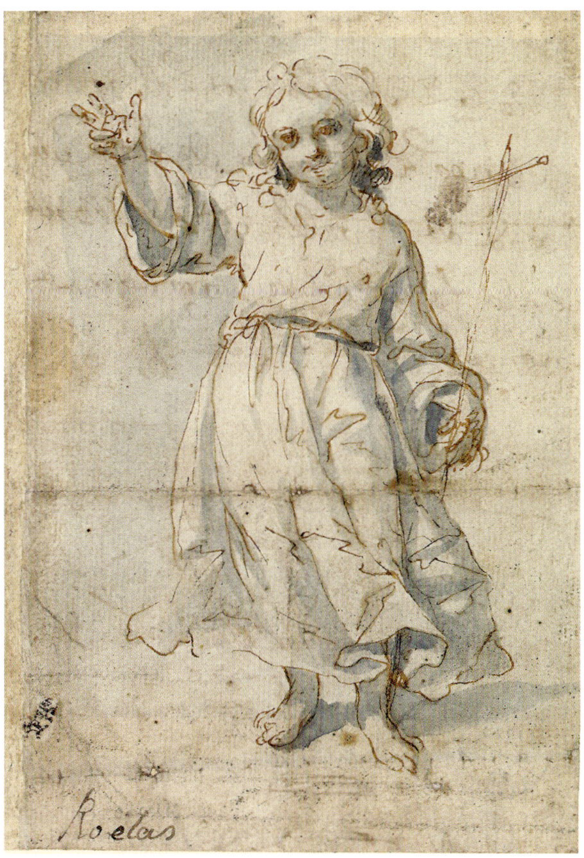

13
Attributed to Juan de Roelas
The Infant Christ, 1600–25
Pen and brown ink and blue wash, 155 x 106 mm
British Museum, London
1920,1116.22

14
Attributed to Francisco de Zurbarán
Saint Agatha, *c.*1640–60
Pen and brown ink and brown wash over black chalk, 243 x 147 mm
British Museum, London
1973,0915.32

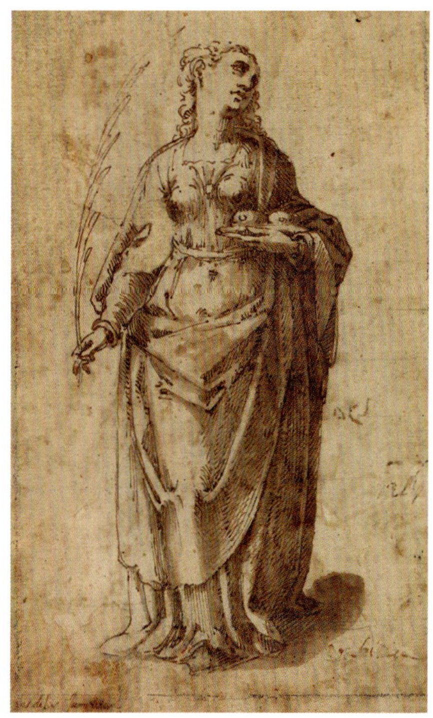

15
Francisco de Zurbarán

Head of a Monk, *c.*1635–55

Black chalk, grey wash with traces of pen and ink, 277 x 196 mm
British Museum, London
1895,0915.873

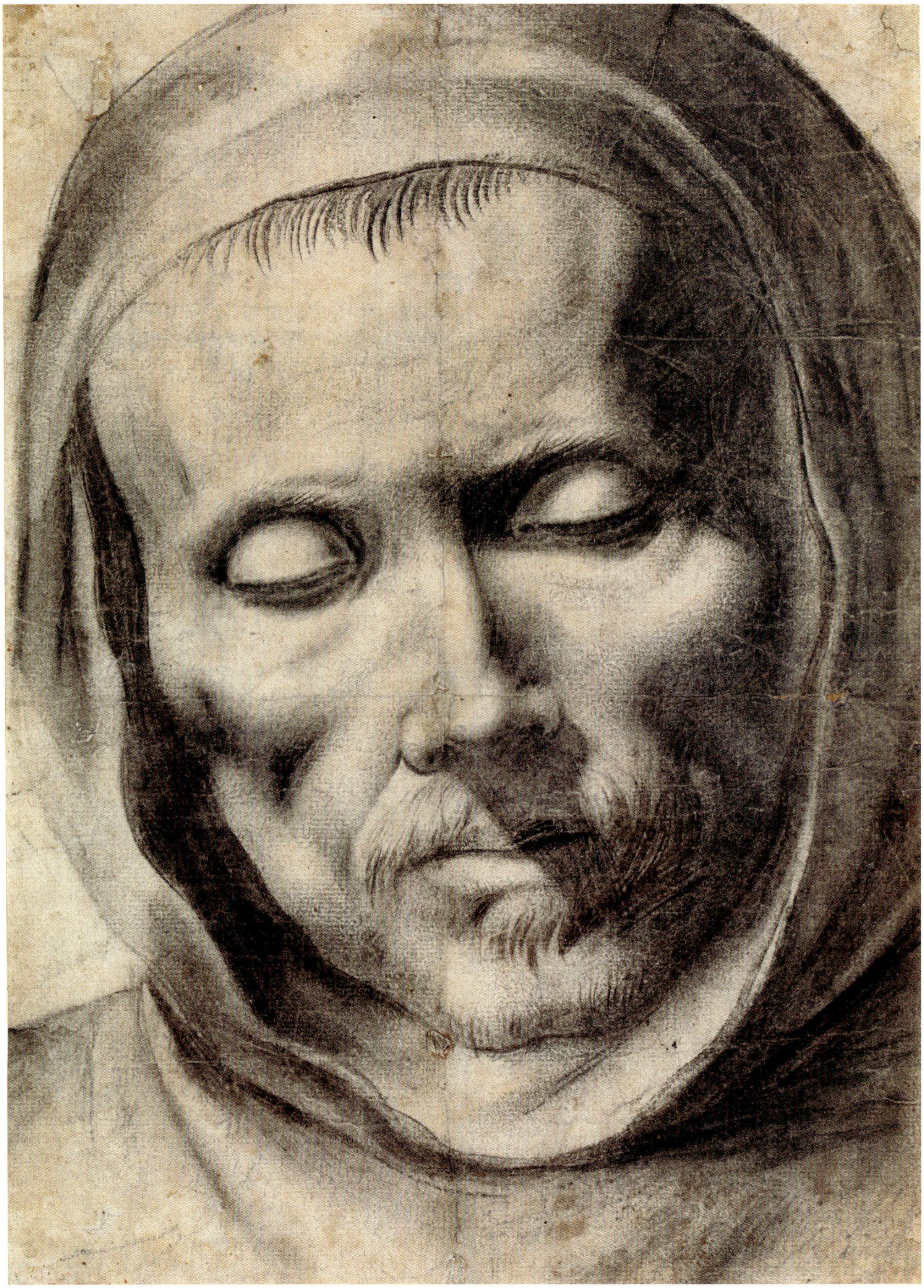

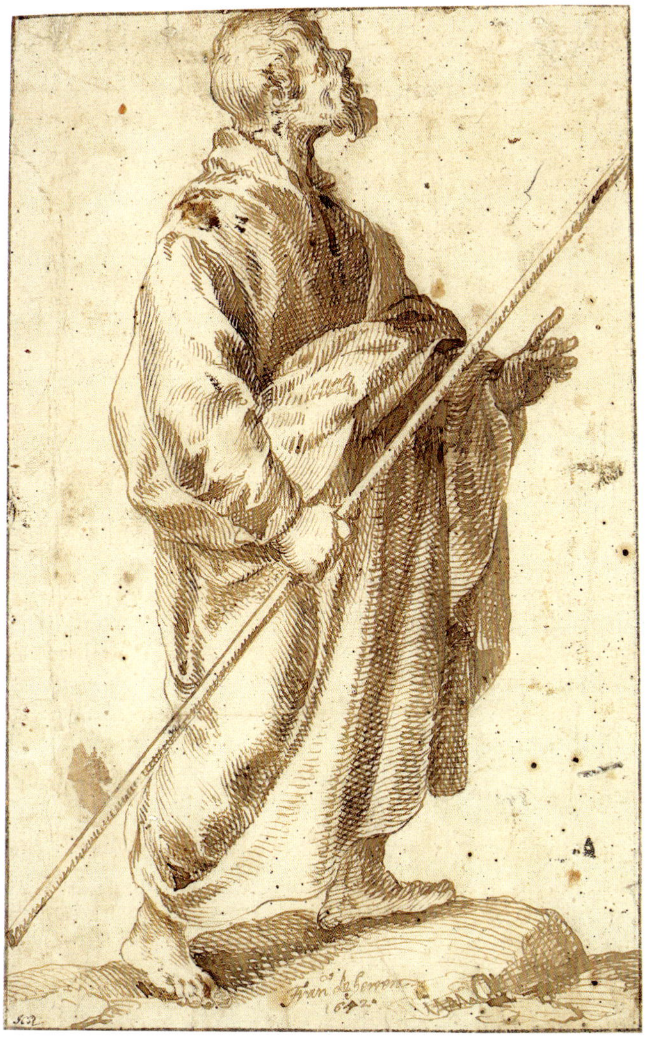

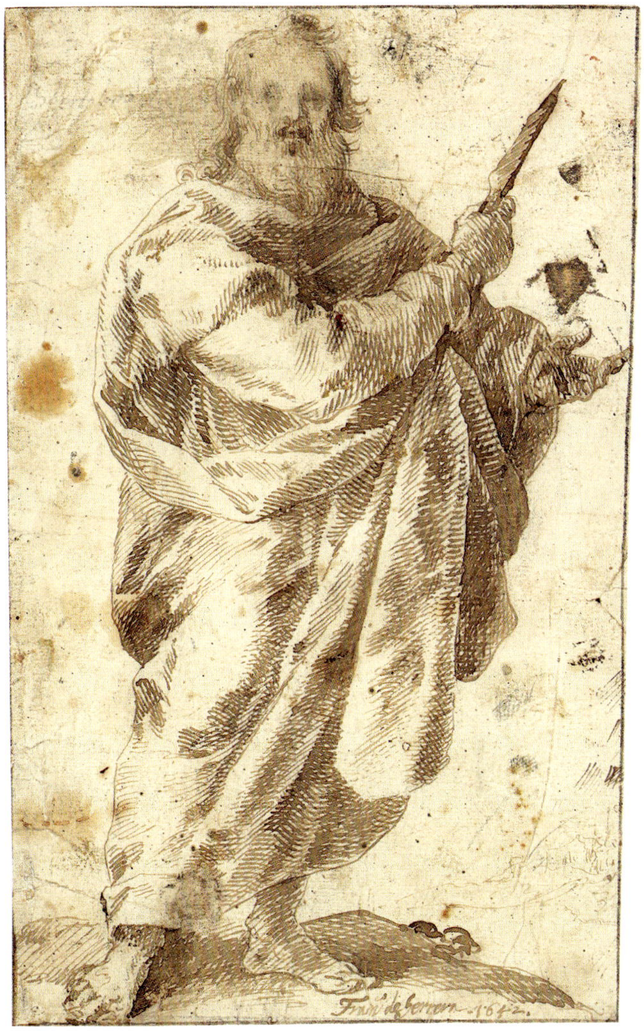

copper plates he engraved. The first of these, *The Elevation of the Cross*, is signed and dated 1597; the second, *The Virgin of Sorrows* after a sculpture by Juan de Juni, was made when Roelas was in Valladolid between 1598 and 1602.[54]

A number of chalk drawings and others in pen and ink have been associated with Francisco de Zurbarán (1598–1664) on the basis of their similarity to the single monumental figures that characterize his paintings.[55] Among these, *Saint Agatha* (fig. 14) is inscribed with the painter's name in a seventeenth-century hand and has more of a claim than most to be firmly identified as by Zurbarán, being typologically similar to his many paintings of virgin martyrs; furthermore, it was believed at the time to be by Zurbarán. The best-known drawing attributed to Zurbarán is the *Head of a Monk* (fig. 15), which perfectly reflects the sensibility of his paintings of saints and monastic figures; this also has elements in common with Pacheco's post-mortem portraits in his *Libro de retratos*, some of which were later engraved.[56]

The drawing practice of Francisco de Herrera the Elder (*c.* 1590–1654), Zurbarán's main competitor in Seville during the 1630s, is better understood. His drawings are relatively abundant and their variety suggests he was a keen draughtsman. The earliest sheets, from around 1626, are preparatory studies

16
Francisco de Herrera the Elder
Saint Thomas, 1642
Pen and brown ink, 298 x 184 mm
British Museum, London
1895,0915.871

17
Francisco de Herrera the Elder
Saint Bartholomew, 1642
Pen and brown ink, 304 x 189 mm
British Museum, London
1895,0915.872

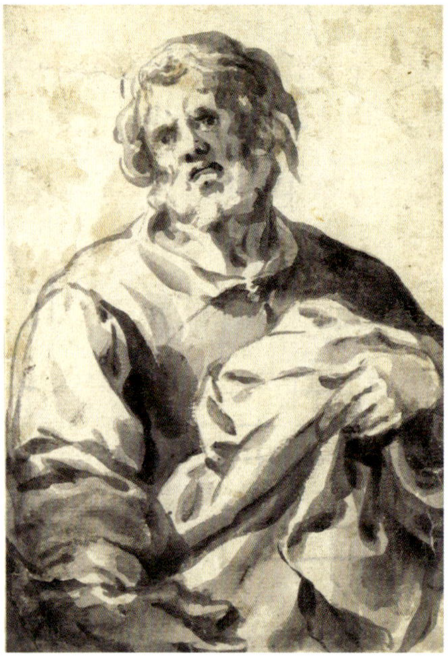

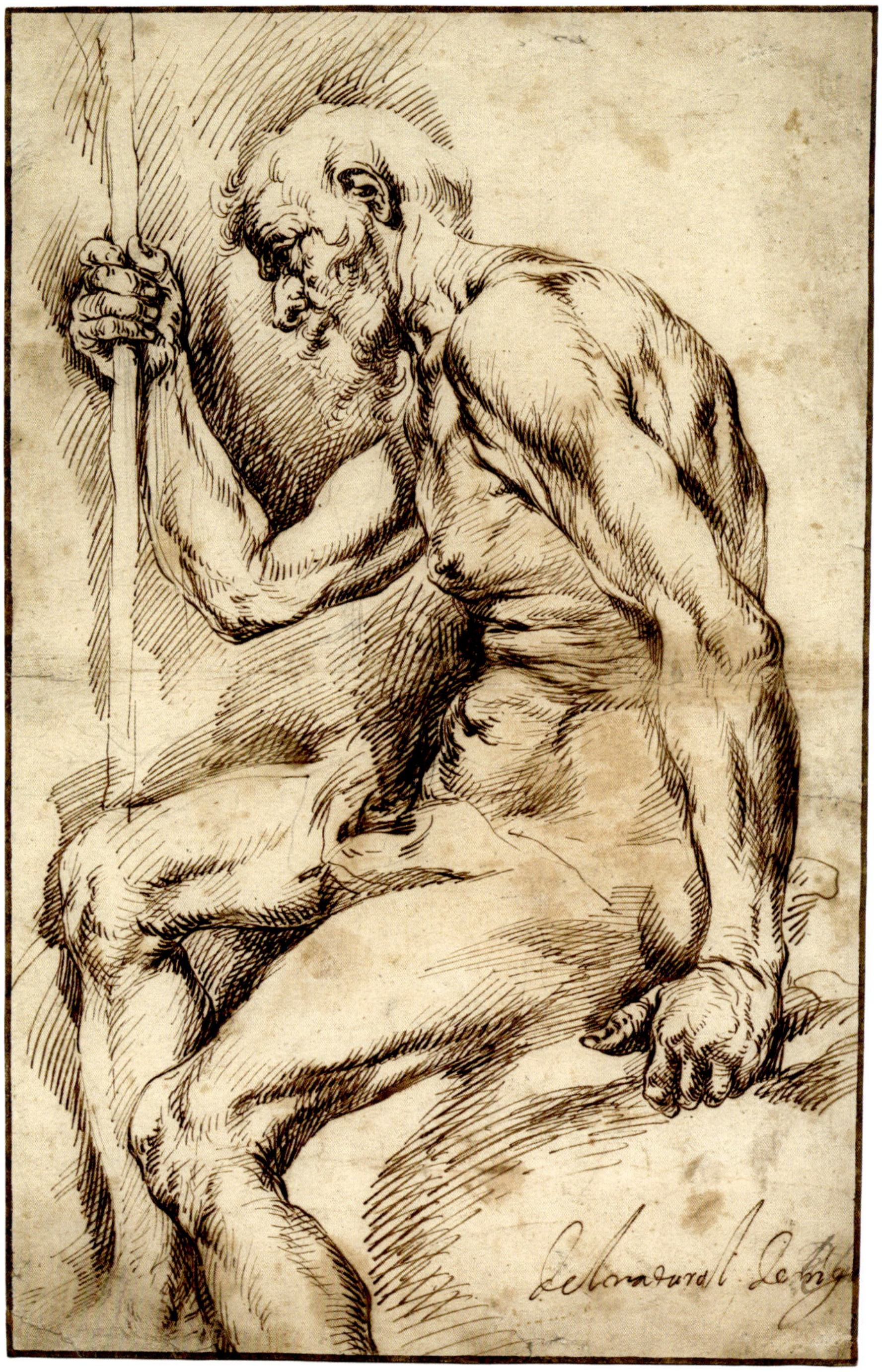

18
Francisco de Herrera the Elder
An Apostle (Peter?), c.1620–40
Brush with grey wash, 153 x 102 mm
Hamburger Kunsthalle 38563

19
Circle of Francisco de Herrera the Elder
Study of a Seated Male Nude, c.1640–50
Pen and brown ink over black chalk, 418 x 263 mm
British Museum, London
Pp,4.54

for the decoration of the nave and cupola of the church of San Buenaventura in Seville. Discovered bound into a 1562 edition of Vignola's treatise on architectural orders and other miscellaneous prints, these include a pen-and-wash elevation of pilasters framing an arch, above which is space for a painting and other details of the cupola decoration.[57] From a series depicting the Apostles, of which eight sheets are known, *Saint Thomas* and *Saint Bartholomew* (figs 16–17) are drawn in the distinctive medium of pen and ink with hatching giving the figure a sense of monumentality.[58] The technique, drawn border, date and signatures on these sheets suggest that they were intended to be engraved. The drawings are abraded and several are badly damaged,

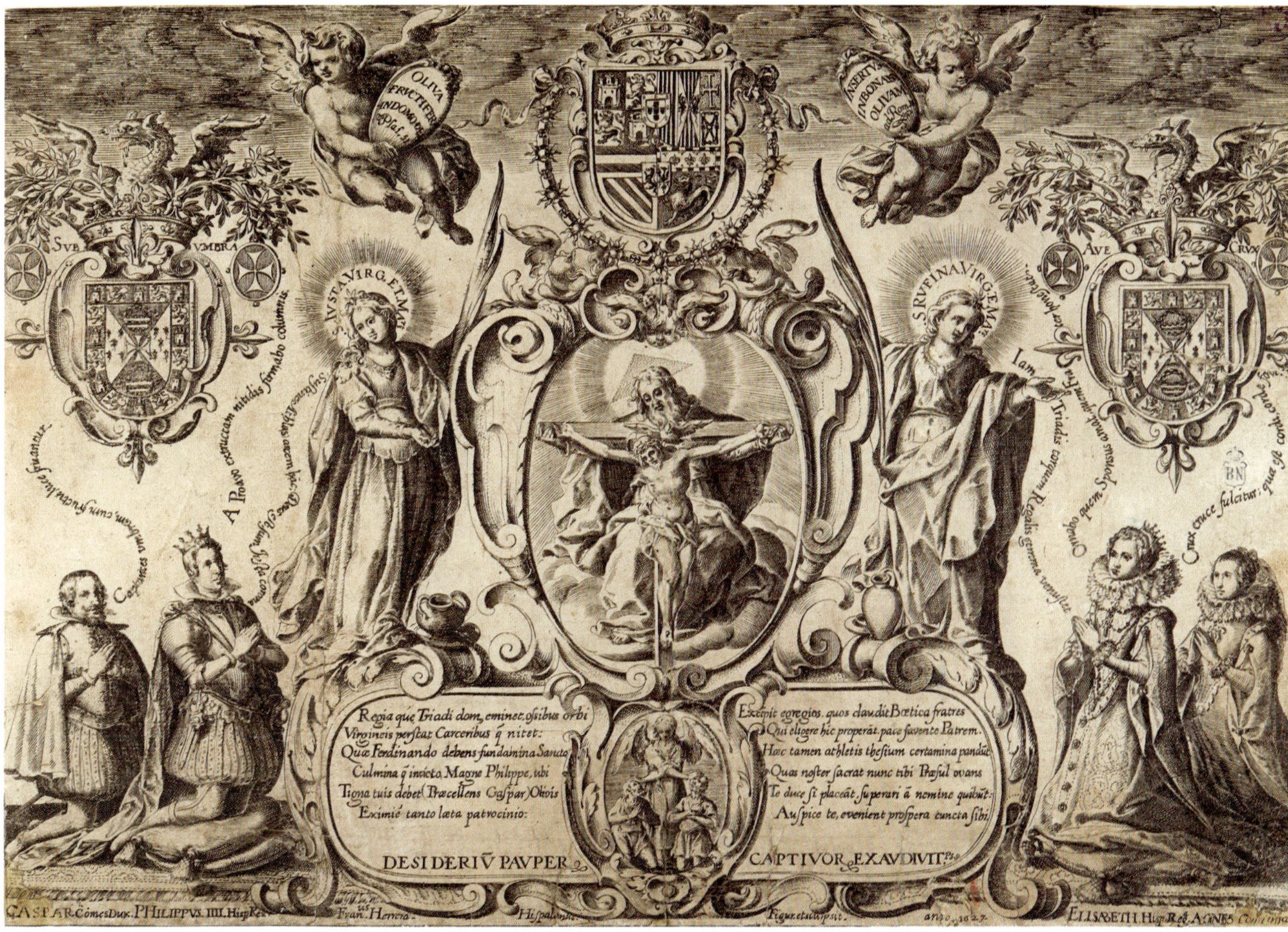

presumably because they were used in the studio as models from which to copy. No other signed drawings by Herrera are known, but a group of wash studies of Apostles (fig. 18) and saints, probably from an earlier point in his career, corresponds to his paintings.[59] A further group of three studies for a Deposition of Christ in pen, ink and brown wash provides a link between the hatched pen-and-ink sheets and those in brush and wash.[60] Herrera's drawing style was based on the naturalism that developed in Seville in the early decades of the seventeenth century. His wash drawings reflect the techniques of those around him, especially Pacheco – with whom, according to Palomino, Herrera served his apprenticeship – and Alonso Cano, whose influence is most evident in Herrera's painting.[61] A number of extant drawings from Herrera's immediate circle show the influence of his distinctive drawing technique. A large pen-and-ink study of a seated naked man made around the middle of the century is inscribed 'from life' (*del natural*) and reflects academic drawing practice occurring in Seville (fig. 19).

Herrera was the first artist in Seville to have also produced prints throughout his career. His earliest was an engraved title page after a design by Diego López dated 1609.[62] In 1627 he was commissioned by the Trinitarians of Andalusia to produce a single-sheet etching dedicated to the Count-Duke of Olivares, who is shown kneeling alongside Philip IV at bottom left (fig. 20); this large print survives in a unique impression.[63] Olivares was an

20
Francisco de Herrera the Elder
The Holy Trinity Flanked by Saints Justa and Rufina and Others Kneeling in Adoration, 1627
Engraving and etching, 294 x 412 mm
Biblioteca Nacional, Madrid 14547

21
Juan Méndez
Print commemorating the Foundation of the Cartuja de la Cuevas, Seville, 1629
Engraving and etching, 380 x 250 mm
Biblioteca Nacional, Madrid
40840

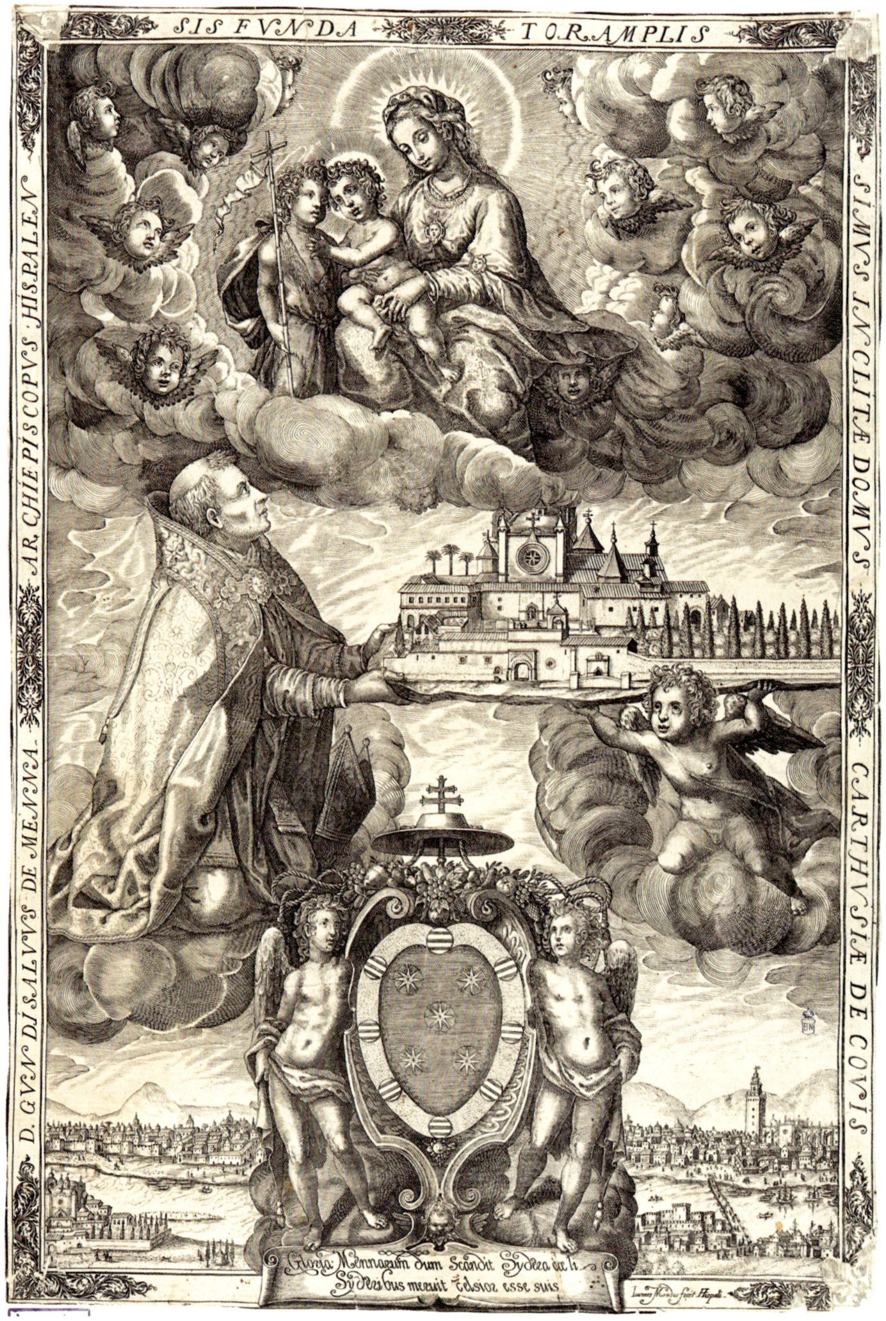

important figure for printmaking in Spain, recognizing as he did the capacity of the medium for disseminating images (fig. 60, p. 118);[64] no doubt the Trinitarians were eager to secure his favour. Herrera both designed and engraved the plate; although the place of publication is not recorded, it was probably Seville. The extent of his activity as a printmaker appears to have been greater than his few surviving prints suggest. Ceán Bermúdez, for example, mentions several etchings, and there is record of an illuminated engraving by Herrera.[65]

A print by Juan Méndez from 1629 made as a book illustration commemorating the foundation of the Cartuja de las Cuevas was also sold as a single sheet (fig. 21). The size of this print and Herrera's Trinitarian commission demonstrates that there were presses in Seville at this date able to deal with large plates.[66]

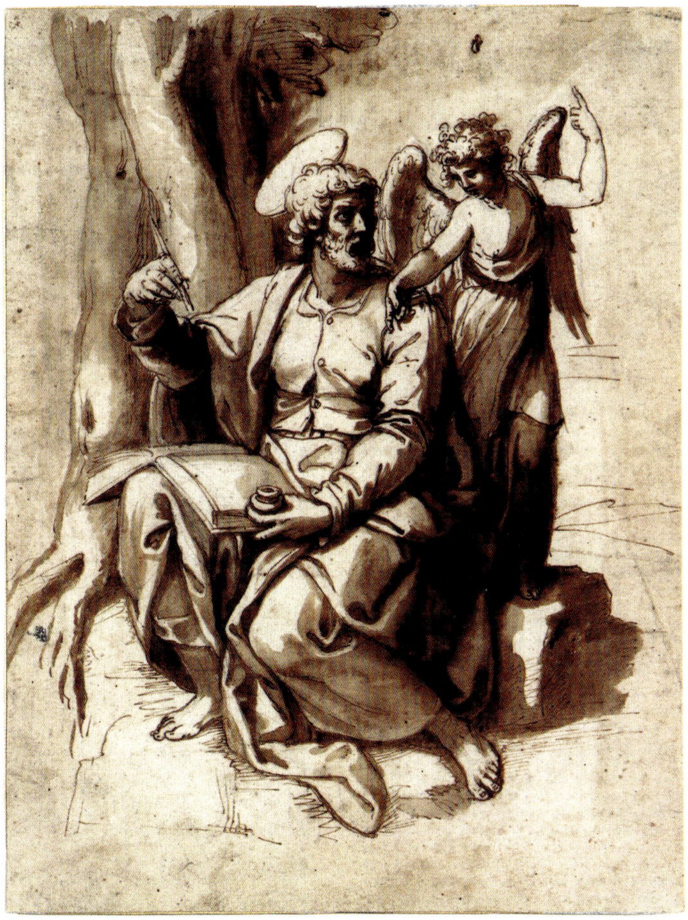

22
Alonso Cano
Saint Matthew and the Angel, *c.*1625–35
Pen and brown ink and wash over black chalk, 275 x 206 mm
The Apelles Collection, London

Alonso Cano: from Granada to Madrid

Alonso Cano (1601–67) stands out among artists in seventeenth-century Spain for his versatility as a draughtsman, painter, sculptor and architect, qualities long admired by his biographers.[67] Born in Granada, he moved with his family to Seville in 1614; about two years later he entered the workshop of Francisco Pacheco to learn drawing. Here he met Velázquez and the two became lifelong friends.[68] Cano was also apprenticed for a short time to the sculptor Juan Martínez Montañes in Seville.[69] He remained in Seville until 1638, when he was called to Madrid to work as a painter and attendant to the privy chamber for the Count-Duke of Olivares. Cano's drawings survive in considerable numbers, revealing a range of subjects far broader than most of his contemporaries. Drawing was fundamental to all aspects of his work, an attitude no doubt impressed on him by Pacheco. Few drawings from his years in Seville are known, but *Saint Matthew and the Angel* (fig. 22) of about 1625–35 clearly shows Pacheco's influence.[70] Compared with Pacheco's 1622 treatment of the subject (fig. 11), Cano's composition is much more dynamic and integrated, his penwork more liberated as he elegantly differentiates between solid and suggested forms.

Cano's time in Madrid was not an unqualified success. When Olivares fell from power in early 1643, Cano also lost his position. The following year his wife was brutally murdered; although Cano was a suspect, charges were never brought against him. He then moved to Valencia but returned to Madrid by late 1645; he moved to Granada in 1651 when he was appointed prebendary to the cathedral, only returning to Madrid for a short period in 1657–60.

The Madrid drawings form an important group that show Cano's maturing style and the influence of other artists working around him. In *Saint Ildephonsus Adoring the Virgin and Christ Child and the Miraculous Chasuble Carried by Three Putti* (fig. 23) of about 1645–52 the figures are carefully drawn in pen and ink and then filled with wash, reflecting his early training.[71] The drawing has scale gradations running along the bottom and it is squared in black chalk, indicating that it was a study for a painting that was either not carried out or has not survived. Occasionally Cano executed drawings in mixed media, such as the study of *Christ in Limbo* (fig. 24) of about 1652, in pen and black ink with brown wash and reddish-white highlights.[72] The composition derives from a print by Giulio Bonasone and shows Cano interpreting a print source through a drawing that he further modified in the final painting.[73]

It is as an architectural draughtsman that Cano excelled, and some of his most striking sheets are for projects that were not realized or have been destroyed.[74] He blended precise architectural drawing, sometimes incised to

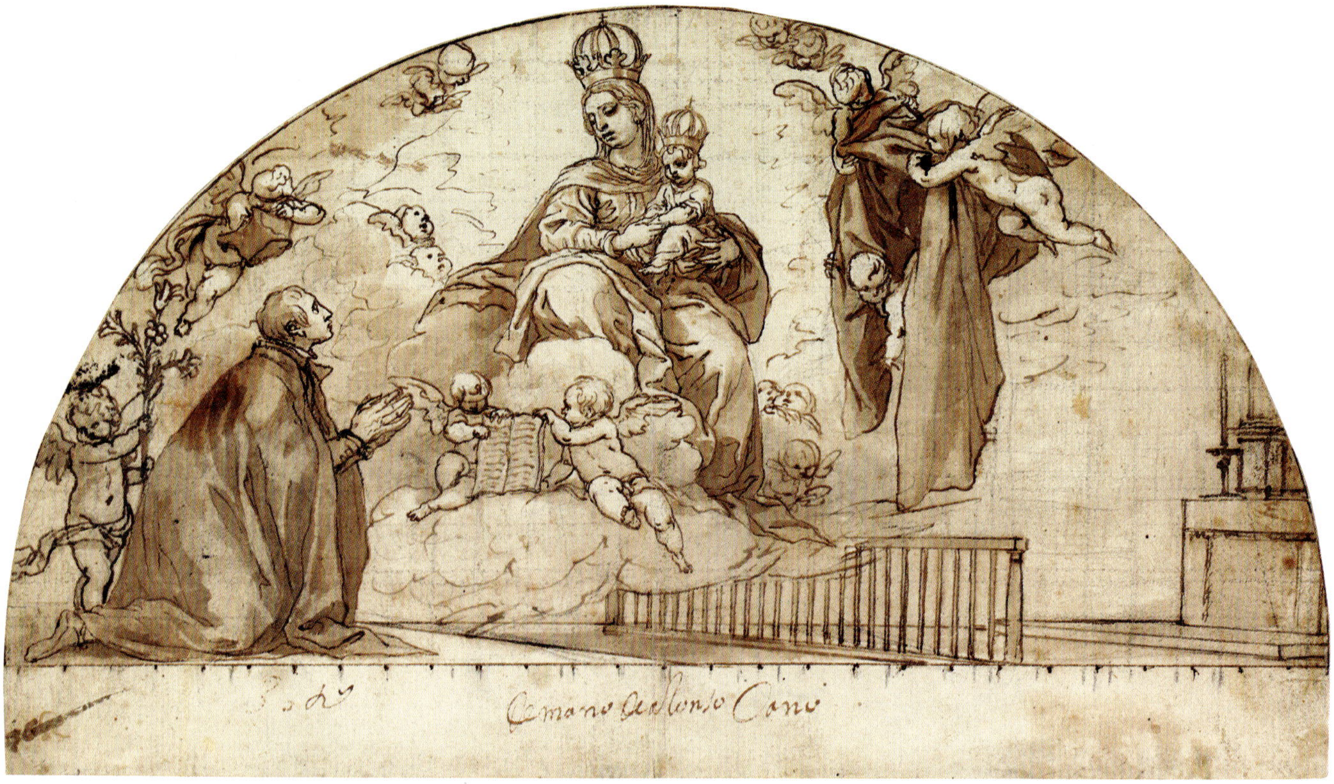

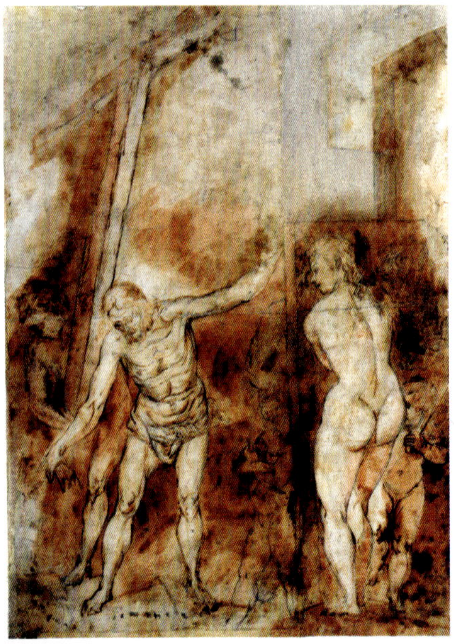

23
Alonso Cano
Saint Ildephonsus Adoring the Virgin and Christ Child and the Miraculous Chasuble Carried by Three Putti, c.1645–52
Pen and brown ink and brown wash over black chalk, squared for transfer, 183 x 311 mm
British Museum, London
1895,0915.877

24
Alonso Cano
Christ in Limbo, c.1652
Black chalk, brown and red wash, 272 x 192 mm
Museo de la Real Academia de Bellas Artes de San Fernando
D/2114

guide the design, with indications of the painted and sculpted decoration. His design of the altarpiece for the now destroyed chapel of San Diego de Alcalá in the convent of Santa María de Jesús at Alcalá de Henares (1657–8) was one of the most important commissions of his career.[75] Made from seventeen joined pieces measuring 1176 x 629 mm, the drawing (fig. 25) shows the projecting architectural elements and the full decorative programme. The delicate application of blue wash helps define forms and give compositional depth. Cano's technique of joining sheets to map the composition echoes Pacheco's *Last Judgement* discussed earlier (fig. 10). Cano's smaller *Design for an Altarpiece* (fig. 26), made around 1660–5, possibly for a client in Malaga, demonstrates his ability to integrate a multi-figure composition with sculpture and an architectural frame.[76] Alternative designs for pilasters, acanthus and fluted, are provided on either side of the sheet for the patron to choose his preference.

The ink-and-wash *Assumption of the Virgin* (fig. 27) of about 1661–2 is one of Cano's finest drawings, made after he had moved to Granada.[77] The drawing is a record of his painting in Granada Cathedral (fig. 28) rather than a

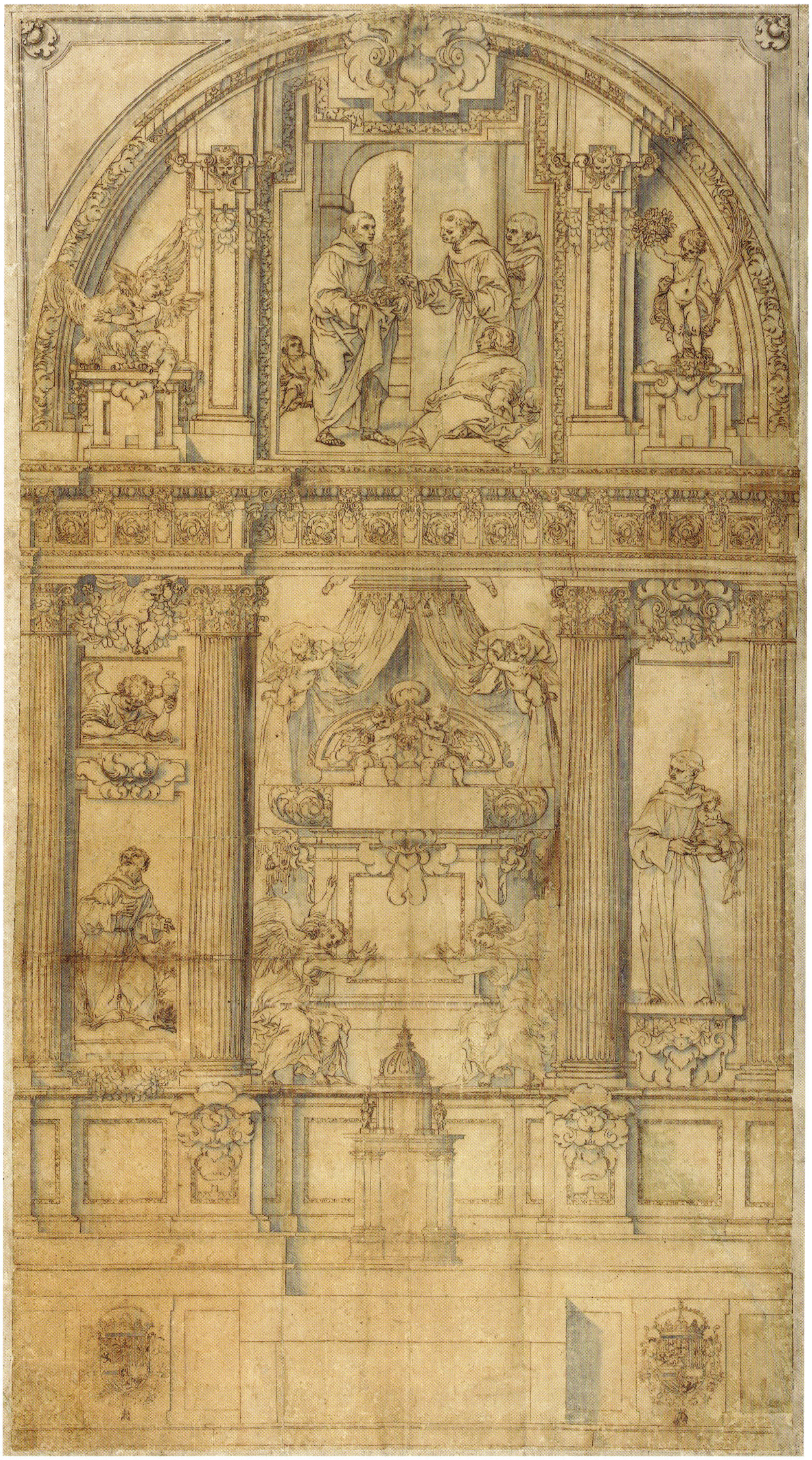

25
Alonso Cano

Design for the Chapel of San Diego de Alcalá in the Convent of Santa María de Jesús at Alcalá de Henares, 1657–8

Pen and brown ink, with brown and blue wash, selectively incised, 1176 x 629 mm
The Pierpont Morgan Library, New York
1986.46

26
Alonso Cano
Design for an Altarpiece, c.1660–5
Pen and brown ink, brown wash over black chalk, 309 x 232 mm
British Museum, London
1950,0211.16

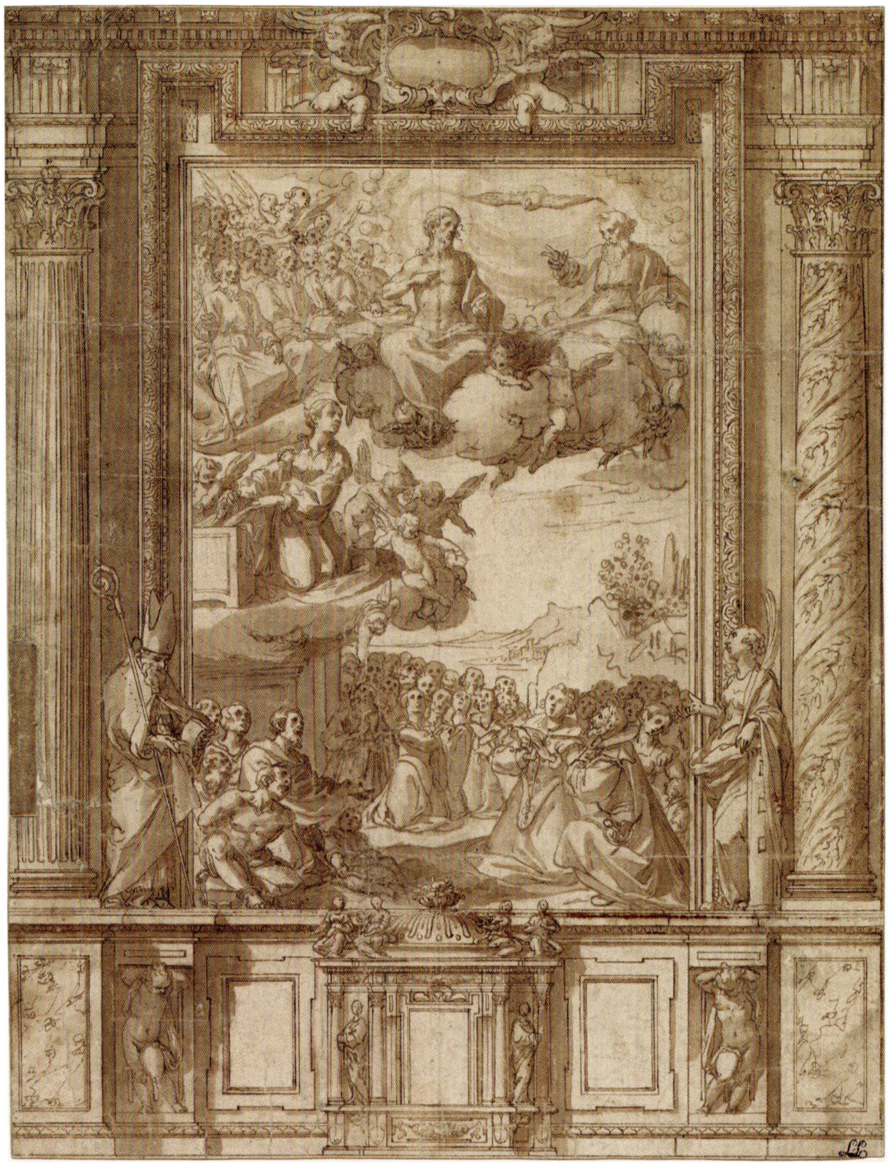

preparatory sketch: there are no marks on the sheet to indicate transfer, and in order to maximize its legibility the arch is shown without the projecting side entablature. Copies of this drawing exist, providing evidence of its value as a model. Also made in Granada, a group of designs made in the early 1660s for paintings of the life of Saint Dominic in Santa Cruz la Real are among Cano's most technically ambitious drawings, and were once owned by Palomino. Their compositions are structured on a geometrical framework of lines incised with a stylus and rule, reflecting the lifelong interest in perspective that is evident in so many of his drawings.[78]

The variety and number of surviving drawings by Cano supports the observation of Ceán Bermúdez, an enthusiastic collector of his work, that he never executed anything in the three fine arts without first making a careful drawing.[79] He also had an interest in printmaking and is known to have assembled a considerable collection of prints and drawings by other artists.[80] He collaborated with the Madrid printmakers Diego and Pedro de Obregón, who

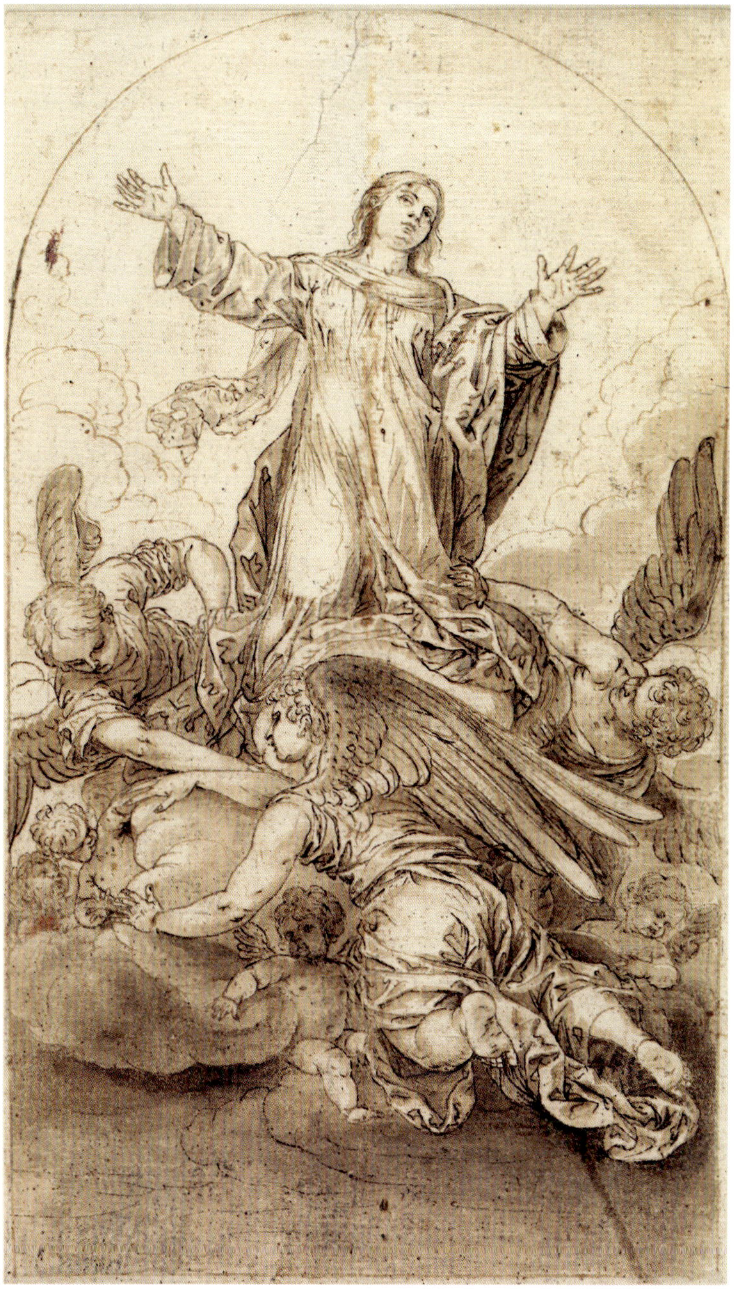

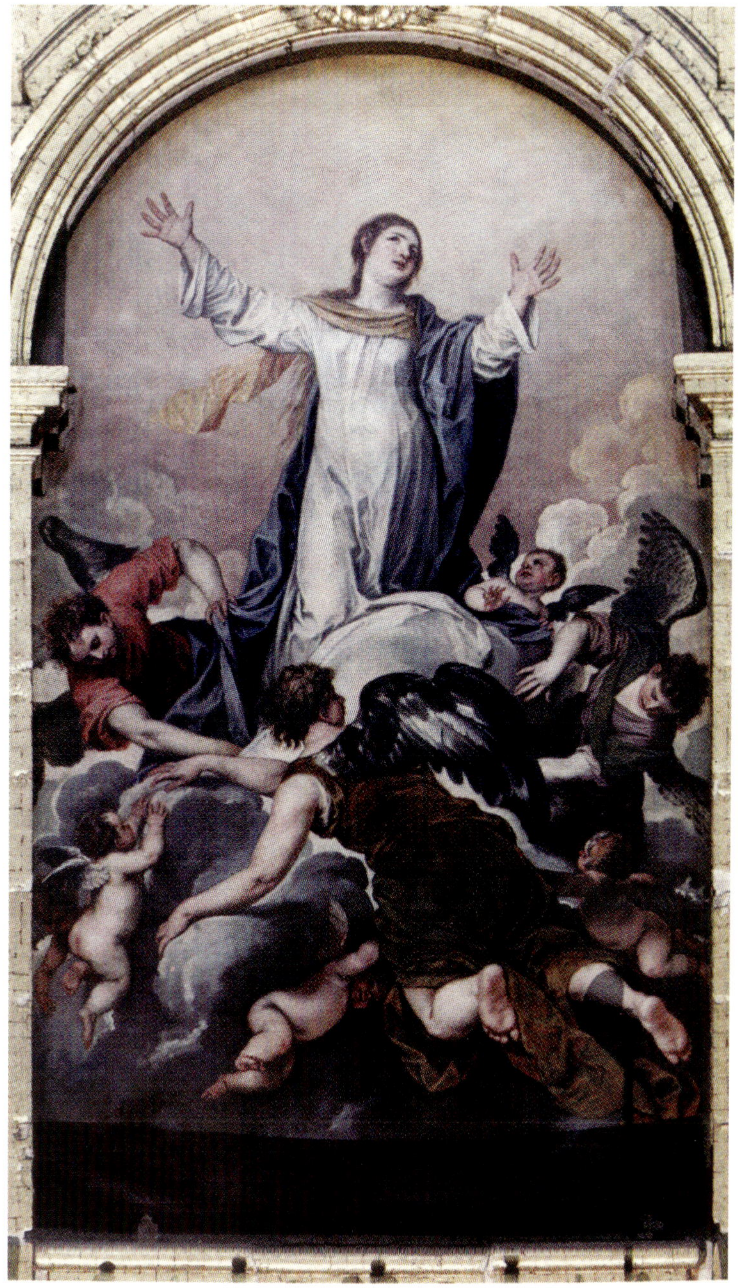

made several prints after his drawings.[81] An etching by Diego de Obregón of *Saint Catherine of Alexandria*, which survives in a unique impression (fig. 29), reproduces a drawing Cano prepared for a painting in the church of San Miguel, Madrid, which was destroyed in 1790.[82] The drawing includes the architectural surround, whereas the print only shows the central image.

Cano's powerful artistic personality had a tremendous influence on artists in Madrid and Granada. As a result it is difficult to differentiate between his work and that of his collaborators and followers, including Sebastían de Herrera Barnuevo (see Chapter 4). The drawing of *The Virgin and Child appearing to Saint Francis of Assisi and Saint Teresa of Avila* (fig. 30) attributed to Pedro Atanasio Bocanegra (1638–89), for example, shows a close connection with Cano's style.[83] Drawings by minor artists working in Granada indicate

27
Alonso Cano
The Assumption of the Virgin, 1661–2
Pen and brown ink and brown wash over black chalk, 234 x 130 mm
British Museum, London
1910,0212.43

28
Alonso Cano
The Assumption of the Virgin, 1661–2
Oil on canvas, 4510 x 2520 mm
Granada Cathedral

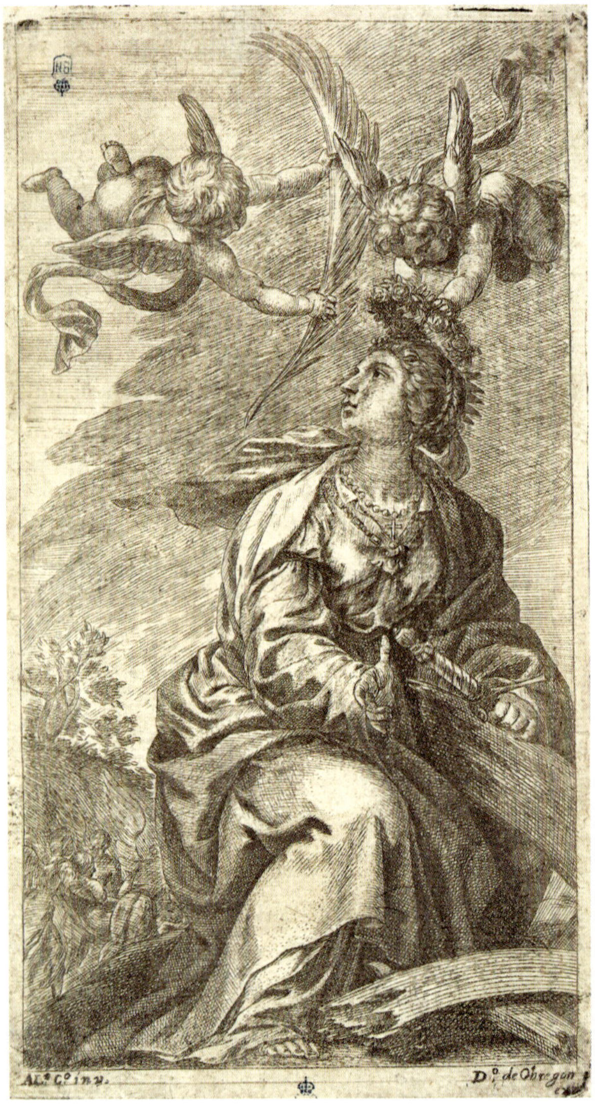

29
Diego de Obregón
Saint Catherine of Alexandria, c.1658–68
Etching, 206 x 111 mm
Biblioteca Nacional, Madrid
41251

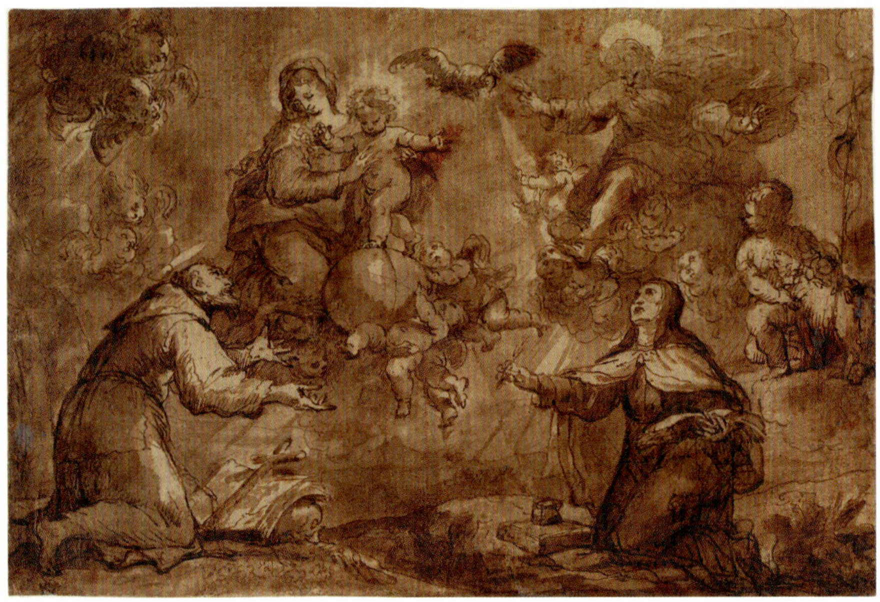

30
Pedro Atanasio Bocanegra
The Virgin and Child Appearing to Saint Francis of Assisi and Saint Teresa of Avila, c.1660–8
Pen and brown ink and brown wash over black chalk, 195 x 286 mm
British Museum, London
1846,0509.183

more widespread activity. Pedro de Moya (*c.*1610–74), who is reported to have worked in Van Dyck's workshop and subsequently in Granada and Seville, is known only through a couple of sheets, none of which is signed.[84] *The Visitation of the Virgin to Saint Elizabeth*, for example, entered the British Museum under his name, where it remains.[85] Two drawings by the sculptor Pedro de Mena (1628–88), made around 1673–4 for the polychrome cedar-wood statues of Queen Isabel (fig. 31) and King Ferdinand in the main chapel transept arch of Granada Cathedral, are the only seventeenth-century contract drawings from Spain to have survived.[86] The contract specifies that Pedro de Mena execute the statues using the drawings previously sent to Granada, which had been adjusted and signed by himself and the cathedral authorities in order to avoid confusion between the two sets of designs submitted.[87] There were evidently four alternative designs (two for each sculpture), which were sufficiently similar to warrant confusion. The fact that there are considerable differences between the present drawings, the contract and the finished sculpture indicates that they are the pair that were rejected, hence their survival.

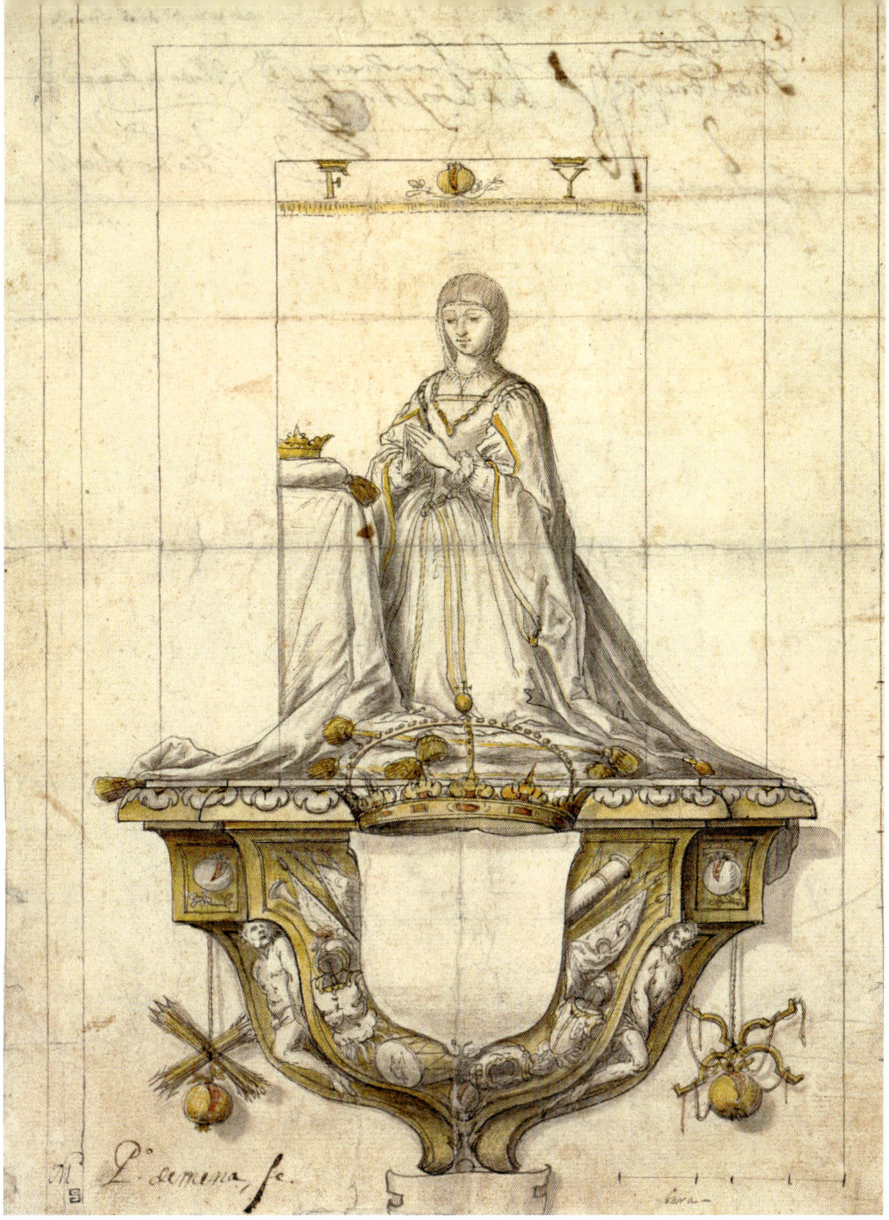

31
Pedro de Mena y Medrano
Study for a Statue of Queen Isabel, c.1673–4
Black chalk, pen and brown-grey ink, yellow, grey, and red wash, 344 x 234 mm
The J. Paul Getty Museum, Los Angeles
94.GA.82

Córdoba

Antonio del Castillo y Saavedra (1616–88) spent his entire career in Córdoba and was the most prolific draughtsman in Spain during the seventeenth century. Around two hundred drawings by his hand survive, mostly in pen and ink but some in red chalk and occasionally wash.[88] His drawings have long been appreciated: both Palomino and Ceán Bermúdez owned examples and praised his abilities as a draughtsman.[89] Many of Castillo's drawings are details of his paintings, effectively forming a library of images, which explains their large numbers. The majority are small, but some were executed on larger sheets and show variations on the same subject. The *Study of Seven Heads* (fig. 32) is one of a number of sheets inspired by pattern prints, in particular those of Frederick and Abraham Bloemaert. Castillo here follows the same arrangement as plate 15 of Frederick's *Tekenboek* (fig. 33);[90] his drawing may have been intended to form a compilation to be engraved.[91]

A number of lesser-known artists working in Córdoba during the seventeenth century were also active draughtsman. The drawings of Castillo's student Juan Alfaro y Gámez (1643–80), who apparently worked in Velázquez's

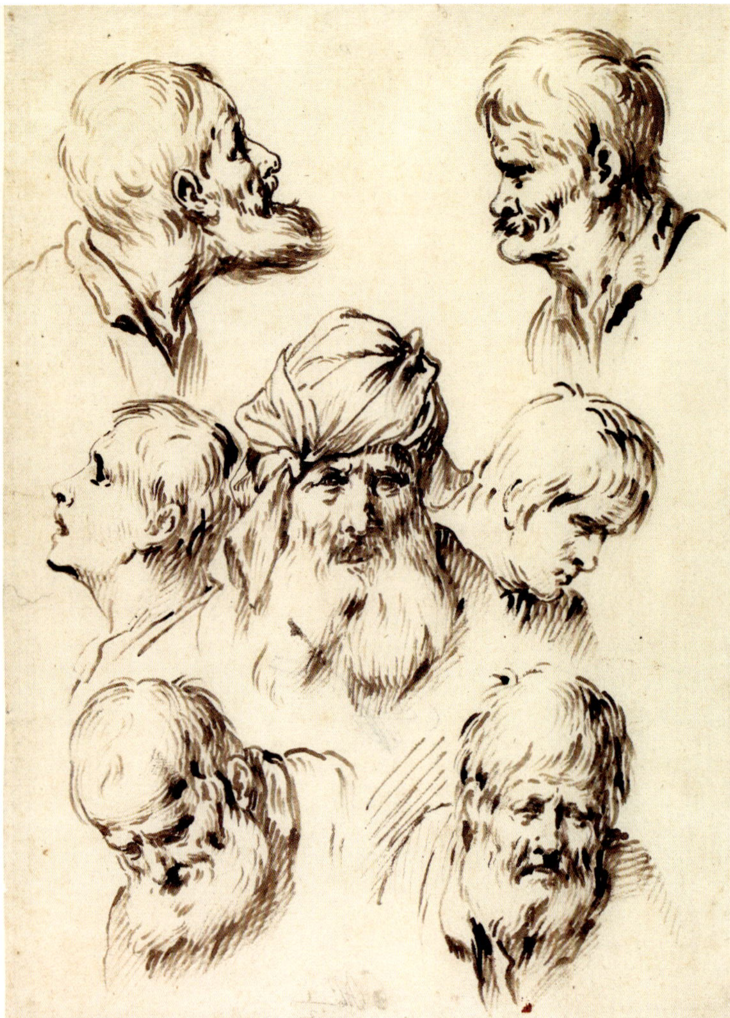

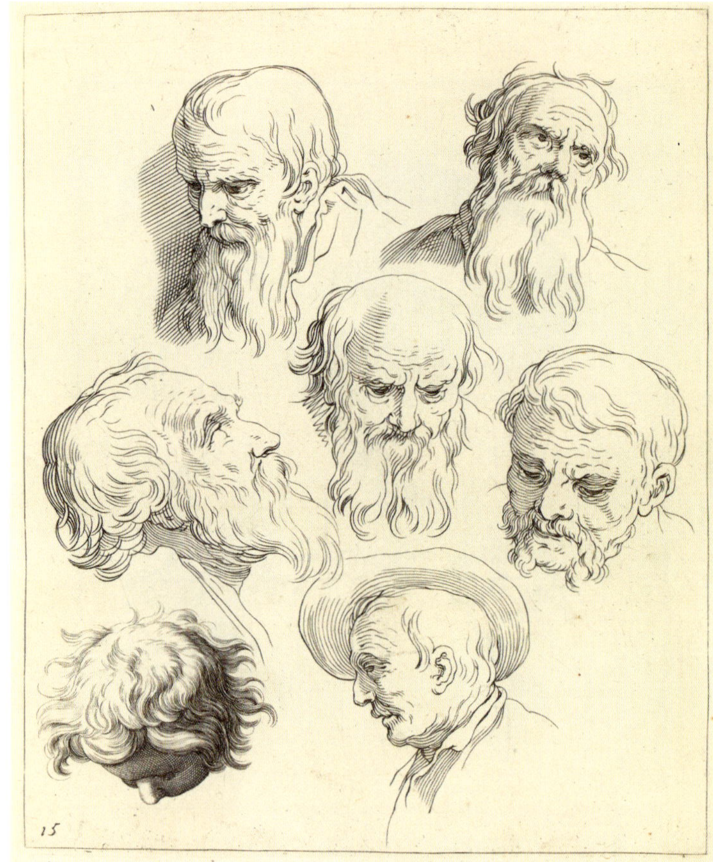

32
Antonio del Castillo y Saavedra
Study of Seven Heads, c.1650–68
Brush and brown ink over black chalk, 286 x 204 mm
British Museum, London
1946,0713.1308

33
Frederick Bloemaert after Abraham Blomaert
Study of Seven Heads from *'Het Tekenboek'*, 1650–6
Engraving, 212 x 171 mm
British Museum, London
L,83.16

studio, have been described as being midway between the schools of Córdoba and Madrid.[92] Antonio García Reinoso (1623–77) helpfully signed and dated a number of his sheets. Born and trained in Granada, García Reinoso later worked in Jaén, Malaga and, towards the end of his life, in Córdoba. Palomino describes his 'great facility of invention' and that he made several studies for the same composition, referring to an abundance of drawings in pen, wash, charcoal and pencil.[93] Although not as prolific as Cano or Castillo, García Reinoso was an able draughtsman, as demonstrated by one of his largest sheets, a spirited drawing in red wash and red and black chalk of figures (fig. 34), signed and dated 1647.[94] An album containing ten drawings of angels holding the instruments of the passion in the Biblioteca Nacional, Madrid, once thought to be by Castillo, are executed with García's characteristic lightness of touch and expressive use of wash.[95] Several other drawings show architectural projects, with alternative details for the patron to choose, a frequent practice at this period.[96]

Andalusia: the second half of the seventeenth century

The bubonic plague of 1649 is estimated to have halved Seville's population and the city began to lose much of its power as a trading centre. The

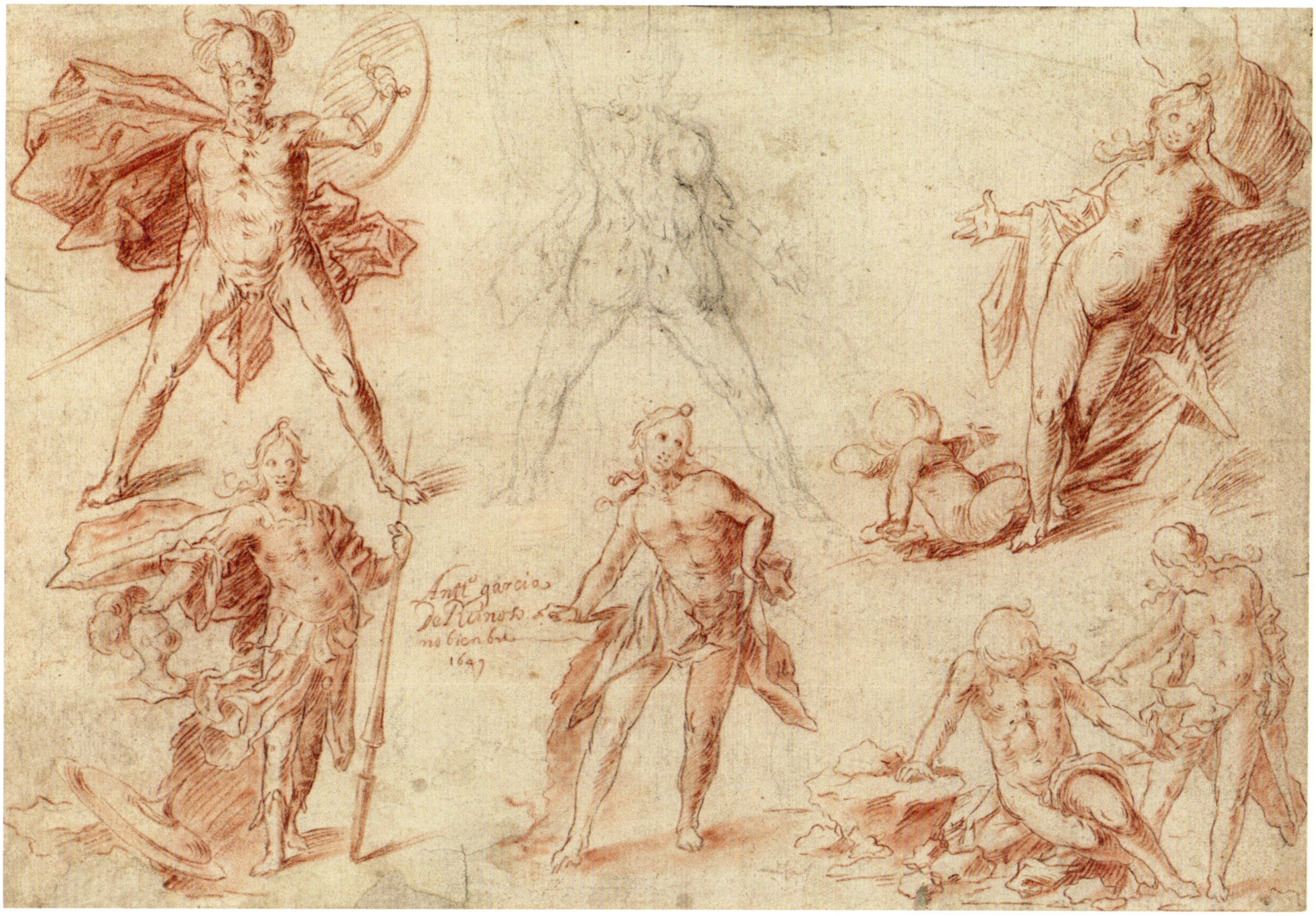

economic constriction had a devastating effect on artists working in the city: Francisco de Zurbarán, for example, ran a thriving workshop until 1640, after which productivity dwindled.[97] But as so often is the case, out of a crisis arises opportunity, and in the second half of the century new artists emerged and markets receptive to their work developed.

Zurbarán's greatest competitor during the 1650s was Bartolomé Esteban Murillo (1617–82), who became the dominant and most successful artist in Seville. The styles of the two artists are diametrically opposed: where Zurbarán's work is characterized by his clear compositions and monumental figures with dramatic lighting, Murillo represents an altogether softer palette and more integrated compositions. An equally clear division can be observed in their drawings. The uncertainty surrounding Zurbarán's drawings contrasts with those of Murillo, who was one of the most prolific draughtsmen working in Spain during the seventeenth century.[98]

Murillo is thought to have served his apprenticeship with the painter Juan del Castillo (*c.*1590–*c.*1657), to whom few drawings have been attributed, and there is nothing to suggest that he had a lasting influence on his pupil.[99] More significantly, Francisco Pacheco, Francisco de Herrera the Elder and Alonso Cano were all active in Seville when Murillo was serving

34
Antonio García Reinoso
Sheet of Figure Studies, 1647
Red and black chalk,
214 x 303 mm
The Courtauld Institute of Art, London
D.1952.RW.4204

35
Bartolomé Esteban Murillo
Saint Anthony of Padua and the Miracle of the Irascible Son, 1645–6
Pen and brown ink and brown wash over black chalk, 345 x 265 mm
British Museum, London
1920,1116.20

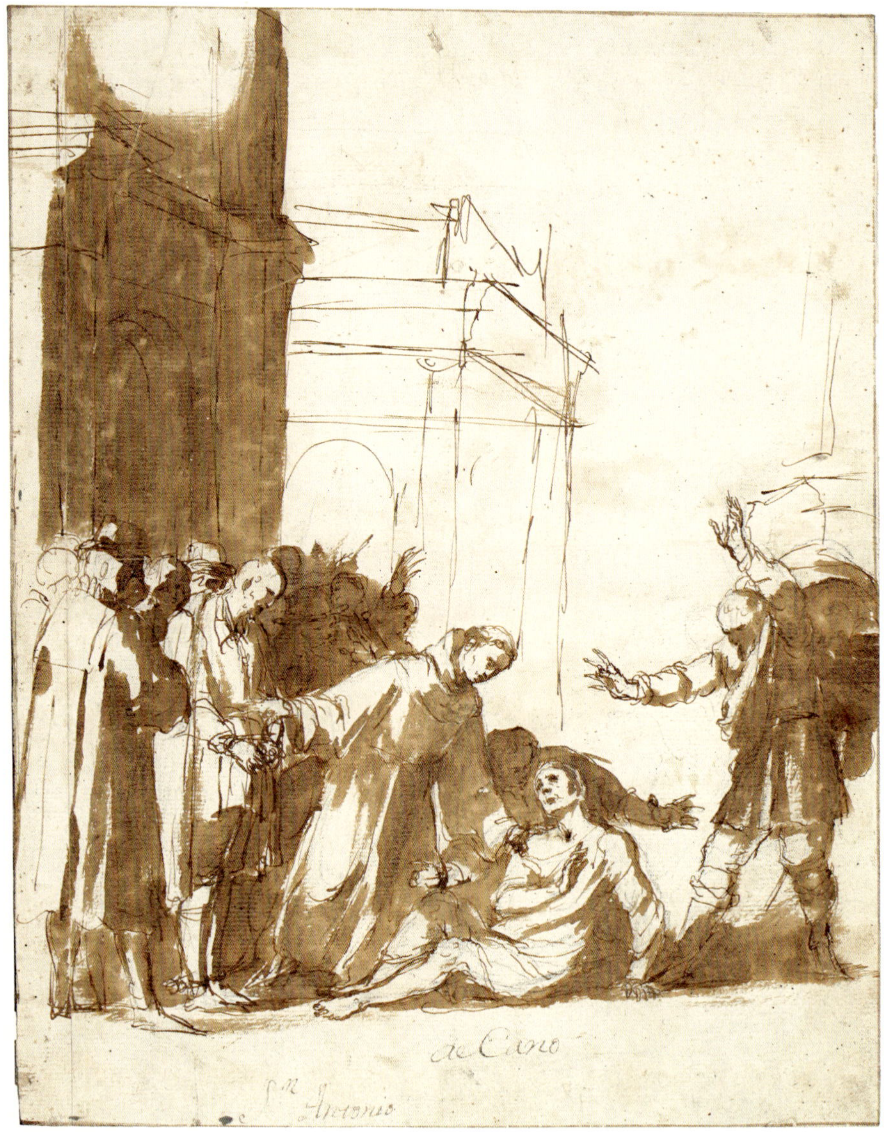

his apprenticeship, and elements of their work can be detected in his drawing. A sheet that is key to understanding his early style, *Saint Anthony of Padua and the Miracle of the Irascible Son* of 1645–6 (fig. 35), was once attributed to Cano on the basis of the inscription: the use of pen to outline the figures and then wash to fill their form was a technique favoured by Cano (fig. 23), who inherited it in turn from Pacheco (fig. 9). The drawing is related to a commission Murillo received for paintings depicting miracles or episodes from the lives of the Franciscans for the Claustro Chico (Small Cloister) of the convent of San Francisco el Grande in Seville.[100]

The Archangel Michael (fig. 36 and detail p. 122), from the mid-1650s, is one of Murillo's most accomplished sheets.[101] The energetic, rapid penstrokes that define the wings and garments impart a sense of great movement to the figure, while the delicate shading of the face draws attention to his intense gaze. No surviving painting by Murillo corresponds to this drawing, but a painting in a private collection in La Paz (Bolivia), thought to date from the end of the seventeenth century and stylistically close to Juan Simón Gutiérrez (*c.*1645–1724), seems to be a copy of the lost canvas by Murillo for which the drawing was a preparatory study.[102]

Early in 1660 Murillo and Francisco Herrera the Younger established an academy of drawing in Seville.[103] Its organization and matters relating to its operation are recorded in the various minutes.[104] Nightly meetings were held in the merchants' exchange, the Casa de la Lonja, where students undertook life drawing. A student could only attain the status of academician once his drawing was judged to be of sufficiently high standard. In 1674 financial problems resulted in the closure of the academy. Yet in fourteen years many students had passed through its doors, guaranteeing the continued role of drawing as the basis of artistic practice. The academy spawned similar operations in Seville. Domingo Martínez (1688–1749), a follower of Murillo, ran a school from his home, using the prints and drawings in his own substantial library as teaching aids.[105] Ceán Bermúdez records that when Martínez died,

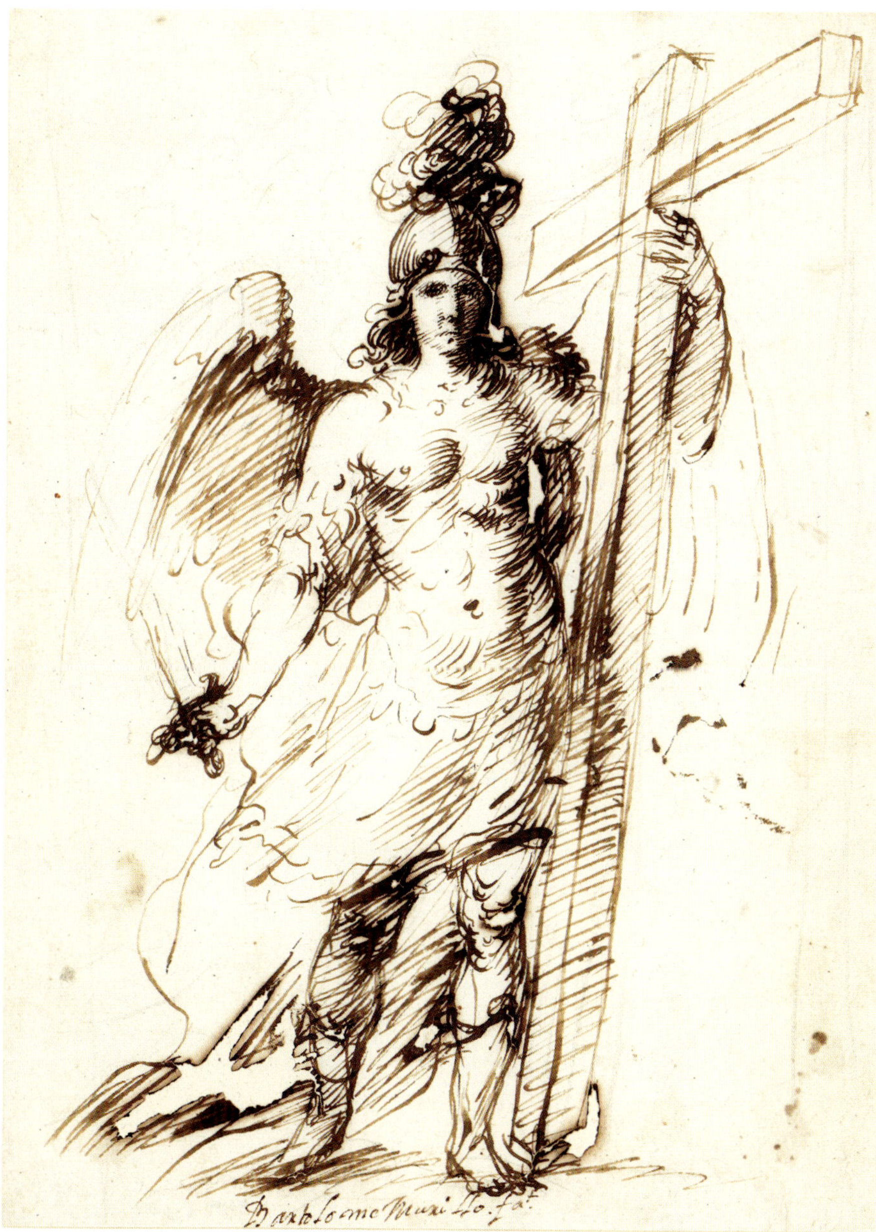

36
Bartolomé Esteban Murillo
The Archangel Michael, c.1655–60
Pen and brown ink over black chalk, 268 x 189 mm
British Museum, London
1873,0614.216

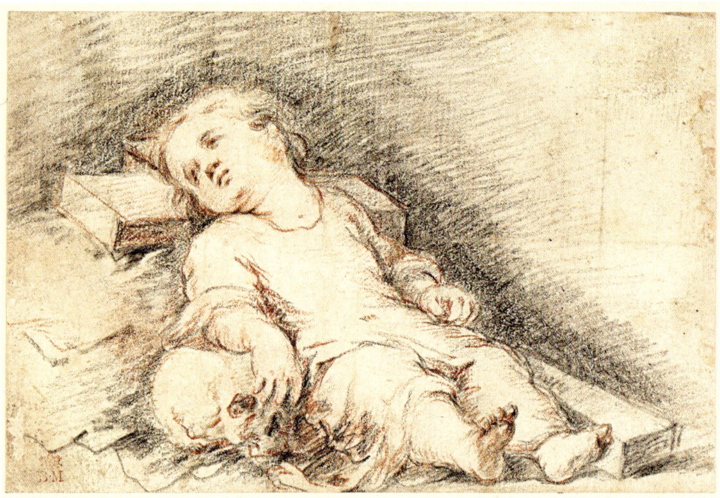

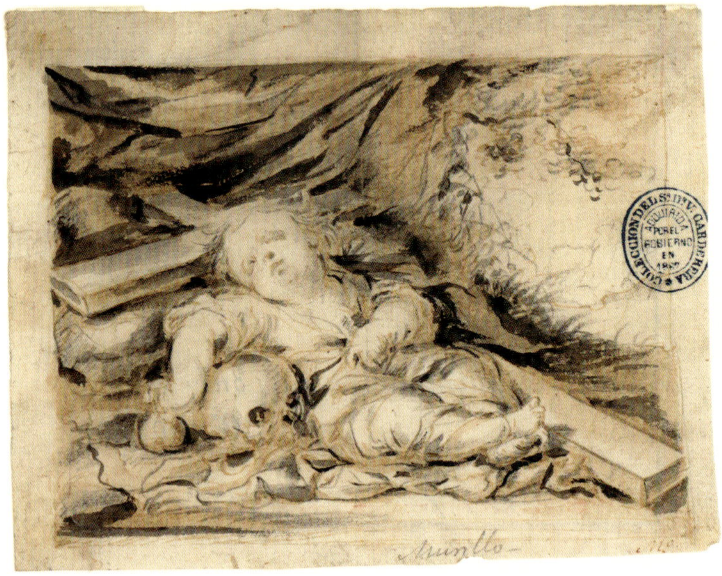

37
Bartolomé Esteban Murillo
The Christ Child Sleeping on the Cross, c.1665–80
Black and red chalk, 94 x 138 mm
British Museum, London
1858,0724.1

38
After Bartolomé Esteban Murillo
The Christ Child Sleeping on the Cross, c.1665–80
Brush with brown and black ink over black chalk, 110 x 139 mm
Biblioteca Nacional, Madrid
DIB/16/40/8

his son-in-law, the painter Juan de Espinel, inherited his 'copious study of drawings, models and prints'. The inventory of Martínez's goods reveals the breadth of his collections: among them were a number of pattern print compilations and books of prints, including engravings after Rubens, the lives of the saints and prints of Roman statuary.[106]

The large number of Murillo's surviving sheets, copies after his works and those imitating his style, and the many studies by students at the Seville drawing academy, where practice sheets were kept because they provided a valuable resource, reveal the impact of the academy on drawing in Seville. A brush-and-ink copy of Murillo's chalk drawing of *The Christ Child Sleeping on the Cross* is the same size as the original (figs 37–8) and even carries an abbreviated form of his name, 'M^{o}', with his full name in pencil in another hand. The drawing shows how closely students copied the master's work, either to improve their own skills, or to make a record of Murillo's compositions.[107] A disbanded album, originally of around 315 drawings now dispersed in collections across the United States, is largely a compilation from one of the Seville academies, although it is not known which one.[108] The sheets include copies of works after Murillo, Alonso Cano and Valdés Leal, demonstrating that drawing was taught not only though copying individual anatomical features from sources such as pattern prints, but also using entire compositions as models.[109]

Murillo drew in different media – occasionally on both sides of the sheet – to study the same or closely related compositions. *Saint Isidore of Seville* (fig. 39) is one of two drawings he prepared for his painting (fig. 40), donated with its companion, *Saint Leander*, to Seville Cathedral in 1655 by the Archdeacon of Carmona, Juan de Federigui.[110] The second drawing (fig. 41), now in Paris, was executed in pen, ink and wash in a style similar to others he made around the same time, such as *The Archangel Michael* (fig. 36) or the *Studies for Saint John the Baptist* (fig. 42).[111] The differences between the two drawings of Isidore have resulted in conflicting opinions as to their precedence and possible function. Angulo suggested that they were for different paintings,[112] yet the British Museum drawing seems to be a development on the Paris sheet, reflecting changes that may have been requested by the patron – or possibly Murillo's own revisions. Here there is more emphasis on Isidore as a scholar as he concentrates on the open book, while his office as archbishop is indicated by his crozier and mitre. The painting retains some elements of the Paris sheet, including the column base and plinth and the books on the table in the background.

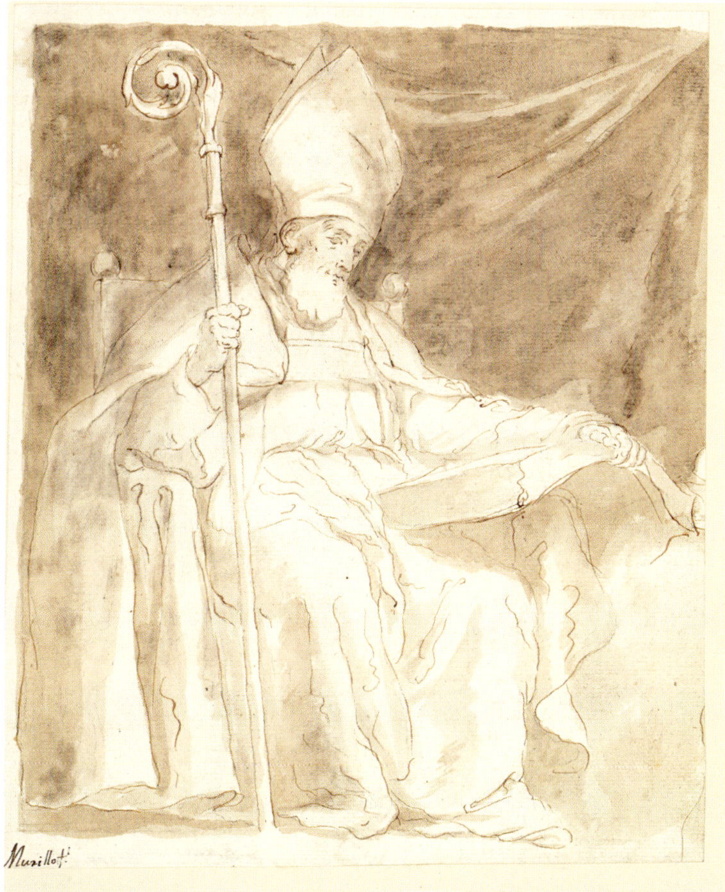

39
Bartolomé Esteban Murillo
Saint Isidore of Seville, 1655
Pen and brown ink, brown and grey wash over black chalk, 260 x 208 mm
British Museum, London
1873,0614.214

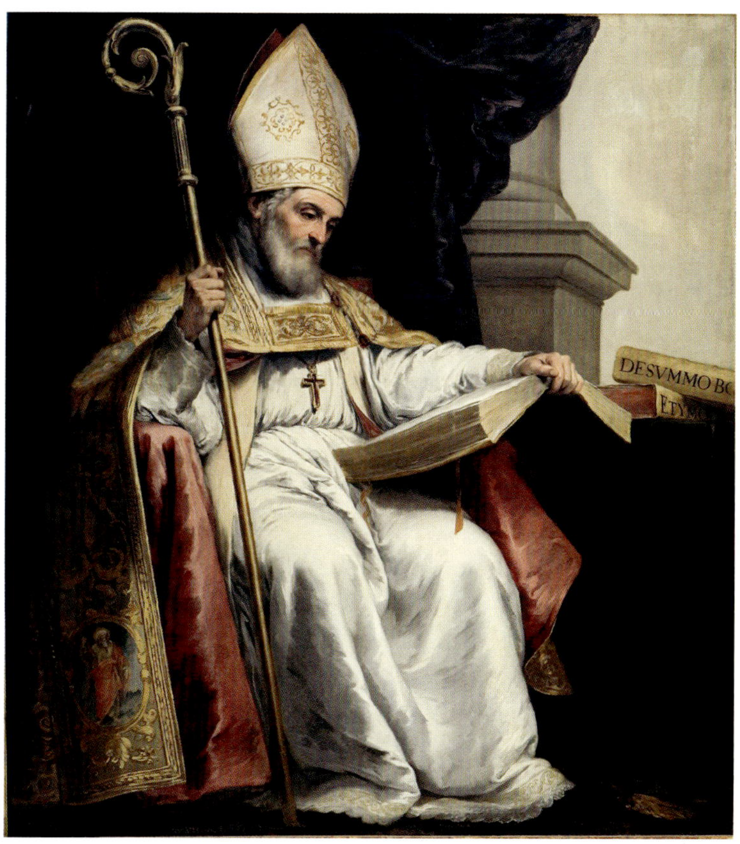

40
Bartolomé Esteban Murillo
Saint Isidore of Seville, 1655
Oil on canvas, 1930 x 1650 mm
Seville Cathedral

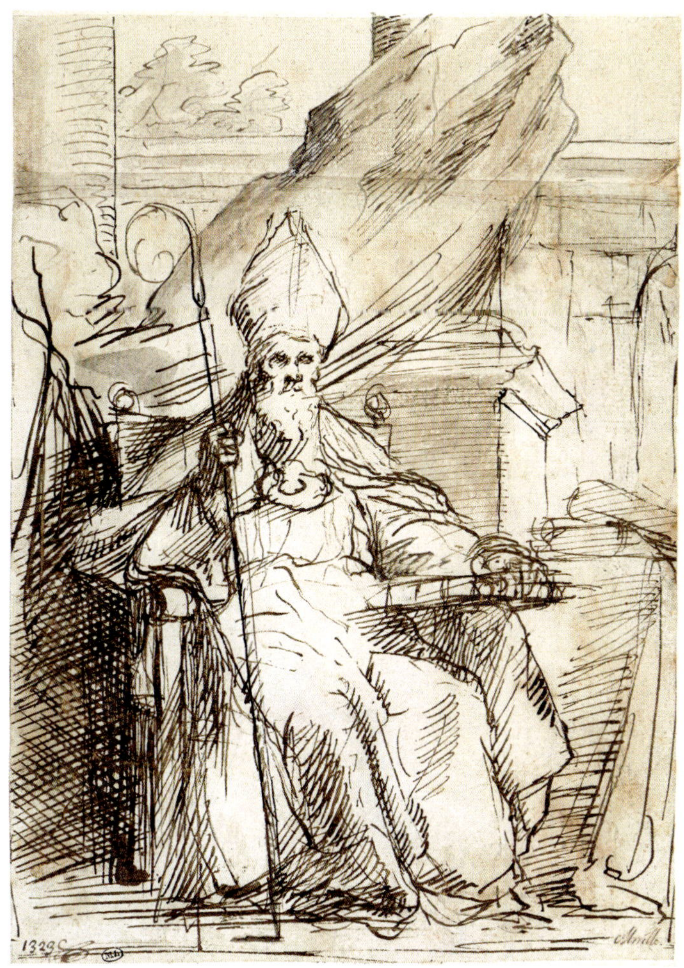

41
Bartolomé Esteban Murillo
Saint Isidore of Seville, 1655
Pen and brown ink with brown wash, 238 x 167 mm
Musée du Louvre, Paris
18445

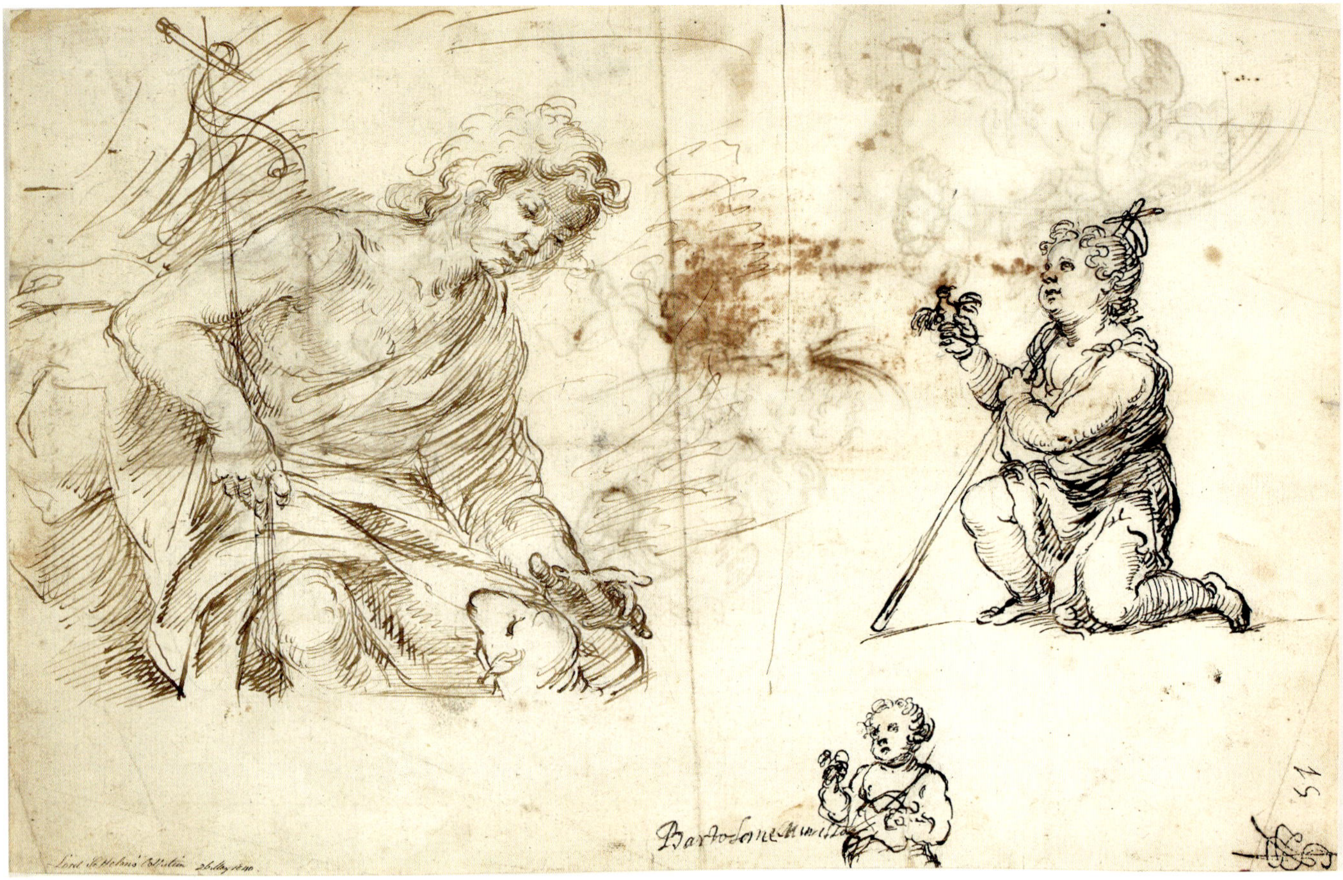

42
Bartolomé Esteban Murillo
Studies for Saint John the Baptist (verso), c.1650–5
Pen and brown ink over black chalk, 220 x 338 mm
British Museum, London
1873,0614.212

Not all Murillo's drawings were preparatory studies. The highly finished black and red chalk *Saint Francis of Paola* (fig. 43) was probably made not in preparation for the painting, thought to date from the last decade of his life, but as a record of its composition.[113] The figure type of a bearded elderly saint occurs in a number of Murillo's paintings. The drawing may have been a presentation piece to demonstrate his skill, in which case exploiting a character type associated with his work would have promoted his creativity. His *Penitent Saint Peter* (fig. 44), also from the 1670s but with quickly drawn lines and a concentration of ink defining the figure, has none of the finish of *Saint Francis*.[114] Both sheets show Murillo's sophisticated approach to drawing, his technique corresponding closely to its purpose.

One of Murillo's closest followers, Francisco Meneses Osorio (*c.*1640–1721), was (like most artists in Seville) a member of the drawing academy[115] and had a particular interest in graphic art. He is recorded buying prints and drawings in an auction of goods from the estate of the sculptor José de Arce in 1666.[116] After Murillo's death in 1682 Meneses used his master's drawings to complete the commission for the high altar of the church of the Capuchin convent in Cádiz.[117] A black chalk drawing, *Saint Joseph Kneeling before the Virgin and the Christ Child* (fig. 45), attributed to Meneses is one of a number of sheets inscribed with Murillo's name because of its clear relationship to his work.[118] Murillo's pervasive influence is evident in other drawings of this period, such as an Immaculate Conception (fig. 46) by an anonymous draughtsman of considerable ability.

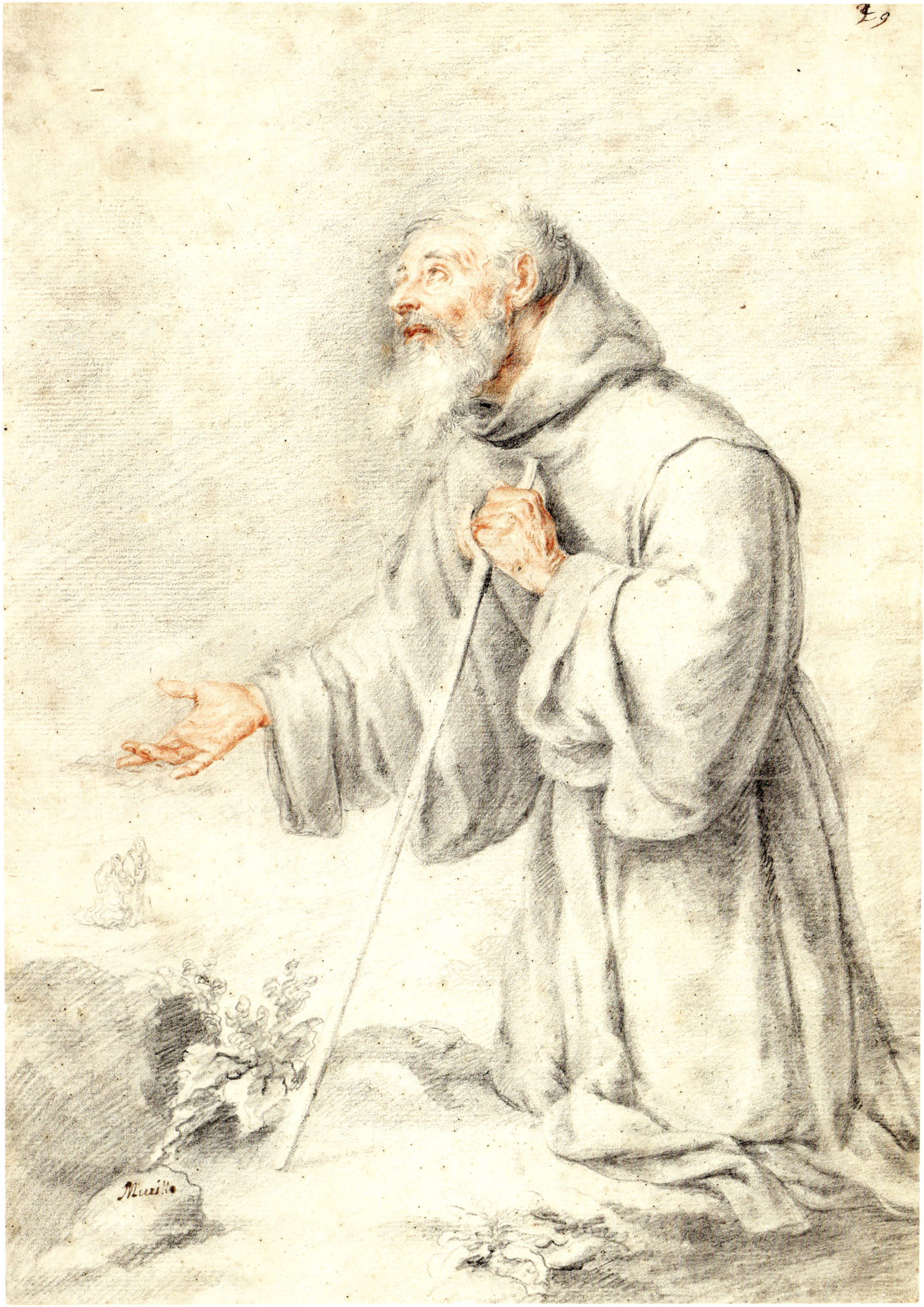

43
Bartolomé Esteban Murillo

Saint Francis of Paola, *c.*1665–75

Black and red chalk, 332 x 232 mm
British Museum, London
1850,0713.2

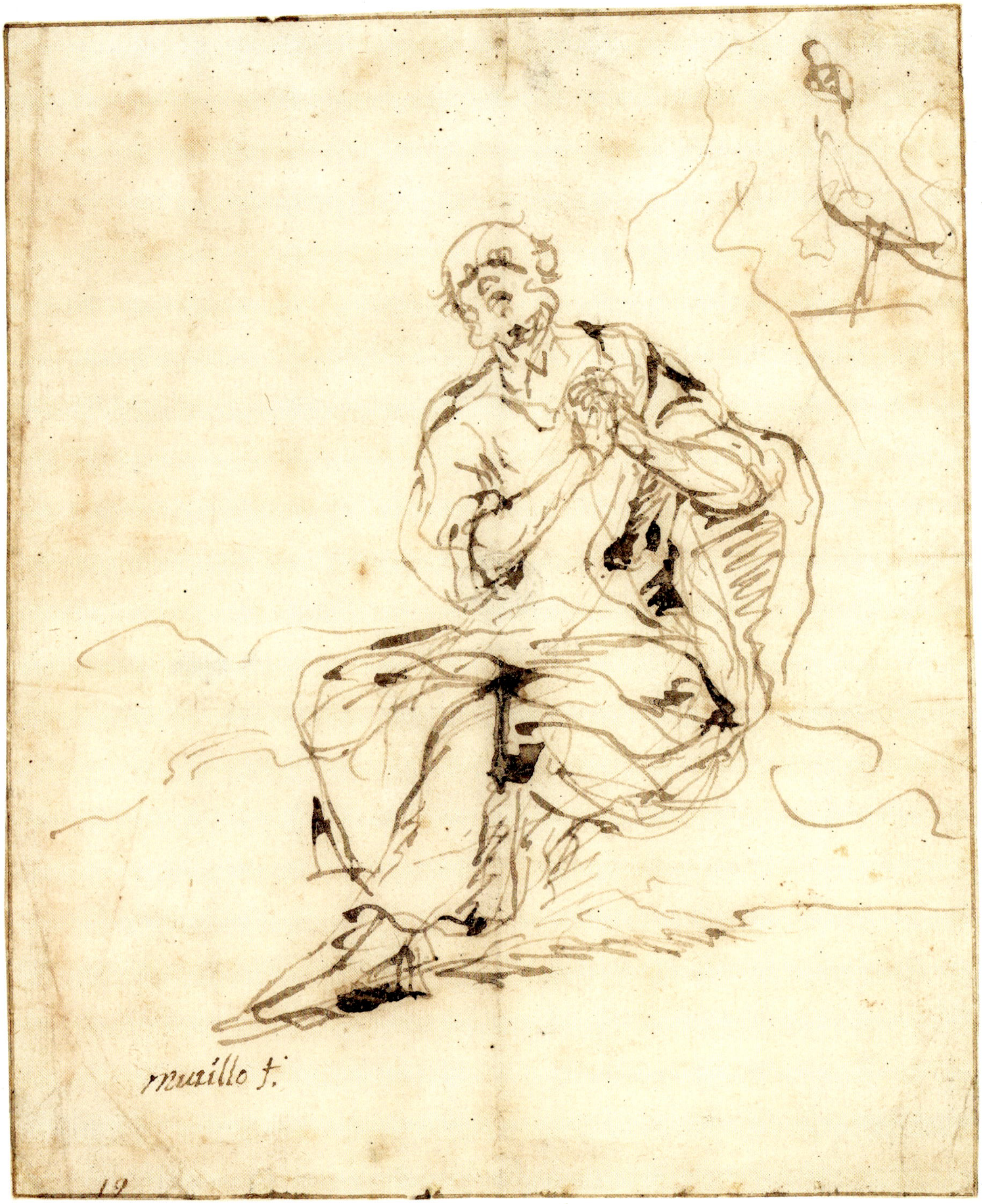

44
Bartolomé Esteban Murillo
The Penitent Saint Peter, c.1670–80
Pen and brown ink, 190 x 153 mm
British Museum, London
1946,0713.1155

Further evidence of a continued demand for paintings in the style of Murillo long after his death can be found in the work of Alonso Miguel de Tovar (1678–1752), who is known to have copied Murillo.[119] Tovar found considerable success in Seville and Madrid, and in 1725 was appointed by Philip V as painter to the Privy Chamber.[120] The Murillo-like cherubs in his paintings have distinctive small wings, their ends terminating at right angles (fig. 47).[121] These can be seen in his drawing of cherubs (fig. 48) cut from an Immaculate Conception, probably from the first decade of the eighteenth century.

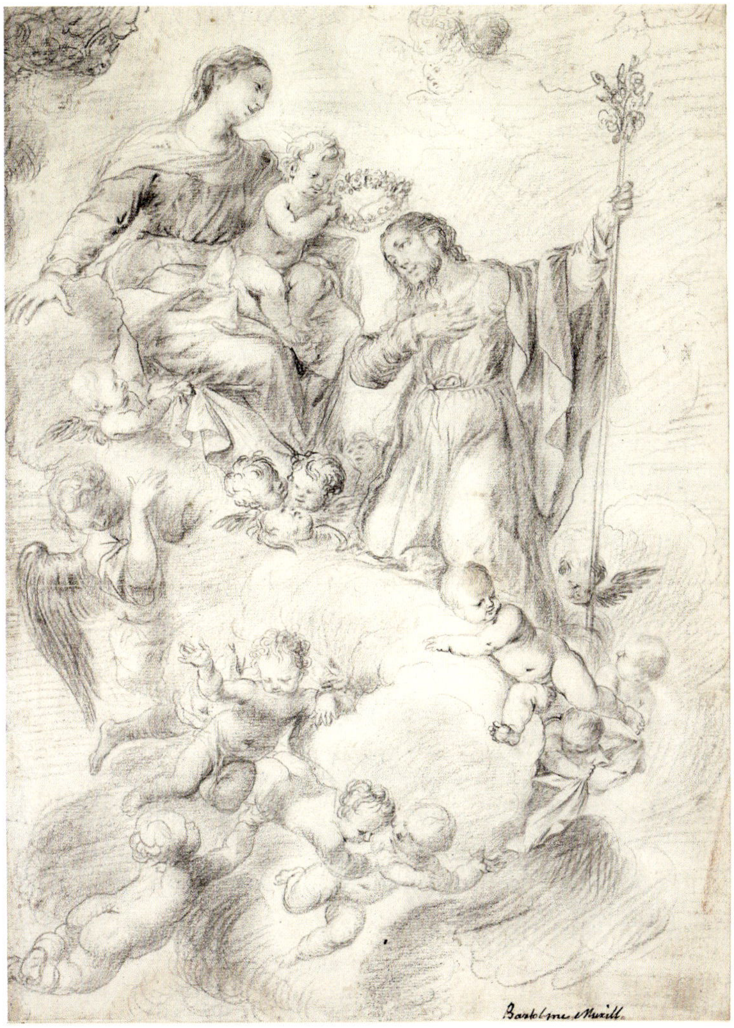

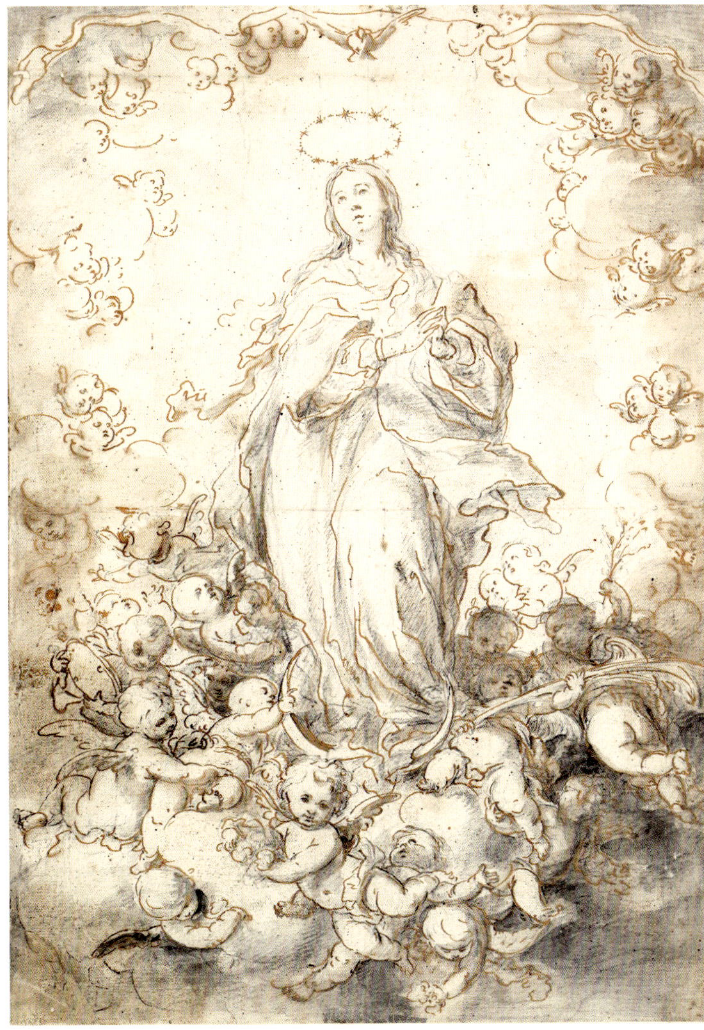

45
Attributed to Francisco Meneses Osorio
Saint Joseph Kneeling before the Virgin and the Christ Child, *c.*1665–1700
Black chalk, 403 x 282 mm
British Museum, London
1895,0915.884

46
Circle of Bartolomé Esteban Murillo
The Virgin of the Immaculate Conception, *c.*1665–85
Pen and brown ink, with black chalk and grey wash, 299 x 206 mm
British Museum, London
1910,0212.46

The Flemish-born Cornelio Schut (*c.*1629–85) was the nephew and disciple of the prolific printmaker with the same name (1597–1655) from Antwerp, who travelled to Spain where his brother Pedro worked as an engineer to Philip IV. Schut the Younger is known to have been in Seville by 1653, where he established his own workshop.[122] He was a founding member of the drawing academy, occupying the posts of treasurer, consul and president between 1670 and 1674.[123] Palomino writes that 'he was a great draughtsman, on account of which he usually presided over the Academy, giving everyone very good lessons, both by his words and by his works'.[124] Schut's drawings are carefully planned and executed compositions, most having pen-and-ink borders, as can be seen in his *Seated Ecclesiastic* (fig. 49). The careful finish of Schut's drawings suggests that they may have provided material to be copied by students.[125]

But not all artists working in Seville during the second half of the seventeenth century fell under Murillo's spell. His influence was persistent because of the drawing practices he promoted, the number of practitioners who passed though the academy and the popularity of his style. Another well-known Sevillian artist, Juan de Valdés Leal (1622–90), developed a very different style of painting and drawing. Having worked for a time in Córdoba,

47
Alonso Miguel de Tovar
Saint Joseph and the Christ Child, c.1700–10
Oil on canvas, 875 x 790 mm
Seville Cathedral

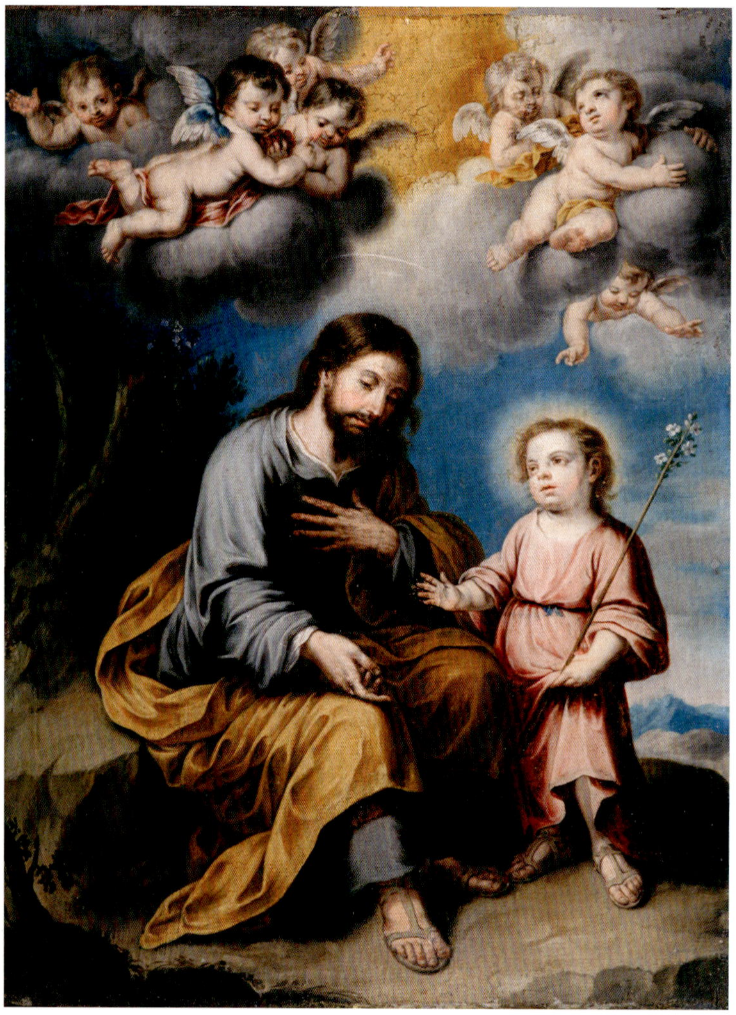

48
Alfonso Miguel de Tovar
Putti beneath the Virgin of the Immaculate Conception, c.1690–1720
Red chalk, pen and brown ink with red-brown wash, 125 x 187 mm
British Museum, London
1846,0509.191

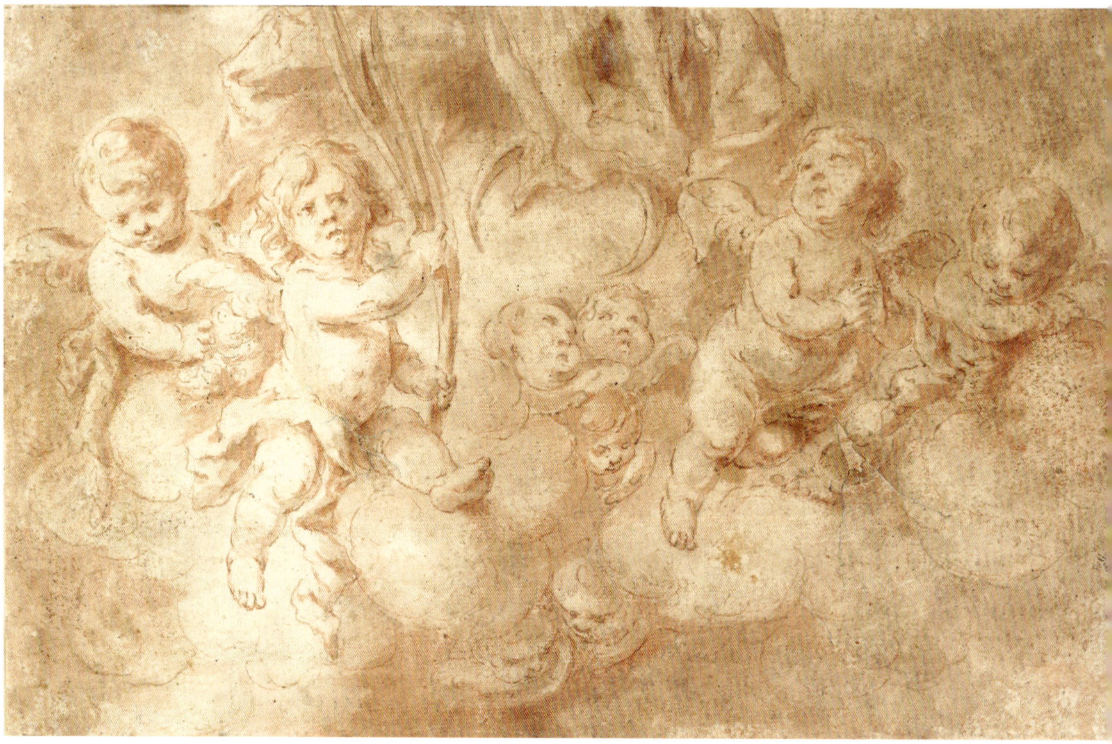

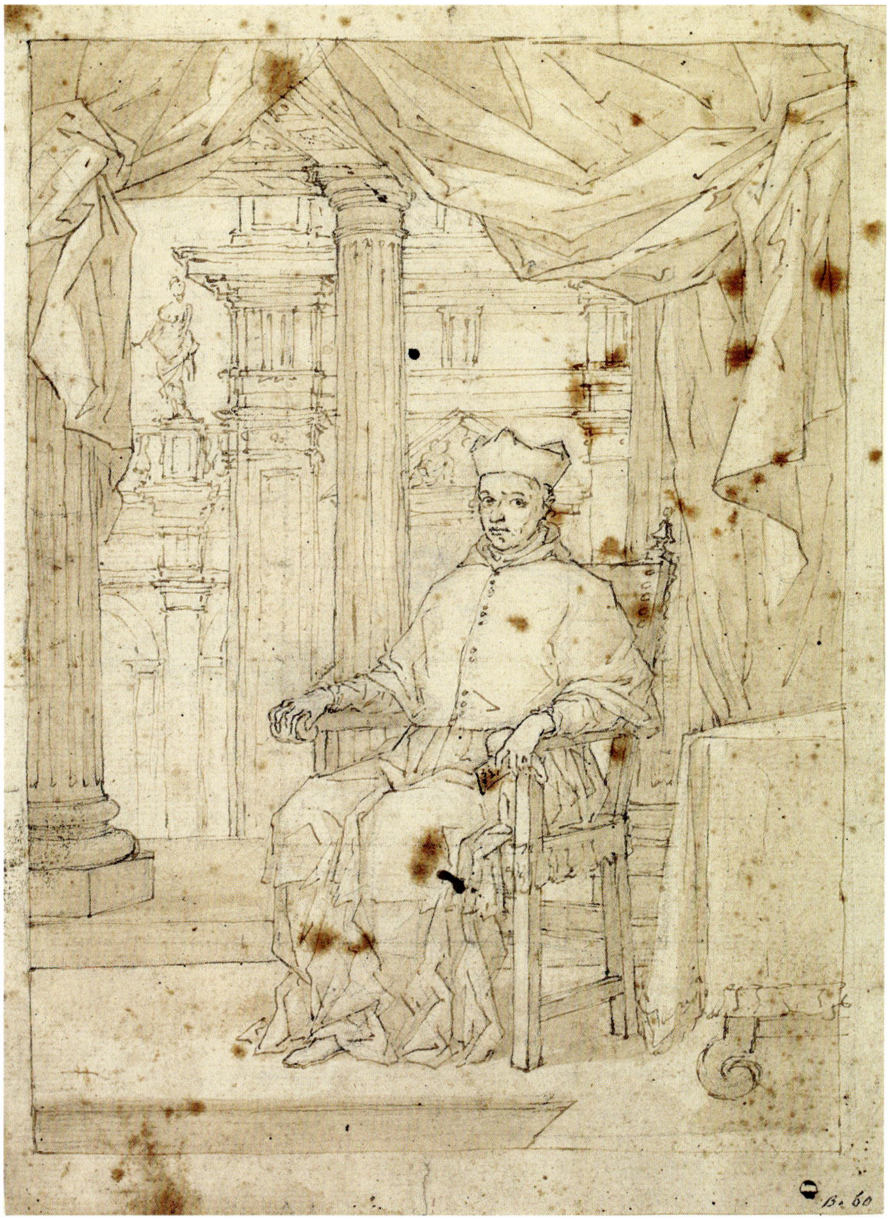

49
Cornelio Schut
A Seated Ecclesiastic, *c.*1660–80
Pen and brown ink and brown wash over black chalk, 273 x 196 mm
British Museum, London
1946,0713.825

Valdés Leal settled in Seville in 1656 where he received his most important commissions.[126] From 1663 to 1666 he was the third president of the academy, where Palomino describes him as the outstanding draughtsman. Valdés Leal shares with Murillo a dedication to drawing that was possibly fuelled by their competitive relationship.[127] One of his most striking sheets, the *Head of Saint John the Baptist* of 1658–60 (fig. 50), shows how he modulated the chalk to achieve contrasting effects of surface and texture. The drawing is very close to his painting on the high altar in the Carmelite convent at Córdoba and was probably not a preparatory study, but rather presented to the client.[128] Valdés Leal's *Vision of Saint Francis in the Porziuncola* (fig. 51), a highly finished work of about 1672 in pen and brown wash with touches of highlight, records his painting at the Colegio de la Escolapias in Cabra (Córdoba) and seems to have served the same function.[129] Of the drawings that are securely attributed to Valdés Leal, none in fact appears to be a study for a composition. It is possible that he did not regard preparatory sheets worthy of preservation,

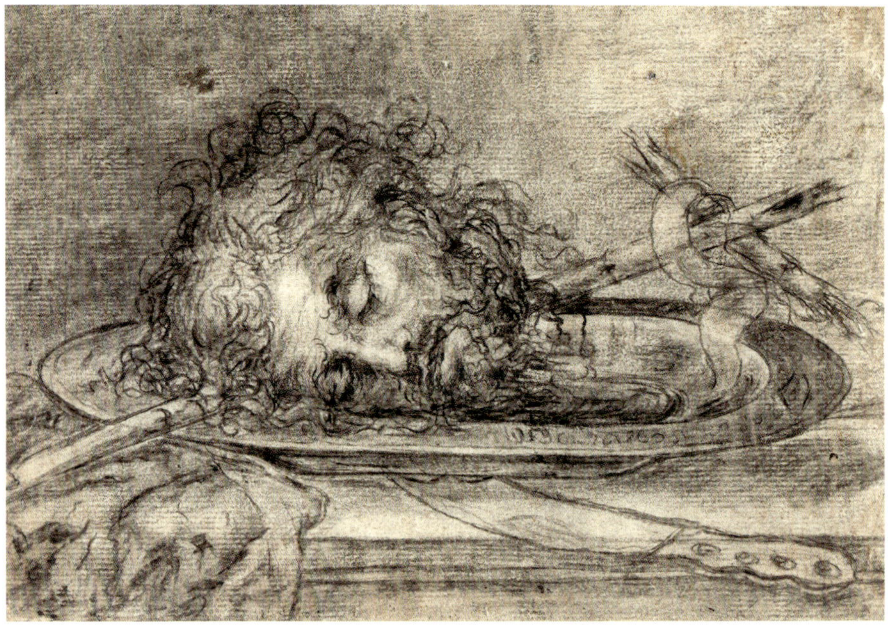

50
Juan de Valdés Leal
Head of Saint John the Baptist, 1658–60
Black chalk, 163 x 230 mm
Hamburger Kunsthalle
38620

but that his finished drawings demonstrated his skill as a draughtsman and provided lasting records of his paintings.

Other lesser-known Sevillian artists who were active draughtsmen and worked into the eighteenth century are Juan de Valdés Leal's son Lucas Valdés (1661–1725) and Domingo Martínez, a colleague of Miguel Alonso Tovar. Lucas's drawings reflect the style of his father, whereas Martínez worked in the style of Murillo.[130] A group of drawings in Córdoba showing Old Testament scenes by Lucas, probably made as book illustrations, were executed in reddish-brown ink and grey wash, a technique similar to the Immaculate Conception mentioned above (fig. 46).[131] This combination of media became popular in Seville during the later decades of the century. Lucas's considerable ability as an architectural draughtsman and designer is demonstrated by a large elevation and plan for a Holy Week monument, signed and dated 1695, now in the Seville Cathedral archive.[132]

The majority of artists working in Seville during the second half of the seventeenth century were involved to some degree in printmaking. Despite the extensive use made of prints in planning painted compositions, printmaking was not part of the syllabus at the academy and prints by academy members are few.[133] In Seville, as elsewhere in Spain, the establishment of a local industry was hampered by the influx of prints from other parts of Europe. Pedro Rodríguez (see Chapter 4) moved to Seville sometime after 1638, where the only record of his activity is a number of landscape etchings of different sizes published by Pedro Campolargo, a painter associated with the academy (fig. 63, p. 120).[134] Nothing is known about the circumstances of their execution except that they were copied after Northern prototypes and might have been made around 1660.[135]

Ceán Bermúdez attributes to Murillo 'a small S. Francis in half-length in etching' and another print, the *Virgin and Child*, has since been attributed to him.[136] In his biography of Cornelio Schut the Elder, Ceán lists a number of his prints, describing them as:

51
Juan de Valdés Leal
Vision of Saint Francis in the Porziuncola, c.1672
Pen and brown ink and wash, with white highlight, over black chalk, 226 x 185 mm
Ecole nationale supérieure des beaux-arts, Paris
308

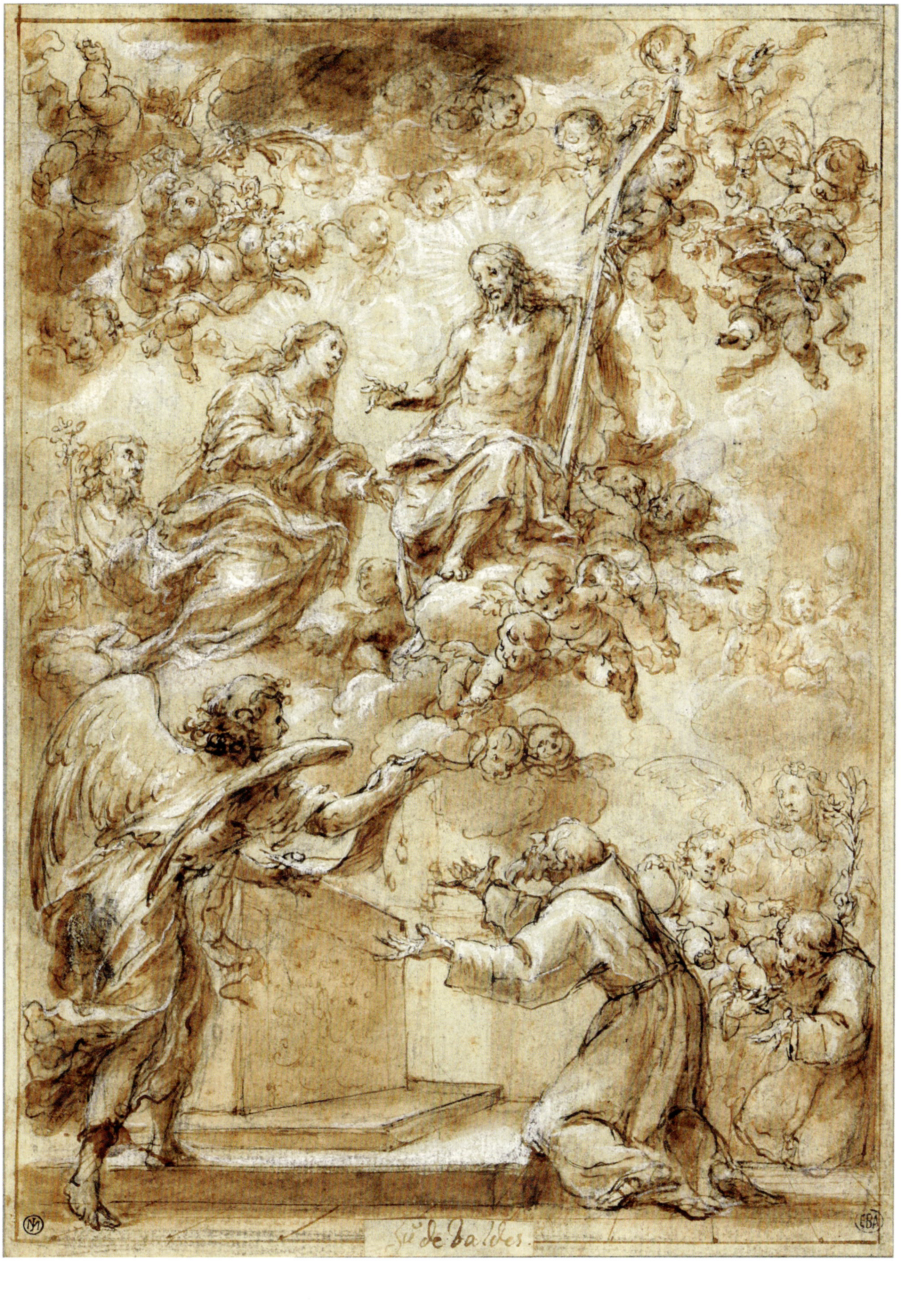
de Baldes.

etched with great pictorial taste with exactitude of drawing and nobility of character. From his hand are prints of the martyrdom of S. Lawrence, of various saints in glory, Venus, Mars, Flora, the Liberal Arts and a portion of small Our Lady's with the Christ Child and infant S. John, and playful children.[137]

Prints by Schut's nephew are not well known but an etched counterproof of *The Virgin and Child* (fig. 52), signed and dated 'Cornelio Schutt in.tor f 1680', comes from his time in Seville.[138] He also provided designs for book illustrations, mainly it seems after his own painted portraits.[139]

The most lavish book published in Seville during the second half of the seventeenth century was Canon Fernando de la Torre Farfán's *Fiesta de la S. Iglesia metropolitana y patriarchal de Sevilla*, an account of the canonization of Ferdinand III, King of Castile, in 1671 by Pope Clement X.[140] The design of the structures and decorations for the celebrations on 25–30 May were the most elaborate ever seen in the city, the result of collaboration between the leading artists in Seville. The cathedral was transformed into a baroque theatre that is described in great detail by Torre Farfán.[141] Several of the artists involved also provided etchings for publication in the *Fiesta*. With the exception of some of the hieroglyphs, all the prints were much larger than the folio-size book and were inserted near the appropriate text. Some of them are dated 1672, the year after the *Fiesta* was published, and were sold as single sheets, which is how the majority have survived.

52
Cornelio Schut
The Virgin and Child, 1680
Etching, 200 x 145 mm
Biblioteca Nacional, Madrid
2882

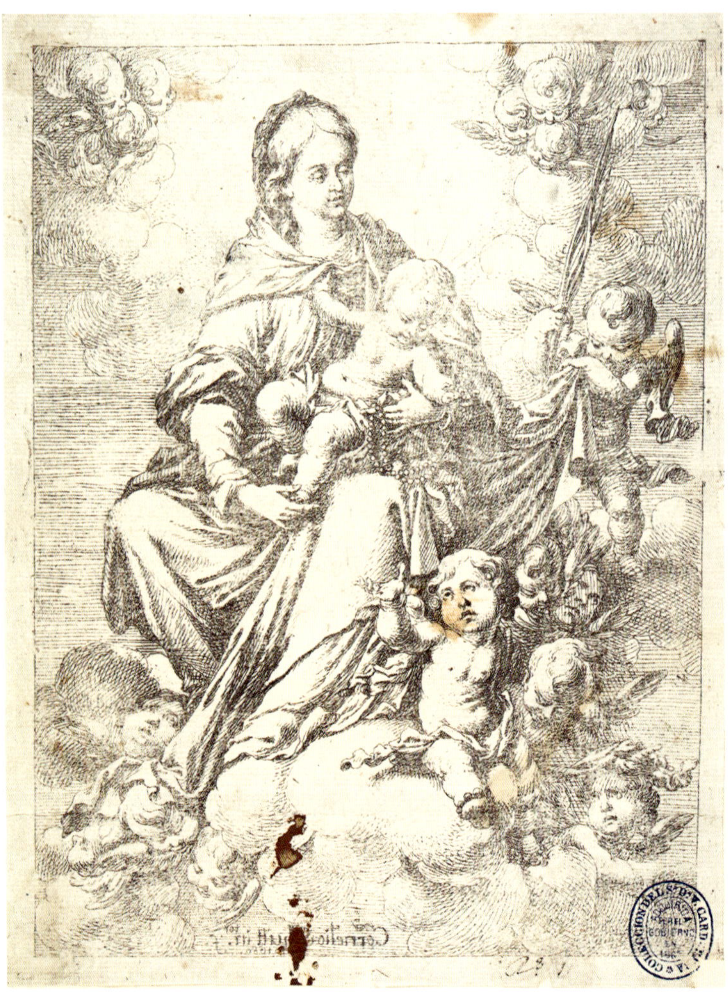

Juan de Valdés Leal was an active printmaker as well as a draughtsman, and from around the mid-1660s he turned increasingly to prints and sculpture as a means of making money. His *Ephemeral Structure in Seville Cathedral* (fig. 15, p. 33) records the structure that he is credited also with designing. It shows a three-tiered wooden octagonal tower 134 feet high, flanked by projecting arches richly decorated with allegorical figures, painted scenes and emblems relating to Ferdinand. A statue of Ferdinand by Pedro Roldán, more than 10 feet high and holding a sword and crown, stands on top, beneath a canopy of putti tumbling in clouds. Valdés Leal depicts himself in the lower centre, discussing a plan of the structure with a group of ecclesiastics (fig. 53). He also produced an etching showing the interior of the main entrance façade of the cathedral, again depicting himself at lower right.[142] Valdés Leal's daughter, Luisa Morales, and his son Lucas also etched the hieroglyphs. Lucas was only eleven years old in 1672, a fact he proudly notes on one of them.[143]

53
Juan de Valdés Leal
An Ephemeral Structure in Seville Cathedral (detail of fig. 15, p. 33), 1671
Etching, 542 x 342 mm
British Museum, London
1868,1114.399

54
Matías Arteaga y Alfaro after Bartolomé Esteban Murillo
Ferdinand III, 1672
Etching, 440 x 277 mm
British Museum, London
1868,1114.390

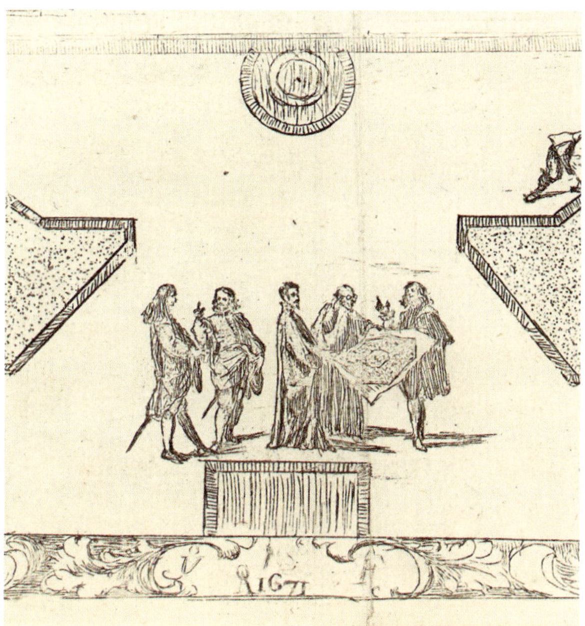

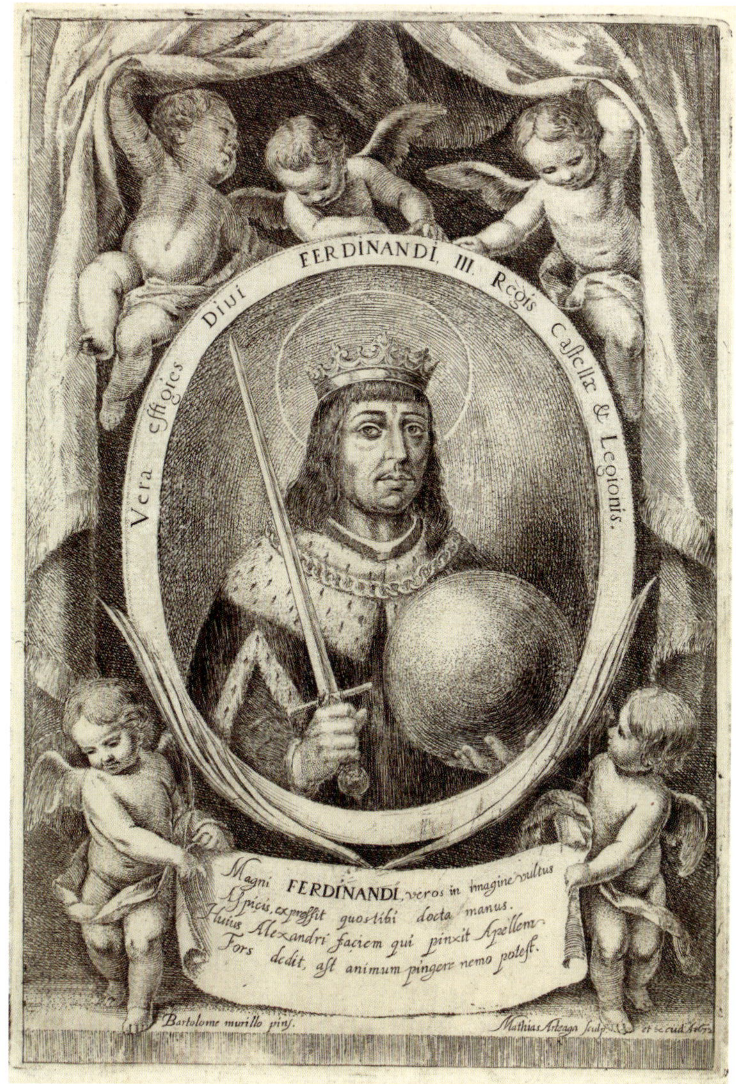

Matías de Arteaga y Alfaro (1633–1703), also a member of the drawing academy, was one of the best printmakers of the day in Seville, and he contributed the largest number of prints to the *Fiesta*.[144] These included a title page after a design by Francisco de Herrera the Younger and a portrait of Ferdinand III after Bartolomé Esteban Murillo (fig. 54). Murillo had seen Ferdinand's corpse on at least two occasions (in 1649 and 1671), confirming the claim on the print that it was a 'True Portrait'.[145] Arteaga continued working as a printmaker until his death, engraving mainly title pages and book illustrations.[146]

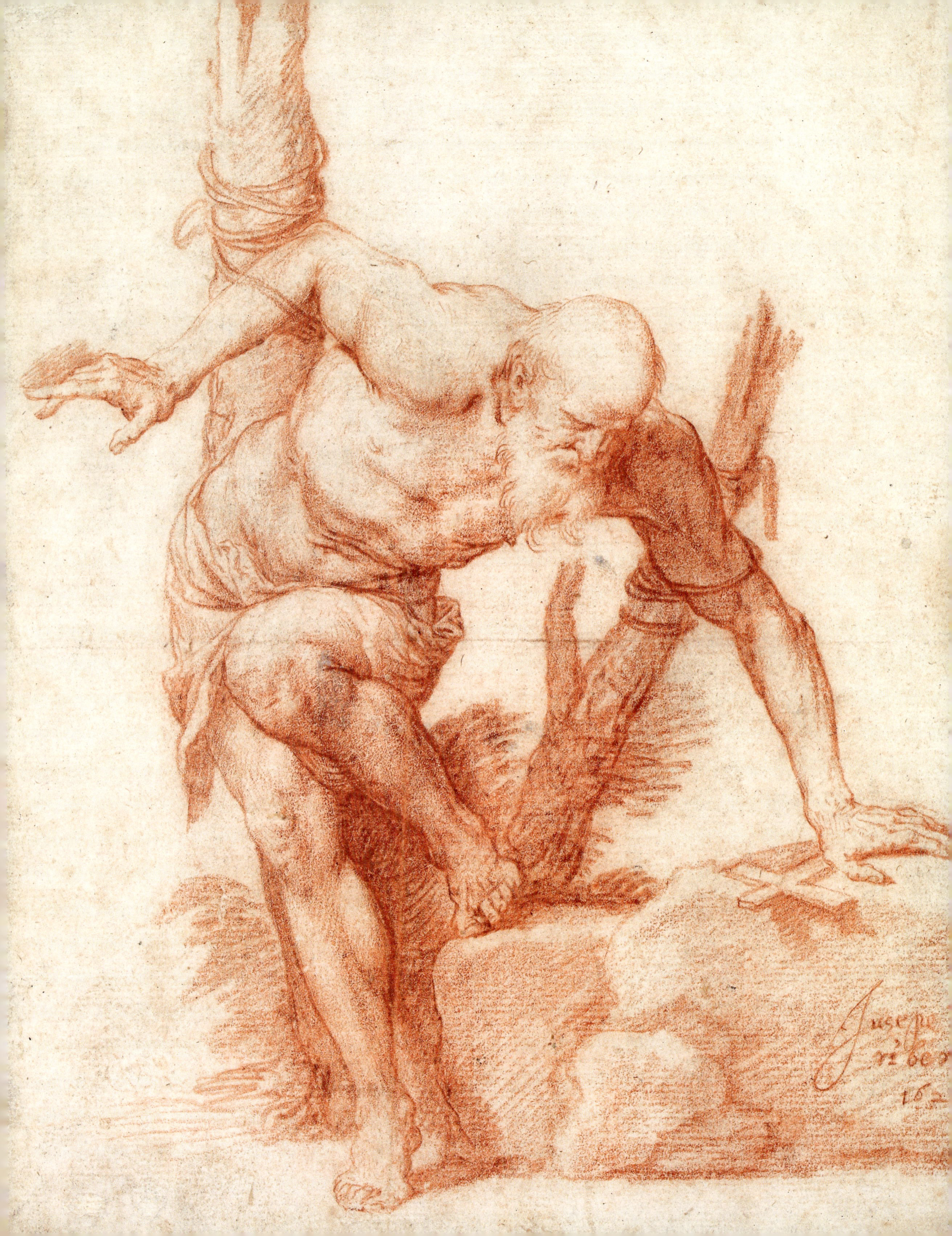
Jusepe

CHAPTER 6

Valencia 1500–1700 and Ribera in Naples

During the fifteenth and sixteenth centuries the city of Valencia, on Spain's eastern seaboard, controlled a thriving commercial trade in the Mediterranean. For many merchants and travellers it was the point of entry before moving to other parts of the Peninsular. Valencia's wealth and cosmopolitan nature were expressed from the fifteenth century through extensive artistic patronage. Valencian artists initially reflected the many strands of Northern art, sometimes described as 'International Gothic', and later Roman and Tuscan painting, transformed into a distinctive local manner.[1]

As discussed in Chapter 2, evidence for prints and drawings in Spain before 1500 is patchy, and Valencia was one of the first places where graphic practices associated with Renaissance Italy took hold. Three of the most significant Spanish artists working in Valencia in the early sixteenth century, were Fernando Yáñez de la Almedina (*c.*1465/70–1536), Fernando Llanos (*c.*1465/70–*c.*1525) and Vicente Macip (*c.*1475–1550), all of whom spent time in Italy. Notorial documents in Florence dating from April and August 1505 record payments made to 'Ferrando Spagnolo' for collaborating with Leonardo da Vinci on the *Battle of Anghiari*; there has been much debate as to whether this refers to Fernando Yáñez or Fernando Llanos.[2] Recent discussion leans toward Llanos, because his compositions and figures show a greater dependency on Leonardo than those of Yáñez, whose work is filled with references to the work of Filippino Lippi, especially his frescos in the Carafa Chapel, Santa Maria sopra Minerva in Rome (1488–1503).[3] It is not known exactly when these three Spanish artists set out for Italy, nor whether they went individually or together, but they were back in Valencia by the end of 1506, their styles powerfully reflecting the influence of their time abroad.

While it is likely that Fernando Llanos did make drawings, none seems to have survived. However, a number of extant studies by Yáñez on prepared paper in metalpoint and others in sanguine wash demonstrate that he was an active draughtsman.[4] Yáñez's metalpoint studies are the earliest evidence of the technique being used in Spain, and they derive from the drawings by Lippi and his circle (fig. 1).[5] Yáñez's delicate manner is revealed by his *Standing Woman in Profile Facing Left* (fig. 2), a chalk-and-wash drawing with touches of metalpoint, possibly from about 1518–19. He subsequently used this in more than one composition, such as the Virgin's companion in the *Visitation* in the Peso Chapel of Cuenca Cathedral, dated around 1531–6.[6] Recycling in this way is very much in keeping with the tradition of pattern-book images, the value of the motif resting as much in the quality of invention as the possibilities of revising it in diverse contexts. There are documentary references to other drawings by Yáñez that no longer survive, for example a

Detail of fig. 32, see p. 186

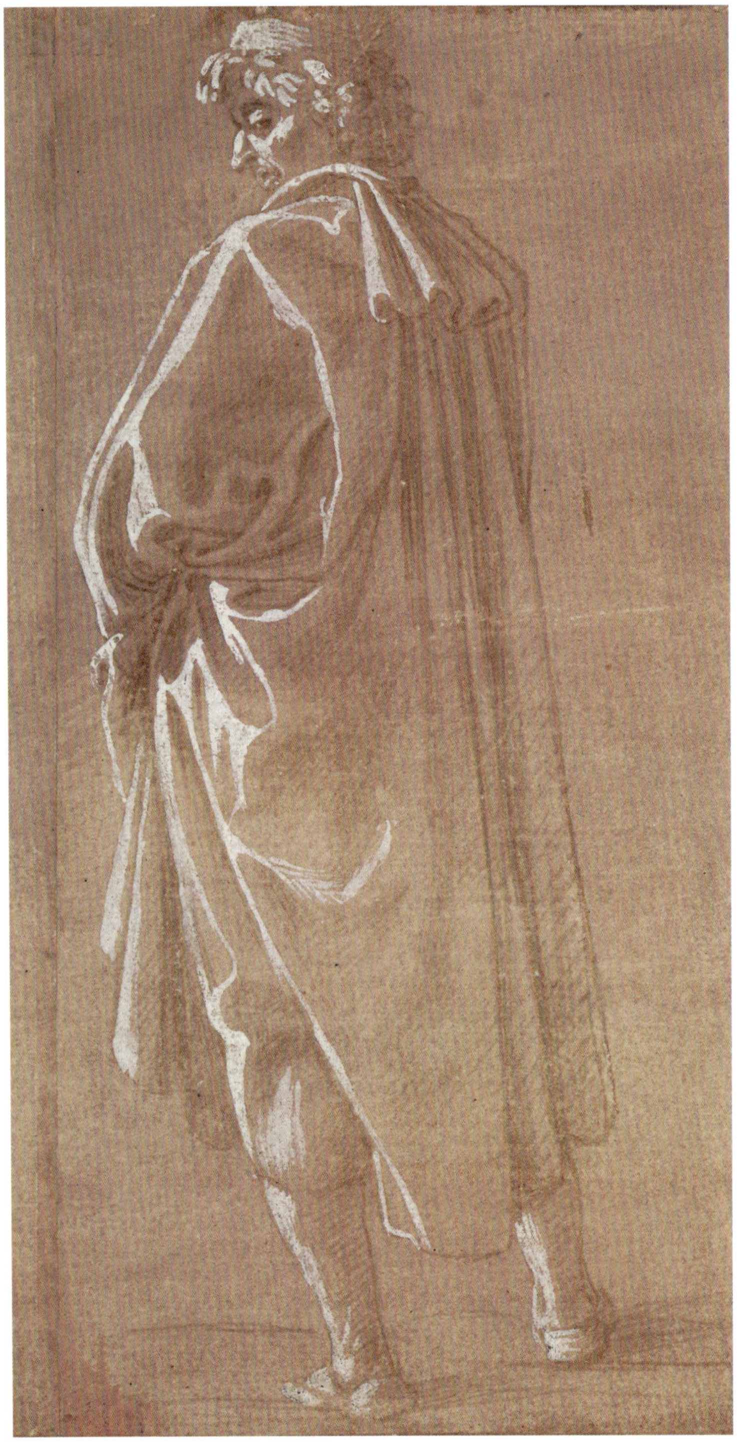

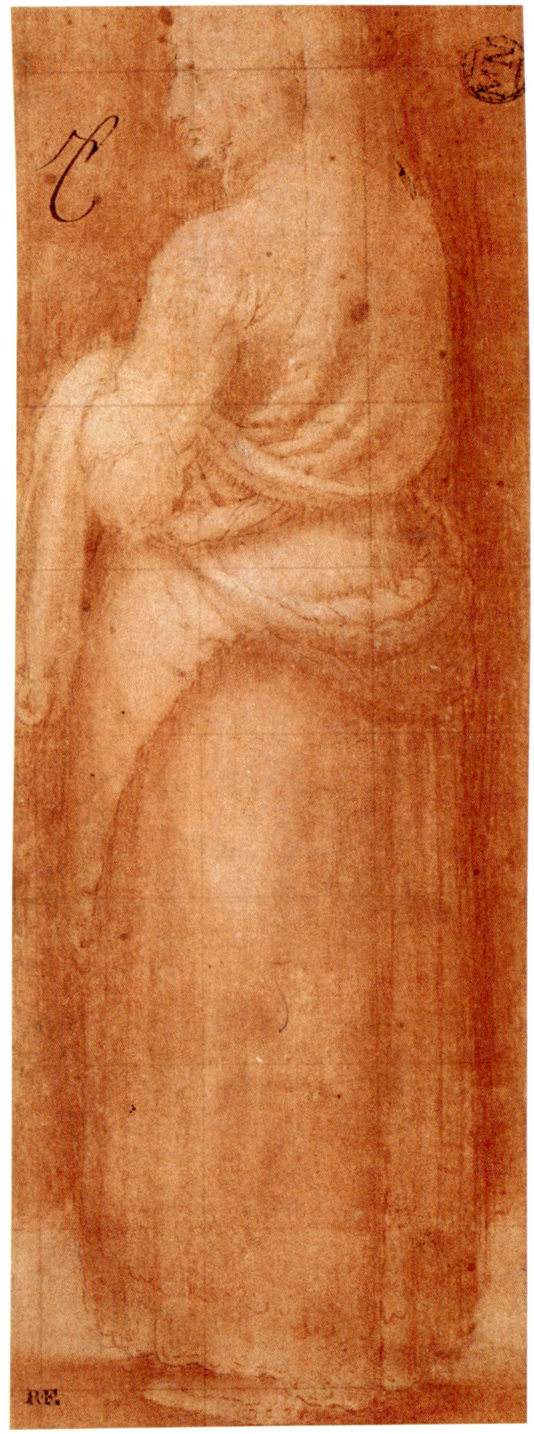

design for the altarpiece of Saint Eloy in Valencia (1509–10) and other studies for decorative panels on the organs in Valencia Cathedral (1513).[7]

Vicente Macip was the founder of an artistic dynasty that dominated Valencia until the 1600s.[8] His style was formed in Italy and influenced by the paintings of Sebastiano del Piombo in Valencia.[9] Vicente was involved in an attempt in 1520 to form a college of painters in Valencia to encourage professional recognition and to regulate painters' work.[10] Nothing is known of Vicente's drawings, but a number of sheets have been attributed to his son,

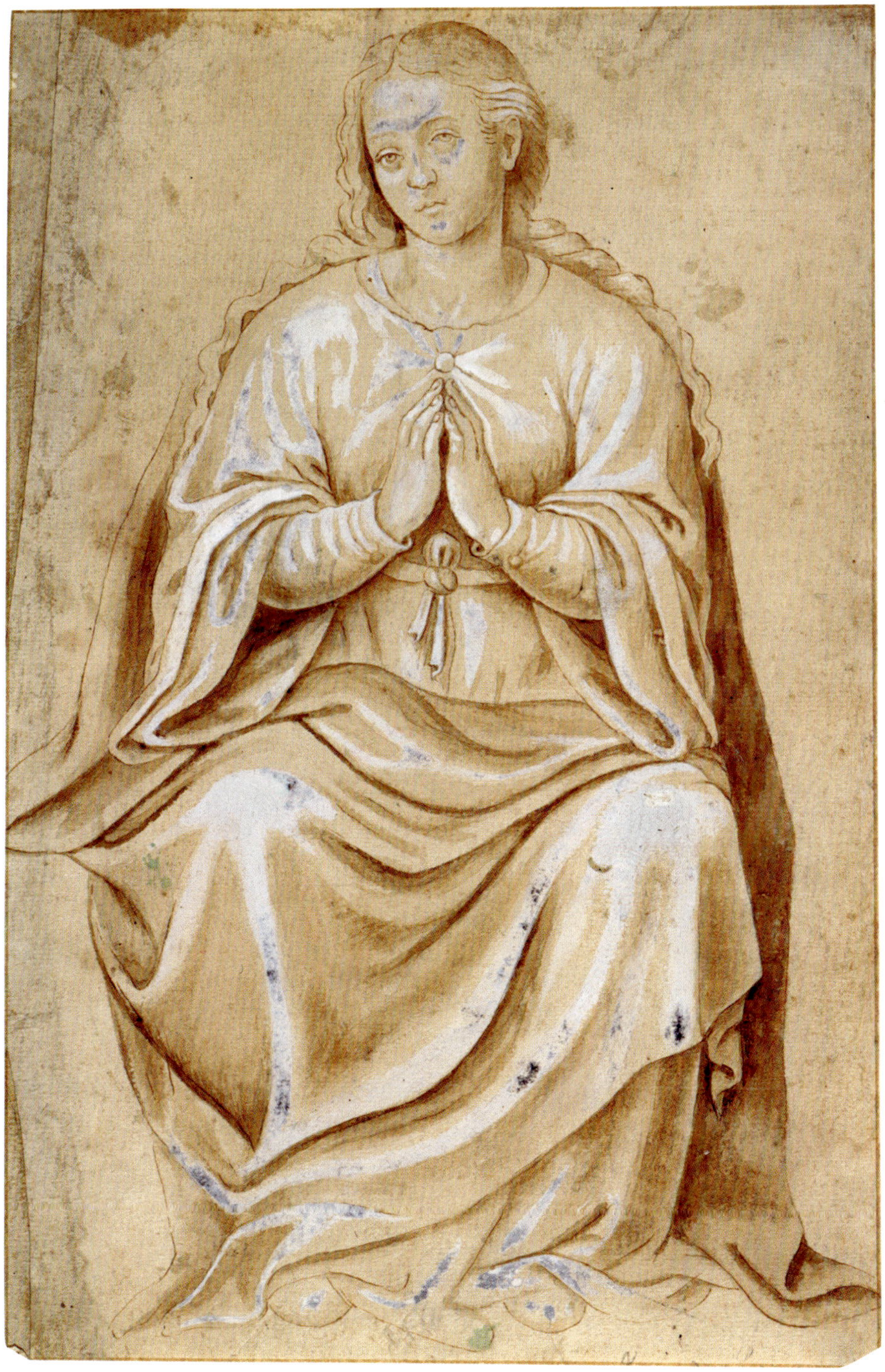

1
Circle of Filippino Lippi
A Standing Man Seen from Behind (detail of recto), 1472–1504
Metalpoint, heightened with white, on two conjoined sheets of pink-grey prepared paper, 265 x 251 mm
British Museum, London
Pp,1.13

2
Fernando Yáñez de la Almedina
Standing Woman in Profile Facing Left, c.1518–19
Red chalk with red wash on red prepared paper, touches of metal point, squared for transfer, 198 x 72 mm
Musée du Louvre, Paris
10805

3
Juan de Juanes
The Virgin Seated, c.1555
Pen and brown ink and wash with white hightening, 285 x 185 mm
Museo del Prado, Madrid
D.11

the best-known member of the family, Juan de Juanes (Joan de Joanes, *c.*1510–79).[11] These provide the most substantial evidence for drawing practice in Valencia around the mid-sixteenth century.[12] Most of Juanes' sheets are large and carefully drawn in pen, ink and wash with areas of white heightening to give the figures a sculptural solidity, as for example his *Virgin Seated* (fig. 3). This corresponds to the coronation scene in the upper section of the altarpiece of the Trinity in the church of San Nicolás de Bari and San Pedro Mártir, Valencia.[13] The sheet is very carefully finished, probably intended as a model for future compositions as well as serving as a preparatory study.[14]

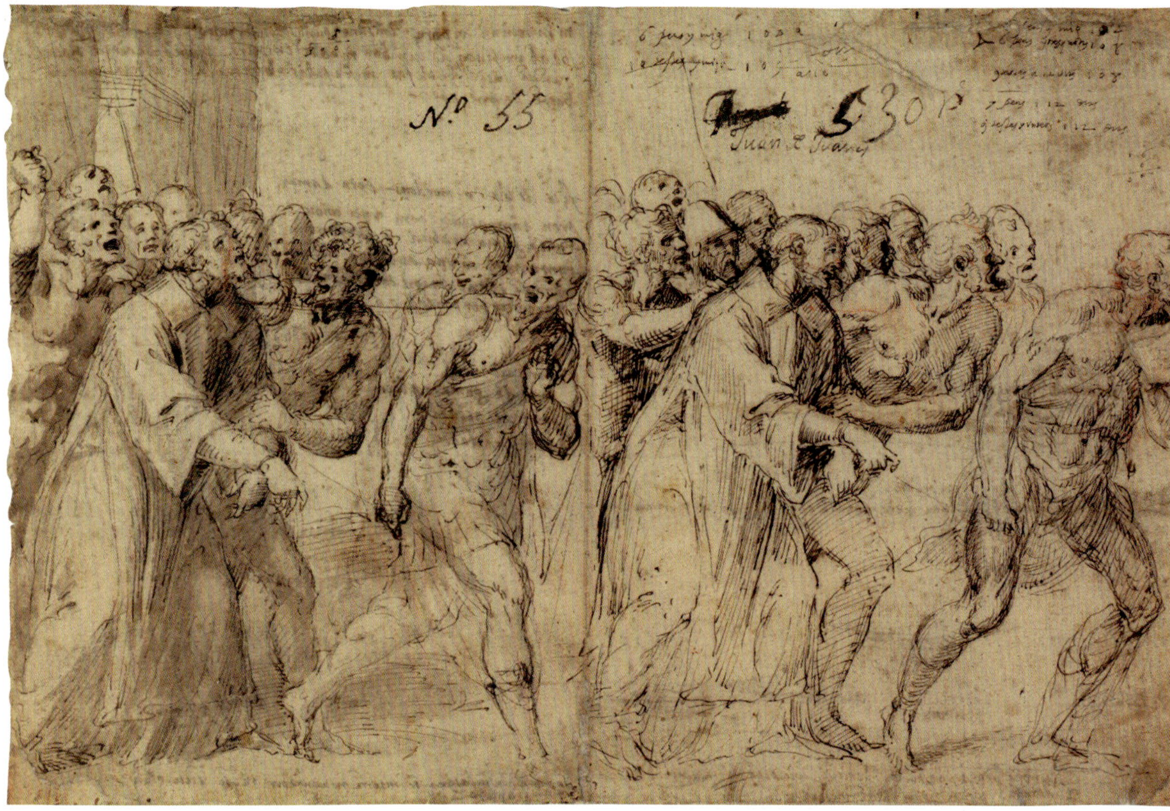

4
Juan de Juanes
Saint Stephen Being Led to his Execution, late 1550s
Pen and brown ink, grey wash and traces of red chalk, 217 x 315 mm
Courtauld Institute of Art, London
D.1963.WF.4730

5
Juan de Juanes
Saint Stephen being Led to his Execution, late 1550s
Oil on panel, 1600 x 1230 mm
Museo del Prado, Madrid
P.840

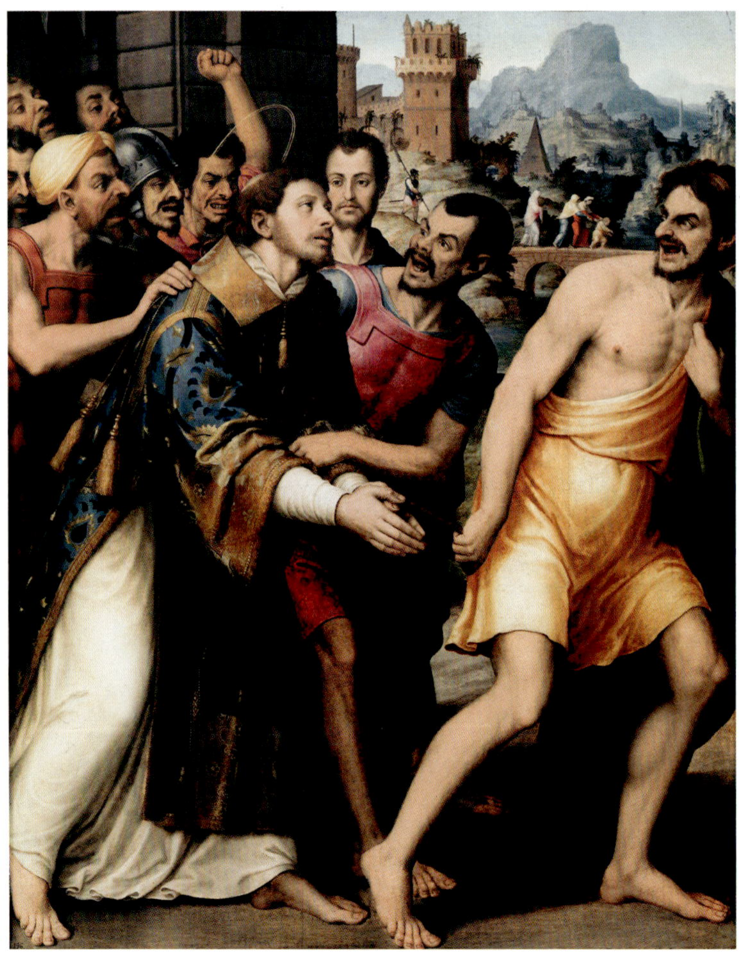

A very different drawing by Juanes, *Saint Stephen Being Led to his Execution* (fig. 4) in pen, ink and wash, is a preparatory study for one of the panels in the altarpiece from the church of Saint Stephen, Valencia, of the late 1550s (fig. 5). The sheet records the artist's preliminary thoughts for the procession through two rapidly drawn studies of the subject. Juanes settled on the study on the left-hand side, where Stephen directs his gaze upwards while his persecutors glare directly at him to emphasize their cruelty. There are a number of inscriptions by Juanes on both sides of the sheet, including a recipe for mordant for gilding, an explanation of how to measure distance across a river, prices to be charged according to the number of heads depicted, and a Latin epigram about love.[15] This unusually large sheet, unlike anything else that survives from Spain during the early second half of the sixteenth century, provides unique evidence of how Juanes planned his composition. Three other drawings by the same artist and related to the altar also survive: the *Predication of Saint Stephen Before the Sanhedrin*, *Saint Stephen being Lowered into the Tomb* and *The Last Supper*.[16] These are different from the two studies of Saint Stephen in that they represent a much later stage of drawing and correspond closely to the finished paintings. Furthermore, they appear to record the compositions for later reference. In the panel of *The Last Supper*, Juanes modified the background by setting Christ against a window aperture rather than the curtain seen in his drawing. The drawing later served as a model for a painting by his son, Vicente Joanes (*c.*1555–*c.*1623).[17]

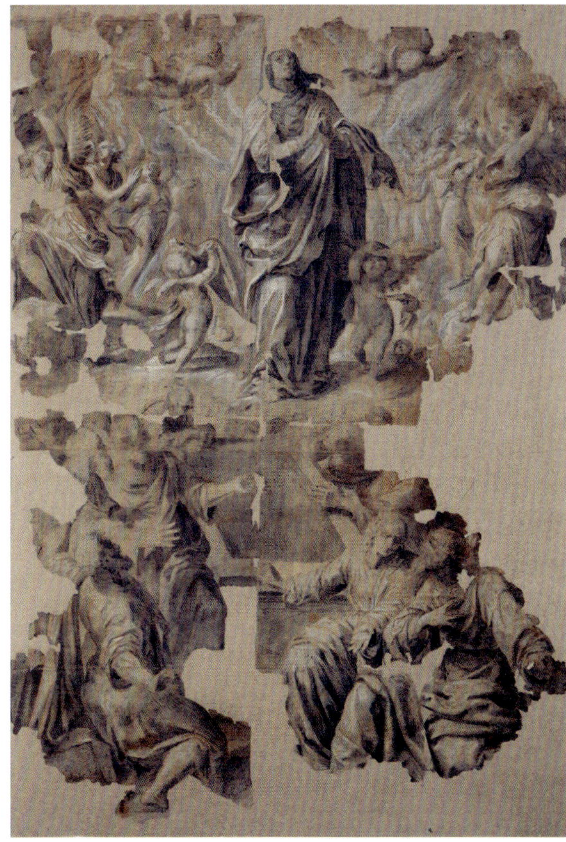

6
Roland de Mois
The Assumption of the Virgin, *c.*1571
Pen and brown ink, brush with grey and brown wash, oil, white heightening, 510 x 350 mm
Museo de Bellas Artes, Valencia 8542

Drawings by other sixteenth-century artists in Valencia are scarce. Nicolás Borrás (1530–1610), a student of Juan de Juanes, seems to have continued his master's drawing style.[18] The Flemish-born Roland de Mois (active 1571–90), who worked in Valencia under the protection of the Duke of Villahermosa, mainly painted portraits of the local nobility.[19] His only known drawing is a large *Assumption of the Virgin* (fig. 6) of about 1571, composed in pen, brush and wash, oil and white highlight on prepared paper for a painting on the high altar of the Monastery of Oliva, today in the Recoletas convent, Tafalla (Navarra).[20] The sheet is badly damaged but achieves an effect close to grisaille or a chiaroscuro print.

There is sufficient evidence to prove that drawing in sixteenth-century Valencia was not an exceptional practice. The surviving sheets generally appear to be finished records of a design rather than first thoughts or preparatory sketches for working out individual details within compositions. The higher survival rate of these drawings corresponds with that of patterns elsewhere in Spain during the same period. While Joanes' *Saint Stephen Being Led to his Execution* might normally have been discarded, the fact that it is annotated on the verso with a lot of information gives it a secondary purpose and context.

The seventeenth century: 1600–1650

Like other large cities in Spain in the early decades of the seventeenth century, Valencia suffered a reversal of fortunes. The expulsion of the Moors in 1609 had a devastating long-term effect on its economy, exacerbated by the pressures

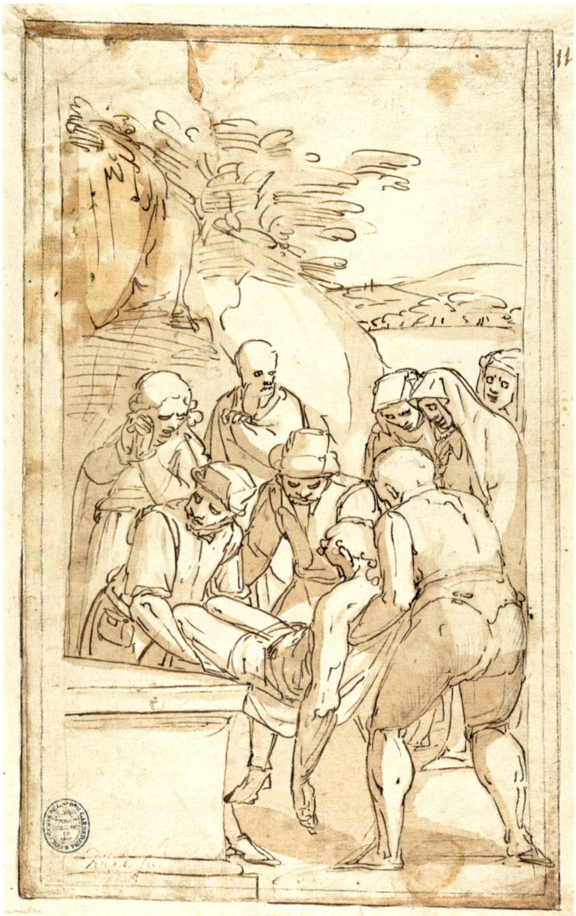

7
Attributed to Francisco Ribalta

The Entombment of Christ, c.1582–1600

Pen and brown ink and wash over black chalk, 345 x 212 mm
Biblioteca Nacional, Madrid
DIB/13/1/17

caused by military unrest throughout Catalonia during the 1640s and 1650s as well as demands made by the government in Castile.[21] Despite her difficulties, Valencia remained a centre of trade and commerce where artistic patronage flourished, supported by religious institutions and wealthy individuals.

Many more drawings are known from the first decades of the seventeenth century, although only a few artists can be identified through their work with any certainty. One of them is Francisco Ribalta (1565–1628), who moved from Barcelona to Madrid around 1582 where, like so many Spanish artists, he fell under the spell of the Italians at the Escorial.[22] Ribalta remained in Madrid until 1599 when he moved to Valencia and established himself as a successful artist. Drawings by his hand are few but, although difficult to fit with specific phases of his career, they are sufficient to indicate a distinctive style. *The Entombment of Christ* (fig. 7) has long been recognized as a Spanish copy of a sheet by Luca Cambiaso but its authorship is disputed, although the inscription 'Ribalta fec', in the same ink as the drawing, suggests that it is by Francisco Ribalta.[23] Elements in the drawing such as the triangular tapered feet recur in his later work. Only a handful of drawings, several of which can no longer be traced, are regarded as preparatory for his paintings.[24] Two examples are *The Apparition of Christ to Saint Vincent Ferrer* (*c.*1604–5) and *Saint Bruno* (*c.*1625–7).[25] The *Apparition*, which is preparatory for Ribalta's painting in the chapel of Saint Vincent in the College of Corpus Christi, Valencia, dates from soon after his arrival in the city and clearly shows his dependency on Italian models. *Saint Bruno* (fig. 8) is a key work in understanding his more simplified drawing style later in his career. The abbreviated penstrokes over lightly drawn lines in black chalk are supported by delicate wash to indicate the folds of the saint's habit. Ribalta also uses the wash to study the dramatic effects of light and dark in his paintings.

Ribalta is said to have introduced etching to Valencia through a print after his painting *The Sacrifice of Isaac* (1599), but no impressions of it survive.[26] The verso of a painting on copper of *The Adoration of the Shepherds* – once attributed to Francisco but now thought to be by his son, Juan Ribalta – is etched with a scene of the predication of Saint Luis Beltrán.[27] If Ribalta was himself a printmaker, his engagement in the process was erratic, but he certainly relied on prints as source material for a number of compositions and was aware of their efficacy in reproducing works of art.[28] Michel Lasne (1597–1667), a French engraver active in Spain, made a print after Ribalta's drawings of scenes from the life of Francisco Simó (1578–1612), a priest of the parish of San Andrés, Valencia.[29]

Evidence for drawing activity linked to Ribalta is fragmentary. An artist in his circle made a finished copy of his 1622–6 painting of the Virgin of Porta Coeli.[30] Ribalta's outstanding disciple was his son Juan (*c.*1596–1628), who died soon after his father.[31] Palomino notes that their close collaboration makes their work hard to distinguish.[32] The few drawings that have been associated with Juan are problematic, because none can be directly connected

8
Francisco Ribalta
Saint Bruno, *c.*1625–7
Pen and brown ink and wash over black chalk, 315 x 180 mm
Museo de Bellas Artes, Valencia
1640

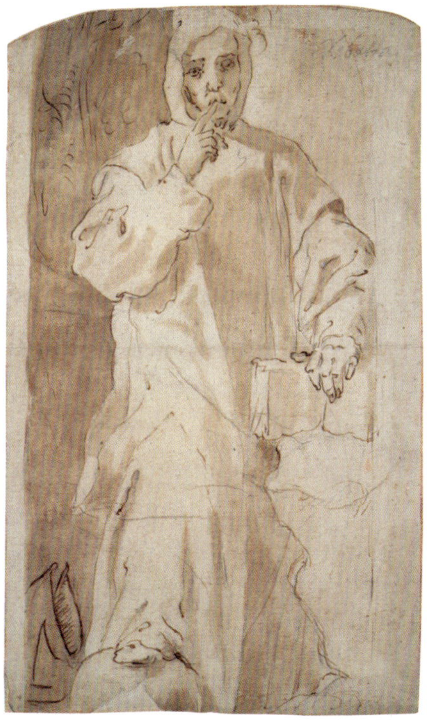

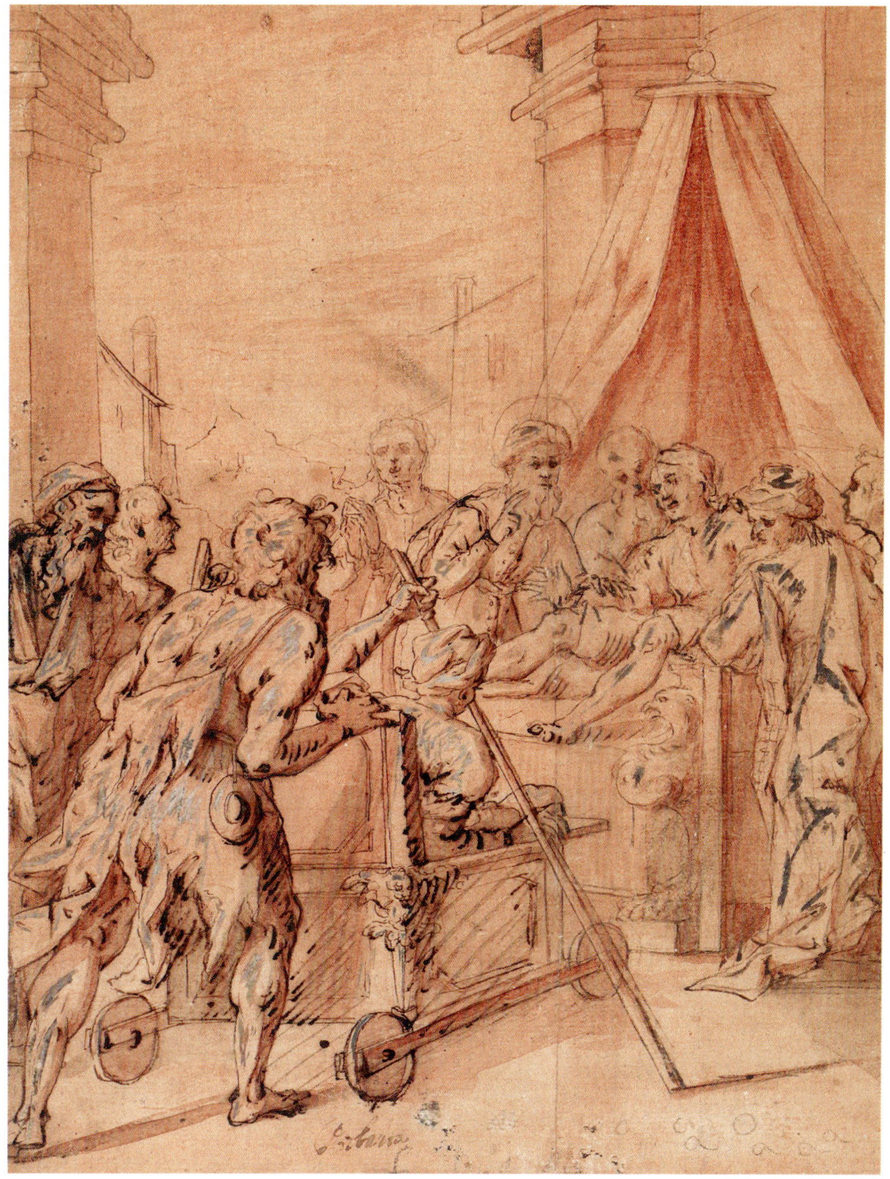

9
Juan Ribalta
A Miraculous Healing by a Saint, *c.*1610–28
Pen and brown ink and brush with brown wash over black chalk, heightened with white on red-prepared paper, 307 x 230 mm
British Museum, London
1846,0509.174

with a painting.[33] For example, a drawing in brown wash of *Christ Being Nailed to the Cross* is related to a work by Juan Ribalta from around 1615–16, but it is not entirely clear whether the drawing is by Juan or his father.[34] A pen-and-brush drawing of *A Miraculous Healing by a Saint* (possibly Saint Vincent Ferrer; fig. 9) has been attributed to Juan Ribalta on the basis of the inscription; the red wash is similar to other drawings thought to be by him.[35] Ribalta also used warm tones for the ground of his paintings, a practice thought to have been influenced by Pedro Orrente, who arrived in Valencia around 1616,[36] and his compositions were informed by Albrecht Dürer's prints.[37] The composition of Ribalta's *Miraculous Healing* drawing, for example, is very similar to Dürer's *Small Passion* and *Life of the Virgin* woodcuts: both have a circle of figures, with a single figure in the foreground seen from the back, those in the background being executed more lightly, some just showing their heads, to suggest depth.[38] The Renaissance-style columns used to frame the composition also occur in Dürer's prints.

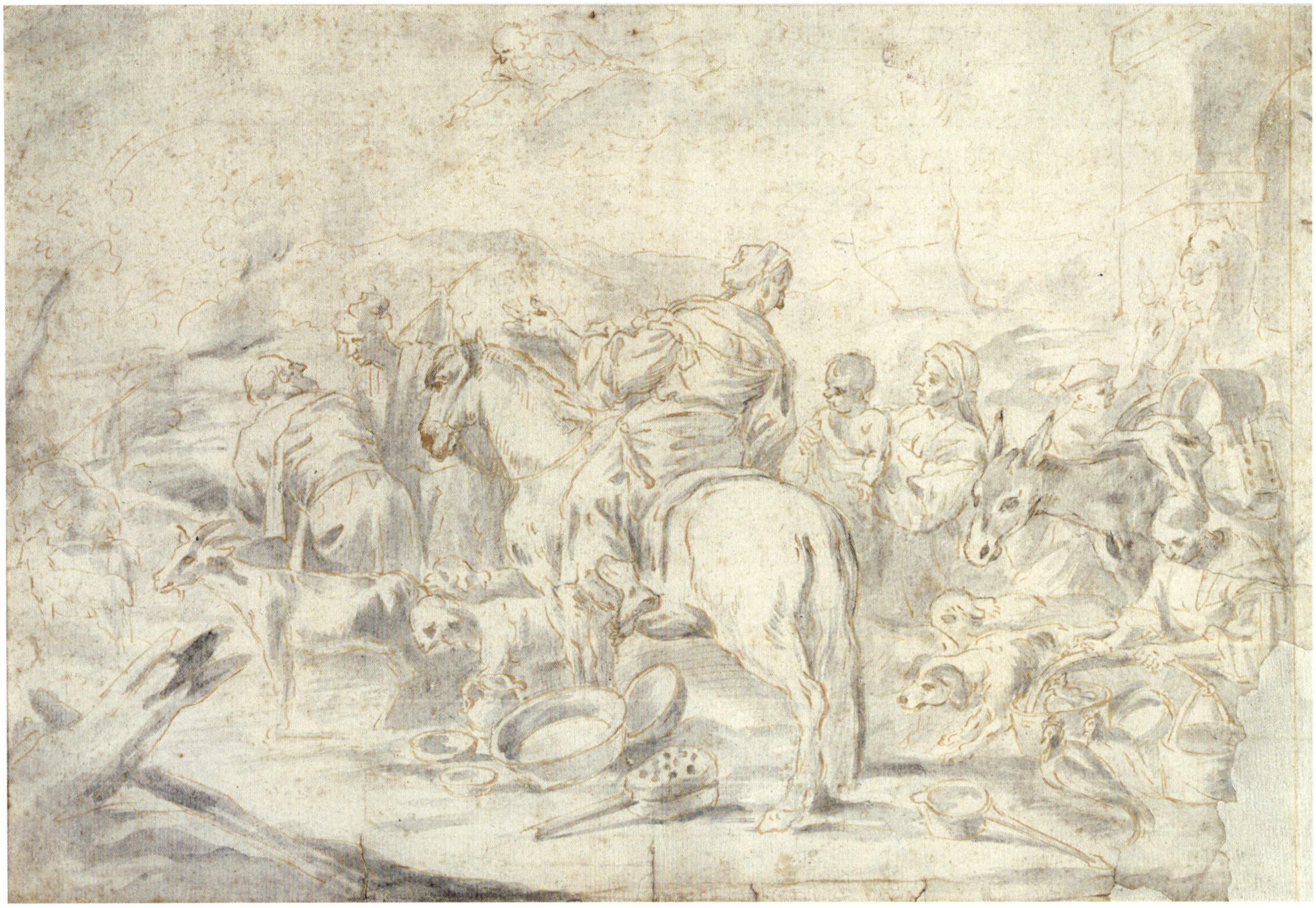

10
Pedro Orrente
Abraham Departing for Caanan, 1627
Pen and brown ink, grey wash over black chalk, 285 x 405 mm
Museo de Bellas Artes, Valencia
8609

11
Pedro Orrente
Saint Bruno and the Duke of Calabria, c.1625–45
Brush and red ink with wash over black chalk, 398 x 285 mm
Biblioteca Nacional, Madrid
DIB/13/1/11

12
Esteban March
Doge Francecso Donato before the Virgin and Other Saints, 1651
Brush and brown wash over black chalk, 410 x 560 mm
Museo de Bellas Artes, Valencia
3449

Of the artists working in Valencia during the first half of the seventeenth century the most prolific draughtsman was Pedro Orrente (1580–1645). He divided his time between Murcia (his birthplace), Toledo and Valencia. Documented in Toledo in 1600, Orrente visited Rome and Venice between the end of 1602 and 1607, possibly working in the studio of Leandro Bassano – indeed, his debt to the Venetian painter has led to him being called the 'Spanish Bassano'.[39] All Orrente's known drawings seem to have been made after his return to Spain. His pen, ink and wash drawing of *Abraham Departing for Caanan* (fig. 10), made in 1627 when he was in the vicinity of Toledo,[40] is a careful copy after Jacopo and Francesco Bassano's painting sent by Philip II's ambassador in Venice, Diego Guzmán de Silva, to the Escorial in 1574. Often large, his surviving drawings are all executed in pen and brown ink, red chalk, or brush and red or brown wash. *Saint Bruno and the Duke of Calabria* (fig. 11), in bright red wash applied with a brush over very faint black chalk outlines, is unrelated to any known painting and seems to be one of Orrente's many independent sheets.[41]

Francisco Ribalta and Pedro Orrente broadly define the parameters of drawing in Valencia during the first half of the seventeenth century. The degree to which they used wash differentiates them from artists working in other parts of Spain. A comparison of Orrente's *Saint Bruno and the Duke of Calabria* and Vicente Carducho's version of the subject made around the same time makes this point clearly (fig. 12, p. 88).

A number of other artists perpetuated Ribalta and Orrente's styles. Judging from what survives, Jerónimo Jacinto Espinosa (1600–67) was a prolific draughtsman.[42] Orrente's student Esteban March (1610–68), who spent most of his career in Valencia, is best known for his battle paintings. His technique of pen, ink and wash and the subjects of his drawings are close to those of his teacher, and their work has sometimes been confused.[43] March's most impressive sheet, the *Doge Franceso Donato before the Virgin and Other Saints* (fig. 12), is copied from a print after Titian.[44] The inscription along the bottom records that March made the drawing when he was in Madrid on 1 June 1651, a level of detail rarely found on drawings.[45] March's reasons for copying the print are not known and may have been clarified in the section of the inscription that has been erased, but Titian's work was very well known and admired in Madrid. Several lesser-known Valencian artists of this period have also had drawings attributed to them. Two sheets by Pablo Pontóns (1630–91) survive, of which one, a black chalk drawing of the *Martyrdom of Saint John the Evangelist*, shows close similarities to his painting now in the Museo de Bellas Artes, Valencia.[46]

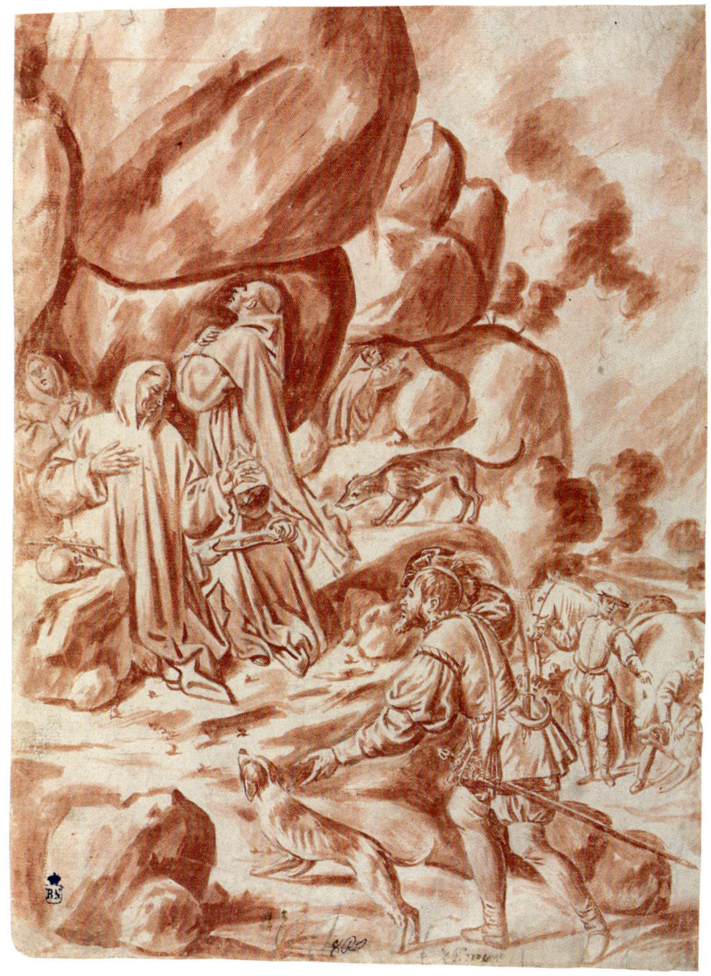

Over 150 drawings probably dating from the late 1630s by Gregorio Bausá (1590–1656) are preserved in the Lassala collection, Valencia.[47] Bausá was possibly apprenticed to Francisco Ribalta and worked in his circle around the 1620s.[48] Some of the drawings can be related to specific passages in Bausá's paintings: for example, he made no fewer than seven studies of the anatomy, fabrics and gestures for his *Arrest of Christ* (1645; Museo Provincial de Bellas Artes, Castellón).[49] As a corpus preserved in an album, his drawings function in a way similar to pattern sheets, providing examples that could be copied and used for future reference.

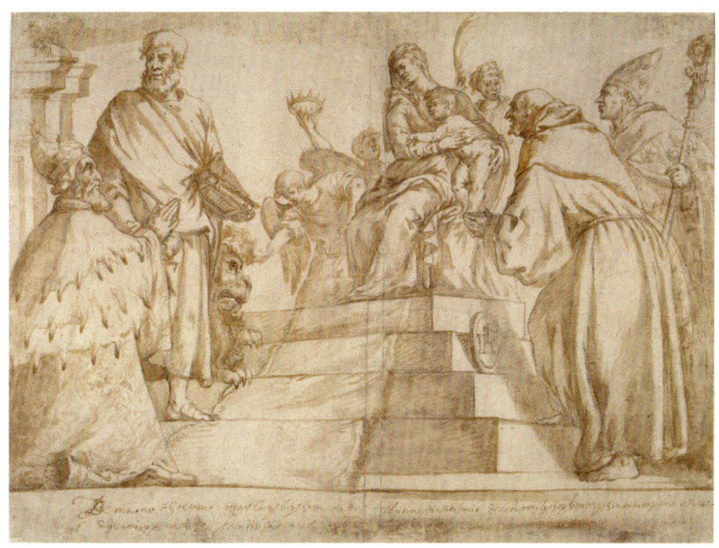

1650–1700

Artistic developments in Valencia during the later decades of the century are not as well studied as those during the first half. Two of the most active artists were Vicente Salvador Gómez (1637–*c*.1680) and Juan Antonio Conchillos y Falcó (1641–1711). Salvador Gómez was appointed Director of the Academy of Santo Domingo in Valencia in 1670 and his earliest surviving drawings date from around this time. It is very unlikely, however, that he began to draw so late in his career: more probably his early work was discarded,

13
Vicente Salvador Gómez
Saint Joseph and the Christ Child, 1674
Pen and brown ink and grey wash, 262 x 170 mm
British Museum, London
1846,0509.186

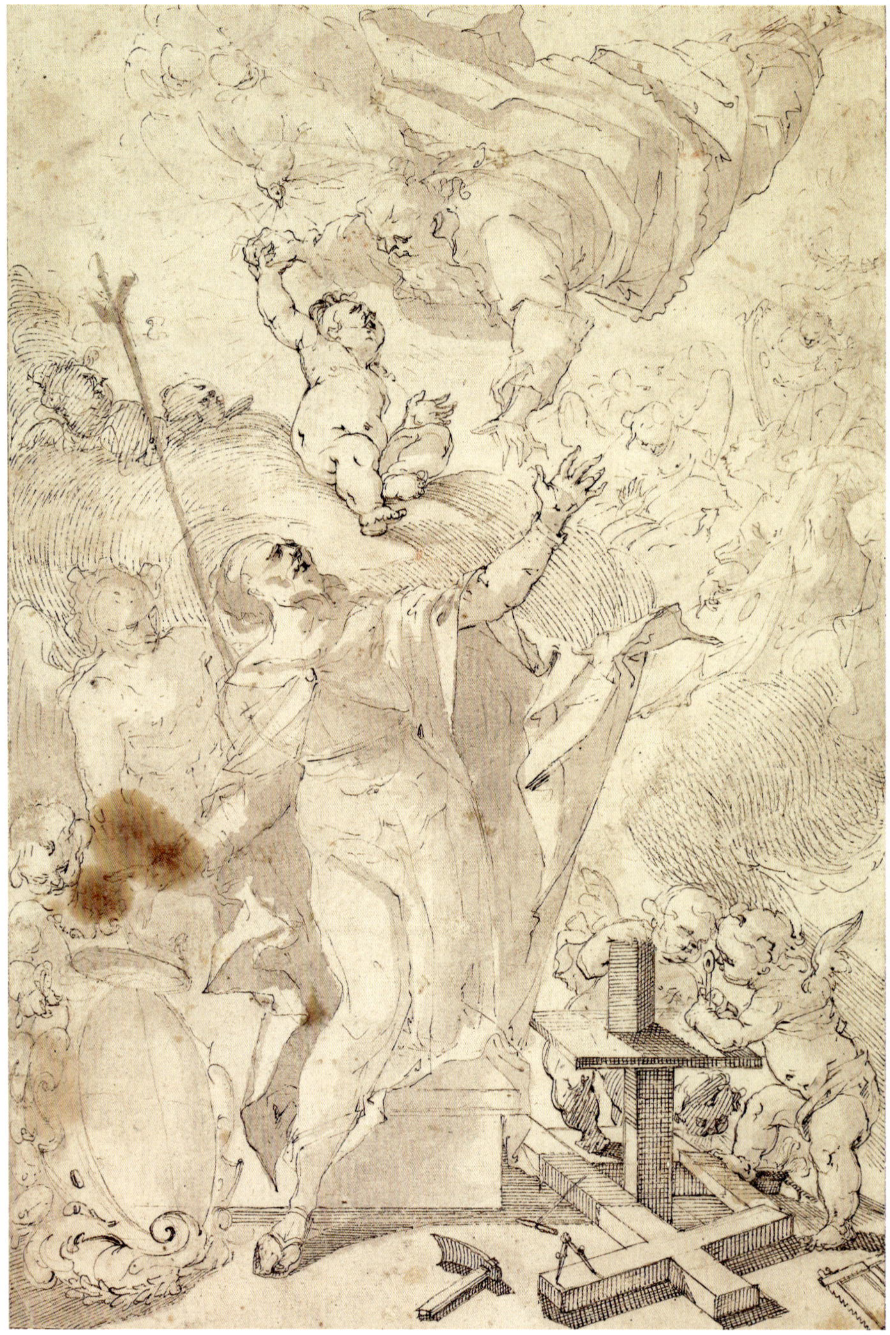

while his mature drawings became valued after he had made his name. In 1673 Salvador Gómez paid the prior of the convent and monastery of the Virgin Mary of Porta Coeli for 'models, prints and drawings' left there by Alonso Cano when he was in Valencia in 1644–5.[50] A year later Gómez produced a manuscript that was to contain his theories on painting, the 'Cartilla y fundamentales reglas de la pintura'. Fragments still survive in manuscript form, although the treatise was clearly intended to be published.[51] According to the introduction the text was to be divided into four dialogues no doubt including the rules of symmetry, anatomy, physiognomy, geometry and perspective.

The title page describes its author, his association with the Office of the Inquisition and his role as censor: 'Vicente Salvador y Gómez, familiar of

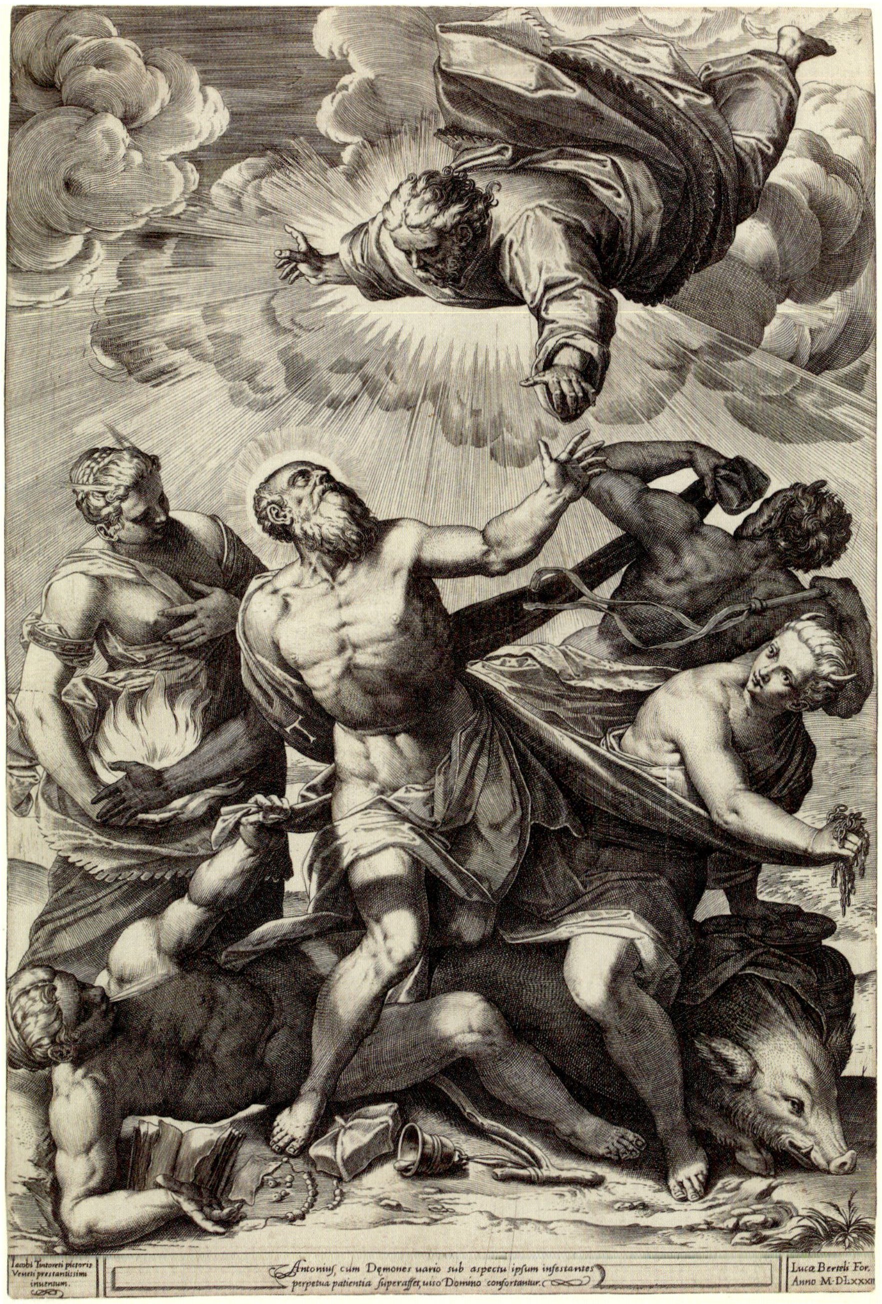

14
Agostino Carracci after Tintoretto

The Temptation of Saint Anthony, 1582

Engraving, 493 x 328 mm
British Museum, London
U,2.93

the Holy Office of the Inquisition and Censor of paintings according to the decency and learning of the said Tribunal. Made at the age of 37 in the year of our Lord's redemption 1674 in Valencia.' As an adjudicator, Gómez was charged with gauging the appropriateness of iconography and its interpretation. The 'Cartilla' contained eleven drawings of parts of the human body to be copied by students, with the text on each page to explain what is shown. The intention was probably also to include complete compositions to show the iconography appropriate to particular subjects, of which one may have been Gómez's drawing of the *Immaculate Conception*, which is of similar size.[52] The 'Cartilla' was to continue the tradition of pattern drawings by Bausá, and Salvador Gómez must also have known Ribera's pattern etchings of 1622 (see below).

At about the same time Salvador Gómez made four drawings of *Saint Joseph and the Christ Child*, of which the British Museum version (fig. 13) is the most dynamic.[53] With his left knee on a plinth, Joseph swings his arms back to release the Christ Child into the hands of God the Father, who enters from the upper right. The figures of Joseph and God were based on Agostino Carracci's 1582 print, the *Temptation of Saint Anthony* after Tintoretto (fig. 14).[54] The complex interconnected perspective of the cross and plinth in the right foreground reflects Salvador Gómez's interest in the careful arrangement of each object, while the compass pinned to the cross draws attention to his accuracy. It is possible that he travelled to Italy, where he would no doubt have seen the architectural and perspective work of Michelangelo Cerquozzi and Viviano Codazzi.[55] These four drawings seem to be connected with the 'Cartilla', perhaps not explicitly to be included, but reflecting the artist's quest for an iconography appropriate to his subject. Each one contains a medallion for a coat of arms, probably that of the individual to whom the drawing was dedicated. The sheet now in Michigan is pricked for transfer but no engraving is known.

Although he was a prolific painter, very few of Salvador Gómez's drawings correspond to known paintings. It is possible that, given his role within the academy, the drawings were intended as iconographic examples for students rather than preparatory studies for his own work. His drawing of *Saint Francis of Assisi Embracing the Crucified Christ* (fig. 15), signed and

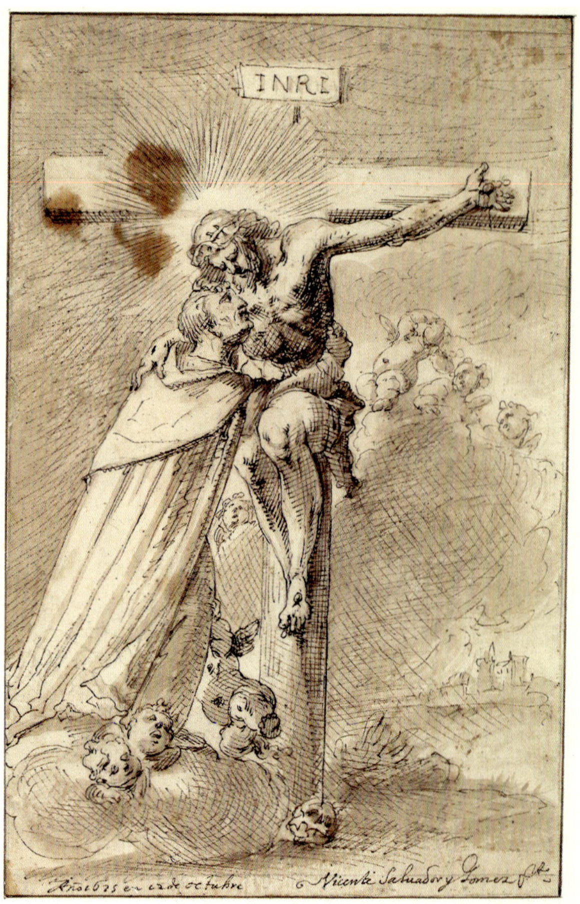

15
Vicente Salvador Gómez
Saint Francis of Assisi Embracing the Crucified Christ, 1675
Pen and brown ink and brown wash, 238 x 150 mm
British Museum, London
1846,0509.185

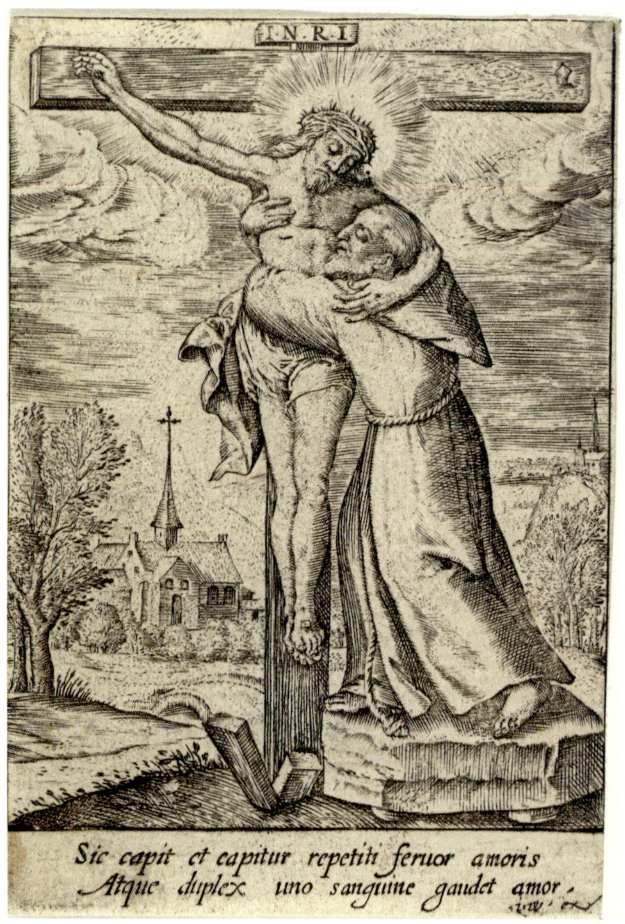

16
Wierix workshop
Saint Francis of Assisi Embracing the Crucified Christ, before 1585
Engraving, 82 x 54 mm
Rijksprentenkabinet, Rijksmuseum
RP-P-1904-1252

dated 12 October 1675, is a case in point. Salvador Gómez would have known Francisco Ribalta's painting of *Christ Embracing Saint Bernard* from around 1620 for the Capuchin monastery of Sangre de Cristo in Valencia, but differences between the two indicate that Ribalta was not the source.[56] A print from the Wierix workshop (fig. 16) seems much closer, although Salvador Gómez intensified the interaction between the saint and Christ by bringing their heads much closer together. His interest in prints can be seen from the inventory of his extensive library, drawn up after his death, which records a large number of examples by artists such as Dürer and Lucas van Leyden, as well as others with generic descriptions: 'trenta estampes fines de paper de diferents Sants and Santes usadas' or 'Metamorfosis de Ovidio con estampas'.[57]

A number of artists working in Valencia during the second half of the seventeenth century are known more from written records, such as those of the Valencian biographer Marcos Antonio de Orellana, than from what has remained of their work. For example, Orellana describes Mosén Domingo Saura (*c.*1650–1715) as follows:

> [he] was very inventive and studious, a great draughtsman whose diligence issued from his genius. He always carried on him the instruments to further his studies, and he made the most of those he had, since he was often in possession of inkpot, pencil, brush, paper, and even a saucer for colours, so that he would not miss the chance to draw any object worth drawing that appeared within sight. For this reason, whenever he went out to have a good time or to enjoy the company of his friends, they, aware of his talent, would ask him to draw something, and he, who could not help himself, would get out his pencils and other instruments to draw, either what appeared before him, or any episode from the life of the saint to whom he had been praying that day.... And being the said Saura so industrious, an endless number of drawings by his hand existed, and still exist, in Valencia.[58]

There is no reason to doubt Saura's dedication to drawing, but few can be identified with certainty today.[59] Orellana describes Saura's drawings of the Old Testament story of Queen Esther thus: 'King Ahasuerus [represented] in the act of proclaiming his decree, with Queen Esther fainting at the feet of the throne, falling in her maids' arms while the said king holds out his sceptre and his golden baton as a sign of mercy'.[60] Two drawings of this story believed to be by Saura entered the British Museum but were later reattributed.[61] That of *Queen Esther Fainting* (fig. 17) corresponds closely with Orellana's description. In view of their Spanish provenance, supported by Orellana's account and their similarity to known drawings by Saura, they are likely to be by him and reveal his refined use of pen and wash.[62]

Another little-known Valencian artist of evident ability, Agustín Gasull (active 1689–1710), is reported to have studied in Rome with Carlo Maratta.[63] *The Adoration of the Magi* (fig. 18), signed and dated 15 November 1689, is the only known sheet by him. The pen-and-wash technique of this drawing reflects the earlier practice of Francisco and Juan Ribalta and Pedro Orrente.

The most prolific draughtsman working in Valencia during the latter decades of the seventeenth century was Juan Antonio Conchillos y Falcó, one

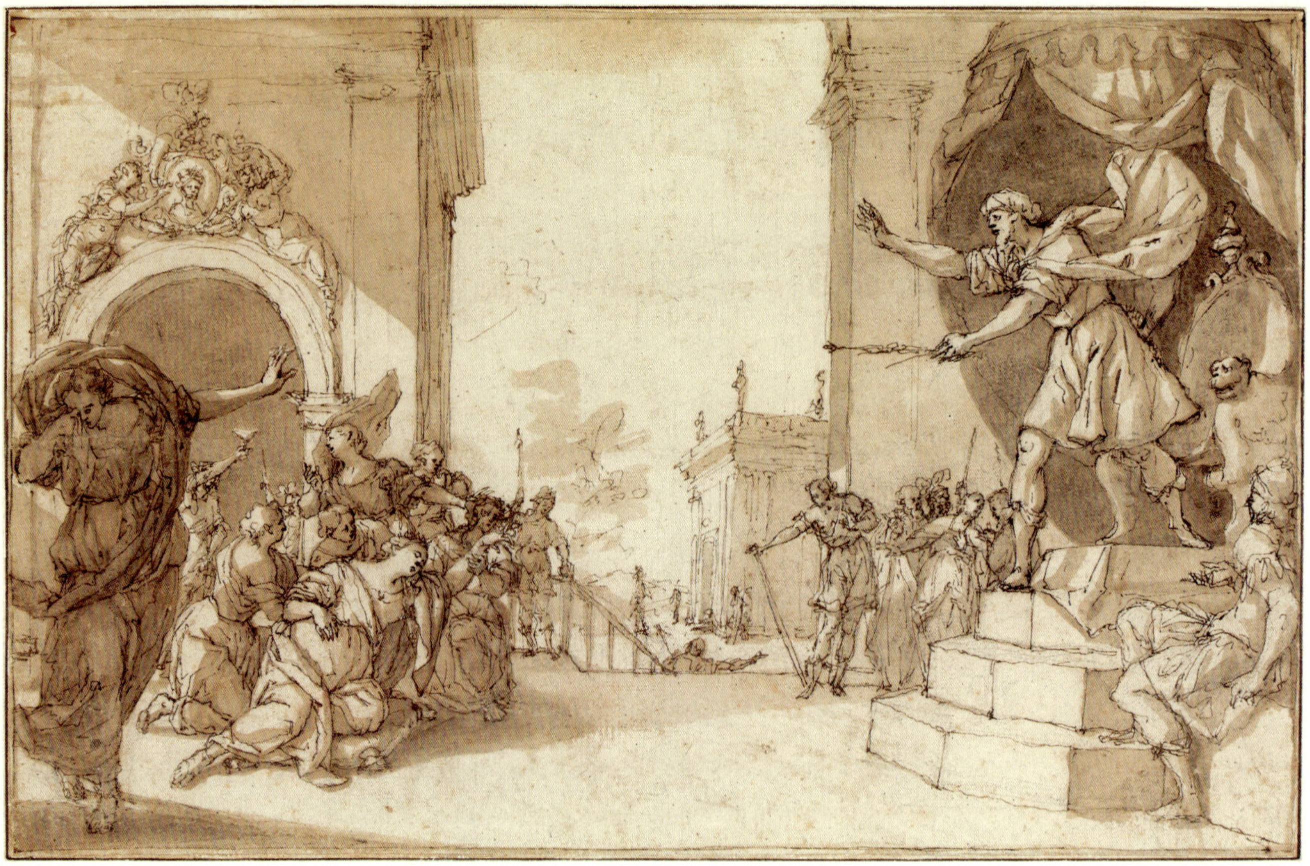

17
Mosén Domingo Saura
Queen Esther Fainting, *c.*1660–80
Pen and brown ink and brown wash over black chalk, 176 x 266 mm
British Museum, London
1846,0509.202

of the few Spanish artists better known for his drawings than for his paintings. After training with Esteban March he moved to Madrid where, supported by José García Hidalgo, he worked as a painter from 1662 to 1667. The exposure to collections at the court had a profound influence on his work; Palomino observes that when Conchillos returned to Valencia, he had 'very much improved in his colouring and no less so in drawing, for he attended very punctually and with great frequency the academies that existed then in the Court and copied the best paintings he could …'.[64] A number of Conchillos' sheets are dated late in his career, between 1691 and 1704; nothing is known of his drawing practice before the 1690s, but it is very unlikely that he only took it up at the age of fifty. He was previously active as a printmaker, as revealed by his etching of *The Lamentation of Christ* (fig. 19), signed and dated 1672.[65] The figure of Christ in the print reappears in two of Conchillos' drawings dated 1693 and 1703.[66]

Antonio Palomino describes Conchillos' drawing practice in detail, since it was such an important part of his activity:

> … he tried to establish an academy in Valencia, and he even had one for many years in his house where he was already of very advanced age, without missing a single evening's attendance and doing a figure in charcoal every night, so that he had innumerable ones, and for any invention that presented itself he would pull out a sheaf of academy figures and easily find what he needed and adjust it to his purpose, composing his story with very good nudes and handsome attitudes.[67]

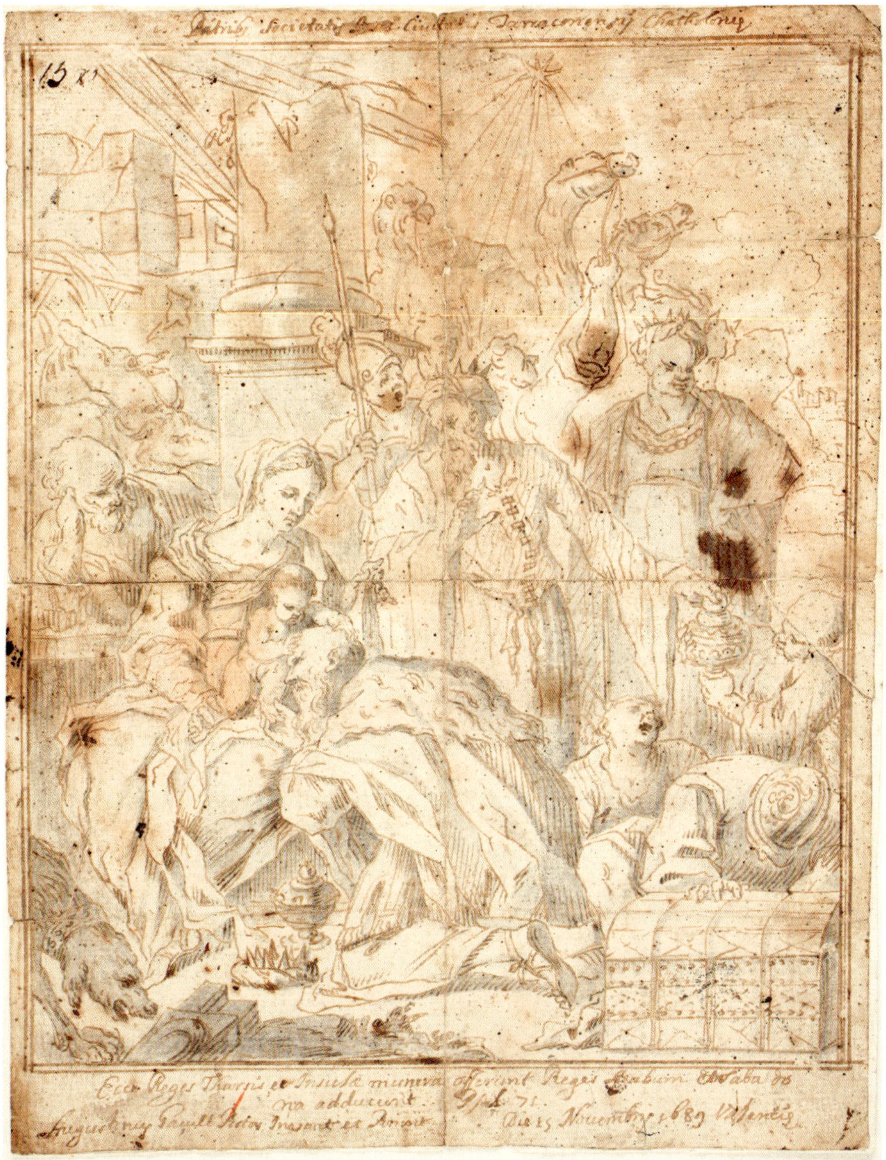

18
Agustín Gasull
The Adoration of the Magi, 1689
Pen and brown ink, brown and blue wash, 252 x 190 mm
Museo del Prado, Madrid
F.D.1194

19
Juan Antonio Conchillos y Falcó
The Lamentation of Christ, 1672
Etching, 120 x 162 mm
Biblioteca Nacional, Madrid
12887

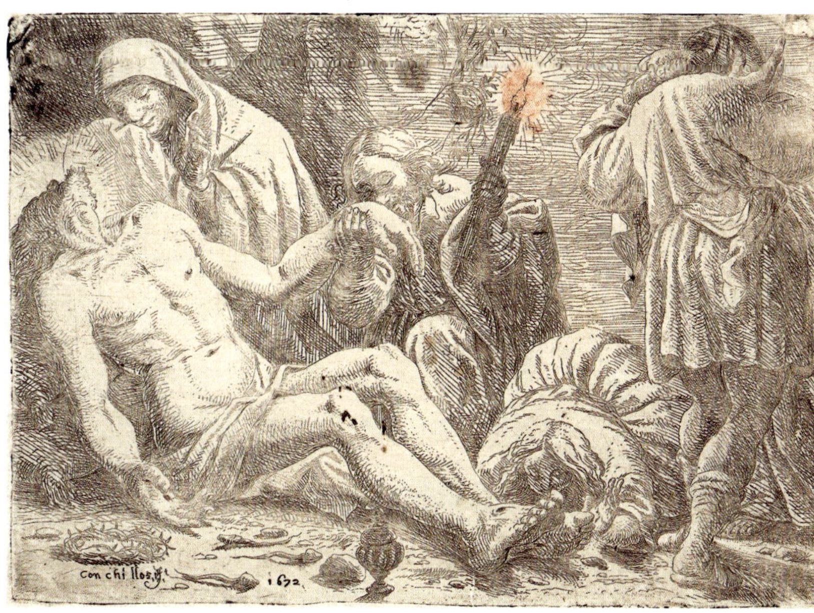

20
Juan Antonio Conchillos y Falcó

Study of a Partly Kneeling Male Nude, 1690–1705

Black charcoal and white chalk on blue prepared paper, 393 x 251 mm
British Museum, London
2011,7065.1

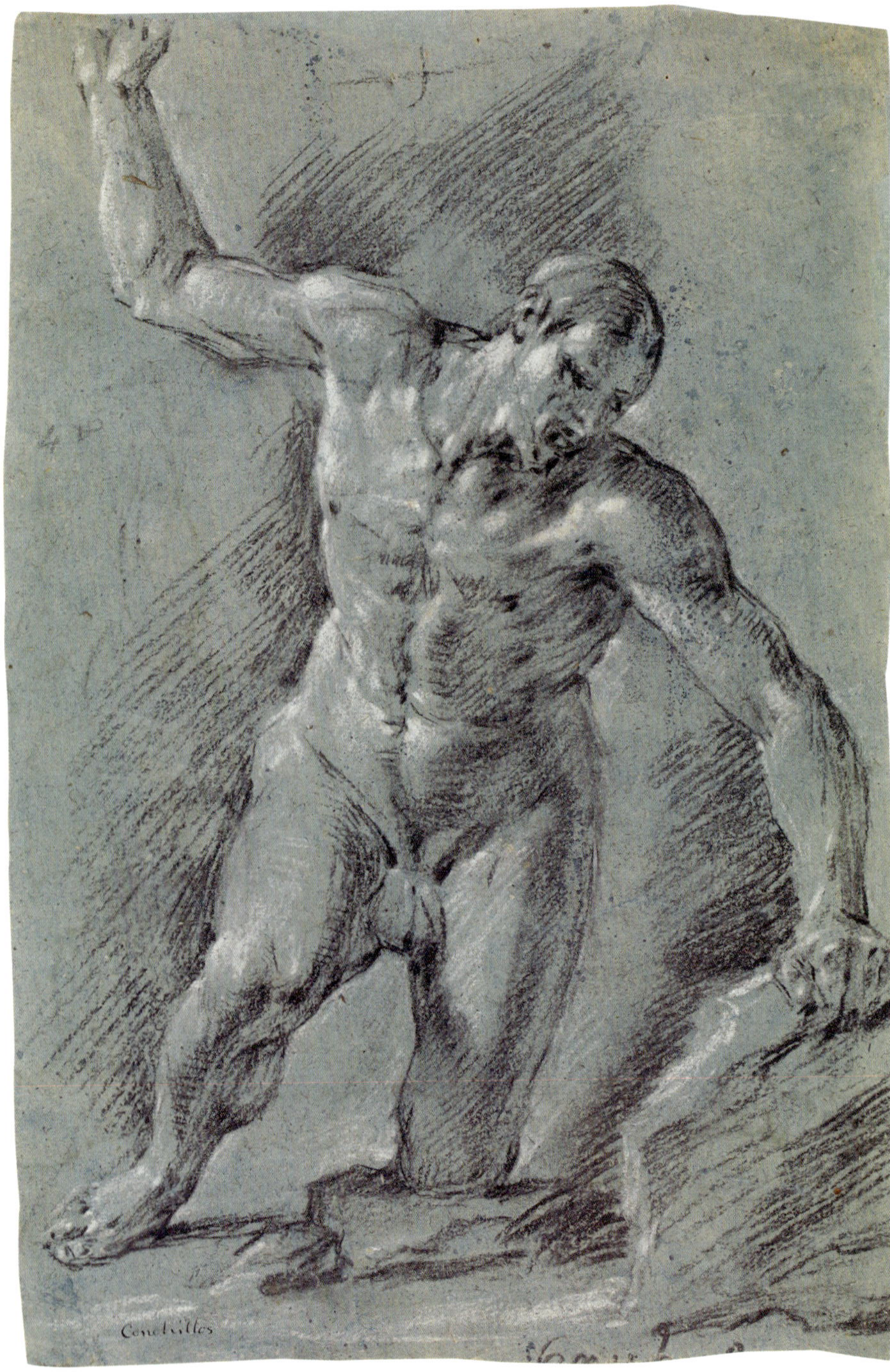

The fact that many of Conchillos' sheets have suffered damage seems to confirm this use of his drawings. His academic ambitions, like those of Salvador Gómez, might explain why after a certain date – when presumably he felt he had some standing as an artist – his drawings are carefully signed and dated. An example of the sort of sheet Palomino describes is the charcoal nude on blue prepared paper (fig. 20), an unevenly cut sheet with the remains of a date in the lower right corner.

Palomino also reports that Conchillos 'had great facility for doing wash drawings of whatever he had to or of any picturesque place he had seen'. He relates how they once met at a roadhouse near Valencia in 1697 and Conchillos made a wash drawing to show those present, including Palomino embracing his student Dionisio Vidal.[68] Another drawing by Conchillos from a group described by Palomino depicts a view of Paterna and the bridge over the river Tura from the village of Cuart de Poblet (fig. 21). Executed in pen and brown ink with pink and brown wash, the sheet is monogrammed and dated 15 October 1690 on a stone in the foreground.[69] Landscape drawings are uncommon in Spain until the eighteenth century (fig. 4, p. 194). All of Conchillos' landscape studies are similar in size and were made over at least a ten-year period from the early 1690s. They may have been part of a project to record the typography of the region of Valencia, hence the careful labelling of buildings and locations.

José de Ribera: printmaker and draughtsman

José (Jusepe) de Ribera (1591–1652) requires special attention here because of his outstanding activity as a draughtsman and printmaker. Born in Játiva, south of Valencia, according to Palomino he trained first with Francisco Ribalta.[70] There is neither stylistic nor documentary evidence to support this, but given that Ribalta was the most established artist working in Valencia during the period, Palomino's assertion has been generally accepted. Ribera was in Italy by 1611, visiting Parma and, from 1613, Rome, where his name appears in May 1616 on the roll of members of the Academy of Saint Luke. Later that year he settled in Naples, where he remained for the rest of his life:[71] Naples was at that time a Spanish territory governed by Viceroys.[72] Ribera often signed his works with his name followed by 'español', indicating pride in his origins and a continued identification with his homeland, which played well with Spanish patrons in Naples.

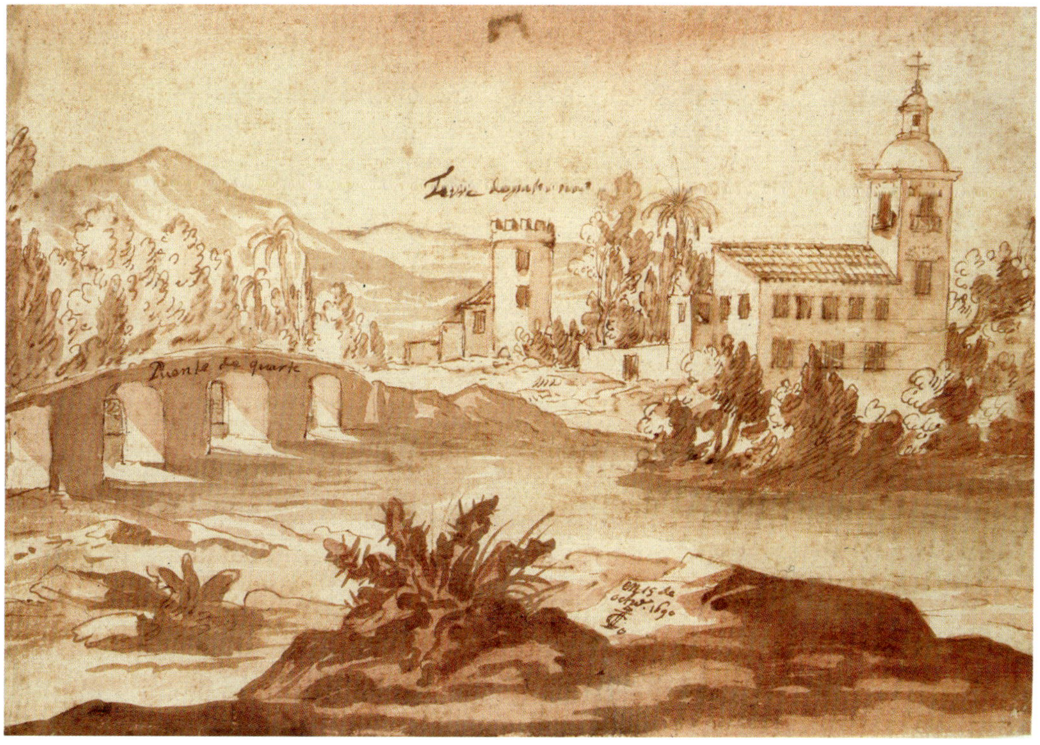

21
Juan Antonio Conchillos y Falcó
View of Paterna, 1690
Pen and brown ink and pink and brown wash, 210 x 290 mm
Museo de Bellas Artes, Valencia
38.A.E

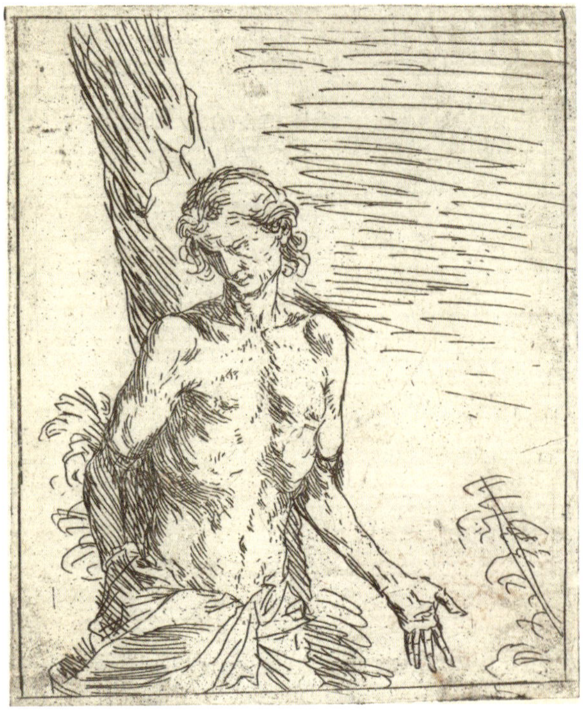

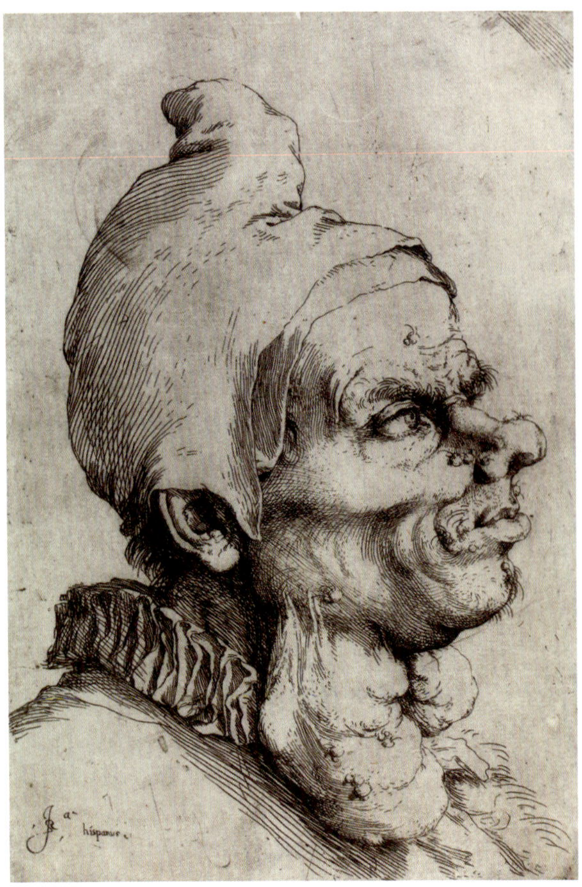

Ribera's prints and drawings have been well studied.[73] Rather than trying to identify distinctly Italian or Spanish characteristics in his graphic work, it is more important to note that his dedication to drawing and printmaking, as well the originality of his work, sets him apart from his peers in either country. His exposure to Italian drawing and printmaking practices had the greatest impact on his own endeavours. His career as printmaker was short lived; only eighteen etchings are known and, with the exception of one, all were made before 1630 and most of them from the early to mid-1620s. Although few in number, they display his inventiveness and skill and are regarded as among the most remarkable prints of the seventeenth century. Nothing specific is known to have inspired Ribera to take up etching. In a letter written in July 1635, his patron, the Duke of Alcalá, observed that the artist learned etching in Rome at the time the duke arrived there, in 1625.[74] The year is incorrect, because his earliest dated prints are from 1621, but that Rome was where he learnt to etch is entirely plausible. Printmaking here in the early decades of the seventeenth century was highly organized, with publishing houses serving an eager and ever-expanding market. The fact that most of Ribera's prints were made during a short period suggests that they were a way of making money at a time when he was establishing himself as an artist.

Ribera's earliest prints, *Saint Sebastian* (fig. 22) and *Saint Bernardino of Siena*, do not show the skill of an experienced artist: his use of the burin is very similar to his earliest pen-and-ink drawings of the early 1620s.[75] Both prints, which survive in few impressions, were experimental and probably made in 1613–16, either in Rome or shortly after Ribera settled in Naples. His first large-scale etched compositions, *Saint Jerome and the Trumpet* and the *Penitent Saint Peter*, both signed and dated 1621, mark the beginning of his serious engagement with printmaking.[76] The following year he made his first pattern prints for the instruction of students in the elements of drawing. He made just three of these – of eyes, mouths, noses and ears (fig. 19, p. 37). The print depicting ears is dated 1622, the year in which Ribera etched the *Small Grotesque Head*; its companion, the *Large Grotesque Head* (fig. 23), was made around the same time. Both seem to be related to Ribera's pattern prints and present types rather than portraits of specific individuals. But their striking appearance sets them apart from earlier pattern prints that rely entirely on didactic demonstrations of linear forms, shading or complete figures. Ribera's etching of *The Poet* (fig. 24) may have been intended as a title page for a proposed compilation, the face of the stone providing space for a title.[77] However, if Ribera's intention was to produce a pattern-book compilation, the project never reached completion for reasons that are not known; this is echoed by similar aborted projects by Pedro de Villafranca and Vicente Salvador Gómez.

Ribera etched *The Martyrdom of Saint Bartholomew* (fig. 25) in 1624, during his most intense period of printmaking.[78] It is his first multi-figured etched composition and his last print with a religious theme, and a subject to which Ribera returned to throughout his career in his drawings and paintings. Technically the *Martyrdom* is one of his most remarkable prints, with a wide variety of strokes and dots to convey diverse textures and surfaces. The print carries a dedication to Prince Philibert Emmanuel of Savoy, nephew of Philip III and Viceroy of Sicily from 1620. The practice of dedicating prints to prominent individuals was a way of flattering them to secure patronage.[79] The dynamic composition and the quality of this print would surely not have failed to impress, but whatever patronage Ribera hoped to gain was thwarted because the prince died on 4 August the same year.

There could be no greater contrast between Ribera's religious prints and his *Drunken Silenus* (fig. 26) of 1628.[80] The print, demonstrating Ribera's

22
José de Ribera
Saint Sebastian, c.1613–16
Etching, 89 x 70 mm
Rijksprentenkabinet, Rijksmuseum
RP-P-OB-21.267

23
José de Ribera
Large Grotesque Head, c.1622
Etching with engraving, 215 x 140 mm
British Museum, London
W,6.111

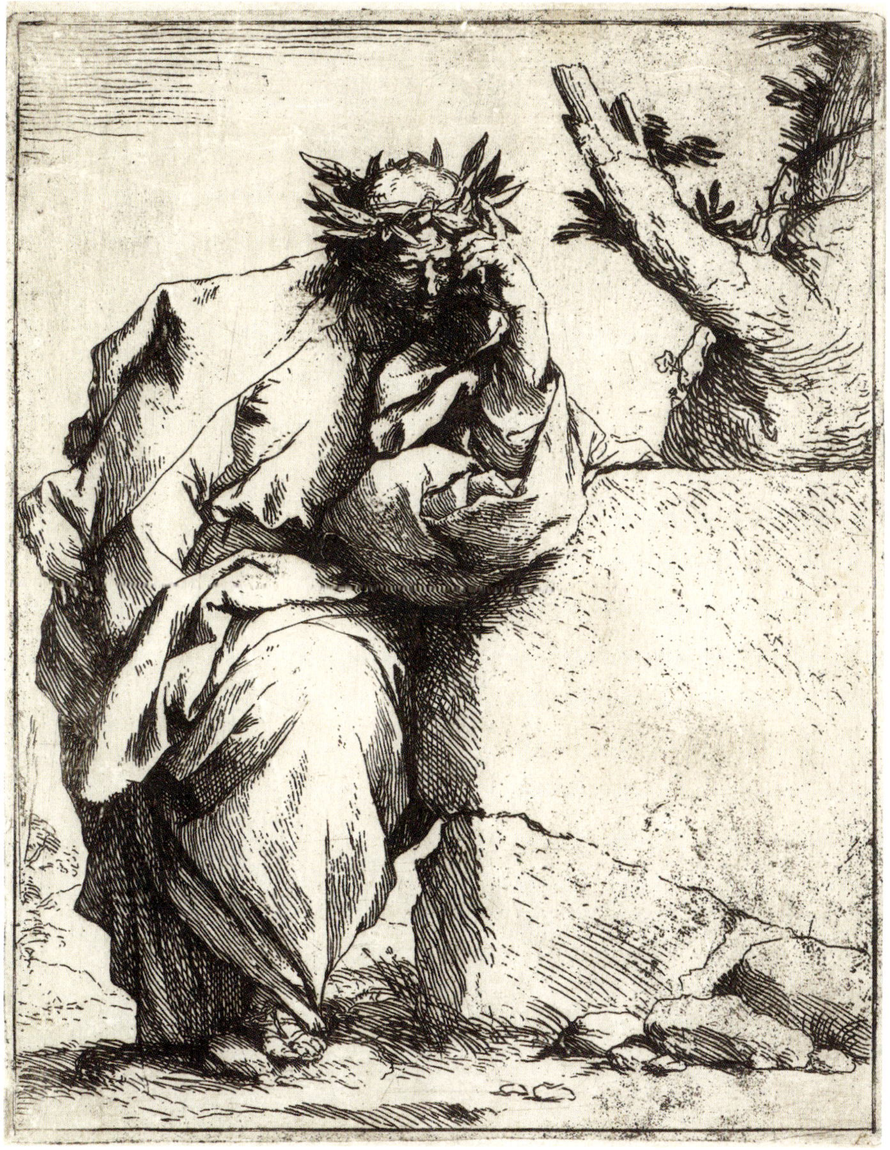

24
José de Ribera
The Poet, c.1620–1
Etching, 161 x 124 mm
British Museum, London
W,6.113

25
José de Ribera
The Martyrdom of Saint Bartholomew, 1624
Etching with engraving, 314 x 241 mm
British Museum, London
1874,0808.746

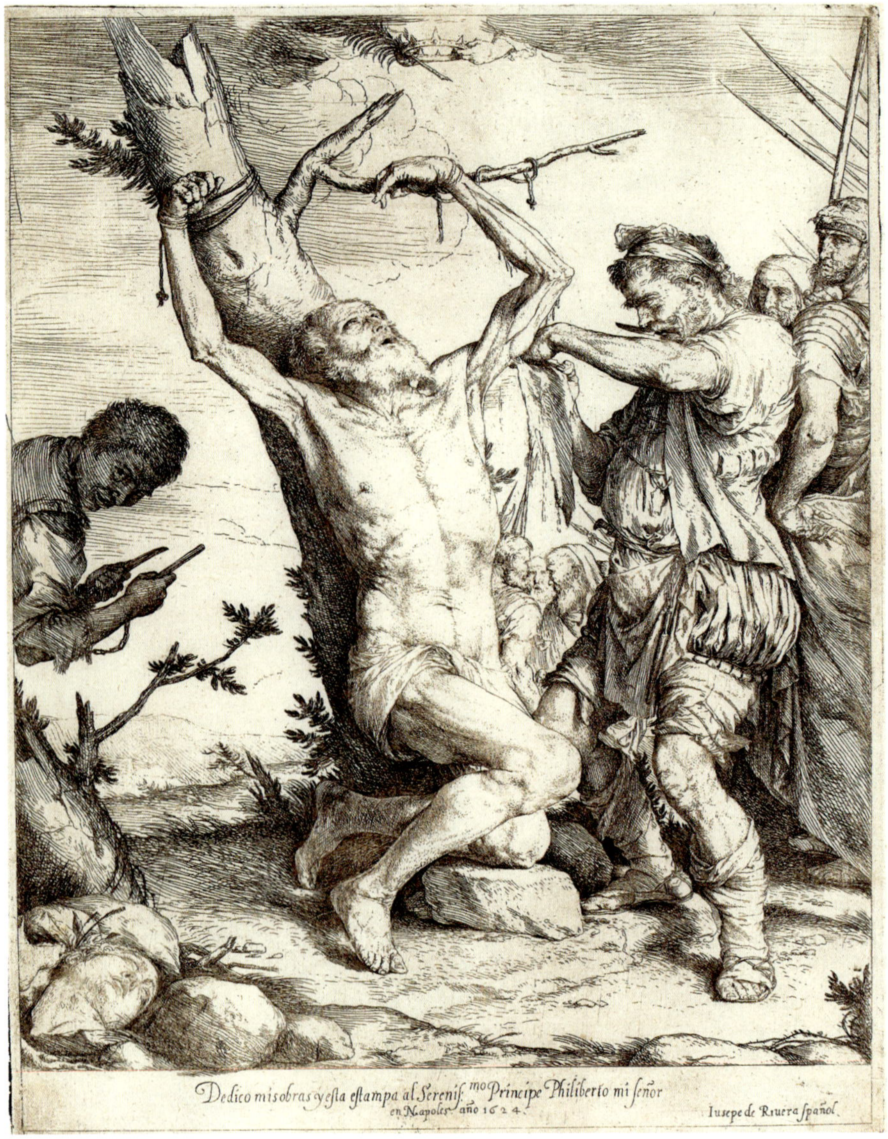

technical ability and his extraordinary powers of invention, is an adaptation of his 1626 painting for Neapolitan artist Giacomo de Castro (fig. 27). The print was so admired that two later editions were printed during the seventeenth century by the Roman publishers Giovanni Orlandi and Giovanni Rossi. For unknown reasons, *Silenus* was the last print he made for twenty years. Brown suggests that he may have taken up printmaking for no other reason than vanity, wishing his art to become better known.[81] His decision to stop printmaking might be explained if that strategy then failed. Yet Ribera's prints demonstrate his commitment to developing his technique to a virtuoso level – not the attitude of an artist who had no more than a shallow interest in the medium. The 1630s were Ribera's busiest decade as a painter, and it seems most likely that he turned his back on printmaking because painting consumed all his energies and was more profitable.

The *Equestrian Portrait of Don Juan of Austria* (fig. 28), dated 1648, marks Ribera's return to printmaking and demonstrates that his ability had in no way diminished. The print commemorates the arrival in Naples in October 1647

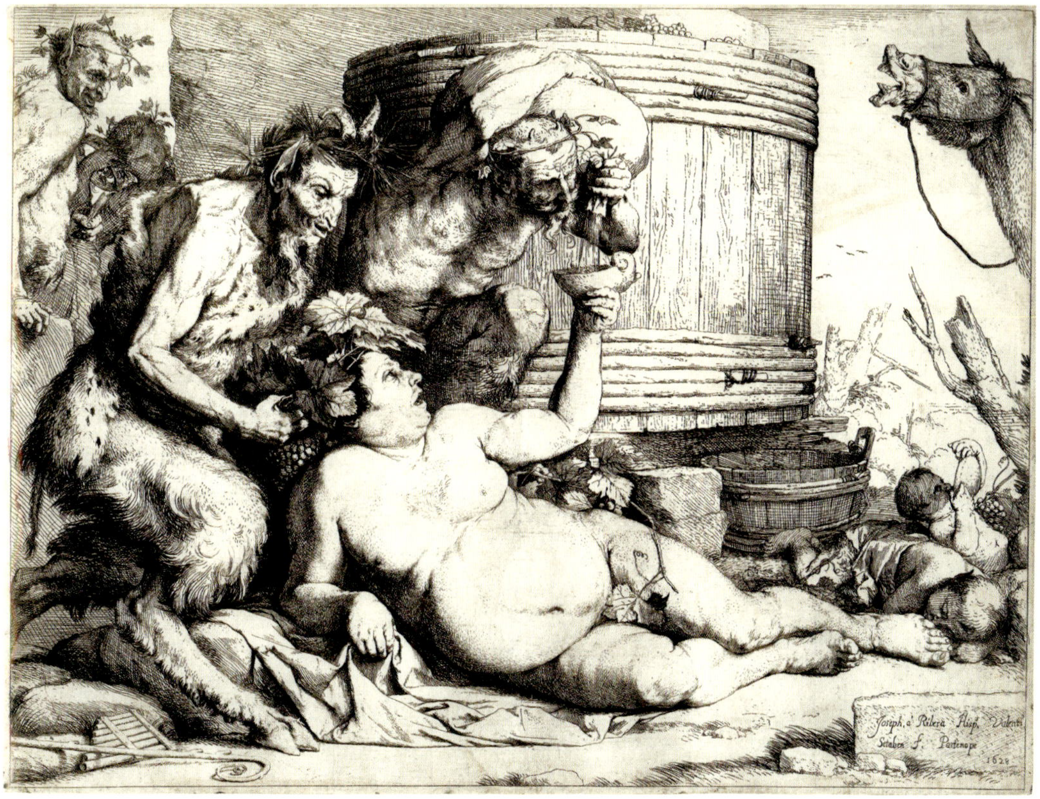

26
José de Ribera
The Drunken Silenus, 1628
Etching with engraving,
274 x 349 mm
British Museum, London
1862,0712.534

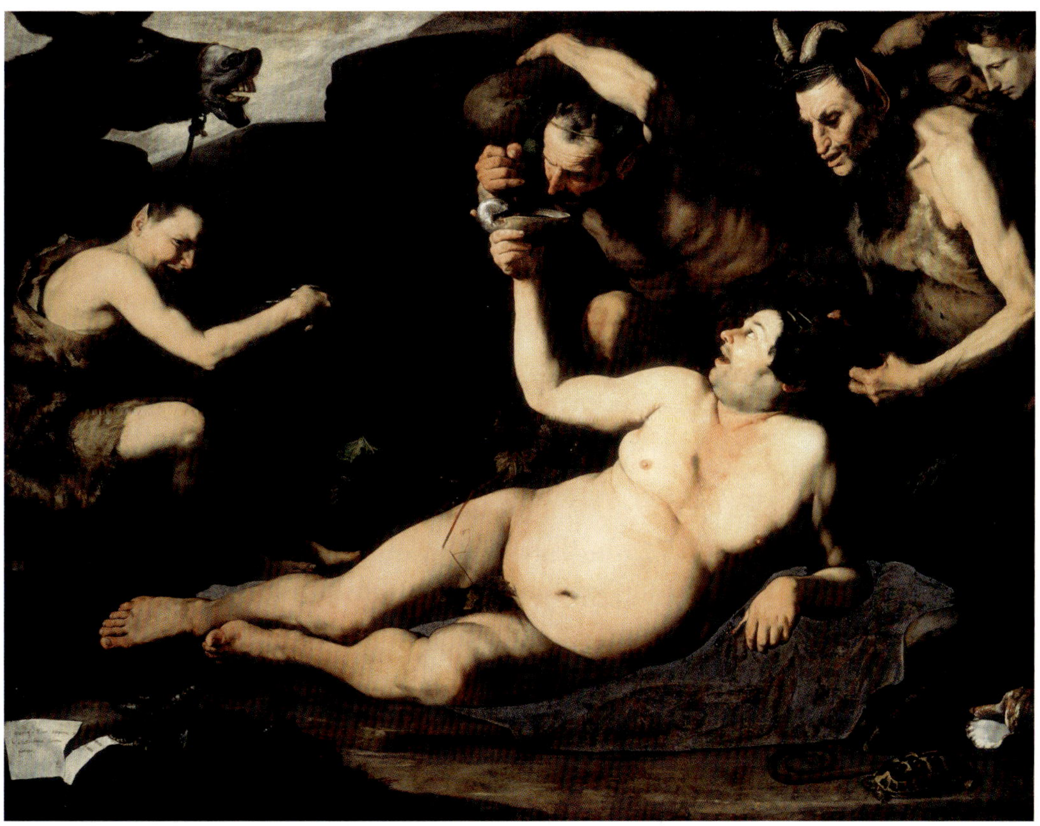

27
José de Ribera
The Drunken Silenus, 1626
Oil on canvas,
1810 x 2290 mm
Museo e Gallerie Nazionale
di Capodimonte, Naples
298

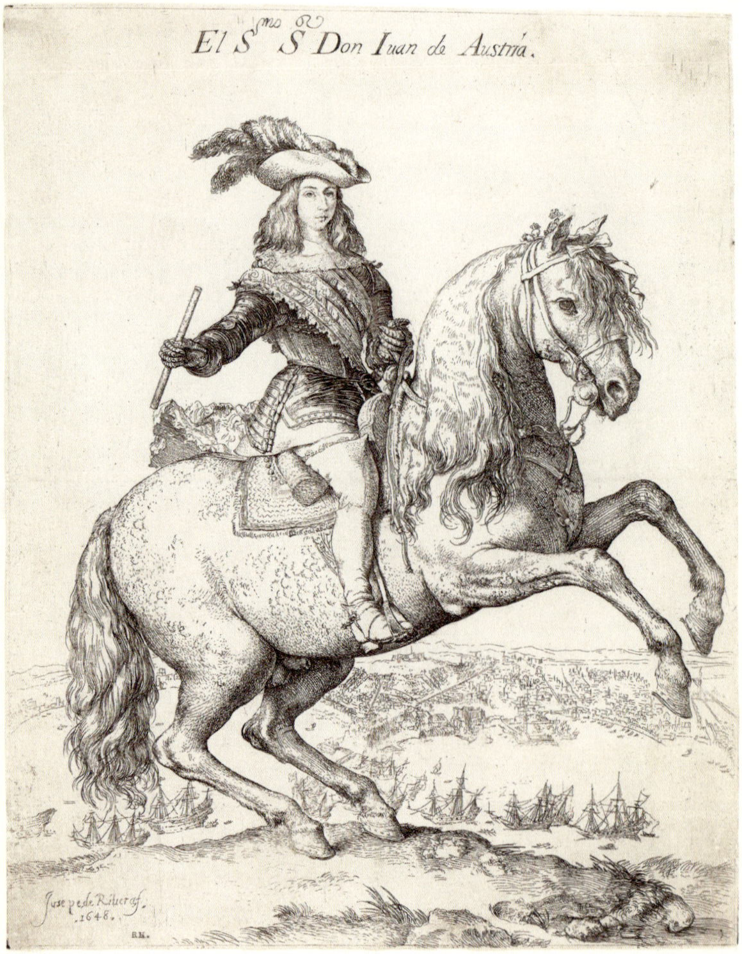

28
José de Ribera
Equestrian Portrait of Don Juan of Austria, 1648
Etching, 350 x 270 mm
British Museum, London
W,6.92

of Don Juan of Austria, the illegitimate son of Philip IV, accompanied by twenty-two Spanish galleons to quell the rioting Neapolitans. The revolution, led by Tomasso Aniello da Amalfi (Masianello), had begun on 7 July prompted by the pressures of increased taxation and inflation. The print is related to a painting now in the Royal Palace, Madrid, commissioned by Don Juan that shows him on a rearing horse, a formula that had long been used to assert the authority of the sitter and reflect notions of good government. The print follows the composition of the painting but considerably opens up the background, including much more detail in order to give a precise historical context. The fleet is anchored in the bay and the buildings along the shoreline can be identified: the Castel San Martino, the Royal Palace, Arsenal, and the Torre di San Vicenzo. At the extreme right is the Piazza Mercato, the hub of the anti-Spanish revolt. As Ribera's last-known print, this marks an end to his remarkable career as a printmaker.

Whereas Ribera's printmaking activity was sporadic, he produced drawings throughout his career. Over a hundred have been identified as by him, and more continue to emerge.[82] The extent to which Ribera drew as an independent, formal exercise is becoming increasingly clear. Many of his sheets are not related to his paintings or prints, and their unconventional subjects suggest that for him drawing was a means to explore themes not suited to other media. Little is known of his early drawings; several sheets have been dated to the 1620s when he was already in his thirties. His drawing activity is mentioned by biographers such as Bernardo De Dominici, who in his *Lives of the Neapolitan Painters, Sculptors and Architects* (1742–5) wrote:

> in the evening he also used to made drawings of what he would paint the following day, and, as soon as he had decided what he wanted to do, he made finished drawings either in pen or with wash and watercolour, and more often with red chalk, although sometimes he used black chalk. And then he painted that figure from a live model … His continuous study [of drawing] is witnessed by the large number of drawings that can be found.[83]

Although De Dominici was writing almost a century after Ribera's death, from the evidence we have his account seems credible. His comments relate specifically to Ribera's finished drawings, in which category the majority of his red chalk sheets, for example, belong. Several of these were owned by Ceán Bermúdez, who described them as 'leaving nothing to be desired'.[84]

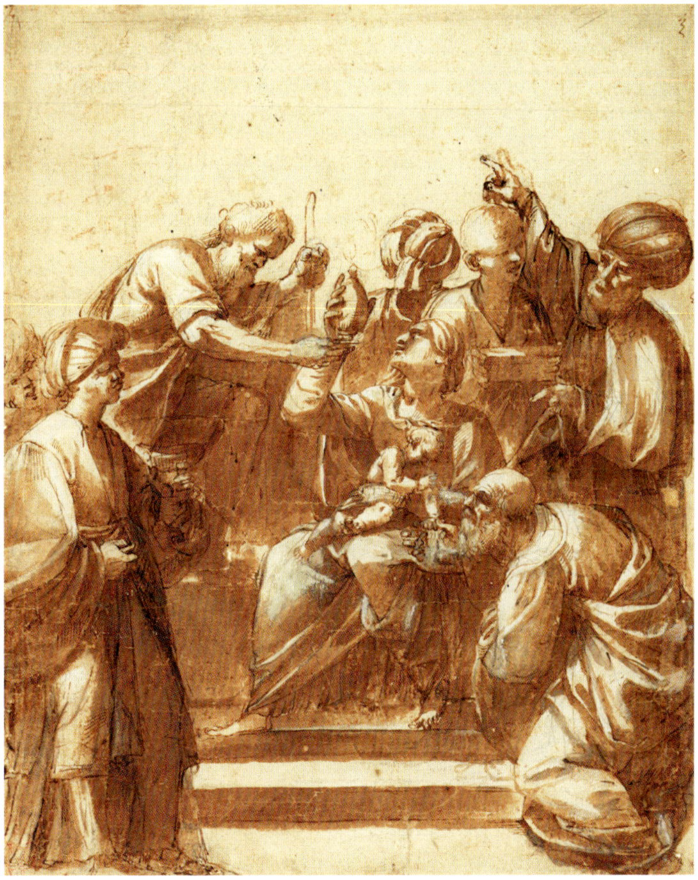

29
José de Ribera
The Adoration of the Magi, *c.*1613–18
Pen and brown ink and brown wash over black chalk, heightened with white, 278 x 219 mm
The J. Paul Getty Museum, Los Angeles
97.GG.52

30
José de Ribera
The Martyrdom of Saint Bartholomew, *c.*1620–4
Pen and brown ink, 133 x 100 mm
British Museum, London
T,13.111

31
José de Ribera
Tityus or Prometheus, *c.*1620–5
Pen and brown ink and wash, 227 x 165 mm
British Museum, London
1937,1008.29

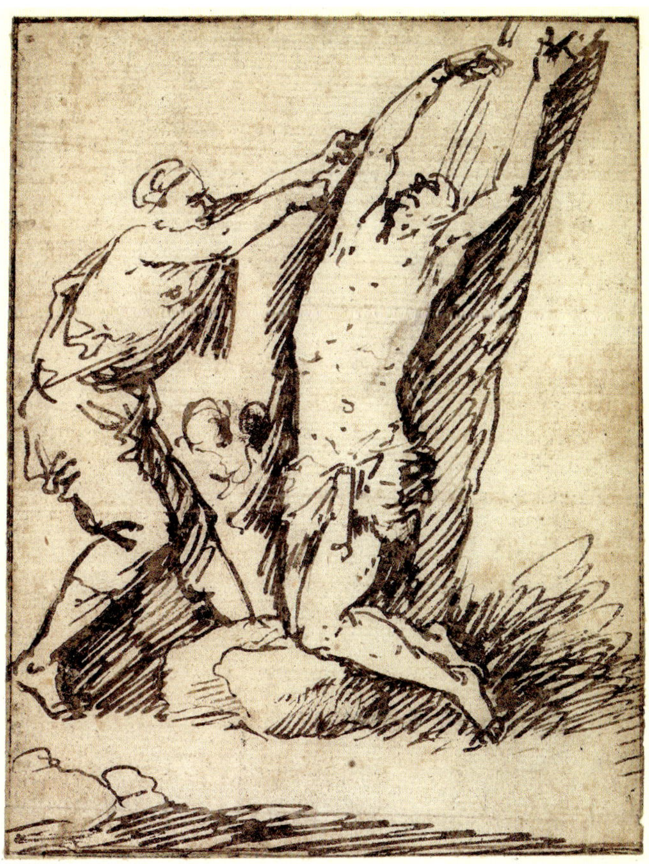

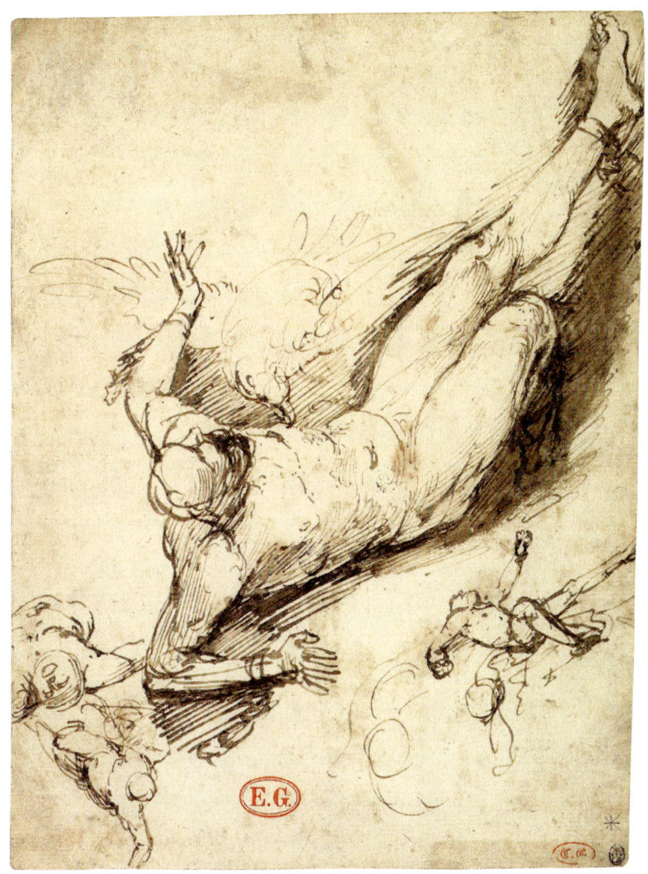

Ribera's earliest-known drawing is *The Adoration of the Magi* of around 1613–18 (fig. 29).[85] Executed in pen and brown ink and brown wash over black chalk, the carefully arranged composition contains the unusual motif of a background figure shown from behind, turning away from the Virgin and Child. More evidence of his work as a draughtsman comes in the 1620s. The pen and ink *Martyrdom of Saint Bartholomew* (fig. 30) is his preliminary study for the central figures in his 1624 etching discussed above, although the differences are significant, indicating that the drawing was made at an early stage, while he was still exploring the subject. There is far greater physical tension in the drawing, as the saint strains against the ropes binding him to the tree while the executioner uses his full weight to strip away his skin. In the print, resigned to his fate, the saint gazes toward heaven and receives the crown of martyrdom. Several of Ribera's drawings of around the same time focus on individual figures. For example, the main figure in *Tityus or Prometheus* (fig. 31) is surrounded by other studies that, viewed from different angles, appear to be tumbling in space, an effect Ribera achieved through turning the sheet to work on it from different sides.

During the 1620s Ribera made highly finished red chalk drawings in the Italian tradition of chalk drawing as an independent exercise. Signed and dated 1626, *A Saint (Albert?) Tied to a Tree*, is one of his most remarkable sheets, made toward the end of his first decade in Naples (fig. 32 and detail p. 162). Another red chalk drawing from around the same time, *Christ Beaten by a Tormentor* (fig. 33), seems to have been inspired by Annibale Carracci's 1606 etching of the same subject.[86] While it is not entirely clear why Ribera made these finished drawings, there is no doubt that they demonstrate his brilliance as a draughtsman. The signature, date and annotation 'fecit' ('made this') commonly appear on prints, and Ribera might have had this in mind. Furthermore, the verso of

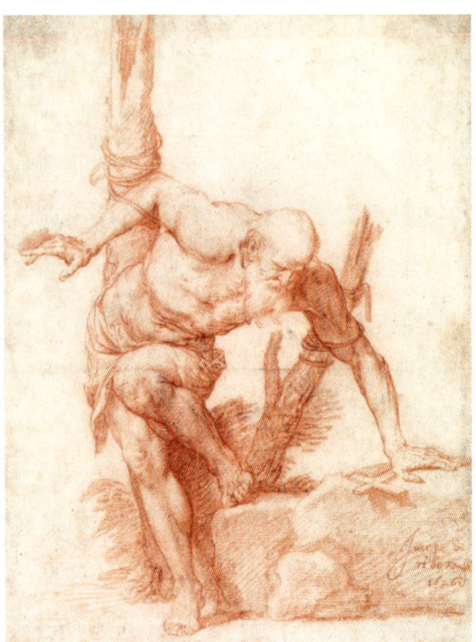

32
José de Ribera
A Saint (Albert?) Tied to a Tree, 1626
Red chalk, 232 x 170 mm
British Museum, London
1850,0713.4

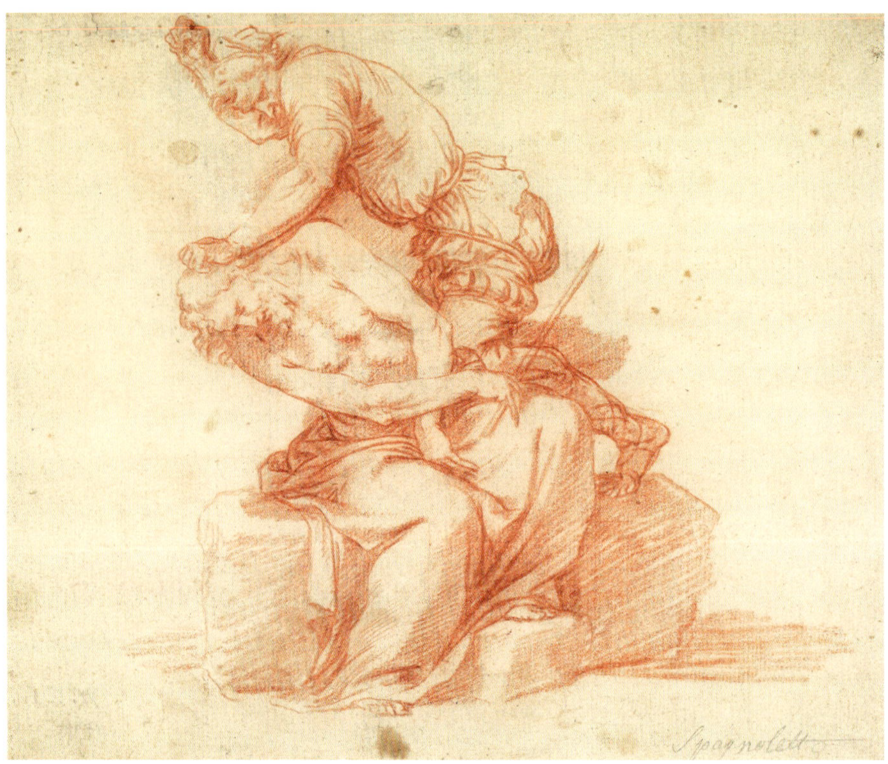

33
José de Ribera
Christ Beaten by a Tormentor, c.1625–30
Red chalk, 184 x 215 mm
British Museum, London
1946,0713.1411

Christ Beaten by a Tormentor is blackened with chalk, suggesting that its design was intended for transfer, for a print or to make a copy. Ribera's interest in finished chalk drawings seems to have been short lived; his later drawings in the medium are executed more quickly.

The 1620s through to the mid-1630s were Ribera's most productive years, during which he explored a great variety of subjects in different media through drawing. Many of these drawings cannot be linked to a painting and are difficult to date, and a number of them depict some of the bizarre, barbaric or grotesque subjects found also in his etchings, the product of his fertile imagination.[87] The *Oriental Potentate Accompanied by his Halberd Bearer* (fig. 34) of about 1625–30, drawn in vivid carmine ink (possibly from cochineal), demonstrates his skilful creation of an engaging and somewhat humorous character through the economical use of line. His interest in caricature fits with the work of late sixteenth- and early seventeenth-century artists in Rome and Bologna, including the Carracci, Pier Francesco Mola and Guercino.

Ribera also uses his drawings to explore extreme physical conditions and violence. A sense of impending violence is palpable in his *Saint (Albert?) Tied to a Tree*, while his *Christ Beaten by a Tormentor* is a more direct image of suffering. One of his most brutal images from the mid-1630s shows a man tied by his arms and legs and stretched between stakes, about to be split by an axe. Another shows a victim suspended from gallows by his hands, resulting in dislocated shoulders, while two men, probably priests, address him from below.[88] These images have been explained as reflecting the reality of daily life in Naples, but Ribera also carried this over into his religious paintings (such as Saint Bartholomew). In keeping with the counter-reformation emphasis on encouraging the viewer to reflect on the suffering of saints, Ribera no doubt regarded violence as an appropriate means of conveying emotional intensity.[89]

From about 1640 Ribera's activity as a draughtsman diminished, probably due to his declining health. From this point cursory penmanship and a greater dependency on wash becomes increasingly noticeable in his drawings:[90] his *Adoration of the Shepherds* and the *Martyrdom of Saint Bartholomew*, on which someone later inscribed his name and the date 1649, both show this looser style.[91] Ribera's commitment to drawing and its range sets him apart from his Neapolitan contemporaries. At the end of seventeenth century Filippo Baldinucci wrote that Ribera was made the head of the Academy of Saint Luke in Rome because he was such an able draughtsman.[92] This assertion was in fact incorrect, but it does demonstrate the high regard in which Ribera was held by his peers in an area of artistic practice regarded as a measure of quality.

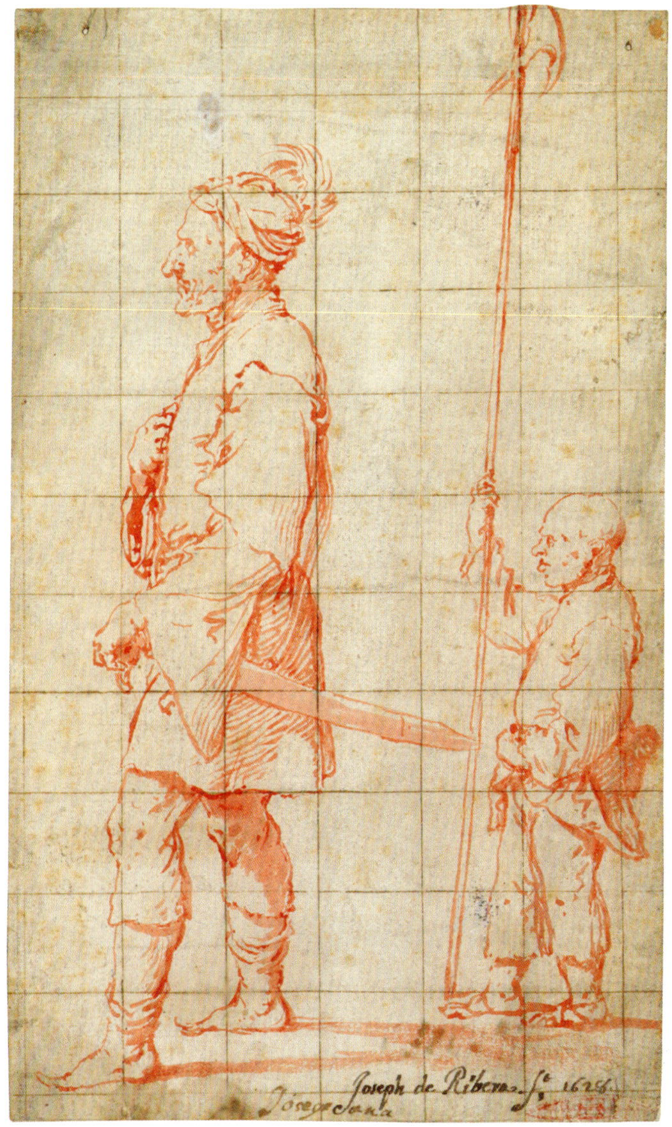

34
José de Ribera
An Oriental Potentate Accompanied by his Halberd Bearer, c.1625–30
Brush and carmine ink, squared for transfer, 231 x 139 mm
The J. Paul Getty Museum, Los Angeles
91.GA.56

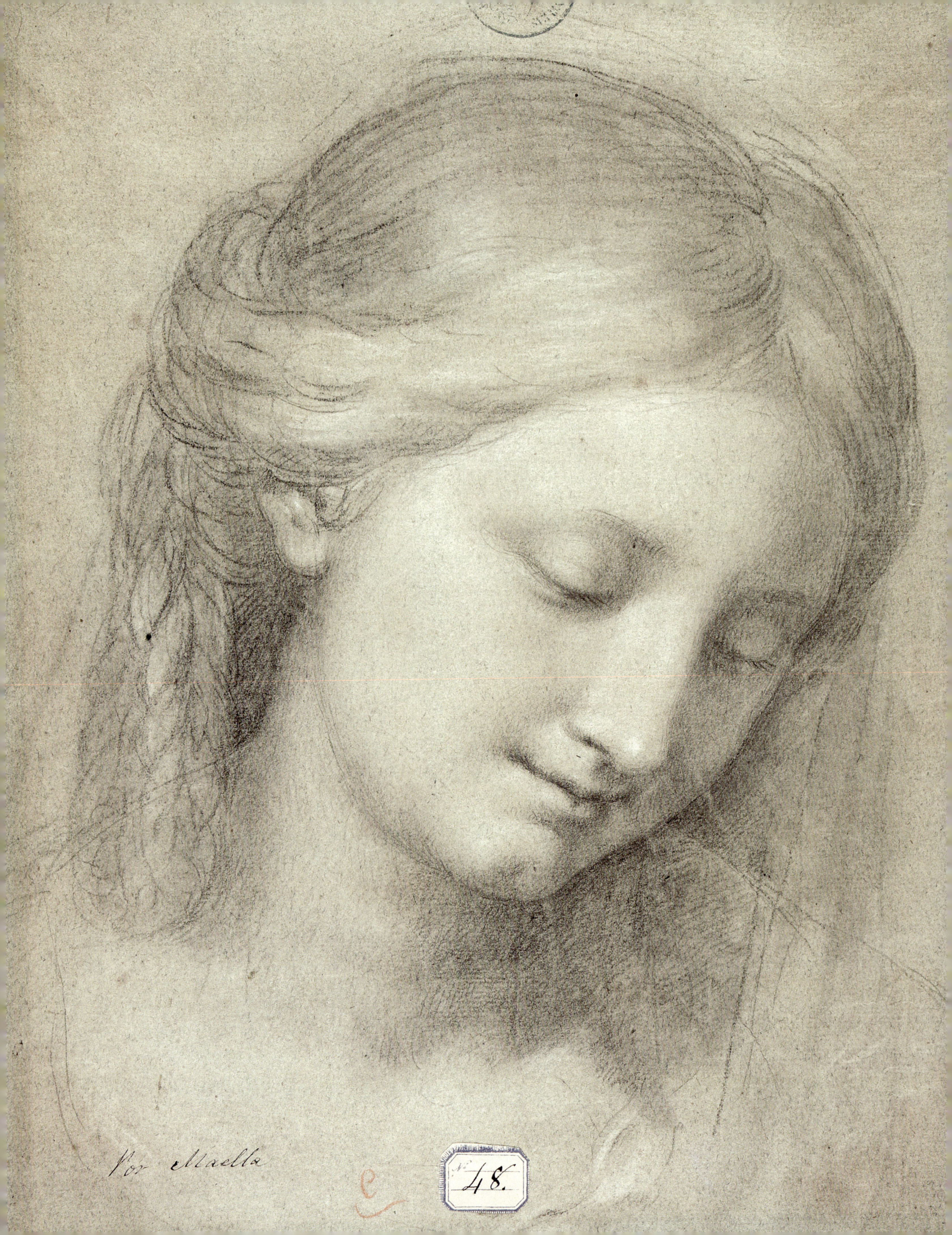
Por Maella
Nº 48.

CHAPTER 7

The eighteenth-century reinvention of the graphic arts

Discussion of art in Spain during the eighteenth century is generally separated into two halves. The first is focused on the court in Madrid and the prevailing French and Italian taste up to 1750, and the second on the emergence of new styles and artists, the most important of whom is Francisco de Goya.[1] Whereas Goya's graphic work forms a corpus unequalled amongst his peers, the artistic context from which he emerged is sometimes not given due credit.[2] The fact is that the development of prints and drawings during the eighteenth century in Spain transformed graphic practices, giving them a much wider cultural significance than is often acknowledged.

Philip V was the first Bourbon and the longest-serving king in the history of modern Spain. He came to the throne in 1700 and married his first wife, Princess María Luisa of Savoy, in 1701; after her death he married Isabel de Farnesio (Elisabetta Farnese) in 1714. Philip was strongly influenced by Louis XIV's taste and wished to replicate the French court style in Madrid. As the aesthetic ambitions of monarchs were expressed through the artists they employed to renovate and decorate their residences,[3] the accession of the Bourbon monarchy was one of a number of factors that brought about artistic change in Madrid – and throughout Spain. Another factor was the deaths of major late seventeenth-century Spanish artists and their followers, such as Claudio Coello in Madrid (1693) and Murillo in Seville (1682), which resulted in a scarcity of native artists able to continue their traditions.

Printmaking during the first half of the eighteenth century continued to suffer from the absence of an apprenticeship system. Prints were mainly made for book illustrations and, with few exceptions, were not of high quality. In Madrid the printing presses were generally old and worn, and the change in monarchy did little to improve the situation. However, printmaking during the second half of the century underwent dramatic transformation, reflecting Enlightenment attitudes and a new awareness of its significance and potential uses. The range of subjects represented in both prints and drawings greatly expanded and the pattern prints, devotional images and records of processions of the previous century were augmented by scientific and anatomical illustration, architectural, costume, landscape, popular and reproductive prints, leading to a national manifestation of eighteenth-century modernity.[4] The epicentre of this visual revolution was Madrid, as the regional centres failed to maintain the importance they had achieved during the previous century.

Drawings and prints *c.*1700–1750

Drawings of the first half of the eighteenth century can broadly be divided into two categories, work that continued the high baroque style and work that

Fig. 22, see p. 206

1
José Benito de Churriguera
Elevation and Plan for the Retable of Saint Francis Xavier in Nuevo Baztán, c.1709–13
Pen with brown and black ink, grey and brown wash over black chalk, 530 x 250 mm
Museo del Prado, Madrid
D.3904

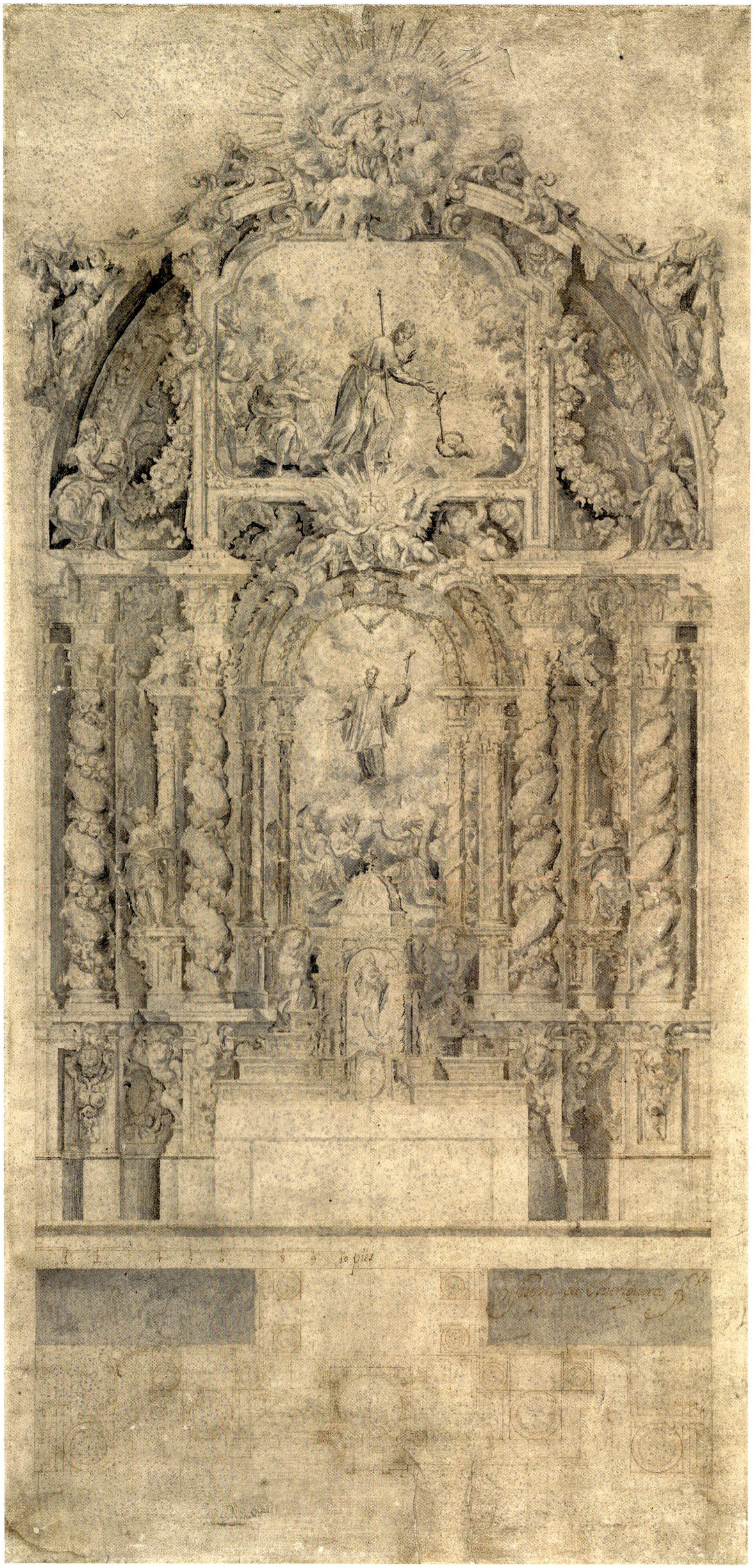

reflected the change in artistic sensibilities brought about by the arrival of the Bourbon court.[5] The two most significant artists working in the baroque style in Madrid were almost exact contemporaries José Benito de Churriguera (1665–1725) and Teodoro Ardemans (1664–1726).

Churriguera's architectural projects, some of which are only known through drawings, show his highly ornate style.[6] He worked mainly for private clients; but one of his few royal commissions (for Charles II), was the catafalque for María Luisa de Orleans in 1689, installed in the church of the Encarnación in Madrid (for which Antonio Palomino also submitted a design, fig. 48, p. 111). Churriguera's catafalque is recorded in an engraving by Francisco Ignatio for the published account of the exequies by Juan de Vera Tassis y Villarroel (fig. 61, p. 119). Churriguera's most significant private client was Juan de Goyeneche, who sponsored building projects in the town of Nuevo Baztán, south-east of Madrid. The elevation and plan for the high altar in the church of San Francisco Xavier (Nuevo Baztán) of around 1709–13 encapsulates Churriguera's architectural style and drawing process.[7] Executed in wash over pen and ink, it depicts the decorative programme of the altarpiece, including the position and subject of the paintings and a scaled floor-plan in the bottom part of the sheet (fig. 1). The drawing is not entirely preparatory, although it might have provided a point of reference for its construction. Its purpose is to preserve the design presented to the client for approval.

The lesser-known Teodoro Ardemans trained as a painter with Antonio de Pereda and probably also Claudio Coello, but throughout his career he worked mainly as an architect.[8] Continuing the pattern of professional versatility of earlier artists such as Francisco Rizi and Sebastian de Herrera Barnuevo, Ardemans devised royal entries and funeral exequies. He designed and decorated entry arches in Madrid for Mariana of Neuburg in 1690, Philip V in 1701 and the exequies of Louis XIV in 1715.[9] From early in his career Ardemans also prepared book illustrations. He is named as designer of an allegorical portrait of Charles II, on the title page to the *Historia de la Conquista de México* (1684) by Antonio de Solís, and two decades later of an equestrian portrait of Philip V engraved by Gerard Edelinck for the *Sucesión del Rey D Felipe V* (1704).[10] Ardemans amassed a considerable library and a rich collection of prints and drawings.[11]

The majority of Ardemans' drawings are signed and relate to architectural projects in Madrid and nearby towns. Their careful execution demonstrates that drawing was key to planning, realizing and documenting such structures.[12] One of his most striking sheets records a project from around the first decades of the century for the exaltation of Saint Francis of Assisi (fig. 2), probably inspired by a print of Bernini's chair of Saint Peter in the Vatican.[13] It is difficult to imagine Ardemans' drawing representing an actual structure; it was possibly made for a print, a painting or a large scenographic screen connected with the celebration.[14]

Most of the French artists called to the court in Madrid had been trained at the Royal Academy of Painting and Sculpture in Paris. The most influential in Spain were Michel-Ange Houasse (1680–1730), who arrived in 1715; Jean Ranc (1674–1735), who arrived in 1722; and Louis-Michel van Loo (1707–71), who arrived in 1737 and stayed until until 1752.[15] Ranc and Van Loo participated in discussions over the creation of the Academy of San

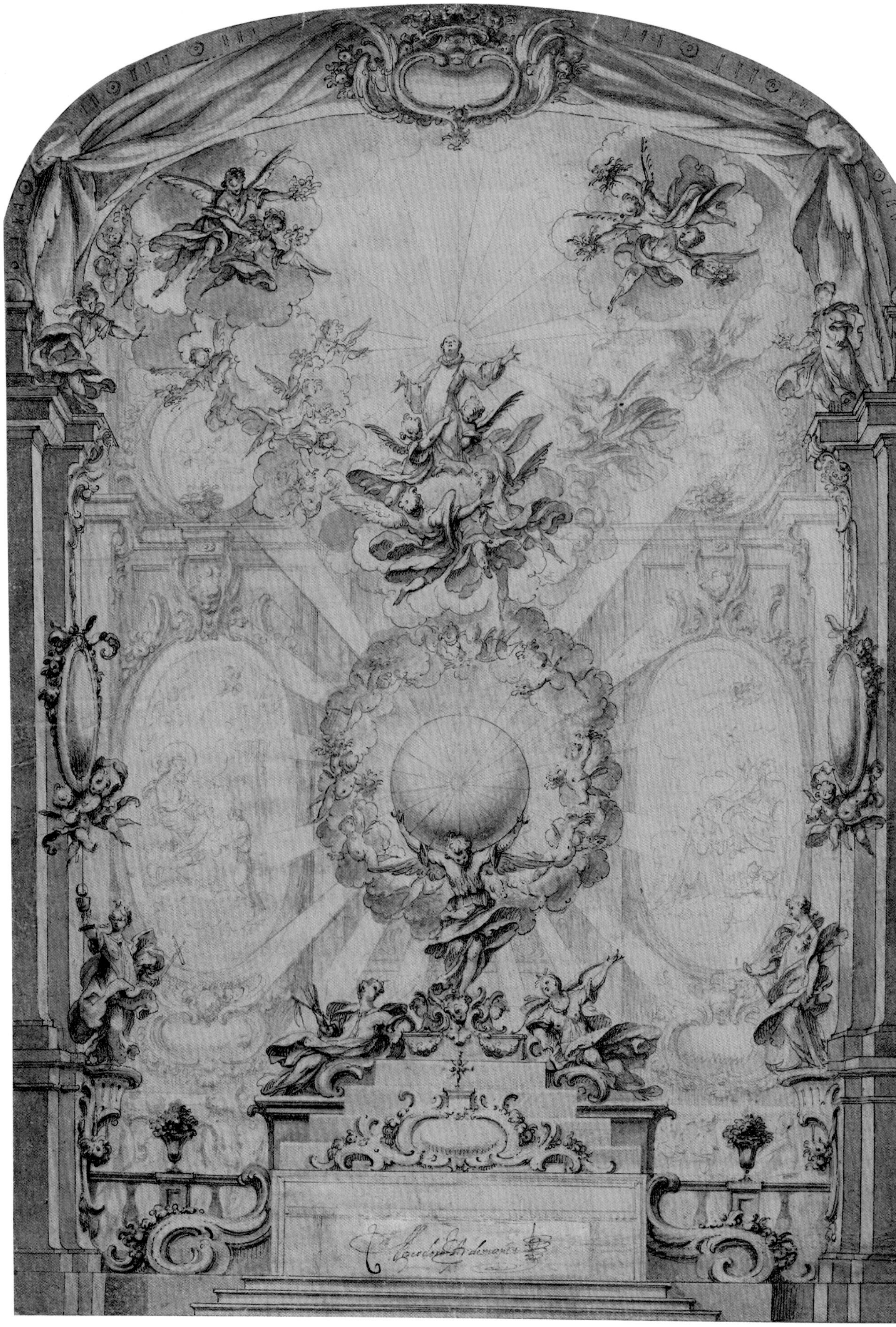

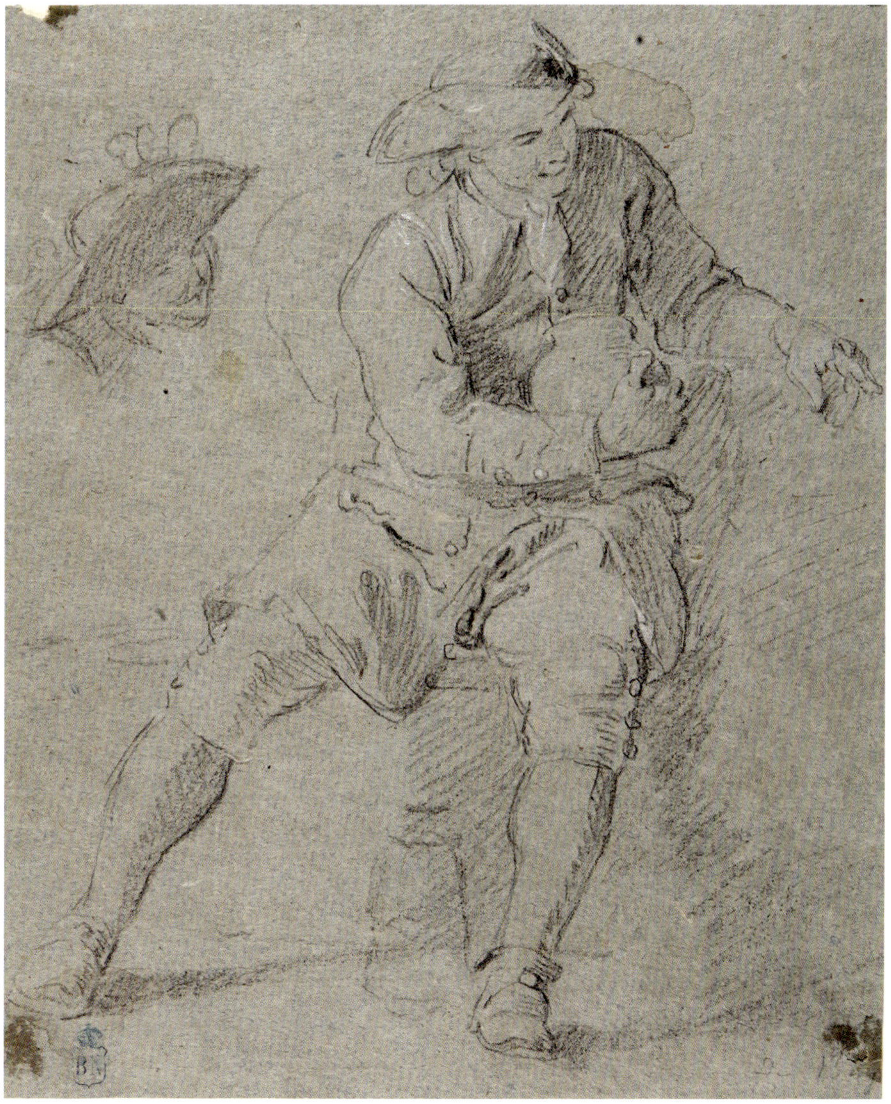

2
Teodoro Ardemans
Design for the Exaltation of Saint Francis of Assisi, c.1700–26
Pen and brown ink and grey wash over black chalk, incised, 477 x 324 mm
British Museum, London
1846,0509.175

3
Michel-Ange Houasse
A Seated Man Holding a Jar, 1722–30
Black chalk and white heightening, 230 x 183 mm
Biblioteca Nacional, Madrid
DIB/13/4/80

Fernando in Madrid (see below), where Van Loo was appointed Director of Painting in 1752.[16] Nothing is known of Ranc's drawing practice in Spain; Van Loo is better understood, as is Houasse, whose drawings reflect the powerful influence of Antoine Watteau (1684–1721).[17] Most are chalk studies of individual figures for his painted compositions. For example, his drawing of a seated man (fig. 3) executed in black chalk with white highlights on blue-grey paper is a study for the central figure in his painting *Villagers in the Forest*.[18] Houasse's drawings have long been admired in Spain; Ceán Bermúdez owned several and described their accomplished execution, gracious and correct drawing.[19]

Houasse was one of the first artists arriving in Spain to paint outdoor views with prominently arranged figures in contemporary dress. A number of his paintings depict royal residences near Madrid (such as the Escorial, Aranjuez and El Pardo), while others are imaginary landscapes. As well as his paintings, several of his landscape drawings survive.[20] The *View of Toledo from across the Tagus River* (fig. 4) is of uncertain authorship, but the formulation of the view, with equal attention given to human activity and the

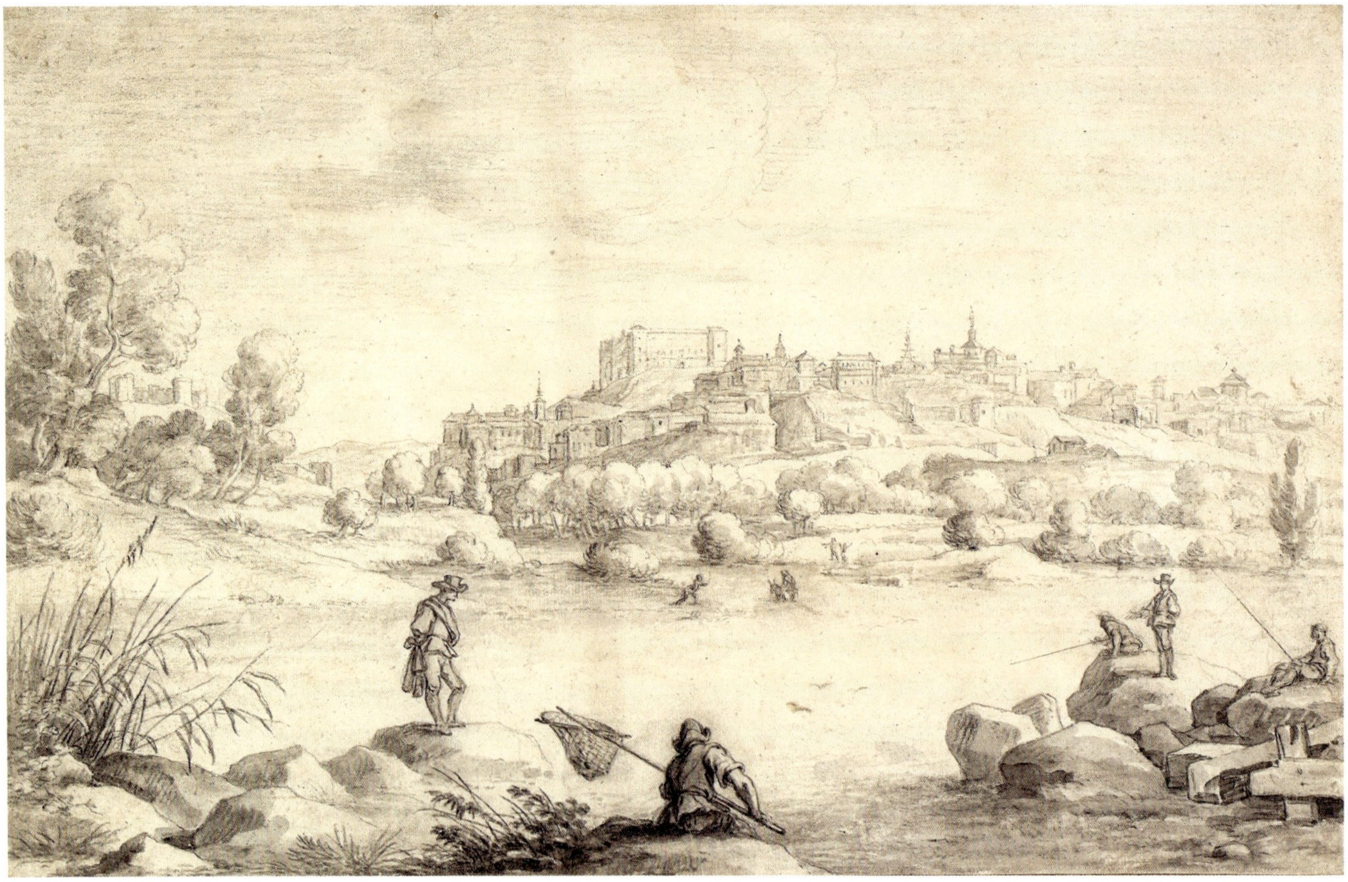

4
Anonymous
View of Toledo from across the Tagus River, c.1750–60
Black chalk and grey wash, 273 x 420 mm
British Museum, London
1846,0509.177

setting, reflects the style Houasse introduced to Spain – and which had also been promoted through landscape prints made outside Spain in the previous century.

Alongside those from abroad, several Spanish artists became extremely successful. Miguel Jacinto Meléndez (1679–1734) gained a considerable reputation at court for his portraits of Philip V and his wife, María Luisa of Savoy, and in 1712 he was appointed Painter to the King.[21] Meléndez stands apart from Spanish artists working in Madrid during the first quarter of the eighteenth century because he managed to combine the portrait style of late seventeenth-century Spain and the French aesthetic promoted by the Bourbon dynasty.[22] Drawing was an important part of his preparation.[23] One of his most striking sheets is a chalk and wash study of Philip's second wife, Italian-born Isabel de Farnesio (fig. 5).[24] In 1714, at the age of twenty-one, Isabel was married by proxy to Philip in Parma; shortly after, she arrived in Spain as Queen Consort.[25] Meléndez's portrait, probably made soon after her arrival, shows Isabel wearing a veil and adorned with jewellery. It does not correspond to a surviving painting, but its many details – dress, the lace trim along her shoulders, earrings and the jewel in her hair – are similar to his other portraits of her and earlier representations of María Luisa of Savoy.[26] For example, her countenance is remarkably similar to Meléndez's 1727 portrait (fig. 6), in which Isabel is shown holding an album of engravings open at a page depicting her husband; the image shown is probably a print by Pierre Drevet based on Hyacinthe Riguad's portrait of 1700.[27] Conveniently, this painting also illustrates the presence of prints in court circles in Madrid: the album rests on a pile of prints and more can be seen at the right.

Isabel de Farnesio was a keen collector and draughtsman herself, who introduced her native Italian taste to the Spanish court.[28] Upon her recommendation a number of Italian artists and architects were called to Madrid during the 1720s and '30s, creating a cosmopolitan and international mix. Among these were the painter Andrea Procaccini, commissioned to decorate her residence at Aranjuez, and later, architects Filippo Juvarra and Giovanni Battista Sacchetti and the painter Francesco Pavona. Despite the presence of these Italians, the French-inspired style continued to dominate in Madrid.[29] A project involving the Italians and closely monitored by the monarchs was the construction of the Royal Palace of La Granja de San Ildefonso, designed by Ardemans and begun in 1721, involving Italian incomers. Modelled on the palace at Versailles, La Granja had to be completed with some urgency after the palace of the Alcázar in Madrid burned to the ground on Christmas Eve 1734. It was only after the accession of Ferdinand VI in July 1746 that court taste turned towards Italian art. In 1753 Ferdinand called to Spain the Neapolitan painter Corrado Giaquinto (1703–66), who subsequently became the dominant artist working in Madrid.

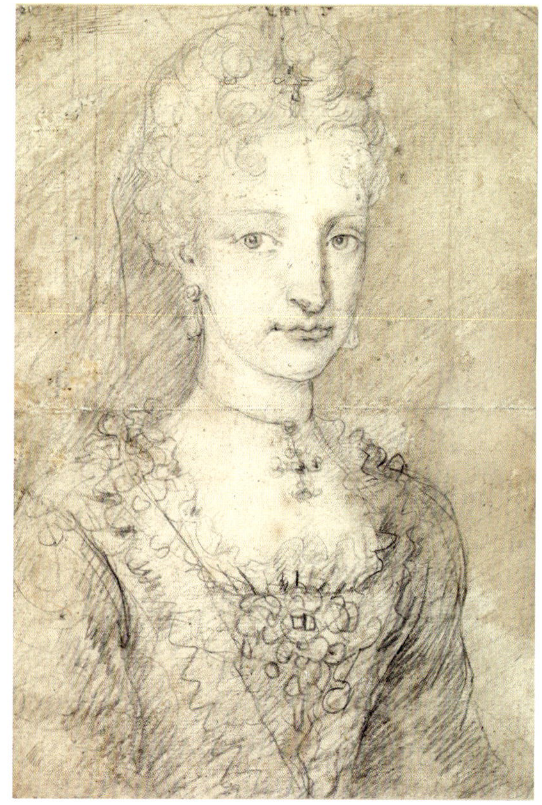

5
Miguel Jacinto Meléndez
Isabel de Farnesio, c.1714–20
Black chalk and brown wash, 195 x 128 mm
British Museum, London
1890,1209.48

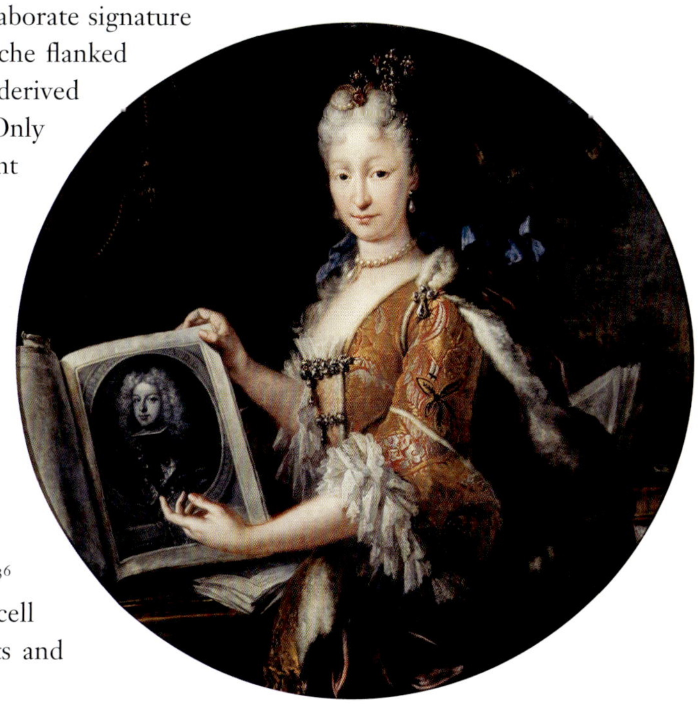

6
Miguel Jacinto Meléndez
Isabel de Farnesio, 1727
Oil on canvas, diameter 1003 mm
Biblioteca Nacional, Madrid
519

Skilled printmakers were rare in Madrid during the first decades of the century. Two stand out in particular: a Franciscan, Matías Antonio Irala Yuso (1680–1753), and Juan Bernabé Palomino (1692–1777).[30] A prolific printmaker, Irala made all his prints from his monastic cell in the convent of the Mínimos de la Victoria.[31] His work dates from the early years of the 1720s and comprised book illustrations, portraits and devotional prints, mainly after his own designs.[32] While many of his prints survive, the *Musical Putti* (fig. 7) is one of few known extant drawings.[33] This was preparatory to plate 35 of his *Método sucinto I conpendioso de cinco simetrías apropriadas a las cinco órdenes de arquitectura adornada con otras reglas útiles* of 1730–9 (fig. 8).[34] The only difference is that the elaborate signature on the drawing has been replaced in the print by a cartouche flanked by musical angels. The *Método* was a compilation of prints derived from earlier works intended as source material for artists. Only three examples of the compilation are known, with different arrangements and with none of the usual apparatus such as an Introduction or Licence, suggesting that it was never intended for wide distribution. The *Método* was dedicated to Prince Fernando (Fernando VI), shown on one of the prints as protector of the liberal arts. Two other prints, the 'Pincel panegírico' and the 'Madrid academy', address the subject of painting as a liberal art.[35]

Irala occasionally made prints from designs by other artists, such as, the allegory of Philip V after José Benito de Churriguera of before 1724, in which the names of the designer and printmaker are prominently inscribed.[36] Ceán Bermúdez wrote that on his death 'Irala left in his cell a large number of engraved plates, drawings, plans, prints and

7
Matías Antonio de Irala Yuso

A Design with Musical Putti, c.1730–9

Pen and brown ink and grey wash over black chalk pricked for transfer, 286 x 189 mm
British Museum, London
1846,0509.167

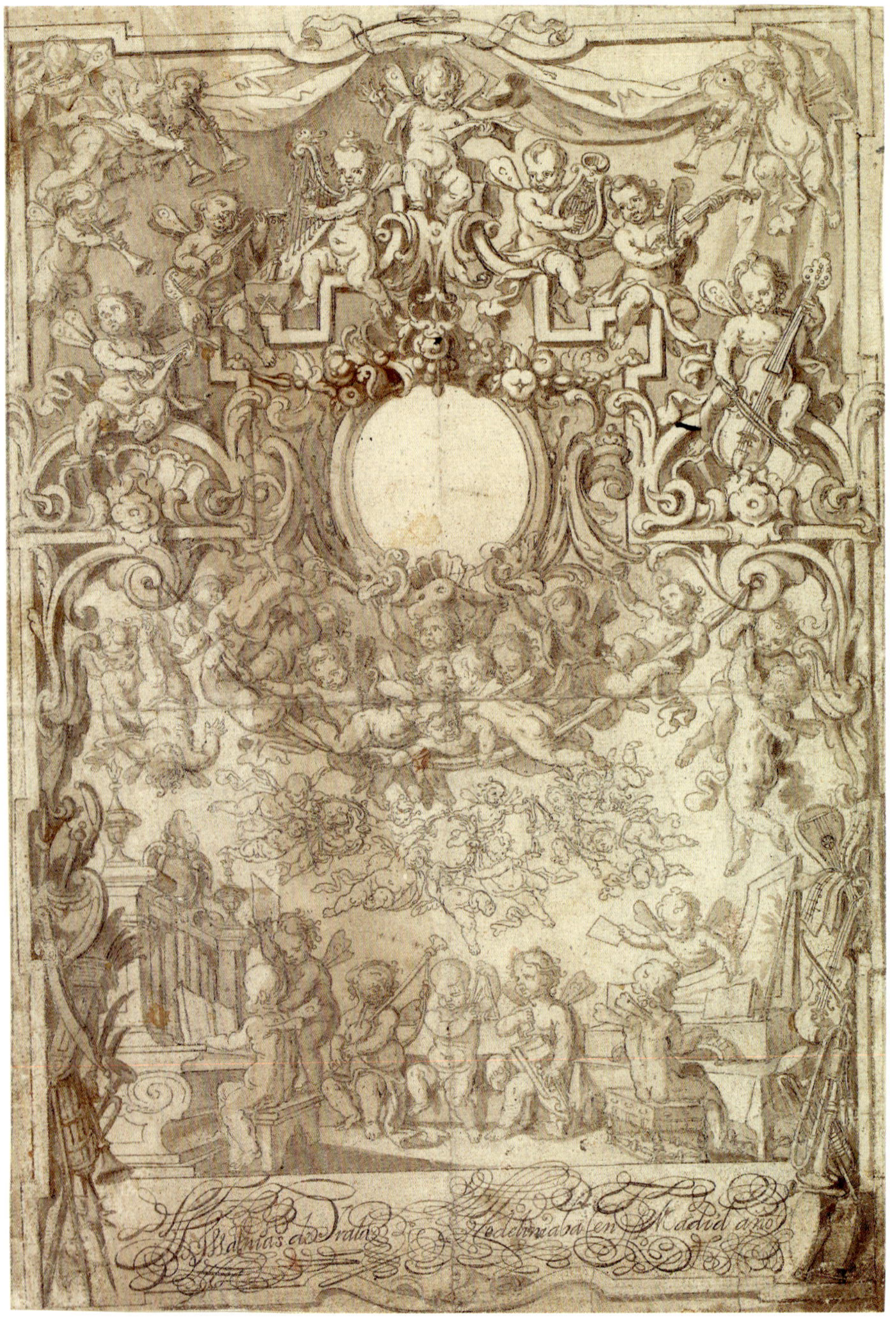

models that were distributed amongst the religious for a cheap price'. This suggests that prints, even by a relatively established printmaker, were not highly valued.[37]

In contrast to Irala, whose earliest-known prints date from when he was around forty years old, there is a more complete record of Juan Bernabé Palomino. He was the nephew of Antonio Palomino, Painter to the King and author of the *Museo pictórico y escala óptica* (see p. 110). It is not known with whom Juan Bernabé served his apprenticeship: Ceán Bermúdez reports that his 'only teacher' was the foreign prints he assiduously copied, but his uncle must have been an important influence and no doubt supported him getting work.[38] His earliest prints from before 1720 reproduce his uncle's drawings and

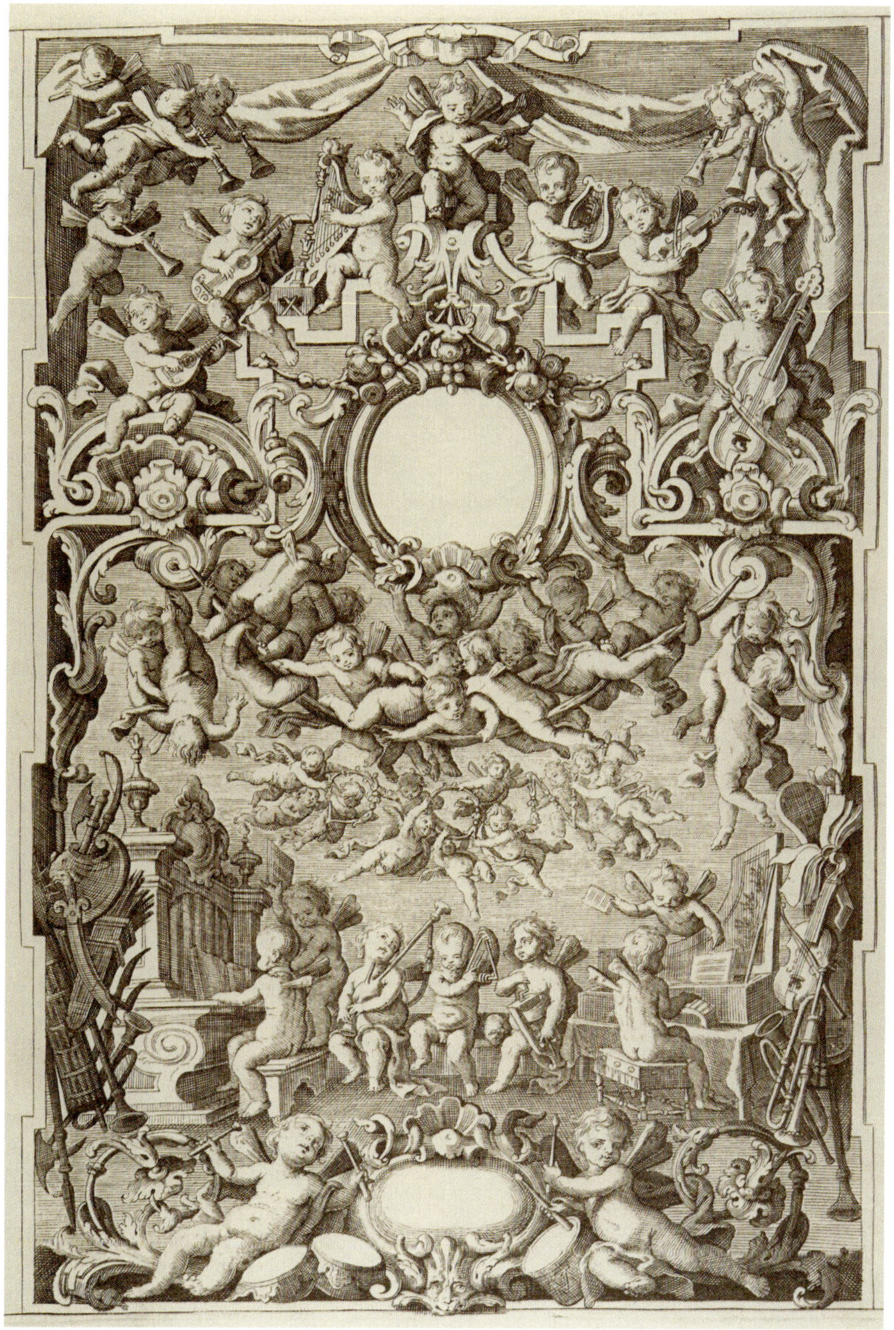

8
Matías de Irala Yuso
Plate 35 from the *Método*, 1730–9
Engraving, 291 x 206 mm
Biblioteca Nacional, Madrid
E.3043

he also made engravings for the second volume of the *Museo pictórico* (1724).[39] Juan Bernabé Palomino's work can broadly be divided into two phases. Before 1752 he engraved mainly portraits for Madrid publishers and was appointed printmaker to the Royal Chamber in 1734 at the age of forty-two. The second phase began in 1752, when he was appointed Director of Engraving at the Academy of San Fernando and his prints became much more varied.[40] The following year he engraved an allegory of the creation of the Academy (fig. 9), based on a painting by his son-in-law, Antonio González Ruiz.[41] The obituary from the Academy on his death in 1777 credits him with 'being the first in Spain to establish with good taste printmaking and to open the way to reach the level that we see today'.[42]

The Academy of San Fernando

The event that had the most profound consequences for artistic practice and the professional recognition of artists in Spain was the founding of the Academy of San Fernando in Madrid in 1744.[43] The need for an academy had long been recognized. In 1740 the Italian sculptor Giovanni Domenico Oliveri arrived in Madrid to work for Philip V, and a year later he opened a private drawing academy in his apartment in the palace of the Buen Retiro.[44] But academic aspirations were voiced even earlier in the century, when in 1726 the painter Francisco Antonio Meléndez petitioned Philip V to establish an academy. Royal approval for the idea was not secured until 1744 and, although an academy operated from that time, it was not officially recognized until 12 April 1752, when it received its royal charter.[45] The Academy of San Fernando was originally located in the Casa Panadería on Madrid's Plaza Mayor; after thirty years it moved to the Goyeneche Palace on the Calle de Alcalá, where it remains to this day.[46]

Printmaking did not feature in the 1744 syllabus or in the statutes of 1751. However, engraving did appear in the programme of 1752, taught by Juan Bernabé Palomino and Tomás Francisco Prieto (1716–82).[47] The 'Distribution of Prizes' in 1754 reports that 'the establishment of the Academy was to procure the necessary advancement of the art of engraving ...'.[48] The promotion of printmaking was motivated by economic considerations and national pride, to curb the considerable expenditure on importing foreign prints and books, which in turn undermined the progress of printmaking in Spain.[49] The issue of what training was appropriate for engravers was raised at government level, and, recognizing that different skills required different types of training, a month after the founding of the Academy the Secretary of State sent a group of four young artists to Paris to learn printmaking. These students were Manuel Salvador Carmona (1734–1820), sent to learn 'portraits and history subjects'; Juan de la Cruz Cano y Olmedilla (1734–90) and Tomás López (1730–1802), to learn 'architectural prints, maps and ornament'; and Alfonso Cruzado (d. 1791), to learn 'engraving in relief', from which medals and seals made of metals or gems were made.[50] The need for foreign expertise was not restricted to engraving: in early 1764 Hipólito Ricarte and Francisco de Espinosa were sent to Paris 'to learn the manoeuvres of printing with perfection'; they returned at the end of June 1766.[51]

Steps were also taken to improve teaching at the Academy itself. The trustees of the Academy petitioned the king for the

9
Juan Bernabé Palomino after Antonio González Ruiz
Allegory of the Creation of the Royal Academy of Fine Arts of San Fernando, 1753
Engraving, 422 x 291 mm
Biblioteca Nacional, Madrid
43637

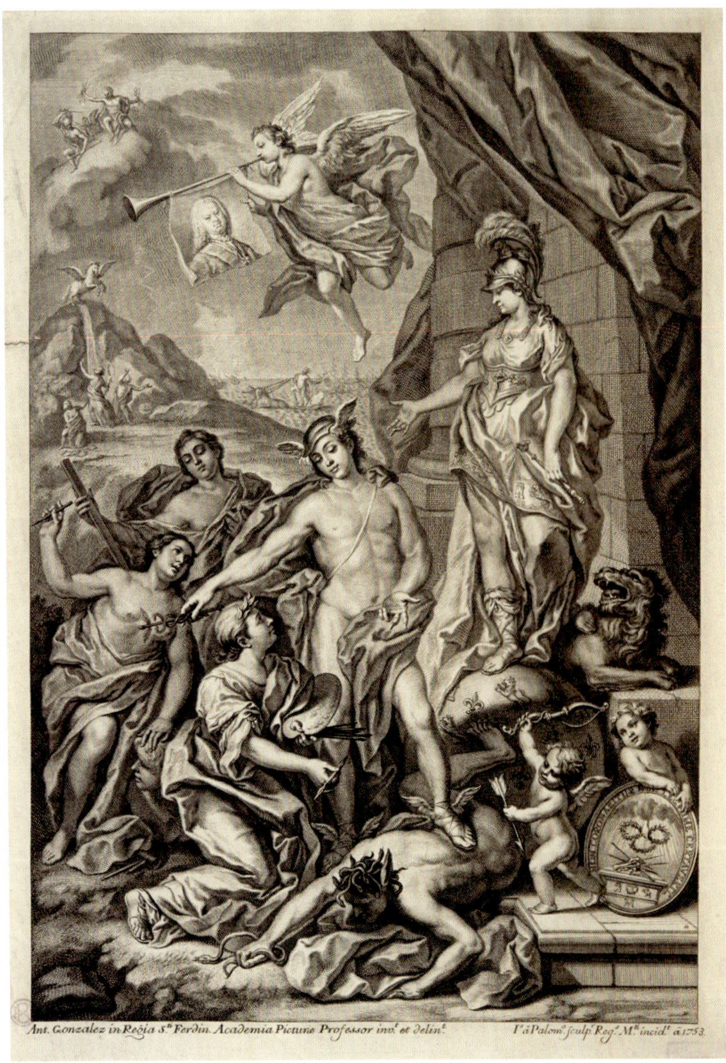

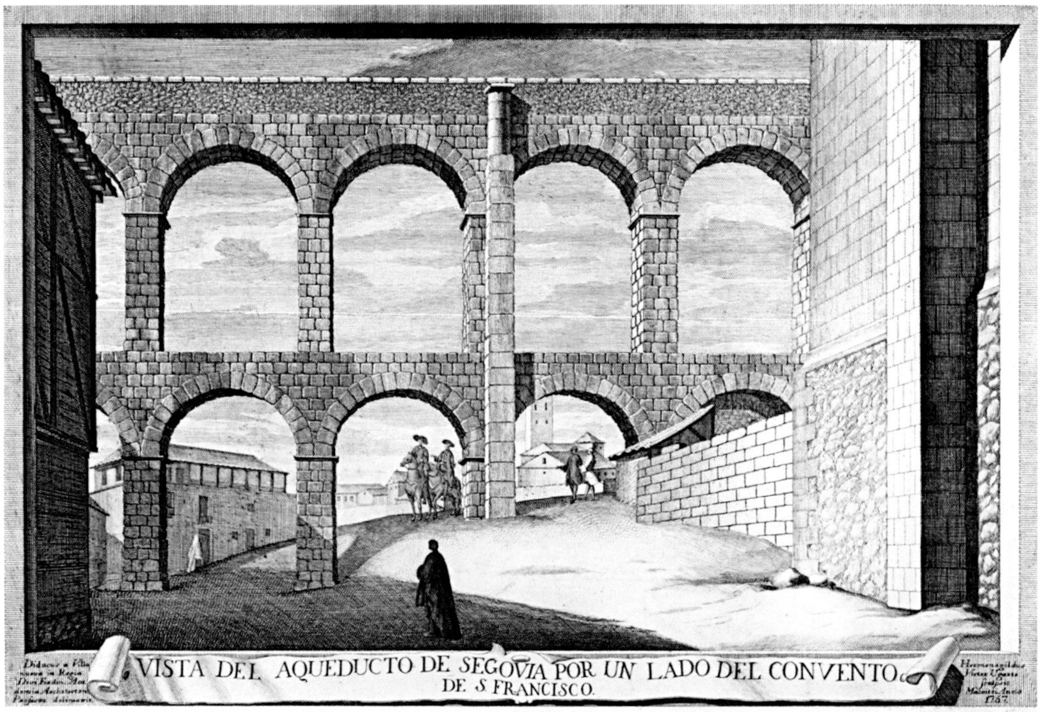

10
Hermenegildo Víctor Ugarte after Diego de Villanueva

View of the Segovia Aqueduct, 1757

Engraving, 300 x 430 mm
Museo de la Real Academia de Bellas Artes de San Fernando
R.3828

establishment of six scholarships of 150 ducats a year to support students from impoverished backgrounds. On 8 August 1753 the king accepted the petition, providing for six students to learn printmaking. Among these were Hermenegildo Víctor Ugarte (1735– after 1768) from Madrid, Juan Minguet (1737–1804?) from Barcelona and José Murgía (1736–76) from Montalvo (Cuenca).[52] From the outset the Academy attracted students from across Spain, and it soon became the national centre for the teaching of art, consolidating Madrid's pre-eminence as artistic capital. The success of printmaking and the recognition of its many virtues resulted in its being included in the Academy prize competitions in 1757.[53] The winner that year was Ugarte, for his print of the façade of the Madrid court jail. Another of his engravings, also of 1757, in a popular new 'optical view' depicted the Segovia aqueduct (fig. 10).[54] This engraving demonstrates the high quality of printmaking in Madrid, which drew favourable comparison with the work of artists trained in Paris. In little over ten years printmaking in Madrid had thus become a highly organized and professional activity.

Whereas printmaking was an important new facet of academic training, drawing had long been cited as the most important element in the petitions for the creation of an academy. In the 1726 petition *diseño* was placed first in the list of subjects to be taught, along with painting, sculpture and architecture, following the 'celebrated examples' of Rome, Paris, Florence and Flanders.[55] From 1752 drawing formed the basis of instruction, in three successive stages: learning the principles (beginner level), drawing from casts, and drawing from life.[56] Teaching was supplemented by prints, a large collection of which had been assembled at the Academy.[57] There is no visual record of the Academy itself, but Houasse's *Academy of Drawing* (fig. 11) of about 1725 gives some idea of how students might have worked.[58] Luis Meléndez (1716–80), who

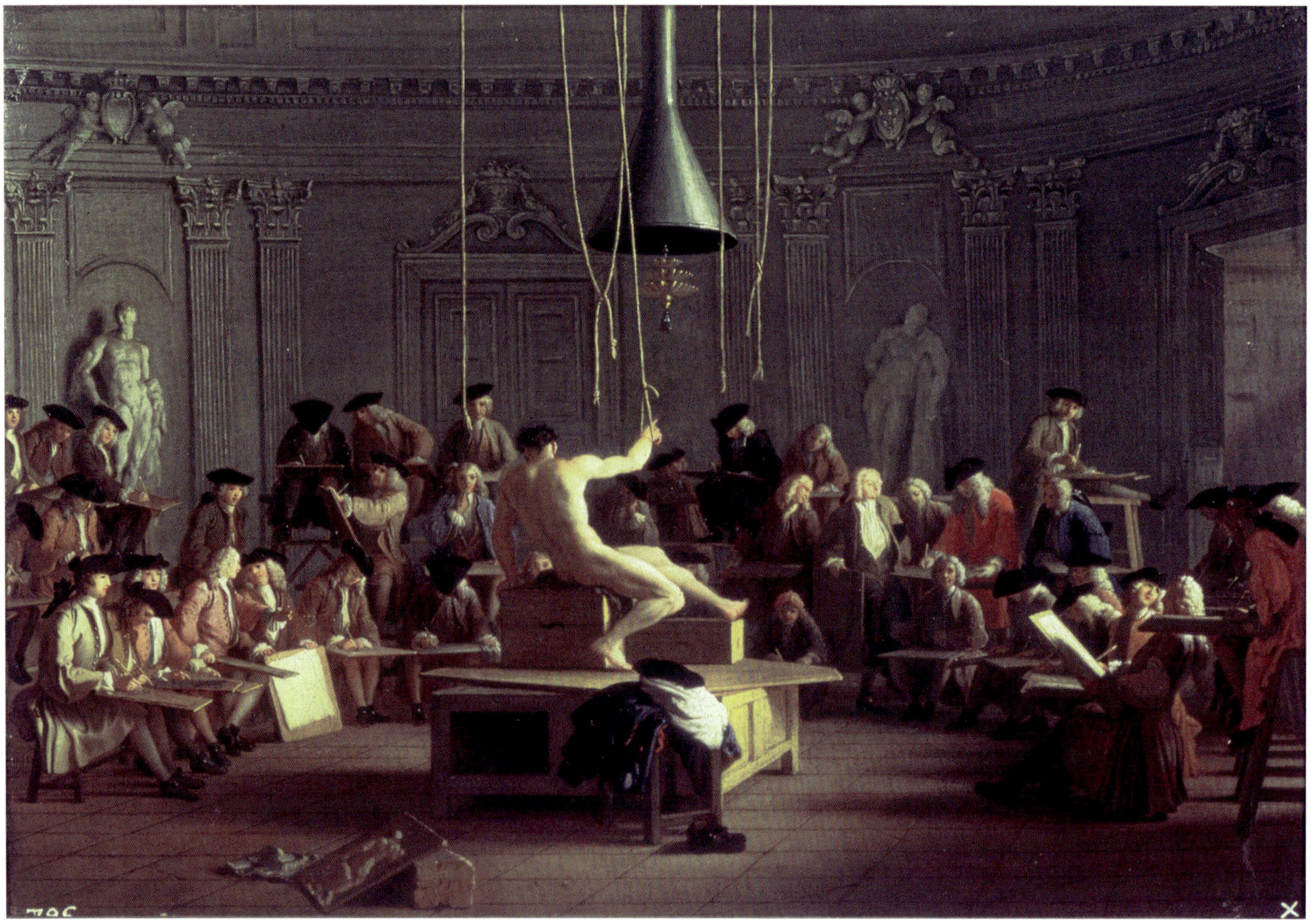

11
Michel-Ange Houasse
An Academy of Drawing, c.1725
Oil on canvas, 610 x 725 mm
Palacio Real, Madrid
10010233

is remembered for his still-life paintings, was among the first students[59] and judged first among his peers in 1745; in the following year he painted his remarkable self-portrait (fig. 12).[60] There could be no clearer demonstration of the value placed on drawing: in his left hand the artist holds a large study of a male nude, its curling edge emphasizing the paper, and in his right a chalk-holder with black chalk in one end and white in the other, for adding highlights.

One of the first directors of the Academy was Antonio González Ruiz (1711–88) who, having been taught with Houasse in Madrid, travelled through Europe, possibly studying in Paris, and returned home in 1737.[61] There is documentary evidence for his reputation as a draughtsman, reinforced by the large number of his drawings that survive.[62] In 1754 he presented the Academy with fifty-four drawings of parts of the human body for the instruction of students. Most of his drawings reflect his knowledge of French work – in particular Watteau and Rigaud – as well as that of Claudio Coello and other later seventeenth-century Spanish artists.[63] Ruiz's large red chalk study of a male nude (fig. 13), very similar to the figure in Meléndez's painting (and of similar date), is one of a group of his finished academic studies.

A competition took place every three years at the Academy, in which prizes were awarded for students' work. There were three categories, of varying degree of difficulty. The first class, *de pensado*, allowed students six months to research a specific subject, often relating to Spanish history, and interepret the theme in a painting or drawing. The second class, *de repente*, involved producing a drawing in a short time, normally a matter of hours. The third class called for a drawing of a classical statue.[64] The competition's significance for consolidating drawing practice hardly needs stating; the many surviving drawings by successful artists provide an incomparable record of graphic practice during the eighteenth century.[65]

Although the French artists in Madrid during the first half of the eighteenth century largely defined artistic taste, artistic allegiances began to dissolve around the middle of the century, with the increasing influence of Italian artists and the growing number of well-trained and talented Spanish practitioners. In August 1752 Ferdinand VI's court painter, the Italian Jacopo Amigoni, died. He had come to Madrid in 1747, having previously worked in England and Venice. Although his drawings made outside Spain are known, his work in Madrid has yet to be recognized.[66] Amigoni was succeeded by another Italian, Corrado Giaquinto, who in 1753 was appointed to three posts: Painter to the King, Director of the Academy of San Fernando and Director of the royal tapestry factory at Santa Barbara, thus securing his artistic supremacy in Spain. At around the same time other directorial posts were also occupied by Italians, such as the sculptor Giovanni Domenico Olivieri and the architect Giovanni Battista Sacchetti.[67]

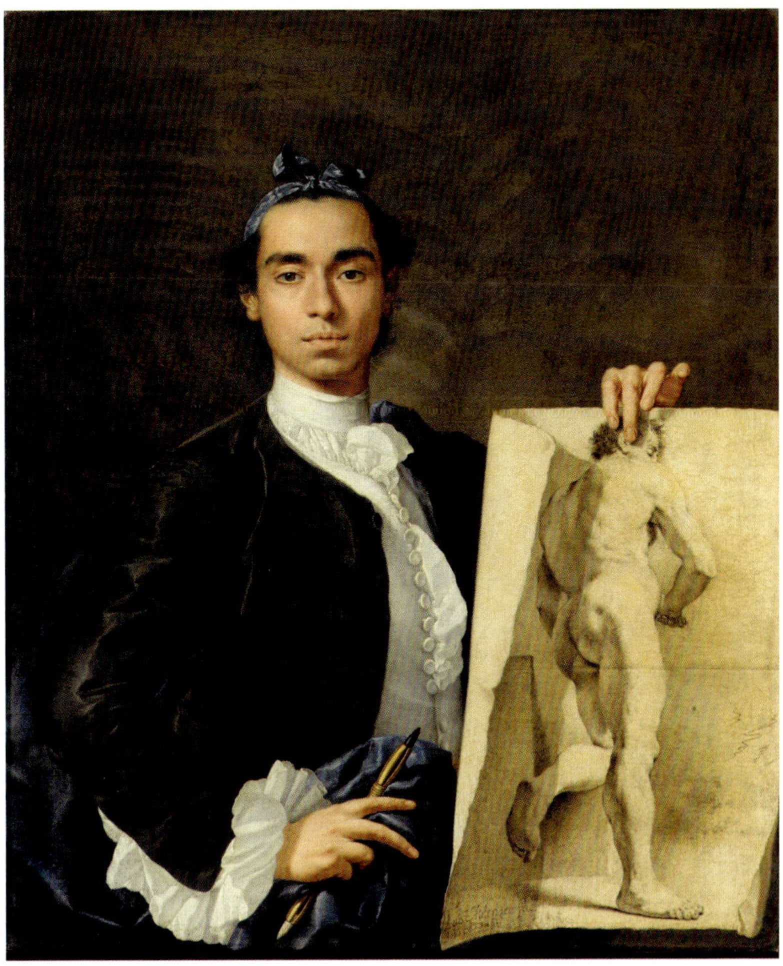

12
Luis Meléndez
Self-portrait, 1746
Oil on canvas, 990 x 820 mm
Musée du Louvre, Paris
RF 2537

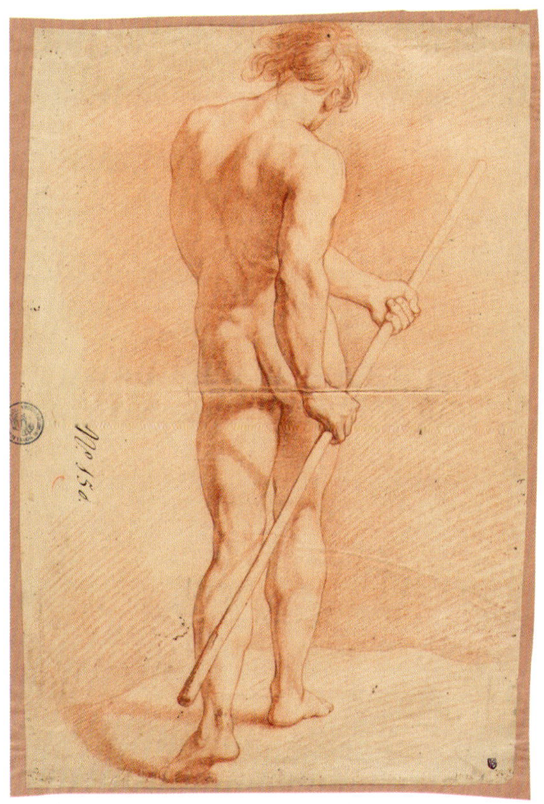

13
Antonio González Ruiz
Study of a Male Nude, *c.*1740–55
Red chalk, 552 x 365 mm
Museo del Prado, Madrid
F.A.407

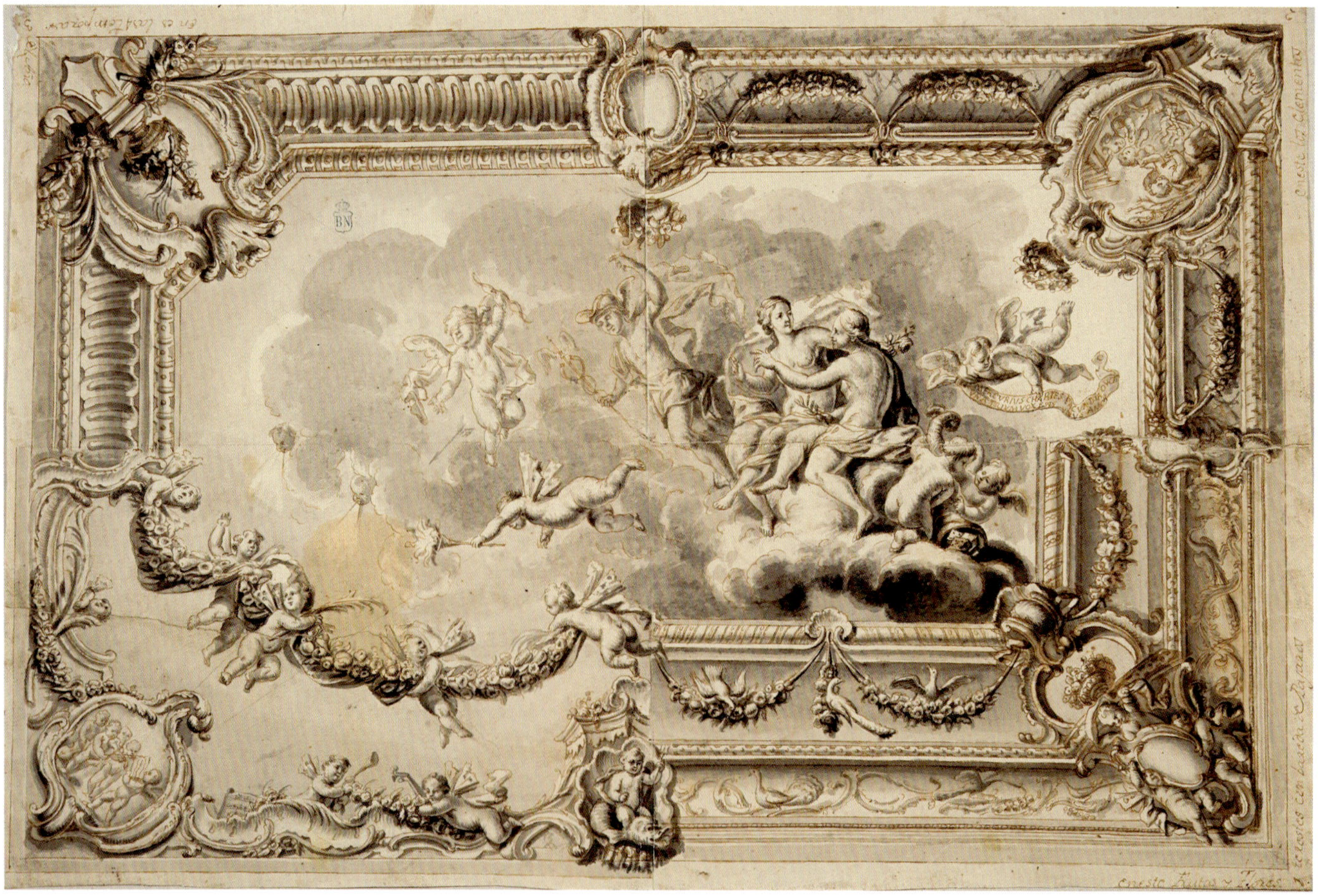

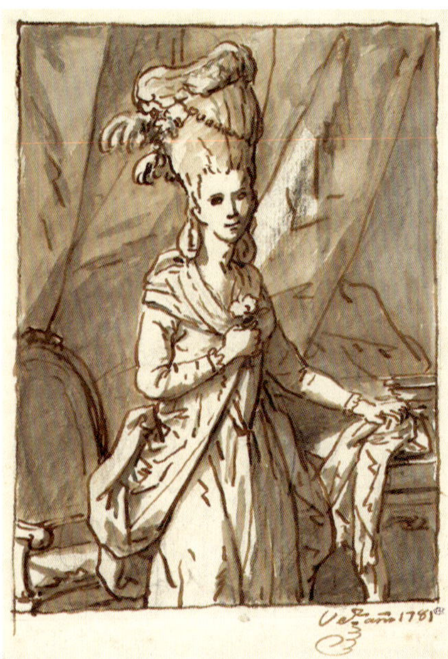

14
Antonio González Velázquez
Design for a Ceiling Devoted to Mercury, c.1760
Pen and brown ink with brush and grey wash over black chalk, 345 x 503 mm (sheet)
Biblioteca Nacional, Madrid
DIB/13/5/58

15
Antonio González Velázquez
A Standing Woman, 1781
Pen and brown ink, brown and grey wash over black chalk, 230 x 158 mm
British Museum, London
1998,0214.4

Giaquinto's nine years in Spain had a tremendous impact on a generation of Spanish artists, the most prominent being Francisco Bayeu and Francisco de Goya.[68] Giaquinto's most important work was at the Royal Palace in Madrid, where he painted three of the largest ceilings. He worked in the Neapolitan drawing tradition, although for him this was integral to preparation rather than simply an academic activity.[69] He produced small sheets of individual figures and studies for large-scale compositions that were rarely fully planned. Evidence of his drawing practice in Spain is not easy to find, and his drawings are sometimes hard to recognize because of the many similar preparatory sheets by his Italian and Spanish followers. But several red chalk sketches of sculptures planned for the staircases of the new Royal Palace in Madrid show his quick and exploratory penmanship.[70]

Giaquinto's influence on Spanish artists can be seen in the work of those who were with him in Rome. Antonio González Velázquez (1723–94) took classes at the Academy in Madrid before travelling to Rome in 1747, where he worked in Giaquinto's studio before returning to Spain in 1752.[71] When Giaquinto travelled from Naples to Madrid in 1753 he visited González Velázquez in Zaragoza, where he was working on frescos in the Basilica of Nuestra Señora del Pilar. Both artists brought to Spain the practice of making preliminary sketches in oil for fresco decorations, which reduced the need for finished preparatory drawings. Several oil studies for the frescos at El Pilar survive.[72] González Velázquez worked under Giaquinto's supervision in Madrid; a drawing of around 1760 for a ceiling devoted to Mercury (fig. 14) reveals his debt to his master.[73] A portrait signed and dated 1781 (fig. 15) demonstrates that throughout his career González Velázquez maintained his distinctive technique of pen and brown ink with contrasting grey wash.[74] It is likely that this sheet was preparatory for a printed illustration: indeed, González Velázquez was praised by Ceán Bermúdez for the drawings he prepared for engravings.[75] During his long career González Velázquez worked as court painter to three consecutive kings of Spain and was appointed to senior positions at the Academy.[76]

Another Spaniard, José del Castillo (1737–93), also worked in Giaquinto's studio in Rome from 1751; two years later they travelled to Madrid, where they continued to work together.[77] As a draughtsman Castillo blended Giaquinto's abbreviated drawing with the more academic style of Anton Raphael Mengs (see below).[78] His dependence on Giaquinto is particularly evident in his red chalk study of Saint Cecilia, signed and dated 23 November 1754 (fig. 16). Four years later the Academy awarded Castillo a grant to study under Preciado de la Vega at the Spanish Academy in Rome; he remained there until he was recalled to Madrid six years later to work at the royal tapestry factory at Santa Barbara.[79] While in Rome he compiled sketchbooks, an Italian practice, as a record of what he had seen and as a repository for his ideas, for future reference.[80]

Giaquinto left Madrid in 1762. His nine years in Spain coincided with the final period of Ferdinand's reign and the first years of his half-brother Charles III, crowned in 1759. Two years later Charles summoned to Madrid the German artist Anton Raphael Mengs (1728–79), whom he had encountered in Naples.[81] Mengs represented a much more sober style of painting than that which flourished in Madrid during Ferdinand's reign. He was appointed Honorary Director of Painting at the Academy in 1763 and Painter to the King following Giaquinto's death in 1766. From the time of his appointment to the Academy Mengs was occupied with the reform of the institution, and in 1766 he produced two theoretical texts: the *Discorso sopra i mezzi per far fiorire le belle arti in Spagna* and the *Ragionamento su l'Accademia delle Belle Arti di Madrid*. He was a controversial figure

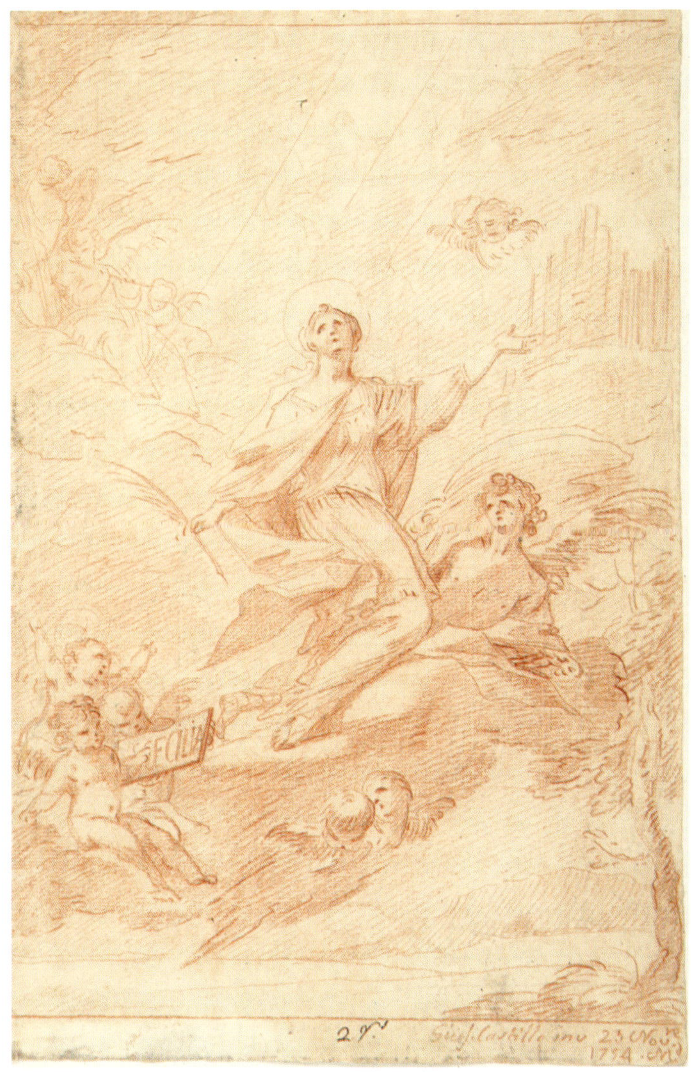

16
José del Castillo
Saint Cecilia in Glory, 1754
Red chalk, 385 x 250 mm
Museo del Prado, Madrid
D.674

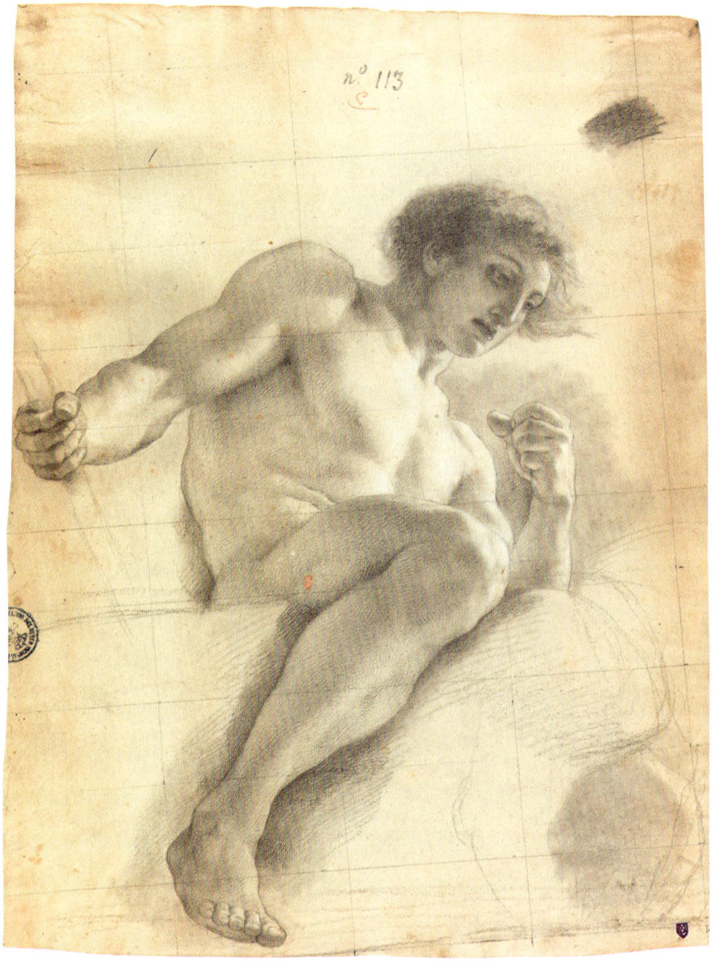

17
Anton Raphael Mengs
A Naked Male Youth Seated, c.1774–6
Black chalk, charcoal and white heightening, squared for transfer, 532 x 398 mm
Museo del Prado, Madrid
D.3071

18
Anton Raphael Mengs
Fame, Putti with the Symbols of the Four Seasons and Other Allegorical Figures, 1774–6
Brush and brown and black ink and oil colour, squared for transfer, 485 x 615 mm
Royal Palace of la Granja de San Ildefonso, Segovia
100 276 86

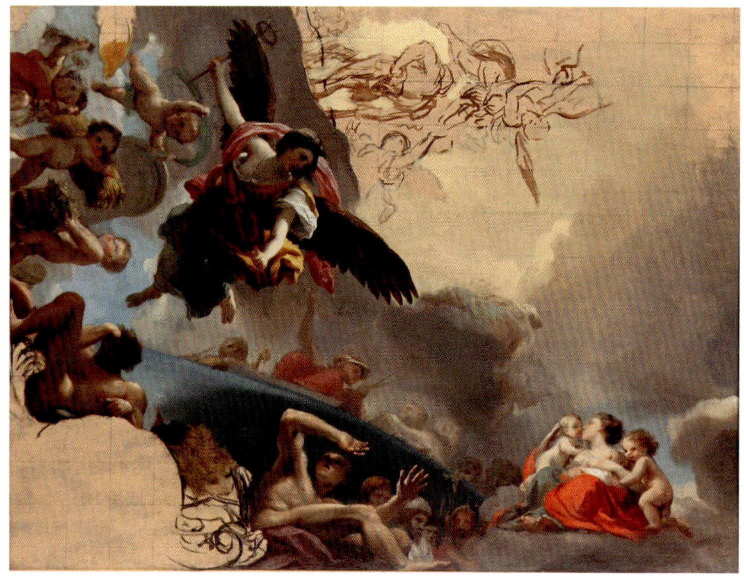

in Madrid, not universally popular although he attracted quite a following.[82] His royal appointment has sometimes been regarded as indicative of Charles III's preference for a more conservative style, in contrast to the dynamism of Giaquinto and his followers. But it is important to remember that Charles also summoned to Madrid the most renowned Italian artist of the eighteenth century, Giovanni Battista (Giambattista) Tiepolo (1696–1770), who arrived from Italy in March 1762 with his sons Domenico and Lorenzo, to carry out a commission to paint three ceilings celebrating Spanish power in the Royal Palace. The Tiepolos' profound and lasting influence on print-making in Madrid is discussed below (pp. 211–2 and Chapter 8).[83]

To return to Mengs, Ceán Bermúdez describes his painstaking drawing practice thus:

> While other painters, satisfied with their facility were content with a simple study, drawing or sketch before starting their paintings, D. Antonio Rafael took months and years to draw each element of each figure, each group and the entire composition, referring to nature and the antique, that there are so many studies from his hand.[84]

Mengs explained the elements he regarded as vital to artistic practice (such as drawing, colouring and invention), in an open letter published by the Spanish painter and writer Antonio Ponz in his *Viaje de España* (*Journey through Spain*, 1776).[85] The many drawings by Mengs that survive support his principles and verify Ceán Bermúdez's comments. They include copies after prints and studies of statuary and paintings, mainly in chalk, but sometimes in wash applied like watercolour.[86] Mengs also prepared cartoons for his frescos, a practice at that time neglected in Spain, which drew praise from both Ceán Bermúdez and Ponz.[87] For his *Apotheosis of Trajan* in the Royal Palace vault of the Saleta (1774–6) studies of different types survive.[88] The naked youth representing self-control (*Dominio de si mismo*, fig. 17) in black chalk with white heightening is a large, carefully drawn study for the figure in the lower left of the fresco, its off-centre squaring conveying how that section of the ceiling would be seen from below. Another planning stage is represented by his squared pen-and-ink study of *Fame, Putti with the Symbols of the Four Seasons and Other Allegorical Figures*, in which Mengs sought to further clarify the design by working some of the figures in oil (fig. 18).[89] His drawings evidently had a profound effect on those around him. The minutes of the Academy from 1764 record Francisco Bayeu requesting 'academic' drawings by Mengs for students to study, and in 1769 Mariano Salvador Maella requested his drawings for the 'Sala de Principios' for students to copy. Such was Mengs' reputation that other of his drawings were sent further afield to Valencia for similar purposes of instruction (see p. 224).[90]

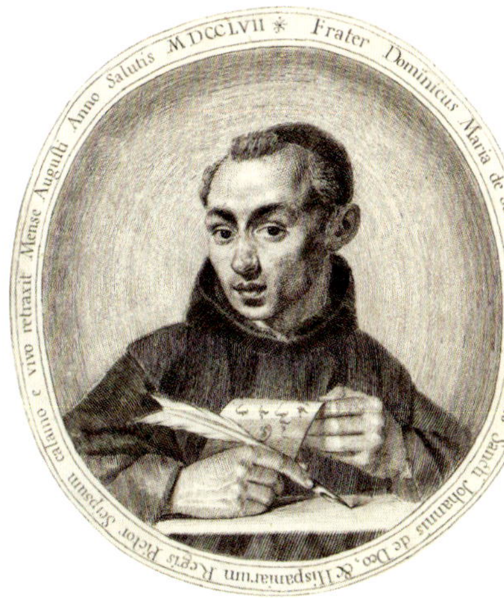

19
Domingo María de Servidori
Self-portrait, 1775
Pen and black ink on parchment, 192 x 170 mm
British Museum, London
1846,0509.198

20
Francisco Bayeu y Subías
Study of a Giant, c.1763
Black and white chalk, 627 x 528 mm
Museo del Prado, Madrid
D.3329

Although drawings produced in Madrid during the eighteenth century were predominantly academic studies and preparatory sketches for paintings or fresco, this was not their exclusive use. Domingo María de Servidori (1724–90), a Dominican who came to Madrid from Rome in 1754, represents a different drawing practice. In 1757 Ferdinand VI granted him an annuity to work as a draughtsman and miniaturist; on a self-portrait dated the same year (fig. 19) Servidori records himself as 'Painter to the King'.[91] The guise in which he portrays himself and the inscription around the portrait emphasize both his religious vocation and his identity as an artist. Although Servidori is referred to elsewehere in documents as a painter and draughtsman, he is best remembered as a writing master and calligrapher,[92] and author of the lavish two-volume *Reflexiones sobre la verdadera arte de escribir* published in Madrid in 1789.[93]

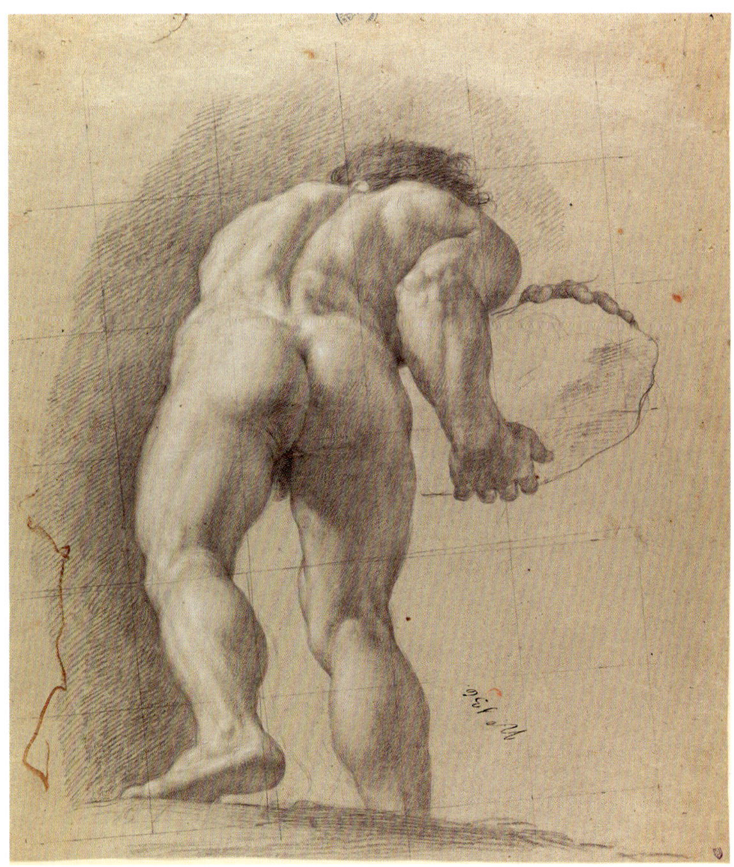

The ascendance of Spanish artists

The teaching programme at the Academy of San Fernando gave rise to a new generation of Spanish artists. Francisco Bayeu y Subías (1734–95), Mariano Salvador Maella (1739–1819) and Luis Paret y Alcázar (1746–99) were among those who achieved great prominence, claiming back some of the national prestige that had diminished since the late seventeenth century.

21
Francisco Bayeu y Subías
Studies of Two Men (petimetres), *c.*1785
Red chalk with white chalk heightening, 314 x 337 mm
Biblioteca Nacional, Madrid DIB/13/4/65.

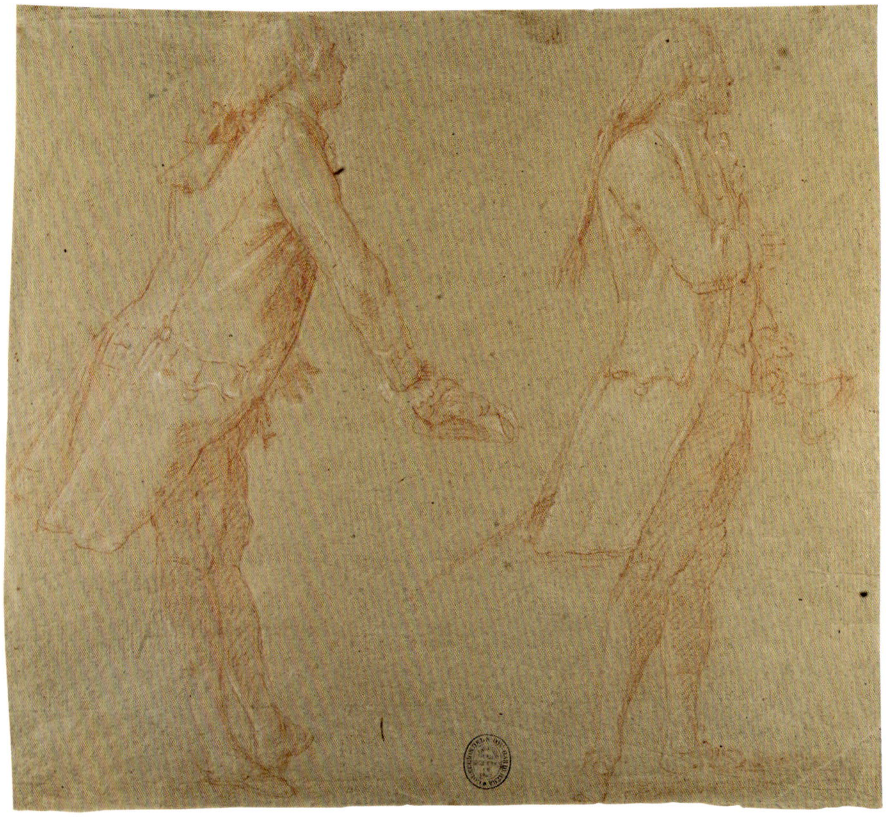

22
Francisco Bayeu y Subías
Head of a Woman, after 1765
Black chalk and white heightening, 356 x 272 mm
Museo del Prado, Madrid D.3503

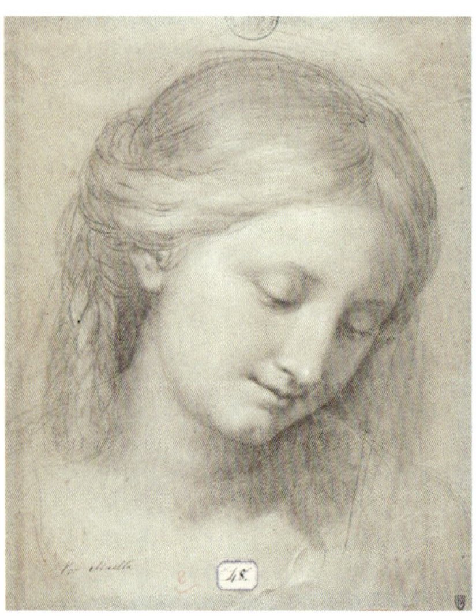

After winning a prize for painting in Zaragoza in 1758, Francisco Bayeu was awarded a scholarship to the Academy in Madrid where his first teacher was Antonio González Velázquez. He returned to Zaragoza a year later, but in 1763 Mengs invited him back to Madrid to work on frescos at the Royal Palace. Bayeu made preparatory studies for each figure in his fresco, the *Fall of the Giants*, to be worked up in oil sketches. Around twenty drawings for the project survive. In its controlled classicism the large finished and squared chalk study of the giant from the lower right section of the fresco (fig. 20) reveals his debt to Mengs.[94]

By the mid 1770s Mengs' influence was in decline. In 1775 the Academy bought a collection of drawings by Carlo Maratta that had belonged to Andrea Procaccini. Bayeu examined these when they were subsequently displayed at the Academy so that students could copy them – several of Bayeu's surviving drawings are very similar to Maratta's.[95]

In 1777 Bayeu was appointed Artistic Director of the royal tapestry factory at Santa Barbara, where he collaborated with his younger brother Ramón (1744–93) and Francisco de Goya on the preparation of tapestry cartoons. Drawings by the two brothers have sometimes been difficult to differentiate, although Francisco's tapestry studies are less academic and more spontaneous. His commitment to drawing is reflected in the enormous number of his surviving sheets, their range demonstrating that he was one of the few artists able to negotiate the predominant styles of drawing in the eighteenth century: the academism promoted by Mengs and the looser, more expressive style of Giaquinto and his followers (fig. 21).[96] Among Bayeu's most accomplished sheets are his highly finished chalk studies of heads on blue paper (fig. 22 and p. 188), once thought to be by Mariano Salvador Maella.[97]

Valencian-born Maella was an artist who was no less dedicated to drawing and with whom Francisco Bayeu occasionally collaborated. He entered the Madrid Academy at the age of eleven; a prizewinning student, he went on to become a senior member of staff.[98] His drawings in different media are typical of an academically trained artist.[99] Like many of his contemporaries, Maella spent time in Rome (1758–65), where he made cartoons after Raphael's *Fire in the Borgo* and the *School of Athens* (fig. 23); these he sent back to Madrid, to great acclaim.[100] On his return to Spain Maella prepared drawings for each stage of his projects. In 1770 he and Francisco Bayeu were commissioned to decorate the Colegiata de La Granja de San Ildefonso, which had remained unfinished following the death of Giambattista Tiepolo earlier that year.[101] Two black chalk drawings for Maella's fresco depicting the choir of angels in the presbytery, now destroyed, indicate the shape of the space with the scene lightly sketched in black chalk.[102] The putti in his fresco *Time Discovering Truth* (1798) in the Royal Palace in Madrid represent the final stage of preparation, after the entire design had been resolved (fig. 24).[103]

Luis Paret y Alcázar also found success with his very distinctive style. Born in the same year as Goya, he is regarded as his most significant Spanish contemporary. Over 250 drawings by Paret survive, many of them independent works on subjects ranging from history, mythology and the court to architecture and fauna.[104] His drawings were highly praised and imitated during his lifetime.[105] He received his initial training in Madrid with the French jeweller Augustin Duflos (active 1722–67); something of a prodigy, he entered the Academy in 1756 as a boy of ten. Here he was taught by Antonio González Velázquez but was more strongly influenced by Giaquinto. In 1760 Paret won second prize in the Second Class of the Academy competition; he narrowly missed winning the major award three years later.[106] Thanks to the patronage of the Infante Luis Antonio Borbón (brother of Charles III), who heard of his controversial failure to secure first prize, Paret was able to travel to Rome in 1763. He returned in 1766 and subsequently found success at the Academy, where historical subjects were favoured: his prizewinning red chalk drawing, *Hannibal Visiting the Temple of Hercules in Cadiz* (fig. 25), with its carefully rendered classical architecture, shows how useful his time in Rome had been.[107]

Paret may have travelled to France or studied French art in Madrid under the guidance of Charles François-Pierre de la Traverse (a pupil of François Boucher), who arrived in Spain in 1759.[108] Their drawings share similar technical qualities, such as dramatic layered shading to create highly atmospheric effects. One of Paret's finest drawings, *The Masked Ball in the Teatro del Príncipe* (fig. 26), made shortly after he returned from Italy, is a study for a painting (fig. 27) and was also reproduced in a print by Juan Antonio Salvador Carmona (fig. 28).[109] This was not a commissioned work; Paret's inscription

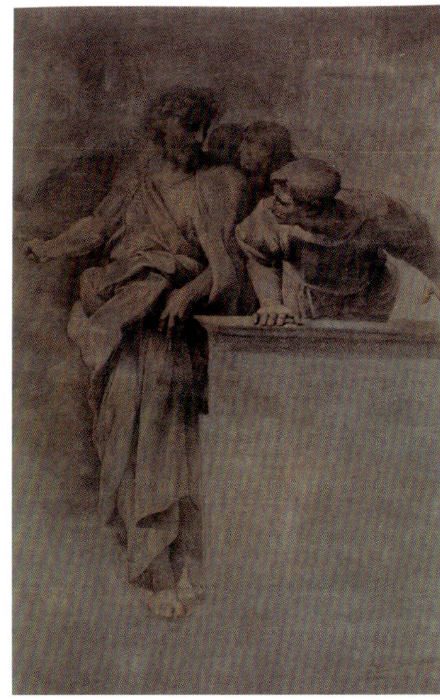

23
Mariano Salvador Maella after Raphael
The 'Disputa' from the School of Athens, 1764
Black chalk, grey wash, and white highlights, 2227 x 1355 mm
Universidad Complutense, Madrid
R-278

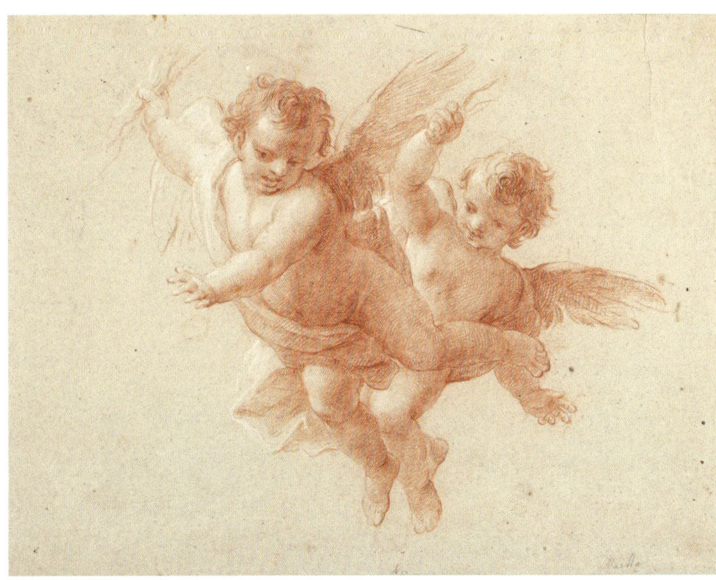

24
Mariano Salvador Maella
Study of Flying Putti, 1798
Red chalk and white heightening, 355 x 460 mm
Museo del Prado, Madrid
D.3104

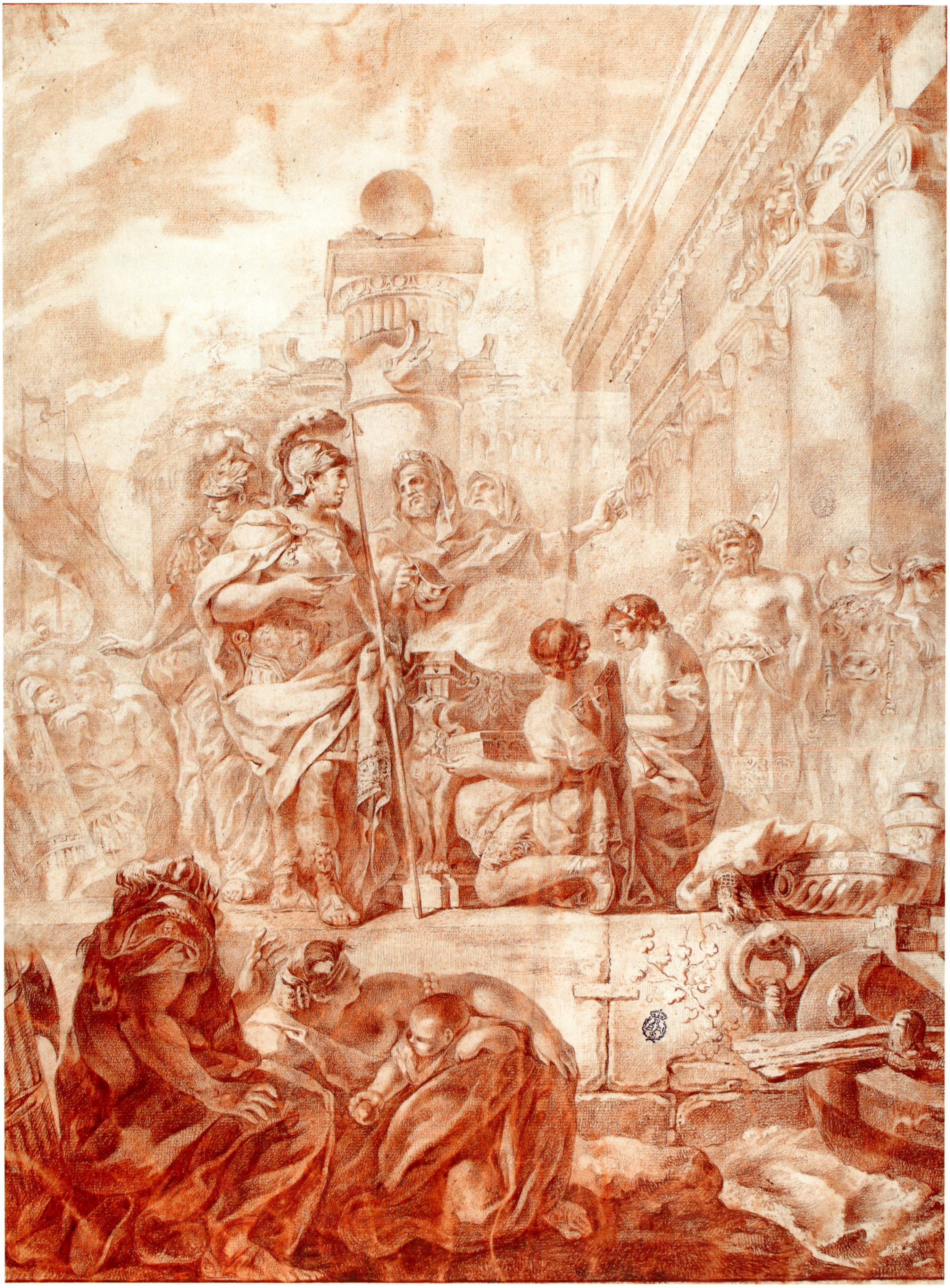

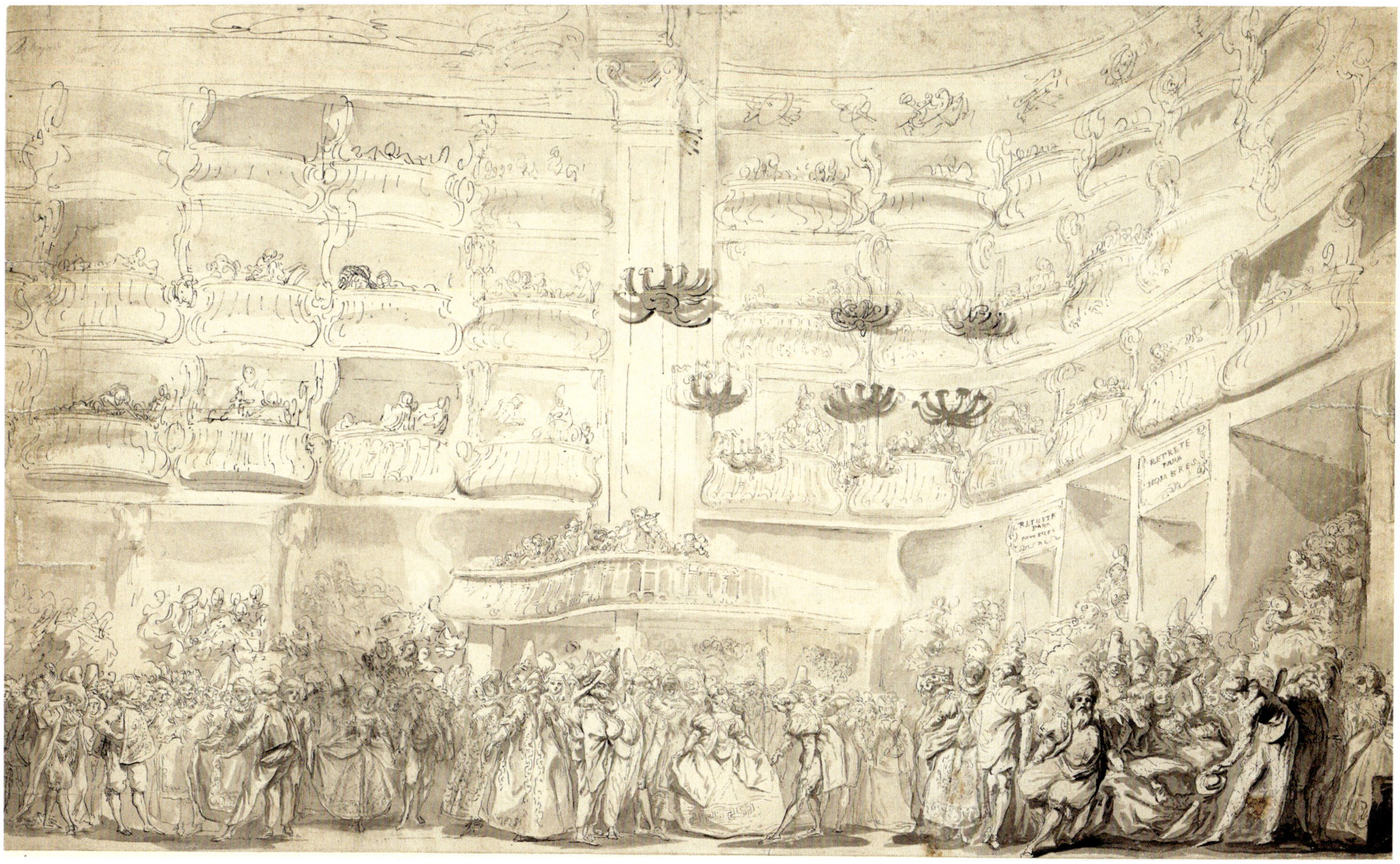

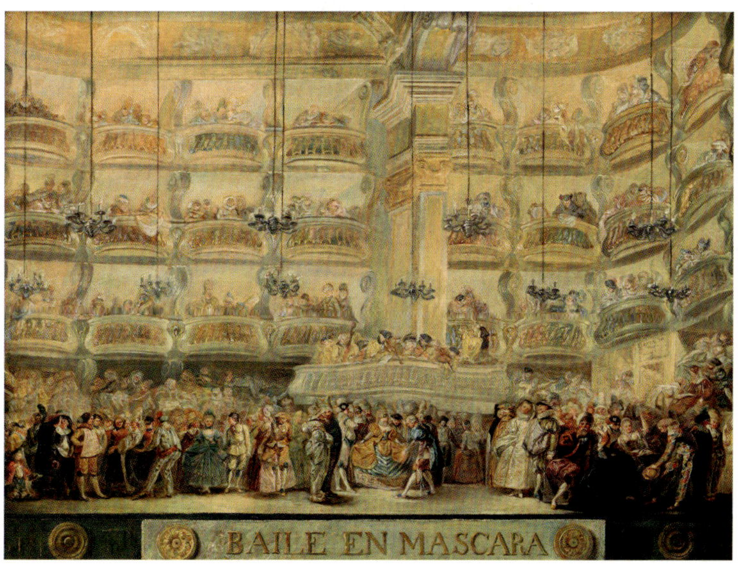

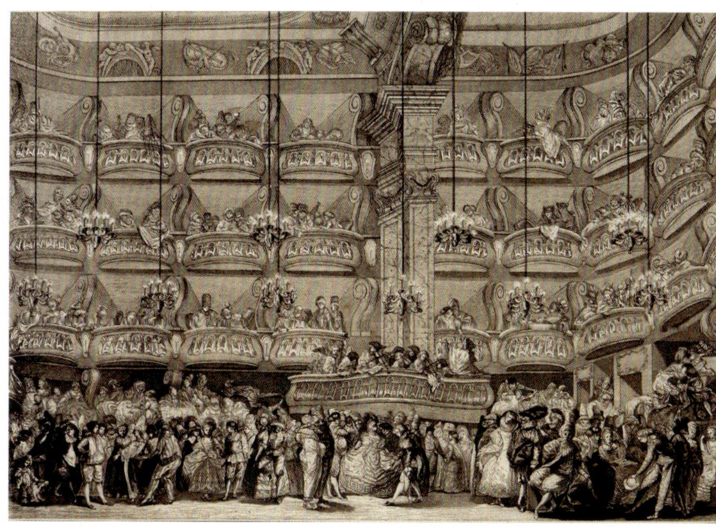

25
Luis Paret y Alcázar
Hannibal Visiting the Temple of Hercules in Cadiz, 1766
Red chalk, 650 x 470 mm
Museo de la Real Academia de Bellas Artes de San Fernando
P/1554

26
Luis Paret y Alcázar
The Masked Ball in the Teatro del Príncipe, *c.*1766
Pen and grey ink and wash over black chalk, 305 x 493 mm
British Museum, London
1890,1209.50

27
Luis Paret y Alcázar
A Masked Ball in the Teatro del Príncipe, 1767
Oil on panel, 400 x 510 mm
Museo del Prado, Madrid
P.2875

28
Juan Antonio Salvador Carmona
A Masked Ball in the Teatro del Príncipe, 1778
Engraving, 386 x 515 mm
Biblioteca Nacional, Madrid
15050

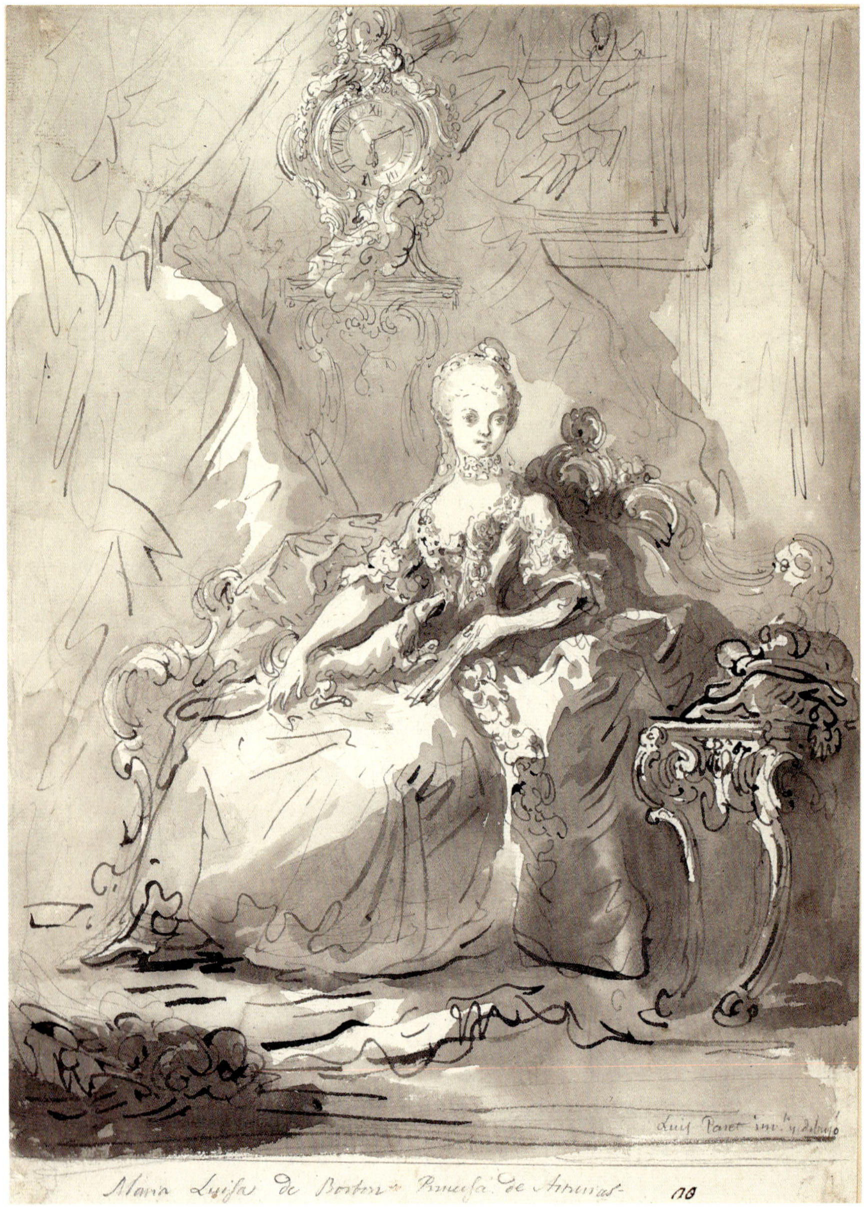

29
Luis Paret y Alcázar
María Luisa de Borbón, c.1766–8
Pen and grey ink and grey wash over black chalk, 350 x 244 mm
British Museum, London
1890,1209.49

on the painting explains that it was his own initiative. The ball was held after a period of mourning for Isabel de Farnesio, who died on 11 July 1766, during which it was forbidden to hold such events.

Paret's portrait of María Luisa de Borbón (fig. 29), of similar date, shows the unmistakable influence of French art.[110] Born and educated in Italy, in 1762 María Luisa became engaged to Crown Prince Charles of Spain (later Charles IV); they married in early September 1765, when María Luisa was fifteen. She is shown here as a young woman, probably a little after her marriage, dressed in the elegant French fashion popular at the Spanish court. The position of Paret's inscription, indicating that he 'designed and drew' the portrait, suggests that it might have been intended for a print. Many of Paret's drawings were for engraving, reflecting how closely artists were involved with printmaking during the second half of the century. In glowing terms, Ceán Bermúdez reports that 'Paret made drawings for engravers that are superior to many foreigners in their invention, in their grace and expressive of the national character, the delicacy of his thought, and in other parts adorned with great taste'.[111] During the late 1770s Paret provided drawings for a series of costume prints etched by Juan de la Cruz Cano (see p. 221), and others of the Muses for the 1794 edition of Palomino's biographical account of Spanish painters, *El Parnaso español*.[112]

Printmaking in the second half of the eighteenth century

From about 1750 two types of printmaker in Spain can be identified: the professional engraver and the painter-printmaker. While the most significant Spanish engravers were trained in Paris and at the Academy in Madrid, the second group were painters who had a subsidiary interest in printmaking. This was a Spanish phenomenon that can be traced to the sixteenth century, with Alonso Berruguete and Juan de Roelas, and others in the seventeenth century such as Vicente Carducho and Juan de Valdés Leal. Most of these painters made etchings rather than engravings, presumably because of the freedom it allowed. Sometimes resembling pen-and-ink drawings, their prints survive in small numbers, further suggesting their experimental nature. Occasionally foreign painters working in Spain also made prints but, as with their Spanish counterparts, it was a secondary activity. An outstanding example is an etching of Fernando VI, Bárbara de Braganza and members of the court by the French painter Charles-Joseph Flipart (1721–97) after a painting by Jacopo Amigoni.[113] Made around the mid-1750s, this very large print (557 x 632 mm) was quite unlike anything else produced in Spain at that time.[114] Another unusual print is Mengs' *Sibyl*, etched in very a controlled manner, similar to engraving.[115]

With their prodigious talent and their commitment to printmaking, the Tiepolo family had the greatest impact on artist-printmakers in Spain. They found an eager market for their prints when they arrived in Spain in 1762. The series of twenty-seven etchings by Domenico Tiepolo (1727–1804) of *The*

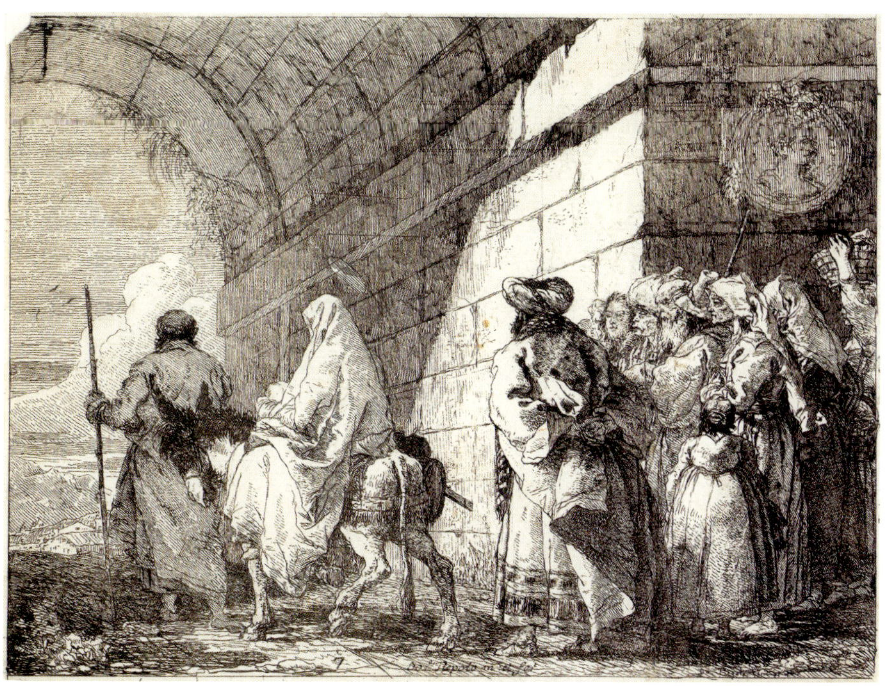

30
Domenico Tiepolo
The Flight into Egypt, 1750–2
Etching, 186 x 240 mm
British Museum, London
1869,0410.2399

31
Lorenzo Tiepolo
Monument to the Priestess Hero, 1750–80
Etching, 690 x 495 mm
British Museum, London
1907,0515.84.88

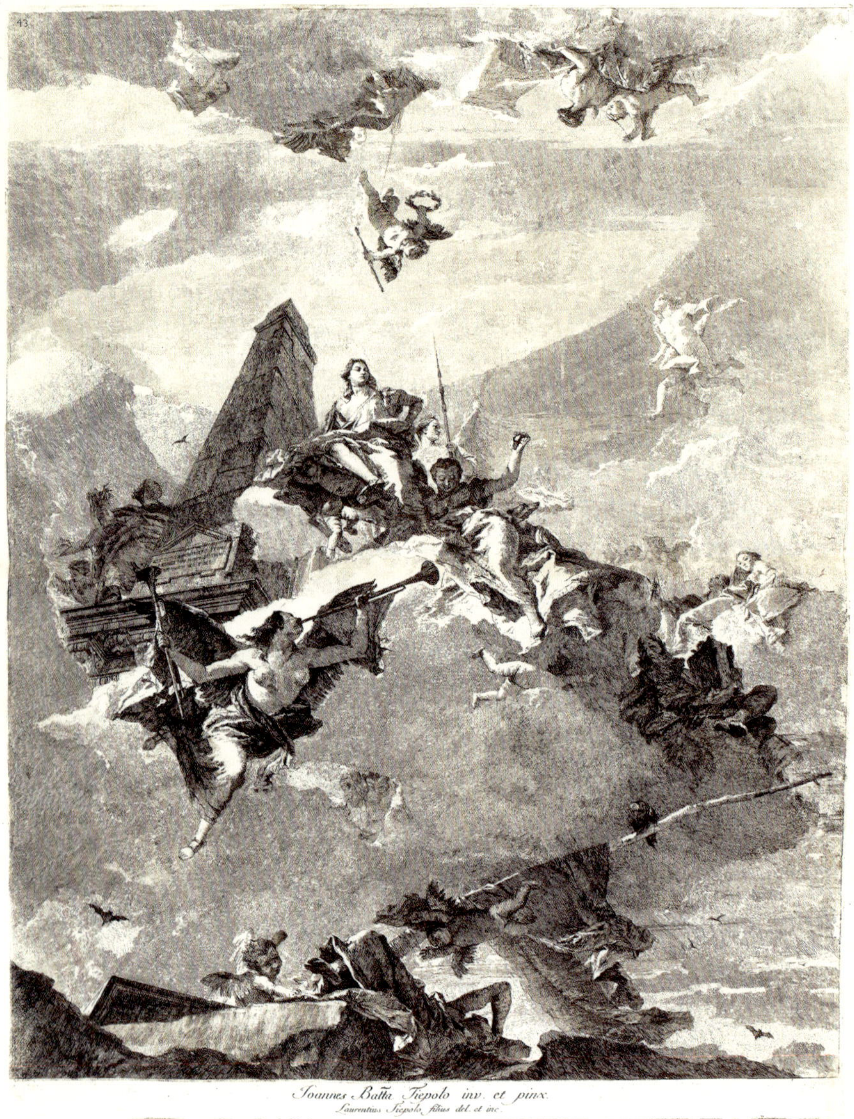

Flight into Egypt of 1750–2 (fig. 30) shows his expressive and open technique, while the much larger *Monument to the Priestess Hero* (fig. 31) by his brother Lorenzo (1736–76) is a *tour de force* of printmaking. Although their fresco commissions in Spain reduced the amount of time the Tiepolo brothers could devote to printmaking, it did not stop their activity. Domenico's *Saint Paschal Bailón Adoring the Eucharist* (fig. 32), after his father Giambattista's painting for the high altar of the Convent of San Pascual de Aranjuez of 1770, was probably published in Venice between 1770 and 1773 and impressions shipped back to Spain.[116]

The Tiepolo prints spawned similar activity in Madrid. José del Castillo is known to have made five prints, all after paintings in Madrid collections.[117] His *Supper at Emmaus* (fig. 33), for example, reproduces Mateo Cerezo's (1637–66) painting then in the Madrid Convent of Agustinos de Recoletos but now lost.[118] It is not known where Castillo learnt to etch, but his prints show an artist completely at ease with the technique, modulating light and dark and using the paper tone to provide contrasts in a way very similar to the Tiepolo.

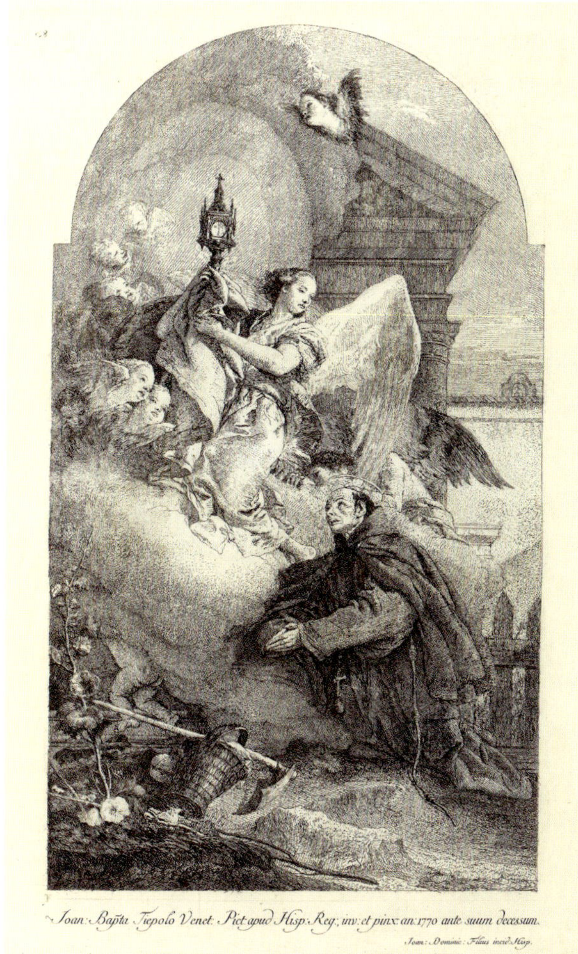

32
Domenico Tiepolo
Saint Paschal Bailón Adoring the Eucharist, 1770–3
Etching, 510 x 288 mm
British Museum, London
1907,0515.84.74

33
José del Castillo after Mateo Cerezo
The Supper at Emmaus, 1778
Etching, 268 x 319 mm
British Museum, London
1848,1125.237

34
Mariano Salvador Maella
The Rest of the Holy Family on the Flight into Egypt, c.1780–90
Etching, 205 x 149 mm
British Museum, London
1860,0414.33

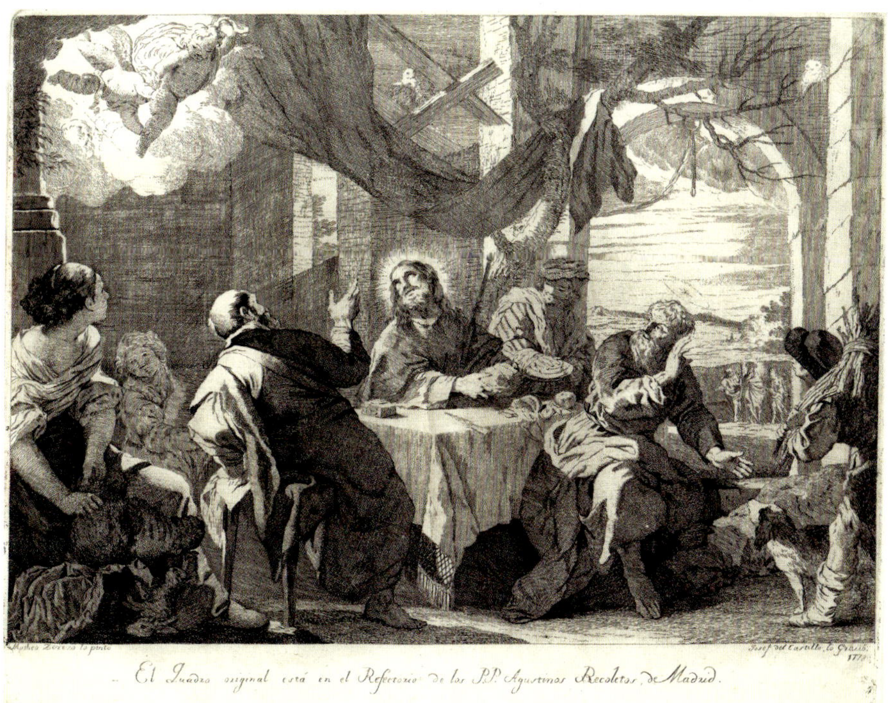

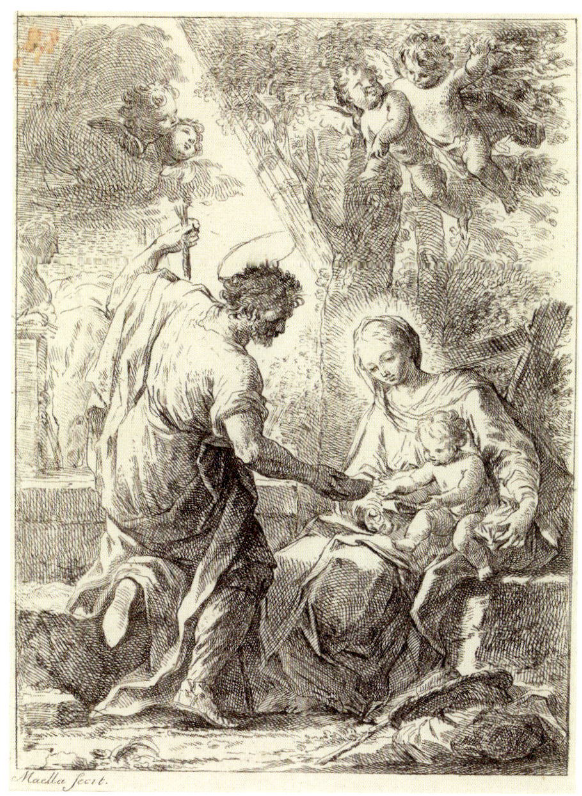

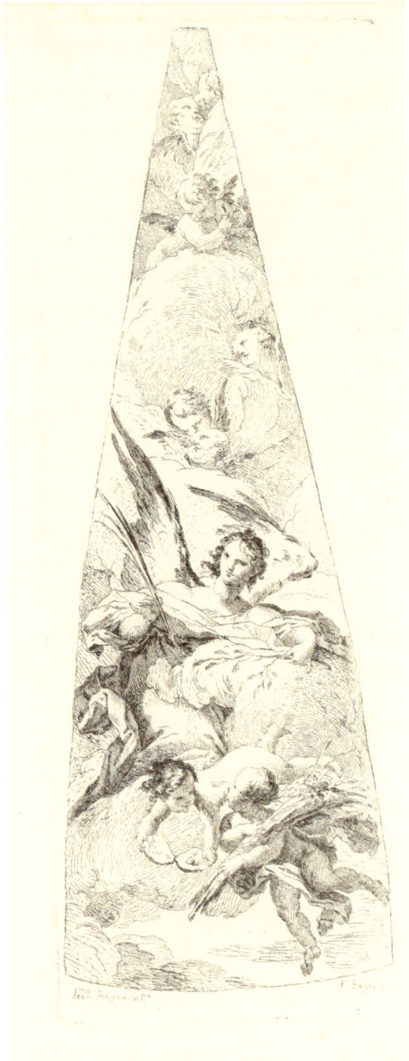 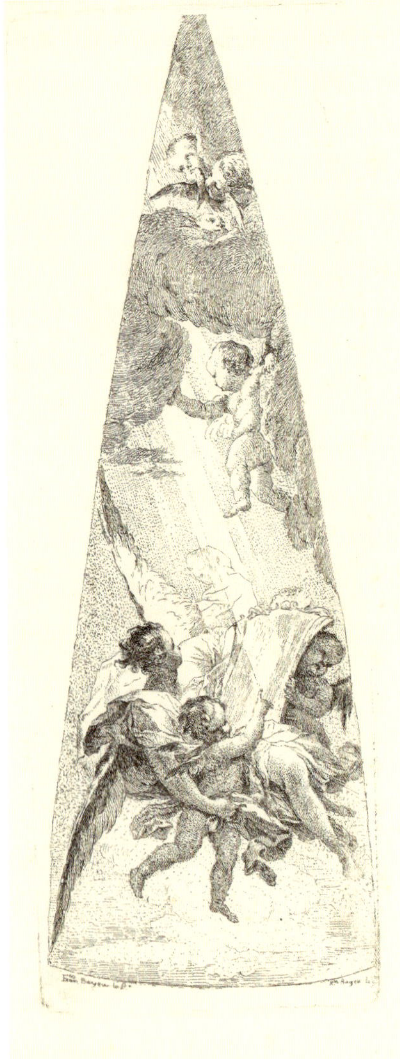 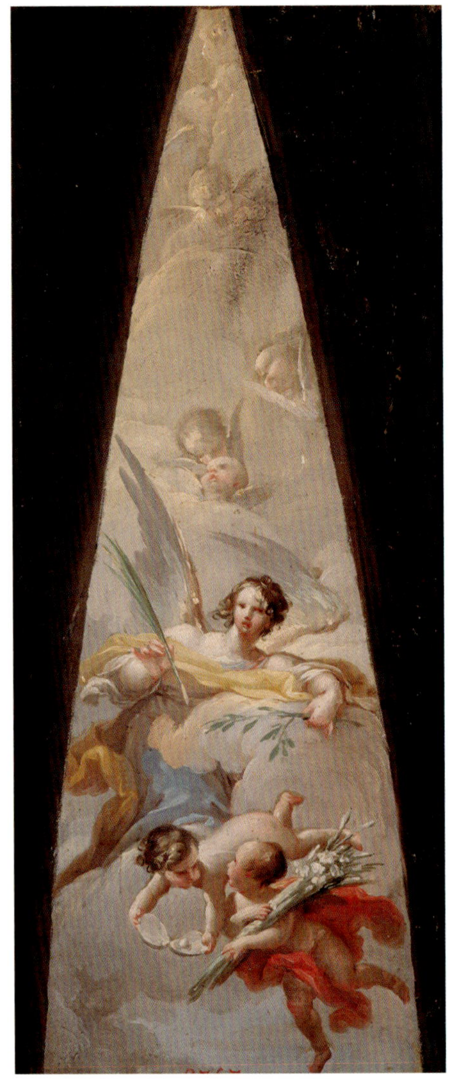

35
Ramón Bayeu y Subías
The Attributes of the Virgin, after 1780
Etching,
289 x 95 mm
British Museum, London
1929,1021.2

36
Ramón Bayeu y Subías
The Attributes of the Virgin, after 1780
Etching,
289 x 98 mm
British Museum, London
1929,1021.3

37
Francisco Bayeu y Subías
The Attributes of the Virgin, c.1778
Oil on canvas,
460 x 190 mm
Museo del Prado, Madrid
P.2952

As a draughtsman Castillo mainly made drawings for prints. He provided a number of designs for the 1780 edition of *Don Quijote* published by the Royal Academy (see p. 219).[119] His contemporary Mariano Salvador Maella is known to have made only one etching, *The Rest of the Holy Family on the Flight into Egypt* (fig. 34), of which three impressions are known.[120]

Ceán Bermúdez observes that Ramón Bayeu made thirteen etchings, significantly more than any of his contemporaries in Madrid.[121] None is dated, and most reproduce paintings in Madrid collections by artists such as Guercino (fig. 14, p. 32).[122] His brother Francisco, whom Ramón assisted in fresco painting and preparing tapestry cartoons (see p. 206),[123] owned etchings by Domenico Tiepolo, including his *Raccolta di Teste* published as a set in Venice around 1774. Two of Ramón's etchings, *The Attributes of the Virgin* (figs 35–6) of after 1780, reproduce Francisco's oil studies for frescos in the apse over the presbytery of the Queen's Oratorio in the Palace at Aranjuez (fig. 37).[124] Ramón's prints show the clear influence of the Tiepolo, but the lightness of his technique is also remarkably close to Goya's early etchings such as the *Blind Guitarist* of 1778 (fig. 4, p. 237).

Professional engravers in Madrid

The growing appreciation of printmaking in Spain after it was made part of the programme at the Academy is reflected in the first manual for printmakers published in Spanish: Manuel Rueda's *Instrucción para grabar en cobre, y perfeccionarse en el grabado a buril, al aguafuerte, y al humo, con el nuevo método de grabar las planchas para estampar en colores, a imitación de la pintura* (Joaquín Ibarra, Madrid 1761).[125] The title indicates its scope, and the advice it contains recognizes that to engrave within a single print such disparate features as architecture, landscape and clouds, requires specialist skills.[126] Rueda's manual was dedicated to the Academy and was based on Abraham Bosse's *Traicté de manières de graver en taille-douce* … (1645 and later editions).

The reproduction of paintings provided the main employment for engravers in Madrid. Manuel Salvador Carmona (1734–1820) is the outstanding Spanish engraver of the second half of the century. His earliest prints date from his time in Paris, where he was elected to the Academy in July 1759.[127] Salvador Carmona returned to Madrid in 1762, and in January 1764 he was awarded the first of his titles, Academician of Merit at the Academy of San Fernando. The *Allegory of Charles III* (fig. 38) after Francesco Solimena, begun in Paris in 1761 and finished in Madrid, demonstrates the benefit of his training: the subtlety of the engraved lines brilliantly conveys the effect of the many surfaces and the depth of the composition.[128] The death in 1777 of Juan Bernabé Palomino, who had been Director of Engraving at the Academy since 1752, meant that the role of Printmaker to the Privy Chamber now became vacant. To ensure his succession, Carmona presented Charles III with a summary of his considerable achievements as an engraver, including his experience in Paris and his election to French academies. He was initially unsuccessful, but eventually secured the position in December 1783, the announcement signed by the Count of Floridablanca describing him as one of the 'foremost printmakers of Europe'.[129]

After the new palace in Madrid had been completed in 1769, Charles III wished to decorate it with the best paintings from the royal collections. By 1772 almost a thousand works had been hung. Four years later Antonio Ponz described in his *Viaje de España* (*Journey through Spain*) the treasures that could be seen in the palace.[130] Although the quality of the Madrid collections greatly impressed him, Ponz laments the lack of reproductive prints that would make them better known and thought it disgraceful that printmakers did not seem to be applying themselves to this work. A man of strong opinions, he also decries the time, money and copper wasted on engraving ridiculous carved altars that he describes as so ugly that they should be kept away from worshippers.[131] Ponz was not alone in promoting professional engraving: in a lengthy open letter reproduced in the *Viaje*, Mengs praises the Spanish Old Masters, above all Velázquez, urging students to copy them in order to understand their methods.[132] In his memoirs the British dramatist Richard Cumberland, who was in Spain in 1780–1, observed that Charles III greatly encouraged English artists to come and copy his paintings, that he would give them access and 'maintain them at free cost', which clearly indicates how eager he was to promote quality reproductive printmaking.[133]

At the beginning of his service for Charles III in 1777, the Count of Floridablanca supported a project to publish reproductive engravings of

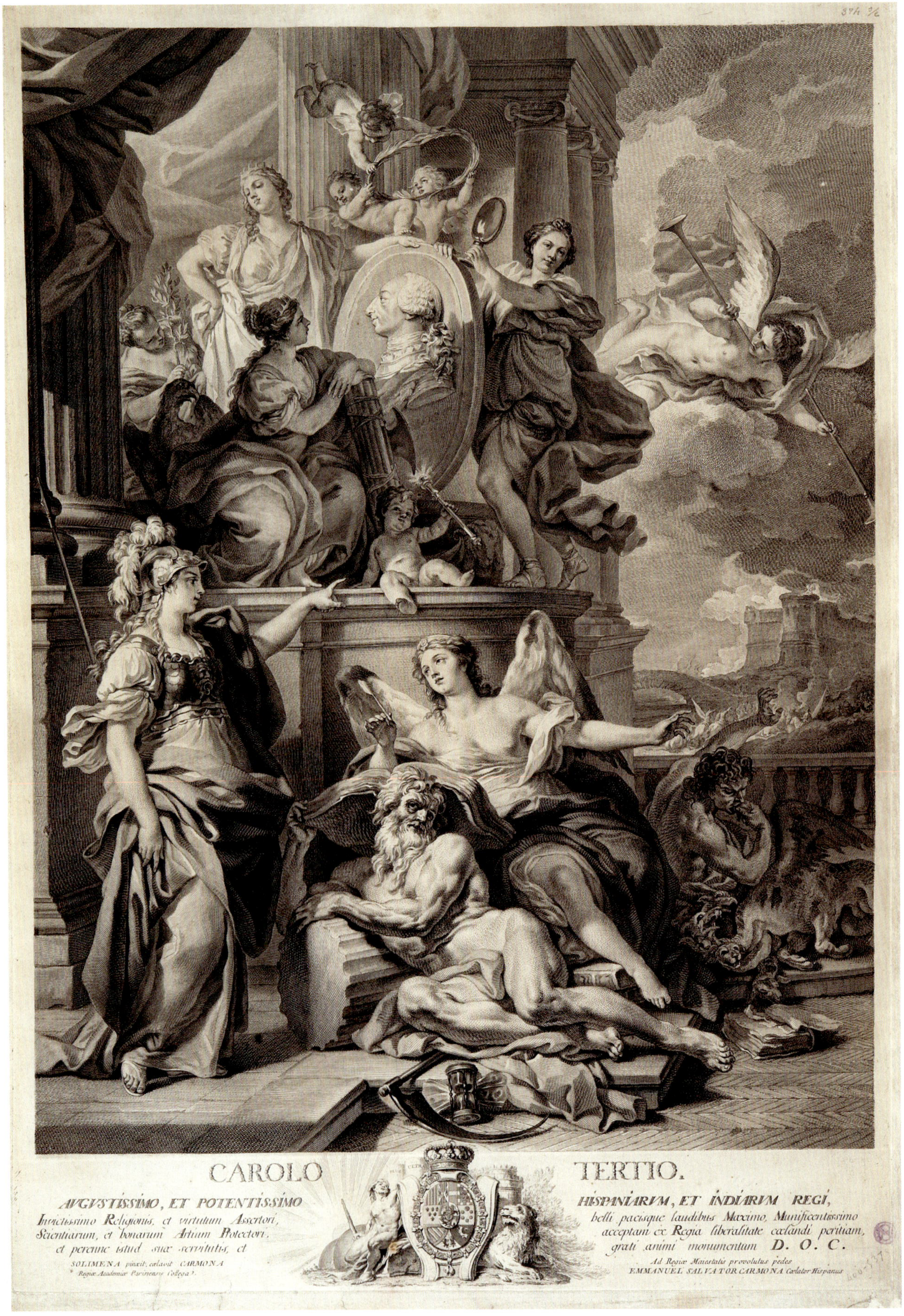
CAROLO TERTIO.
AVGVSTISSIMO, ET POTENTISSIMO
HISPANIARVM, ET INDIARVM REGI,
Invictissimo Religionis, et virtutum Assertori,
Scientiarum, et bonarum Artium Protectori,
belli pacisque laudibus Maximo, Munificentissimo
et perenne istud suæ servitutis, et
acceptam ex Regia liberalitate cælandi peritiam,
grati animi monumentum D. O. C.
SOLIMENA pinxit; cælavit CARMONA
Regiæ Academiæ Parisiensis Collega.
Ad Regiæ Maiestatis provolutus pedes
EMMANUEL SALVATOR CARMONA Cælator Hispanus

masterpieces from the royal collections. This ran aground because of financial problems,[134] but over the next few years engravings reproducing royal works were published in some numbers. For example, Juan Antonio Salvador Carmona (1740–1805), brother of Manuel, made twelve engravings and in 1778 Goya etched his famous series after paintings by Velázquez (see pp. 238–9).[135] The following year sixteen engravings were published after Luca Giordano's frescos of the *Labours of Hercules* in the Buen Retiro (destroyed during its nineteenth-century remodelling). José del Castillo provided the intermediary drawings for these and the plates were engraved by Juan Barcelón (1739–1801) and Nicolo Barsanti (active 1779).[136]

The growing artistic and commercial success of printmaking during these years was among the factors that led to the creation of Royal Chalcography (Real Calcografía) in 1789. Its aim was to provide a location annexed to the Royal Printers (Imprenta Real) where printmaking could be centralized.[137] In the same year – following the failed project of 1777 – a company was formed to publish paintings in the royal collection (Compañía para el grabado de los cuadros de los Reales Palacios). This was supported by Manuel Godoy, Prime Minister of Spain from 1792, who later explained the need 'throughout the kingdom to promote the study of the national and foreign models and spread the news and the glory of the Spanish Old Masters that are little or not at all known through Europe'.[138] In November 1789 Charles IV approved the project, allowing access to the paintings so that they could be drawn for the engravings.

The company operated for a decade and published ninety-five prints, involving many of the leading draughtsman and printmakers in Spain, Rome and Paris.[139] Beset by financial difficulties and heated arguments over the poor quality of some of the drawings produced, the venture was not entirely successful, but it demonstrates the importance of printmaking and reveals which works were regarded as most worthy of reproduction. Manuel Salvador Carmona, for example, made six engravings after Spanish masters:[140] his 1793 engraving (fig. 39) reproduces Velázquez's *The Drunkards* (fig. 40), then hanging in the Royal Palace in Madrid.[141] Each print recorded production details, the size and location of the original painting and biographical information relating to the artist.

Salvador Carmona's outstanding student was Fernando Selma (1752–1810), one of the second generation of professional Spanish engravers. Selma received his earliest training at the academy in Valencia, before being awarded a scholarship in 1768 to study in Madrid.[142] For the

38
Manuel Salvador Carmona after Francesco Solimena
Allegory of Charles III, 1761–3
Engraving, 641 x 442 mm
Biblioteca Nacional, Madrid
IH/1711/64 G

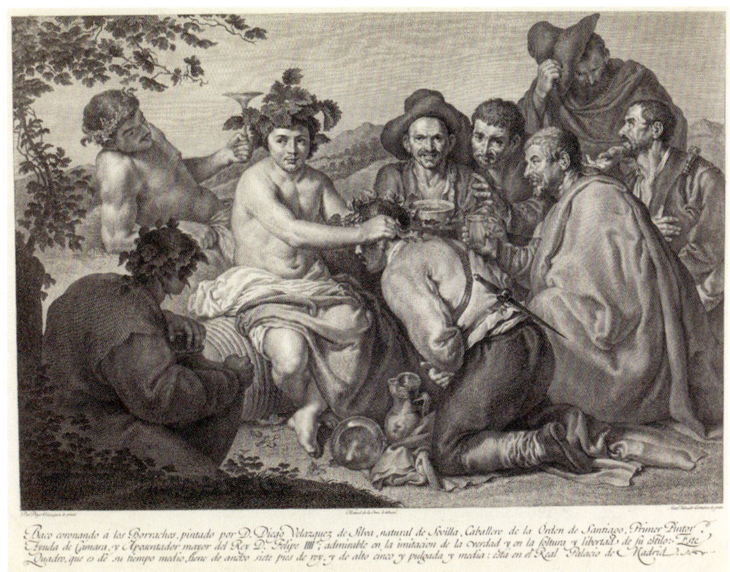

39
Manuel Salvador Carmona after Diego Velázquez
The Drunkards or *The Triumph of Bacchus*, 1793
Engraving and etching, 470 x 610 mm
British Museum, London
1845,1223.7

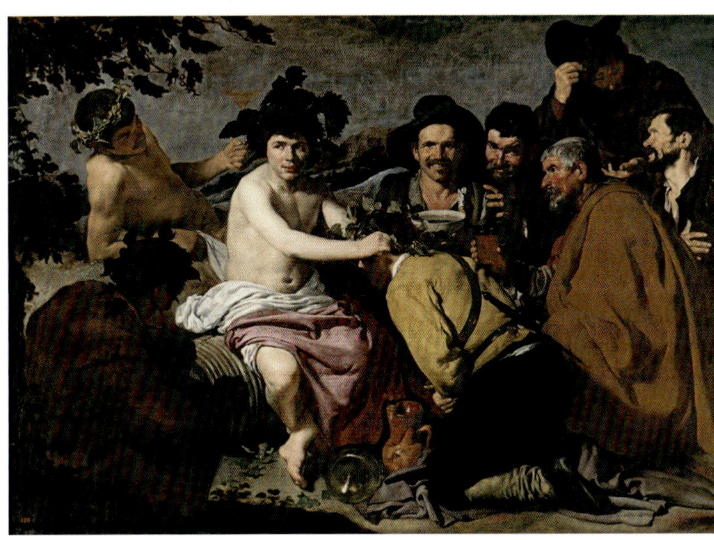

40
Diego Velázquez
The Drunkards or *The Triumph of Bacchus*, 1628–9
Oil on canvas, 1650 x 2250 mm
Museo del Prado, Madrid
P.1170

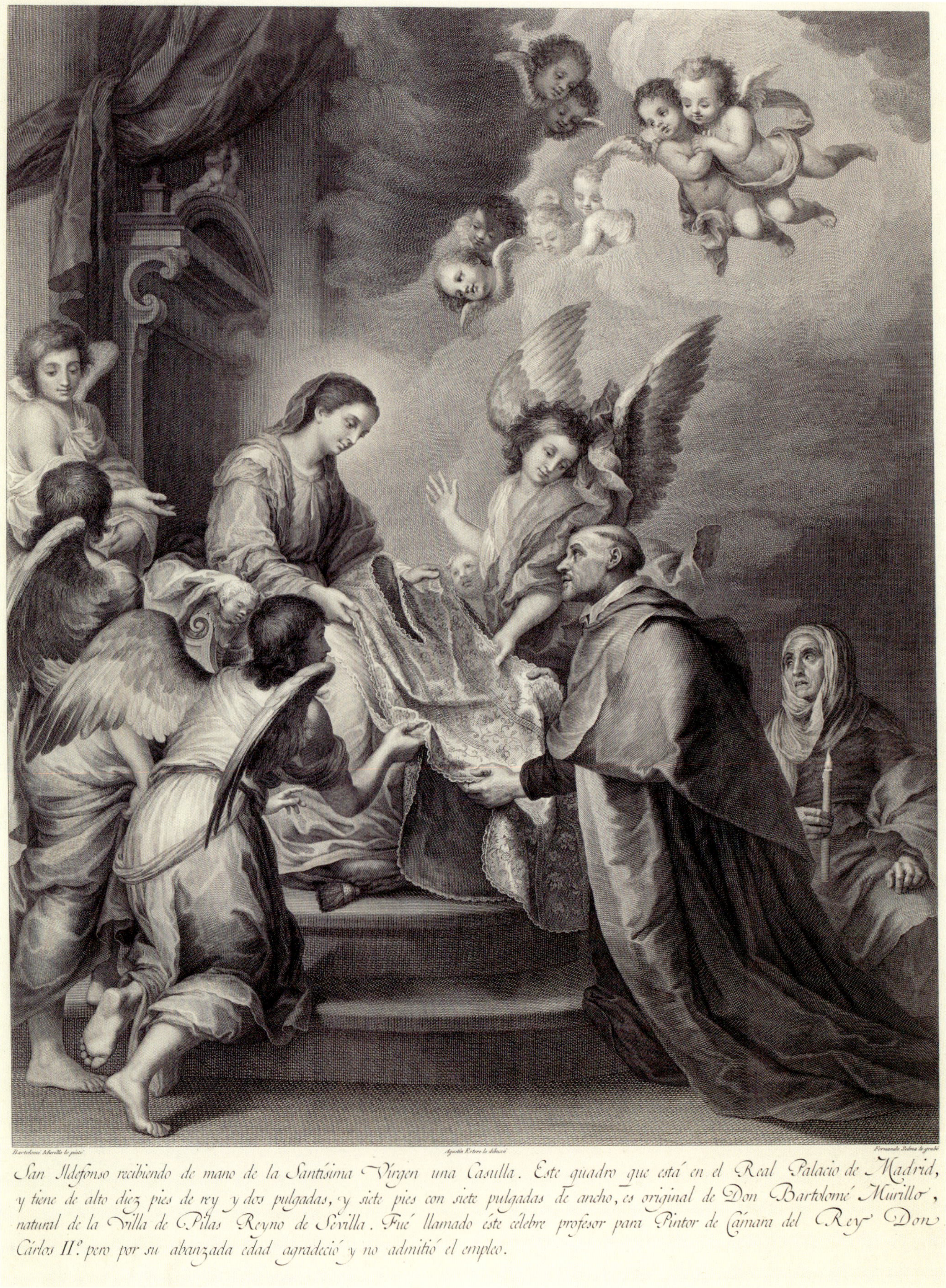
Bartolome Murillo lo pintó
Agustin Estere lo dibuxó
Fernando Selma lo grabó
San Ildefonso recibiendo de mano de la Santísima Virgen una Casulla. Este quadro que está en el Real Palacio de Madrid,
y tiene de alto diez pies de rey y dos pulgadas, y siete pies con siete pulgadas de ancho, es original de Don Bartolomé Murillo,
natural de la Villa de Pilas Reyno de Sevilla. Fué llamado éste célebre profesor para Pintor de Cámara del Rey Don
Cárlos II.º pero por su abanzada edad agradeció y no admitió el empleo.

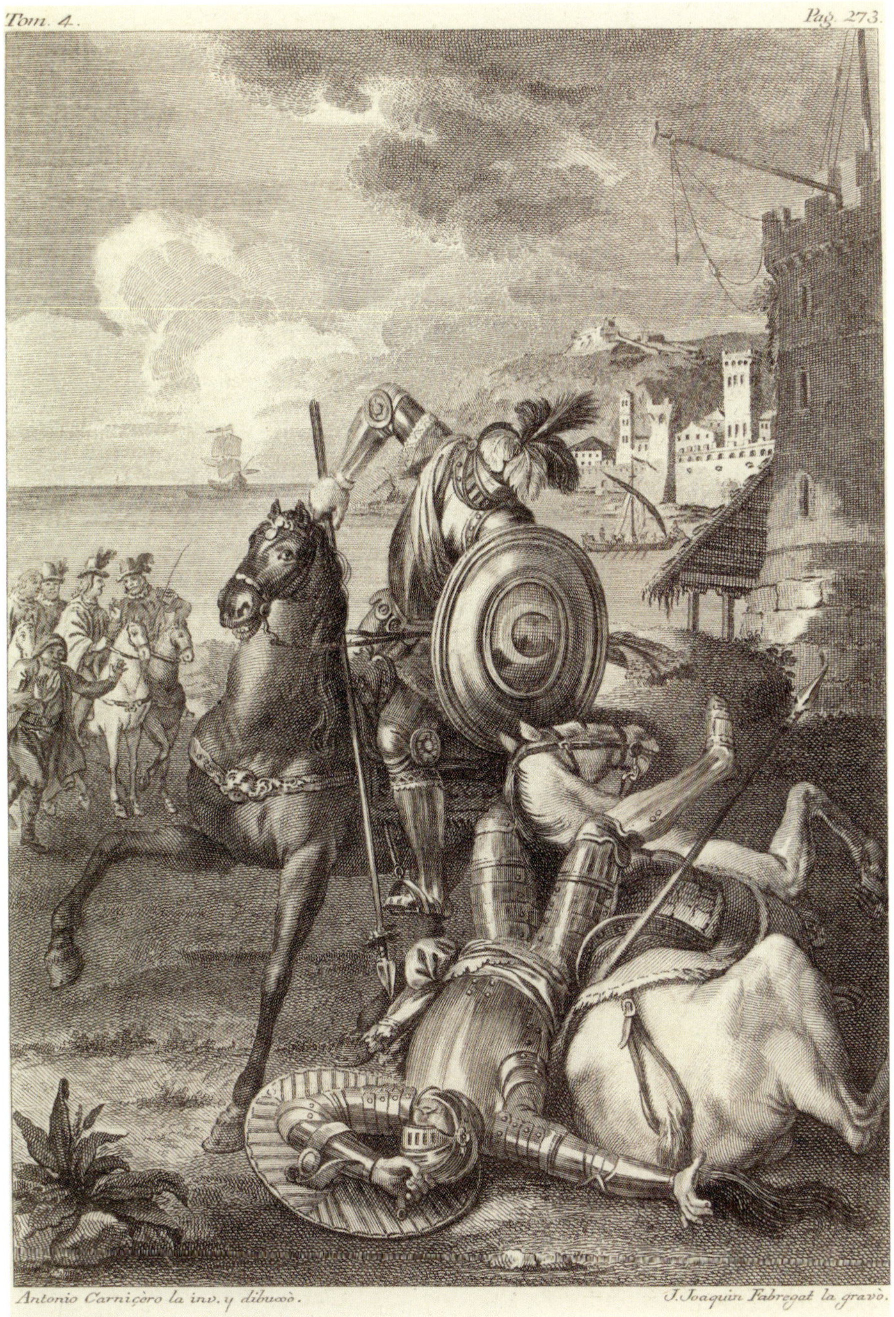

41
Fernando Selma after Bartolomé Esteban Murillo

Saint Ildephonsus Receiving the Chasuble from the Virgin, 1789–1800

Engraving and etching, 662 x 522 mm
British Museum, London
1845,1223.5

42
José Joaquín Fabregat after Antonio Carnicero

Don Quijote Defeated by the Knight of the White Moon, 1780

Etching and engraving, 207 x 142 mm
British Museum, London
1849,1208.85

company Selma engraved Murillo's painting of *Saint Ildephonsus Receiving the Chasuble from the Virgin* (fig. 41).[143] Reproductive prints made before this time were fairly small, but the large size of this print (660 x 522 mm) demonstrates unprecedented ambition and quality that came to characterize printmaking in Spain.

Of the new subjects that appeared through of the expansion of printmaking, many appeared in book illustrations. Book projects engaged the services of many prominent artists, often working collaboratively. In 1780, for example, the Royal Academy of Spain (Real Academia Española) published an illustrated edition of *Don Quijote*. The project was conceived early in 1773, when the Academy identified the need for a magnificent edition engraved by the best printmakers and appointed a commission dedicated to the project.[144] The book comprised four parts and contained thirty-five high-quality engraved illustrations. Eight artists provided drawings to be engraved by ten printmakers. The episodes chosen for illustration were those that best expressed the character of Don Quijote. In 1774 José del Castillo provided the first of his drawings; his eventual eight included *Don Quijote Beaten by Two Men in a Forest*, engraved by Pedro Pascual Moles. Several drawings for this composition survive, as well as a proof impression of the print and the copper plate.[145] Three years later the Academy decided to dispense with Castillo's services, stating that he was too expensive, and then had to find a replacement. Seven artists presented designs, among them Francisco de Goya. The commission settled on Antonio Carnicero (1748–1814),[146] who provided nineteen final designs for the book, a greater number than any other artist. His drawing of *Don Quijote Defeated by the Knight of the White Moon* (fig. 42), for example, was engraved by José Joaquín Fabregat (1748–1807).[147] The prints were also sold as loose impressions to offset the considerable cost of the edition.

Popular prints

The growth of the printmaking industry gave rise to the publication of collections of prints, some of which, for example the engraved views of royal residences, had political significance in promoting the prestige of the court.[148] Others can be best described as popular prints – implying wide appeal rather than necessarily cheap production values. The appetite for printed images, especially during the last third of the century, was enormous, with subjects

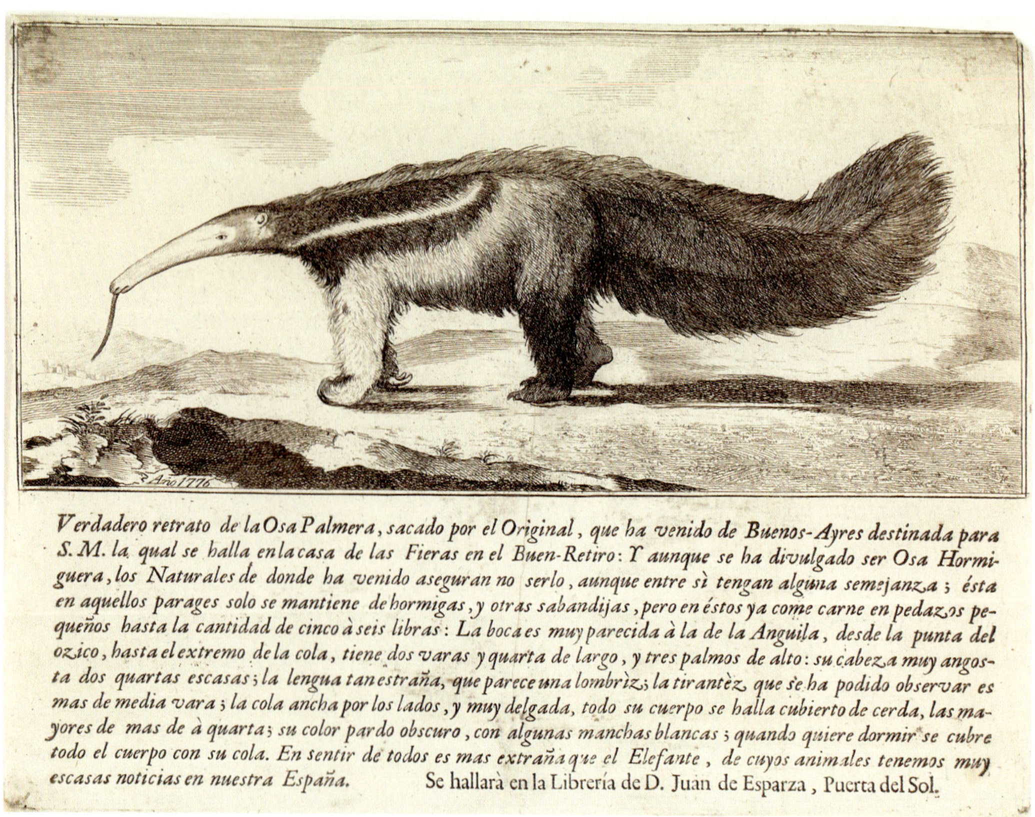

43
Anonymous after Francisco de Goya
The True Portrait of a She Ant-bear (anteater), 1776
Etching and letterpress, 214 x 276 mm
British Museum, London
1917,1208.455

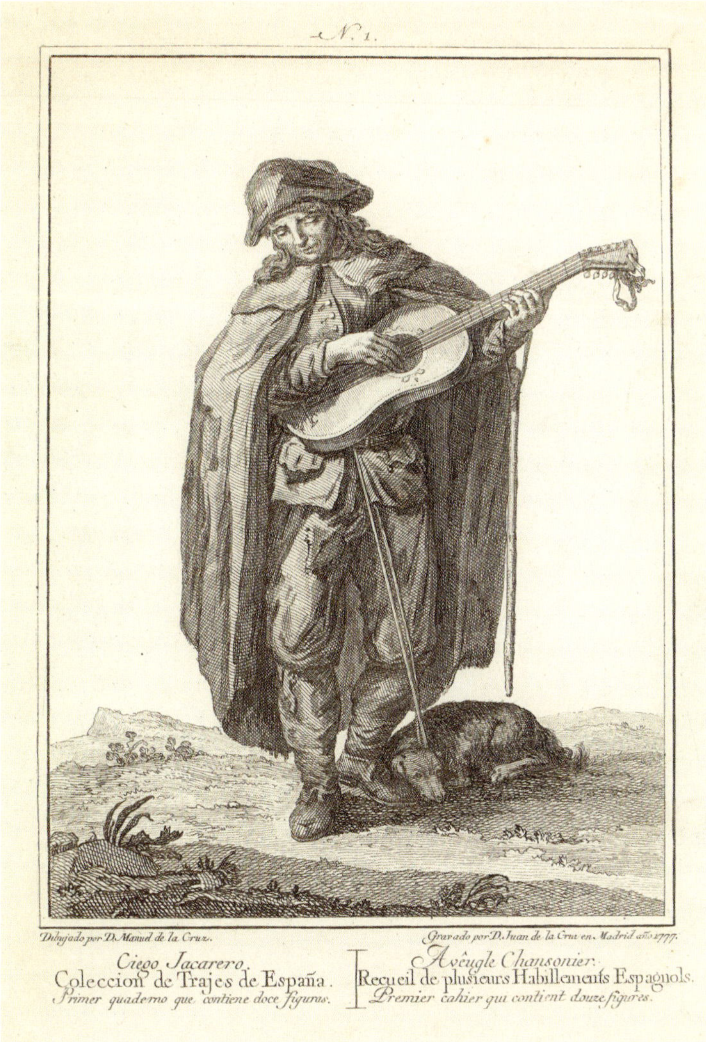

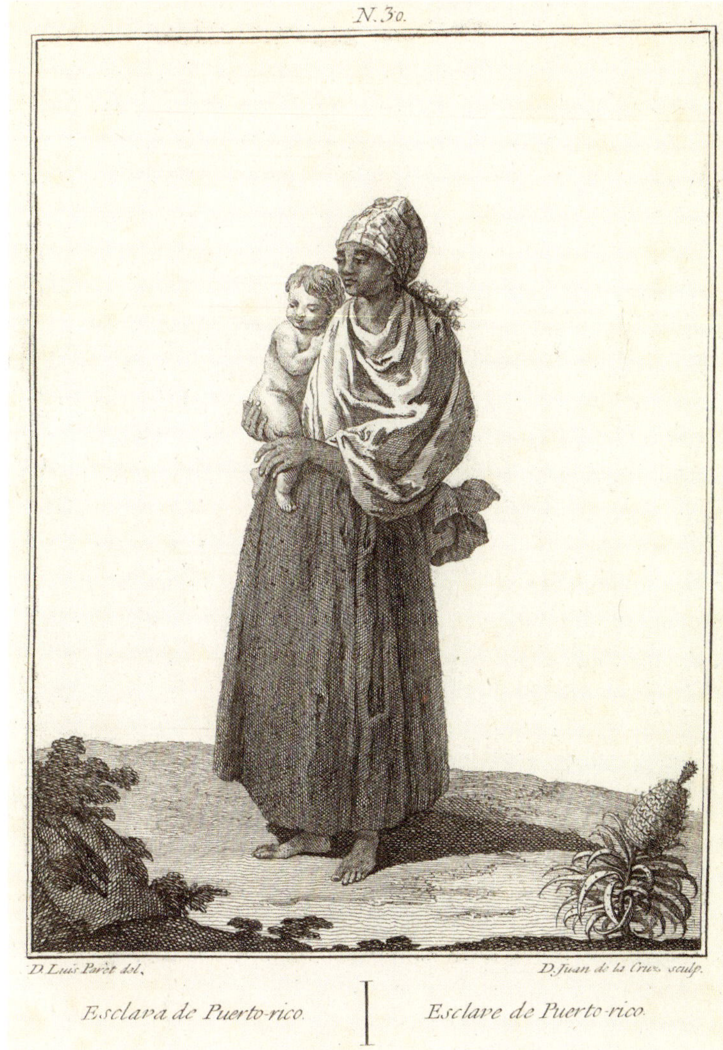

such as dress, customs, popular pastimes, unusual or remarkable creatures and events becoming staples of production.[149]

Advertised for sale in the *Gazeta de Madrid* on 10 September 1776, an etching entitled *The True Portrait of a She Ant-Bear* (fig. 43) depicts an anteater brought from Buenos Aires and paraded before Charles III and the court. The creature was kept in the gardens of the Buen Retiro and aroused enormous interest, resulting in a royal commission to have a painting made of it, under the direction of Mengs; the painting has been attributed recently to Goya.[150] The text below the image describes its unusual features, colouring and size – such exotic animals were little known in Spain.

The *Collection of Spanish Costume* (*Colección de trajes de España*), engraved by Juan de la Cruz Cano, represents a sort of print series that became very popular in Spain.[151] Cruz Cano was among the group of artists sent to Paris in 1752 in order to learn engraving (p. 198). The title page of the *Colección* describes its encyclopaedic ambition: it was to be divided into two volumes with eight *cuadernos* (gatherings) of twelve prints each. The first volume depicted familiar costumes from Spain (fig. 44), while the second illustrated those which were less well known, from across the entire empire and including

44
Juan de la Cruz Cano y Olmedilla after Manuel de la Cruz
The Blind Guitarist, 1777
Etching and engraving, 304 x 224 mm
British Museum, London
1896,0511.131

45
Juan de la Cruz Cano y Olmedilla
A Slave from Puerto Rico, 1777
Etching and engraving, 291 x 215 mm
British Museum, London
1917,1208.31(15)

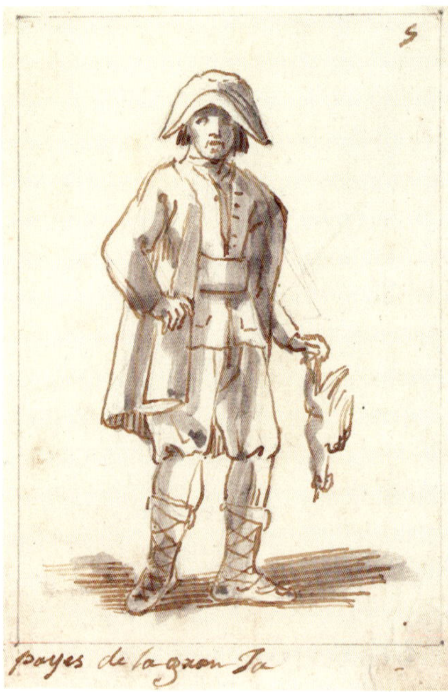

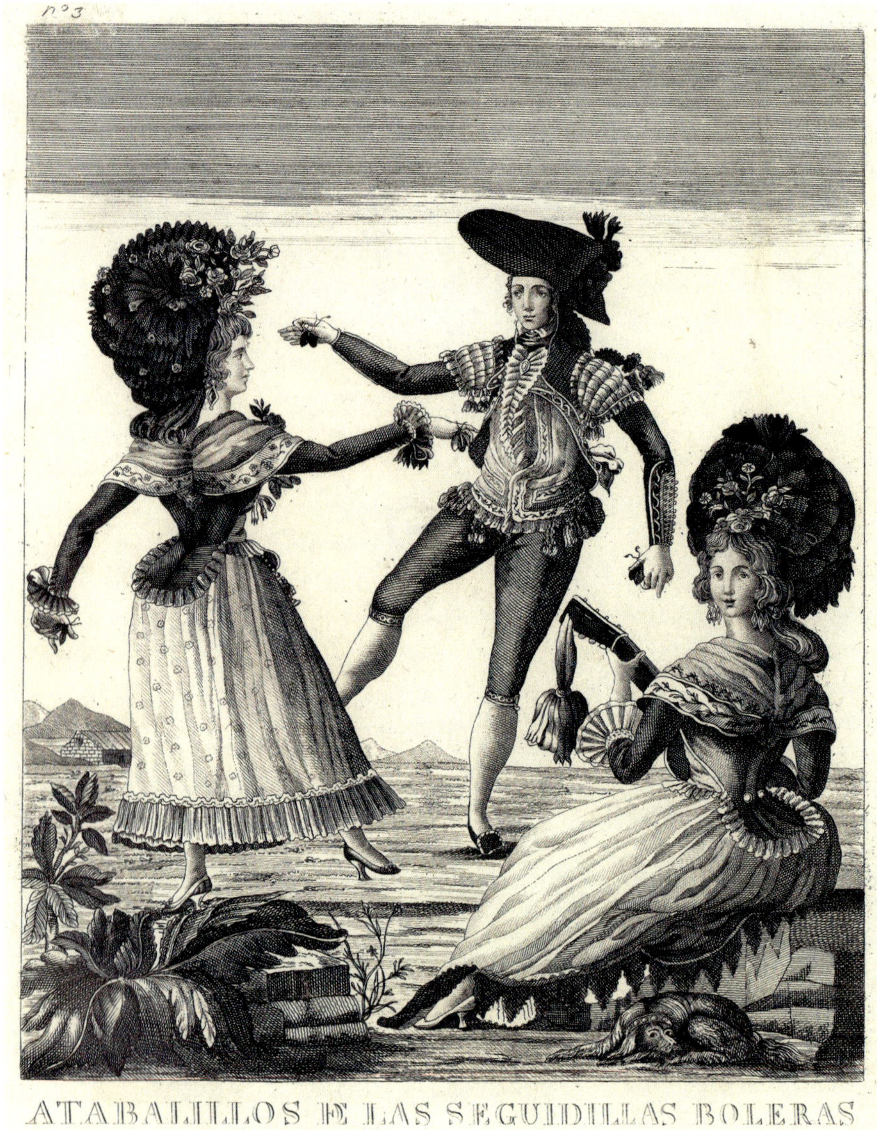

46
Anonymous
Man from La Granja Holding Game, c.1770–90
Pen and brown ink with grey wash over black chalk, approx. 139 x 91 mm
British Museum, London
1985,0608.46

47
Marcos Téllez Villar
Spanish Dances (plate 3), c.1780–90
Etching and engraving, 287 x 218 mm
Biblioteca Nacional, Madrid
ER.3439(3)

different professions and social positions – such as, for example, a slave from Puerto Rico (fig. 45). The project was not completed: only six *cuadernos* containing twelve figures were published between 1777 and 1788; Cruz died in 1790. Among those artists who provided drawings for the prints were Antonio Carnicero and Luis Paret. The prints have lettered descriptions in Spanish and French, in order to appeal to different audiences; their remarkable success was sufficient for Cruz to denounce the existence of fraudulent editions.[152] A group of anonymous drawings from the second half of the eighteenth century has also survived: these were presumably made for prints and depict people from different regions of Spain (fig. 46).

Series of popular prints were often of high quality. A set of prints of about 1780–90 depicting Spanish dances (*seguidillas boleras*), for example, were expertly etched by Marcos Téllez Villar and carefully printed (fig. 47). Dance and other forms of recreation were popular subjects during the later part of the century and depicted by many artists, from the tapestry designers at Santa Barbara to Francisco de Goya and José Camarón y Bonanat. Antonio

Carnicero's twelve etchings of bullfighting, the *Collection of the Principal Manoeuvres of Bullfighting* (*Colección de las principales suertes de una corrida de toros*), published in both black-and-white and hand-coloured editions in Madrid between 1787 and 1790, were enormously popular.[153] Copies and variants were also popular outside Spain.[154] The series begins with the bull being led into the ring, followed by images of the principal manoeuvres of the engagement, until the bull is killed and dragged away by horses (fig. 48–9). The series had a specific relevance beyond broadly celebrating the art of bullfighting: it was conceived in homage to the famous toreador Pedro Romero, who had triumphed over his rivals Joaquín Costillares and Pepe Hillo during celebrations for Charles IV's coronation in 1789. Pedro Salanoba's poetic composition, *Tauromaquia Hispania*, published in the *Diario de Madrid* on 8 November 1790, identifies Romero as the bullfighter in plate XI of the series.[155] In the following year Carnicero added another, much larger print of the public spectacle at the bullring near the Puerta de Alcalá in Madrid, paid for by Ferdinand VI, where the first bullfight was held on 3 July 1749.[156]

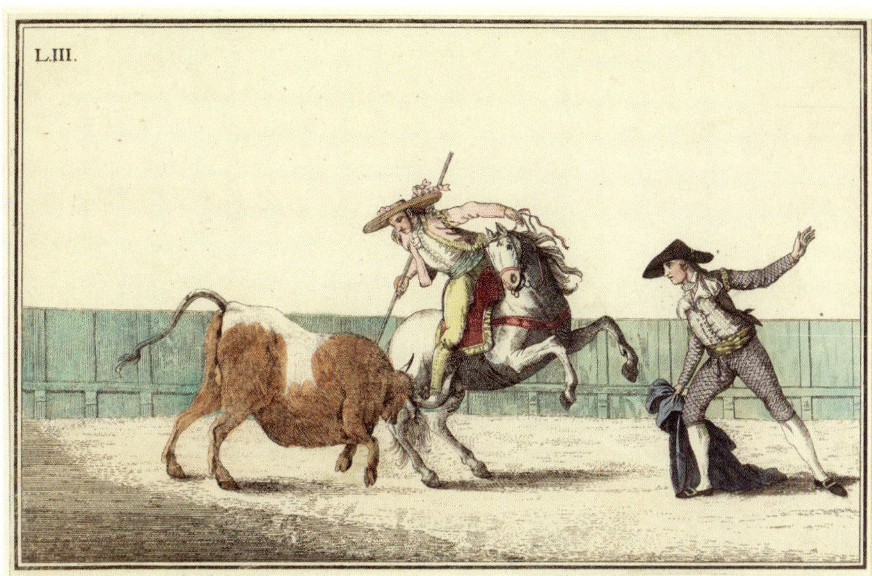

48
Antonio Carnicero
A Picador Leaves the bullring after Stabbing the Bull, c.1789
Hand-coloured etching, 177 x 280 mm
British Museum, London
1871,0812.4514

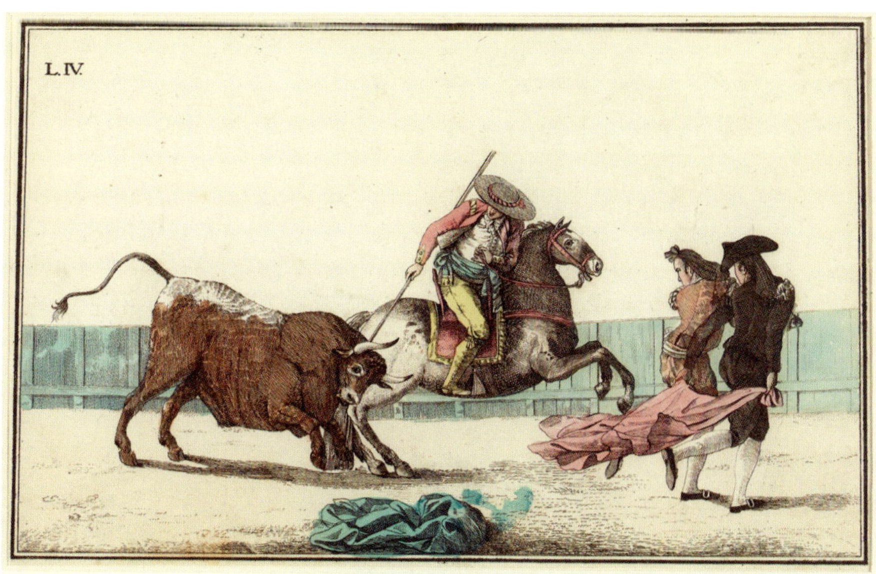

49
Antonio Carnicero
A Picador on Horseback Stabbing a Bull, c.1789
Hand-coloured etching, 177 x 267 mm
British Museum, London
1871,0812.4515

Prints and drawings in the regional centres of Spain

The dominance of the Academy and the patronage of the court, religious and private clients in Madrid had a detrimental effect on the artistic survival of the regional centres (Valencia, Barcelona, Seville and Granada).[157] Yet these towns did not fall into complete decline, as can be seen by the activity of their art academies and drawing schools, a number of them established during the second half of the eighteenth century.[158] Different bodies were responsible for their establishment: councils, the church, societies (*sociedades económicas*) and individual patrons. There were attempts to formalize training in an academic context in Valencia, Zaragoza and Valladolid; while the Madrid Academy was not involved in their foundation in every case, it provided a powerful model to be emulated.[159]

The movement of artists, motivated by employment opportunities, had long been a feature of the history of art in Spain and continued during the eighteenth century. Those who remained in their home towns are often overlooked because they were not part of established networks of patronage connected in some way to Madrid. Their work is also hard to reconcile with the dominant artistic trends because it was parochial, made for local audiences and confined mainly to book illustration and devotional prints.

In early 1753 artists in Valencia created their own academy, under the patronage of Santa Barbara.[160] (In the previous century provincial artists such as Juan Conchillos and Evaristo Muñoz ran drawing schools from their own homes; see Chapter 6).[161] The Academy of Santa Barbara was modelled on the Madrid Academy: in the early years it was run entirely by artists, with the emphasis almost exclusively on drawing.[162] In February 1768 an Academy of Fine Arts (San Carlos) was officially founded in Valencia, following careful consultation with colleagues in Madrid and the conferment of royal approval in 1765. The teaching programme was based on the syllabus of the Madrid Academy, which sent drawings to Valencia for students to copy, together with replica casts of antique statues to illustrate Mengs' neoclassical theories.[163] Printmaking was also part of the programme. A consequence of artistic exchange was that many artists who began their careers in Valencia eventually settled Madrid – as, for example, Maella, Fernando Selma and José Joaquín Fabregat. The most important printmaker associated with the Valencia Academy in its early days was Carlos Francia (active 1741–62), who was also a painter and architect.[164] He designed and etched a number of prints, several of which record celebrations associated with the festival of Saint Vincent Ferrer in Valencia in 1755, and later, an ephemeral monument for the proclamation of Charles III as king in 1759.[165]

The most significant eighteenth-century Valencian artist was José Camarón y Bonanat (1731–1803).[166] After his early education in Segorbe, Camarón moved to Valencia by 1749 and Madrid by 1752, where he was associated with the Academy. He was back in Valencia by 1754, when he was nominated Academician of Merit and appointed teacher of painting at the Academy of Santa Barbara. In 1762 he was elected Academician by the Madrid Academy.[167] Camarón is one of the most prolific draughtsmen of the eighteenth century. The 1805 Acts of the Valencia Academy records that he 'drew with consummate intelligence and taste a great number of subjects, in wash and pencil, on biblical history, profane and fabulous subjects'.[168] He

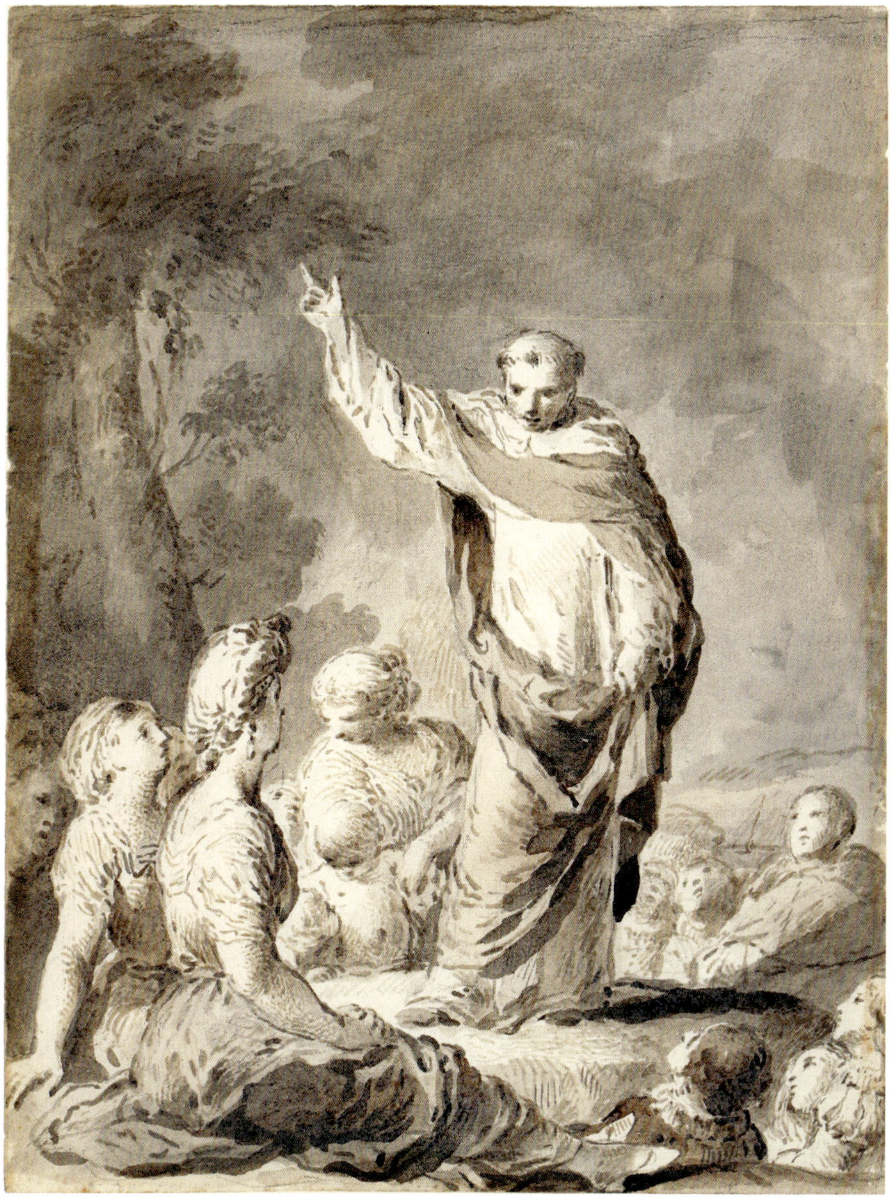

50
José Camarón y Bonanat

Saint Vincent Ferrer Preaching, c.1752–60

Brush drawing in grey and brown wash over black chalk, 205 x 151 mm
British Museum, London
1973,0120.5

51
Michel-Ange Houasse

Saint Francis Regis Preaching, before 1722

Oil on canvas, diameter 158 mm
Museo del Prado, Madrid
P.4196

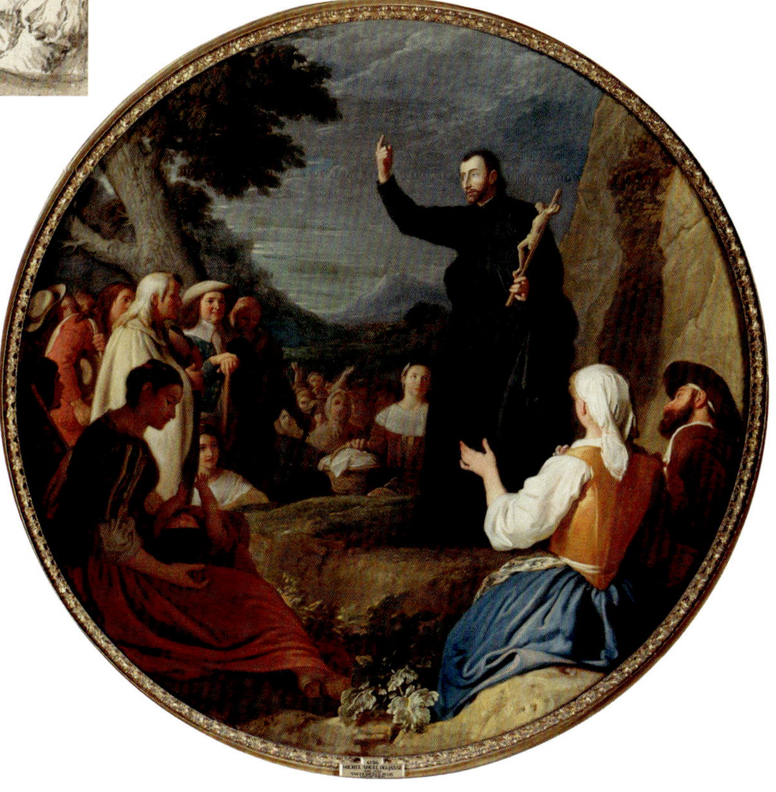

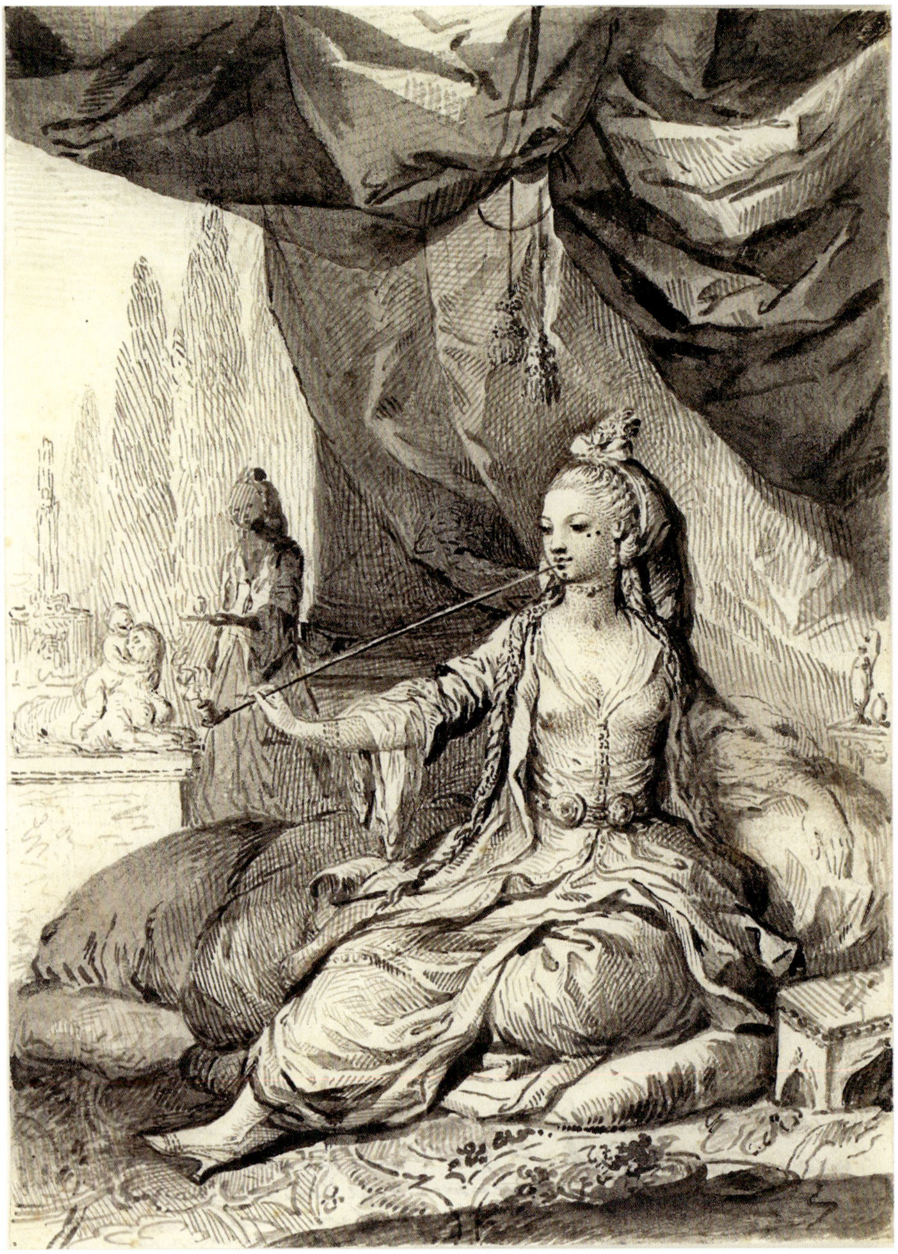

52
José Camarón y Bonanat
An Algerian Woman Seated Beneath a Canopy, c.1771–80
Brush drawing in grey ink and wash, 214 x 149 mm
British Museum, London
1973,0120.4

made preparatory studies for paintings, book illustrations and independent sheets, many it seems forming sketchbooks that have since been separated. He prepared so many drawings in different media that it is difficult to determine a clear chronology; drawings from early in his career in particular, are hard to identify.

In his drawing of Saint Vincent Ferrer (fig. 50) Camarón was depicting a greatly venerated local saint. Vincent Ferrer (d. 1419) was born in Valencia and renowned for his evangelizing zeal. Camarón depicts him preaching to a group of seated figures in eighteenth-century dress, reinforcing the continued relevance of the saint's message. The drawing seem to have been based on Michel-Ange Houasse's *Saint Francis Regis Preaching* (fig. 51), commissioned by the Jesuit Capilla del Noviciado in Madrid and painted before 1722.[169] Camarón made another almost identical version of this drawing (Biblioteca

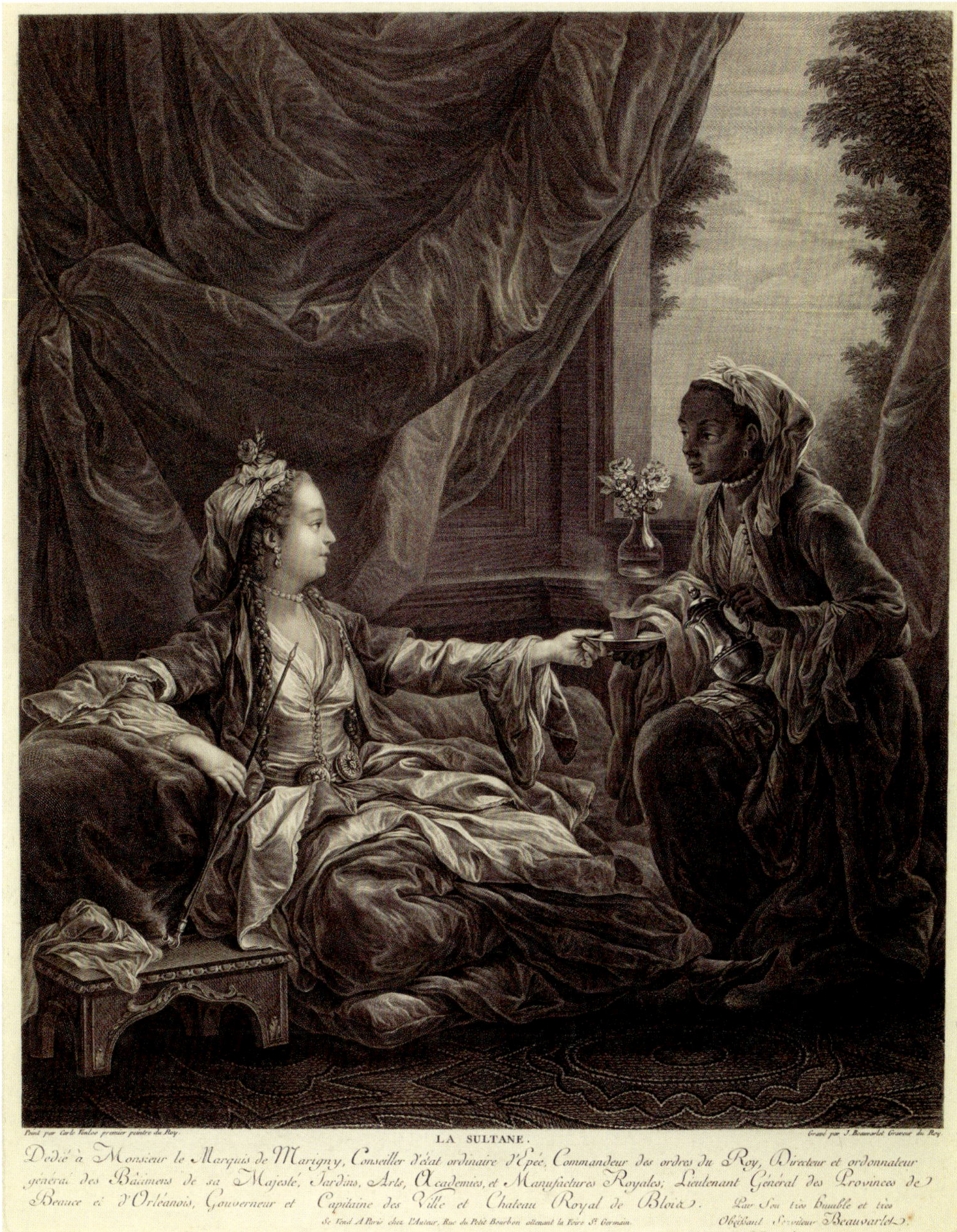

53
Jacques Firmin Beauvarlet
The Sultana Taking Coffee, c.1771
Engraving and etching, 480 x 368 mm
British Museum, London
1917,1208.2094

Nacional, Madrid) and repeated the figure of the saint, as the angel of the Apocalypse, in the mural medallion in the apse in the church of San Vincent Ferrer de Algimia (Castellón) around 1776.[170] Given the close connection between his drawing and Houasse's painting it might have been made when Camarón was in Madrid in the early 1750s.

One of Camarón's most striking sheets is his brush drawing of an Algerian woman (fig. 52), which has notes on the verso describing the colours to be used for the various elements in a painting that does not seem to have materialized.[171] The drawing is based on Carle Van Loo's *Sultana Taking Coffee* (Hermitage, St Petersburg) of the early 1750s.[172] Camarón would certainly have known of the painting, through the print by Jacques Firmin Beauvarlet published around 1771 (fig. 53).[173] The majority of Camarón's drawings were for book illustrations. José Esteve writes in a letter (1795) that 'his passion for

54
José Camarón y Bonanat
Saint Mary Magdalene in the Desert, c.1760–90
Pen with grey and brown ink and wash, 204 x 150 mm
British Museum, London
1973,0120.9

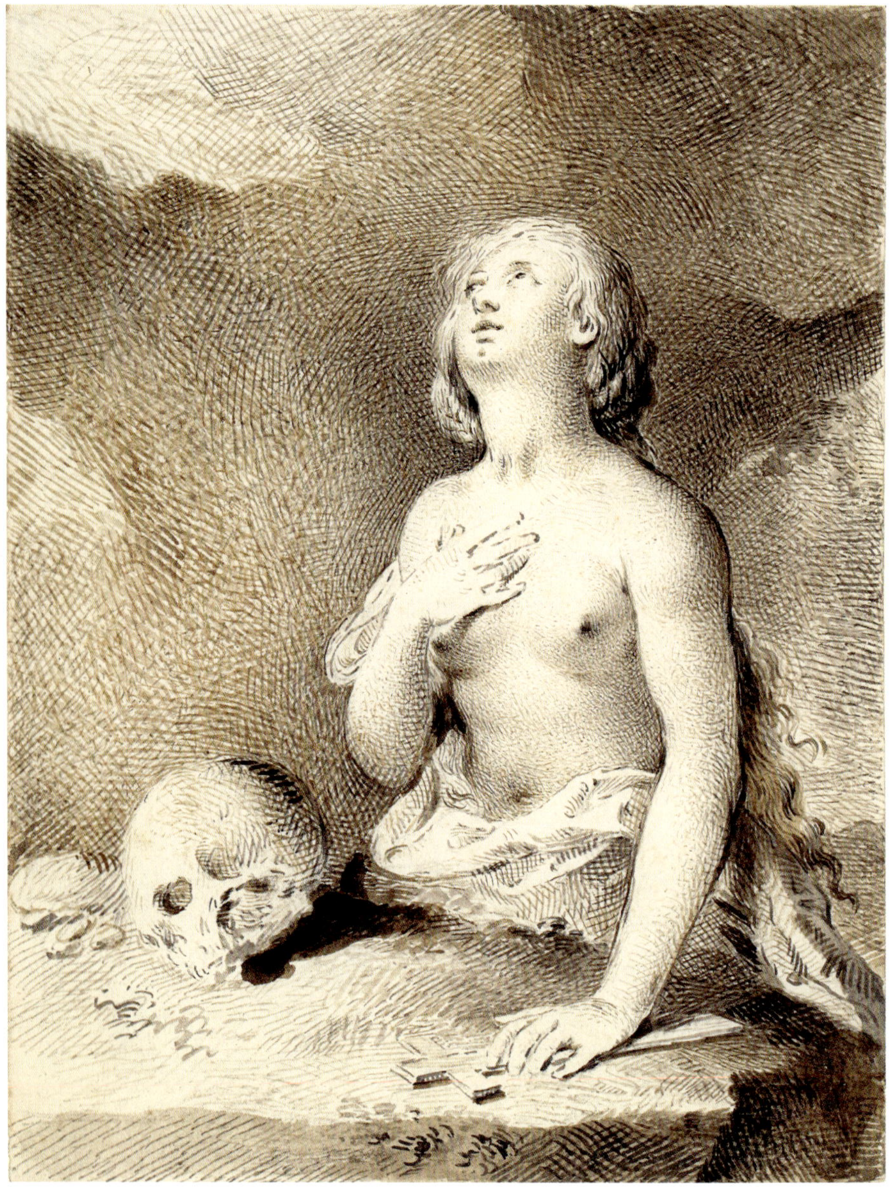

drawing was such that following his work during the day devoted to painting, he spent most of the night making drawings for engravings'.[174] In 1771 Camarón produced thirty-four drawings for a lavish edition of *Don Quijote*, and three years later twenty-four scenes for a life of Saint Joseph and more for another edition of *Don Quijote* published in 1797–8.[175] In a number of his drawings the hatched pen-and-ink technique resembles engraving, probably to facilitate the easy translation of areas of light and dark into print: this can be seen, for example, in his *Saint Mary Magdalene in the Desert* (fig. 54).

José Vergara (1726–99) and Luis Antonio Planes (1742–1821) are regarded as Camarón's most significant contemporaries. Vergara was closely involved in establishing the Valencia Academy. He was a prolific draughtsman from whose hand many sheets survive, mainly studies of individual figures and details for painted compositions.[176] Planes was the more talented draughtsman, but fewer of his drawings survive.[177] His great skill is demonstrated by the remarkably well-preserved study of the Last Supper for the high altar in the

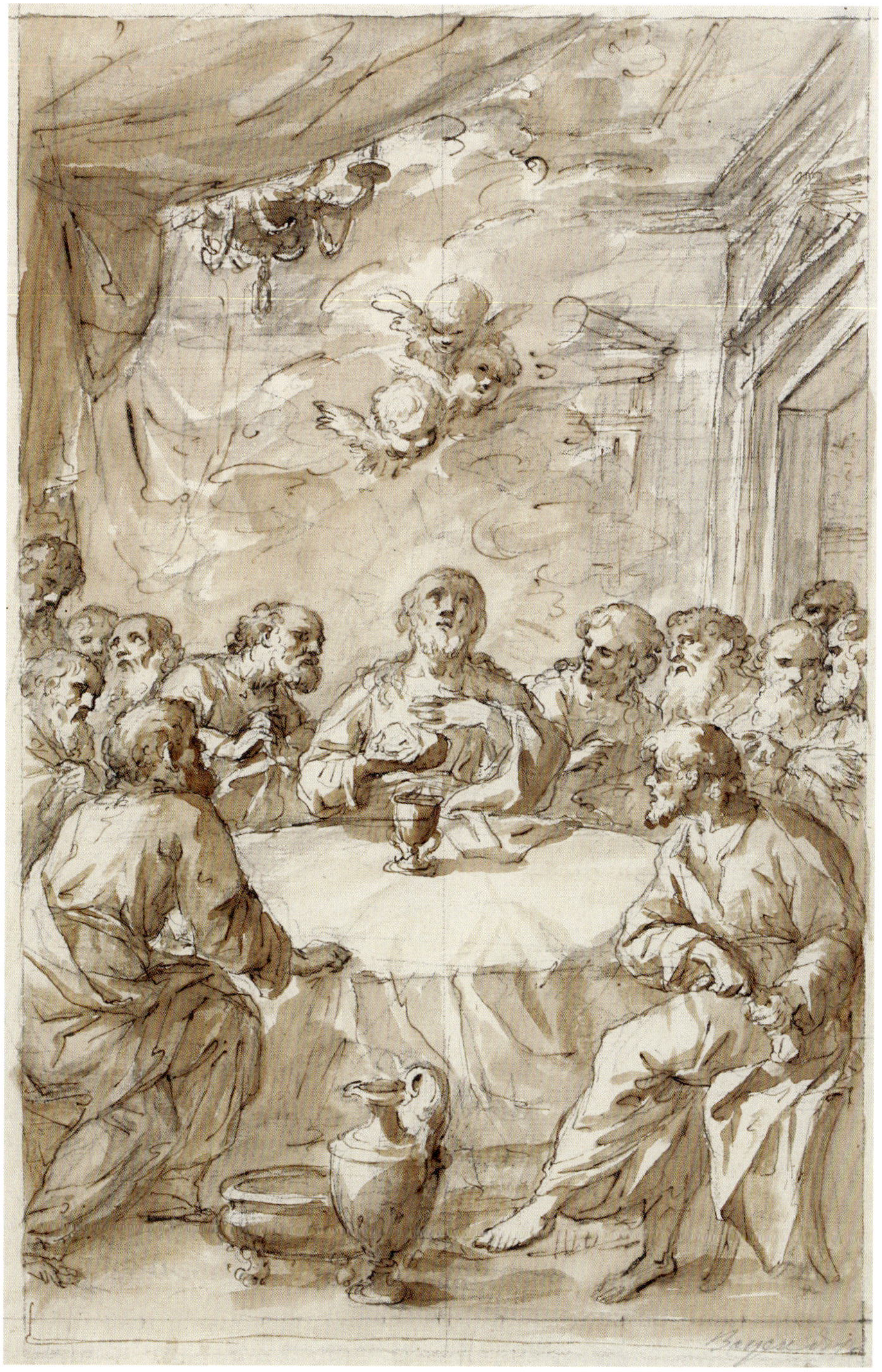

55
Luis Planes
The Last Supper, 1802–4
Pen and brown ink and brown wash, over black chalk, scaled for transfer, 356 x 247 mm
British Museum, London
1946,0713.1507

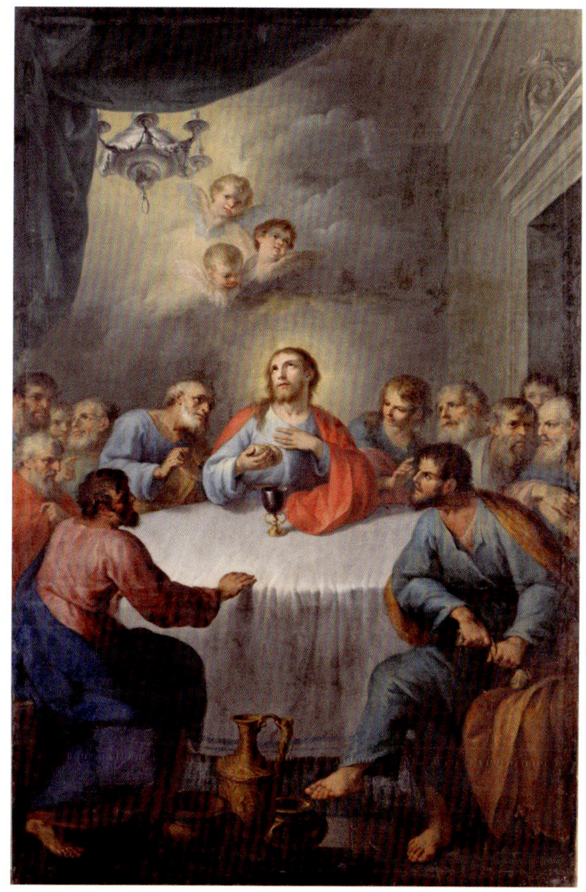

56
Luis Planes
The Last Supper, 1804
Oil on canvas,
2520 x 1615 mm
Santa María La Mayor de Rubielos de Mora. Teruel

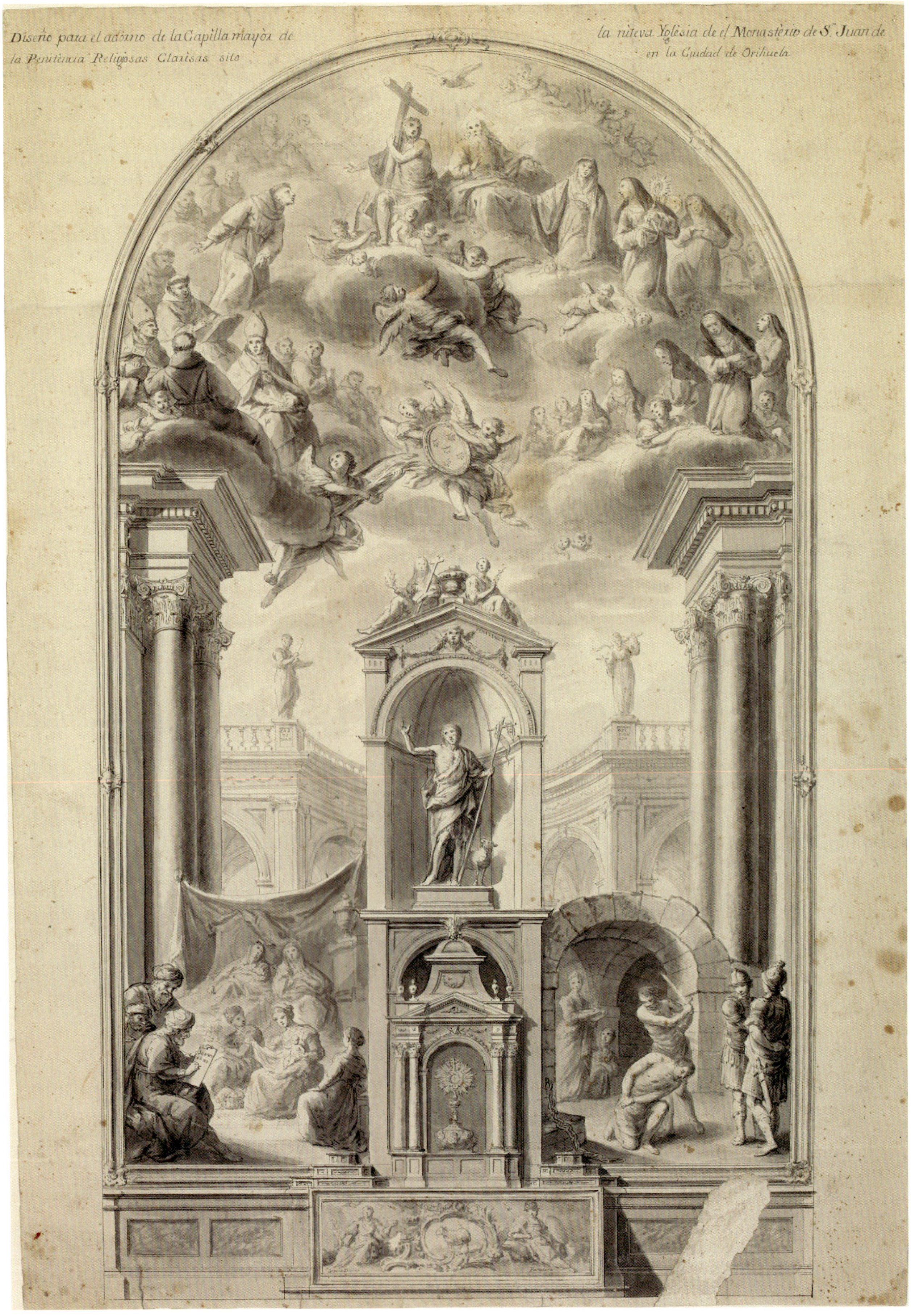
Diseño para el adorno de la Capilla mayor de
la Penitencia Religiosas Clarisas sito
la nueva Yglesia de el Monasterio de Sn. Juan de
en la Ciudad de Orihuela

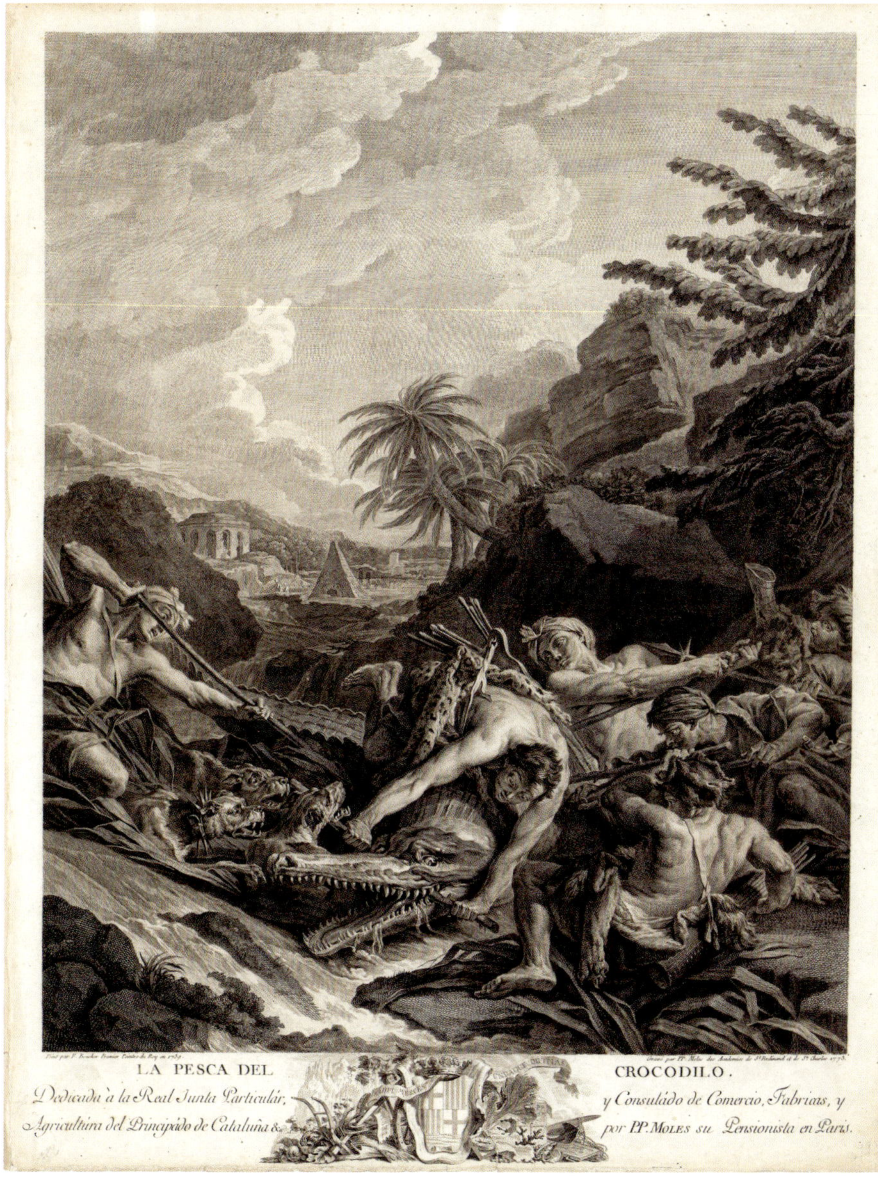

57
Antonio Villanueva
Design for an Altar Wall Dedicated to Saint John the Baptist, c.1780
Pen and grey ink and grey wash, 524 x 356 mm
British Museum, London
1946,0713.1519

58
Pedro Pasucal Moles after François Boucher
The Crocodile Hunt, 1773
Etching and engraving, 634 x 462 mm
British Museum, London
1875,0710.2653

chapel of the Communion of the Colegiata de Rubielos de Mora (Teruel) of 1804 (fig. 55).[178] The drawing corresponds closely to the painting and its light squaring indicates that it was used to transfer the design; only the position of Christ's head has changed. The painting (fig. 56), originally thought to have been painted by Maella but now known to be by Planes, exemplifies the influence of the pictorial style in Madrid at the end of the eighteenth century.

Numerous drawings survive by lesser-known artists working in the province of Valencia. Antonio Villanueva (1714–85), for example, was creator of a drawing of around 1780 showing scenes from the life of Saint John the Baptist and a Franciscan allegory (fig. 57), which was preparatory to a painting that once covered the entire back wall of the presbytery in the church of San Juan de la Penetencia in Orihuela.[179] The majority of the painting was destroyed in the Civil War and today only the top section, representing the allegory, remains. Villanueva's composition – especially the section depicting the Trinity – is close to the work of Giaquinto, which he probably knew

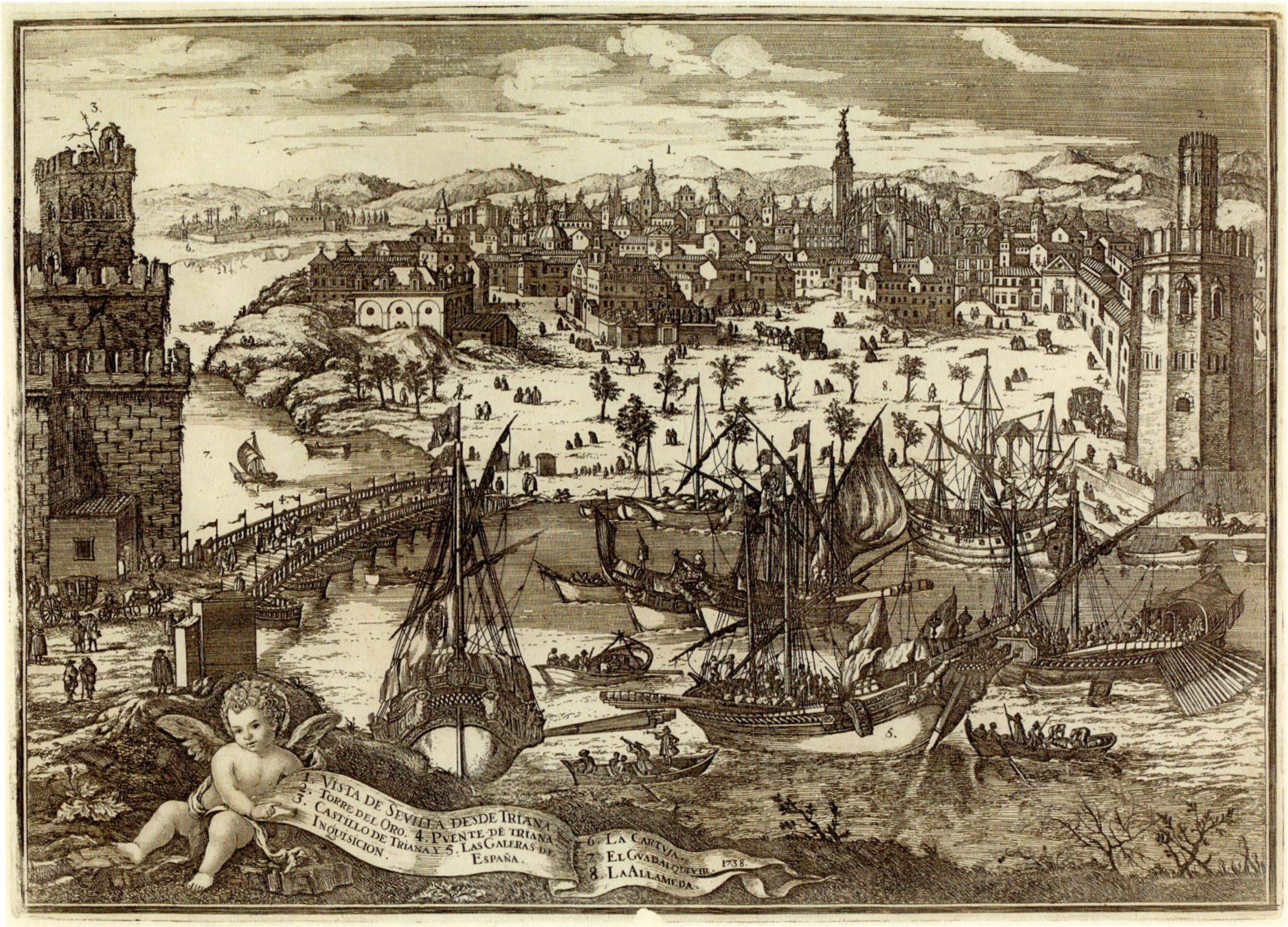

59
Pedro Tortolero
View of Seville from Triana, 1738
Etching and engraving, 352 x 485 mm
British Museum, London
1917,1208.4276

through prints and the work of his followers.[180] Orellana refers to the many architects who carried out work based on Villanueva's drawings:[181] no doubt these were architectural drawings, which would have been destroyed in the process of realizing the designs. Unlike these, the drawing for the presbytery wall was not produced as a stage in the planning of a work in another medium, but to show how the painting would ultimately appear. The careful lettering in the upper section, the resolved composition, its equivalence to the surviving painted section, and the detailing of the frame present the design as an agreed solution to what must have been Villanueva's most important commission towards the end of his career.

The Valencian-born artist Vicente López y Portaña (1772–1850) trained with Villanueva until his master's death in 1785. Four years later he won first prize at the Academy in Valencia and was granted a scholarship to study in Madrid, where he trained for three years under Maella. His rigorous drawing practice is reflected by the many surviving preparatory studies for his paintings. For his most ambitious compositions López drew individual features such as hands and fabrics, in addition to complete and partial figures and fully resolved compositions.[182] In 1792 he returned to Valencia, becoming General Director of Painting at the Academy of San Carlos in 1801. He remained in Valencia until 1814, when he succeeded Goya as court painter to Ferdinand VII. López's drawings, mainly in pen, ink and wash, are entirely typical of an academically trained artist and show that by the end of the eighteenth century the methods and techniques promoted by the academies resulted in a degree of standardization across Spain, diminishing the sharp stylistic divisions of the past.[183]

In Barcelona Pedro Pascual Moles (1741–97) was a key figure in printmaking.[184] In 1754–8 he studied at the Academy of Santa Barbara in Valencia, and by 1762 he had settled in Barcelona. Two years later he was appointed Printmaker to the Royal Council and Commercial Consulate of Cataluña. In 1766 he requested a grant from the Consulate to enable him to complete his training in Paris; here he remained for eight years, working with Nicolás Gabriel Dupuis and Charles Nicolás Cochin.[185] His return to Barcelona in 1774 coincided with the founding of the School of Drawing (Escuela gratuita de Diseño) in early 1775, where he was appointed Director General and the first Professor of Printmaking.[186] The benefit of his time in Paris is demonstrated by his 1773 print, *The Crocodile Hunt* (fig. 58), after François Boucher. Moles was named Academician of Merit by the Madrid Academy in 1770 and in 1774 contributed engravings to the Royal Academy of Spain's magnificent illustrated edition of *Don Quijote* (see p. 219).[187]

The school of art in Barcelona was sponsored by the Commercial Council and provided funding for artists to study in Madrid. Blas Ametller Rotllan (1768–1841) was one such artist, whose initial training was with Moles in Barcelona before he moved to Madrid in 1790. Here he spent five years studying under Manuel Salvador Carmona and took part in the project to publish prints after paintings in the royal collection (see p. 217).[188]

Seville was reinvigorated in 1729 when Felipe V, his wife Isabel de Farnesio and the entire court moved there and remained until 1733. Their presence gave rise to elaborate festivals, celebratory events that resulted in published descriptions and prints documenting their splendour.[189] For example, a large etching by Pedro Tortolero (*c.*1700–66) – the leading printmaker in the city during first half of the century – depicts the royal entourage entering Seville.[190] In 1738 Tortolero engraved a group of prints including scenes of the celebration of the feast of Corpus Christi in Seville, the redemption of child slaves from the Barbary Coast, and a view of Seville across the river from Triana (fig. 59). The latter includes significant contemporary details such as the presence of the royal Armada and the renovated royal Seminary of San Telmo.

As in other regional centres, drawing schools were established in Seville during the eighteenth century. One of these operated from the house of the silversmith Eugenio Sánchez Reciente in 1759. Ten years later another was set up under the patronage of Charles III, demonstrating the continued need for tuition in the techniques of drawing as the basis of artistic practice.[191]

Eighteenth-century Spain saw a transformation in the technical production of prints and drawings, their uses and their public perception. The spread of academic study and the desire for artistic practice here to be on a par with that other parts of Europe ensured that drawing and printmaking became firmly established. Students benefited from travelling and studying abroad, mainly in Paris and Rome. By the final decades of the century artists born in Spain had a thorough knowledge of the broader history of art – due in no small part to the availability of reproductive prints – as well as of the latest artistic trends. From this context emerged the best-known Spanish artist of all, Francisco de Goya, a product of Madrid's artistic environment of the late eighteenth century.

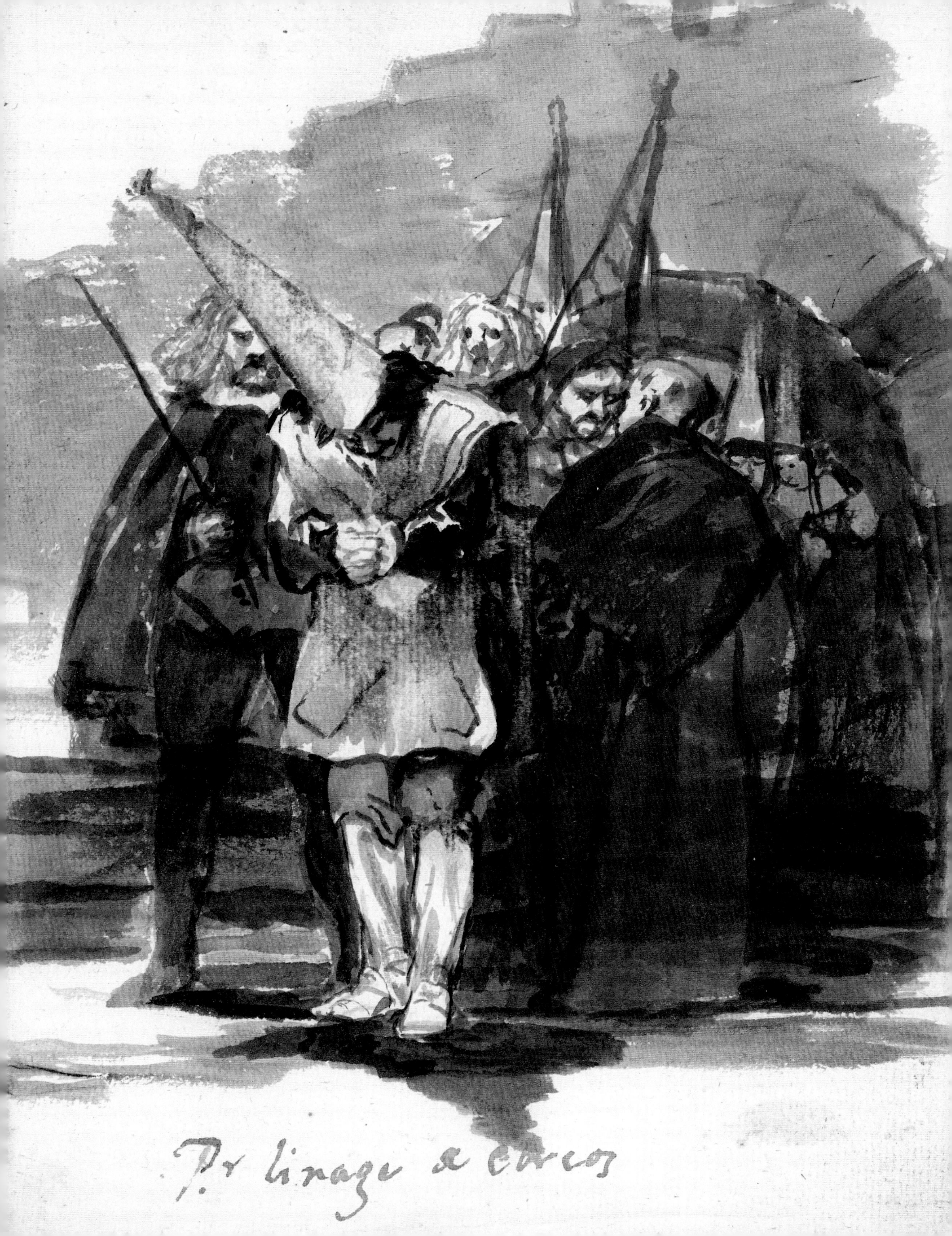
P.r linage de ebreos

CHAPTER 8

Francisco de Goya (1746–1828)

Francisco de Goya's death in Bordeaux on 16 April 1828, at the age of eighty-two, brought to an end a career during which he produced a body of work remarkable for its imagination, artistic vision and profound humanity. Goya's prints and drawings are among his most compelling works. Because they were not commissioned, they allowed him to explore fantastic subjects, human beliefs and behaviour, often creating complex meaning through series of images. He witnessed momentous social and political change, including the French occupation of Spain and the horrific effects of the Inquisition. His political liberalism, criticism of superstition and distaste for intellectual oppression reflected eighteenth-century Enlightenment ideals.[1] But to view Goya as an artist who merely embodied Enlightenment ideology is simplistic: as Janis Tomlinson observes, 'the Enlightenment in Spain is defined just as much by the limits imposed upon its ideas as by the contradictions that arose in society as a result of their diffusion'.[2]

Goya created almost three hundred prints and about nine hundred drawings.[3] The selection featured here demonstrates the range of his graphic abilities and the subjects that absorbed him. Although his dedication to drawing and printmaking sets Goya apart, he was very far from being a 'lone genius' unaffected by his contemporaries, and his art should be seen in the context of the unprecedented scientific, social and artistic developments that were taking place in Spain and the rest of Europe during the eighteenth century. Much attention has been given to Goya's print series but less to the albums – or more accurately, sketchbooks – of drawings, which he did not begin until he was fifty. Before this time, drawing seems to have played a conventional role in his practice. The albums allowed Goya to express his most private thoughts and are a rich repository of imagery, providing extraordinary insight to his imagination and creative process. Comprising a personal iconography, many drawings have captions that sometimes elucidate their meaning, but often deepen their complexity. Goya numbered many of the drawings in the albums, sometimes renumbering them later, indicating that their sequence was important to him. He worked on more that one project at the same time, revisiting his various preoccupations in new and evocative ways. Goya's prints and drawings worked together and are discussed here chronologically.[4]

Earliest graphic work to the mid-1790s

Francisco Goya y Lucientes was born in Fuendetodos near Zaragoza, in the province of Aragon. He began his artistic training with José Luzán Martínez (1710–85), who also taught Francisco and Ramón Bayeu (see Chapter 7). Goya's lifelong interest in prints no doubt began at this time, copying them

Detail of fig. 35, see p. 255

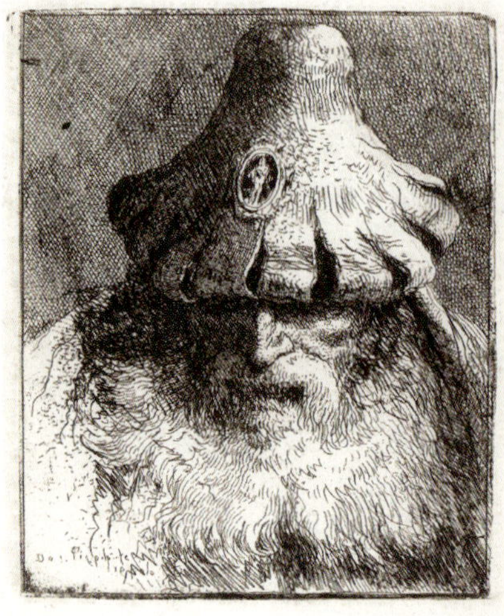

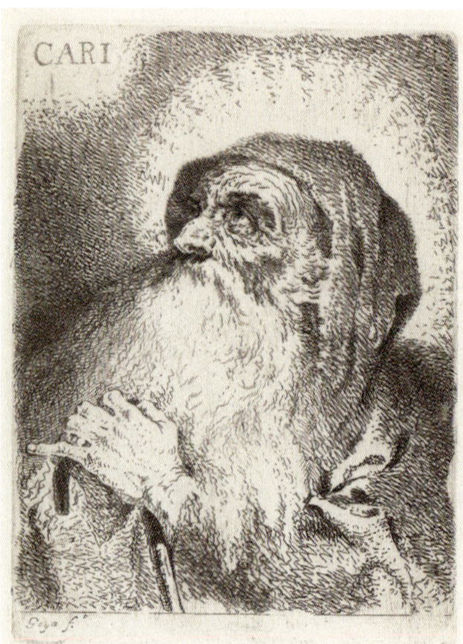

1
Domenico Tiepolo
Head of an Old Man, *c.*1757–70
Etching, 127 x 100 mm
British Museum, London
1869,0410.1863

2
Francisco de Goya
Saint Francis of Paola, *c.*1776–8
Etching and drypoint,
132 x 95 mm
British Museum, London
1975,1025.12

as an educational exercise. In 1764 and 1766 he entered the competitions at the Academy in Madrid but on both occasions failed to secure a vote. Eager to expand his knowledge, like many before him he went to Italy; during this time he recorded what he saw in a notebook. This is the only surviving bound compilation that pre-dates his albums of drawings, and it disproves the view of some scholars that in his early years Goya was not interested in drawing or that it formed a negligible part of his practice.[5] On folio 39 of the notebook he lists the places he visited in Italy: from Rome he travelled east, then up to Venice across to Parma and beyond.[6] As he travelled he bought prints, presumably reproducing the works of art that interested him.[7] The notebook provides valuable insight to Goya's early drawing style: a number of his red chalk studies are reminiscent of those by José del Castillo, who also compiled sketchbooks in Italy in the early 1750s (see p. 203). Thus Goya was firmly rooted in contemporary graphic practices and style.

By June 1771 he was back in Zaragoza; in late 1774, along with other artists, he was summoned by Mengs to work at the royal tapestry factory in Madrid under the direction of Francisco Bayeu.[8] Earlier, when Goya entered the painting competition organized by the Fine Arts Academy in Parma in 1771, he declared himself to be 'a disciple of Francisco Bayeu' – indeed, he and his wife lived in Francisco's house after he returned to Spain until the birth of their second son in December 1775.[9] Goya's few surviving drawings for tapestry cartoons, mainly figure studies executed in black and white chalk on blue paper, are entirely in keeping with those of his fellow artists, especially Bayeu, a committed and prolific draughtsman (fig. 21, p. 206).[10]

Towards the end of the 1770s Goya turned his attention increasingly to printmaking.[11] The atmosphere of enlightened artistic discussion and the growth of print publishing (see Chapter 7) provided fertile ground for his first attempts. We do not know whether he was directly involved in the 1776 print that reproduces the painting recently attributed to him of the anteater brought from Buenos Aires (fig. 43, p. 220), but he would certainly have known it – and there can be no doubt that he understood the value of prints for reproducing paintings. His early technique was profoundly influenced by the prints that had such currency in Madrid, bringing him into contact with the work of diverse Italian masters such as the Tiepolo family (figs 30–2, pp. 211–13). The etched heads from Domenico Tiepolo's series *Raccolta di Teste* (fig. 1) clearly influenced Goya's early work, in particular, the technique of short, wavy strokes, the densely worked background and the use of the paper ground to provide contrasts (fig. 2).[12]

Because of their dedication to marketing their work, prints by the Tiepolo family were widely available in Madrid, those by Old Masters possibly less so. Goya, however, had access to the remarkable print collection of his close friend Ceán Bermúdez, who encouraged him to explore printmaking. Ceán's collection included works by both Old Masters and contemporary artists: Dürer, Rembrandt, Callot, Parmigianino, Ribera, Vicente Carducho and Manuel Salvador Carmona, among many others.[13] In Ceán's unfinished *Historia de la Pintura* (1824) he recalls giving Rembrandt etchings to Goya while he was working on the *Caprichos*.[14] Goya especially admired Rembrandt's use of light and his handling of complex compositions. A little after Goya died, his son Javier remarked on his father's veneration of the Dutch artist.[15]

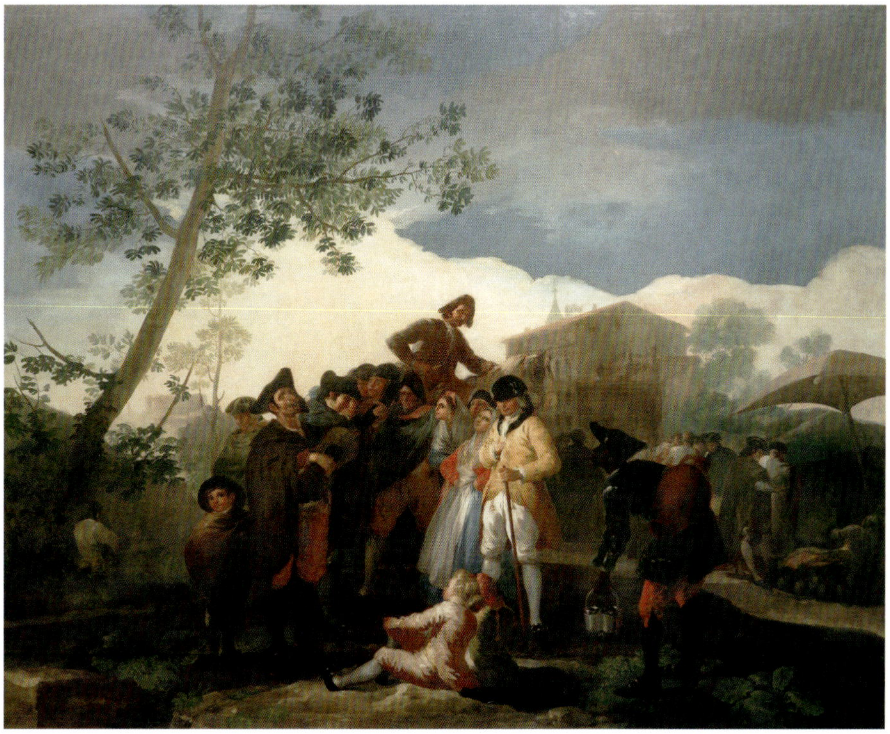

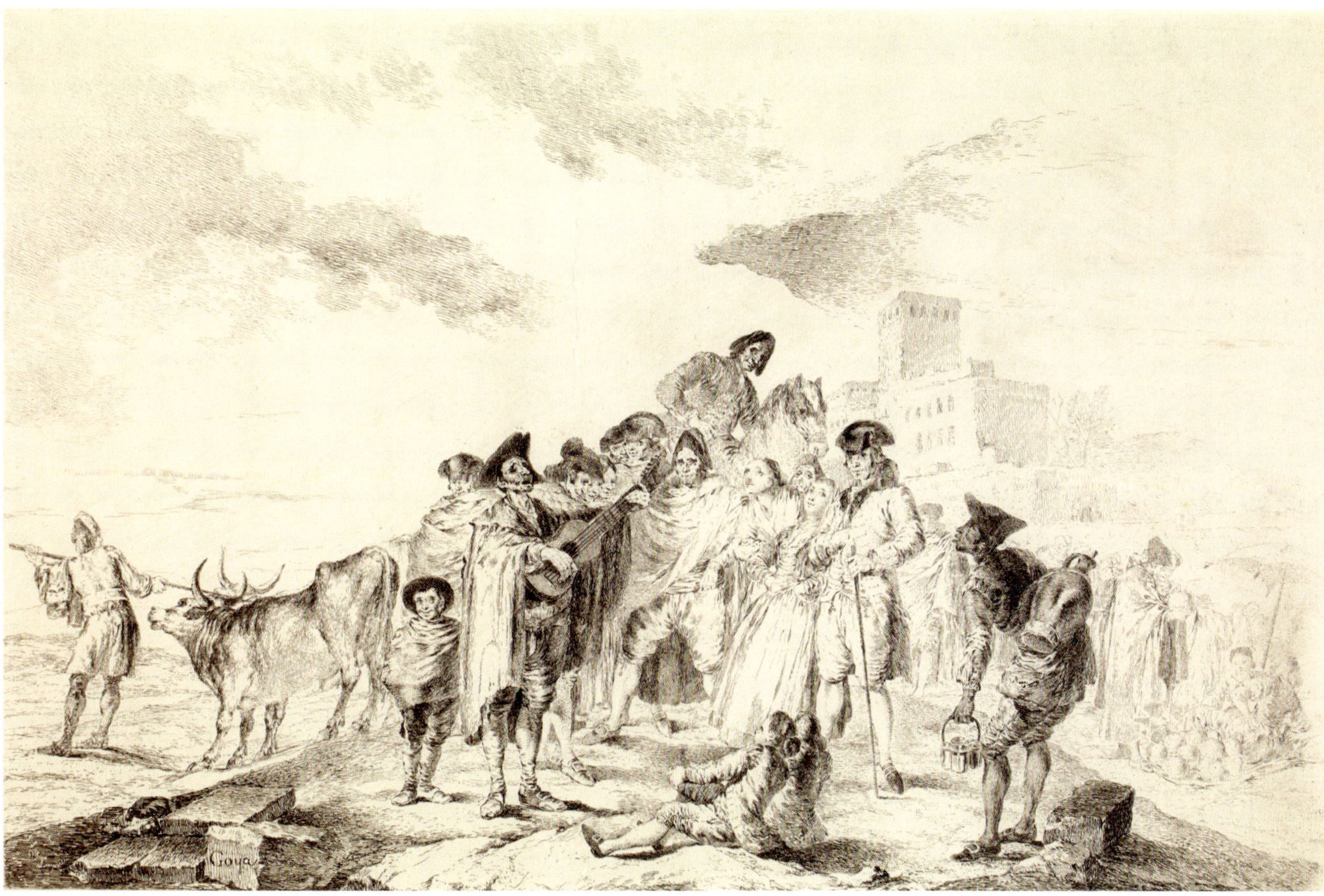

3
Francisco de Goya
The Blind Guitarist, 1778
Oil on canvas,
2600 x 3110 mm
Museo del Prado, Madrid
P.778

4
Francisco de Goya
The Blind Guitarist, 1778
Etching, 355 x 535 mm
British Museum, London
1854,1020.17

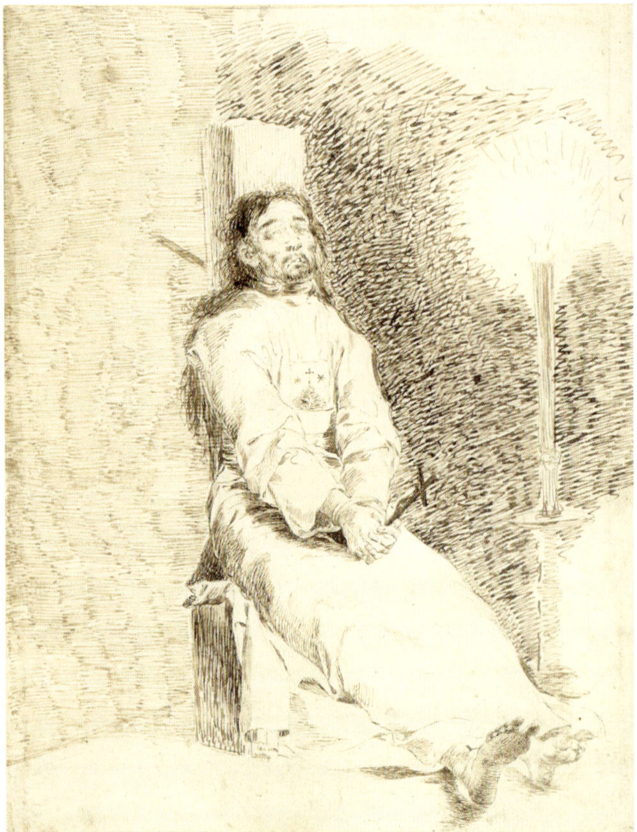

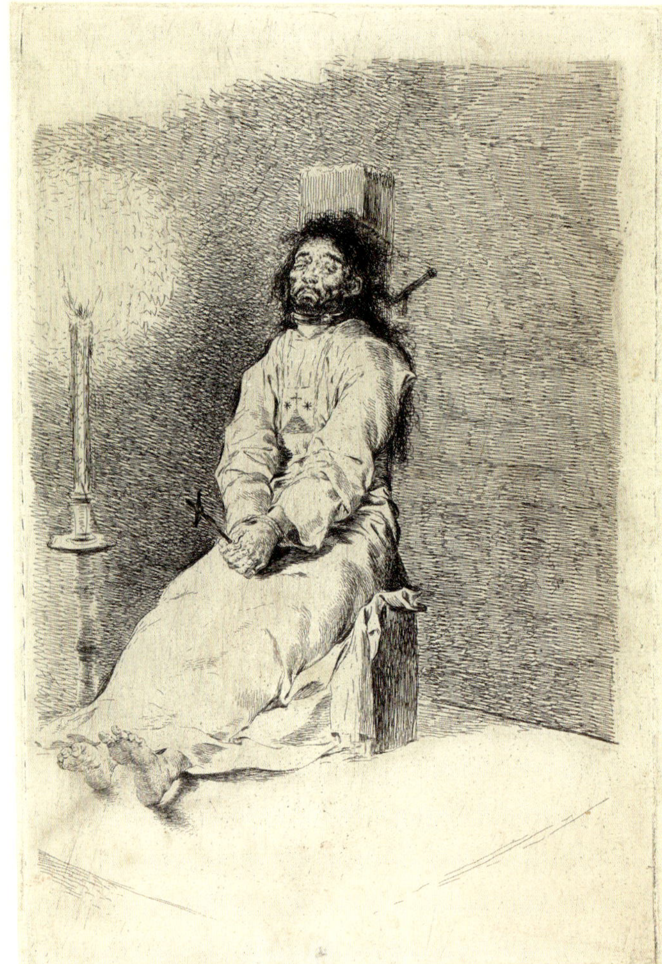

5
Francisco de Goya
The Garroted Man, c.1778
Pen and brown ink, incised, 264 x 200 mm
British Museum, London
1850,0713.11

6
Francisco de Goya
The Garroted Man, c.1778
Etching, 327 x 211 mm
British Museum, London
1875,0612.95

Goya's 1778 tapestry cartoon of the *Blind Guitarist* (fig. 3) provided the basis for his largest etching (fig. 4). This print, the only one he made after one of his own paintings,[16] shows the composition of the original cartoon: Goya subsequently had to modify the design because the weavers found it impossible to interpret. Recognizing the ability of the medium to convey minute detail, in the etching Goya emphasizes the expressions of the figures gathered around the guitarist. In his earliest prints his technique is an extension of drawing: as with many artists' first attempts at etching, the lines have the fluidity of pen and ink. His *Garrotted Man* (figs 5–6) is from the same period, its design transferred from the black chalk rubbed on the verso of the drawing to the plate using a stylus. Although this is a common method of transfer, Goya used it infrequently: his preferred method was more unusual and involved dampening the sheet, placing it face down on the plate and then applying pressure, thus registering the design while preserving the drawing.

Similar in technique but remarkably different in subject and scale, Goya's early etchings are entirely experimental. He began his first systematic series of etchings after Velázquez – probably encouraged by Ceán – at a time when the demand for prints after the Spanish Old Masters was very much part of Enlightenment attitudes and the desire to reproduce and disseminate knowledge of these works (see Chapter 7).[17] On 28 July 1778 the

Gazeta de Madrid advertised 'nine prints drawn and engraved in etching by Don Francisco Goya, Painter', after Velázquez. These included equestrian portraits of the royal family, court dwarfs and figures of philosophers, and they were available from two Madrid booksellers, Antonio de Sancha and Manuel Barco.[18] In December the same year two more prints by Goya, *Don Baltasar on Horseback* and *Los Borrachos* (*The Drunkards*), were offered for sale. Because he was not yet entirely familiar with the etching technique, Goya discarded a number of the plates, admitting in a letter to his friend Martín Zapater: 'you cannot imagine the thousand difficulties I have had with them.'[19]

Two of Goya's prints, the *Infante Don Fernando* (fig. 7) and *Barbarroxa*, not published until later, are partly executed in the relatively new technique of aquatint that allows for rich tonal effects.[20] The prints exist in numerous proofs showing Goya experimenting, revising and finally mastering aquatint; he would use the technique to create astonishing effects in his later prints. Whereas his etchings convey the painterly sensibility of Velázquez's technique (fig. 40, p. 217), he did not feel confined by his source and freely interpreted the figures. This can be seen in *The Drunkards* (fig. 8), where Goya's figures are more rustic. Further comparison with an engraving of the same subject by Manuel Salvador Carmona (1793) shows how idiosyncratic Goya's approach was (fig. 39, p. 217): Carmona is a faithful translator while Goya is a creative interpreter. The etchings after Velázquez attracted immediate attention in Madrid. Several foreign officials are known to have sent impressions abroad: Lord Grantham, the English ambassador to Spain (1771–9), for example, sent five sets back to England in 1778.[21] What Goya learnt through the difficult genesis of the prints after Velázquez laid the ground for his first series of original prints, *Los Caprichos*.

By around 1780 Goya had gained a considerable reputation as a painter. In 1785 he was appointed Deputy Director of Painting at the Madrid Academy

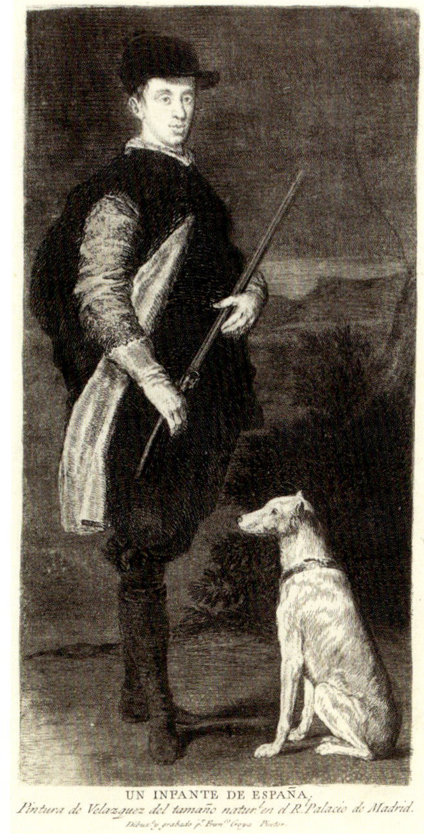

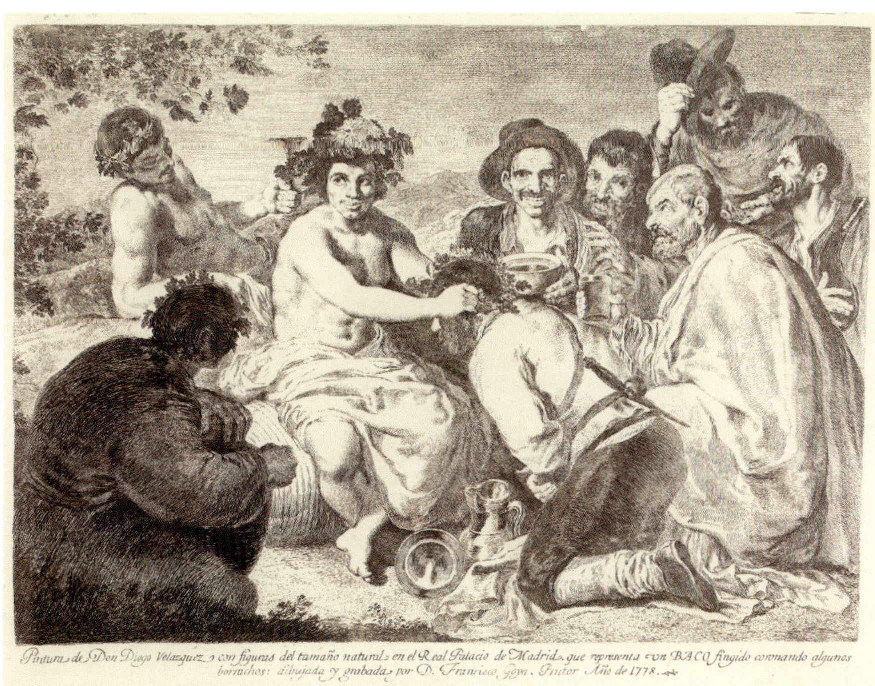

7
Francisco de Goya after Diego Velázquez
The Infante Don Fernando, 1778
Etching, aquatint and drypoint, 282 x 170 mm
British Museum, London
1848,1125.236

8
Francisco de Goya after Diego Velázquez
The Drunkards or *The Triumph of Bacchus*, 1778
Etching, 320 x 434 mm
British Museum, London
1862,0712.178

and Director five months later. In May 1787 he became Painter to the King and in 1789, after the accession of Charles IV and his wife María Luisa, First Painter to the Privy Chamber. Despite his public success, his attitudes to art and its practice seemed at odds with those traditionally promoted by the Academy. In his submission to the Academy dated 14 October 1792 regarding revisions to its teaching programme, Goya wrote at length about artistic liberty, observing that

> the Academies should not be exclusive, or serve more than as an aid to those who freely wish to study in them, banishing all servile subjection of the primary school, mechanical precepts, monthly prizes, financial aid, and other trivialities that degrade, and effeminate an Art as liberal and noble as painting…[22]

He went on to reinforce the importance of allowing students to develop their abilities unencumbered by any one dogma. Goya's dedication to artistic freedom is reflected in his own practice and is important for appreciating the directions he took as an artist. He was not alone in promoting reform: his views broadly agreed with several – but by no means all – of his colleagues.

After persistent poor health, Goya travelled to Seville in early 1793 where he fell gravely ill. He continued to Cadiz to recuperate with his friend and art collector Sebastián Martínez Pérez and remained for several months.[23] As a result of his illness he suffered a total loss of hearing. Upon his return to Madrid later that year he was too weak to continue work on the large tapestry cartoons. On 4 January 1794 Goya wrote to his friend Bernardo de Iriarte, Vice Protector of the Academy of San Fernando, that he was sending him a set of cabinet pictures in which 'I have managed to make observations for which there is normally no opportunity in commissioned works which give no scope for fantasy or invention'. In another letter, of 7 January, he describes one of the pictures as 'a yard with lunatics'.[24] Goya's submission to the Academy and his personal correspondence is important for understanding his artistic preoccupations during his convalescence, which underpinned his future projects. Around this time he made his first albums, motivated surely by the fact that they were manageable, allowing him to create freely on a small scale.[25]

9
Francisco de Goya
Young Woman in a Maja Costume, c.1794
Brush and grey ink wash, 172 x 97 mm
Museo del Prado, Madrid
D.4342

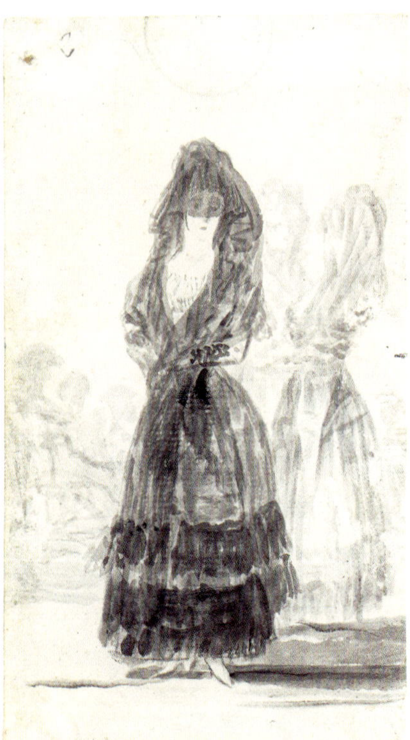

A now dismembered small album (17 x 10 cm) known as the Sanlúcar Album (A), containing eighteen compositions on both sides of nine pages and three more known through copies, are among his earliest wash-and-ink work.[26] Traditionally dated to the end of 1796, the Sanlúcar Album was so named because it was previously thought that Goya made it during his stay on the estate of the Duchess of Alba at Sanlúcar de Barrameda, before he returned to Madrid (it is now believed, however, that he made the drawings in Madrid, from around 1794).[27] In August of 1794, he received a commission to portray the Duchess. Two drawings in the Sanlúcar Album relate to the portrait, while others depict women in various postures (fig. 9). Several are naïve and sometimes awkward, as Goya grappled with this new medium, but they convey a strong feeling for form. Others, such as the woman fixing her hair (page C), have a simple elegance, beautifully capturing a private moment. In contrast to the later albums, the images are not numbered and have no captions, making it impossible to determine their original order.

Several of the drawings in the Sanlúcar Album, such as that showing a woman sweeping the floor, with the head of a bull on the wall behind her, anticipate subjects in another, more ambitious and larger compilation, the Madrid Album, which Goya began working on around the same time.[28] Almost a hundred drawings on double-sided pages have witty and satirical imagery, and the captions from p. 55 onwards identify the scenes as 'masquerades' or 'caricatures' (fig. 10).[29] The album has long been considered the most significant in Goya's development, not only for its thematic richness but because it signals his commitment to drawing as an essential means of personal expression. In their subject matter these sheets reflect the series of prints planned as *sueños* (dreams) and their expansion into the prints known as *Los Caprichos*. The remarkable variety of compositions suggests that the album was made over a number of years, some of the later drawings – for example, 'Jesus, what a wind' – directly providing material for a print in the *Caprichos* series.[30] This was the last album in which Goya drew on both sides of the sheet, marking a turning-point in the way he perceived their composition and function.

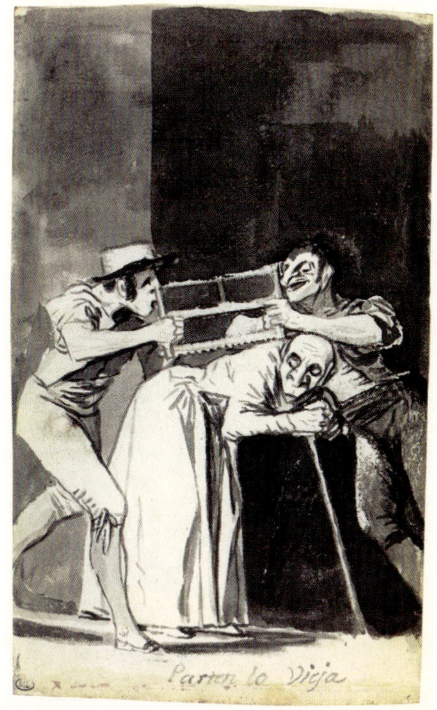

10
Francisco de Goya
They are Cutting the Old Woman in Two, c.1794–7
Brush and Indian ink with scraping, 209 x 125 mm
Musée du Louvre, Paris
RF 6914

Los Caprichos (1799)

Goya's return to etching after almost two decades, *Los Caprichos* were created during a period of personal upheaval, political intrigue at the court and economic crisis in Spain. He continued to suffer from poor health, forcing him to give up his salaried position as Director of Painting at the Academy in 1797. Queen María Luisa's lover, Manuel Godoy, had been promoted to a high position at court in 1792, and several of Goya's liberal-minded friends were subsequently appointed to senior ministerial posts. Goya may have felt that the atmosphere was now sufficiently permissive for him to create a series of prints that reflected the liberalism of the writings of his friends who were committed to reforming Spanish society. In 1798, however, Godoy was forced to resign, and enlightened ministers with him; by the time the *Caprichos* were published in 1799 the atmosphere had greatly changed.

On 17 January 1799 Goya signed a receipt for four books of the *Caprichos* acquired by the Duke and Duchess of Osuna for their collection.[31] Almost a month later, on 6 February, the *Diario de Madrid* formally announced the publication of *Los Caprichos*, Goya's collection of eighty prints of 'capricious' (or whimsical) subjects created from the mid-1790s to 1798. Withdrawn from sale soon after the series was advertised, the prints were certainly known to his friends, some of whom he must have consulted when considering their content. In 1803 he offered the etched plates, along with 240 unsold sets, to the Royal Chalcography (set up in 1789, later the Calcografía Nacional) in exchange for a pension for his son. In his request he reported that most purchasers of the prints were foreigners:[32] in the four years since their publication he had managed to sell only twenty-seven sets. Years later, in exile in Bordeaux, Goya wrote that he had been denounced to the Inquisition even though he had donated the plates to the king.[33]

The advertisement in the *Diario de Madrid*, thought to have been written by Goya's friend, the Spanish playwright Leandro Fernández Moratín, carefully masks the potentially volatile meaning of the *Caprichos* and emphasises that the author did not 'have the intention to mock the particular faults of

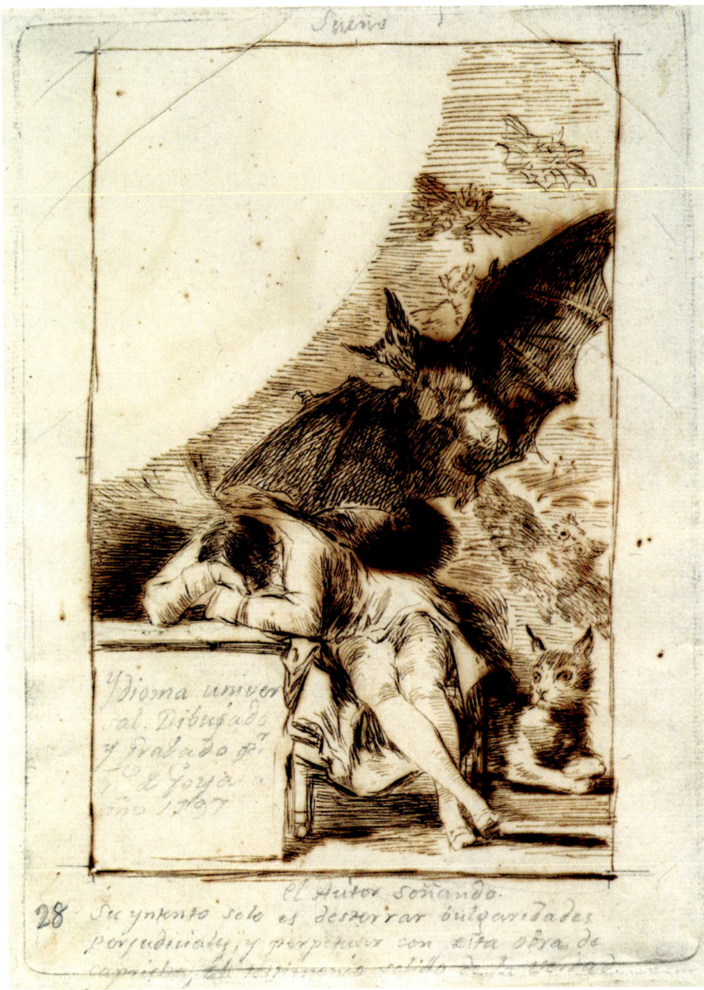

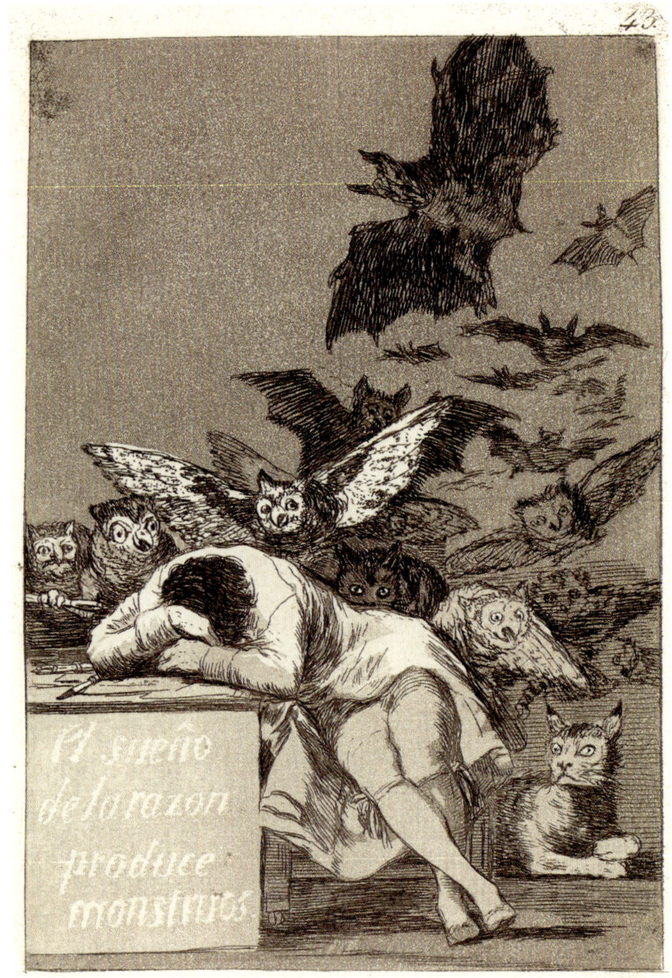

11
Francisco de Goya
Universal Language ('Idioma Universal'), 1797
Pen and brown ink over black chalk, 240 x 172 mm
Museo del Prado, Madrid
D.3923

12
Francisco de Goya
The Sleep of Reason, c.1797–8
Etching and aquatint, 215 x 150 mm
British Museum, London
1975,1025.124

one or another individual' in a single one of the compositions.[34] The *Caprichos* were Goya's personal declaration that the chains of social backwardness had to be broken if humanity was to advance, attesting to his political liberalism and his contempt for ignorance and intellectual oppression. They mirror his ambivalence towards authority – both Church and State – and contain political caricatures of individual stupidity, vanity, superstition, corruption and greed, themes he continued to explore in later work.[35]

Goya first conceived the series as dreams (*sueños*), a device widely used to make veiled criticisms of society. His original *sueños* were drawn in pen and ink, whereas the drawings for the greatly expanded project were in red chalk, for easier transfer to the plate. The drawn frontispiece to the *sueños* carries three inscriptions: the series title and number over the drawing: '1st Dream'; a brief title, 'Universal Language. Drawn and engraved by Francisco de Goya in the year 1797' on the face of the table lower left; and along the bottom, the more discursive 'The author dreaming. His only intention is to banish harmful beliefs commonly held and to perpetuate with this work of *caprichos* the solid testimony of truth' (fig. 11).[36] These inscriptions provide a valuable indication of Goya's original intentions for the series. He abandoned the concept of dreams for the published title page, preferring his self-portrait, and the first drawn *sueño* became plate 43, *The Sleep of Reason* (fig. 12).

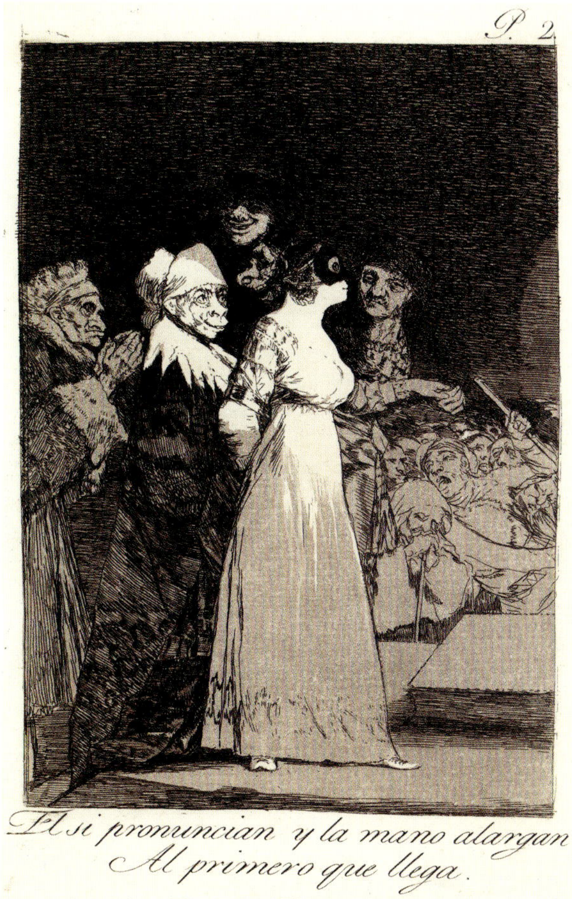

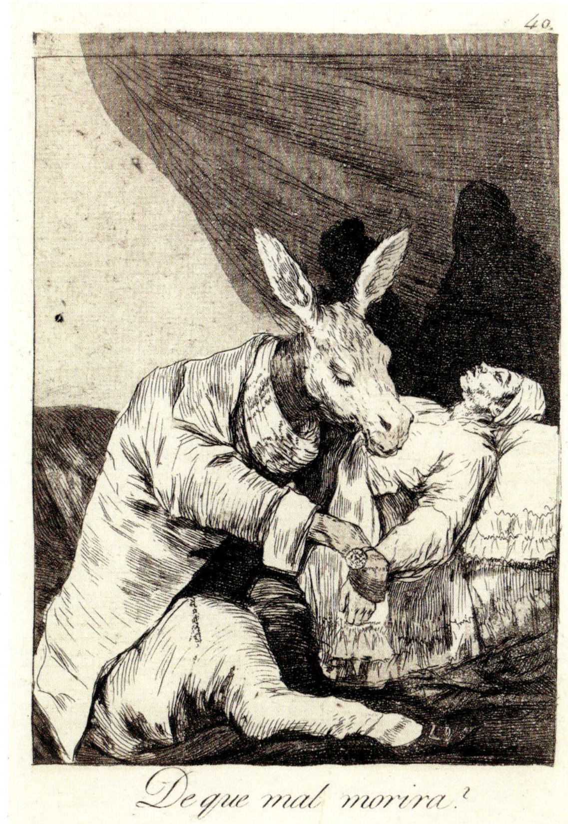

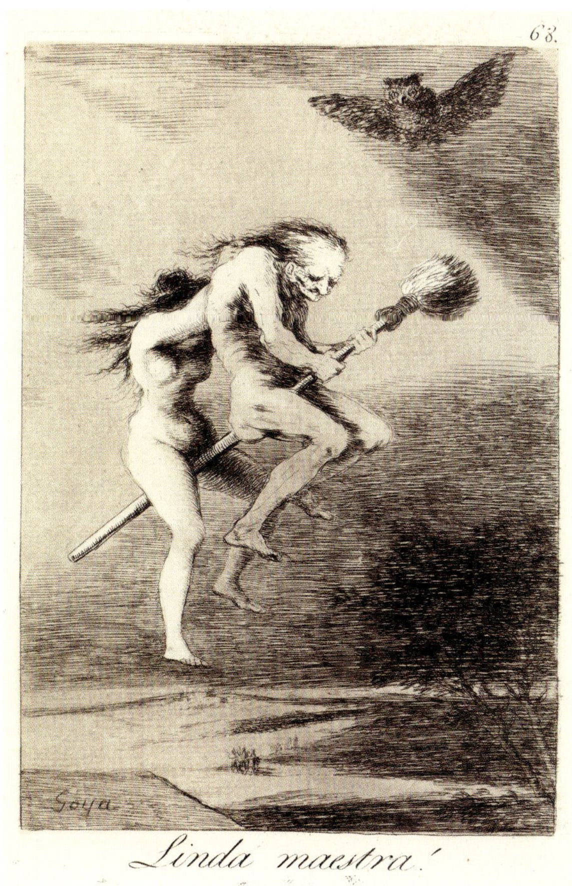

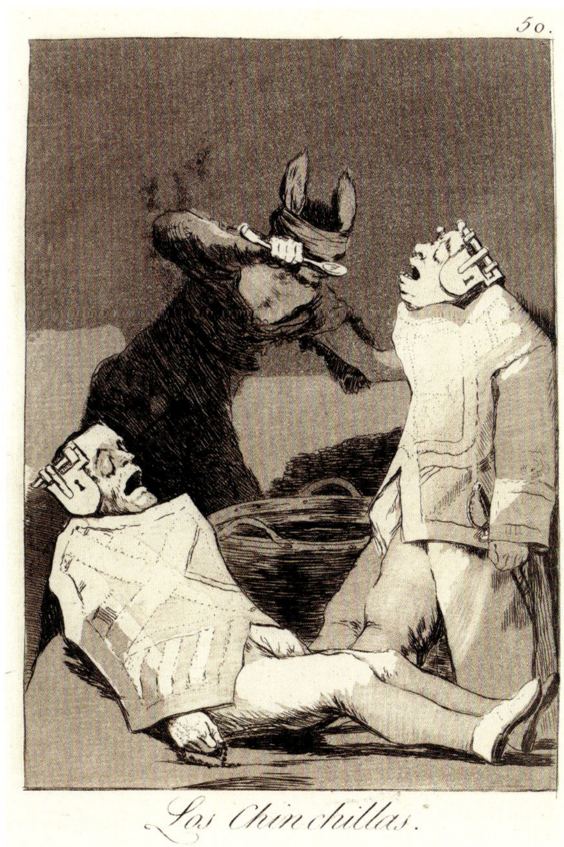

13
Francisco de Goya
They Say Yes and Give their Hand to the First Comer, c.1797–8
Etching and burnished aquatint, 216 x 153 mm
British Museum, London
1975,1025.61

14
Francisco de Goya
Of What Ill Will He Die?, c.1797–8
Etching and aquatint, 215 x 149 mm
British Museum, London
1975,1025.118

15
Francisco de Goya
Pretty Teacher!, c.1797–8
Etching, burnished aquatint and drypoint, 210 x 148 mm
British Museum, London
1975,1025.170

16
Francisco de Goya
The Chinchillas, c.1797–8
Etching, burnished aquatint and burin, 205 x 150 mm
British Museum, London
1975,1025.138

In the *Caprichos*, goblins, witches, priests, prostitutes and nobility occupy the same world. Goya undermines the traditional boundaries between these groups as each individual takes part in the web of deceit: young women take the hand of the first man who comes along and accept advice from old hags (fig. 13), parrots preach to scholars, an ass-doctor takes the pulse of a dying man (fig. 14), witches suck the marrow of babies and learn to fly on broomsticks (fig. 15), withered hags admire themselves in mirrors, and intellects are padlocked (fig. 16). Goya's imagery combines material from emblem books, age-old traditional iconography, linguistic puns and popular sayings.[37] Many of his preparatory drawings and proof impressions have inscriptions that reveal the genesis of his ideas. The final titles on the prints are much reduced, possibly to mask their meaning or at least not make them so explicit in the increasingly repressive society that had developed by the time they were published.

Soon after the *Caprichos* appeared reactions seem to have been mixed, as far as we know from surviving evidence. A manuscript (of about 1799–1803) that belonged to the dramatist Adelardo López de Ayala identifies categories of people and names individuals (Godoy and Queen María Luisa), whereas the best-known account in the Prado from around the same time provides very general explanations of each plate, in the same tone as the circumspect advertisement in the *Diario de Madrid*.[38] However, their popularity at the time is beyond question. Goya's colleague at the court in Madrid, Gregorio González Azaola, published an article in March 1811 that is key to understanding their reception: he observes that 'from the ambassadors down to the artists and travellers, there is no recent arrival in Madrid who has not tried to meet Goya and obtain a copy of his work'. Earlier in the same piece, he notes that 'their subtlety is such that even the sharpest minds do not perceive the whole of their moral point at the first perusal'.[39]

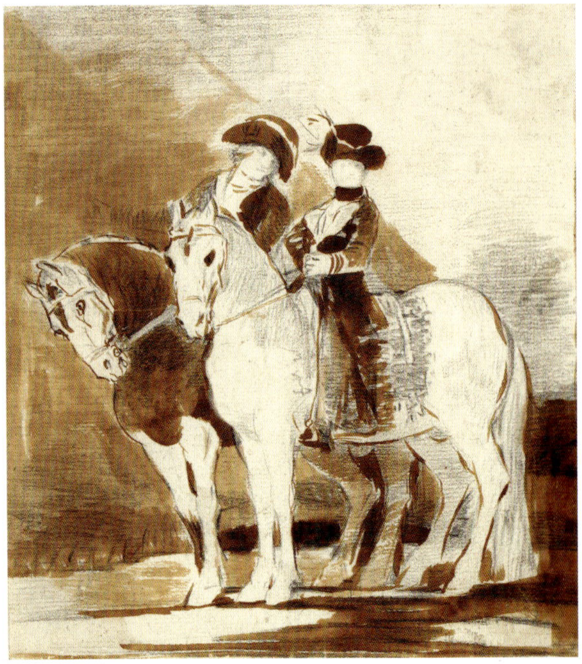

17
Francisco de Goya
Charles IV and María Luisa, 1799–1801
Graphite and brush and brown ink, with brown wash, 240 x 206
British Museum, London
1895,0915.892

Goya was enormously productive during last years of the century. Around 1797–8 he painted a series of six small paintings on the subject of witchcraft for the Duke and Duchess of Osuna's country palace of La Alameda, and in four months during 1798 he created the fresco decorations of the hermitage of San Antonio de la Florida.[40] An important source of income for him during the period was portrait commissions, a remarkable example of which is his 1798 painting of his friend Gaspar Melchor de Jovellanos, a prominent Enlightenment intellectual.[41] A brush-and-ink double equestrian portrait of Charles IV and María Luisa (fig. 17), possibly a study for an unexecuted painting,[42] would be one of a number of royal commissions that culminated in the vast *Family of Charles IV*, the highpoint of Goya's career as a court painter.[43] He also prepared portrait illustrations in chalk for Ceán Bermúdez's dictionary of artists, the *Diccionario de los más ilustres profesores de las Bellas Artes*,[44] among them the portrait of the Spanish sculptor Pedro Roldán (fig. 18). The *Diccionario* was first published in 1800, but without any illustrations.

In the early years of the new century Goya's personal circumstances further deteriorated. The Duchess of Alba died in 1802, and Martín Zapater, his closest childhood friend, the following year. Many of his friends left Madrid

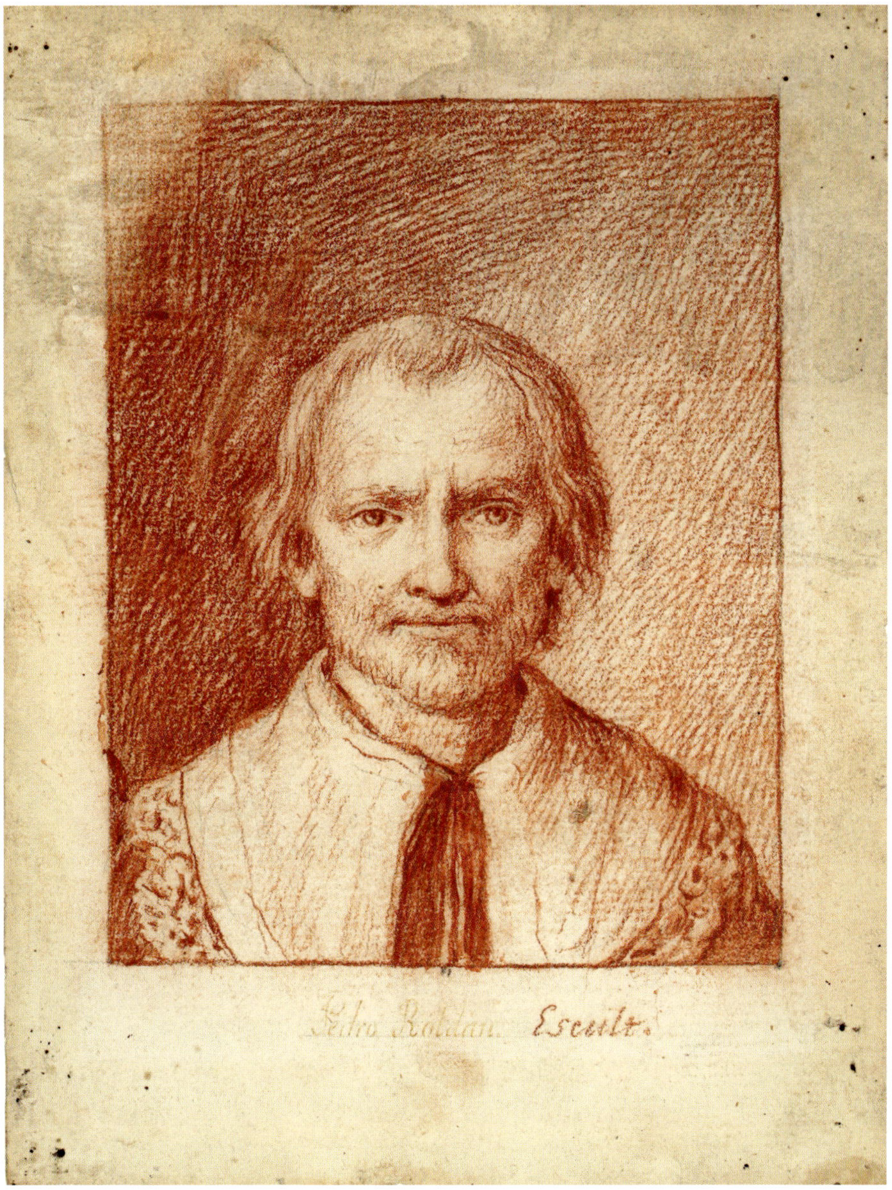

18
Francisco de Goya
Pedro Roldán, 1798–9
Red chalk over black chalk, 173 x 126 mm
British Museum, London
2007,7077.4

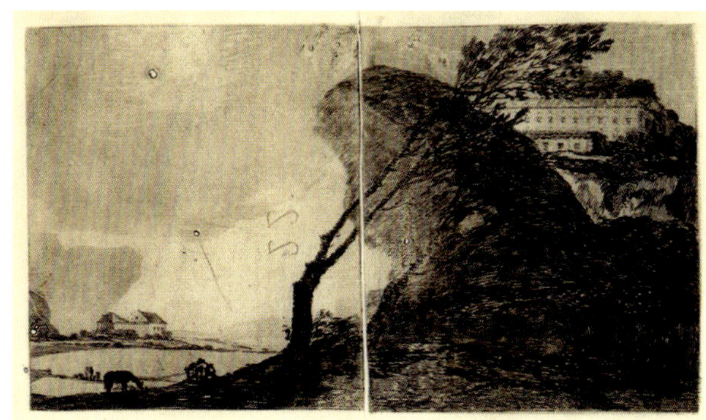

19
Francisco de Goya
Rocky Outcrop and Leaning Trees, before 1810
Etching and burnished aquatint, 168 x 278 mm
British Museum, London
1975,1025.32

or were exiled,[45] including the liberal minister Gaspar Melchor de Jovellanos, who was banished to Mallorca and imprisoned there until 1808. When Goya stood for election for the post of Director General of the Madrid Academy in 1804 he secured very few votes. He increasingly distanced himself from the court and received no further royal commissions. He continued to earn an income from portraits and to express his innermost thoughts in drawings. Between the *Caprichos* and his next series of prints, known as the *Disasters of War*, the only prints Goya appears to have made were possibly the *Seated Giant* or *Colossus*[46] and two beautiful etched and aquatinted landscapes, probably made in the first years of the century, whose plates he later cut in half in order to use the versos for four of the *Disasters of War* prints (fig. 19).[47]

The Disasters of War (*c.*1810–15; published 1863)

Goya's series of eighty aquatint etchings, the *Disasters of War*, were made in response to the Napoleonic invasion of Spain in 1808–13 (plates 2–47), the

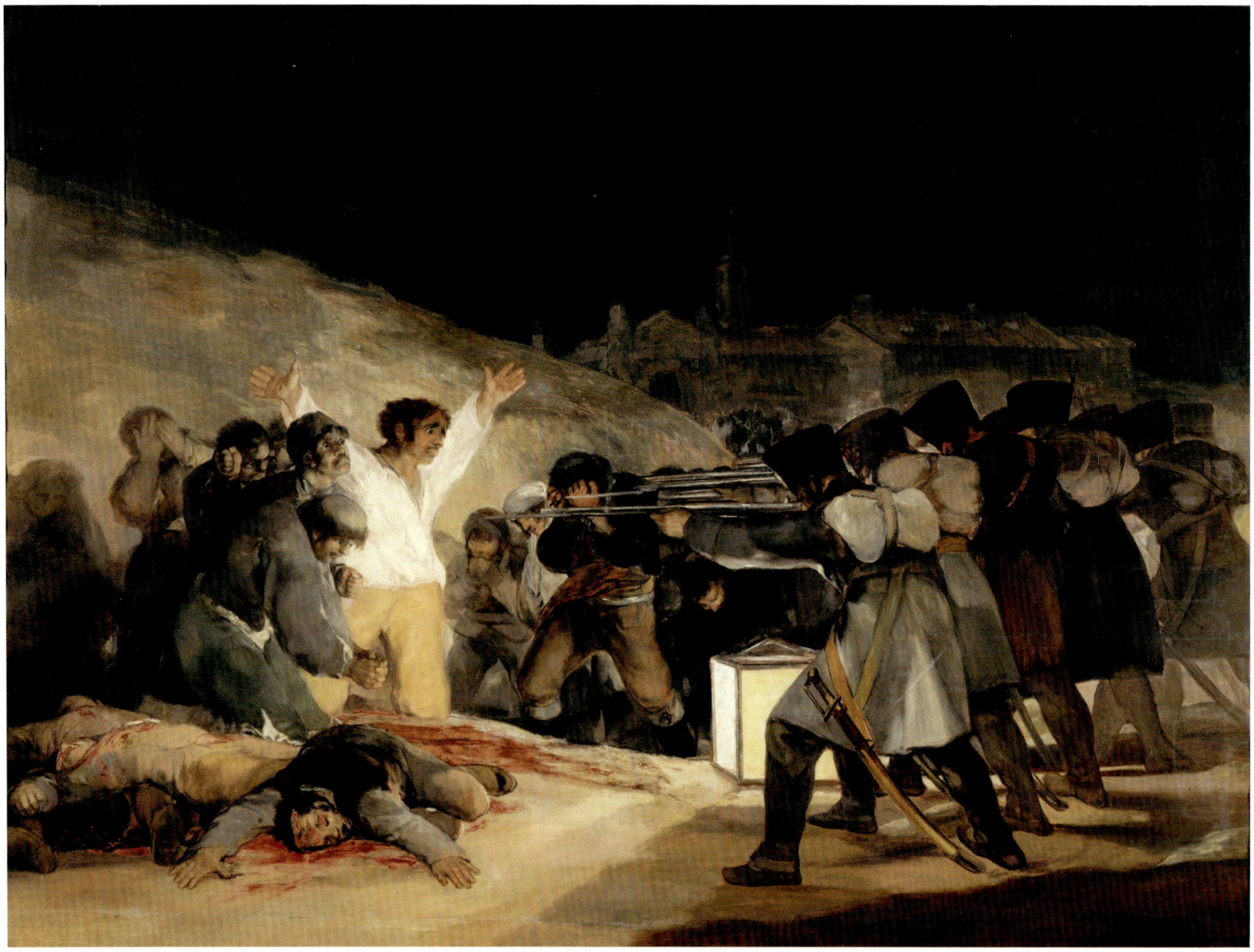

20
Francisco de Goya
The Third of May 1808, 1814
Oil on canvas,
2680 x 3470 mm
Museo del Prado, Madrid
P.749

famine in Madrid of 1811–12 (plates 48–64) and the repressive government of Ferdinand VII (plates 65–80); they were published posthumously in 1863.[48] The etchings express Goya's reaction to the 'Fatal consequences of the bloody war in Spain with Bonaparte', the oppression and threat to individual freedom and the violation of the codes of conduct that govern war. For Goya the fault lay at the feet of the invaders, reflecting a widespread sentiment in Spain that 'given that it is absolutely necessary to shed blood, better to offer it in a holocaust to the fatherland than to a tyrant's ambition'.[49]

The Peninsular War (1808–14) began when French and Spanish armies invaded Portugal in 1807; the following year France turned against Spain, her former ally.[50] The best-known events, early in the conflict, were the uprising in Madrid on 2 May, which led to a massacre on the following day, the horror of which was captured in Goya's painting (fig. 20).[51] News of the events spread quickly and throughout Spain the provinces rose up against the French, beginning a long and bloody conflict. On 15 June 1808 the French army laid siege to Zaragoza. They were fiercely opposed by thousands of Spaniards led into the city by General José Palafox y Melci, whose bravery made him a national hero. The assault lasted until mid-August, when the French were forced to lift the siege and retreat, having destroyed large parts of the city. Goya was summoned to Zaragoza by General Palafox in order to 'examine the ruins of that city and to portray the glories of its citizens'.[52] He arrived in October but was forced to withdraw to his birthplace of Fuendetodos when the French troops again besieged the city in late December; he was back in Madrid by early May 1809.[53] What Goya witnessed provided the material for the *Disasters of War*, which he began in 1810.[54]

Although Goya's original intentions for the *Disasters of War* are not well understood, they were not without precedent. Jacques Callot's etched series, the *Miseries of War* (1633–4), which Goya knew through the collections of Ceán Bermúdez and Sebastián Martínez, must have provided an important precedent, especially the close-up views and tight narrative focus of Callot's prints. Goya's drawings for his prints are on different papers, and work on the etchings was carried out over five or so years, using batches of copper plates of varying sizes and quality. Groups of working proofs also vary in the types of paper and ink used. These variations no doubt reflect the way in which Goya modified his approach and ideas as events in Spain unfolded. The earliest prints are dated 1810 in the copper plates (plates 20, 22 and 27) and on the versos of the cut landscapes (plates 13–15 and 30). Fifty-six plates are numbered in the lower left corner. This probably indicates Goya's intention to publish his original wartime 'disasters', perhaps as early as August 1812, following the British victory over the French on 22 July 1812. Led by Arthur Wellesely, the future Duke of Wellington, the British Army routed the French at the Battle of Arapiles and at Alba de Tormes near Salamanca, arriving in Madrid on 12 August as the French, who had occupied the city since 1808, began to leave. Alternatively, Goya's project may have followed the final expulsion of the French in 1813, before the reversal of the liberal constitution and the return to Spain of Ferdinand VII as a self-proclaimed absolute monarch in May of the following year, by which time Goya would have added the famine scenes (plates 48–64). There is still disagreement as to the dating of the allegorical *caprichos enfatícos* (see below) that completed the series (and are numbered only in the upper left corner).

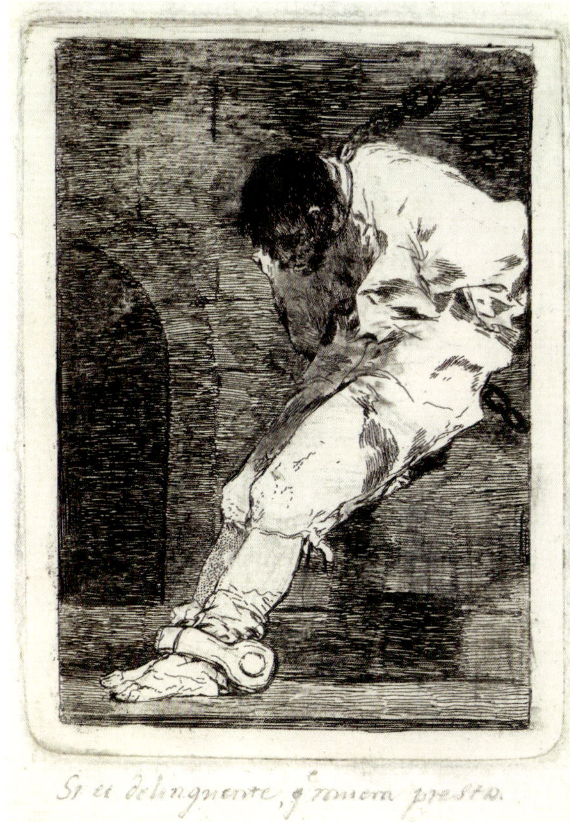

21
Francisco de Goya
If he is Guilty let him Die Quickly, c.1810–15
Etching touched with graphite, 120 x 86 mm
British Museum, London
1975,1025.421.85

An album of proof impressions (now in the British Museum) assembled by Goya for his friend Ceán Bermúdez provides valuable information. The impressions have manuscript titles that are the only record of how Goya conceived of the series by the time he had completed and intended to publish it as a book of eighty-five prints,[55] to include the later *caprichos enfáticos*, and three 'Prisoners'.[56] The man restrained by a leg clamp and chains in the Ceán Album (fig. 21) is captioned in Goya's hand 'If he is guilty let him die quickly' – in the biting tone of his other prints. The title page carries a neatly written inscription, probably devised by Goya to be engraved: 'Fatales consequencias de la sangrienta guerra en España con Buonaparte y otros caprichos enfaticos, en 85 estampas' ('The fatal consequences of the Bloody War in Spain with Bonaparte and other *caprichos enfatícos* in eighty-five prints').

More proofs for the *Disasters of War* survive than for any other of Goya's print series, which may indicate that they were made in batches to

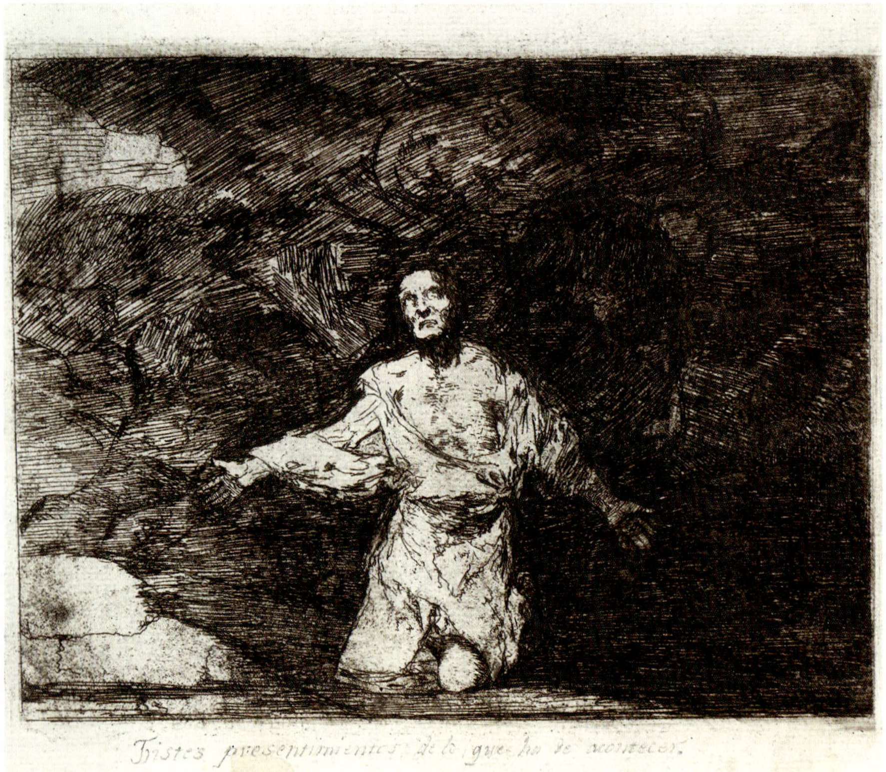

22
Francisco de Goya
Sad Presentiments of What is to Come, c.1810–15
Etching, burin, drypoint and burnisher, 176 x 217 mm
British Museum, London
1975,1025.421.3

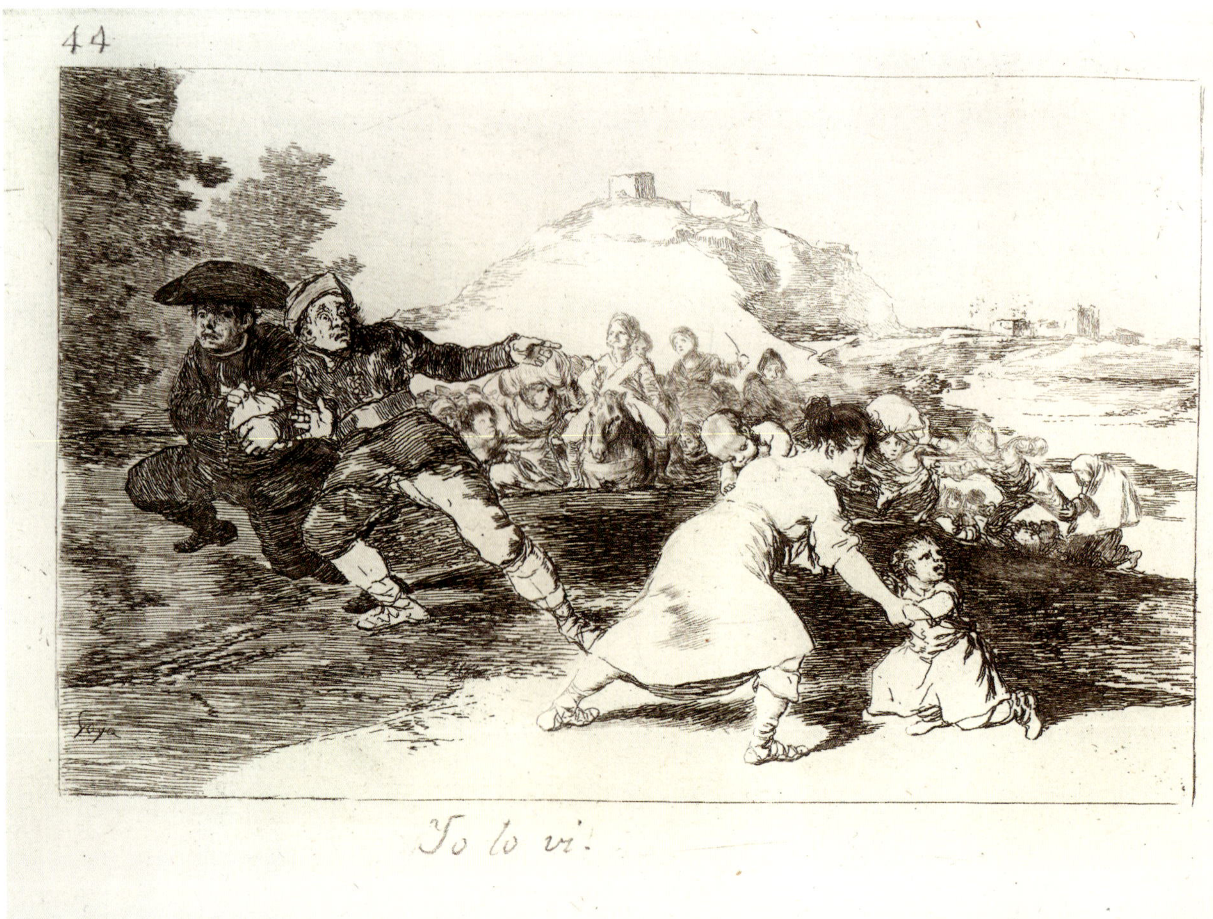

23
Francisco de Goya
I Saw It, c.1810–15
Etching, drypoint and burin, 157 x 235 mm
British Museum, London
1975,1025.421.46

show friends.[57] The return of the despotic Ferdinand VII in 1814, and Goya's decision to leave Spain in 1823 because of the political oppression, prevented the series from being published in his lifetime in Spain. Ceán's daughter gave the album to the art historian and collector Valentín Carderera,[58] who lent it to the Academy of San Fernando in 1862 so that the titles could be engraved on copper plates; the published edition was issued a year later. The prints in the published edition are very different from Goya's proofs: a film of ink was left on the surface of the plates giving tone to the entire print, whereas in the proofs Goya carefully contrasted the whiteness of the paper with the printed lines to create dramatic effect.

The *Disasters of War* opens with *Sad Presentiments of What is to Come* (fig. 22), in which a disconsolate figure kneels with his arms wide before a darkened background, reflecting the tragedy predicted by the title. The prints that follow have a tight narrative focus that conveys an intimacy with the subject and provokes a strong emotional response. The mass graves, generic murderers and nameless victims are templates for the indiscriminate effect war has on all people. The plates dated 1810 must be based on the scenes Goya witnessed on this journey to Zaragoza: plate 44, showing peasants fleeing in terror, is entitled *I saw it* and testifies to the artist's first-hand experience (fig. 23). In the famine of 1811–12 more than 20,000 people in Madrid

24
Francisco de Goya
Unhappy Mother!, c.1811–15
Etching, burnished aquatint and drypoint, 155 x 205 mm
British Museum, London
1975,1025.421.52

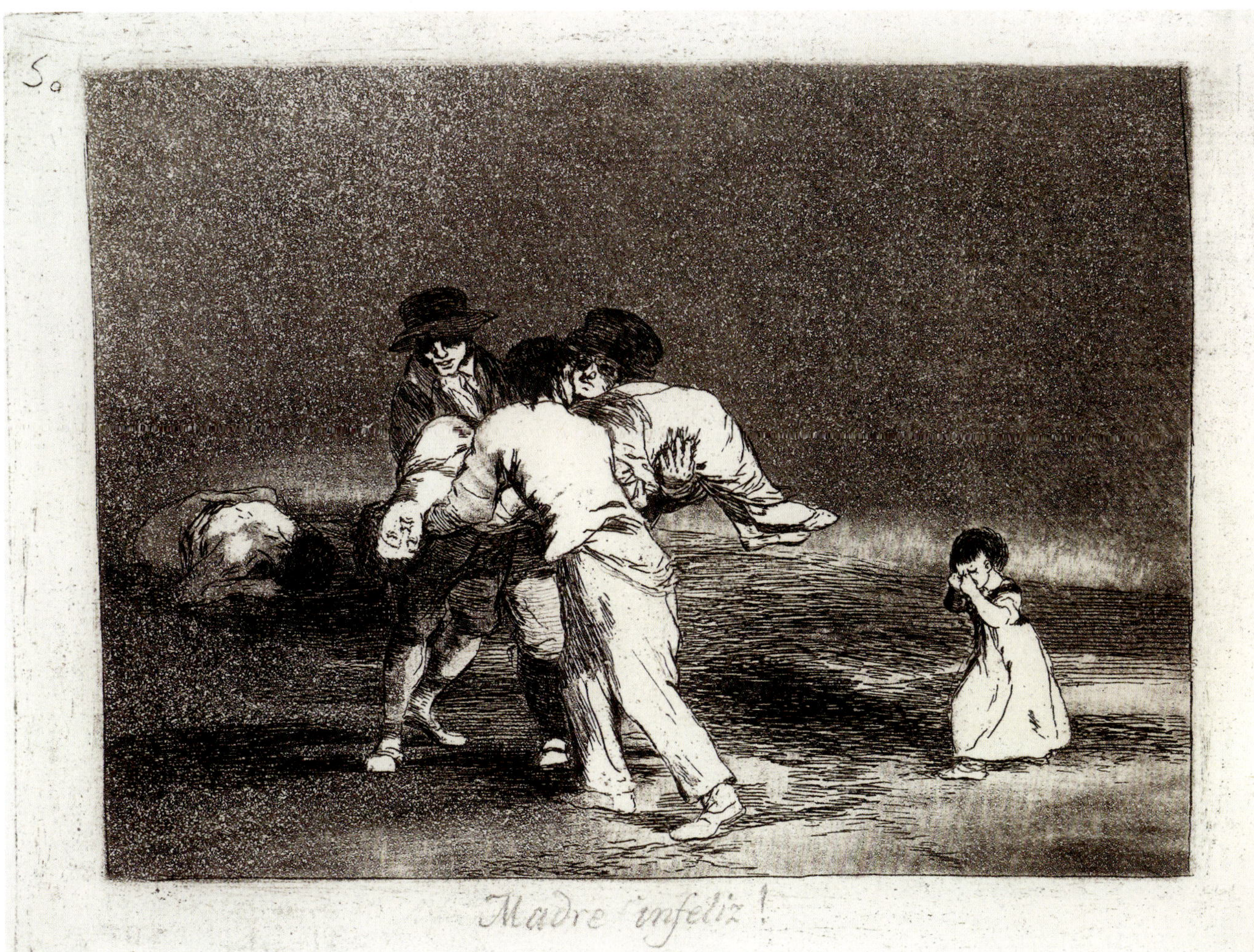

died. Goya's prints on this subject include scenes of charity, beggars, and the dead being removed. In the print *Unhappy Mother!* (plate 50) a small child follows as its dead mother is carried away (fig. 24). One of the men looks at the young woman, another back to the child, forming a powerful continuum of sorrow.[59] At times Goya uses captions to convey cinematic intensity by creating narrative links within subgroups of prints. For example, three visually distinctive scenes (plates 9–11) are entitled 'They don't like it' – 'nor do these' – 'or these either'. By the time he was working on the series he clearly regarded captions as indispensable for linking individual atrocities to the universal horror of war.

To the 'fatal consequences' of war, Goya added the *caprichos enfáticos*, images that have most recently been understood as a reaction to the repression initiated by Ferdinand VII on his return to Spain in May 1814 after a six-year absence, and are thus a finale to the images of war and famine.[60] Earlier interpretations saw them as a response to royal and ecclesiastical repression under Ferdinand VII, made during a three-year period following a liberal revolution in 1820 that obliged the king to re-adopt the constitution and suppress the Inquisition.[61] As a result, the *caprichos enfáticos* were placed after the *Tauromaquia* (1816) and *Disparates* (*c.*1816–24) discussed below.[62] A number of the *caprichos enfáticos* are satires against the Church, which had allied itself with the vindictive monarchy. Plate 76 depicts a large carnivorous vulture apparently excreting an ecclesiastical figure while trying to take flight (fig. 25). Other scenes show animals in human guise, such as a monstrous scribe (plate 71), its feet resting on a globe, possibly an allegorical figure representing the domination of the world by such creatures (fig. 26).[63] A pair of prints towards the end of the series, *Truth has Died* and *Will She Rise Again?* unambiguously point to Goya's bitter resentment at the loss of freedom of the Spanish people (fig. 27).

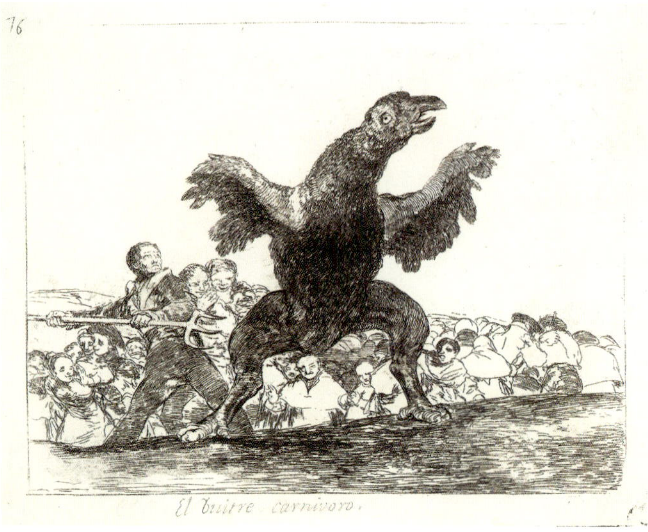

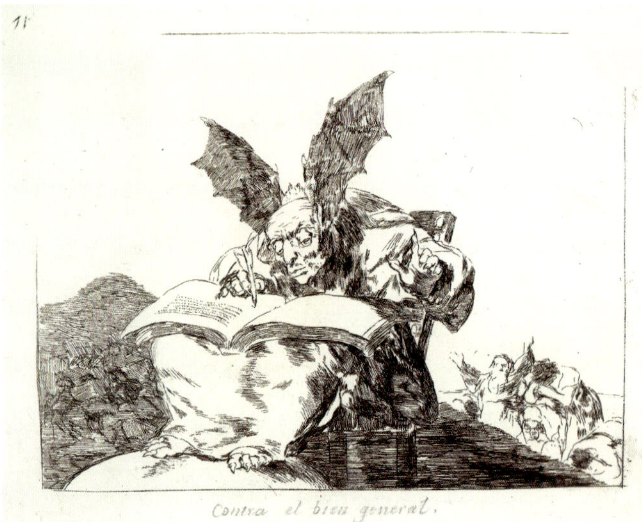

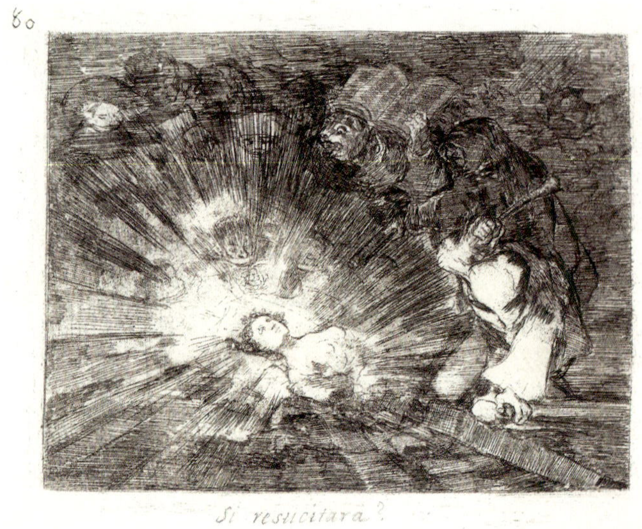

25
Francisco de Goya
Large Carnivorous Vulture, c.1814–15
Etching, burin and burnisher,
175 x 216 mm
British Museum, London
1975,1025.421.78

26
Francisco de Goya
Against the Common Good, c.1814–15
Etching and burnisher,
174 x 218 mm
British Museum, London
1975,1025.421.73

27
Francisco de Goya
Will She Rise Again?, c.1814–15
Etching and burnisher,
177 x 217 mm
British Museum, London
1975,1025.421.82

An ongoing project, Goya's work on the *Disasters of War* was punctuated by commissions for official portraits of those involved in the war on both sides. A remarkable red chalk study depicts Arthur Wellesely, the future Duke of Wellington, who led the British army to victory at the Battle of Arapiles (fig. 28). Goya's drawing, showing him exhausted from the campaign, was preparatory to his equestrian portrait (fig. 29) now at Apsley House, London, speedily painted over one of Manuel Godoy or perhaps Joseph Bonaparte while Wellington was in Madrid.[64] The study also served as the basis for a portrait of Wellington (National Gallery, London), and Goya evidently also intended to use it for a print, since the paper shows a strong platemark (the result of the sheet being wrapped around the plate), while the space below the drawing would allow for an inscription.

The degree to which Goya documented his reaction to the war marks him unique, but he was not alone in addressing its consequences.[65] Fernando Brambila (1763–1834) and Juan Gálvez (1773–1846) were among the artists who went to Zaragoza to record the destruction of the city after the French

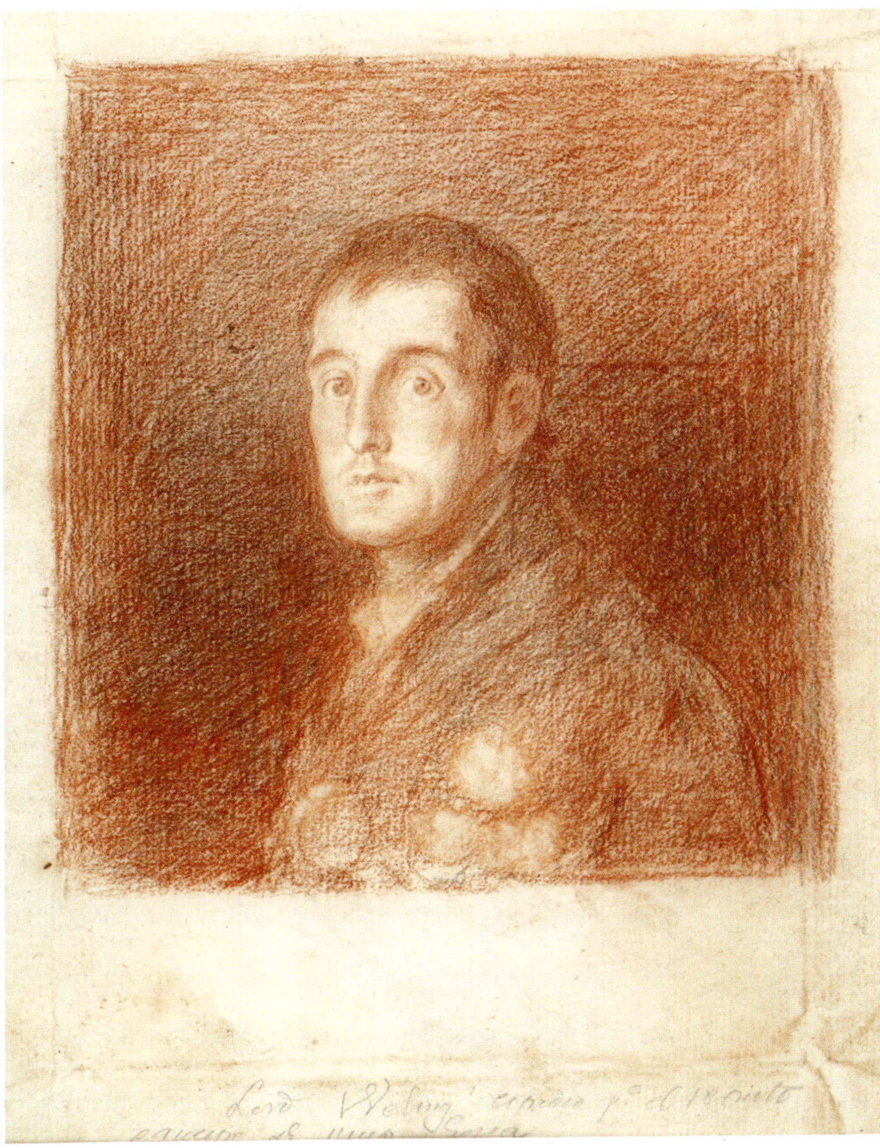

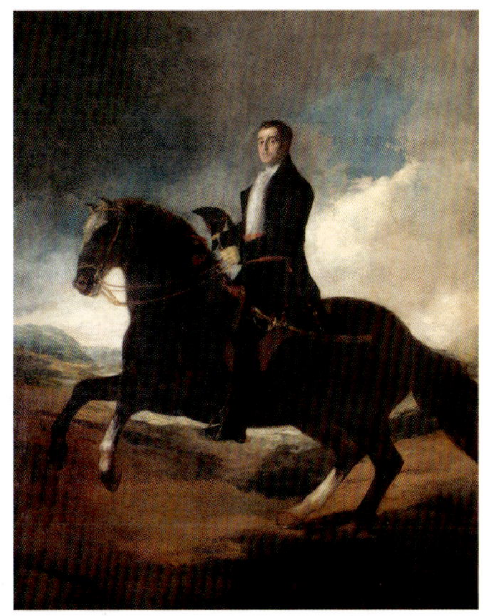

28
Francisco de Goya
Arthur Wellesley, 1st Duke of Wellington, 1812
Red chalk over black chalk and graphite, 235 x 177 mm
British Museum, London
1862,0712.185

29
Francisco de Goya
Equestrian Portrait of the Duke of Wellington, 1812
Oil on canvas, 2940 x 2400 mm
Apsley House, London

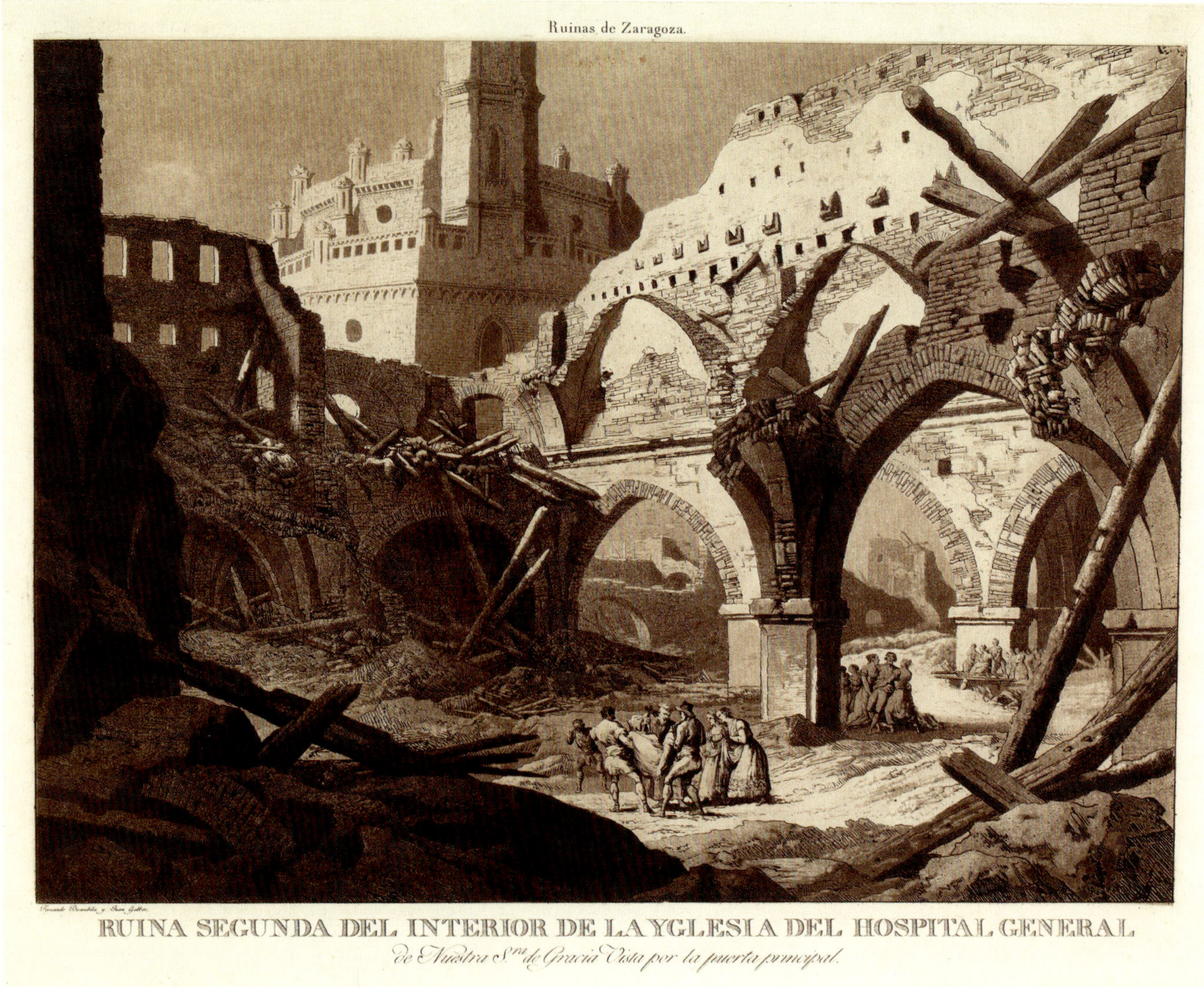

30
Fernando Brambila and Juan Gálvez
Ruins of the Church of the General Hospital, 1808–14
Etching and aquatint, 434 x 551 mm
British Museum, London
1899,0713.165

troops had left. They were in the city at the same time as Goya, returning to Madrid in November 1808 to work their material into a series of prints. Progress was interrupted by the second French occupation of the city, at which point they moved to Cadiz where their project was taken up by the Academy of Fine Arts. The series consisted of thirty-six prints of different sizes, the first of which were published in 1812 in instalments of three on the last day of each month.[66] The smaller prints celebrate the actions of individuals, emphasizing that the resistance was fuelled by their bravery. These include a countess who risked her life many times to get provisions to her comrades, and 'Uncle Jorge', an honourable worker who died from fatigue. The larger prints, such as *Ruins of the Church of the General Hospital* (fig. 30), mainly show the destroyed city. The series is remarkable for the Romantic aesthetic of the sublime horror they convey, with the ruins themselves an expression of the violence wrought on Spain by the occupying forces.

Goya based details in several of his *Disasters of War* series on the prints by Brambila and Gálvez. The central figures in his famine scene *Cartloads to the Cemetery* (plate 64), for example, seem to have been based on figures in

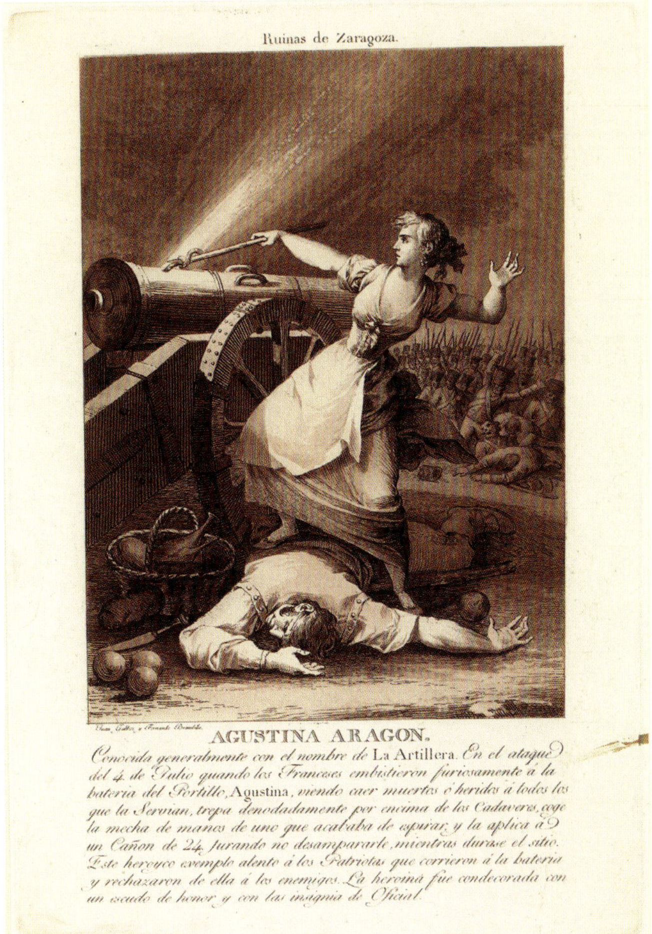

31
Fernando Brambila and Juan Gálvez
Agustina of Aragon, 1808–14
Etching and aquatint, 355 x 235 mm
British Museum, London
1899,0713.177

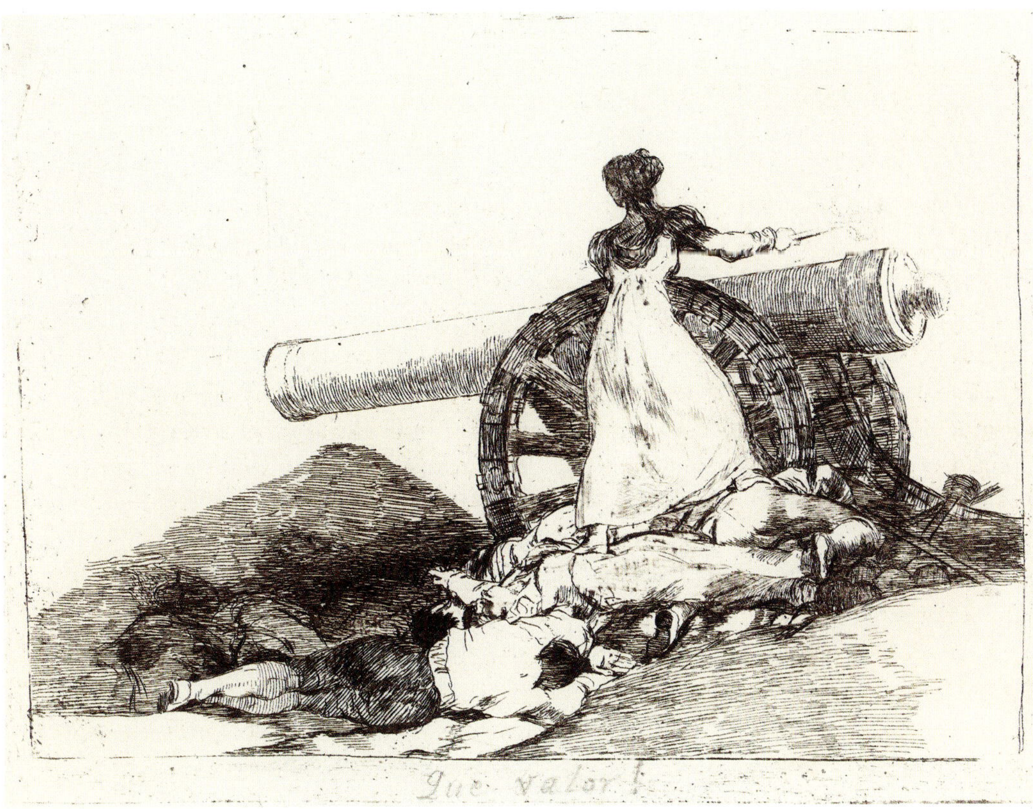

32
Francisco de Goya
What Bravery!, 1810–12
Etching, drypoint, burin and burnisher, 155 x 205 mm
British Museum, London
1975,1025.203

33
Henry Meyer
Manuela Sancho, 1811
Mezzotint, 513 x 406 mm
British Museum, London
1902,1011.3486

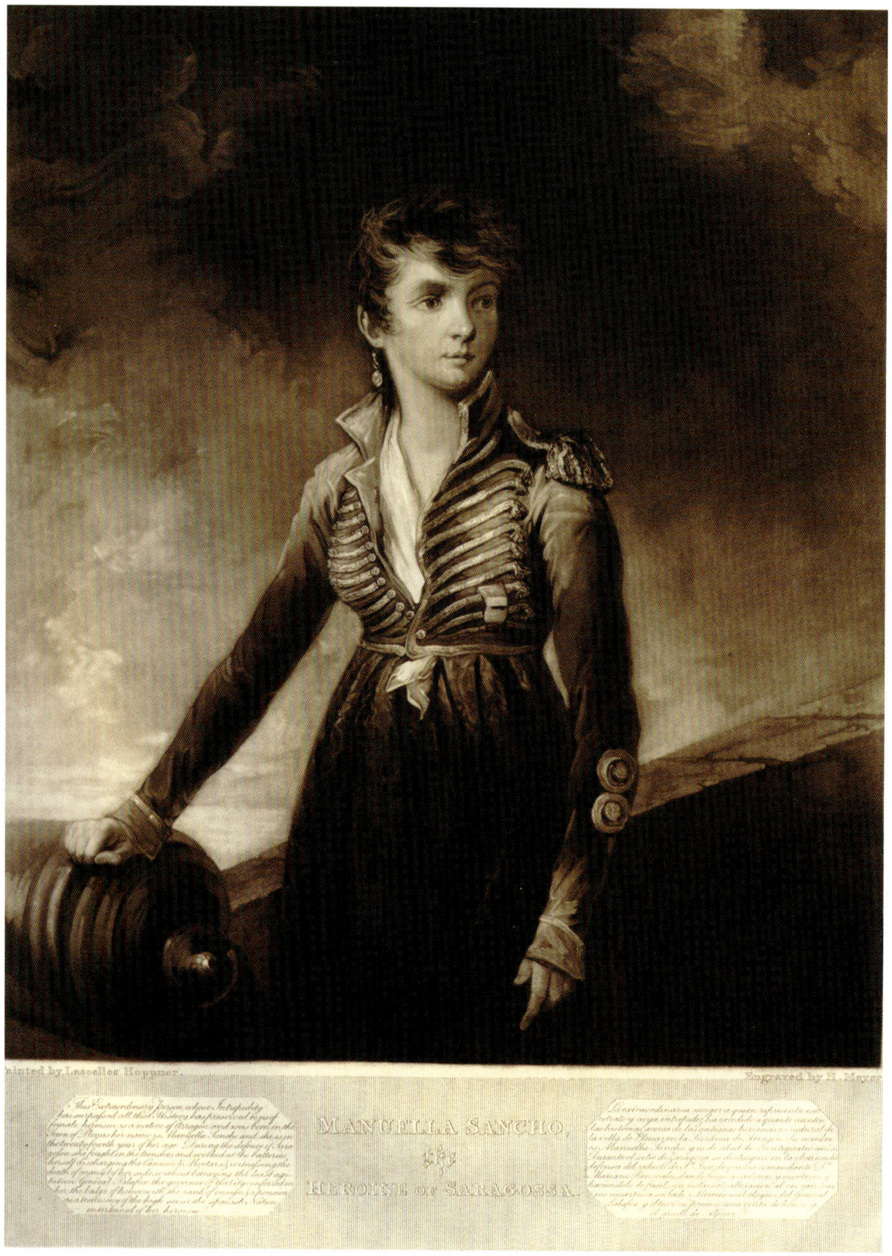

the nocturnal view of the *Ruins of the Seminary*.[67] The clearest connection is the image of a young woman lighting the fuse of a cannon, who in Brambila and Gálvez's print is identified as Agustina of Aragon (fig. 31). On 4 July 1808 the French soldiers stormed the Portillo, a gateway to the city of Zaragoza defended by cannons manned mainly by volunteer Spaniards. The 22-year-old Agustina arrived carrying food for those defending the gate. She saw her comrades being slaughtered, whereupon she clambered on their corpses, loaded a cannon and lit the fuse that blasted the invaders at close range. Inspired by her actions, comrades who had fled the gate returned to fight the enemy, who shortly after gave up the assault.[68] Goya does not identify her as Agustina in *What Bravery!* (fig. 32): instead, she is a lonely figure turned from the viewer, standing on corpses and lighting the fuse, representing the courage of the ordinary Spaniard who was responsible for defeating Napoleon's army.

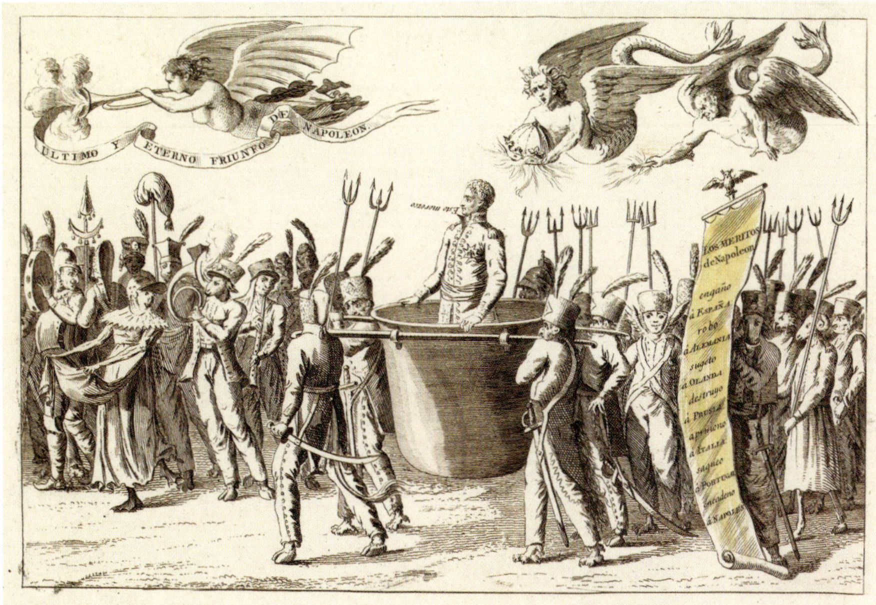

34
Anonymous
A Satire on Napoleon's 'Ultimate Triumph', c.1810
Etching with yellow hand-colouring, 151 x 224 mm
British Museum, London
1878,0112.28

The notoriety of individuals was celebrated well beyond Spain. Manuela Sancho, who in the 1808 siege discharged cannons 'without betraying the least agitation', is shown in a mezzotint by Henry Meyer published in London in 1811: she stands calmly beside her cannon, dressed in a hussar-inspired unbuttoned tunic and wearing an earring (fig. 33).[69] Napoleon's character and political ambitions were mocked in satirical prints throughout Europe.[70] A print representing his 'ultimate triumph' shows him standing in a cauldron being carried by an army of sheep and birds of prey. Issuing from his mouth are the words 'I deserve this' ('Esto Merezco'); on the right is a banner inscribed with his 'merits', including deceiving Spain, robbing Germany, destroying Prussia and sacking Portugal (fig. 34).[71]

The Inquisition (*c.*1808–14) and Images of Spain (*c.*1812–20) albums

The order in which Goya produced his albums of drawings has been the subject of much discussion. Working on several projects at the same time, he turned his attention to diverse subjects. Two albums that illustrate this point are roughly contiguous to the *Disasters of War*: the Inquisition Album (C) and the Images of Spain Album (F).

The Inquisition Album is the longest of Goya's albums and originally comprised 133 loose sheets assembled around 1808–14, from the outbreak of the war in 1808 to after the establishment of the liberal Spanish government in 1812.[72] The drawings are executed in brush and ink, on subjects similar to the *Disasters of War*: fate and destiny, human misery, visions, anti-clericalism, victims of the Inquisition and the restitution of liberty. Many have captions that indicate their subject. For example, *For Having Jewish Ancestry* (fig. 35 and detail p. 234) is one of a large group addressing the Inquisition and judicial abuse, in which Goya concentrates on the condition of individuals to express his sympathies.[73] Condemned figures in penitential garments emerge from a prison and file between a priest and an officer of the Inquisition. The tragedy of the scene is underscored by the first figure clasping his hands, his head

35
Francisco de Goya
For Having Jewish Ancestry, c.1808–14
Brush drawing in brown ink and wash, 205 x 142 mm
British Museum, London
1862,0712.187

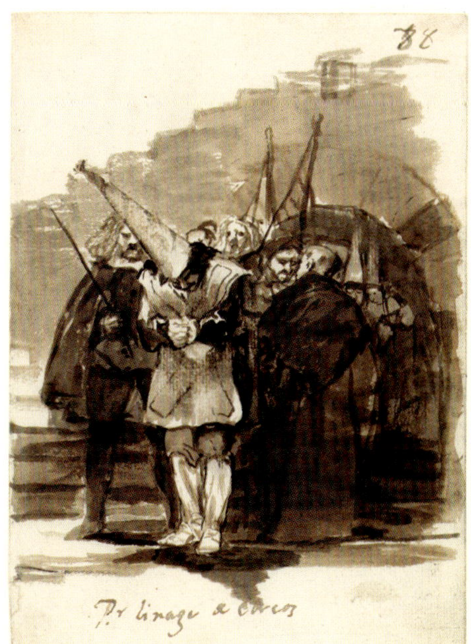

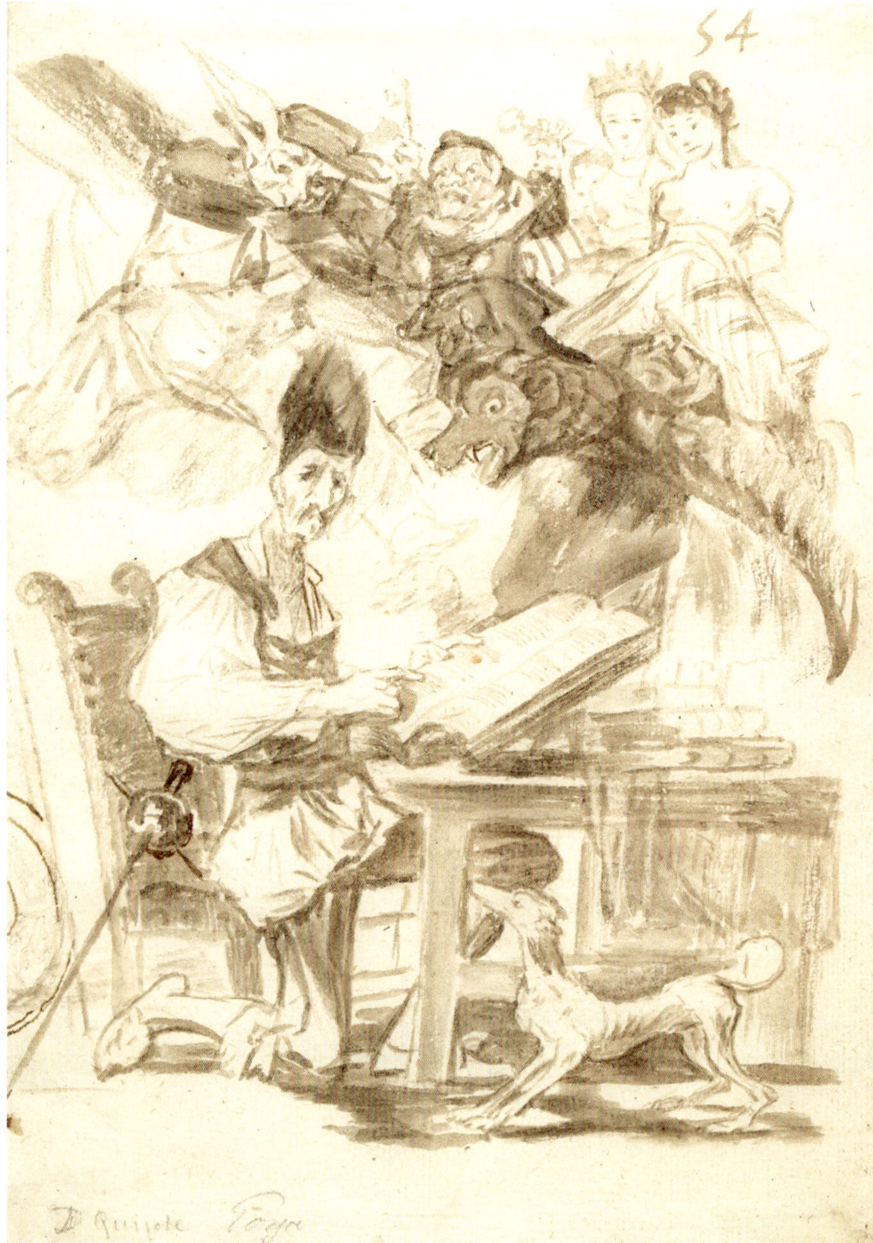

36
Francisco de Goya
Don Quijote Beset by Monsters, c.1812–20
Brush drawing in grey-brown ink and wash, 207 x 145 mm
British Museum, London
1862,0712.188

hung in shame. Goya might have been encouraged to make the Inquisition drawings in response to two publications by Juan Antonio Llorente, who had been Secretary to the Inquisition in Madrid from 1789 until 1791, in which he attacks its history and practices.[74] Towards the end of the album a number of drawings celebrate the restoration of the Constitution and liberty to Spain, emphasized by their titles: *Divine Liberty*, *May the Joy Last* and *Light from Darkness*.[75]

The Images of Spain Album was made from a disbanded and re-used album, suggesting that it was begun during the war when new materials were in short supply, and has been dated to the period 1812–20.[76] The drawings are in the same type of writing ink as the Inquisition Album. Their wide range of subjects makes it difficult to find a linking theme and supports the broad date range. All the drawings have human subjects – there are no witchcraft or diabolical scenes, for example – and only three have captions in Goya's hand. By turns violent, humorous, erotic and enigmatic, there are drawings of games, duels, violence, poverty and crowds, and the album ends with a group of hunting scenes. Eighty-nine sheets survive from an album that originally had up to 106 numbered sheets. The sheet numbered 54 depicts Don Quijote beset by demons and figures from his imagination (fig. 36), a subject closer to themes in *Los Caprichos* and the *Disparates* than to other drawings from this album.[77] The drawing comes in the middle of a group of scenes that deal broadly with violence. Writing in 1830, Goya's friend Bartolomé José Gallardo recalled that the artist sent him a message in London 'saying that he had thought of producing some original *Caprichos* with the title *Don Quijote's Visions*, in which he painted the fantasies of the mad knight of La Mancha in a new style'.[78] The project did not materialize, but the subject resonates with Goya's interests and the drawing of Don Quijote in the Images of Spain Album may have been part of the aborted project.[79]

Towards the end of the album are a number of sheets that have been identified as relating to Constitutional Spain; these provided the ideological source for two prints in the *caprichos enfáticos* discussed above.[80]

The *Tauromaquia* (1816)

Even in his later years nothing seems to have impeded Goya's imagination or dampened his desire to create. At the age of seventy he completed a series of thirty-three aquatint etchings of bullfighting subjects, later entitled *La Tauromaquia*. They were advertised for sale in the *Diario de Madrid* on 28 October and 31 December 1816, described thus:

> [a] collection of prints, invented and etched by Don Francisco Goya, Court Painter to his Majesty, wherein are represented diverse manoeuvres with bulls ... an idea being given in the series of prints of the origins, the growth, and present state of the said fiestas in Spain, which will be self evident without an explanation solely by looking at the plates...[81]

Goya's intentions in creating the series are not known but have been subject to a number of interpretations. In the nineteenth century the *Tauromaquia* were described as reflecting his enthusiasm for bullfighting and thus regarded as a documentary work. Since then the series has been seen variously as a respite from satire and the horrors of war; a satire on or criticism of bullfighting in Spain, where published sources have been identified; and a reflection of Goya's ambivalence to the national pastime, both as *aficionado* and as an enlightened critic.[82] Most commentators note the influence of Nicolás Fernández de Moratín's *Carta histórica sobre el origen y progresos de la fiesta de toros en España* (1777) and agree that the prints themselves mitigate against a straightforward interpretation.

Understanding the series has been complicated by the existence of variant titles and changes in the order of the prints. The prints themselves have no titles engraved on the copper plates, perhaps because Goya assumed that anyone who knew bullfighting would recognize the subjects and those involved, as suggested in his advertisement. However, complete first-edition

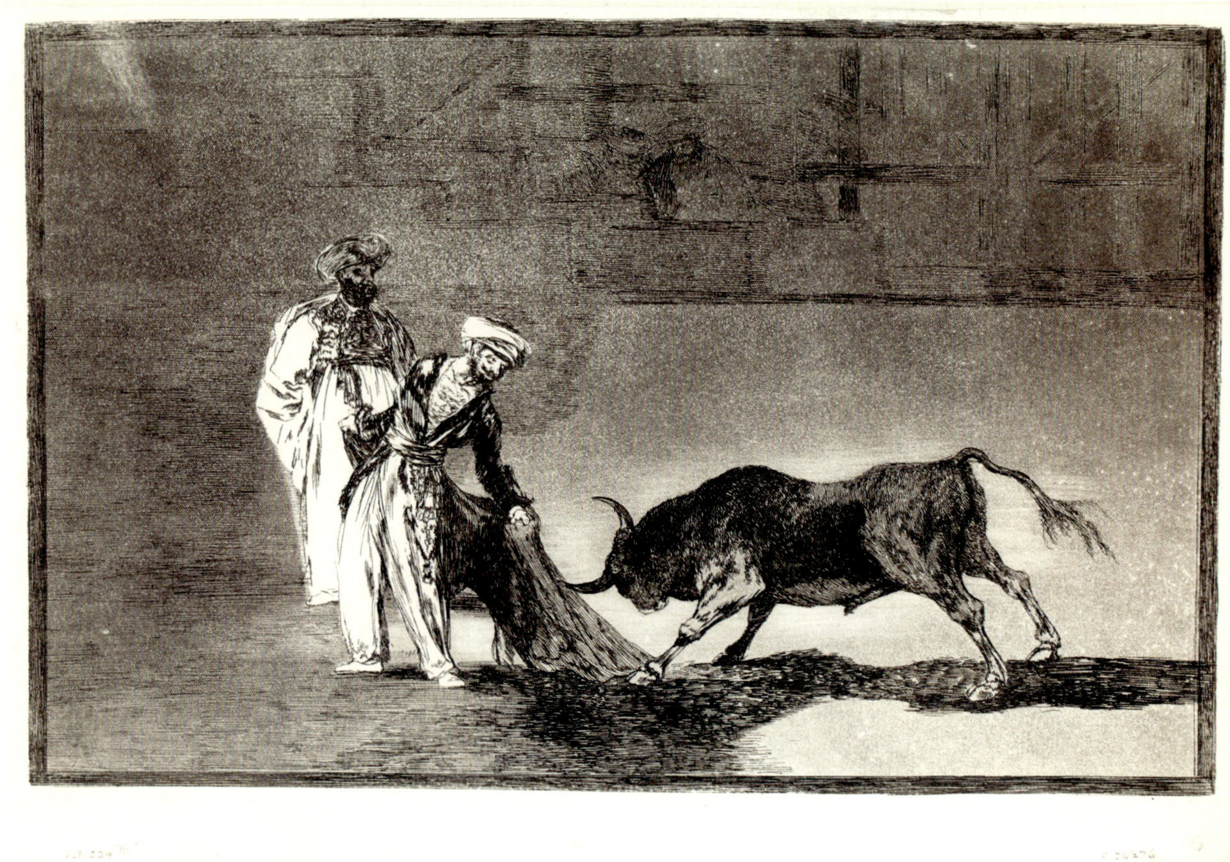

37
Francisco de Goya
The Moors Made a Different Play in the Ring Calling the Bull with the Burnous, 1816
Etching, burnished aquatint and drypoint, 224 x 324 mm
British Museum, London
1975,1025.311

38
Francisco de Goya
Dreadful Events in the Front Rows of the Ring in Madrid and the Death of the Mayor of Torrejón, 1816
Etching, burnished aquatint, wash, drypoint and burin, 245 x 355 mm
British Museum, London
1862,0712.161

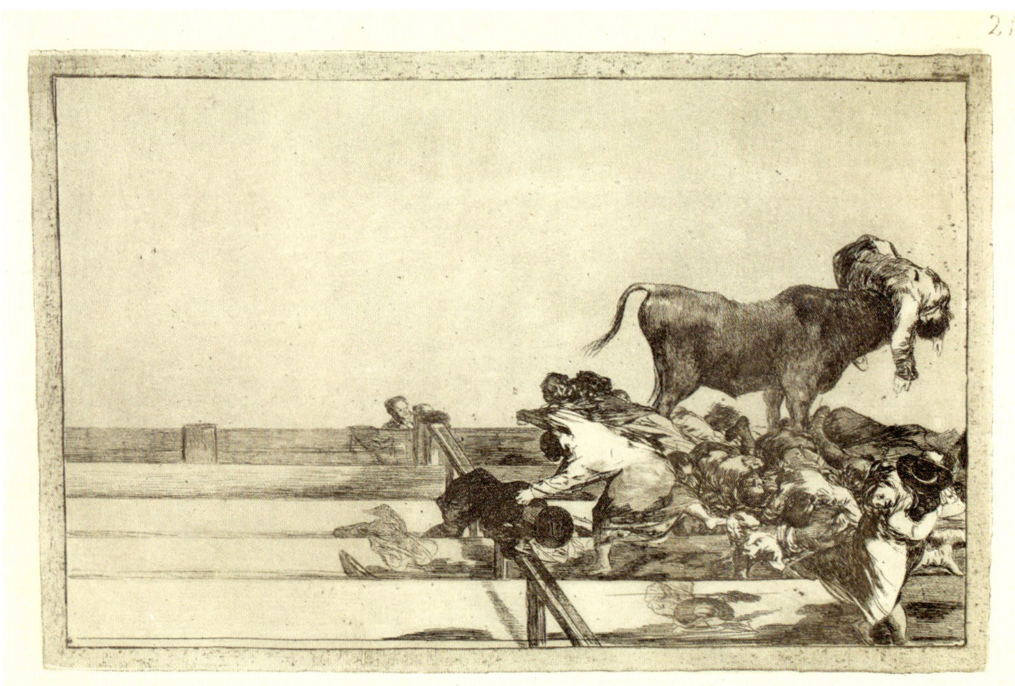

sets of prints are usually accompanied by an explanatory list of subjects, drafted with help from one or more of the artist's friends.[83] Goya's own handwritten titles appear on a unique set of the prints (Boston Public Library): these are brief and often do not identify a specific subject.[84] He gave a set of proofs (now in the British Museum) to his friend Ceán Bermúdez; a note by Valentín Carderera, who later owned them, explains that Goya asked Ceán to draft explanations for the prints, and that these were dictated by Ceán to his son. Ceán rearranged the prints in chronological order, scratching out Goya's etched numbers and renumbering them on pasted paper tabs.[85] A professionally calligraphed inscription, intended as a model for an engraved title page, described an additional print, *A Way of Flying*. A further etching was added later, facing the list of plates: depicting a blind guitarist caught up on the horns of a bull, this is inscribed, probably in Goya's hand, 'Barbaro diversion!' ('Barbarous entertainment!'). In the 1816 published edition of the *Tauromaquia* Goya's original numbering was unchanged, the titles were simplified in the printed list and the prints of the blind guitarist and *A Way of Flying* were not included.

The numbered series progresses from scenes of the origins of bullfighting and its historical development to contemporary figures and actual events that Goya may have seen. Plate 6, *The Moors Made a Different Play in the Ring Calling the Bull with the Burnous* (fig. 37), is one of the group depicting its origins in Spain, whereas plate 10 shows Charles V on horseback lancing a bull during a fiesta in 1527 in Valladolid. Plate 21 depicts an event

39
Francisco de Goya
The Daring Martincho in the Ring at Zaragoza, 1816
Etching, burnished aquatint and drypoint, 248 x 355 mm
British Museum, London
1862,0712.158

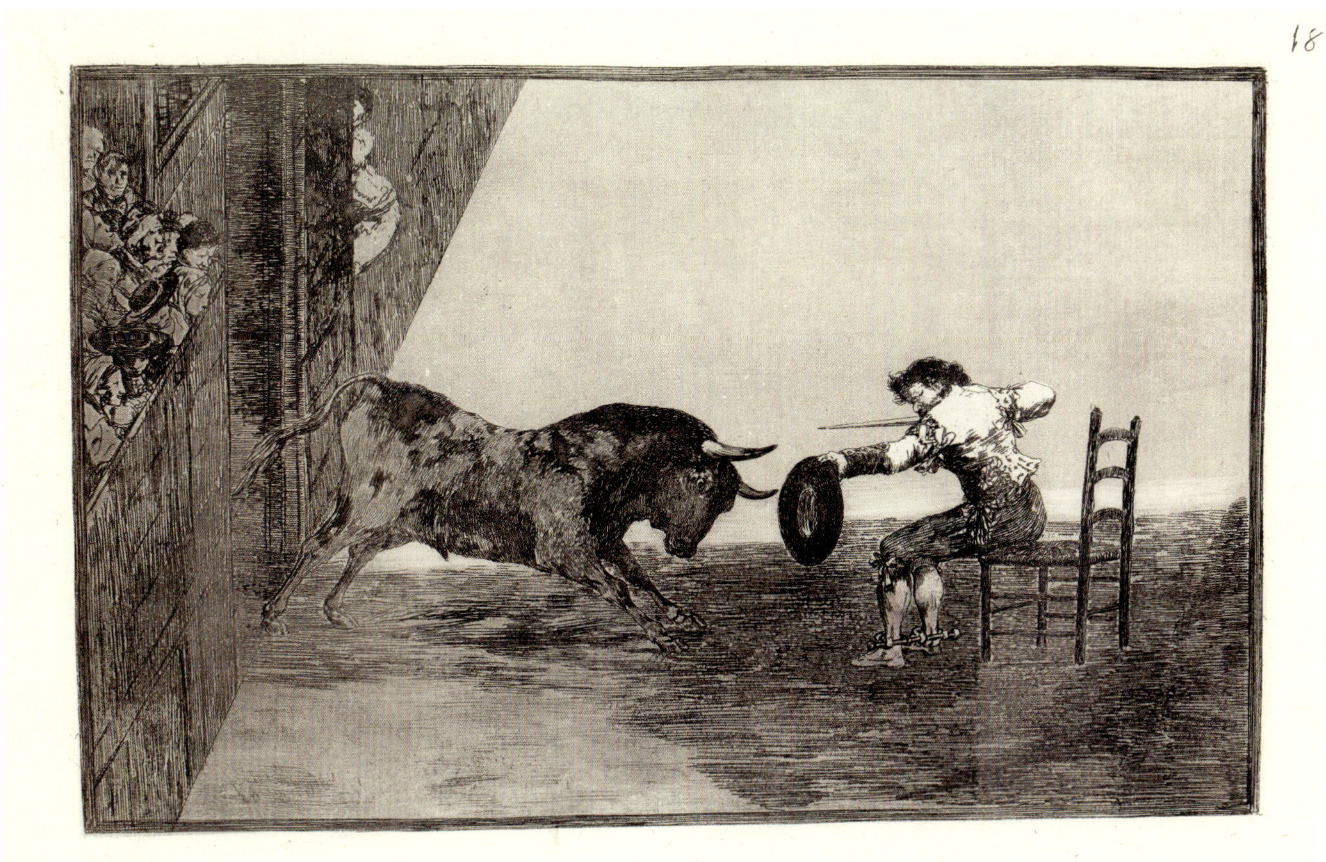

said to have occurred in the Madrid bullring, when a bull jumped into the front row of the bleachers and impaled the Mayor of Torrejón on its horns (fig. 38). Goya included some of the most famous bullfighters of his day. Pedro Romero, who retired in 1799, was renowned for his composed style (plate 30), while Pepe Hillo (José Delgado Guerra) was known for his daring manoeuvres that ultimately resulted in his death (plates 29, 33). The famous Argentinian Mariano Ceballos, known as 'The Indian', is shown killing a bull from his horse (plate 23) and the foolhardy 'Martincho' (Francisco Antonio Basson), sitting on a chair, his legs in shackles, as he lances the charging animal in the ring in Zaragoza (plate 18, 19; fig. 39). Three of the contemporary scenes (plates 19, 29 and 31) are signed and dated 1815, while the historical scenes are mainly on the versos of discarded or damaged plates of contemporary scenes, providing evidence that the historical 'early' scenes in fact came later, replacing defective or otherwise unsatisfactory plates.[86] For the third edition of 1876 another seven prints were added, printed from the rejected versos, and labelled A to G.[87]

Goya completely mastered the aquatint technique in the *Tauromaquia*, achieving remarkable theatrical effects through contrasting light and dark. Many of the prints have a concentrated simplicity, where the background serves to emphasize the action. Spectators form an indistinct mass and, with the exception of a couple of plates, are not meaningfully connected to the principal action. Goya's intentions in creating the series will probably never be known, but it is worth noting that almost all the *Tauromaquia* show acts of cruelty, which was condemned around this time by members of his circle, such as the print historian José de Vargas Ponce.[88] If we regard the *Tauromaquia* as Goya's critical response to bullfighting, then they may be seen as broadly in line with the preoccupations expressed in his series highlighting human failings, the *Caprichos* and especially the *Disasters of War*. The *Tauromaquia* had little commercial success and were not nearly as popular as Carnicero's colourful series of 1799 (figs 48–9, p. 223).

The Black Border (E, *c.*1816–20) and Witches and Old Women (D, *c.*1819–23) albums

Around the time of the publication of the *Tauromaquia* Goya was making drawings with very different subjects. The Black Border Album of about 1816–20, named for the ruled lines around each drawing (also known as Album E), was possibly never bound.[89] Forty-two sheets are known at present; the highest number inscribed on a sheet is 50. The sheets are unusually large, and the drawings, in brush and Indian ink, concentrate on figures, either single, in pairs or small groups. The drawing technique and inked borders may be linked to Goya's interest in lithography, suggesting that he planned to publish them – the first lithographic press was established in Madrid in 1819, around the time he was working on them. They are brilliantly executed and among the most engaging he ever produced. Several are full of humour, with witty captions: an old woman happily dancing (no. 2), midgets taunting a well-dressed bourgeoise (no. 16); others are tremendously powerful: the crippled victim of the war (no. 11), a bandit holding a dagger leading a woman and child to a cave (no. 41); or nightmarish: the screaming old hag riding a flying bull (no. 20). The hag is also related to an unfinished album of smaller

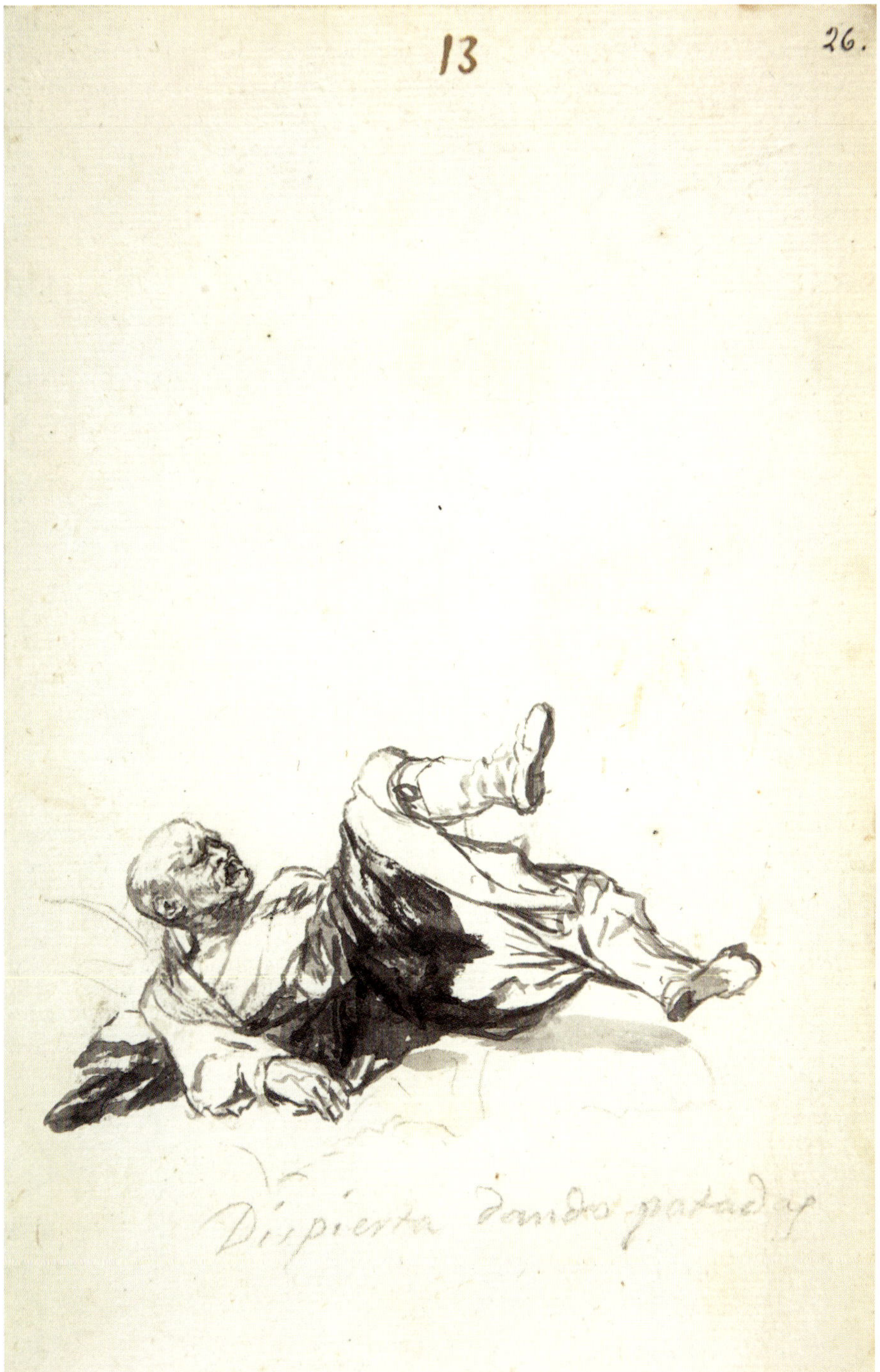

40
Francisco de Goya
He Wakes Up Kicking, *c.*1819–23
Brush and grey wash, 236 x 146 mm
Metropolitan Museum of Art, New York
35.103.26

ink-wash drawings showing witches and old women (Album D) dated to about 1819–23.[90] These drawings share compositional simplicity and directness with the Black Border Album, but they are not so carefully finished; few of them have a background, encouraging the viewer to concentrate on the figures. Those that have a nightmare quality suggest a connection with Goya's 'Black Paintings', the murals he painted from 1820 in his house on the outskirts of Madrid. Visions emerge from dreams, or in the case of *He Wakes Up Kicking* (fig. 40), we see the confused moment where an old man appears to be trying to free himself from a blanket.

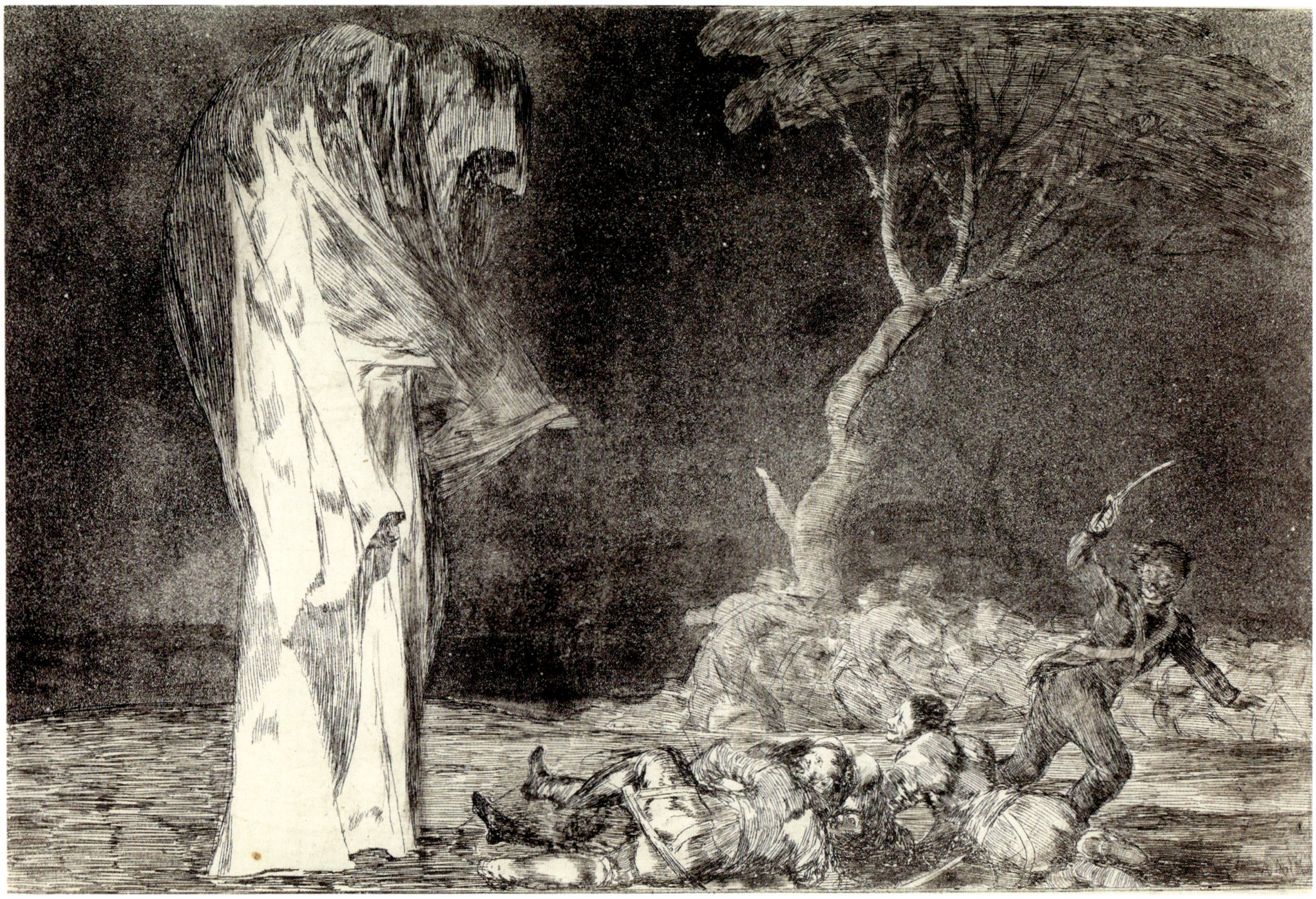

41
Francisco de Goya
Soldiers Fleeing a Phantom, c.1816–24
Etching, burnished aquatint and drypoint, 245 x 353 mm
British Museum, London
1975,1025.325

The Disparates (*c.*1816–24, published 1864 as *Los Proverbios – The Proverbs*)

Goya probably began working on this unfinished series of etchings as he was completing and preparing his *Tauromaquia* prints for publication in 1816; he continued working on the prints, using the same large English copper plates, until he abandoned it, either 1819 (when he moved to his house outside Madrid) or 1824 (when he left for France).[91] One of the prints included in the *Tauromaquia* set that Goya gave to Céan Bermúdez was *A Way of Flying* (see p. 259), in a pure etching state, before the addition of aquatint, and this has generally been regarded as one of the earliest prints in the new series. Very few contemporary working proofs are known – none at all of some of the plates – and on some Goya wrote his enigmatic 'Disparate' titles.[92]

The series was never published in Goya's lifetime. Eighteen plates were printed privately in Madrid, possibly in 1848 or 1849 but more likely after the death of Goya's son Javier, in May 1854, when they passed to Jaime Machén Casalins. In 1862 they were acquired by the Academia de San Fernando, together with the eighty plates of the *Disasters of War*.[93] The first edition was published two years later, as *Los Proverbios*, with a dated title page and explanatory introduction. The titles given to the prints have long been the subject of discussion. On proof impressions in the final state with aquatint, manuscript titles generally accepted as in Goya's hand all begin with the word 'Disparate'. Although they were published under the title *Los Proverbios*, there

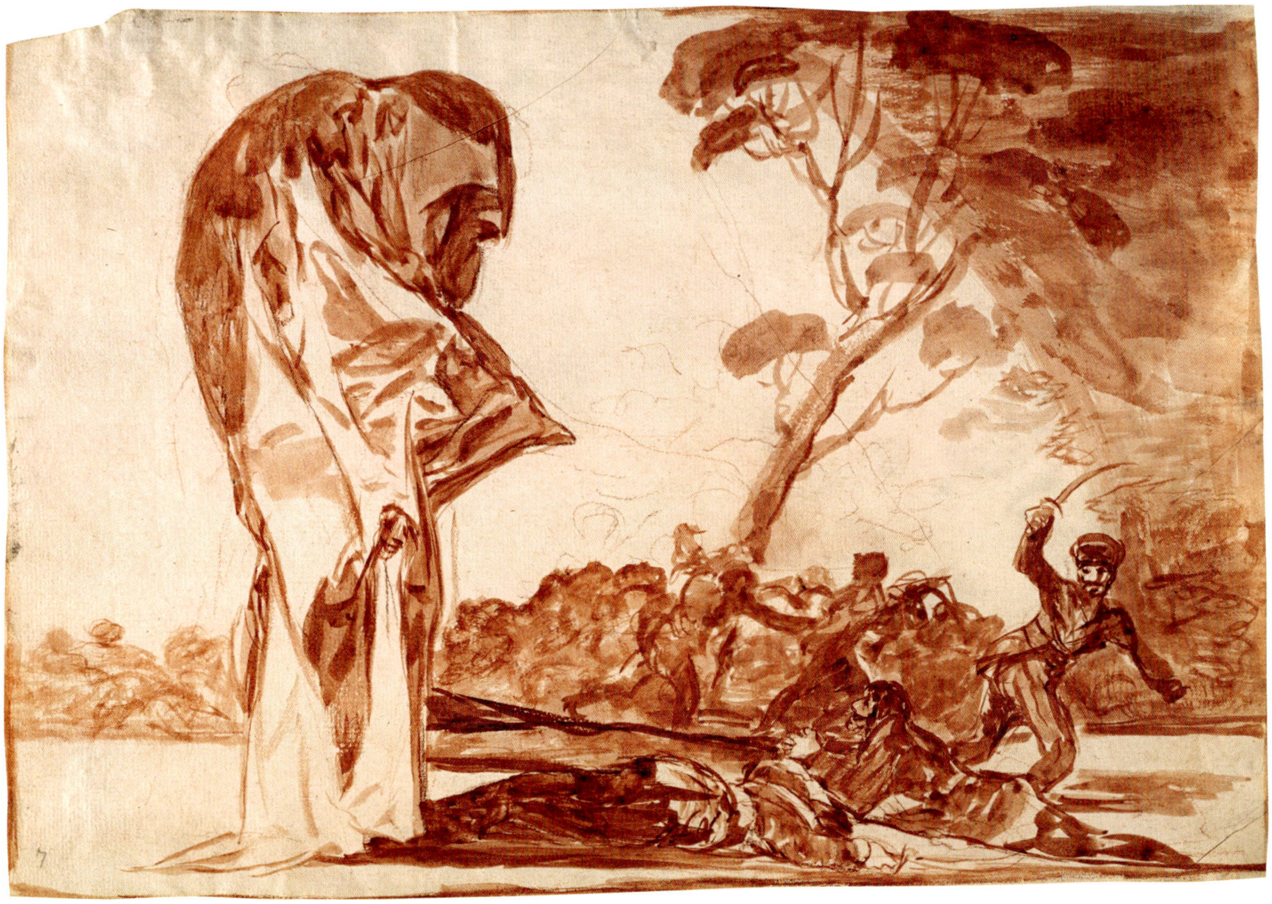

is no evidence to suggest that Goya intended them as illustrations of proverbs – although collector and scholar Tomás Harris attempted to provide a proverbial equivalent for each one.

A number of preparatory drawings survive, very freely brushed in sanguine wash, while others that were not turned into prints confirm that a more ambitious project was left unfinished.[94] *The Disparates* is Goya's most enigmatic print series and has provoked many interpretations. Described as pessimistic, dark and ominous, like the 'Black Paintings' murals, they are marked by violence, superstition, and nightmare-like visions – subjects that also dominate the *Caprichos* and particularly the *Disasters of War*. Many writers have recognized the carnival associations evident in the series, reflecting a world upside down, where roles are reversed, the irrational is presented in human form and beliefs and institutions are open to mockery.[95]

Plate 2, in which soldiers fall away from a huge phantom, suggests irrational fear and the ease with which men are deceived as the mask or head peeking out from the phantom's sleeve reveals it to be an illusion (fig. 41). Soldiers in the background huddle around a tree while others recede into the distance. The preparatory drawing in vivid red wash over red chalk (fig. 42) shows that the original intention was to extend the line of figures all the way across the horizon to the left.[96] The hooded spectre appears earlier in the *Caprichos* (plates 3, 52) and the soldiers in the *Disasters of War*, but combined in this print they powerfully convey different meaning.

42
Francisco de Goya
Soldiers Fleeing a Phantom, c.1816–24
Red wash over red chalk, 233 x 331 mm
Museo del Prado, Madrid
D.4274

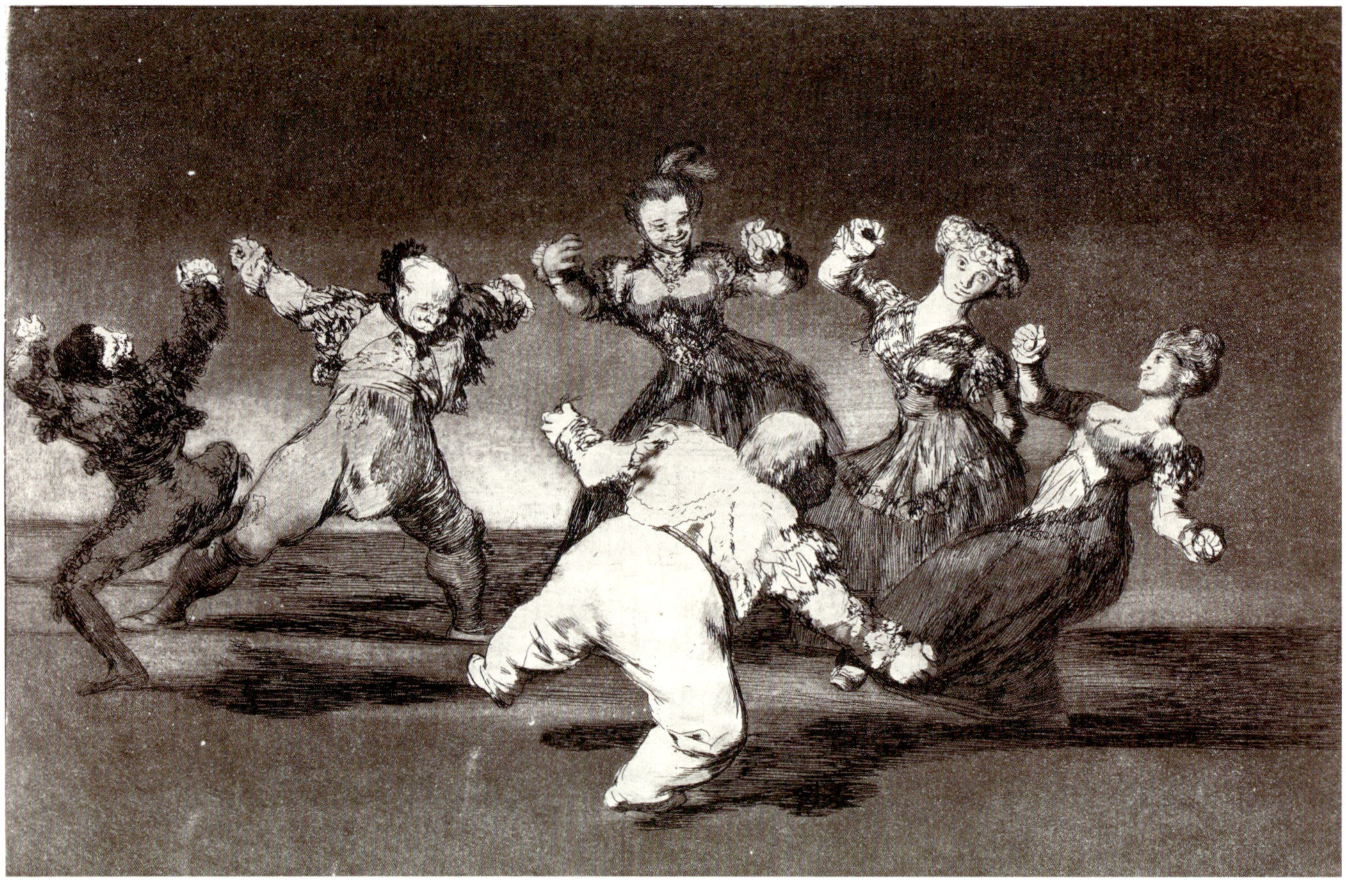

43
Francisco de Goya
Figures Dancing in a Circle, c.1816–24
Etching, burnished aquatint and drypoint, 245 x 355 mm
British Museum, London
1975,1025.363

44
Francisco de Goya
Burial of the Sardine, c.1814–16
Oil on panel, 825 x 620 mm
Museo de la Real Academia de Bellas Artes de San Fernando
676

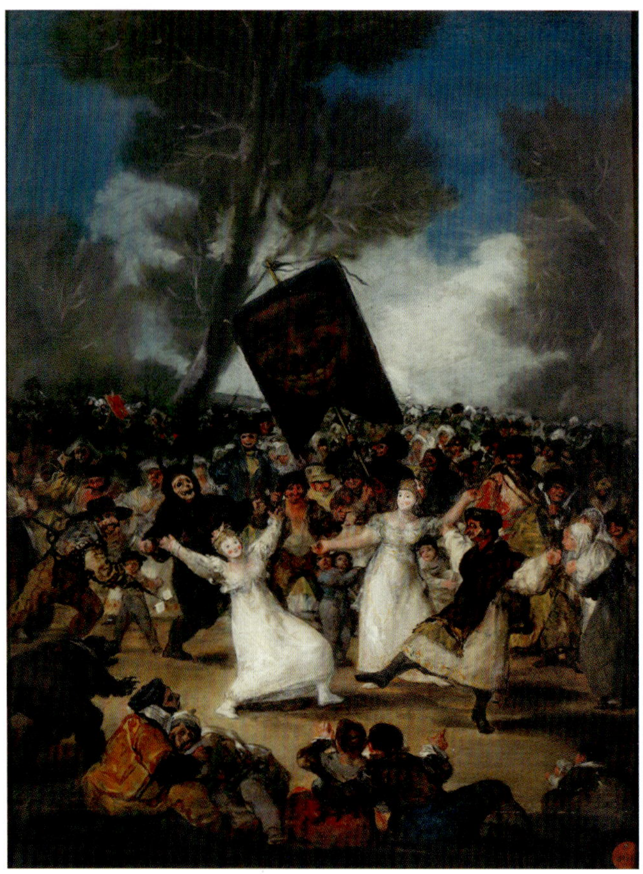

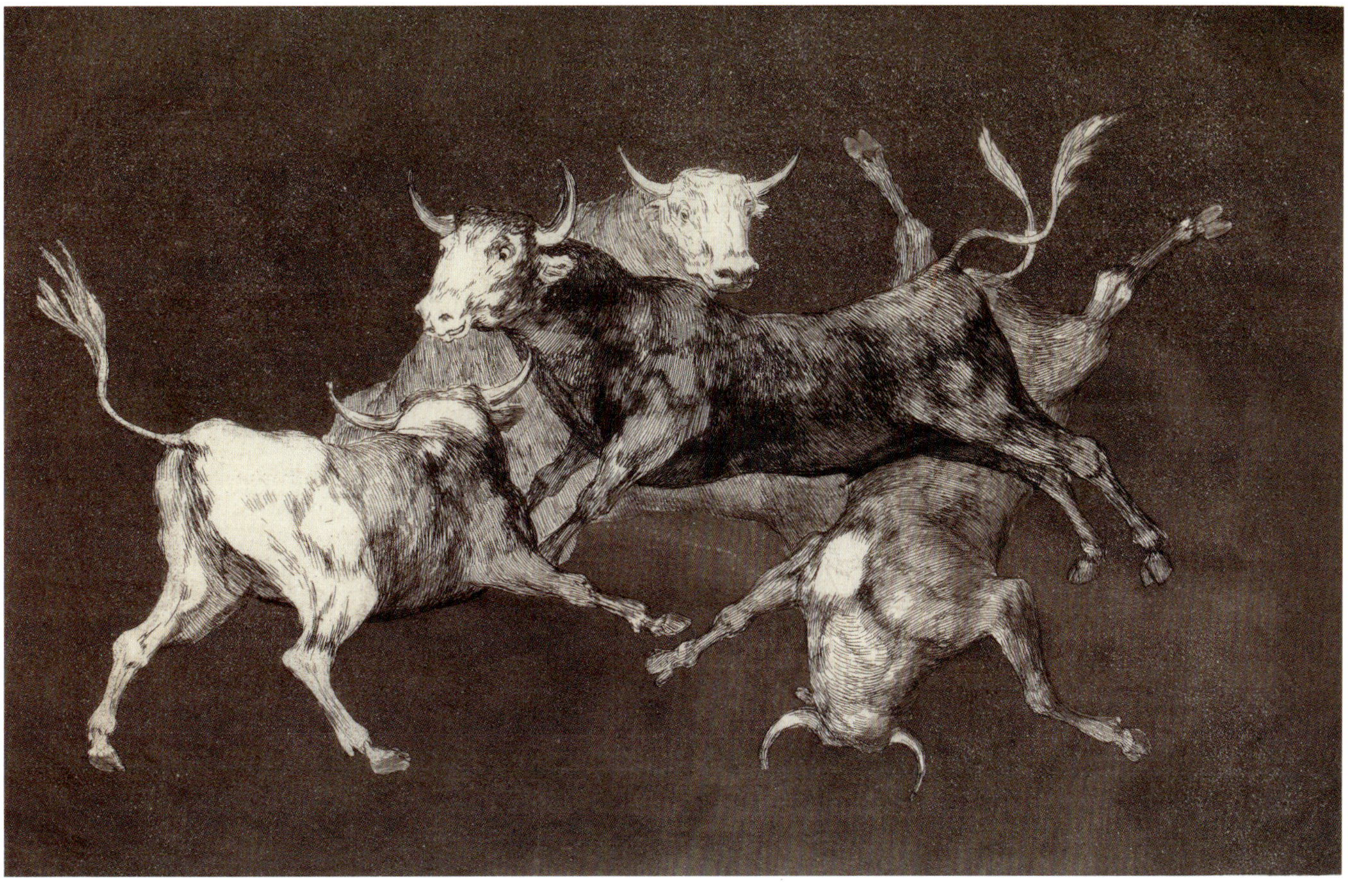

45
Francisco de Goya
Fools' Folly, c.1816–24
Etching, aquatint and drypoint, 245 x 355 mm
British Museum, London
1931,1012.7

The giddy world of the carnival is evoked in plate 12, where six well-dressed figures of different ages and physical conditions dance with great energy in a circle, arms raised to play castanets (fig. 43).[97] Conveying nothing of the grace of Goya's 1777 tapestry cartoon, *Dance on the Banks of the Manzanares*, the stiffness of their movement and mask-like expressions convey an air of demented abandonment similar to the *Burial of the Sardine* (fig. 44) of around 1814–16.[98] Four additional plates for the series became separated from the eighteen published in Madrid and were not published until 1877 in France.[99] One of these prints shows four suspended bulls tumbling in limitless space (fig. 45). The bulls, while superficially similar to those in the *Tauromaquia*, resonate more with Goya's last series of prints, the *Bulls of Bordeaux*.

The subjects of the *Disparates* invite further study. Appreciating the remarkable technical effects Goya achieved in the series does not resolve their meaning: he wished to engage the viewer through their daring formal qualities. Throughout the *Disparates* the use of aquatint, for example, creates an unearthly, glutinous light from which figures emerge while others dissolve, instilling the prints with a corrosive, nocturnal, dreamlike quality. Often a horizon is indicated but implies an unstable, shifting mass rather than a separation between earth and sky. If Goya intended specific meaning that still eludes us, despite the efforts of generations of scholars, perhaps these mysterious prints will continue to resist logical analysis.

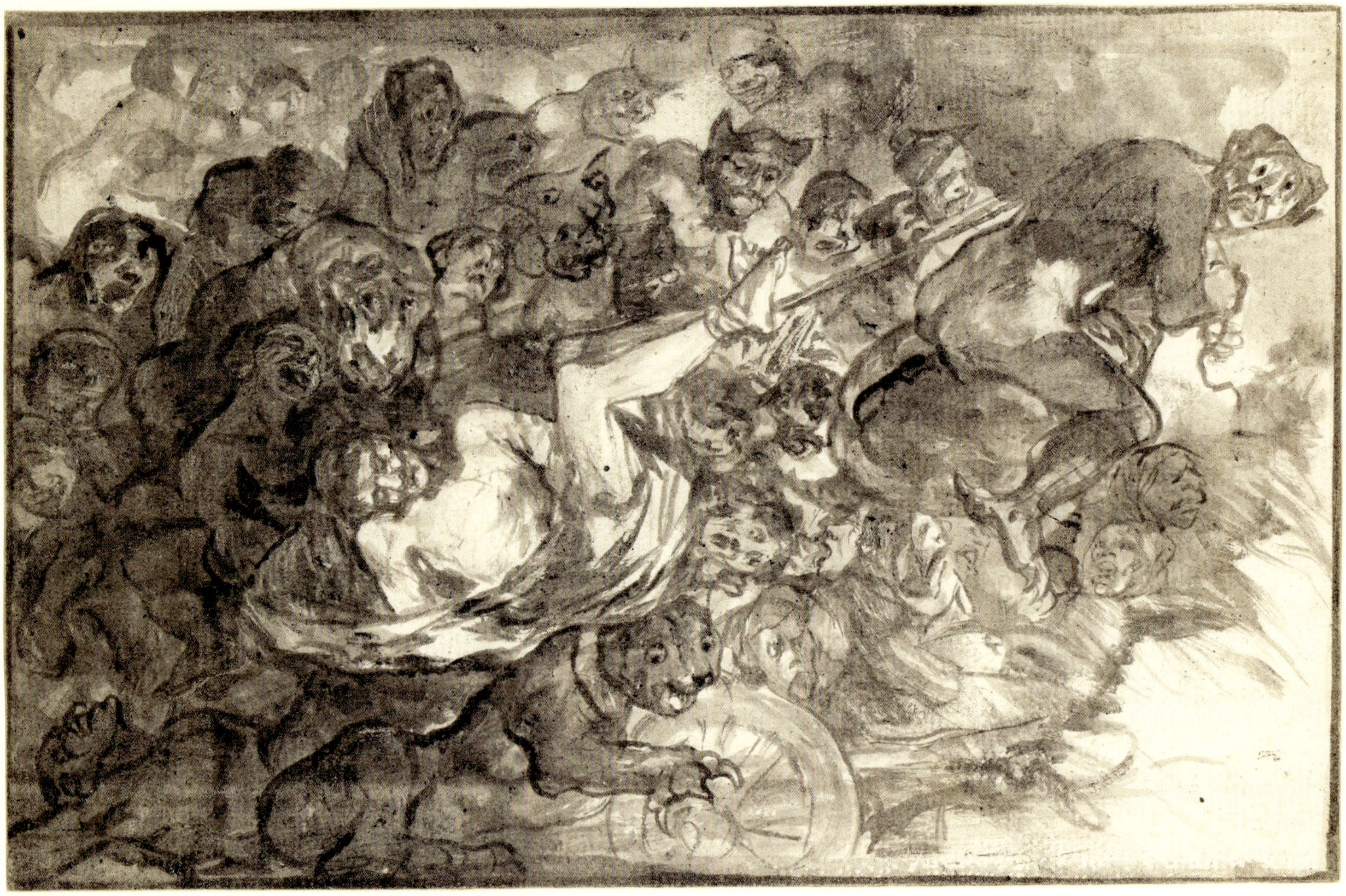

46
Francisco de Goya
Inferno, *c.*1818–19
Lithographic ink-wash, 154 x 234 mm
British Museum, London
1876,0510.374

Goya and lithography

Goya was always willing to embrace new techniques. His eagerness and determination to master their difficulties sets him apart from his contemporaries. In 1819, at the age of seventy-three, he made his first lithographs.[100] Lithography had been invented between 1796 and 1799 by Aloys Senefelder in Munich as a cheap way of circulating musical scores. Its advantage was that an image could be drawn directly onto the stone or on a special paper that could be transferred to the stone, thereby dispensing with the many technical difficulties of etching and aquatint. José María Cardano, who had studied the technique in Senefelder's workshop in Munich and then in Paris, founded the first lithographic workshop in Madrid in 1819. Goya's first lithographs are printed on the versos of Cardano's discarded proofs.[101] His unfamiliarity with the technique meant that he initially had difficulties with the transfer process he may have used for his very first attempt, *An Old Woman Spinning*, dated in another hand 'Madrid Febrero 1819'. The brush-and-wash drawing for the transfer lithograph of the *Inferno* (fig. 46), of around the same time, did not transfer entirely successfully to the lithographic stone, and is known only from a unique, unevenly printed proof (fig. 47) in which the lower area corresponding to the drawing is lacking, possibly because it had been removed from the stone.[102]

Goya made ten lithographs in Madrid, impressions of which are rare.[103]

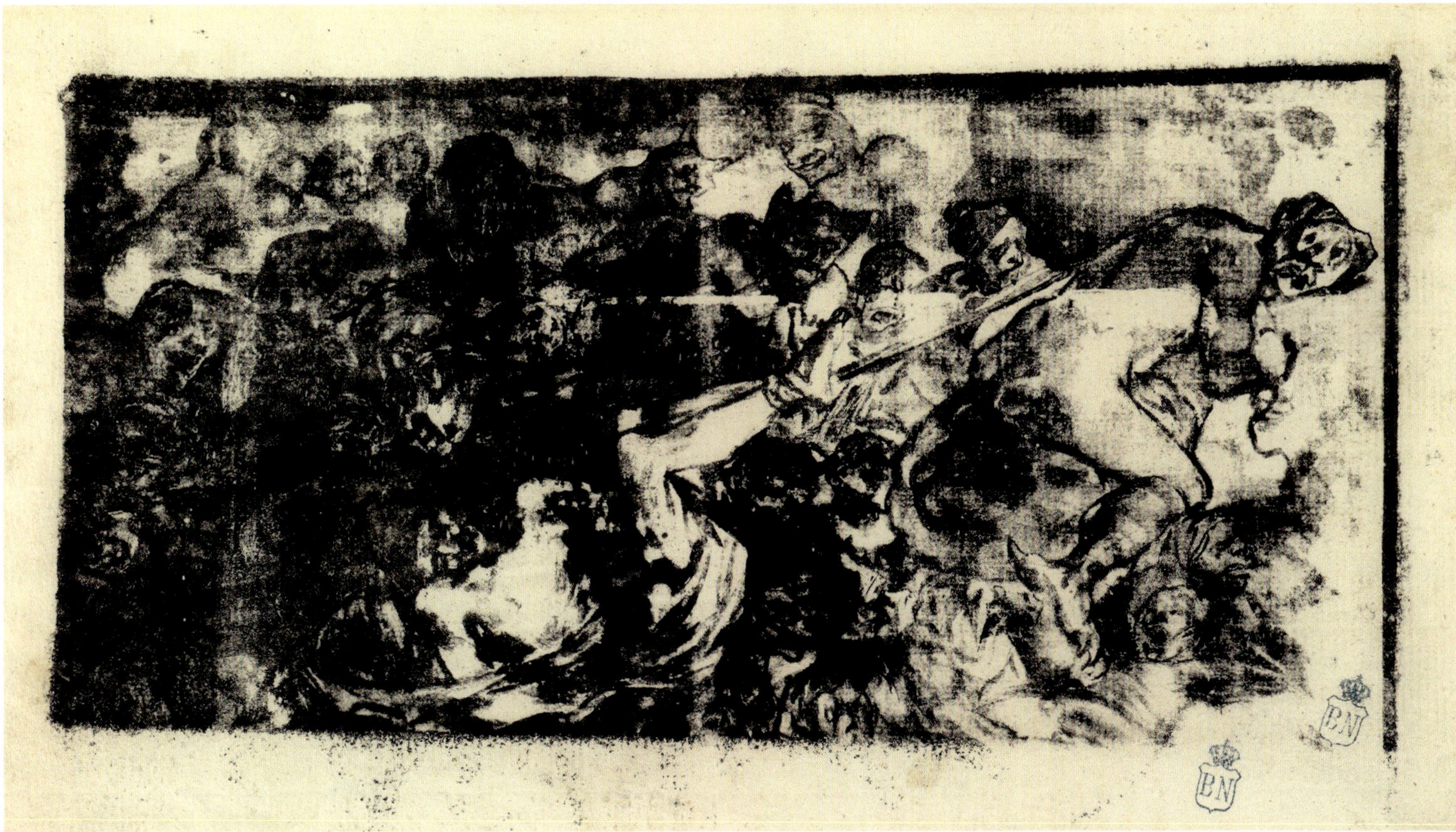

47
Francisco de Goya
Inferno, *c.*1818–19
Lithograph, 126 x 235 mm
Biblioteca Nacional, Madrid
45629

Based on a drawing from his Images of Spain Album, the *Old Style Duel* (fig. 48) exists in five known impressions, all of them retouched in ink.[104] Recent research on the papers Goya used to print his lithographs has reclaimed for his production in Spain a number of prints previously attributed to the Bordeaux years, and it is now clear that he had already tried working directly on the stone, using a lithographic crayon and scraper, sometimes combining them with pen and ink or ink wash. Prints he made in Madrid using these direct methods include the *Woman Reading to Two Children* (fig. 49) and the *Bull Attacked by Dogs*, a reversed copy, with some changes, of plate 25 from the *Tauromaquia*, both previously thought to have been printed in France.[105] It is uncertain whether a very accomplished bullfighting print, known from a unique proof in Berlin, was made in Spain or in France.[106]

In early 1823 France again invaded Spain, this time to help Ferdinand VII suppress the Liberal government, marking the beginning of the 'ominous decade', ten years of absolutist reign. In this atmosphere of betrayal, mistrust and repression – and possibly fearful of repercussions – Goya went into hiding for three months in 1824, from late January to the middle of April. He then took advantage of an amnesty for Liberals to request six months' official medical leave (in order to preserve his full salary). He left for France in June, on the pretext of poor health, to consult medical specialists and to take the

48
Francisco de Goya
Old Style Duel, *c.*1819
Lithograph, 117 x 230 mm
British Museum, London
1875,0612.98

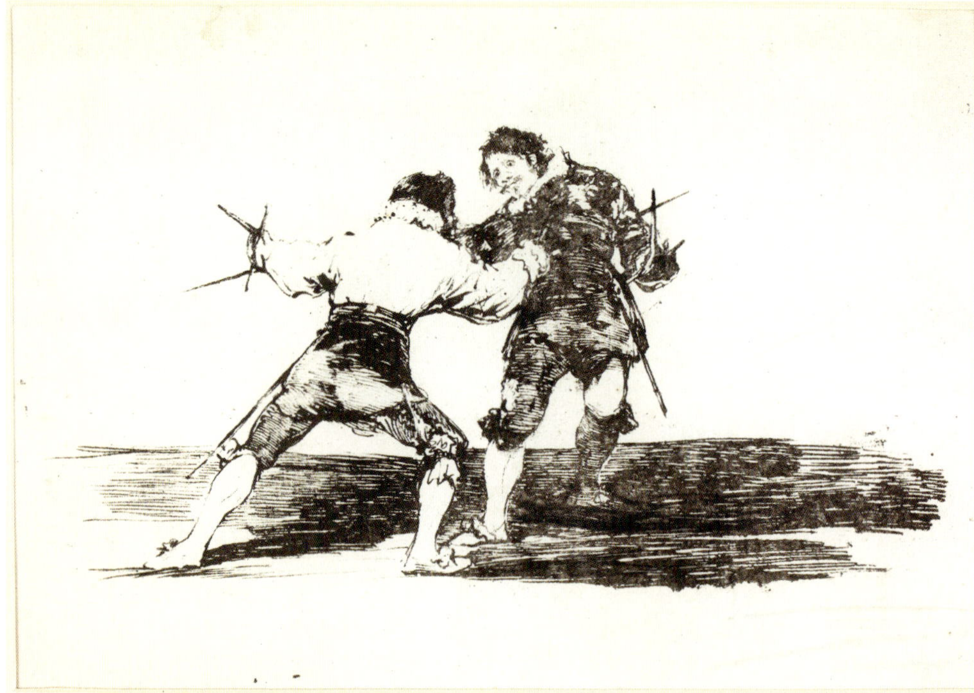

waters at Plombières. He reached Bayonne on 24 June and Bordeaux three days later, and continued straight on to Paris where he met up with Cardano. He remained in Paris for two months, returning to the community of Spanish émigrés in Bordeaux, including his old friend Leandro Fernández de Moratín.[107] Goya seems to have settled quickly with his companion Leocadia Weiss and her children and resumed his artistic activity with renewed vigour. One of his neighbours in Bordeaux was Cyprien Charles Gaulon, a calligrapher and expert lithographer, who had set up his establishment there in 1818 and of whom Goya made a superb lithographic portrait, known in only three impressions.[108]

No doubt encouraged by Gaulon, and anxious to provide for his life in Bordeaux, Goya resumed his experiments with lithography and adopted a novel way of working on the stone described by the young Spanish artist Antonio Brugada, who acted as a companion to the elderly artist:

> The artist worked at his lithographs on his easel, the stone placed like a canvas. He handled his crayons like paint brushes, and never sharpened them. He remained standing, walking backwards and forwards from moment to moment to judge the effect. Usually he covered the whole stone with a uniform, grey tint, and then removed the areas that were to be light with the scraper ... The crayon was then brought back into play to reinforce the shadows and accents, or to indicate the figures and give them a sense of movement ... People might laugh if I said that Goya's lithographs were all executed with a magnifying glass. The fact is that it was not in order to do detailed work, but because his eyesight was failing.[109]

Goya's four prints known as the *Bulls of Bordeaux*, published by Gaulon, were made by drawing directly on the stone with a lithographic crayon, as described

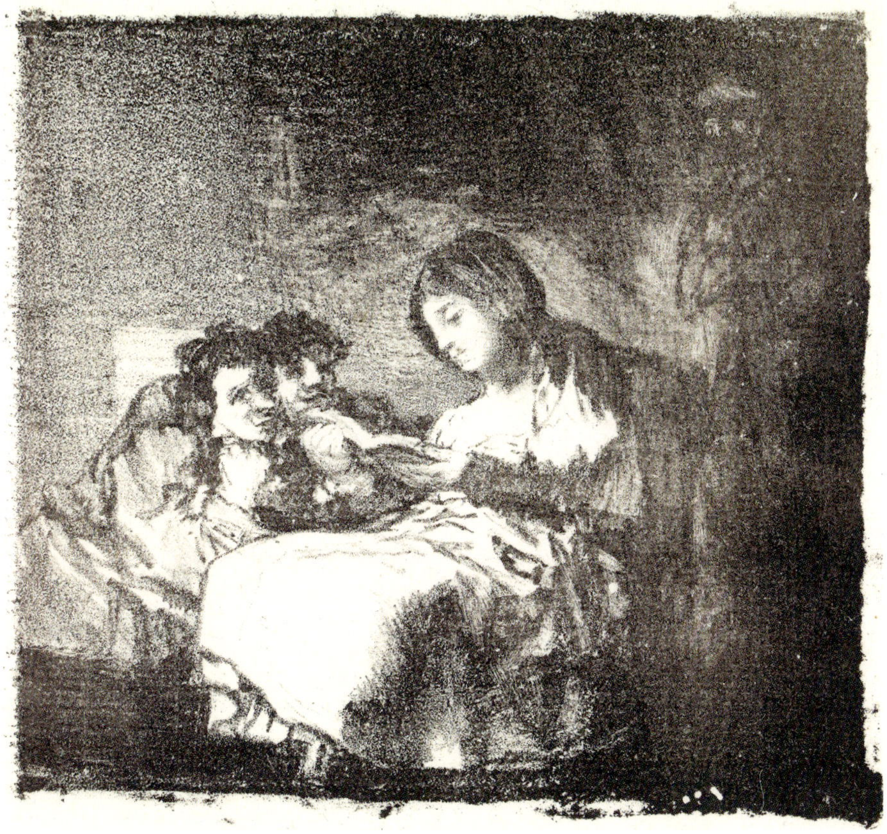

49
Francisco de Goya
Woman Reading to Two Children, c.1819
Lithograph, 123 x 125 mm
British Museum, London
1876,0510.356

by Brugada, and creating brilliant highlights with a knife or razor.[110] These reflect Goya's complete mastery of the technique and are among the finest lithographs ever made. On 6 December 1825 he wrote to Joaquin Ferrer, a Spanish émigré friend in Paris, asking if he would look at a proof impression of a bullfight with young bulls and show it to Cardano to see if it was saleable. Goya's response on 20 December to Ferrer's now-lost reply implies that he was not encouraged and that Ferrer suggested that Goya issue another edition of the *Caprichos* instead.[111] Ferrer's advice should be seen in light of the popularity of the *Caprichos* in France, demonstrated by the set of lithographic copies published by Charles Motte in Paris in 1824.[112] A hundred impressions each of two lithographs of a *Course de Taureaux* were registered with the Dépôt Legal in Bordeaux (on 17 and 29 November), and two further prints were registered on 23 December.[113] The print referred to by Goya in his letter must be the *Spanish Entertainment* (*Dibersion de España*; fig. 50).[114] The setting is an amateur ring at the start of a fiesta, when the bulls are allowed to run free. The wide grins of the spectators, as a bull exposes and sniffs at a participant's backside, indicate that they are unconcerned by the trampled figures at lower left.

Last years in Bordeaux

Alongside the *Bulls of Bordeaux* around 1825–8 Goya was working on new albums of drawings now referred to as Bordeaux Albums I (G) and II (H). These contain his last drawings and demonstrate that his advanced age did not impair the sureness of his hand or his tremendous imagination. The drawings from both Bordeaux Albums are in black chalk or crayon, a choice that may

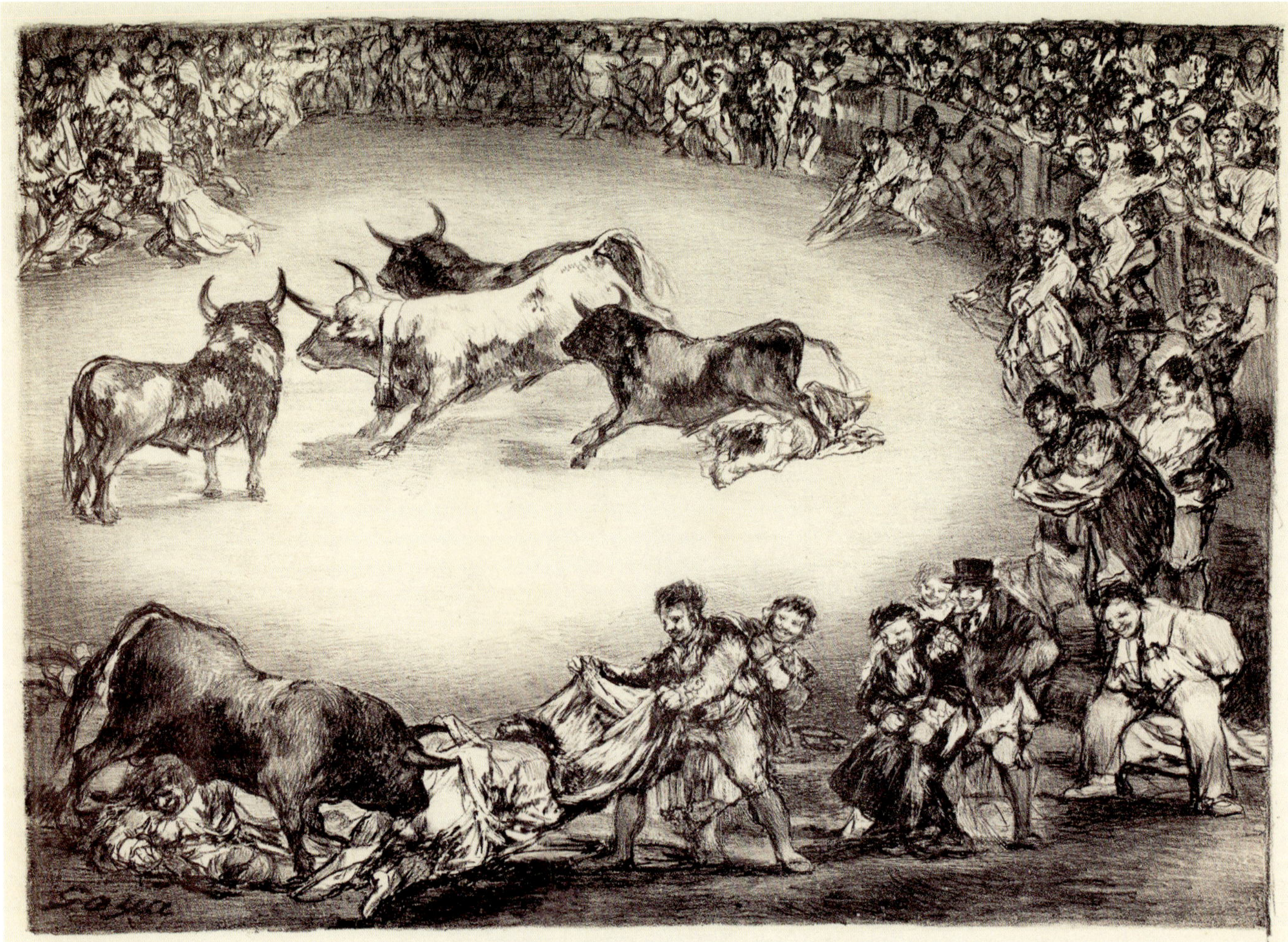

50
Francisco de Goya
Spanish Entertainment, 1825
Lithograph, 300 x 410 mm
British Museum, London
1975,1025.425

have been prompted by his lithographic work, on French paper. Album G originally comprised drawings numbered up to 60, of which fifty-five are now known, with subjects including modes of transport for beggars, cripples, madmen and punishment.[115] One of the most moving drawings, which may be understood as a metaphorical self-portrait, shows a heavily bearded and stooped old man before a dark background, walking with the aid of two sticks and gazing at the viewer. Goya inscribed the sheet 'Aun Aprendo' ('I am still learning').[116] In another drawing, *Lunatics* (fig. 51), from a group of sheets relating to mad people, an amusing game is being played: a figure crawls under the legs of another, who wears an inane grin and has his jacket pulled up to his head. Goya gave a pithy title to all the drawings in this series, several of them longer and more descriptive – possibly intended as the basis for a new set of prints, prompted by Ferrer's suggestion for a re-issue of the *Caprichos*.

The second Bordeaux Album (H) is possibly slightly later. This has pages numbering up to 63, of which sixty drawings are known. These are more sober than those in the first album but cover similar subjects and only six have captions. There are fewer complex compositions and the figures take up more of the page. The sheet numbered 22, depicting a fashionably dressed young woman, returns to themes in the *Caprichos*. This sheet provided the basis for one of four small etchings Goya made in his final years. One of the last drawings from the album shows a dancing phantom set against a dark

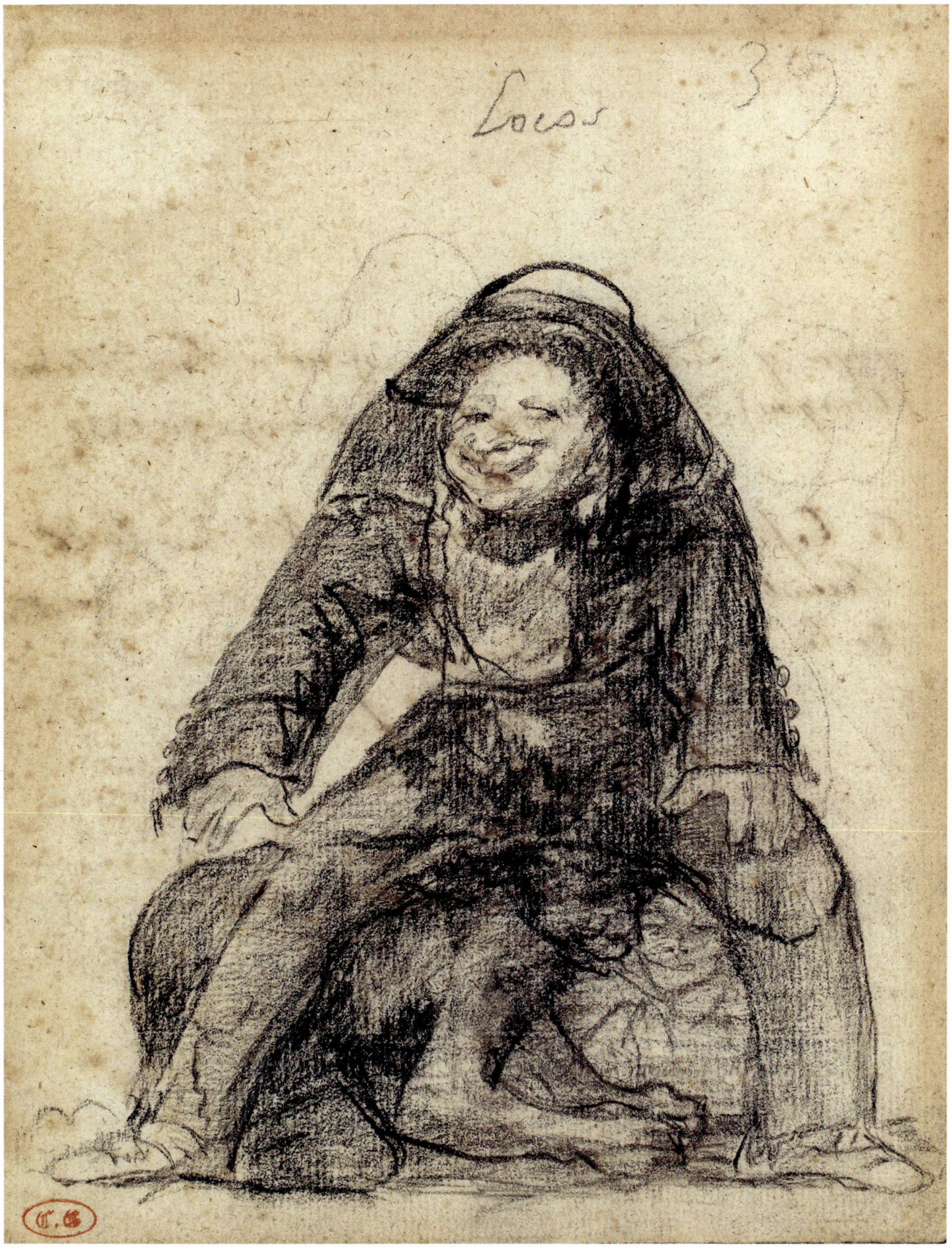

51
Francisco de Goya
Lunatics, *c.*1825–8
Black chalk and crayon,
191 x 147 mm
British Museum, London
1980,0628.56

52
Francisco de Goya
A Phantom Dancing with Castanets, *c.*1825–8
Black chalk, 191 x 151 mm
Museo del Prado, Madrid
D.4123

53
Francisco Goya
Old Man on a Swing, *c.*1827–8
Etching and aquatint, 185 x 122 mm
British Museum, London
1975,1025.48

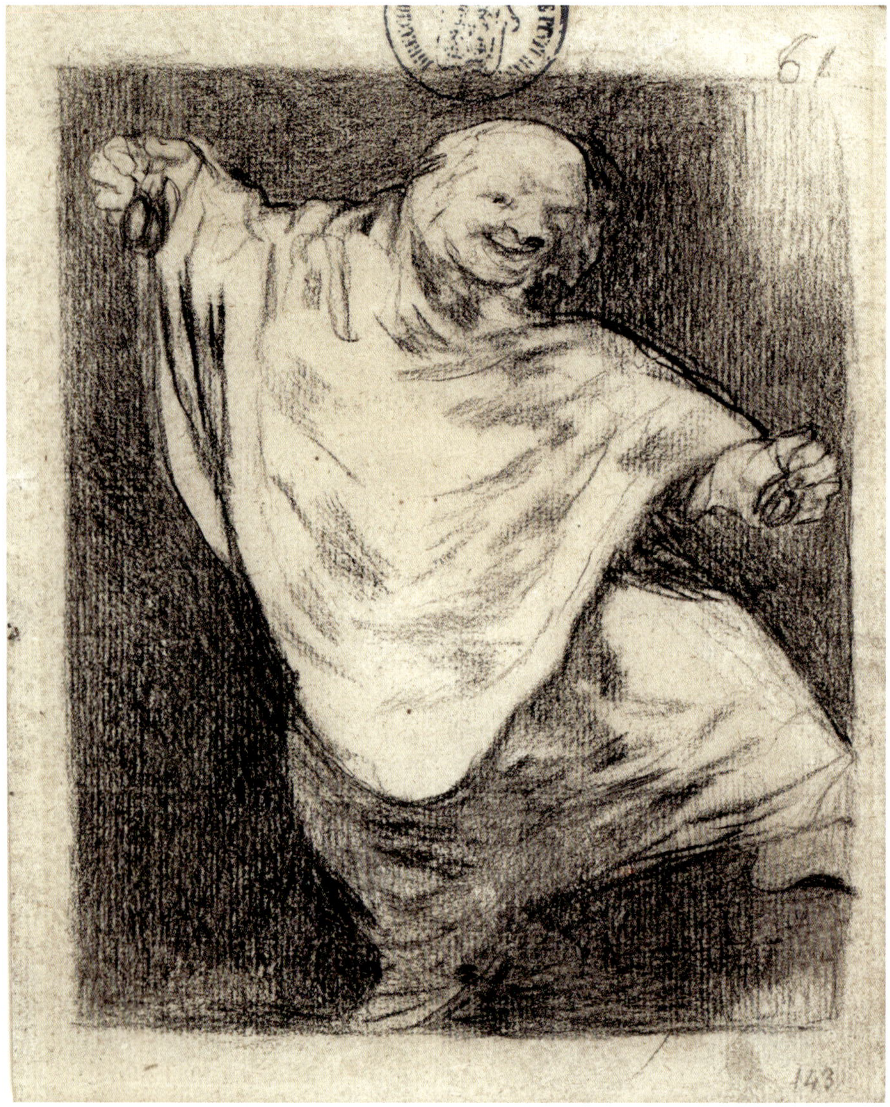

background, his left foot raised, grinning as he plays castanets in his oversized hands (fig. 52).[117] This strangely eerie and unsettling fusion of contradictory elements, in this case humour and menace, is typical of Goya. The drawing recalls earlier sheets, such as the dancing giant in plate 4 of the *Disparates* and the old woman dancing from the Black Border Album.[118] Together the drawings in both of the Bordeaux Albums seem to enter the realm of fantasy. Although several are roughly drawn, they have all the intensity of Goya's earlier sheets.

As he became increasingly infirm Goya was unable to maintain the physical demands of lithography. Instead he turned his attention to drawing, producing small etchings with single figures based on those in the second Bordeaux Album (H). Four subjects are known, in etching and aquatint, with etchings on the versos of three of the copper plates.[119] The *Old Man on a Swing* (fig. 53), after the drawing numbered 58 in Album H, possibly made in the last year of Goya's life, provides a fitting epitaph. Wearing a manic smile, the man clings to the rope, unaffected by the clamouring demons in the background, shooting out his prominent bare feet in front of him with the careless abandon of a happy child.[120]

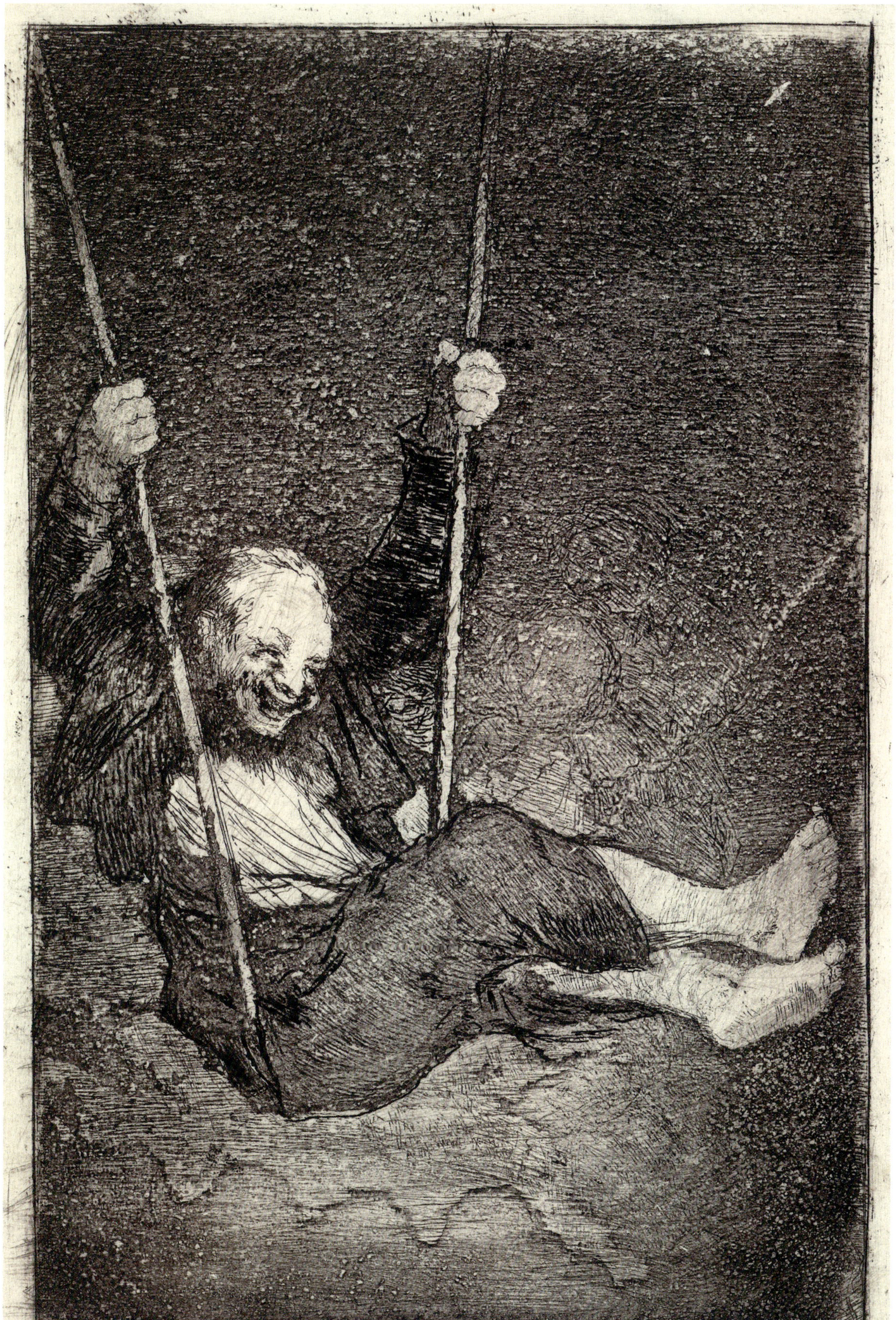

APPENDIX

Paper and papermaking in Spain

Clara de la Peña Mc Tigue

The collection of Spanish prints and drawings at the British Museum provides an excellent resource to explore the types of papers available to and used by artists and printmakers in Spain. During the Middle Ages, Spanish paper was exported by Geniza (Jewish) merchants throughout the Byzantine Empire, the Islamic world and Europe. By the fifteenth century Spain relied mainly on imported paper to supply the administrative needs of its rapidly growing empire. There was also a growing papermaking industry in Spain, although it was not supported by the government through incentives such as tax relief. Papers made both locally and abroad reflect the innovations introduced in European papermaking before the nineteenth century.

Spanish paper in the late Middle Ages, from the zig-zag mark to *papel con senyal*

Paper was first imported into Europe in the ninth and tenth centuries, via Spanish territories under Muslim rule. In Al-Andalus the laws of the *convivencia*, the coexistence of Jews, Arabs and Christians under relatively tolerant Muslim rule, provided the ideal circumstances for the development of paper-making and other crafts.[1] Paper was probably manufactured close to the flourishing cities of Córdoba and Granada. The first documented account of paper made in Spain comes, however, from Xátiva (Játiva), described by the geographer al-Idrisi in 1150 as 'a pretty town with a castle ... where magnificent paper is made ... and exported to the East and the West'.[2] In 1237, during the reconquest of Valencia, James I of Aragon annexed the neighbouring Xátiva and its Muslim papermakers. For centuries, Mudéjar enclaves provided Aragonese monarchs with paper, a relatively inexpensive material on which to record legal and diplomatic information for their growing political and administrative needs. Aragon became the first Christian territory in Europe to favour paper over parchment.[3]

Following Islamic practices, papermakers in Spain used linen and hemp rags as raw materials; these were the basis of European papermaking until the nineteenth century. The wet rags were cleaned in streams and then beaten with a stone mortar, either by hand or with trip hammers powered by humans or animals, a process that resulted in the separation of fibres and the production of lightly beaten pulp. This was poured into a vat of water and the pulp was collected (scooped) with a screen or a wooden sieve known as a paper-mould in order to produce individual sheets of paper. During the drying process the sheets were sized with a solution of wheat or rice starch and then burnished.[4] This basic process could be carried out by a single individual, making it possible to produce paper wherever fresh and clean water was available. The ease of the operation no doubt contributed to the expansion of papermaking in the Iberian Peninsular.[5] Some Islamic papers produced here and in the North of Africa often have a distinctive zig-zag mark, probably added during the stacking of the sheets of paper: after the sheets had been grouped and folded into sections, the outer sheet was probably marked with a blunt tool when the papers were slightly damp. This was perhaps an attempt to reduce the bulk of the thick sheets as making a pressure mark close to the bulkier spine area would help to flatten the fold, or a way of counting the pages to then be sold.[6]

Fourteenth-century papers with zig-zag marks now in the Archivo de la Corona de Aragón were soon replaced by thinner papers bearing Italian watermarks. These first papers were produced in regions such as Fabriano, Camerino and Pioraco in Italy and slowly made their way to cities in Castile. The Italian papermaking industry was supported by a cost-effective trade and efficient distribution. Successful Italian traders such as Francesco Datini, who sent paper to Spain from Venice, Perugia and Florence, soon established strategic points of distribution in Barcelona, Majorca, Valencia and Muslim Granada.[7]

Spanish Arabic paper could not compete with Italian imports, and as a result Islamic papermaking techniques were rendered obsolete. Paper mills in the Italian Marches quickly adapted to the increased demands of paper for printing: most importantly, they attached stamp hammers to water-powered mills in order to produce a more effective and finer beating of the rags. Thinner sheets of paper were also achieved using moulds with parallel and crossed lines of wire instead of wooden structures.[8] Italian papermakers also incorporated gelatine as a sizing agent, which was better suited to oil-based inks than the heavily starch-sized and burnished sheets of Islamic manufacture. For several decades in Spain both types of paper were often bound together in the same document, until Islamic papers were eventually used only for paper seals and blotting paper. There is some evidence of papers probably made in Spain that display characteristics of both Eastern and Western papermaking. These were sized with starch and

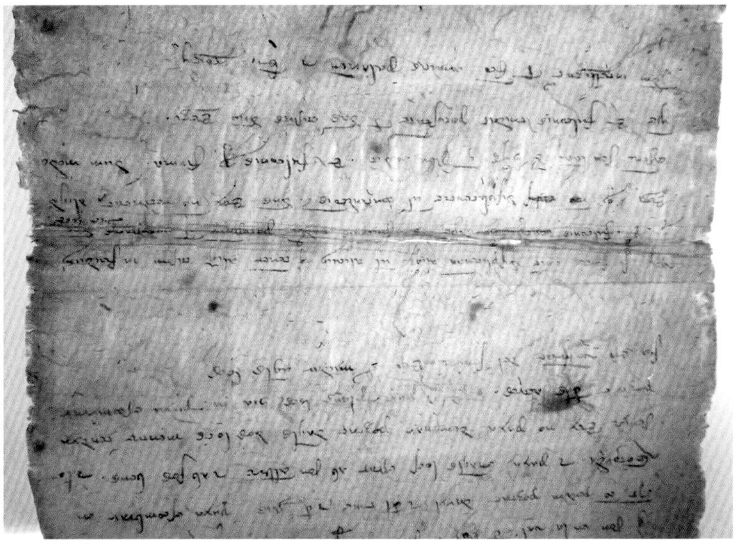

1 Transmitted light image of a zig-zag mark in Spanish Arabic Paper. Instituto del Patrimonio Histórico Español

burnished, as with Islamic papers, but they were made with Western wire moulds.[9]

Printing and Western paper production in Spain

With the gradual expulsion from Spain of the Muslim papermakers and Jewish traders, Islamic production decreased and had largely disappeared by the mid-fifteenth century.[10] The Castilian and Aragonese authorities relied on Italian paper and Western paper mills were established in Spain at a much slower pace than elsewhere in Europe: they struggled financially, there were too few to meet demand, and they often produced paper of inferior quality that was hard to sell. These factors contributed to the delayed growth of printing in the Iberian Peninsular (see Chapters 2 and 3): with poor quality local materials and expensive Italian imports, the first itinerant printers struggled to become established.[11]

In some cases the Spanish monarchy granted royal privileges to Italian master papermakers who established businesses in Spain under private or monastic patronage.[12] They were part of the Italian diaspora of papermakers, who brought with them the skills and organization they had learnt from the paper mills of Voltri (Cartieri di Voltri) – an influx that continued until the mid-eighteenth century.[13] Italian papermakers such as the Guerço brothers from Genoa, who had spent time in France, settled in Catalonian mills in 1477. Among the first regions in Spain to register master papermakers in the fifteenth century were La Rioja, Cuenca and Catalonia, where oil and grain mills were frequently converted into paper mills.

The *senyal* or watermark is a characteristic of Western papers that can provide information about date and origin. Mould makers would weave curved pieces of wire into their moulds in order to create personalized marks, perhaps with the aim of making papers identifiable as the industry grew. The earliest-known Spanish watermark, probably made in 1371, bears the heraldic shield of Xátiva, suggesting that Italian papermakers were already established on the east coast of Spain by the fourteenth century.[14] However, replicating popular European watermarks was common practice, making it difficult to differentiate between Spanish papers and those made elsewhere. An early contract from the Catalan paper mill of Jonqueres, dated 1500, describes a paper '*del palegri o de la mà*' ('with pilgrim or hand watermarks'), which confirms the use of popular foreign watermarks.[15] The most common watermark found in late fifteenth-century Spanish incunabula is the glove or hand, and can be seen, for example, on one of the earliest single-sheet printed images found in Spain, a fifteenth-century print of Death (p. 52, fig. 10).[16]

The growth of printing in the sixteenth century created an increased demand for paper from emerging Spanish paper mills associated with monastic orders. Hieronymite monks produced cheap, and poor-quality *papel de Bula* (paper for Bulls) for Charles V to grant indulgences to Crusaders. The order owned two mills in El Escorial and twelve in Valladolid, employed Italian master papermakers and soon became the most important manufacturers in Castile. However, the demand for paper was so great that they had to supplement their production with paper imported from France.[17]

Of even lower in quality than paper for the royal Bulls was the brown paper known as *papel de estraza*, which contracts between mills and traders reveal was produced in large quantities. This second-rate product was cheap and easy to manufacture: sacks, cloth, string, even straw were lightly beaten with linen and hemp rags to produce a darker and low-quality pulp, processed in imperfect moulds and unclean facilities. This brown paper was sturdy, adequate for wrapping and could be layered to make cardboard.[18] In Spain it was used by printers as early as the fifteenth century for pamphlets and ephemera, such as an uncut sheet of playing cards printed in Toledo in the late sixteenth century (fig. 21, p. 39).

The Italian artists employed to decorate the monastery of El Escorial used Renaissance drawing techniques that they passed on to their co-workers (see Chapter 3): one group, for example, pricked a large number of blue sheets in order to transfer their drawn designs to embroideries.[19] Among these is a drawing attributed to Miguel Barosso and López de Escuriaz, *Christ Distributing Bread to his Disciples after his Resurrection*, executed on a coarse and uneven sheet of blue paper with no visible mould structure (fig. 2 and fig. 25, p. 74). The paper has similar characteristics to other drawings for embroideries.[20] Blue paper had a similar composition to brown paper but incorporated dyed rags to add colour.[21] Although blue paper was sometimes imported in small quantities from Italy, it was made in large quantities in the Catalan mills, as can be seen from orders detailed in surviving sixteenth-century contracts.[22] Certain foods were wrapped in blue paper – no doubt to contrast with the whiteness of sugar or flour, for example –

which may in turn explain why reams of white paper imported from Italy were often packaged in blue.[23] Blue paper also became popular among artists such as Bartolomé Carducho, who used it for finished drawings such as *Saint Lawrence Baptising the Prisoners* (fig. 11, p. 65).

Whereas affluent printers and booksellers in sixteenth-century Spain used fine imported paper for books, paper for high-quality prints was very hard to come by. Pedro Perret's engravings after Juan de Herrera's designs of the Escorial are printed on lightly sized thick paper ideally suited to engraving. In 1584 Herrera asked Cristóbal de Salazar, the Spanish ambassador in Venice, to send him good paper to print Perret's plates, observing 'I cannot find paper here [in Spain] to fit this purpose'.[24] The consignment was to be packed and shipped with stained glass for the king. Although most of the paper used for the Escorial prints was Italian (some possibly French) and of high quality, there is no evidence that it was from this batch or that it was ever dispatched. Significantly, Italian printers based in Madrid were commissioned to print the plates (see Chapter 3). In the first prints of the Escorial engravings bound in an album now in the British Library, which once belonged to the Roman collector Cassiano dal Pozzo, the watermarks show either a crown or an encircled diamond (fig. 29, p. 77).[25] When examining paper under transmitted light it is possible to measure the distance between the chain and laid lines formed on the sheet during manufacture. Although the distance between chain and laid lines remains consistent in all the prints in the dal Pozzo album, half-way through the set (from plate no.7 onwards) the watermark becomes a larger, more elaborate crown or a six-pointed star within a circle,[26] perhaps due to a change of moulds during the papermaking process.[27] Herrera commissioned 52,000 impressions from the first edition, a huge undertaking for which a single order of paper, as suggested in Herrera's request to Salazar, may not have been sufficient.[28]

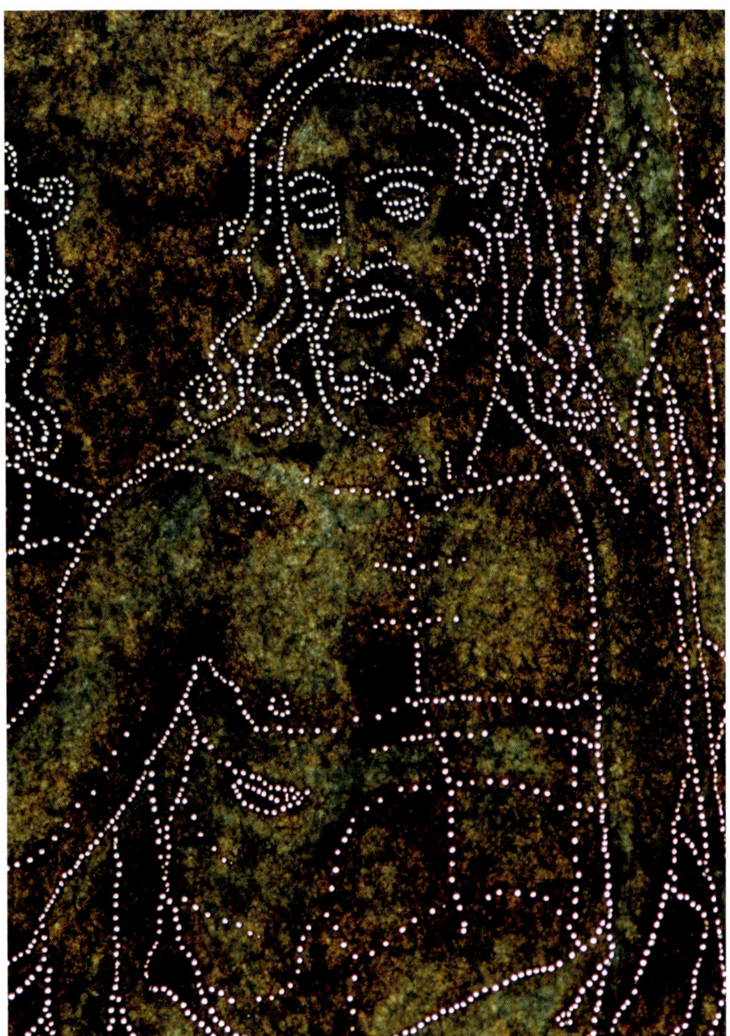

2 Transmitted light detail of *Christ Distributing Bread to his Disciples after his Resurrection* showing the pricked drawing on blue paper with an uneven sheet formation and fibre clumps (see also figs 25–6, page 74)

The Genoese paper monopoly versus French and Spanish papers

Throughout the sixteenth century Spanish artists trained in Italy, influenced by Italian artists, often used *papel blanco* (white paper) for their drawings. The buff white tone of these papers relies on the purity and quality of carefully selected linen and hemp rags and the cleanliness of the papermaking process. These drawings bear a wide range of Italian watermarks indicating different origins: an example is the *Assumption of the Virgin* on Italian paper by Alonso Berruguete (fig. 14, p. 67), who spent time in Italy. By the late sixteenth century paper imports from Italy were monopolized by Genoese merchants and watermarks became more standardized. The Genoese jealously controlled both the production and the distribution of paper exported to Spain and her colonies. They were often granted tax relief and guaranteed free trade in lieu of payment of the debt amassed by the Spanish court and local governments. The Genoese produced enough paper to supply most of the printing needs of Spain and the New World, with demand growing as record-keeping and printing images were essential to maintaining Spain's vast Empire. Until the mid-eighteenth century up to a half of all paper produced in Genoa serviced Spanish and Latin American markets.[29] The *tre mundi* (three circles) watermark identifying paper imported from Genoa was soon imitated by French and Catalan papermakers attempting to break into their market. The Genoese bylaws reacted by using symbols and acronyms in their watermarks to indicate provenance, quality and paper formats. The *tre mundi* watermark is commonly found in seventeenth- and eighteenth-century Spanish prints and drawings[30] such as *A Melancholic Pope* attributed to Cornelio Schut and drawn on fine, thin paper with a clear and regular structure (figs 3–4). In the top circle a Lombard cross replaces the Islamic symbol of the crescent moon, while in the second circle an A followed by a either a B (for *carte bianca*, white paper) or an R (*reale*, a large format) indicates that this rare and expensive paper was available in seventeenth-century Seville.[31] The high-quality papers used by Bartolomé Esteban Murillo also frequently bear the *tre mundi* watermark.[32]

Standardized paper formats first recorded on a stone slab known as the 'Bologna stone' were followed closely by the Genoese papermakers.[33] Spanish papermakers, on the other hand, did not closely follow these formats: their papers are often inconsistent in their mould size, wire structure and sheet thickness.[34] Unlike foreign imports, where a ream had a specific weight, the sizes and quantity of sheets in a ream in Spain had never been officially regulated. This contributed to an irregular trade, since the buyer would know neither the exact size nor the quantity of paper contained in the reams they ordered.[35]

From the 1640s, under severe economic pressure, the Spanish court began to tax goods such as paper destined for the Americas. A revenue stamp placed on the edge of the sheets indicated that it was '*papel sellado*' (sealed paper) and that it should be taxed.[36] Further taxes were imposed by regional authorities as the paper travelled from its point of origin to its destination.[37] These multiple taxes made it prohibitively expensive for Spanish papermakers to sell their product across regional borders. In 1673 the Genoese offered to rid the coasts of Naples, Sicily and Spain of pirates in exchange for the paper tax franchise; but the Spanish government declined. Most of the Genoese paper was therefore exported to the Spanish colonies, only small amounts being retained for everyday use by printers in Spain. They often resorted to contraband French paper smuggled through the Pyrenean border with Navarra.[38]

Seventeenth-century printers in Madrid had access to French imports as well as papers from local mills. The pages in the book published in Madrid in 1662, the *Difiniciones de la Orden y Cavalleria de Alcantara con la Historia y Origen Della*, which are imperfect and irregular, are watermarked with a five-petal flower, similar to those found in other books printed

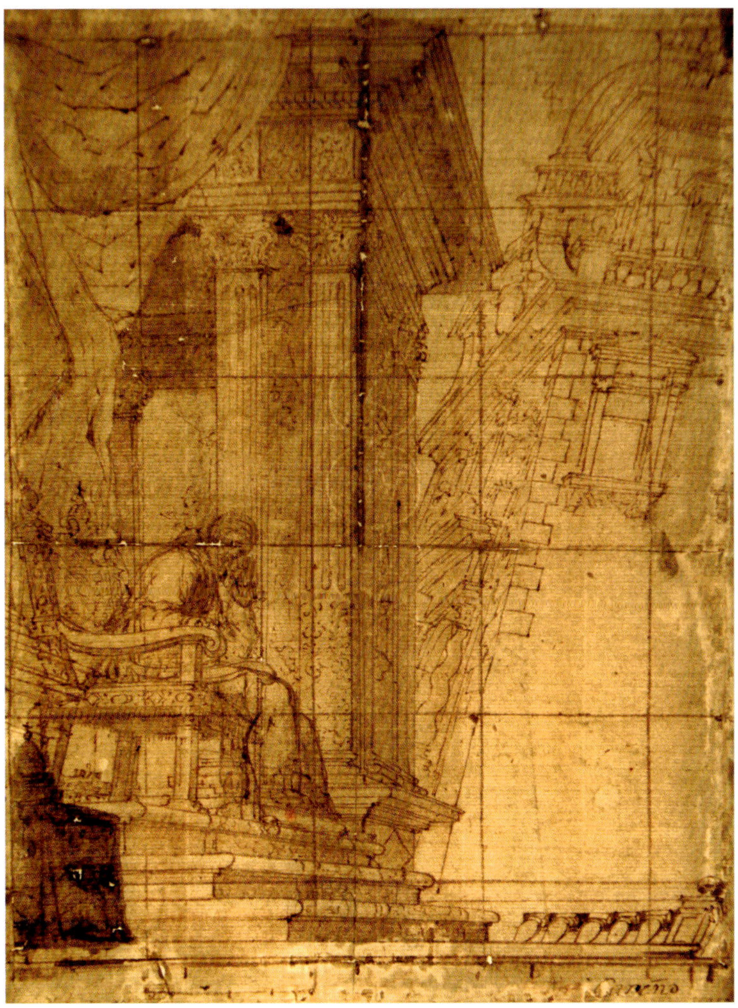

3 *A Melancholic Pope,* 1614–84, attributed to Cornelio Schut, is drawn on high-quality imported Italian paper with a *tre mundi* watermark in the centre of the sheet. The transmitted light image shows the clear and regular sheet formation.

Pen and brown ink, with grey wash and black chalk; squared for transfer, 270 x 195 mm
British Museum, London 1948,1231.1

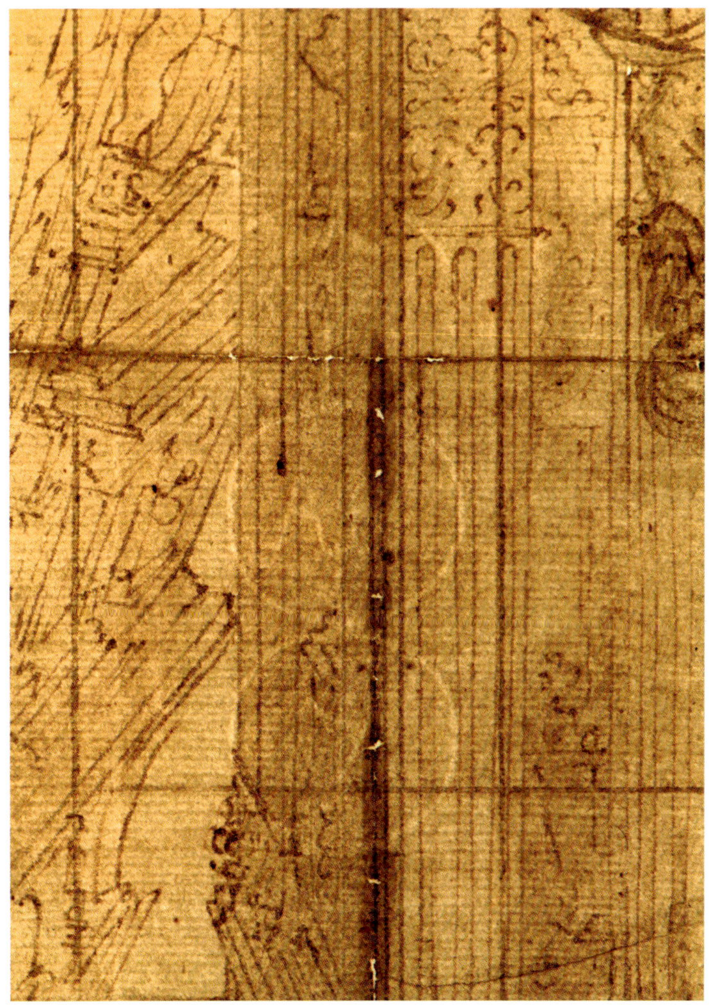

4 Inverted detail of fig. 3 showing the *tre mundi* watermark

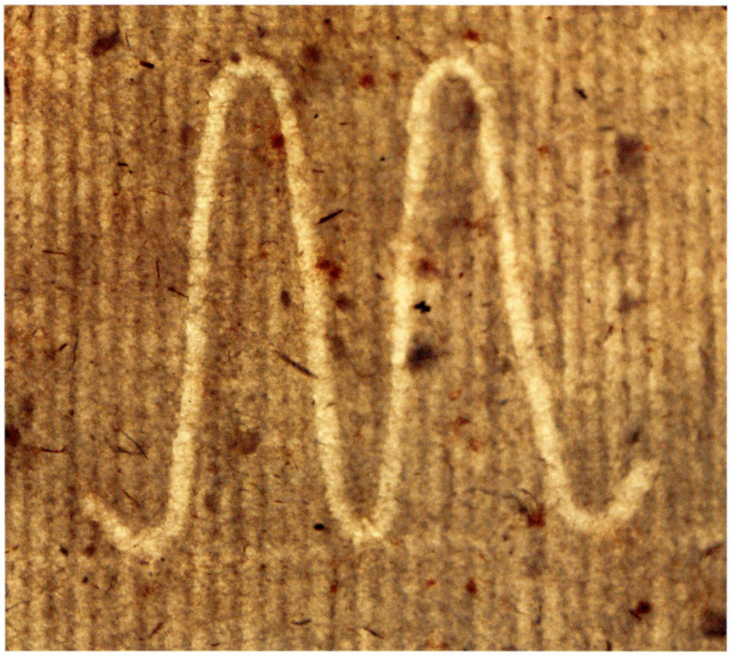

5 Transmitted light detail of the Spanish watermark from the Castilian mill of El Paular on the end sheet of the book *Difiniciones de la Orden y Cavalleria de Alcantara con la Historia y Origen Della*
British Library, London 4625.f.6

in Madrid and identified as French papers of medium to low quality.[39] The thick endpaper next to the title page, however, bears a watermark associated with one of the most renowned Castilian mills of the seventeenth and eighteenth centuries, El Molino del Paular between Madrid and El Escorial, which was run by Carthusian monks. The watermark, an M between two chain lines, resembles other Paular watermarks recorded in the early 1670s (fig. 5).[40] Paper from this mill was used for the first edition of Cervantes' *Don Quijote*, as well as by other printers in Alcalá de Henares and Madrid from the fifteenth to the eighteenth centuries.[41] The thicker endpaper was probably inserted by the bookbinder after the book was printed. The book and its paper perfectly demonstrate the collaboration between printers and bookbinders at the time.

Generally cheaper than Italian paper, French paper had been exported from the ports of Bordeaux and Bayonne to Spain and its new world colonies since the sixteenth century (in addition to the contraband smuggled in to Spain via the Pyrenees).[42] Artists working in Madrid may also have acquired small quantities of paper from these sources. The bunch of grapes watermark, originally Italian but more widespread in French papers, is commonly found in Spanish drawings by artists at the court in Madrid and can be seen, for instance, in the drawing of an *auto da fé* attributed to Diego Velázquez (fig. 13, p. 31). Drawings by earlier court artists such as Vicente Carducho also bear this watermark.[43] Carducho briefly mentions paper in his *Diálogos de la Pintura*: 'drawings are done on white paper with chalk, quill or washes … and white highlights are applied when the paper is blue'.[44] This is revealing in relation to his drawings – and those of his father, Bartolomé, mentioned above – which are mostly on cream or blue papers, but are often discoloured, with an irregular structure and a cloudy appearance under transmitted light.[45] These papers frequently have no watermark. They are made with inferior rags and defective moulds, an indication that Carducho had little concern for the quality of the supports used for his drawings. There are similar examples among the work of his contemporaries: *Saint Ildephonsus at the Tomb of Saint Leocardia* (fig. 7, p. 86) by Eugenio Cajés, for example, is on a similarly irregular paper.

The use of paper for Spanish baroque drawings

The examination of prints and drawings by Spanish baroque artists reveals the use of different papers according to their style, technique and financial means, from foreign imports to locally produced Spanish papers. Brown paper became increasingly common in late seventeenth-century Spanish drawings: sold to chemists and haberdashers for wrapping goods, it was cheap and ideally suited as a material for ephemeral structures created for processions and royal events, together with cloth and wood.[46] Antonio Palomino describes how pieces of walnut wood used for charcoal were cut, tied together and then wrapped in brown *papel de estraza* before charring in an oven.[47] He also suggests using a simple version of *papier mâché* consisting of damp brown paper to dress a sculpture and create a lifelike model as a substitute for figure drawing.[48] Palomino used a poorly formed sheet of brown paper for his own drawings, such as *Ahimelec Giving to David the Sword of Goliath* (fig. 6). The use of brown paper in this period is probably best demonstrated by many surviving drawings of Juan Carreño de Miranda (see Chapter 4). The Valencian artist Juan Antonio Conchillos y Falcó also used a full sheet of rough-textured *papel de estraza* for his study, *A Partly Kneeling Male Nude* (fig. 7). The brown coarse fibres retain the full density of the black chalk, whilst knots and clumps of pulp in the paper break the drawn line for quick, expressive strokes; a blue wash was applied beforehand to provide contrast with the white chalk highlights.[49]

Thin white papers were more appropriate for subtle chalk drawings. For example, the diffused chalk in Murillo's *Saint Francis de Paola* (fig. 43, p. 153) and the refined and detailed shadowing in the red chalk drawings by José de Ribera are complemented by the clean, fine paper with a lightly textured surface, the dry technique uninterrupted by the delicate laid lines (figs 32–3, p. 186). In contrast, some artists took advantage of the pronounced laid texture of paper to guide their lines. Alonso Cano used thick, high-quality papers for his 'technical' compositions and favoured the wire side of the sheet, which had been in contact with the mould during the manufacturing process and often had a more pronounced laid structure. Ruled quill lines in his drawings align perfectly with the laid lines of the paper, such as in his *Design for an Altarpiece* (fig. 8).[50]

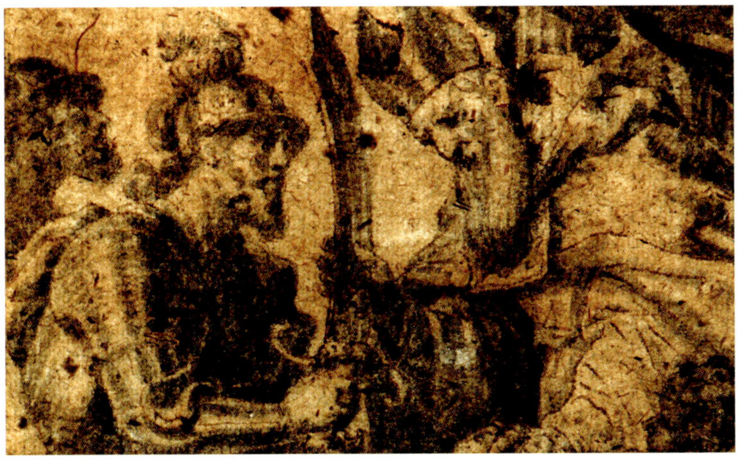

6 Detail of a transmitted light image of *Ahimelec Giving to David the Sword of Goliath* by Antonio Palomino showing uneven distribution of fibres and blurred chain lines in a brown paper (see fig. 49, page 112)

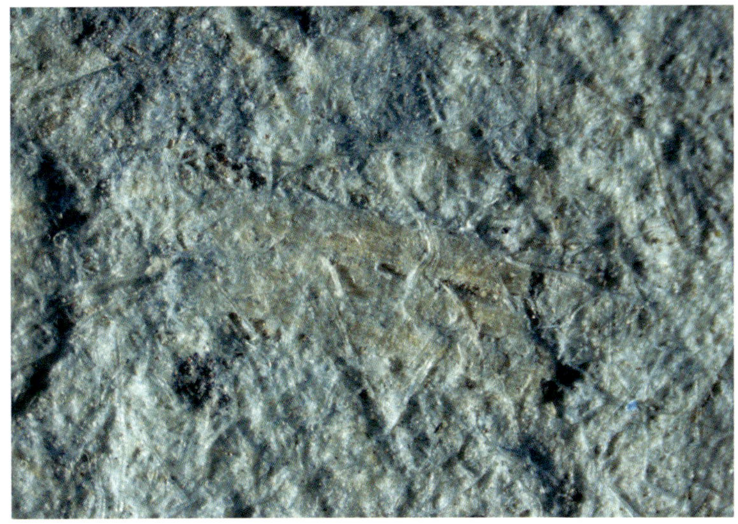

7 Microscopic detail of unbeaten coarse fibres and drops of blue wash in *Study of a Partly Kneeling Male Nude* by Juan Antonio Conchillos y Falcó (see fig. 20, page 178)

Spanish paper, the Hollander beater and the eighteenth century

By the mid-eighteenth century, legislation introduced by the Bourbons greatly affected the production of paper in Spain. In 1757 a national law prohibited the trade of Genoese paper in Spain; although paper from Genoa continued to be imported in smaller quantities until the nineteenth century, the breaking of the monopoly hugely benefited Spanish paper production. Through royal privileges, individual Catalan papermakers during the early eighteenth century were granted tax relief on their mills and the sale of papers. By 1780 the government had extended individual tax privileges on domestic rags and paper to all Spanish papermakers, and in the 1790s it set out a standard for formats and types of papers.[51] As a result the quality of paper produced in Spain improved and entered the competitive Latin American market.[52] Throughout the eighteenth century, areas of Spain with scattered mills, such as Capellades in Barcelona, Alcoy in Valencia or Molinos de Papel, in Cuenca, now developed into important papermaking centres.[53]

Papermaking processes in Spain remained unaltered until the end of the eighteenth century with the continued use of water-powered hammers to beat the rags.[54] The shadows along the laid lines can be seen clearly on the surface of the paper. Antique laid papers that display a pronounced shadow around the chain lines indicating pulp accumulation are common in Spanish prints and drawings until the early nineteenth century, but paper composition in the eighteenth century improved until the uneven quality of earlier papers gradually disappeared. The *tre mundi* watermark that had been imitated in Catalonia since the seventeenth century now developed into personalized patterns, and by the eighteenth century papermakers in Spain were creating their own marks with the names of Catalan and Valencian papermakers sewn into the moulds.[55] The British Museum print of *A Satire on Napoleon's Political Ambitions*

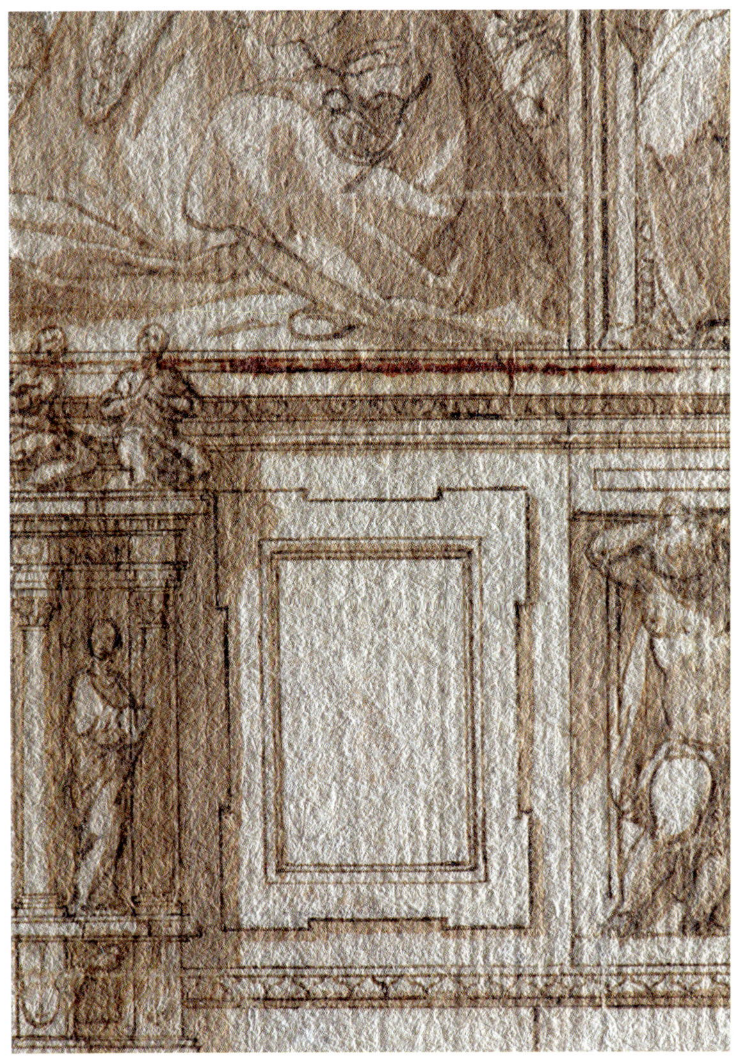

8 Architectural lines aligned with the pronounced laid texture of the paper in Alonso Cano's *Design for an Altarpiece* (see fig. 26, page 142)

contains a watermark similar to those on papers produced in Alcoy.[56] Paper for printing now became thicker, with the felted side having a quality similar to textile, as can be seen, for example, in, Ramon Bayeu y Subias' *The Attributes of the Virgin* (figs 35–6, p. 214).

Imported papers were still common at this time, especially high-quality sheets from Holland and France. By the mid-eighteenth century Dutch and French paper mills had begun to use new technology in the form of the Hollander beater, a large tub with metal blades which allowed finer and faster beating of the pulp.[57] As a result the finer pulp accumulated less around the chain lines. Together with a new kind of mould that had a wider pattern and allowed the water to run through much faster, the formation of the sheets became much quicker. The paper had a more regular appearance, with thicker and more clearly defined laid and chain lines. The Hollander beater was known in Spain by the end of the eighteenth century thanks to the 1779 Spanish translation of Joseph de Lalande's *L'art de Faire le Papier*, although it was not used for papermaking here until the 1790s.[58] It is possible to identify Dutch and French papers used for prints and drawings in Spain at this period by the structure of the paper, as can be seen in a photograph using transmitted light of Antonio González Velázquez's *A Standing Woman* (fig. 9). Watermarks, too, continue to offer clues as to paper origins: the portrait of *María Luisa de Borbón* by Luis Paret y Alcázar (fig. 29, p. 210), for example, has a large fleur-de-lis watermark suggesting a French or Dutch paper.[59]

Lighter, ivory-toned papers become more common in Spanish eighteenth-century prints and drawings, such as Camarón's *An Algerian Woman Seated Beneath a Canopy* (fig. 52, p. 226) or *Saint Mary Magdalene in the Desert* (fig. 54, p. 228). The Hollander beater eliminated the need for fermenting rags for paper pulp and the result was a whiter paper.[60] On the other hand, cotton, regarded by some scholars as essential for producing whiter paper, was used in greater quantities. Cotton had become widely available in Spain through extensive plantations in the colonies. In 1756, well before the Hollander beater had been introduced to Spain, Catalan papermaker and scholar Francisco de Mora, mentions the addition of cotton rags as essential to achieving whiteness in high-quality papers.[61]

New publications on the subject of papermaking also had an effect on the use of alternative raw materials in Spain. In the 1770s Father Martín Sarmiento described how to make 'incombustible' paper from Mexican pita, and by 1787 the Real Fábrica de Papel in San Fernando de Henares (Madrid), a paper mill commissioned by the king to compete with private initiatives, applied his methods successfully to make a very dark yet resistant cardboard. Other unusual materials such as esparto (a coarse grass native of Spain and America), or the bark of the banana tree (used to make paper in the Canary Islands and Cuba) were encouraged by the growing scarcity of rags.[62]

Francisco de Goya's use of papers

The papers Goya used for his prints and drawings deserve particular attention. In the catalogue of his prints in the Biblioteca Nacional in Madrid, Carmen Hernández analyses and describes the watermarks in this collection.[63] Goya's use of Catalan watermarked papers from the Romaní, Romeu and Serra paper mills in his first-edition prints in the *Disasters of War* (*c.*1810–15) and *Tauromaquia* (1816) series coincides with the reputed quality and easier distribution of papers from these mills in the early nineteenth century. In Goya's earlier prints, such as the etchings of 1778 after Diego Velázquez (figs 7–8, p. 239), his papers vary in composition and manufacture, from antique non-watermarked papers to high-quality imports bearing Dutch watermarks. Goya was experimenting with printing techniques in the 1770s and may have tried out several papers in order to test their receptivity to inks and the effects they created.[64]

The paper used for the first edition of *Los Caprichos* (1799) in the British Museum shows characteristics very similar to the other two first editions examined in the Museo Nacional del Prado and the Biblioteca Nacional de España.[65] The distance between the chain lines are not always consistent along the sheet. Although they do indicate repeated patterns in spacing, they are not necessarily distributed in the same order in every sheet. Additionally, the cut edges of the individual sheets indicate that the paper was made in a larger format. None of the sheets in any of the three sets examined has a watermark, so it is impossible to be certain of the provenance of the paper.[66] A letter from Manuel Ezquerra Trábaga dated 1798 states that Goya had received from him three orders of a half-ream of paper '*de marca mayor, imperial*', the last of which was '*papel imperial de Génova*', thick, large-format papers suitable for printing which may relate to the types of paper used for *Los Caprichos*.[67]

The availability and cost of handmade papers used for printing in Spain dictated the quality of the final impression, but with the development of the papermaking industry the commercial expectations of the printer became an increasingly important factor. Antonio Carnicero's etchings of bullfighting (*Colección de las principales suertes de una corrida de toros*; *c.*1789), depicting bullfighting manoeuvres, were printed on medium-quality papers with a darkened composition, irregular pulp accumulation and numerous water droplets, which occur when the sheet of paper is carelessly lifted from the vat (fig. 48–9, p. 223).[68] By contrast, Goya's later series, *La Tauromaquia*, was printed on high-quality papers from flourishing Catalonian mills.[69]

Recent examination of Goya's pen-and-ink drawing of *The Garrotted Man* (*c.*1778) provides new information on his working process of preparing a drawing for a print (figs 5–6, p. 238). Conservation has revealed previously hidden chalk markings rubbed on the verso of the paper as a means of transfer to the metal plate.[70] Two red chalk drawings, the *Portrait of Pedro Roldán* (1798–9) and the *Study for an Equestrian*

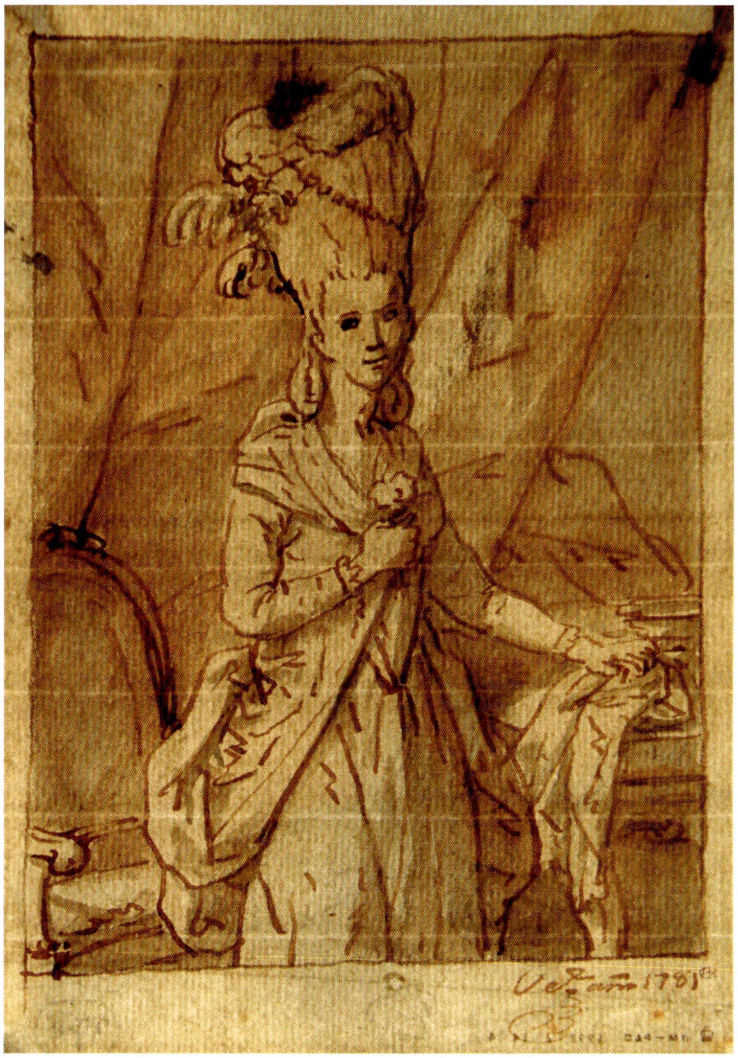

9 Transmitted light image of a study by Antonio González Velázquez showing eighteenth-century paper with thick, marked chain lines and a regular sheet formation, characteristic of papers made with the Hollander beater (see fig. 15, page 202)

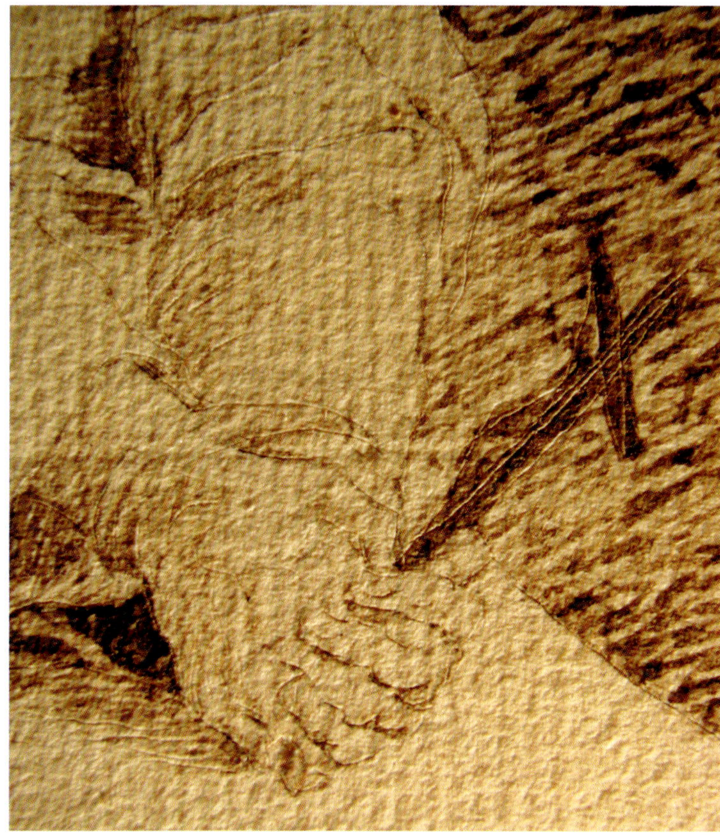

10 Raking light detail showing how the incision marks for transfer are embedded in the paper of *The Garrotted Man* by Francisco de Goya (see fig. 5, page 238).

Portrait of Arthur Wellesley (1812), were executed by Goya on textured laid Hollander beater papers. The watermark on the portrait of Arthur Wellesley (fig. 28, p. 251) may be of Dutch origin.[71] Other developments in papermaking in Europe, such as wove paper with a uniform surface, would not make their way into Spanish paper mills until the mid-nineteenth century, although Goya did sometimes draw on thin wove papers possibly imported from abroad by stationers and art suppliers in Madrid and widely used for letter-writing.[72]

From the earliest years of printing in Spain through to the eighteenth century the lack of government protection meant that Spanish papermakers found it very difficult to compete with foreign imports. Spanish baroque artists demonstrated great creativity and resourcefulness in adapting papers produced both locally and abroad. By the mid-eighteenth century, as papermakers were granted official privileges and tax exemptions, Spanish papermaking began to flourish.

Meanwhile, the innovations introduced in paper mills across Europe can be seen in the papers used by artists. Thus the Spanish prints and drawings in the British Museum collection reflect the evolution and changes in Western papermaking while at the same time providing a better understanding of the often complex circumstances surrounding the creation of art in Spain during this period.

I would like to thank José Carlos Balmaceda (paper conservator, CAHIP), María del Carmen Hidalgo Brinquis (Head of Paper Conservation, Instituto del Patrimonio Histórico Español, IPHE), M. Carme Sistach (Chemist of the laboratory of Conservation, Archivo de la Corona de Aragón), Isabel Ortega and Isabel García-Toraño (Department of Prints and Drawings, Biblioteca Nacional de España), Department of Prints and Drawings at the Museo Nacional del Prado, Marjorie Shelley (Head of Paper Conservation, The Metropolitan Museum of Art, New York), Dr Richard Mulholland and Elisabetta Zandarin. Birthe Christensen (Head of Conservation and Preservation, Royal Museums Greenwich) and the Paper Conservation Section at Royal Museums Greenwich. Joanna Kosek, Jenny Bescoby and Judith Rayner of the Department of Paper Conservation (WAP) at the British Museum.

Notes

Introduction

1 For the significance of Isabel and Ferdinand as cultural promoters, see Yarza Luaces 1993.

2 Many excellent studies have been devoted to the subjects outlined above. For the English reader accessible historical studies include Elliott 2009; Kamen 2005; Kamen 2002; Braudel 1992. For a good bibliography with emphasis on work published in English, see Kamen 2005, pp. 296–311. Important Spanish studies are cited in the books listed. Studies on the art of Spain are cited in the chapters that follow.

Chapter 1

1 Brief surveys have been written by Gallego Gallego 1979 (prints) and Pérez Sánchez 1986 (drawings). More substantial overviews of printmaking in Spain appear in vol. 31 of *Summa Artis*: see Bozal 1987; Carrete Parrondo 1987; Checa Cremades 1987. Catalogues of major drawing collections include: Barcia 1906; García-Toraño Martínez 2009; Santiago Páez 1991 (Biblioteca Nacional, Madrid); Sánchez Cantón 1930 (reprinted 1970; various collections); Pérez Sánchez 1972 and 1977; Arnáez 1975 (Museo del Prado); Espinós Díaz 1979 and 1984 (Museo de Bellas Artes, Valencia). Catalogues of major print collections in Spain include Vega 1992 (Museo del Prado) and Páez Ríos 1981–3 (Biblioteca Nacional, Madrid). For catalogues of individual artists, see subsequent chapters in the present volume.

2 E.g. Vega 2010; essays in Santiago Páez 2004; Portús and Vega 1998. For broader artistic context, see e.g. Kasl 2009.

3 Chennevières 1880, pp. 32–4.

4 Gradmann 1946, pp. iii, iv (published in English, French and German).

5 Gómez Sicre 1949, p. 5 (published in English, French and German).

6 For Cuban curator and critic Gómez Sicre, see Fox 2010.

7 Sánchez Cantón 1964, p. 12.

8 Rodriguez-Moñino 1954.

9 For a concise summary of scholars who have worked on Spanish drawings and their publications, see Boubli 1999, pp. 349–50; earlier review by Muller 1976a.

10 McKim Smith 1974, p. 11; Pérez Sánchez 1970, p. 5.

11 Pérez Sánchez 1972a; Stubbe 1966.

12 Ainaud quoted by Checa Cremades 1987, p. 82.

13 McDonald 2006b.

14 British Museum, 1871,0812.788 and 1912,0131.1.

15 See e.g. studies by Bury 2001 (Italy); Van der Stock 1998 (Antwerp); Landau and Parshall 1994, pp. 103–61.

16 Brakensiek 2003; McDonald 1998; González de Zárate 1992–4.

17 Brown and Elliott 1980, p. 123.

18 Véliz 2008, pp. 424–32. For broad discussion, see Trusted 2007, pp. 25–30.

19 Trapier 1941, p. 1.

20 Nash 2008, pp. 27–36.

21 On this subject, Boubli 2003, pp. 211–12.

22 Trapier 1941, p. 4.

23 Martínez 2006, p. 295; Brown 1989, pp. 178–9; Calvo Serraller 1981, p. 523.

24 Quoted by Glendinning 1988, p. 69.

25 Martínez 2006, p. 188.

26 For treatises and documents, see Gutiérrez Pastor 2008; Calvo Seraller 1981.

27 Brown 1989, p. 184, n. 11. The 1624 document was published by Volk 1979, p. 627. The text of the document can be found in Volk 1977, Appendix v, Document 49, pp. 398–413.

28 Volk 1977, pp. 405–7.

29 Brown 1989, p. 182; Brown 1976, pp. 44–6.

30 Navarrete Prieto, Zapata Fernández de la Hoz and Martínez Ripoll 2008; Navarrete Prieto 1998; Navarrete Prieto 1994.

31 Goltzius print: Hollstein VIII.12 (Dutch and Flemish).

32 Calvo Serraller 1981, pp. 297–302. See especially Carducho's Dialogue v, 'Trátase del modo de juzgar de las pinturas, singularidad de la perspectiva; que es dibujo, y qué el colorido …', Carducho 1979 edn, pp. 217–56.

33 'Del debuxo y de sus partes', in Pacheco 1990, pp. 341–51.

34 León Tello and Sanz Sanz 1979, pp. 204–5.

35 Véliz 2008, p. 420; Palomino 1988, II, pp. 74, 114.

36 Summary by Portús and Vega 1998, pp. 202–5.

37 Caturla 1968–9, pp. 177–221.

38 Agulló y Cobo 1994–2006, I, p. 124.

39 Marías and Bustamente García 1981, Appendix II, p. 223.

40 Banner 2007.

41 Navarrete Prieto and Pérez Sánchez 2009, pp. 18–21, 296–9; Navarrete Prieto 2006, pp. 13–28.

42 Palomino 1987, p. 248.

43 For Carpio, see López-Fanjul 2010. Also Ph.D. dissertation by the same author submitted to the Courtauld Institute of Art, London in 2011. For Monterrey, see Pérez Sánchez 1977a.

44 See also the case of Manuel de Porras, a collector of limited means. Agulló y Cobo 2003.

45 Carducho 1979, p. 435.

46 Ceán Bermúdez 1800, I, pp. liv–lv. For his print collection, see Chapter 8 in the present volume.

47 The standard work on cartoons and transfer of drawings is Bambach 1999. There exists no comprehensive study of the technical aspects of drawings in Spain.

48 Angulo Iñiguez and Pérez Sánchez 1975, no. 38.

49 Destroyed in the fire of 1734. Escobar 2004, p. 21; Wilkinson-Zerner and Brown 1990, p. 9.

50 There are many studies on architectural drawings in Spain. See e.g. García-Toraño Martínez 2009; Fernández Martín 2003; Santiago Paéz 1991.

51 Delfín Rodríguez Ruiz in García-Toraño Martínez 2009, no. 111.

52 Trusted 2007, pp. 94–8.

53 José Manuel Barbeito in García-Toraño Martínez 2009, no. 271.

54 Angulo Iñiguez and Pérez Sánchez 1975, no. 500.

55 Chapman and Faietti 2010, p. 25.

56 Kasl 1993.

57 *Noticia del Recibimiento i Entrada de la Reyna Nuestra Señora Doña María-Ana de Austria en la muy noble i leal coronada villa de Madrid*, Madrid 1650. Print: Páez Ríos 1981–3, no. 2252-10; drawing: Brown 1973, p. 376.

58 Navascués Palacio 1986.

59 Landau and Parshall 1994, p. 162.

60 Páez Ríos 1981–3, no. 230.12.
61 Gallego Gallego 1979, pp. 19–23.
62 Páez Ríos 1981–3, no. 2252-72.
63 Popular prints run through most of the print categories discussed here. See Duran i Sanpere 1971 and Chapter 7 in the present volume.
64 Brown 1973, nos 7–9 (*ears* no. 7).
65 Mendoza Díaz-Maroto 2010, no. 2, p. 10. Playing cards were made elsewhere in Spain, for example Barcelona in the early sixteenth century. See Rubió i Balaguer 1986, p. 101.
66 For others in the series, see Banner 2005; José Manuel Barbeito in García-Toraño Martínez 2009, no. 70.
67 Portús and Vega 1998, fig. 16, p. 61.
68 Páez Ríos 1981–3, no. 331.18. British Museum, 1878,0112.360. An impression of an eighteenth-century etching on silk of Our Lady of the Heather is accompanied by the explanation that if the beholder recites an 'Ave Maria' or 'Salve' in front of the image they will be granted 200 days indulgence. The print was once framed or fastened to a rigid support. British Museum, 1878,0112.361.

Chapter 2

1 Boubli and Pérez Sánchez 1991, pp. 14–15
2 Angulo Iñiguez and Pérez Sanchez 1975, p. 10. On the connection between Spain and Flanders, see Nash 2008, pp. 101–11; Silva Maroto 2002; Yarza Luaces 1993; Silva Maroto 1990. For Italy and Córdoba, see Urquízar Herrera 2001, pp. 32–54. For Italy, France and Spain, see Natale 2001.
3 Sánchez Cantón 1964, pls 1–5, 8–9, 12–13, 16.
4 Holcomb 2009, pp. 3–34; Bambach 1999, pp. 137–41.
5 See Vasari's description of *disegno* in Vasari 1966–87 edn, I, pp. 111–21.
6 Chapman in Chapman and Faietti 2010, pp. 48–9; Scheller 1995; Elen 1995.
7 Heriard Debreuil 1987, I, chap. 3, pp. 113–56 and II, figs 308–9, 314, 317, 327, 332 etc.
8 A number of attributions have been proposed. For Starnina (alias the 'Maestro del Bambin Vispo'), see Gómez Frechina 2007, pp. 24–36; Andrea de Marchi in Natale 2001, nos 4a–b, 5a–b and (by Joan Aliaga) 10; Scheller 1995, no. 31, pp. 317–30; Van Waadenoijen 1974.
9 See the comparisons made by Heriard Debreuil 1987 (note 7 above).
10 None of the model books described by Scheller (1995) is from Spain.
11 Yarza Luaces 2003, p. 164: 'molts papers ab imatges deboxadas … de poch valor'.
12 Espanyol Bertran 1997, p. 85: 'Item un plec de papés deboxats … Item molts altres papés deboxats … Item un caxó poc, ab pany e clau, vell, amb molts papers deboxats e mostres … Item molts papés pintats e deboxats de pocha valor'.
13 Cited by Joan Aliaga in Natale 2001, p. 188.
14 By contrast, in Italy there is evidence of a different value placed on drawings, see Chapman in Chapman and Faietti 2010, pp. 21–3.
15 Francesca Español in Natale 2001, no. 1.
16 Dalmases 1992, II, p. 318: 'Item vna veronica de nostre senyor ab lo peu nou daurat de fust deboxada sobre paper blanquit E primo en los pits ha sinc seraphins de argent daurats ab vnes bolletes de argent E sobre dita guarnicio ha vna fresa de obra de lima ab vnes coronets …'.
17 Angulo Iñiguez and Pérez Sanchez 1975, no. 1; Ainaud, Gudiol and Verrié 1947, I, p. 88, II, figs 596 and (detail) 597.
18 Drawings survive that are similar but from a much earlier period. See, for example, Italian works in Degenhart and Schmitt 1968–80, and the design drawing of the façade of Strasbourg Cathedral (1260s) in Holcomb 2009, no. 38.
19 Lacarra Ducay 1983, pp. 556–7 and figs 1, 2.
20 Ibid., fig. 6.
21 Bambach 2005 and 2005a.
22 Pérez Sánchez 1986, p. 112 (as Guas? or Anequín Egas Cueman?); Pérez Sánchez 1972, I, pp. 17–18. Sánchez Cantón 1928.
23 Ibid.
24 Angulo Iñiguez and Pérez Sanchez 1975, nos 2–4; Wethey 1937, p. 381.
25 Yarza Luaces 2003; Angulo Iñiguez and Pérez Sanchez 1975, no. 6a–g.
26 Finaldi and Garrido 2006; Bambach 1999, esp. chap. 2.
27 I am making a distinction between a preparatory drawing made for a painting and the use of model books. For Gallego's underdrawing see Finaldi and Garrido 2006, nos 10, 11.
28 Alvarez 1998, pp. 49–56.
29 Silva Maroto 2004, pp. 242–90.
30 Anderson, Dotseth and Roglán 2008, no. 22.
31 Dotseth 2008.
32 Bambach 1999, pp. 79–80; d'Andrea Cennini 1960 edn, p. 75.
33 Drawing on parchment continued into the sixteenth century, it seems, mainly for drawings that had a similar purpose to the works mentioned above; but they are not common survivals. See e.g. design for a fountain by Diego de Tiedra that accompanies a contract dated 1558. Tiedra was probably a Castilian sculptor who worked in Cuenca (active 1538–58). Angulo Iñiguez and Pérez Sanchez 1975, no. 247; Rokiski Lázaro 1968.
34 Yarza Luaces 1993, pp. 95–100.
35 For summary, see Vega 1992b, Lyell 1976.
36 Checa Cremades 1987, pp. 23–30; Garcia Vega 1984, I, pp. 27–32; Gallego Gallego 1979, pp. 23–32.
37 Garcia Vega 1984, II, pp. 7–8.
38 Ibid., pp. 151–4.
39 For the Crombergers, see the seminal study by Griffin (1988). Also, Portillo Muñoz 1980. A summary of the printers and their publications can be found in Checa Cremades 1987, pp. 30–7; also Garcia Vega 1984, II, pp. 91–3.
40 Checa Cremades 1987, pp. 27–9. Gallego Gallego 1979, chaps 1, 2.
41 López Serrano 1973, p. 27; Bland 1969, p. 191.
42 Illustrated in Checa Cremades 1987, fig. 11, p. 28.
43 Garcia Vega 1984, II, no. 245.
44 See 'El Grabado', in Garcia Vega 1984, I, pp. 95 ff., and map I p. 98, map II p. 99.
45 Cosin was of French origin and provided the technical expertise while Gómez, who was Secretary to the Privy Chamber (Escribano de Cámara), provided financial backing. Garcia Vega 1984, II, pp. 47, 49–50; Pérez Pastor 1970, pp. xx–xxiii.
46 For metalcuts, see Griffiths 1996, pp. 29–30; Gallego Gallego 1979, 'las estampas sueltas', pp. 19–23; Ainaud 1962, pp. 246–51.
47 Pilar Vinatea Serrano in Madrid 2001, no. 56.
48 Also known as Carlos IV de Navarra (1421–61), titular king of Navarra 1441–61.
49 See the drawn copy of this print attributed to Juan de Juanes. Garín Llombart 1979, no. 43. Albi 1979, II, pp. 81–2, III, pl. CXLII.
50 Checa Cremades 1987, p. 45. The impressions in the Biblioteca Nacional Madrid and the Museo de Bellas Artes, Valencia, are nineteenth-century. See Silvestra Visa and Tomas Sanmartin 1982, no. 139.
51 Biblioteca Nacional (42.367). This impression was reprinted in 1651. The lower margin carries the publication details 'En Valencia / En casa de Fuster, por Geronimo Vilagrasa, junto a S. Martin. Ano 1651'.
52 McDonald 2004.
53 Ibid., I, pp. 75–84.
54 Ibid., II, nos 1035, 2452.
55 The inventories of Mencía's collections are being transcribed as part of the Mencía de Mendoza Research Project (International Museum Institute, University of Southern California, Los Angeles). The material discussed here derives from an unpublished paper given by the author in Oaxaca, Mexico, in April 2006 as part of the Research Project.
56 Goris and Marlier, 1971; Rupprich 1956.
57 The descriptions are taken from the inventories of Mencía's collections cited in note 55.

58 ‘1 padronzillo en papel de la jaula de breda del jardin del principe que se saco al natural / costo felipus al pintor 8.8.4’ (122–3r).
59 For explanation of early print terminology, see McDonald 2004, I, pp. 75–98.
60 ‘más otro cajón con muchos papeles de dibujos’ (122–46v).

Chapter 3

1 The population in 1558 was 20,000; by 1595 it had increased to 60,000. Alvar Ezquerra 1989, pp. 15–104.
2 Mulcahy 2004; Checa Cremades 1992.
3 Kamen 2010, pp. 46–85; Mulcahy 1994, p. 2; Kubler 1982, pp. 12–13.
4 Cano de Gardoqui y García 1994, pp. 108–20; Kubler 1982, p. 20.
5 Wilkinson-Zerner 1993, pp. 10–13.
6 Most of the known documents have been published by Bustamente García 1994.
7 For Titian’s association with Spain, see Checa 1994, pp. 37–87.
8 Mulcahy 2004, pp. 3–50; Checa Cremades 1992, pp. 242–5. For the formation and development of Philip’s taste for Venetian art, see Checa 1994, pp. 15–23.
9 For general discussion, see Falomir Faus 1998, pp. 203–27; Brown 1991, pp. 53–5.
10 Mulcahy 1994. For synthesis, see Brown 1991, pp. 52–67.
11 For introduction to the types and function of Italian Renaissance drawing, see Chapman in Chapman and Faietti 2010, pp. 15–75.
12 Newcome Schleier 1995, p. 18.
13 Wilkinson-Zerner 1993, p. 51.
14 For Castello’s drawings in Spain, see Angulo Iñiguez and Pérez Sánchez 1975, nos 109–15. For *Apollo and Mars*, see Turner 2008, no. 16. Redín Michaus 2007, figs 161, 162, pp. 234–5. For his drawing style in Italy see e.g. Clifford 1975.
15 García-Frías in di Giampaolo 1995, pp. 61–83.
16 For the frescos, see Carofano 1993; Angulo Iñiguez and Pérez Sánchez 1975, (*Judgement of Solomon*) nos 249–70, (others) nos 271–95.
17 For this category of drawing, see Bambach 1999, pp. 249–82. Other Italian artists at the Escorial such as Romulo Cincinnato (*c.*1540–*c.*1597) also made highly finished preparatory drawings. García-Frías 1995a.
18 Angulo Iñiguez and Pérez Sánchez 1975, no. 253.
19 For this category of drawing see Bambach 1999, pp. 283–95.
20 Angulo Iñiguez and Pérez Sánchez 1975, nos 266–70.
21 Ibid., no. 288.
22 Newcome Schleier 1995, pp. 19–34; Mulcahy 1994, pp. 43–4, 68–99.
23 Beguin 1995, p. 85.
24 Mulcahy 1994, pp. 116–36.
25 Gere and Pouncey 1983, no. 274.
26 Ibid., no. 275.
27 Mulcahy 1994 pp. 100–115.
28 Mulcahy 1995a, pp. 101–19.
29 Popham and Wilde 1984, no. 1046.
30 Angulo Iñiguez and Pérez Sánchez 1975, nos 89–106.
31 Barcia (1906) catalogues a number of drawings under Bartolomé, but notes that they are more likely to be by Vicente.
32 Boubli and Pérez Sánchez 1991, no. 6.
33 Kitaura 1995, pp. 148–9.
34 Davies 2007, pp. 113–14; Marías and Bustamante 1981, p. 227.
35 Marías and Bustamante García 1981, p. 236. On the importance of Michelangelo’s art for El Greco, see Boubli 2003, pp. 215–17.
36 Turner 2007, p. 291; Davies 2003, nos 18, 19 (by Xavier Bray), 20, 41 (by Gabriele Finaldi).
37 Wethey 1962, II, p. 151.
38 The drawing was once part of Giorgio Vasari’s *Libro de’disegni*. He inscribed it ‘Domenico Greco’. For El Greco and Florence, see Marías 1997, pp. 82–3.
39 For El Greco, Tintoretto and Titian, see Marías 1997, pp. 62–72. Wethey suggested that the drawing may have been copied from a model in Tintoretto’s studio (Wethey 1962, II, pp. 151–2).
40 Hellwig and Zeitler 2006, pp. 26–30; Kitaura 1995, pp. 145–58; Kehrer 1935.
41 Gabriele Finaldi in Davies 2003, no. 20.
42 Davies 2007, pp. 114–20.
43 For the drawings, see Kitaura 1995, pp. 145–62; Angulo Iñiguez and Pérez Sánchez 1975, nos 155–63. For a problematic attribution, see Marías 2007. Questionable attributions to El Greco have also been proposed by Nicholas Turner (2007).
44 On this subject, see Redín Michaus 2007, pp. 15–26.
45 Waldman 2002, pp. 22–7.
46 Vasari 1991 edn, p. 889.
47 Espinós Díaz 2010, no. 158; Espinós Díaz 1979, no. 6; Angulo Iñiguez and Pérez Sánchez 1975, no. 66. For Berruguete and Michelangelo, see Boubli 2003, pp. 212–17.
48 Heredia Morena 2005; Boubli 1994; Martín González 1981.
49 Boubli 1994, pp. 19–21.
50 Boubli 2002, no. 7; Boubli 1994, figs 32–4.
51 Parrado del Olmo 2002.
52 Mulcahy 1999; Mulcahy 1994, pp. 14–43. Navarrete’s fellow countrymen Luis de Carvajal and Diego da Urbina, who also worked at the Escorial, are not discussed here. No drawings by Urbina are accepted as autograph and the two by Carvajal (Angulo Iñiguez and Pérez Sánchez 1975, nos 107,108) are uncertain attributions.
53 Redín Michaus 2007, pp. 304–9; Mulcahy 1999, pp. 5–8; Sigüenza 1988, p. 343.
54 For Navarrete’s drawings, see Fernández Pardo 1995. Three drawings catalogued by Barcia (1906) as Navarrete (nos 76–8) have all been assigned to other artists: B.76 = F. Ribalta (DIB/16/39/6); B.77 = F. Ribalta (DIB/16/39/7); B.78 = G.B. Castello (DIB/16/39/8).
55 A highly finished drawn copy of Navarrete’s 1576 painting of *Abraham and the Three Angels* now in the Instituto Valencia de Don Juan, Madrid, has sometimes been regarded as by his hand. Mulcahy (1999, p. 47) sensibly suggests that it is a late sixteenth-century copy.
56 The British Museum sheet is not dissimilar to *Christ at the Column* inscribed ‘Navarrete el Mudo’ but now attributed to Ribalta (Biblioteca Nacional, Madrid. DIB/16/39/6); Fernandéz Pardo 1995, p. 224; Robinson 1876, no. 418.
57 Martínez de la Peña y González 1968, pp. 297, 300.
58 For Becerra in Italy, see Redín Michaus 2007, pp. 159–217; Fracchia 1999; Mulcahy 1999, pp. 70–1.
59 Gallerie dell’Accademia, Venice. Published by Davidson as Navarrete, but it is by Becerra. See Boubli 2003, p. 218 for further references and corrections; Davidson 1993, pp. 93–6.
60 Becerra’s drawing is remarkably similar to Michelangelo *Risen Christ* (*c.*1532–3) in the British Museum (1895,0915.501 recto). For Volterra and Michelangelo, see Chapman 2005.
61 For the drawings, see Capel Margarito 1998, pp. 31–4; Pérez Sánchez 1972, p. 22 (fragments of the Last Judgement, Museo del Prado F.A.2;). Also, Biblioteca Nacional, Madrid, DIB/13/1/24. The drawings are not copied from the fresco or drawings by Michelangelo as has been proposed, but from prints, possibly by either Nicolò della Casa (1543–8) or Giulio Bonasone (1546–50). For the prints see Moltedo 1991, nos 6, 10.
62 Redín Michaus 2007, pp. 208–17. It is thought that the engraved illustrations in the book were also designed by Becerra. *Historia* (British Library, London, C.112.f.10).
63 Serrano Marqués 1999; Fracchia 1998.
64 For the Alcázar, see Checa 1994a (and other studies in the same volume). For El Pardo, see García-Frías 2005, pp. 107–11; Escobar 2004, p. 28.
65 Boubli 2002, no. 1.
66 Pacheco 1990, pp. 438–9. See also *The Beheading of Medusa* for El Pardo. García-Frías 2005, pp. 72–4, 125.
67 Adela Espinós Díaz in Madrid 1998, nos 79.1, II; Angulo Iñiguez and Pérez Sánchez 1975, no. 38.

68 The altar was destroyed by fire in 1862. For the drawing, see Capel Margarito 1998, pp. 36–8; also Adela Espinós Días in Madrid 1998, no. 173.
69 Arias Martínez 1998, pp. 275–8.
70 Armenini quoted by García-Frias 2005, note 1, p. 132; Carducho 1979, p. 179.
71 Bambach 1999, pp. 368–71.
72 Angulo Iñiguez and Pérez Sánchez 1975, nos 309–85; Junquera 1963.
73 Not recorded by Angulo Iñiguez and Pérez Sánchez 1975.
74 British Museum, 1846,0509.171 and 172; Angulo Iñiguez and Pérez Sánchez 1975, no. 232; Brown 1968.
75 Palomino 1987, p. 47.
76 Angulo Iñiguez and Pérez Sánchez 1975, no. 207.
77 Schroth and Baer 2008, p. 292; Angulo Iñiguez and Pérez Sánchez 1969, p. 212.
78 Schroth and Baer 2008, p. 294; Angulo Iñiguez and Pérez Sánchez 1969, p. 86.
79 Evelyn Lane in Wilkinson-Zerner and Brown 1990, p. 63.
80 Bury 2001, no. 56.
81 See selection in Ollero 1993, pp. 123–99.
82 Bécares Botas 1999; Macías Rosendo 1998; Pérez Castro and Voet 1973; Rekers 1972 pp. 46–8.
83 See recent studies on Montano in Maestre Maestre et al. 2006; also Hänsel 1999.
84 Brakensiek 2003; McDonald 1998; González de Zárate 1992–4.
85 For Montano's *Divinarum nuptiarum conventa* ... engraved by Galle, see Mellion 2009, pp. 39–51; Bataillon 1942.
86 Marías 2005. For other drawings at the Escorial, see Deswarte-Rosa 2004, p. 258; Andrés 1968.
87 See essays in Varey et al. 2000.
88 Garcia Vega 1984, I, p. 67.
89 See, for example, details regarding the costs of moving the Giunti (Junta) press from Salamanca to Madrid, Pettas 2005, p. 68.
90 Garcia Vega 1984, I, p. 86, II, pp. 270–1, 349–52; López Serrano 1963.
91 For the prints, see Sáenz de Miera 1998, pp. 114–31; Wilkinson-Zerner and Brown 1990. For Herrera, see Wilkinson-Zerner 1993; Bury 1986.
92 Bury 1991, p. 77.
93 Matilla Rodríguez 1994, pp. 461–4
94 Witcombe 1992, p. 177; Cervera Vera 1988, pp. 35–6, 38–40; Cervera Vera 1984.
95 The *Sumario* has been published by Wilkinson-Zerner and Brown 1990, pp. 12–13. Also Santiago Páez 1985, pp. 230–53.
96 For Testa, see *Dizionario* 1977, p. 248; Cervera Vera 1988, pp. 43–6 (Testa and Gaeta). Bury notes that suitable paper would have been bought from Italy (presumably on the advice of Gaeta and Testa) and that several editions were printed on silk and white and yellow satin. Bury 1991, p. 78 note 5; Cervera Vera 1988, pp. 49–50.
97 Wilkinson-Zerner 1993, p. 50.
98 Villalpando 1990. First volume of text by Jerónimo Pardo published in 1595 and the second, with architectural reconstructions, in 1604. Luciano Rubio in Villalpando 1990, pp. 73–99.
99 For a list of printmakers, see Villalpando 1991, I, pp. 521–2.
100 Cherubino Alberti as the engraver in Villalpando 1991, I, p. 522.
101 Wilkinson-Zerner 1993, pp. 50–1, also p. 182 note 10.
102 Hollstein XVII (Dutch and Flemish), no. 127.
103 Fernando Bouza Álvarez in Madrid 1998, no. 307.
104 Hollstein XVII (Dutch and Flemish), no. 35; Biblioteca Nacional, Madrid, 37082.
105 Gallego Gallego 1979, p. 124.
106 Pettegree 2010, pp. 260–3; Checa Cremades 1987, pp. 37, 81.
107 The criteria for including publishers varies from source to source. The figure of sixteen is taken from Garcia Vega 1984, II, p. 211.
108 For the Giunti dynasty in Spain, see Pettas 2005; Checa Cremades 1987, p. 39; Garcia Vega 1984, II, p. 51.
109 Pérez Pastor 1970 edn, p. xxxi and note 1 on same page.
110 Roteta de la Maza 1985, pp. 131–44.
111 For the painting, see Gabriele Finaldi in Davies 2003, no. 46.
112 Roteta de la Maza 1985, pp. 233–4. Ceán Bermúdez 1800, I, pp. 80–1. The lettering on Astor's print of Saint Francis follows conventions established outside Spain: the printmaker's name and date and the painter's name in the lower left.
113 *Dizionario* 1977, pp. 70–1.
114 *Regla de las cinco órdenes de architectura de Iacome de Vignola Agora nuevo traduzido en Romance por Patritio Caxesi florentino* (Madrid 1593, Biblioteca Nacional, Madrid, ER/2534).
115 Ceán Bermúdez 1800, I, p. 307.

Chapter 4

1 Banner 2009; Schroth 2008.
2 Schroth 2008, p. 88.
3 Ollero 1993, pp. 201–45.
4 Defourneaux 1979, p. 47.
5 Jordan 2005, pp. 30–1.
6 Marías and Cruz de Carlos Varona 2009, p. 63.
7 Kusche 2007, p. 61; Angulo Iñiguez and Pérez Sánchez 1975, no. 212.
8 Kusche 2007, p. 125.
9 For a survey of Rubens' practice as a draughtsman, see Logan and Plomp 2005, pp. 3–35.
10 The painting is in the Museo del Prado, Madrid (P.03137); the drawings are in the Musée du Louvre, Paris (20.185), and the Staatliche Graphische Sammlung, Munich (1983.84).
11 Vignau-Wilberg 2001, pp. 24, 56.
12 Vosters 1990, pp. 41–9, esp. p. 49.
13 Schroth 2001, pp. 34–5, 62.
14 Angulo Iñiguez and Pérez Sánchez 1969, pp. 86–109
15 Ibid., pp. 212–26.
16 De Lapuerta Montoya 2002, pp. 61–70; Volk 1977, p. 38.
17 De Lapuerta Montoya 2002, pp. 374–83.
18 Ibid., pp. 100–102; Boubli and Pérez Sánchez 1991, no. 5.
19 The drawing of the Virgin in the tabernacle in the centre, by another hand, is on the sheet of paper that has been glued on.
20 For history of the commission, see Virginia Tovar Martín in Santiago Paéz 1991, no. 75. For Mora's career in Madrid, see Tovar Martín 1986, pp. 1–162.
21 Angulo Iñiguez and Pérez Sánchez 1969, nos 67–70.
22 Beutler 1997.
23 Úbeda de los Cobos 1989a.
24 Pérez Sánchez 1982a.
25 Brown 1989; Volk 1977, Appendix V, Document 49.
26 Calvo Serraller in Carducho 1979, pp. lxvii–lxix; Volk 1977, pp. 74–83.
27 Brown 1991, p. 95.
28 Many important passages relating to artistic practice have been translated and quoted by Orso (1993, esp. chap. 2). For an annotated edition in Spanish, see Carducho 1979.
29 Jordan 2005, p. 39; Pérez Sánchez 1999, pp. 36–7.
30 Brown 2005.
31 Vergara 1999, pp. 57–112.
32 The drawing might represent the Infante Don Carlos, but it must have been executed in Madrid. See Vergara 1999, pp. 61–5 and for his reputation in Spain, especially after his first trip until his second, pp. 19–56; Held 1986, no. 173.
33 Alpers 1971.
34 Orso 1993, pp. 40–96; Brown 1986, pp. 43–5; Harris 1982, pp. 57–74.
35 Santiago Morán the Elder (*pintor de cámara*), Eugenio Cajés, Vicento Carducho, Bartolomé González and Francisco López (*pintores del rey*).
36 Vergara 1999, pp. 59–60; Orso 1986, p. 18.
37 For the most sensible comment on the subject, see McKim Smith 1980.
38 Mena Marqués 1999; Pacheco 1990, p. 528.
39 McKim Smith 1980, p. 5.
40 Brown 2005, p. 45. For the Count-Duke and Velázquez, see Elliott 1986, pp. 141, 172–4.
41 Brown 1986, pp. 60–1.
42 Museo del Prado, Madrid, D.3055. Illustrated in Boubli and Pérez Sánchez 1991, no. 34.
43 Orso 1993, pp. 46–9.

44 Carducho 1979, pp. 274–5 and note 208.
45 Orso 1993, p. 70.
46 Quoted in translation by Orso 1993, p. 68; Carducho 1979, pp. 270–2.
47 Brown and Elliott 1980.
48 Úbeda de los Cobos 2005; Brown and Elliott 1980, pp. 141–92.
49 For painting, see Úbeda de los Cobos 2005, no. 20.
50 Úbeda de los Cobos 2005, nos 17, 21.
51 Boubli and Pérez Sánchez 1991, no. 36.
52 Brown 1991, pp. 147–8. Little is known about Cuevas, other than that he was born 1568, died in 1644 and apparently had many students. Palomino 1987, p. 93.
53 For painting, see Úbeda de los Cobos 2005, no. 24; Orso 1993, pp. 143–4.
54 Pérez Sánchez 1972a, no. 49.
55 For the painting, see Úbeda de los Cobos 2005, no. 18; for the drawing, McKim Smith 1980, no. 2.
56 Palomino 1987, pp. 205, 207 note 1; Pérez Sánchez 1978.
57 Úbeda de los Cobos 2005, no. 15; Jordan 2005, p. 33. For Crescenzi, see Cherry 1999, *passim*.
58 Boubli and Pérez Sánchez 1991, p. 104; Pérez Sánchez 1972b, pp. 152–4.
59 Ribera's prints of Saint Jerome, one dated 1621 (Brown 1973b, no. 4), the other from around the same time (Brown 1973b, no. 5). On Ribera's wider influence, see Brown 1989a pp. 43–4.
60 For a survey of 1650–1700, see Sullivan in Sullivan and Mallory 1982, pp. 7–35.
61 Salort Pons 2002, pp. 149–82.
62 García Cueto 2005.
63 Feinblatt 1992, pp. 112–15.
64 García Cueto 2005, figs 21, 28–30; Salort Pons 2002, pls 164–5, 168–70; Feinblatt 1992, figs 13.2–13.4.
65 García Cueto 2005, pp. 135–6 (a Spanish follower); Salort Pons 2002, pp. 176–7 (Mitelli and Colonna).
66 Pérez Sánchez 1986a, pp. 64–90.
67 Palomino 1987, pp. 308–9; Sullivan 1986, p. 36.
68 Sanz Ayán 2005.
69 Greer 1991, pp. 12–15; Brown and Elliott 1980, pp. 206–13.
70 Palomino 1987, p. 267.
71 Boubli and Pérez Sánchez 1991, no. 78.
72 Report of the entry with the print: *Noticia del recibimiento I entrada de la Reyna nuestra Señora Doña Maria-Ana de Austria en la muy noble i Leal Villa de Madrid*, 1650 (British Library, London, RB.23.b.4568). See also Sáenz de Miera Santos 1986; López Torrijos 1985a, pp. 148–56; for the drawing, Brown 1973, p. 376.
73 In the context of decorations for celebrations, see also the drawings from Rizi's circle in the British Museum: *Meleager and Atalanta Hunting the Calydonian Boar* (1846,0509.192) and *Venus in her Carriage Approaching the Deceased Adonis* (1846,0509.193).
74 Pérez Sánchez 1986a, p. 58.
75 Orso 1986, pp. 68–70.
76 Those responsible for decorating the Hall are described in detail by Palomino in his biography of Velázquez, including the specific scene shown in this drawing (Palomino 1987, pp. 167–8). See also García Cueto 2005, pp. 118–46; Pérez Sánchez 1986a, p. 71.
77 For a reconstruction of the fresco programme, see García Cueto 2005, fig. 23, p. 138.
78 Boubli and Pérez Sánchez 1991, no. 76; Harris 1961, pp. 101–5.
79 Angulo Iñiguez 1971, pp. 378–9.
80 Pérez Sánchez 1985, pp. 46–7.
81 Palomino 1987, p. 275.
82 Hellwig 2007, pp. 354–5; Pérez Sánchez 1986a, pp. 30–54.
83 Boubli and Pérez Sánchez 1991, no. 50; Lunn and Espinosa Carrión 1979, no. 3.
84 See, for example, *Studies for an Assumption* (Metropolitan Museum of Art): Lisa Banner in Brown 2010, no. 25; Bambach 1999a, p. 412. *The Visitation* (Getty Museum): Turner, Hendrix and Plazzotta 1997, no. 105. Also, the unpublished study for a ceiling decoration on verso of *Studies of Saint Ildefonso* (Biblioteca Nacional, Madrid, DIB/16/40/1).
85 Angulo Iñiguez 1959a, pp. 90–2.
86 Palomino 1987, p. 220.
87 Harris 1960.
88 Angulo Iñiguez 1959a, pl. xi.
89 For example, *Virgin and Child with Saint Teresa and Other Saints* (Museo del Prado, Madrid, FD.1397): Boubli and Pérez Sánchez 1991, no. 44.
90 Boubli and Pérez Sánchez 1991, no. 45.
91 Museo del Prado, Madrid, FD.1204 (375 x 234 mm).
92 For his work in Segovia, see Collar de Cáceres 1986.
93 No painting corresponding to the drawing is known, but *Saint Felix with the Virgin*, from before 1657, is mentioned by Díaz de la Valle. See Angulo Iñiguez 1959a, p. 105. For other of his paintings, see Angulo Iñiguez 1965, pp. 59–61.
94 Wethey 1958, pp. 19–23.
95 Palomino 1987, p. 217. There is evidence for drawings that no longer survive, see Barrio Moya 1983, pp. 409–10.
96 Díaz Garcia 2005, pp. 53–4; Tovar Martín 1975, pp. 101–8.
97 Pérez Sánchez 1986, p. 253.
98 Orso 1989, pp. 60–1; Marías and Bustamente 1985. The drawing is in the Metropolitan Museum of Art, New York. *Descripción de las honras que se hicieron a la Catholica Mag[d]. de D. Phelippe quarto Rey de las Españas y Nuevo mundo* …, Francisco Nieto, Madrid 1666 (British Library, 605.e.31).
99 Wethey 1958, pp. 22–3; Robinson 1876, no. 427.
100 Angulo Iñiguez 1959; Angulo Iñiguez 1958, p. 341, pl. iv.
101 For his architectural work, see Tovar Martín 1975, pp. 108–19.
102 Palomino 1987, p. 217.
103 For comparison, see the *Study for an Altar with Virgin and Child*, Biblioteca National, Madrid (DIB/16/35/10), where the image of the Virgin and Child is on a separate sheet and pasted on.
104 Wethey and Wethey 1966, fig. 5.
105 Palomino 1987, pp. 270–4; Pérez Sánchez 1986a, pp. 92–101.
106 Brown 1975, no. 3, pl. 3. The drawing is very close to a painting attributed to Herrera the Elder, see Pérez Sánchez and Navarrete Prieto 1996, fig. 27 (private collection).
107 Brown (1974, p. 133) dated the drawing to the 1660s, but the re-dating of *Saint Hermenegild* places the drawing in the mid-1650s (Brown 1975, p. 236).
108 Fernández-Santos Ortiz-Iribas 2005.
109 Brown 1975, no. 14; Pérez Sánchez 1972, p. 150, pl. lxiii (as anonymous but, according to Brown, verbally accepted by him as by Herrera).
110 Oesterreichische Nationalbibliothek, Vienna, Cod. Vindob. 13.217. For a description of the MSS, see Kraft 1957, p. 43. For the drawings, see Shergold and Varey in Vélez de Guevera 1970, pp. xxxvii–xliii.
111 Ceán Bermúdez 1800, II, p. 281.
112 Sullivan 1986, pp. 201–49.
113 The *Altar of the Immaculate Conception* has been dated to after 1665. See Boubli and Pérez Sánchez 1991, no. 60; Sullivan 1986, no. D43.
114 Drawings thought to be related to the entry survive. See Zapata Fernández de la Hoz 1993; Zapata Fernández de la Hoz 1991; Sullivan 1986, no. D19; López Torrijos 1985, pp. 239–50.
115 British Museum, 1860,0414.24. Páez Ríos 1981–3, no. 494.1. The same book contains two other prints, probably also by Coello. Sullivan 1986, no. E2.
116 Boubli and Pérez Sánchez 1991, no. 62; Sullivan 1986, no. D35.
117 Zapata Fernández de la Hoz and Carlos Gómez Argüete 2012, p. 31. The painting is not illustrated and the drawing is very different from others securely attributed to him.
118 León Tello and Sanz Sanz 1979a.
119 Virginia Tovar Martín in Santiago Paéz 1991, no. 91; Boubli and Pérez Sánchez 1991, no. 71.
120 Navarrete Prieto 2011, pp. 61–3.
121 Taylor 1950, p. 34 and Document 12, p. 55.
122 Zapata 2000; López Torrijos 1985. For his paintings, see Pérez Sánchez 1965.
123 Zapata 2000, pp. 126, 133–6 (as Torres); Sullivan 1986, no. D12 (as Coello).

124 Castañeda Becerra 2000, p. 63; Céan Bermúdez 1800, I, pp. 330–1.
125 Castañeda Becerra 2000, no. 6, pp. 100–2; Palomino 1987, p. 319.
126 Urrea Fernández 1975, fig. 3 (painting in the Museo de Arte de Cataluña) and fig. 5. The drawing is in the Casa de la Moneda, Madrid (Durán González-Meneses 1980, no. 28).
127 Cerezo is better known. See Piedra Adarves 2000; Buendía and Gutiérrez Pastor 1986, nos D.1–D.11; Pérez Sánchez 1972, pp. 81–2. For Escalante, see Pérez Sánchez 1972a, nos 127–8.
128 Hermoso Cuesta 2008, pp. 83–127.
129 Ibid., pp. 186–201; Ferrari and Scavizzi 1966, I, p. 203. Blas, Cruz de Carlos Varona and Matilla 2011. This book appeared too late for it to be fully cited in the present volume.
130 Biblioteca Nacional, Madrid, DIB/16/40/3.
131 Blas, Cruz de Carlos Varona and Matilla 2011; For summary, see Gallego Gallego 1979, pp. 149–70.
132 Courbes returned to France from 1622 to 1627, during which time he was closely associated with the workshop of Parisian printmaker Léonard Gaultier. For Courbes' work made during this trip, see Matilla 1991, pp. 1–4.
133 Vetter 1972, pp. 83–9 (Courbes), 72–8 (Popma), 78–82 (Schorquens) (British Library, 467.d.7.)
134 Ollero 1993, no. 216; Garcia Vega 1984, II, pp. 365–70; Páez Ríos 1981–3, no. 2009-4. The *Viage*... was printed in Madrid by Tomas Giunti.
135 Garcia Vega 1984, I, pp. 86–7; Hollstein XXVI (Dutch and Flemish), no. 25. Gallego suggests that Schorquens may have been part of Philip III's entourage in Portugal. Gallego Gallego 1979, p. 151.
136 McDonald 2000a.
137 Ceán Bermúdez 1800, V, pp. 246–7.
138 Brown 1988, pp. 137–54.
139 For Velázquez's influence on book illustration, see López Serrano 1960.
140 Antonio León Pinelo, *Pompa Funeral Honras y Exequias en la muerte De la muy Alta y Catolica Señora Doña Isabel de Borbón Reyna de las Españas y del Nuevo Mundo* ..., Diego Díaz de la Carrera, Madrid 1645. See Orso 1990.
141 Published in Francisco de los Santos, *Descripción breve del monasterio de S. Lorenzo*, Imprenta Real, Madrid 1657. For Velázquez's painting that provided the model, see López-Rey 1996, II, no. 120. For the print, see Ollero 1993, no. 251; Páez Ríos 1966–7, III, no. 2948-42.
142 Hollstein XVII (Dutch and Flemish), no. 82; Lafuente Ferrari 1960.
143 Páez Ríos 1966–7, II, no. 4219 (1-27).
144 Judson and Van de Velde, I, 1978, pp. 73–4.
145 Céan Bermúdez 1800, IV, p. 42.
146 Diego de Silva y Pacheco, *Commentaria theologica in primam partem Divi Thomae* (Biblioteca Nacional, Madrid, 3-76222).
147 *Descripcíon ... publica Entrada, que hizo la Reyna Nuestra Señora Doña Luisa de Borbón* ..., Madrid *c.*1680 (Biblioteca Nacional, Madrid, VE/126/73).
148 Carrete Parrondo 1987, p. 345.
149 Biblioteca Nacional, Madrid (*Saint Jerome*, 41259; *Cain and Abel*, 41260). Páez Ríos 1981–3, no. 423 1-2.
150 For the prints, see Kubler 1965.
151 The painting is mentioned by Ceán Bermúdez (1800, I, p. 254).
152 Carrete Parrondo 1987, fig. 500, p. 343.
153 *Saint Lawrence* after Lucas Vorsterman I, after Rubens (Biblioteca Nacional, Madrid, 12977; Hollstein XLIII, no. 88.g (Dutch and Flemish)); *Saint Bartholomew*, after Ribera (12976; Brown 1982, no. 12); Páez Ríos 1981–3, nos 1871.1-2.
154 *Vida del Don Juan de Palafox y Mendoza* ..., Lucas de Bedmar, Madrid 1671; Páez Ríos 1981–3, nos 2252-26 and 48.
155 Ceán Bermúdez 1800, I, p. 343.
156 Biblioteca Nacional, Madrid, 14519 and 45843. Carrete Parrondo 1987, fig. 545, p. 377; Páez Ríos 1981–3, no. 434; Ceán Bermúdez 1800, I, p. 266.
157 See essays in García Hidalgo 2006, vol. I. Also, García Hidalgo 1965.
158 On the subject of pattern prints and teaching, see Vega 1989a, pp. 7–12.

Chapter 5

1 Lleó Cañal 1996, p. 23.
2 Salort Pons 2006, pp. 57–64.
3 Valdivieso 1991, pp. 3–9.
4 Brown 1991, p. 115.
5 Pérez Sánchez and Navarrete Prieto 2006, pp. 19–52.
6 With regard to Córdoba, see Urquízar Herrera 2001.
7 Different dates have been given for Vargas' trips to Italy. See Redín Michaus 2007, pp. 282–7; Dacos 2004, pp. 17–21; Serrera 1984, pp. 391, 403 note 115. For Salviati's influence on Vargas, see Navarrete Prieto 2009, pp. 115–26.
8 Painting: National Gallery of Art, Washington, DC (K-1621). Drawing: Angulo Iñiguez and Pérez Sánchez 1975, no. 297.
9 Pérez Sánchez and Navarrete Prieto 1995, nos 1–3.
10 For Vargas in Italy, see Redín Michaus 2007, pp. 286–7. For these drawings and others, see García de la Torre 1997, pp. 42–6; Pérez Sánchez and Navarrete Prieto 1995, no. 2.
11 Pacheco 1990 edn, pp. 348, 415, 436, etc.
12 Ibid., p. 418; Camón Aznar 1970, p. 406.
13 For drawings, see Dacos 2004, figs 4, 10, 12; for the painting, Redín Michaus 2007, p. 283. I am grateful to Benito Navarrete for this information.
14 Rubio Lapaz 1993, pp. 21–3.
15 Ibid., pp. 27–33.
16 Ceán Bermúdez 1800, I, pp. 323–4.
17 Angulo Iñiguez and Pérez Sánchez 1975, nos 120–7.
18 Ibid., no. 121A. Boubli attributes another sheet to him (Boubli 2003, fig. 10.6).
19 Pacheco 1990 edn, p. 436.
20 Ibid., p. 440, trans. in Véliz 1986, p. 39.
21 The letter was published by Ceán Bermúdez 1800, V, pp. 273–315. See also Rubio Lapaz 1990, pp. 20–7; Brown 1978, pp. 45–6.
22 Muller identifies the influence of Taddeo Zuccaro in a drawing of the *Adoration of the Magi* attributed to Céspedes (Muller 2006, no. 5).
23 See revised chronology by Valdivieso 2008, pp. 40–5; also Serrera 1989, pp. 1–3; Dacos 1980; Camón Aznar 1970, pp. 391–402.
24 Navarrete Prieto and Pérez Sánchez 2009, no. 2; Valdivieso 2008, pp. 173–83; Pérez Sánchez and Navarrete Prieto 1995, nos 5–8; Serrera 1989, pp. 6–8; Dacos 1987.
25 Pérez Sánchez and Navarrete Prieto 1995, no. 6; Durán González-Meneses 1980, no. 14. Another drawing for the same commission depicts the *Visitation*: Pérez Sánchez and Navarrete Prieto 1995, no. 5. For discussion of the altar, see Valdivieso 2008, pp. 113–32.
26 A sheet Dacos attributes to Campaña and regards as preparatory for *Saint George and the Dragon* in the Metropolitan Museum of Art is not in fact by him: it is a drawn copy of part of a print by Philips Galle after Stradanus, published in his series of *Hunts and Animal Scenes* made around 1578–80. New Hollstein III, no. 423 (Stradanus). See Dacos 1987, pp. 363, 365.
27 Benito 1995, pp. 49–51.
28 Longhi 1953; Dacos (1984) attributes a number of drawings to Machuca. Lizzie Boubli sensibly regards the Louvre sheet to be a questionable attribution (Boubli 2002, no. 16; Boubli 1999, p. 354).
29 Boubli 2002, no. 12; Boubli and Pérez Sánchez 1991, no. 13.
30 A painting of this composition is not known. Boubli 2002, no. 13; Boubli and Pérez Sánchez 1991, no. 14.
31 Boubli 2002, nos 17, 18; Espinós Díaz 1979, no. 4.
32 Brown 1978, pp. 21–43.
33 Cacho Casal 2011; Cacho Casal 2010, p. 384; Carrete Parrondo 1986.
34 The bulk of the drawings are in the Museo Lázaro Galdiano, Madrid. Angulo Iñiguez and Pérez Sánchez 1975, nos 131–95.
35 Ibid., no. 144.
36 Pacheco 1990 edn; Brown 1978, pp. 44–62.
37 Pacheco 1990 edn, p. 349.
38 Ibid., pp. 433–45, trans. in Véliz 1986, pp. 35–43.

39 Pacheco 1990 edn, pp. 435–6.
40 Ibid., pp. 265–8.
41 Ibid., p. 126.
42 Pérez Sánchez and Navarrete Prieto 1995, no. 10.
43 Biblioteca Nacional, Madrid, DIB/13/1/65/2. López Torrijos 1982.
44 Cherry 1997; Cherry 1996.
45 For context, see Trusted 2007, pp. 72–4.
46 Kunoth 1964.
47 Pérez Sánchez and Navarrete Prieto 1995, no. 11.
48 Navarrete Prieto 2010 (the painting is the Musée Goya, Castres).
49 Pacheco 1990 edn, p. 309.
50 Angulo Iñiguez and Pérez Sánchez 1985, nos 102, 103, 109, 110.
51 Serrera 1996, fig. 4.2, p. 37; Valdivieso and Serrera 1985, no. 194.
52 Pacheco's drawing of *Envy* (Biblioteca Nacional, Madrid, DIB/16/3/14) has a thicker sheet of paper at the back, of exactly the same size, as does the *Torso* discussed above.
53 Pérez Sánchez and Navarrete Prieto 1985, no. 52 (as anonymous 'Zurbaranesque'); Valdivieso and Serrera 1985, nos 17, 20 (paintings); Valdivieso 2006.
54 The *Elevation of Cross* is in the Calcografía Nacional, Madrid, and the *Virgin of Sorrows* in the Museo Colegio de San Gregorio, Valladolid. For the *Virgin*, see Margarita de los Ángeles González in Valladolid 2009, no. 53; Carrete Parrondo 1987, pp. 353–4. For the sculpture, see Martín González 1974, pp. 325–31.
55 Angulo Iñiguez and Pérez Sánchez 1985, nos 232–46. Peter Cherry regards several of the drawings as having being studied from dressed models (Peter Cherry 1996, p. 73).
56 Portraits of *Fray Pablo Santa María* and *Pedro de Valderrama* (Cacho Casal 2010, figs 4–6). See also the chalk drawing of a head of a deceased Franciscan monk (Madrid, second half of the seventeenth century), Durán González-Meneses 1980, no. 101.
57 Delenda and Navarrete Prieto 2006, pp. 99–122; Pérez Sánchez and Navarrete Prieto 1996, pp. 366–8.
58 Angulo Iñiguez and Pérez Sánchez 1985, nos 1–8; Martínez Ripoll 1978, D.10-13.
59 Angulo Iñiguez and Pérez Sánchez 1985, nos 9–23; Martínez Ripoll 1978, Da.2–13 (the *Apostle* [St Peter?] is Da.13). Brown (1973, p. 377) suggests that they are by Herrera the Younger, but this has rightly been rejected. For a summary of opinions, see Lisa Banner in Brown 2010, p. 56; Pérez Sánchez and Navarette Prieto 1996, figs 12–23; Martínez Ripoll 1978, p. 230. For corresponding paintings of Apostles, see Pérez Sánchez and Navarrete Prieto 2006, nos 7–10.
60 Boubli and Pérez Sánchez 1991, no. 80; Pérez Sánchez and Navarrete Prieto 1985, nos 34–6; Martínez Ripoll 1978, D.21–D.23.
61 For Cano's influence, see Pérez Sánchez and Navarrete Prieto 1996, p. 382; Palomino 1987 edn, p. 127.
62 Martínez Ripoll 1978, G.1.
63 Páez Ríos 1981–3, nos 1021–3; Martínez Ripoll 1978, G.4; Martínez Ripoll 1973.
64 McDonald 2006, p. 376.
65 Martínez Ripoll 1978, Gp. 1–4; Ceán Bermúdez 1800, II, p. 277. For other printmakers working in Seville around the same time, see Carrete Parrondo 1987, pp. 359–63.
66 Carrete Parrondo 1987, pp. 361–2.
67 For summary, Véliz 2011, pp. 15–28, 565–71; Véliz 2001, pp. 25–30.
68 For documentation regarding his time in Seville, see Aterido Fernández 2002.
69 For Cano as sculptor, see Sánchez-Mesa Martín 2000.
70 Véliz 2011, no. 43 (for other early drawings, see nos 41–2); Zahira Véliz in Pérez Sánchez and Navarrete Prieto 2006, no. 58; Wethey 1952, p. 218.
71 Véliz 2011, no. 52.
72 Ibid., no. 14; Boubli and Pérez Sánchez 1991, no. 110, Wethey 1958, p. 20.
73 Plate 23 from Bonasone's *Passion of Christ*. Bartsch.XV.118.33 (British Museum, H,4.25). For discussion of painting in the Los Angeles County Museum, see Wethey 1955, p. 59.
74 Rodríguez G. de Ceballos 2001.
75 Véliz 2011, no. 120; Lisa Banner in Brown 2010, no. 11.
76 Véliz 2011, no. 101.
77 Ibid., no. 26.
78 Véliz 2007.
79 Ceán Bermúdez 1800, I, p. 214.
80 For Cano's print sources, see Véliz 2001, pp. 35–41.
81 Matilla 2001, pp. 79–92.
82 The drawing is in the Kunsthalle in Hamburg, M-116/38497. Véliz 2011, no. 49.
83 The composition is very close to several of Bocanegra's paintings, for example, the *Mystical Marriage of Saint Catherine* (Orozco Díaz 1937, no. 146).
84 Palomino reports his association with Van Dyck (Palomino 1987 edn, p. 189). Pérez Sánchez 1986, p. 302; Sánchez Cantón 1930, III, no. 245.
85 British Museum 1846,0509.200. A number of minor Granadine artists are discussed by Pérez Sánchez 1986, pp. 302–12; Orozco Díaz 1937, pp. 1–13.
86 Tatsakis and Roglán 2004, no. 11; McDonald 2000.
87 For the contract, see Llordén 1960, pp. 130–3.
88 Navarrete Prieto and García de la Torre 2008; Muller 2008; Muller 1963.
89 Palomino 1987 edn, p. 200; Ceán Bermúdez 1800, I, p. 291.
90 Navarrete Prieto and García de la Torre 2008, no. 120, but it is not a direct copy.
91 McDonald 1998a.
92 García de la Torre in Navarrete Prieto and García de la Torre 2008, pp. 151, 719. His only signed and dated drawing is the 1677 *Adoration of the Shepherds* in the Museo de Bellas Artes, Córdoba, CE0896D. García de la Torre 2006, p. 192; Palomino 1987 edn, p. 249. See also *Christ Entering Jerusalem*, British Museum 1846,0509.187.
93 Palomino 1987 edn, p. 246.
94 Brown 1983a, no. 3.
95 Muller 1963, nos 96–105. Biblioteca Nacional, Madrid, DIB/15/46(1–10).
96 For example, the project for an altar, signed and dated 1663, in the Museo de Bellas Artes, Córdoba, CE0906D.
97 Brown 1991, pp. 241–2.
98 Mena Marqués 1982; Brown 1976; Angulo Iñiguez 1974.
99 For Castillo, see Valdivieso and Serrera 1985, pp. 303–15. For the drawings, see Angulo Iñiguez and Pérez Sánchez 1985, pp. 17–18; Turner, Hendrix and Plazzotta 1997, nos 108–9 (though probably by Giovanni Battista Castello).
100 Pérez Sánchez and Navarrete Prieto 1995, no. 74; Angulo Iñiguez 1981, I, pp. 243–63; II, nos 1–13; Brown 1976, no. 5.
101 Brown 1976, no. 10.
102 Pérez Sánchez 1982, p. 305.
103 Brown 1976, pp. 44–6.
104 Gestoso y Pérez 1916, pp. 66–76.
105 Navarette Prieto and Pérez Sánchez 2009, p. 21; Aranda Bernal 2004, esp. p. 92; Aranda Bernal and Quiles García 2000, p. 121; Ceán Bermúdez 1800, III, p. 74.
106 The inventory was made in 1751; Aranda Bernal 2004, doc. 4, pp. 133–52 and commentary pp. 153–61; Ceán Bermúdez 1800, II, p. 32.
107 For the thorny issues regarding copies after Murillo, see Brown 1983 and further references to those who disagree with his conclusions. Forthcoming studies by Jonathan Brown and Manuela Mena Marqués will no doubt add to the discussion.
108 Pérez Sánchez 1986, p. 299; McKim Smith 1974, no. 40.
109 Cherry 1996, pp. 69–74.
110 Brown 1976, nos 12, 13.
111 Boubli 2002, no. 85; Pérez Sánchez and Navarrete Prieto 1995, no. 76; Boubli and Pérez Sánchez 1991, no. 85.
112 Angulo Iñiguez 1974, pp. 101–2.
113 Brown 1983, pp. 160–3; Angulo Iñiguez 1981, no. 310; Brown 1976, no. 30, painting fig. 57, p. 106.
114 Brown 1976, no. 86.
115 For introduction to Murillo's followers, see Valdivieso 1982.
116 Serra Giráldez 1990, p. 20.
117 Ibid., p. 24; Pemán 1977.

118 No corresponding painting survives, but see his *Apparition of the Virgin to Saint Peter Nolasco* in the Museo de Bellas Artes, Seville (Serra Giráldez 1990, pl. 7).
119 Ibid., pp. 19–21; Quiles 2005, pp. 37–42; Ceán Bermúdez 1800, v, p. 48.
120 Barrio Moya 2000.
121 Quiles 2006, no. 24.
122 Quiles García 2008; Valdivieso 2003, pp. 462–3.
123 For his role at the academy, see Kinkead 2009, pp. 518–28. Alonso de la Sierra and Quiles 1998–9, p. 84.
124 Palomino 1987 edn, p. 234.
125 For his drawings, see Navarrete Prieto and Pérez Sánchez 2009, nos 41–4; Ceán Bermúdez 1800, iv, p. 360.
126 Kinkead 1978.
127 Palomino 1987 edn, p. 303.
128 Pérez Sánchez and Navarrete Prieto 1995, no. 101; Valdivieso 1991, pp. 86–7 and no. 14. Kinkead considers the drawing to be a study for a painting that is a shop piece, now in a private collection in Córdoba (Kinkead 1978, d.3 [drawing], no. 35 [painting]).
129 Valdivieso 1991, no. 71; Angulo Iñiguez 1970.
130 For Martínez, see Pérez Sánchez 2004. For Valdés, see Fernández López 2003, pp. 59–60, 130–40; Boubli 2002, nos 150–4; Pérez Sánchez and Navarrete Prieto 1995, nos 122–5.
131 García de la Torre 1997, pp. 127–32.
132 Morales 1993.
133 Navarrete Prieto 1998.
134 Carrete Parrondo 1987, pp. 366–8; Ceán Bermúdez 1800, i, p. 206.
135 One of the prints, *Noviembre* (Carrete Parrondo 1987, fig. 532), for example, is a copy in reverse after Jan Van de Velde the Younger, Hollstein xxxiii (Dutch and Flemish), no. 56. The suggested publication date, *c.*1660, would significantly extend the working dates traditionally given for Rodríguez (active 1636–8?).
136 Carrete Parrondo 1987, p. 363; Gallego Gallego 1979, p. 217.
137 Ceán Bermúdez 1800, iv, p. 359; Carrete Parrondo 1987, p. 364.
138 Over 200 prints by Cornelio Schut the Elder have been catalogued by Hollstein xxvi (Dutch and Flemish).
139 Quiles García 2008, figs 6, 7.
140 Two copies in the British Library, 487.i.36 (207.e.10; 1871 re-edition). Published by the widow of Nicolàs Rodríguez, Seville.
141 Mulcahy 2010.
142 Páez Ríos 1981–3, no. 2190.2. British Museum, 1868,1114.405.
143 A sheet of four emblems is signed ‘A 1672 Lucas Baldes F^{A} de edad de 11 A^{o}S’. British Museum, 1854,0708.52. See Fernández López 2003, no. 4, p. 142.
144 Roda Peña 2003, nos 10–12; Banda y Vargas 1978.
145 Wunder 2001.
146 Gallego Gallego 1979, pp. 217–8; Carrete Parrondo 1987, pp. 369–74. See also a drawing attributed to Arteaga of the *Presentation of the Virgin in the Temple* (Boubli 2002, no. 36).

Chapter 6

1 Natale 2001. For an introduction to subject, see Falomir Faus 1994.
2 Gaye 1840, ii, pp. 89–90.
3 Benito Doménech 1998, pp. 28–9; Gómez 1998; Ruiz Manero 1996, i, pp. 17–18, 21–2, etc; Ibáñez Martínez 1994, pp. 230–2; Cordellier 1994.
4 Boubli 2002, nos 23–31; Cordellier 1998.
5 In particular, see Yáñez's metalpoint drawing on grey prepared paper, *Studies of Two Figures*, where the head of the woman in profile and the method of hatching to make the figure stand in relief, comes close to Leonardo. Boubli 2002, no. 28.
6 Boubli 2002, no. 26 (and further refs); Cordellier 1998, pp. 228–9; Ibáñez Martínez 1997, p. 140; Cordellier 1994, p. 417.
7 Gavara and Gómez Ferrer 1998; Garín Ortiz de Taranco 1978, Document 26, p. 194.
8 For the Macip family, see Albi 1979.
9 Benito Doménech and Galdón 1997, pp. 19, 27–8; Benito 1995, pp. 56–66.
10 Benito Doménech and Valles Borras 1992.
11 Also known as Joan Macip Navarro; Benito Doménech 2000.
12 Muller 1976; Angulo Iñiguez and Pérez Sánchez 1975, nos 168–78.
13 For the altar, see Benito Doménech 2000, no. 20; for the drawing, Garín Llombart 1979, no. 40. Angulo Iñiguez and Pérez Sánchez 1975, no. 169.
14 See also another drawing of the *Holy Martyrs* for the same commission (Museo de Bellas Artes, Valencia), regarded by Albi, Pérez Sánchez and Garín Llombart as autograph but by Benito Doménech, with better reason, as a careful copy: Benito Doménech 2000, p. 94; Albi 1979, ii, pp. 47–9, iii, pl. cxxvi; Garín Llombart 1979, no. 41; Angulo Iñiguez and Pérez Sánchez 1975, no. 169. Nevertheless, it indicates the drawing activity in the Juanes workshop and the practical use for recording compositions.
15 For an analysis of their meaning, see González García 1999, pp. 39–43.
16 *Predication of Saint Stephen before the Sanhedrin*, pen, ink and wash, 330 x 240 mm. Nationalmuseum, Stockholm (Angulo Iñiguez and Pérez Sánchez 1975, no. 170; Benito Doménech 2000, pp. 153–4). *Saint Stephen Being Lowered into the Tomb*, pen, ink, wash and white highlight, 360 x 275 mm. Uffizi, Florence (Angulo Iñiguez and Pérez Sánchez 1975, no. 172; Benito Doménech 2000, pp. 157–9). *The Last Supper*, pen, wash and touches of highlight, 200 x 420 mm. Museo de Bellas Artes, Valencia. Benito Doménech 2000 pp. 251–2.
17 Vicente Joanes, also known as Vicente Macip Comes. Espinós Díaz 1999, no. 2, pp. 20–23; Benito Doménech 1996, no. 16.
18 Hernández Guardiola 2010. Drawings by him have not been identified with absolute certainty, but a number from the ‘circle of Juanes’ are thought to be by him. Espinós Díaz 1979, no. 3.
19 Espinós Díaz 1979, p. 17.
20 Ibid., no. 5; Espinós Díaz 1975, pp. 411–2.
21 Casey 1979; Elliott 1963.
22 Benito Doménech 1988, pp. 35–6; Fitz Darby 1938, pp. 71–86.
23 Fitz Darby 1938, p. 277 (as Juan Ribalta); Angulo Iñiguez and Pérez Sánchez 1988, p. 73 (as anonymous copy after Cambiaso). The Cambiaso sheet is in the Uffizi, Florence, 13668.
24 For several lost drawings, see Kowal 1984.
25 Drawings: *Apparition of Christ to Saint Vincent Ferrer* (Museo Nacional de Arte de Cataluña, Barcelona, mna/gdg 66118-d), *Saint Bruno* (Museo Bellas Artes, Valencia), Espinós Díaz 1997, nos 4, 7. The painting is in the Museo de Bellas Artes, Valencia, Espinós Díaz 1979, no. 119.
26 Carrete Parrondo 1987, p. 350; Gallego Gallego 1979, pp. 196–7.
27 Benito Doménech 1987, no. 66, pp. 234–5.
28 Kowal 1984, p. 772.
29 Kowal 1985, pp. 84–5, Appendix C, pp. 209–11; Ainaud de Lasarte 1957.
30 Biblioteca Nacional, Madrid. dib/13/1/19. Angulo Iñiguez and Pérez Sánchez 1988, no. 377; Benito Doménech 1987, pp. 186–7; Kowal 1985, no. f-46m(3). In the drawing, the upper section with angels has not been copied and the sheet appears to be unfinished.
31 For Juan Ribalta, see Kowal 1985, pp. 109–18.
32 Palomino 1987 edn, p. 91.
33 See discussion of Juan Ribalta's *Birth of Christ* in Benito Doménech 1996, no. d.4, p. 156; Boubli and Pérez Sánchez 1991, no. 129.
34 Espinós Díaz 1997, no. 2.
35 Boubli 2002, no. 118.
36 Kowal 1985, p. 111.
37 Benito Doménech 1988, pp. 53, 114; Benito Doménech 1987, pp. 216, 232.
38 Dürer's *Presentation of Christ in the Temple* from the *Life of the Virgin* series (Bartsch. vii.132.88) provides a good comparison. See also Juan Ribalta's paintings for

the parish church of Andilla (Valencia). Fernando Francisco Martínez Serrano in Segorbe 2001, no. 134; Kowal 1985, no. J9a–h.
39 Baer 2008, p. 60.
40 On the verso is an autograph inscription, 'En 16 setembre del An 16.7', which has been interpreted as 1627. Espinós Díaz 1997, no. 9; Adela Espinós Díaz in Benito Doménech 1996, no. D.7. For the painting, see Falomir Faus 2001, no. 2, pp. 40–4, 195–7.
41 Espinós Díaz 1997, no. 16.
42 Pérez Sánchez 2002; Espinós Díaz 1997, nos 24–37; Adela Espinós Díaz in Benito Doménech 1996, nos D.5, D.6.
43 Espinós Díaz 1997, pp. 122–3, nos 42–57; Angulo Iñiguez and Pérez Sánchez 1988, pp. 117–43.
44 For the print, see Rosand and Muraro 1976, no. 71.
45 Espinós Díaz 1997, no. 42. The inscription in the same ink as the drawing reads: 'De mano estevan marco ysoylo en Madr[id] el primer día de Junio del año mil y sey cientos y sinquenta y uno en casa de su amigo y maestro francisco de aguirre.'
46 Espinós Díaz 1997, nos 38 (*Saint John*), 39.
47 Benito Doménech and Galdón 1994; Angulo Iñiguez and Pérez Sánchez 1988, nos 149–62 verso; Benito Doménech 1984 (thought to be by Miguel March, p. 277).
48 Kowal 1985, pp. 121–3.
49 See figures in Benito Doménech and Galdón 1994.
50 Navarrete Prieto 1995, pp. 136–7.
51 Angulo Iñiguez and Pérez Sánchez 1988, nos 402–7.
52 Espinós Díaz 1997, no. 61.
53 Angulo Iñiguez and Pérez Sánchez 1988, nos 388–91; McKim Smith 1974, no. 39.
54 DeGrazia Bohlin 1979, no. 101; Bartsch.XVII.69.63. British Museum, U,2.93.
55 López Azorín, Navarrete Prieto and Salort Pons 2001, p. 398; Navarrete Prieto, 1995, fig. 6, pp. 139–40.
56 The painting is in the Museo de Bellas Artes, Valencia. Benito Doménech 1988, no. 19.
57 López Azorín, Navarrete Prieto and Salort Pons 2001, pp. 405–24.
58 Orellana 1930, pp. 353–4.
59 Espinós Díaz 1997, nos 75–8; Angulo Iñiguez and Pérez Sánchez 1988, nos 409–17.
60 Orellana 1930, p. 354.
61 Angulo Iñiguez and Pérez Sánchez 1988, nos 409–10 state that the drawings have inscriptions on the mount that read: 'Sacerdote Mosen Dominco Saura', of which there is no trace. These were given to Flaminio Allegrini by Gere and Pouncey 1983, I, nos 16, 17.
62 See in particular *The Rest on the Flight into Egypt*, signed 'Saura' (Espinós Díaz 1997, no. 75).
63 Orellana 1930, p. 338.
64 Palomino 1987 edn, p. 377.
65 Páez Ríos 1981–3, no. 503-1. Only one other signed print by Conchillo's is known, *Saint Felix of Cantalico*, Páez Ríos 1981–3, no. 503-2.
66 Espinós Díaz 1997, no. 79.
67 Palomino 1987 edn, p. 378; Orellana 1930, p. 201. Conchillos' student Evaristo Muñoz (1671–1737) also established an academy of drawing where many students who developed into successful artists were trained. See Bérchez 1987, pp. 62–3 note 86.
68 Palomino 1987 edn, p. 379.
69 Espinós Díaz 1997, no. 110.
70 Palomino 1987 edn, p. 122.
71 For Ribera between Játiva and Naples, see Milicua 1992.
72 Colomer 2009; Muto 2009.
73 Finaldi 2005. Print entries by Andrea Bayer in Pérez Sánchez and Spinosa 1992, nos 71–88; and drawing entries by Manuela Mena, nos 89–120; see also entries D.1–D.64 in the expanded Spanish edition (1992); Brown 1982; Brown 1973b.
74 Andrea Bayer in Pérez Sánchez and Spinosa 1992, no. 71, p. 174. Saltillo 1940–1, p. 247.
75 Brown 1973b, nos 1, 2.
76 Ibid., nos 4, 6.
77 McDonald 1991.
78 Andrea Bayer in Pérez Sánchez and Spinosa 1992, no. 82; Brown 1973b, no. 12.
79 Bury 2001, p. 78.
80 Andrea Bayer in Pérez Sánchez and Spinosa 1992, no. 84; Brown 1973b, no. 14.
81 Brown 1982, p. 78.
82 Bambach 2009; Finaldi 2005.
83 De Dominici 2008 (1742), pt III, pp. 32–3 , quoted in Brown 1982, p. 79.
84 Ceán Bermúdez 1800, IV, p. 189.
85 McDonald 1999, p. 371.
86 Drawing: Brown 1974a, no. 3; print: DeGrazia Bohlin 1979, no. 21, pp. 468–9. British Museum, 1855,0214.86.
87 Finaldi 2005, pp. 24–7.
88 Teylers Museum, Haarlem, illustrated in Brown 1982, fig. 106, p. 87; Rhode Island School of Design, Providence, Brown 1973b, no. 32.
89 Mena Marques 1992, p. 201.
90 Brown 2010, p. 40.
91 *Adoration*, Brown 2010, no. 10; *Martyrdom*, Brown 1973, no. 35.
92 Cited in Brown 1973b, p. 117.

Chapter 7

1 Bottineau 1962 (1700–46); Morales y Marín 1994 (1750–1808).
2 Kasl and Stratton 1997.
3 For a summary of the French influence in Spain, mainly during the first half of the eighteenth century, see Luxenberg 1997.
4 The recent study by Jesusa Vega places these developments in the context of the Enlightenment. See Vega 2010, esp. chap. 2.
5 Ansón Navarro 2008, pp. 54–8; García-Toraño Martínez 2004, p. 359.
6 For Churriguera, see Blasco Esquivias 2003, pp. 272–9; Rodríguez G. de Ceballos 1971, pp. 17–23, 30–4; García y Bellido 1929.
7 Other members of the Churriguera family who practiced as architects and sculptors were also active draughtsmen. See Rodríguez G. de Ceballos 1971.
8 Blasco Esquivas 2003, pp. 265–72; Blasco Esquivas 1991; Corral 1974. For Coello and Pereda, see Chapter 4 in the present volume.
9 José Manuel Barbeito in García-Toraño Martínez 2009, no. 13; Aterido Fernández 1995–6, pp. 135–7; Zapata Fernández de la Hoz 1991a.
10 *Historia de la Conquista* …: British Library, 9771.f.13.
11 Blasco Esquivas 1991, II, pt 7, pp. 1219–1348; Agulló y Cobo 1977.
12 See drawings in García-Toraño Martínez 2009.
13 Aterido Fernández 1995–6, p. 137; Blasco Esquivas 1991, I, pp. 203–5; Bonet Correa 1989, pp. 147–52.
14 Earlier, in 1686, Ardemans painted *The Apotheosis of Saint Francis* for the ceiling of the sacristy of the Chapel of Christ of Sorrows. See Aterido Fernández 1995–6, pp. 138–9.
15 For summary, see Luna 1995. For drawings, Úbeda de los Cobos 2003; Pérez Sánchez 1986, pp. 335–7; for van Loo, see Luna 1978. For these artists in relation to their Spanish contemporaries, see Luxenberg 1997, pp. 41–5.
16 Luna 1978, p. 332.
17 Luna 1981, pp. 100–1; Held 1968, pp. 194–5.
18 Luna 1981, no. 90; Held 1968, no. Z.20.
19 Ceán Bermúdez 1800, II, p. 301.
20 Luna 1981, nos 108–9.
21 Santiago Paéz 1995.
22 Santiago Paéz 1990, p. 15; Santiago Paéz 1989.
23 Santiago Paéz 1990, nos 44–57; Santiago Paéz 1989a, nos 79–96.
24 Santiago Paéz 1989a, no. 82; Pérez Sánchez 1986, pp. 333–4.
25 Pérez Samper 2003.
26 Examples include the *Portrait of Isabel* formerly in the collection of Lázaro Galdiano (Santiago Páez 1989a, no. 27); *Portrait of Isabel holding Charles III*, 1716 (Santiago Páez 1990, no. 14); *Portrait of María Luisa of Savoy*, 1710, gouache on parchment, Madrid, private collection (illustrated in Morán Turina 2003, no. III.92, p. 502).

27 Santiago Páez 2004a, p. 160, no. B3, p. 488; Santiago Páez 1990, no. 20. Santiago observes that a signed drawing the National Gallery of Scotland was possibly preparatory for the painting, but there are too many differences for this to be possible (National Galleries of Scotland, Edinburgh, NG D4815). For the importance of Rigaud in Spain, see Morán Turina 1990, pp. 21–38; also Úbeda de los Cobos 2003, pp. 89–140. For an impression of the Drevet print, see British Museum 1872,0713.44.
28 Isabel drew herself and was a devoted collector of books. Santiago Páez 2004b. Her own pastels hung on the walls of the royal residence of La Granja. Pérez Samper 2003, pp. 361–83; Lavalle-Cobo 2000.
29 Morales y Marín 1994, pp. 89–96; Bottineau 1962.
30 For survey of the period, see Santiago Páez and Vinatea 2004.
31 Bonet Correa 1979, I, pp. 12–16; Gallego Gallego 1979, pp. 237–41; Ceán Bermúdez 1800, II, pp. 310–12.
32 Páez Rios 1981–3, no. 1056.1-40. *Our Lady of the Rosary* is dated 1721. Matilla Tascon 1982, p. 187.
33 Similar musical angels occur in his drawing for a title page that is completely pricked for transfer. Gutiérrez Pastor 2008, no. 48. Other drawings survive in the Biblioteca Nacional, Madrid. See Gutiérrez Pastor 1982.
34 Bonet Correa 1979, II (facsimile).
35 Illustrated in Carrete Parrondo 1987, figs 586, 587, p. 411; Bonet Correa 1979, I, pp. 41–2.
36 Santiago Páez and Vinatea 2004, pp. 382–3; Morán Turina 1990, fig. 8; Bonet Correa 1979, I, pp. 26–7.
37 Ceán Bermúdez 1800, II, p. 312. For a discussion of minor printmakers, some of who were trained by Irala, see Gallego Gallego 1979, pp. 241–3.
38 Ceán Bermúdez 1800, IV, p. 27.
39 The first volume to the treatise published in 1715 contained engravings by the Valencian painter and printmaker Hipólito Rovira y Brocandel. See Bonet Correa 1973.
40 Carrete Parrondo 1987, pp. 400–2.
41 The painting is in the collection of the Real Academia de Bellas Artes de San Fernando, Madrid.
42 Quoted by Gallego Gallego 1979, p. 247.
43 For a history of the Academy, see Bédat 1989. For the significance of printmaking in the Academy within the context of wider cultural and scientific advances, see Vega 2010, pp. 217–60.
44 Cioffi 1989, p. 186.
45 Bédat 1989, pp. 27–30. There had been attempts to establish an academy in Spain since the early seventeenth century, none of which met success (see Chapter 4).
46 For a list of academic positions in the Academy during the eighteenth century, see Fernández Agudo and Sánchez de León Fernández 1988.
47 Regarding the teaching of engraving in Spain, see Vega 1989, pp. 90–102. For Prieto's early training in Salamanca, see Nieves Rupérez Almajano 1997, pp. 415–41.
48 Carrete Parrondo 1987, p. 439.
49 Bédat 1989, p. 273; Gallego Gallego 1979, pp. 267–8.
50 Of this group, Carmona and Cruz Cano are discussed below; for López, see Líter Mayayo 2002.
51 Bédat 1989, pp. 278–9
52 Villena 1992, p. 85; Carrete Parrondo 1987, p. 440.
53 Vega 2010, pp. 231–3.
54 Ibid., pp. 386–90.
55 Bédat 1989, p. 27.
56 Ciruelos Gonzalo 1994, pp. 134–41.
57 Cánovas del Castillo and Lasarte Pérez-Arregui 1994, pp. 186–8. Regarding the teaching of drawing in Spain, see Vega 1989a, pp. 7–29.
58 Alisa Luxenberg in Kasl and Stratton 1997, no. 5; Luna 1981, no. 82.
59 Cherry 2006, pp. 31–2.
60 Ibid., p. 32; Tufts 1985, pp. 9–11, no. 1.
61 Arrese 1973, pp. 21–59.
62 Pérez Sánchez 1977, pp. 35–49; Arrese 1973, pp. 103–14.
63 Pérez Sánchez 1986, pp. 346–8; for less-known artists, ibid., pp. 349–51.
64 For discussion of the competition and the winners for each year, see Azcárate Luxan et al. 1994.
65 Many are illustrated in Azcárate Luxan et al., 1994; see also Ciruelos Gonzalo and García Sepúlveda 1989.
66 Claye 1974.
67 Helston 1989, pp. 19–23; Bottineau 1962, pp. 520–54.
68 For general discussion, see Morales y Marín 1994; Cioffi 1997
69 Bray 1999, p. 416.
70 Cioffi 1984, pp. 434–40.
71 Arnaiz 1999, pp. 13–22.
72 Ibid., nos 21a, b, c. Morales y Marín 1992a, pp. 239–40; Helston 1989, nos 2 (Palacio Real, Madrid), 3a,b (El Pilar).
73 García-Toraño Martínez 2009, no. 50; Arnaiz 1999, D.8.
74 These are not recorded by Arnaiz (1999).
75 Ibid., nos D.15–46, G.1–52; Ceán Bermúdez 1800, II, p. 222. The inventory made after his death records a large number of drawings, some of which have been identified. Bray 1999, p. 421; see also Arnaiz 1988, nos 1–21.
76 Arnaiz 1999, pp. 41–61.
77 Sambrico 1958.
78 Morales y Marín 1996a, pp. 85–8; Pérez Sánchez 1977, pp. 21–9.
79 For his first work at the Factory in 1756, see Espinós Díaz 1982, p. 188.
80 The Castillo sketchbooks are in the Museo del Prado, Madrid, D.5540–D.5979, D.6024–D.6027.
81 Roettgen 2003, pp. 217–78.
82 Ibid., pp. 260–4; Úbeda de los Cobos 1987.
83 Morales y Marín 1994, pp. 114–35; For summary, see Helston 1989, pp. 13, 15, 17.
84 Ceán Bermúdez 1800, III, pp. 127–8.
85 Ponz 1947, VI, esp. p. 571. See also note 132 below.
86 For drawings, see Roettgen 1999, pp. 419–87; Agueda 1980.
87 Ponz quoted by Pérez Sánchez 1986, pp. 363–4; Ceán Bermúdez 1800, III, p. 127.
88 For a complete analysis of the ceiling, the individual figures in chalk and oil studies, see Roettgen 1999, nos 299–300.
89 Sancho 1997, pp. 515–16.
90 Agueda 1980, p. 84.
91 Urrea Fernández 1977, p. 221.
92 For other calligraphers, see Cotarelo y Mori 1913.
93 British Library, C.119.k.1.
94 Arnáez 1972, no. 139, p. 136.
95 Bray 1996, p. 54, figs 72, 73.
96 The Museo del Prado, for example, has around 450 drawings by him. Arnáez 1975, pp. 17–146. Also Held 1968a.
97 De la Mano 2011, I, p. 484 (as Bayeu); Morales y Marín 1996, no. 75 (as Maella).
98 For biography, see Morales y Marín 1996, pp. 33–92.
99 For drawings, see De la Mano 2011; Morales y Marín 1996, nos 1–186; Pérez Sánchez 1977, pp. 57–78; Mollinedo 1973, pp. 145–57.
100 De la Mano 2011, I, nos II.17, II.18; Morales y Marín 1996, nos 17, 18.
101 De la Mano 1998; Morales y Marín 1996, pp. 46, 105–8; Morales y Marín 1994, pp. 143–4.
102 De la Mano 2011, II , nos VI.1.6, VI.II.7; Morales y Marín 1996, nos 26, 27; Mollinedo 1973, pp.146–8.
103 De la Mano 2011, II, no. V.22.
104 Morales y Marín 1997, pp. 157–204. See entries by Javier Gonzalez de Durana and José Juan González de Txabarri in Bilbao 1991, nos 32–88; Carrete Parrondo 1991.
105 Calvo Serraller 1996, pp. 25–7; Symmons 1987.
106 See relevant years in Azcárate Luxan et al. 1994.
107 Javier Gonzalez de Durana in Bilbao 1991, no. 35; Delgado 1957, no. 3.
108 Morales y Marín 1997, pp. 43–5; Baticle 1966; Delgado 1957, p. 24.
109 Morales y Marín 1997, no. 9 (painting), no. 1 (prints), also p. 111; Delgado 1957, no. 7; Gaya Nuño 1952, no. 6, p. 139.
110 Delgado 1957, no. 8.

111 Ceán Bermúdez 1800, IV, p. 55.
112 See 'series e ilustraciones de libros' in Morales y Marín 1997, pp. 211–24.
113 Flipart had been appointed painter and printmaker to the Privy Chamber (*pintor y grabador de cámara*) in May 1753.
114 Biblioteca Nacional, Madrid, IH/3161/22/IG; Luna 1979.
115 Vega 1995, fig. 104, p. 158. The print is mentioned by Ceán: Ceán Bermúdez 1800, III, p. 128.
116 Madrid 1996b, no. 102. For the painting, see Sánchez Cantón 1927, pp. 3–9; print: British Museum, 1907,0515.84.74.
117 Morales y Marín 1996, nos 1–5; Páez Rios 1981–3, no. 462.1-4.
118 Morales y Marín 1996, no. 1. A preparatory drawing for the print, signed 'José del Castillo lo dibujó 1778', is in the Biblioteca Nacional, Madrid (DIB/13/4/22). Martínez Iborra 1933, p. 137; Buendía and Gutiérrez Pastor 1986, no. 78; Tormo 1927, p. 253.
119 Morales y Marín 1996, nos 37–44; Sambrico 1958, pp. 20–1.
120 Páez Ríos 1981–3, no. 1278.1. For its preparatory drawing, see De la Mano 2011, II, no. VIII.26; Morales y Marín 1996, no. 24.
121 Ceán Bermúdez 1800, I, p. 105. Vega increases Ceán's count by one (Vega 1992, nos 27–40). Páez Rios adds two further possible attributions: Páez Ríos 1981–3, no. 230.1-16 (attributions: 15 and 16).
122 See, for example, the *Liberation of Saint Peter* and the *Incredulity of Saint Thomas*. British Museum, 1929,1021.5 and 6. Páez Ríos 1981–3, no. 230-12, 13.
123 Morales y Marín 1995 pp. 40–2.
124 Ibid., nos 132, 133; Vega 1992, nos 34, 35; Páez Rios 1981–3, no. 230.14; Ceán Bermúdez 1800, I, p. 102.
125 Rueda 1990.
126 Vega 2010, pp. 236–41; Carrete Parrondo and Villena 1990, pp. 133–7; Carrete Parrondo 1989, pp. 14–18.
127 For Carmona in Paris, see Carrete Parrondo 1989, pp. 20–4; Carrete Parrondo 1987, pp. 485–91; Carrete Parrondo 1980.
128 Carrete Parrondo 1989, nos 29, 30 (printed key).
129 Ibid., pp. 28–9.
130 Eighteen vols published 1772–94; vols V and VI, devoted to Madrid, published 1776. See Madrid 1996b, no. 96. Ponz 1947, V, pp. 405–503.
131 Ponz 1947, VI, pp. 555–6, quoted and trans. Sayre 1974, pp. 1, 18.
132 Ponz 1947, VI, pp. 565–82.
133 Cumberland 1806, p. 380.
134 Rose 1981, pp. 173–81.
135 For Juan Antonio, see Páez Rios 1981–3, no. 1968.1-72.
136 Hermoso Cuesta 2008, pp. 139–62; Morales y Marín 1996, nos 16–31; Vega 1992, nos 1108–27.
137 Carrete Parrondo 1987, pp. 525–30.
138 Vega 1992, p. 222; Carrete Parrondo 1987, pp. 564–75.
139 Vega 1992, nos 1139–86.
140 Carrete Parrondo 1989, nos 316–21.
141 Ibid., no. 317.
142 For an account of his career, see Barrena, Matilla and Villena 1993, pp. 23–37.
143 Ibid., no. 146; Vega 1992, no. 1163; Páez Rios 1981–3, no. 2020.46.
144 Santiago Páez 2006a, p. 24.
145 Part I, vol. 1, chap. XV, p. 116. Santiago Paez 2006, nos 7.1–8.
146 Lenaghan 2006, p. 59.
147 Part II, vol. 4, chapter LXIV, p. 273. A number of drawings for the composition and the copper plate survive. Santiago Páez 2006, nos 32.1–5. For Fabregat, see Carrete Parrondo and Villena 1990.
148 Series described by Vega 1992, pp. 215 (Aranjuez), 220 (El Escorial).
149 For survey of subject, see Bozal 1987, pp. 649–711. For a wide range of illustrations of Spanish popular prints, see Tokyo 1999.
150 Jordán de Urríes y de la Colina 2011.
151 For discussion of series, see Bozal 1987, pp. 669–84.
152 Bozal 1988, p. 9.
153 Heckes 2001, p. 51; Vega 1992, pp. 25–6; Carrete Parrondo 1991a.
154 Carrete Parrondo 1991a, pp. 11–16. Carrete Parrondo and Martínez-Novillo 1989. A variant of four small numbered scenes per plate, totalling twenty-three images, is in the Biblioteca Nacional, Madrid (ER/3058).
155 Carrete Parrondo 1991a, p. 20.
156 Facsimile: Carrete Parrondo 1991.
157 For regional centres in relation to painting, see Morales y Marín 1994, pp. 333–78.
158 For academies in Spain outside Madrid, see Bédat 1989, pp. 399–431; Carrete Parrondo 1987, pp. 458–65; Gallego Gallego 1979, pp. 256–66, 308–10. For Valencia, see Rodríguez Culebras 2006, p. 122; for Seville, see Aranda Bernal and Quiles García 2000, pp. 121–4.
159 See discussion of the centrality of Madrid by Úbeda de los Cobos (1989).
160 Garín Ortíz de Taranco 1993, pp. 49–91; Bédat 1989, pp. 399–405; Tramoyeres Blanco 1911; Ceán Bermúdez 1800, V, pp. 197–204.
161 Ceán Bermúdez 1800, V, p. 197.
162 Bérchez 1987, esp. pp. 61–79.
163 For the influence of Mengs at the academy in Valencia, see Úbeda de los Cobos 1987. For the Academy see León Tello and Sanz Sanz 1979.
164 Garín Ortíz de Taranco 1993, p. 56.
165 Bérchez 1987, pp. 67–70, pls 5–7; Llorens and Catalá 1983, pp. 28–35.
166 Espinós Díaz 2006; Rodríguez Culebras 1968.
167 Espinós Díaz 2006, pp. 23–35; Morales y Marín 1994, pp. 336–8.
168 Rodríguez Culebras 2006, p. 118.
169 For the painting, see Luna 1981, no. 8.
170 Biblioteca Nacional, Madrid (DIB/15/89/24). Rodríguez Culebras 2006, no. 18. The medallion is illustrated by Espinós Díaz (2006, p. 70).
171 Another drawing by Camarón in the Biblioteca Nacional, Madrid, *The Wise and Foolish Virgins* (DIB/15/89/36), is also annotated with colour notes. The style of both sheets is similar, the use of dark grey ink and opulent fabrics suggesting that they may have been made around the same time. The Madrid drawing is undated, but discussed by Espinós Díaz in the entry relating to a 1761 painting that shows a related subject (Espinós Díaz 2006, p. 141).
172 For discussion of the painting and theme, see Stein 1994; Stein 1996.
173 For the relation of the drawing to Van Loo's painting, see Cerón 2006, pp. 204–5.
174 Quoted by Rodríguez Culebras 2006, p. 121; also, engravings pp. 229–50.
175 Espinós Díaz 2006, p. 63; Benito Doménech 1987a.
176 Bérchez 1987, pp. 105–7; Espinós Díaz 1984, II, pp. 178–247.
177 Espinós Díaz 1984, I, pp. 137–49.
178 I am grateful to David Montolío Torán for information relating to this painting. Also Montolío Torán in Segorbe 2001, no. 200. Another study for the painting (oil on paper glued to panel) exists in a private collection. See Víctor Marco García in Segorbe 2001, no. 207.
179 McDonald 2006a.
180 Prints were important to the development of Villanueva's art, as pointed out by Orellana 1930, pp. 452–4; Hernández Guardiola 1990, p. 26 note 5.
181 Orellana 1930, p. 458.
182 For discussion of his drawing process, see Bray 2002, pp. 20–7.
183 Díez García 1999.
184 Vega 1992, p. 137.
185 Carrete Parrondo 1987, pp. 461–5; Gallego Gallego 1979, pp. 302–4.
186 Úbeda de los Cobos 1989, pp. 472–3.
187 Santiago Páez 2006, nos 7.1–8
188 Vega 1992, pp. 9–11; Páez Rios 1981–3, no. 103.1-41.
189 See essays in Morales and Quiles García 2010; León 1990, pp. 67–84; León 1989, pp. 360–9.
190 Published as a single sheet (as noted by Ceán) and included in the *Annales eclesíasticos i seglares … de Sevilla*, Florencia Joseph de Blàs y Quesada, Seville, 1647 (British Museum, 1866,1208.638 [165*c.2]). Ceán Bermúdez 1800, V, p. 70.
191 For the drawing school that opened in 1769, see Ceán Bermúdez 1800, II, p. 32.

Chapter 8

I am extremely grateful to Juliet Wilson-Bareau for her generous help with this chapter.

1 The Enlightenment, an eighteenth-century philosophical and cultural school of thought, emphasized the dominance of reason and the belief in human progress. Many studies have focused on different aspects of the Enlightenment in Spain, e.g. Vega 2010; Domínguez Ortiz 2005; Kasl and Stratton 1997; Tomlinson 1992; essays in Pérez Sánchez and Sayre 1989; Glendinning 1972; Sarrailh 1954.

2 Tomlinson 1992, p. 17.

3 The literature on Goya's prints and drawings is vast. Major catalogue studies include Gassier 1973 (albums) and 1975 (all other drawings); Gassier and Wilson 1971 (prints, drawings and paintings); Harris 1964 (prints). Major facsimile publications showing prints (with states), preparatory drawings and copperplates, with full historic bibliographic references have been produced by the Museo Nacional del Prado and the Calcografía Nacional, Madrid. For *Los Caprichos*, see Blas, Matilla and Medrano 1999; for *Los Desastres de la Guerra*, see Blas, Matilla and Aguilar, 2000; for *La Tauromaquia*, see Matilla and Medrano 2001; for *Los Disparates*, see Carrete and Matilla 1996 (without illustrating preparatory drawings).

4 The titles of the drawing albums have been taken from Juliet Wilson-Bareau's revision, which makes their contents clearer. See Wilson-Bareau 2001.

5 Facsimile edition with annotated transcription and essays by Manuela Mena Marqués and Jesús Urrea in Madrid 1994; also Reuter 2008.

6 Cristina Monterde and Raquel Gallego in Sureda 2008, pp. 101–2. Essays in Sureda 2008 examine Goya's journey in detail, his practice and what he saw in Italy.

7 On folio 3 of the Notebook Goya's wrote: 'estampas …76', referring to a quantity of prints. See comment by Manuela Mena on p. 25 of text accompanying facsimile (see Madrid 1994).

8 Goya's journey to Madrid is recorded in the Notebook. See Cristina Monterde and Raquel Gallego in Sureda 2008, p. 102; Madrid 1994, p. 47.

9 On their relationship, see Morales y Marín 1995, pp. 34–9.

10 For Goya's drawings, see Tomlinson 1989, figs 12, 13, pp. 36–7; Gassier 1975, pp. 29–39 (nos 3–11).

11 Wilson-Bareau 1996, pp. 33–41.

12 Los Llanos 2008.

13 Santiago Páez 1996b.

14 Glendinning 1977, p. 257.

15 Canellas López 1981, p. 517, no. CLXXXVI.

16 Tomlinson 1989, pp. 70–2.

17 For the entire series, see Madrid 1996a, nos 5–60; Madrid 1996b, nos 79–94. For discussion of the drawings, see Vega 1995, pp. 153, 156–7; Mena Marqués 1991.

18 The announcement is reproduced in Madrid 1996b, p. 130, no. 95. For discussion, see Vega 1995.

19 Madrid 1996a, nos 57–60; Madrid 1996b, nos 89B–94; Gassier and Wilson 1971, p. 50. For the letter, see Symmons 2004, pp. 82–3, no. 37.

20 Madrid 1996a, nos 43–56; Madrid 1996b, nos 86–9; Sayre 1974, nos 25–9.

21 Wilson-Bareau 2003, p. 142; Glendinning, Harris and Russell 1999, p. 601; Canellas López 1981, p. 216, no. 23.

22 Tomlinson 1992, pp. 38–45 and Appendix 1, pp. 191–4 (text in Spanish and English).

23 Symmons 2004, pp. 232–4, nos 226, 227.

24 For the series of paintings, see Wilson-Bareau and Mena Marqués 1994, pp. 189–209, pls 32–43; for the letters: Symmons 2004, pp. 237–8, nos 232, 234; Canellas López 1981, pp. 314–15, docs 188, 189.

25 For brief overview, see Andrew Schulze in Brown 2010, pp. 119–26.

26 Mena Marqués and Mühle-Maurer 2006, esp. pp. 27–46; Wilson-Bareau 2001, pp. 37–46. Gassier 1973, pp. 17–44, nos 1–18 (copies 19–21).

27 Vega 1996, pp. 53–4; Vega 1996b, p. 152.

28 Mena Marqués and Mühle-Maurer 2006, p. 133.

29 Wilson-Bareau 2001, pp. 47–78; Gassier 1973, pp. 45–137, nos 3–94 (lost drawings nos 91–2).

30 Drawing p. 81 from the Madrid Album, *Caprichos* plate 36 ('Mala noche').

31 The document is illustrated in Madrid 1996b, p. 178, no. 166. Symmons 2004, p. 257, no. 257; Canellas López 1981, p. 327, no. 210; Gassier and Wilson 1971, Appendix V, p. 383 ('Osuna Documents').

32 Symmons 2004, pp. 268–9, nos 269–71; Canellas López 1981, pp. 360–1, nos 223, 224, p. 477, no. CVIII.

33 Sayre 1974, p. 304 and note 5.

34 Wilson-Bareau 1996, p. 36; Sayre 1974, pp. 55–6.

35 For a breakdown of the *Caprichos* content into subjects, see Wilson-Bareau 1992.

36 See Blas, Matilla and Medrano 1999, no. 43; Madrid 1996b, nos 121, 122; Sayre 1974, pp. 59–60 and nos 72–5.

37 Madrid 1996b, nos 154–6; Wolf 1991; Lorenzo de Márquez 1989, pp. lxxxv–xciv.

38 Sayre 1989, pp. ci–ciii; Sayre 1974, pp. 55–8; Helman 1963, p. 50, Appendix II, pp. 219–41.

39 Cited by Glendinning 1977, pp. 60–1.

40 For the paintings, see Wilson-Bareau and Mena Marqués 1994, pp. 211–21 and nos 44–9; Gassier and Wilson 1971, nos 659–63. For San Antonio de la Florida, see Borrás Gualis 2006; Wilson-Bareau and Mena Marqués 1994, pp. 232–7; Gassier and Wilson 1971, nos 717–35.

41 Gudrun Maurer in Madrid 2008, no. 14.

42 Gassier 1975, no. 352 (also no. 353). The attribution of the drawing is uncertain.

43 See studies in Mena Marqués 2002.

44 Gassier 1975, pp. 187–98, nos 149–59. For discussion of their attribution, see Santiago Páez 1996, pp. 63–4, nos 47–51.

45 For the correspondence between Goya and Zapater, see Symmons 2004, pp. 21–33 and letters.

46 See Manuela Mena Marqués in Madrid 2008, no. 28, where this pure aquatint plate is tentatively dated *c.*1800.

47 Madrid 1996b, nos 194–8 (includes the drawings); Sayre 1974, nos 93, 94.

48 The prints were given their present title (*Los Desastres de la Guerra*) in 1863. See Madrid 1996a, no. 176 (where the dated title page is illustrated).

49 Jesusa Vega quoting Manuel José Quintana's *Manifiesto de la Nación Española a la Europa* (Seville 1809), in Pérez Sánchez and Sayre 1989, p. 185.

50 Álvarez Junco 2008.

51 Manuela Mena Marqués and Gudrun Maurer in Madrid 2008, nos 123, 124; Tomlinson 1992, pp. 131–49.

52 Sayre 1974, p. 126.

53 Glendinning 2008, pp. 48–51.

54 Vega 1992a.

55 The complete set is reproduced, with its title page, other proofs and the preparatory drawings by Blas and Matilla 2000. The calf-bound album, labelled 'CAPRICHOS DE GOYA' on the spine, and its title page are illustrated in Wilson-Bareau 1996, figs 43, 44. On the manuscript titles, see Sayre 1974, p. 130.

56 José Matilla in Madrid 2008, nos 120–2; Madrid 1996a, nos 67–70; Mena Marqués in Pérez Sánchez and Sayre 1989, nos 95, 96; Harris 1964, II, nos 26–8.

57 Sayre 1974, pp. 129–30.

58 Vega 1992a, p. 24 note 55. The source of this information is the slip of paper in the volume, with a note by Carderera that is reproduced in Blas and Matilla 2000, following p. 65.

59 Blas and Matilla 2000, no. 50 (drawing and Ceán Album proof); Gassier 1975, no. 199.

60 José Matilla in Madrid 2008, p. 341 and nos 80, 112–19; Vega 1992a, pp. 44–8.

61 Anes 1989, pp. xliv–xlvi.

62 Sayre 1989, pp. cxxii–iv and nos 154–63; Sayre 1974, p. 129, nos 233–47. Changes in the dating of the *Disasters* plates is noted in the analysis of the bibliography

of this series in the Introduction to Blas and Matilla 2000.

63 José Matilla in Madrid 2008, no. 115.

64 Juliet Wilson-Bareau in Madrid 2008, nos 78, 79; Eleanor Sayre in Pérez Sánchez and Sayre 1989, no. 97.

65 See the many works illustrated in Madrid 2008a.

66 Vega 1992, p. 235.

67 Madrid 1996, nos 134, 137.

68 For Juan Gálvez's preparatory drawing for the print, see Navarrete Prieto 2006, no. 71. Gálvez also painted the subject: Díez 2005, pp. 120–1.

69 Manuela Sancho (1783–1863).

70 Madrid 2008a, pp. 249–87.

71 Madrid 1996, no. 13.

72 Wilson-Bareau 2001, pp. 79–89; Sayre 1989, pp. cv–cviii; Gassier 1973, pp. 223–354; López-Rey 1956.

73 Gassier 1973, no. 233: C.88.

74 Margarito Moreno de las Heras in Pérez Sánchez and Sayre 1989, no. 73.

75 Gassier 1973, nos 259: C.115, 260: C.116, 261: C.117.

76 Wilson-Bareau 2001, pp. 91–112; Sayre 1989, pp. cxx–cxxi; Gassier 1973, pp. 385–497, nos 277: F.1–364: F.106a.

77 Wilson-Bareau 2001, no. 59; Gassier 1973, no. 320: F.54.

78 Glendinning 1977, p. 67.

79 The drawing was reproduced in etching by Félix Bracquemond to illustrate an article by Valentín Carderera published in the *Gazette des Beaux-Arts* in 1860. See Paris 2008, no. 237. British Museum, 1900,1231.5438.

80 Sayre 1989, p. cxxi and nos 147 and 151, 148 and 162.

81 Trans. Sayre 1974, p. 197.

82 For summary of these interpretations, see Matilla and Medrano 2001, pp. 15–39. For the historical context, see Martínez-Novillo 1992.

83 Reproduced in Madrid 1996a, no. 311.

84 Sayre 1974, pp. 198–201.

85 Wilson-Bareau 1996, p. 61; Harris 1964, I, pp. 173–4.

86 Wilson-Bareau 1996, p. 64.

87 Madrid 1996a, no. 312.

88 Heckes 2001, p. 52.

89 Wilson-Bareau 2001, pp. 113–33; Gassier 1973, pp. 165–222.

90 For discussion of their dating, see Wilson-Bareau 2001, p. 135; Sayre 1989, pp. cxv–cxvi; Gassier 1973, pp. 139–64.

91 The dating for the series varies. Most recently, Matilla (Madrid 2008, no. 175) argues for 1816–19; Sayre suggested *c.*1816–17 (Sayre 1989, p. cxvii). For the English plates made by William & Russell Pontifex & Co. (London), see Glendinning 1992, p. 19 note 1.

92 Illustrated in Carrete and Matilla 1996.

93 Matilla 2000, pp. 109–10; Vega 1996a, p. 83; Clifford Ackley in Sayre 1974, p. 251 note 3; Harris 1964, II, p. 366, 'Trial Proofs I'.

94 For drawings paired with the prints, see Matilla 2000, nos 33–54. Also (drawings) Gassier 1975, pp. 432–78, nos 290–302, 304–11; (prints) Harris 1964, II, nos 269a–g.

95 Glendinning 1996; Glendinning 1992.

96 José Matilla in Madrid 2008, no. 175; Gassier 1975, no. 291.

97 For an interpretation of this print, see Michael Roche in Pérez Sánchez and Sayre 1989, no. 140.

98 Manuela Mena Marqués and Gudrun Maurer in Madrid 2008, no. 131; Tomlinson 1989, fig. 15, p. 41.

99 Sayre 1974, nos 225, 226–9; Harris 1964, II, nos 266–9.

100 Brown and Galassi 2006, nos 23–7. For a detailed discussion of lithography in Spain, and an analysis and categorization of Goya's lithographs (those made in Spain and those in France), see Vega 1990, pp. 43–53 and (for Goya) pp. 54–64, nos 21–38. A different account is given in Madrid 1996a, pp. 251–63, nos 400–5, Appendix II 'Watermarks', nos 14, 15 (Madrid), pp. 406–12, nos 16–20 (Bordeaux); Wilson-Bareau 1996, pp. 46–9 and nos 313–26, 'Catalogue of Watermarks': nos 41–3 (Madrid), 45–8 (Bordeaux); Harris 1964, I, pp. 213–22, II, nos 270–9 (Madrid), 280–7 (Bordeaux).

101 Wilson-Bareau 1996a, pp. 48–9, figs 51, 52 (Cardano fragments); Vega 1990, pp. 72, 74, fig. 48, no. 61.

102 José Matilla in Madrid 2008, nos 186–8; Wilson-Bareau 1996a, p. 49 and nos 316–18; Gassier 1975, no. 312; Sayre 1974, nos 249, 250; Harris 1964, I, p. 215, illus. pp. 218–19, II, no. 272.

103 Vega 1990, nos 21–30.

104 Wilson-Bareau 1996, p. 47, fig. 50; Gassier 1973, no. 286: F.12; Harris 1964, II, no. 271.

105 Paris 2008, p. 148, fig. 6 and no. 212; Madrid 1996a, nos 404, 405; Madrid 1996b, nos 319, 320; Vega 1990, nos 23, 25; Harris 1964, II, nos 276, 277.

106 Madrid 1996a, Appendix I, no. 8; Vega 1990, no. 30 (as in Madrid); Harris 1964, II, no. 278.

107 Accounts of Goya's departure from Spain and years in France have been based on Núñez de Arenas (1950). Jonathan Brown in Brown and Galassi 2006, pp. 2–9; Sue Welsh-Reed in Sayre 1974, pp. 304–5. For documents and correspondence, see Symmons 2004, pp. 286–7, nos 304–7; Canellas López 1981, pp. 386–7, no. 269 and p. 496, no. CXLV.

108 Sueur-Hermel, 2008, p. 146 and no. 213; Sayre 1974, no. 256; Harris 1964, II, no. 282.

109 As told to Goya's biographer Laurent Matheron: Matheron 1996 edn, pp. 264, 267; Wilson-Bareau and Mena Marqués 1994, p. 333.

110 Jonathan Brown in Brown and Galassi 2006, pp. 147–62. A unique proof of a related bullfight of the same size, signed and dated 'Goya Bo[r]deaux 1825', was probably an abandoned trial for the series. See Madrid 1996a, Appendix I, no. 11; Wilson-Bareau and Mena Marqués 1994, pp. 333, 335, no. 114; Harris 1964, II, no. 287.

111 Symmons 2004, pp. 291–2, nos 312, 313; Canellas López 1981, pp. 389–90, nos 272, 273.

112 Sueur-Hermel 2008, pp. 141–9 and nos 224–34.

113 Harris 1964, I, p. 220.

114 Ibid., II, no. 285.

115 Jonathan Brown in Brown and Galassi 2006, pp. 167–73; ibid., nos 28–51 (not in album order); Wilson-Bareau 2001, pp. 145–58, nos 94–106 (G), pp.159–71, nos 107–17 (H); Sayre 1989, pp. cxxv–cxxvii; Manuela Mena Marqués and Michael Roche, nos 164–72 (G), Teresa Lorenzo de Márquez and Michael Roche, nos 173–8 (H) in Pérez Sánchez and Sayre 1989; Gassier 1973, pp. 499–572, nos 365–418 (G), pp. 573–647, nos 419–476 (H).

116 Gassier 1973, no. 411: G.54.

117 Ibid., no. 473: H.61.

118 Ibid., no. 113: E.2.

119 Madrid 1996a, nos 72–7; Madrid 1996b, nos 327–33; Sue Welsh Reed in Sayre 1974, nos 262–8; Harris 1964, II, nos 30–5.

120 For the drawing, see Jonathan Brown in Brown and Galassi 2006, pp. 226–9; Gassier 1973, no.470: H.58. For the aquatinted etching, see Lorenzo de Márquez 1989, no. 179; Sayre 1974, nos 262–5. The attribution of the verso etching of an old woman (?) on a swing (Harris 1964, no. 33) remains uncertain.

Appendix

1 Montalbán Jiménez 2007, pp. 86–7; Remie Constable 1994, pp. 194–6.

2 Idrisí 1988, p. 182.

3 Sistach 2001, p. 97; Llorca 2009.

4 Loveday 2001, pp. 32–48.

5 The important production of paper in Spain at this time has led some researchers to believe that overshot waterwheels to power the pulp-beating hammers were introduced in order to meet the high demand for paper in Christian territories. Innovations of this kind preceding the Western paper industry are unlikely; see Bloom 2001, pp. 206–8.

6 Sistach and Rabal 2011, pp. 118–20.

7 Balmaceda 2008, pp. 105–6. In Castile, Islamic paper was probably introduced later and was still used in the fifteenth century; see Burón Castro 2003.

8 For an introduction to Western formation of sheets see Robinson 1977, p. 6.

9 For examples of late Islamic paper in Spain, see Llorca 2009, pp. 49–50. For documents with both types of paper bound together, see Sistach 2005, pp. 107–10. For an example of paper made with Western wire moulds but starch sized and burnished see Document 7, Abadía del Sacromonte; Jiménez and Ávila 2007, p. 5.

10 Montalbán Jiménez 2007, p. 87.

11 Millard 2007, pp. 1–2.

12 For a table listing the first Italian papermakers to be established in Catalonia, Valencia, Andalusia and Castile, see Balmaceda 2004, p. 98. In 1571 the Duke of Pastrana brought both Moorish and Milanese workers to Guadalajara in order to improve the paper industry; the Duke also owned a paper mill in Pastrana. The collaboration between Muslim and Christian workers in Spanish papermaking, although likely, is not documented. Gayoso Carreira 2006, vol. 1, pp. 25, 86.

13 Balmaceda 2007, pp. 95–108.

14 Llorca 2009, p. 44.

15 Valls i Subirá 1978–82, vol. 2, pp. 49–51.

16 The watermark, a large-format hand with five open fingers, topped with an eight-petal flower, bears similarities to the Briquet series, perhaps no. 10719 (Briquet 1907, vol. 3, p. 552). For hand watermarks in Spanish *incunabula* see Hidalgo Brinquis 2008.

17 Gayoso Carreira 2006, vol. 1, p. 25. A document dated 1717 by Eugenio de la Llave, prior of the Monastery of El Escorial at the time, mentions that the two mills in El Escorial were closed down because they frightened off the king's hunt. De la Llave requests from the monarch that these mills be reinstated by the monastery, with a wall built round them to resolve the hunting problem (Gayoso Carreira 2006, vol. 1, p. 88).

18 Krill 1987, pp. 51–6. In Spain layered brown paper was called '*papel cartón o papelón*' and its early use can be identified in fifteenth-century Mozarabic bookcovers made with layered Islamic paper. See Jiménez Colmenar 2009, p. 88.

19 Bambach 1999, pp. 34–6, 368–71.

20 See structure of *The Adoration of the Magi* (Metropolitan Museum of Art, New York, 2008.379).

21 Examples of earlier coloured papers made in Al-Andalus are found in the 'Cartas Reales' (1306–10), sent from the Kingdom of Granada to James II of Aragon, where a wash of red lead, ochre or malachite was applied to Islamic paper. Sistach 1997, p. 75. This technique bears no resemblance to the production of blue papers in Western papermaking, where the actual fibres used to make the pulp came from indigo dyed rags, a technique derived from fifteenth-century Italy and commonly used as a support for drawings; see Robinson 1977, pp. 33–5.

22 Although the mills in El Escorial specialized in '*papel de Bula*', Catalan papermakers' contracts from Spanish mills at this period suggest that they probably also made blue and brown paper in white paper mills; see Valls i Subirá, 1978–82, vol. 2, pp. 55–7. For imported brown and blue Italian papers see Balmaceda 2004, p. 25 and table p. 154.

23 Krill 1987, pp. 56–61.

24 Ruiz de Arcaute 1936, p. 99.

25 Pedro Perret's prints of the Escorial after Juan de Herrera in the *Templa Diversa* (British Library, 3.tab.34).

26 Watermarks described in the first pages are also found in prints by Perret, *7th Design – General View of the Monastery of San Lorenzo de El Escorial* (Museo Nacional del Prado, Madrid, G.2976) and typeset 1587 edition, *Designs after Juan de Herrera for the Monastery of San Lorenzo de El Escorial* (Biblioteca Nacional de España, Madrid, 28841-48). Another first edition series of Perret engravings at the Biblioteca Nacional (28860) is printed on thinner, cloudier sheets of paper, bearing a watermark of thirty-six grapes below the letters 'LC', which might suggest that other papers were sourced from different papermakers.

27 For more information on pairs of watermarks and the repeated use of moulds, see Stevenson 1951–2.

28 The number of prints and the size of the paper were detailed in the contract with the printers Testa and Gaeta: fifty prints in '*Imperial*', one hundred in '*Real*' and two hundred in '*medio Real*', following Italian formats. Cervera Vera 1988, p. 45.

29 Balmaceda 2004, pp. 69–84.

30 For a corpus of French and Catalan versions of the *tre mundi* watermarks, see Balmaceda 2004, pp. 128–53. Ongoing examination of Catalan sheets bearing *tre mundi* watermarks indicates a tendency to a single irregular shadow on one side of the chain line, as opposed to Italian papers with accumulation of pulp on either side of the chain lines. See Balmaceda 2004, pp. 229–30.

31 The watermark in this drawing was examined by José Carlos Balmaceda, who kindly deciphered the acronyms and provided a description of the paper.

32 The drawings by Bartolomé Esteban Murillo of the *Annunciation* and *The Good Shepherd* both in the Museo Nacional del Prado, Madrid (D.5598 and D.6319), bear this type of watermark. Drawings by other Andalusian artists, such as Alonso Cano, often display similar watermarks: see e.g. *The Holy Family* (The Morgan Library and Museum, New York, III, 126) and *Putti* (Biblioteca Nacional de España, Madrid, DIB/15/4/32).

33 The Bologna stone indicates the four sizes standardized and followed by Italian papermakers: '*Imperialle*' or '*Imperiale*' (500 x 740 mm), '*Realle*' or '*Reale*' (445 x 615 mm), '*meçane*' or '*mezzana*' (345 x 515 mm), and '*reçute*' or '*rezzuta*' (315 x 450 mm); Bambach 1999, p. 364. For further information on the Bologna stone and later interpretations of formats see Harris 2010 online, 'The Shape of Paper' (http://ihl.enssib.fr/siteihl.php?page=272&aflng=fr). The three first formats were translated into Spanish as '*Imperial*', '*Real*' and '*medio Real*'. Spanish contracts from paper mills and documents on paper imports often used the terms '*marca mayor*', '*marca menor*' and '*marquilla*'. Cabanes Pecourt 1997, p. 125.

34 '*Papel fino*', '*florete*' or '*mónaca*', '*Real*', and '*Real mayor*' all had a *tre mundi* watermark. Other types of paper known as '*blanco ordinario*', '*grezzoto blanco*', '*grezzotto negro*' and '*Real ordinario*' displayed the Genoese shield with a combination of circles. See Balmaceda 2004, p. 154.

35 Valls i Subirá 1978–82, vol. 2, p. 24.

36 A document in the Archivo General de Indias in Seville states that this stamp was also placed on paper made in China and imported to the Spanish Philippine colonies in order to reduce the transport costs of paper from Europe; see Balmaceda 2004, p. 70.

37 Nuevo Ábalos 2005.

38 Ostolaza Elizondo 1997.

39 British Library, London (4625.f.6). Valls i Subirá 1978–82 vol. 3, pp. 18–21; Gayoso Carreira 2006, vol. 3, Corpus p. 60 n. 11.

40 Valls i Subirá 1978–82, vol. 3, p. 104, Paular corpus n. 9; Gayoso Carreira 2006, vol. 3, Paular corpus, p. 48 n. 80.

41 Jurado 2007, p. 71; Gayoso Carreira 2006, vol. 1, pp. 98–9.

42 The French authorities complained about contraband paper smuggled into Spain damaging their export business; see Valls i Subirá 1978–82, vol. 2, pp. 18–19.

43 *The Martyrdom of Father Andres* (The Morgan Library and Museum, New York, 1986.42).

44 Carducho (1633) 1979, p. 133.

45 *Prostrated Carthusian* (Museo Nacional del Prado, Madrid, D.82) by Vicente Carducho is a highly significant example of the use of a white paper of very inferior quality, with a poor fibre composition and an extremely irregular mould pattern.

46 In the fifteenth century, upon the arrival in Valencia of Ferdinand of Aragon, imported white paper and starch were used to create ephemeral sculptures

which were then painted with pigments in workshops. Brasilwood was used for 'fire' papers, sunflower and saffron for yellows, Baghdad indigo for blues. See Cabanes Pecourt 1999.

47 Palomino 1714, p. 12.

48 Ibid., p. 93. Also mentioned earlier by Francisco Pacheco citing Leonardo da Vinci, see Pacheco (1649) 1990, pp. 339–40.

49 The ridge observed in the middle of the paper in this drawing is characteristic of handmade papers and is known as a 'back mark'. This is caused by the hair ropes over which papers were suspended for drying in the loft of the mill. See Krill 1987, p. 28.

50 The opposite side of the paper is generally smoother and is called the felt-side, Krill 1987, p. 21.

51 Nuevo Ábalos 2001, pp. 351–8

52 Spanish paper was sent in large quantities from the port of Malaga to La Habana, Montevideo or Veracruz; see Balmaceda 2004, p. 109.

53 Gayoso Carreira 2006, vol. 1, pp. 26–7.

54 Stamping mills remained in use in Spain until the twentieth century. The region of Beceite in Zaragoza made exquisite handmade writing paper in mills with waterwheels and stamp hammers until the 1970s. The archaeological remains of some of these mills are in good condition and can still be visited in Beceite. See also Gayoso Carreira 2006, vol. 1, pp. 55–6.

55 Watermarks in the eighteenth century tend to be more elaborate and sewn with thinner wires; Nicholson 1982, p. 1. For the evolution of watermarks in Spain in the seventeenth and eighteenth centuries see Gayoso Carreira 2006, vol. 2 (Corpus de Filigranas); for eighteenth-century corpus of Catalan *tre mundi* watermarks see Balmaceda 2004, p. 105.

56 British Museum, 1878,0112.38. Partial Watermark, Gayoso Carreira 2006, Alcoy corpus n. 310 (dated 1786), vol. 3, p. 135.

57 Laurentius 1999, pp. 31–3; Hunter 1957, pp. 162–5.

58 Earlier attempts to introduce the new Dutch Hollander beater in Spain are first mentioned in 1764 in a letter from Valencian papermaker Albors: 'I am assembling a machine with a cylinder ... I will produce more reams at a cheaper cost ... and if I succeed our Kingdom will be the first to have brought this discovery to Spain'. It failed, probably due to lack of skilled staff or appropriate facilities. See Wenger et al. 2011, p. 27.

59 For similar watermarks in Spanish eighteenth-century drawings, see e.g. Camarón's *Christ appearing to Saint Catherine of Siena* (Museo Nacional del Prado, Madrid, D.638).

60 Robinson 1977, p. 21.

61 Castelló Mora 2007, p. 433.

62 Wenger et al. 2011, pp. 23–7.

63 Hernández 1996.

64 Papers in the British Museum bear close similarities in paper structure and composition to some of the prints by Goya examined at the Biblioteca Nacional de España, *The Drunkards* (45534-36) and *Santiago de Morra* (45590)

65 The two 1799 *Los Caprichos* series examined here are bound at the Biblioteca Nacional de España (45653*) and the Museo Nacional del Prado (G.2089 to G.2168).

66 The papers used for the proofs of the first edition at the British Museum seem to be of a lower quality, with darker furnish, impurities in their composition and irregular pulp accumulation.

67 Canellas López 1981, pp. 468–9.

68 Comparative research based on Carnicero's 1787–90 set at the Museo Nacional del Prado (G.969 to G.983).

69 Hernández 1996, p. 275.

70 Condition assessment and conservation performed by Jenny Bescoby, Paper Conservator, Department of Conservation and Scientific Research, British Museum.

71 *Equestrian Portrait of Arthur Wellesley*, possibly D&C Blauw partial watermark bearing an x linked at the bottom; Churchill 1965, p. 171 (similar to acronyms in n. 194).

72 Museo Nacional del Prado, examples of 1797–8 drawings on wove paper made for *Los Caprichos* include *Love and Death* (plate 10, D.3948) and *They are Hot* (plate 13, D.4232).

Bibliography

Agueda, M., 'Dibujos de Mengs en el Museo del Prado', *Boletín del Museo del Prado*, i, 1980, pp. 83–98.

Agulló y Cobo, M., 'La biblioteca de don Teodoro Ardemans', in *Primeras jornadas de bibliografía* (proceedings 1976), Madrid 1977, pp. 570–82.

——, *Documentos para la historia de la pintura española*, 3 vols, Madrid 1994–2006.

——, 'Un curioso coleccionista del siglo xvii: Don Manuel de Porras', *Archivo Español de Arte*, lxxvi, 2003, pp. 235–48.

Ainaud, J., 'Grabado', *Ars Hispaniae: Historia universal del arte hispánico*, xviii, Madrid 1962, pp. 245–320.

——, J. Gudiol and F.-P. Verrié, *La ciudad de Barcelona* (*Cátalogo monumental de España*), 2 vols, Madrid 1947.

Ainaud de Lasarte, J., 'Francisco Ribalta. Notas y comentarios', *Goya*, no. 20, 1957, pp. 86–9.

Albi, J., *Joan de Joanes y su círculo artístico* (*Cuadernos de Arte* xxvii), 3 vols, Valencia 1979.

Alonso de la Sierra, L., and F. Quiles, 'Nuevas obras de Cornelio Schut el Joven', *Norba-Arte*, xviii–xix, 1998, pp. 83–105.

Alpers, S., *The Decoration of the Torre de la Parada*, Corpus Rubenianum Ludwig Burchard, pt ix, Antwerp 1971.

Alvar Ezquera, A., *El nacimiento de una capital europea. Madrid entre 1561 y 1606*, Madrid 1989.

Alvarez, M.-T., 'Artistic enterprise and Spanish patronage: The art market during the reign of Isabel of Castile (1474–1504)', in *Art Markets in Europe, 1400–1800*, eds M. North and D. Ormrod, Aldershot 1998, pp. 45–59.

Álvarez Junco, J., 'La guerra Napoleónica', in Madrid 2008, pp. 15–38.

Anderson, B., A. Dotseth and M. Roglán (eds), *Fernando Gallego and his Workshop: The Altarpiece from Ciudad Rodrigo*, exh. cat., Southern Methodist University, Dallas 2008.

d'Andrea Cennini, C., *The Craftsman's Handbook (Il libro dell' arte)*, trans. D.V. Thompson Jr, New York 1960.

de Andrés, G., 'Catálogo de las colecciónes de dibujos de la Real Biblioteca de El Escorial', *Archivo Español de Arte*, xli, 1968, between pp. 76–7 (no pagination).

Anes, G., 'Freedom in Goya's age: Ideas and aspirations', in Pérez Sánchez and Sayre 1989, pp. xxvi–xlix.

Angulo Iñiguez, D., 'Nuevas obras de José Antolínez', *Archivo Español de Arte*, xxxi, 1958, pp. 341–3.

——, 'Herrera Barnuevo y Antolínez', *Archivo Español de Arte*, xxxii, 1959, pp. 331–2.

——, 'Francisco Camilo', *Archivo Español de Arte*, xxxii, 1959a, pp. 89–107.

——, 'Nuevas obras de Francisco Camilo', *Archivo Español de Arte*, xxxviii, 1965, pp. 59–61.

——, *Cuarenta dibujos españoles* (Academia de San Fernando), Madrid 1966.

——, 'Un dibujo de Valdés Leal en la Escuela de Artes Decorativas de París', *Archivo Español de Arte*, xliii, 1970, pp. 408–9.

——, 'Francisco Rizi. Cuadros de tema profano', *Archivo Español de Arte*, xliv, 1971, pp. 357–87.

——, 'Algunos dibujos de Murillo', *Archivo Español de Arte*, xlvii, 1974, pp. 97–108.

——, *Murillo. Su vida, su arte, su obra*, 3 vols, Madrid 1981.

—— and A.E. Pérez Sánchez, *Historia de la pintura española. Escuela Madrileña del primer tercio del siglo xvii*, Madrid 1969.

—— and A.E. Pérez Sánchez, *A Corpus of Spanish Drawings*. i: *1400–1600*, London 1975.

—— and A.E. Pérez Sánchez, *A Corpus of Spanish Drawings*. ii: *Madrid School, 1600–1650*, London 1977.

—— and A.E. Pérez Sánchez, *A Corpus of Spanish Drawings*. iii: *Seville School, 1600–1650*, London 1985.

—— and A.E. Pérez Sánchez, *A Corpus of Spanish Drawings*. iv: *Valencia 1600–1700*, London 1988.

Ansón Navarro, A., 'El dibujo en españa durante el siglo xviii', in *Dibujo español del renacimiento a Goya. La colección de la Reina María Cristina de Borbón*, eds A. Ansón Navarro and R. Centellas Salamero, exh. cat., Palacio de Sástago y Cajalón, Zaragoza 2008, pp. 53–79.

Aranda Bernal, A., 'La "Academia de Pintura" de Domingo Martínez', in *Domingo Martínez en la estela de Murillo*, exh. cat., Centro Cultural El Monte, Seville 2004, pp. 87–107.

—— and F. Quiles García, 'Las academias de pintura en Sevilla', *Academia (Boletín de la Real Academia de Bellas Artes de San Fernando)*, no. 90, 2000, pp. 119–38.

Arias Martínez, M., 'Gaspar Becerra, escultor o tracista. La documentación testamentaria de su viuda, Paula Velázquez', *Archivo Español de Arte*, lxxi, 1998, pp. 273–88.

Arnáez, R., 'Dibujos de Francisco Bayeu en el Museo del Prado', *Archivo Español de Arte*, xlv, 1972, pp. 119–48.

——, *Museo del Prado: Catálogo de Dibujos*. ii: *Dibujos españoles siglo xviii: A–B*, Madrid 1975.

Arnaiz, J.M., 'El álbum de Vicente Camarón y otros dibujos españoles inéditos', *Academia (Boletín de la Real Academia de Bellas Artes de San Fernando)*, no. 67, 1988, pp. 115–231.

——, *Antonio González Velázquez. Pintor de cámara de su majestad, 1723–1792*, Madrid 1999.

Arrese, L. de, *Antonio González Ruiz* (*Biblioteca de estudios madrileños* xvi), Madrid 1973.

Aterido Fernández, Á., 'Teodoro Ardemans, Pintor', *Anuario del Departamento de Historia y Teoría de Arte (U.A.M)*, vii–viii, 1995–6, pp. 133–48.

—— (ed.), *Corpus Alonso Cano (Documentos y textos)*, Madrid 2002.

Azcárate Luxan, I., V. Durá Ojea, M.P. Fernández Agudo and M.A. Sánchez de León Fernández, *Historia y alegoría: Los Concurso de pintura de la Real Academia de Bellas Artes de San Fernando (1753–1808)*, Madrid 1994.

Baer, R., 'El Greco to Velázquez: Artists of the reign of Philip III', in Schroth and Baer 2008, pp. 41–75.

Balmaceda, J.C., *La contribución genovesa al desarrollo de la manufactura papelera española*, Malaga 2004.

——, 'Italian manufacturers, techniques and manufacturing methods in paper production in Spain', *L'impiego delle techniche e dell'opera dei cartai fabrianesi in Italia e in Europa: The Use of Techniques and Work by Papermakers from Fabriano in Italy and Europe*, Fabriano 2007, pp. 95–108.

——, 'Apuntes para el estudio del papel y las filigranas durante el siglo xv en la Corona de Aragón', *Aragón en la Edad Media*, xx, 2008, pp. 103–16.

Bambach, C.C., *Drawing and Painting in the Italian Renaissance Workshop*, Cambridge 1999.

——, 'Recently acquired Spanish Baroque drawings at the Metropolitan Museum of Art', *Master Drawings*, xxxvii, 1999a, pp. 407–15.

——, 'Christ at the Column: A new acquisition for the Metropolitan Museum of Art', *Apollo*, clxi, 2005, pp. 42–9 (pt 1).

——, 'The Delli Brothers: Three Florentine artists in fifteenth-century Spain', *Apollo*, clxi, 2005a, pp. 75–83 (pt 2).

——, 'A new Ribera drawing among Michelangelos', *Apollo*, clxx, 2009, pp. 50–5.

Banda y Vargas, A. de la, 'Matías de Arteaga, grabador', *Boletín de las Bellas Artes: Real Academia de Bellas Artes Santa Isabel de Hungría*, vi, 1978, pp. 73–131.

Banner, L.A., 'A drawing by Francisco La Vega and a series of fans commissioned for Isabella Farnese', *Fana* (Fan Association of North America Journal), 2005, pp. 7–16.

——, 'Francisco de Solís: A seventeenth-century artist-collector', *Master Drawings*, xlv, 2007, pp. 359–66.

——, *The Religious Patronage of the Duke of Lerma*, Farnham 2009.

Barcia, A.M., *Catálogo de la colección de dibujos originales de la Blblioteca Nacional*, Madrid 1906.

Barrena, C., J.M. Matilla and E. Villena, *Fernando Selma. El grabado al servicio de la cultura ilustrada*, Madrid and Valencia 1993.

Barrio Moya, J.L., 'Sobre un dibujo de Herrera Barnuevo para un trono de plata', *Archivo Español de Arte*, lvi, 1983, pp. 409–10.

——, 'Alonso Miguel de Tovar: un pintor onubense en el Madrid de Felipe V', *Aestuaria: revista de investigación*, no. 7, 2000, pp. 197–204.

Bartsch, A., *Le Peintre-graveur*, 21 vols, Vienna 1803–21.

Bataillon, M., 'Philipe Galle et Arias Montano. Matérieux pour l'iconographie des savants de la renaissance', *Bilbiothèque d'humanisme et Renaissance. Travaux et documents*, II, 1942, pp. 132–60.

Baticle, J., 'Les attaches françaises de Luis Paret y Alcázar', *La revue du Louvre et des musées de France*, no. 3, 1966, pp. 157–64.

Bécares Botas, V., *Arias Montano y Plantino. El libro flamenco en la España de Felipe II* (Humanistas Españoles), León 1999.

Bédat, C., *La Real Academia de Bellas Artes de San Fernando (1744–1808)*, Madrid 1989.

Beguin, S., 'Pellegrino Tibaldi', in *Dibujos italianos para El Escorial*, ed. M. di Ciampaolo, Madrid 1995, pp. 85–100.

Benito, F., 'Sebastian del Piombo y españa', in *Sebastian del Piombo y españa*, exh. cat., Museo Nacional del Prado, Madrid 1995, pp. 41–79.

Benito Doménech, F., 'Una importante colección de dibujos Valencianos del siglo XVII', *Archivo Español de Arte*, LVII, 1984, pp. 277–317.

——, *Los Ribalta y la pintura valenciana de su tiempo*, exh. cat., Museo Nacional del Prado, Madrid 1987.

——, 'Dibujos de José Camarón Boronat sobre la vida de San José', *Archivo Español de Arte*, LX, 1987a, pp. 419–45.

——, *The Paintings of Ribalta 1565–1628*, trans. Suzanne L. Stratton, New York 1988.

——, (ed.) *Cinco siglos de pintura valenciana. Obras del Museo de Bellas Artes de Valencia*, exh. cat., Museo de Bellas Artes, Valencia, Madrid 1996.

——, 'Los Hernandos: pintores hispanos del entorno de Leonardo', in *Los Hernandos: pintores hispanos del entorno de Leonardo*, exh. cat., Museo de Bellas Artes, Valencia 1998, pp. 23–42.

——, *Joan de Juanes. Una nueva visión del artista y su obra*, exh. cat., Museo de Bellas Artes, Valencia 2000.

—— and J.L. Galdón, 'El "Maestro del Álbum Lassala" y Gregorio Bausá. Anotaciones al "Corpus" del dibujo Valenciano del siglo XVII', *Archivo Español de Arte*, LXVII, 1994, pp. 105–18.

—— and J.L. Galdón, *Vicente Macip (h.1475–1550)*, exh. cat., Museo de Bellas Artes, Valencia 1997.

—— and F. Valles Borras, 'Un Colegio de Pintores in Valencia de 1520', *Archivo de Arte Valenciano*, LXXIII, 1992, pp. 62–7.

Bérchez, J., *Arquitectura y academicismo en el siglo XVIII valenciano*, Valencia 1987.

Beutler, W., *Vicente Carducho: der grosse Kartäuserzyklus in El Paular*, Salzburg 1997.

Bilbao. *Luis Paret y Alcázar (1746–1799)*, exh. cat., Museo de Bellas Artes, Bilbao 1991.

Bland, D., *A History of Book Illustration: The Illuminated Manuscript and the Printed Book*, 2nd edn, London 1969.

Blas, J., M. Cruz de Carlos Varona and J.M. Matilla, *Grabadores extranjeros en la Corte Española del Barroco*, Madrid 2011.

—— and J.M. Matilla, *El libro de los Desastres de la Guerra. Francisco de Goya*, I: *Coincidencias y discrepancias en torno a los Desastres. El proceso de creación gráfica: dibujos, pruebas de estado y Álbum de Ceán*, Madrid 2000.

——, J.M. Matilla and I. Aguilar, *El libro de los Desastres de la Guerra. Francisco de Goya*, II: *Elenco de referencias críticas. La difusión de la imágenes: láminas de cobre y estampas de la primera edición*, Madrid 2000.

——, J.M. Matilla and J.M. Medrano, *El libro de Los Caprichos. Francisco de Goya. Dos siglos de interpretaciones (1799–1999). Catálogo de los dibujos, pruebas de estado, láminas de cobre y estampas de la primera edición*, Madrid 1999.

Blasco Esquivias, B., 'Teodoro Ardemans y su entorno en el cambio del siglo (1661–1726). Aspectos de la arquitectura y el urbanismo Madrileños de Felipe II a Carlos III', Ph.D. dissertation, Universidad Complutense de Madrid, Madrid 1991.

——, 'Eliogio del barroco castizo: Ardemans, Churriguera y Ribera', in Morán Turina 2003, pp. 257–88.

Bloom, J.M., *Paper before Print: The History and Impact of Paper in the Islamic World*, New Haven and London 2001.

Bonet Correa, A., 'Láminas de *El Museo Pictórico y escala Óptica* de Palomino', *Archivo Español de Arte*, XLVI, 1973, pp. 131–44.

——, *Vida y obra de fray Matías de Irala grabador y tratadista español del siglo XVIII*, 2 vols, Madrid 1979.

——, 'Proyecto y ostentación barroca en un dibujo de D. Teodoro Ardemans', in *El arte en las cortes Europeas del siglo XVIII* (conference proceedings, April 1987), Madrid and Aranjuez 1989, pp. 147–52.

Borrás Gualis, G.M., *Las pinturas de San Antonio de la Florida de Goya*, with technical discussion by J. Ruiz Pardo, Madrid 2006.

Bottineau, Y., *L'art de cour dans l'espagne de Philippe V (1700–1746)*, Bordeaux 1962.

Boubli, L., '"Magnífico mastre Alonso Berruguete': introduction à l'étude de son oeuvre graphique', *Revue de l'Art*, no. 103, 1994, pp. 11–32.

——, 'The state of scholarship of sixteenth- and seventeenth-century Spanish drawings', *Master Drawings*, XXXVII, 1999, pp. 349–64.

——, *Musée du Louvre. Département de Arts Graphiques. Inventaire générale des dessins, École espagnole, XVI–XVII siècle*, Paris 2002.

——, 'Michelangelo and Spain: On the dissemination of his draughtsmanship', in *Michelangelo's Effect on Art and Artists in the Sixteenth Century*, eds F. Ames-Lewis and P. Joannides, Aldershot 2003, pp. 211–37.

—— and A.E. Pérez Sánchez, *Dessins espagnols. Maîtres de XVIe et XVIIe siècles*, exh. cat., Musée de Louvre, Paris 1991.

Bozal, V., 'La estampa popular en el siglo XVIII', in *El grabado en España (siglos XV al XVIII). Summa Artis. Historia General del Arte*, eds J. Carrete Parrondo, F. Checa Cremades and V. Bozal, Madrid 1987, pp. 647–756.

—— (ed.), *Colección de trajes de España. Tanto antiguos como modernos* (facsimile edn), Madrid 1988.

Brakensiek, S., *Vom 'Theatrum mundi' zum 'Cabinet des Estampes': Das Sammeln von Druckgraphik in Deutschland 1565–1821*, Hildesheim and New York 2003.

Braudel, F., *The Mediterranean and the Mediterranean World in the Age of Philip II*, trans. Siân Reynolds, abridged by Richard Ollard, London 1992.

Bray, X., 'Review of exhibition of Bayeu drawings at the Prado, Madrid', *The Burlington Magazine*, CXXXVIII, 1996, pp. 54–5.

——, 'Drawings by Giaquinto's Spanish followers: Antonio González Velázquez and José del Castillo', *Master Drawings*, XXXVII, 1999, pp. 416–28.

——, *Vicente López. La invención de un cuadro de historia 'Ciro el Grande ante los cadáveres de Abradato y Pantea'*, Bilbao 2002.

Briquet C.M., *Les filigranes: dictionnaire historique des marques du papier*, Paris 1907 (http://www.ksbm.oeaw.ac.ac.at).

Brown, J., 'Algunas adiciones a la obra de Blas de Prado', *Archivo Español de Arte*, XLI, 1968, pp. 29–33.

——, 'Spanish baroque drawings in the Sperling Bequest', *Master Drawings*, XI, 1973, pp. 374–9, 430–9.

——, 'Notes of Princeton drawings, 9: Bartolomé Eséban Murillo', *Record of the Art Museum, Princeton University*, XXXII, 1973a, pp. 28–33.

——, *Jusepe de Ribera: Prints and Drawings*, exh. cat., Art Museum, Princeton, NJ 1973b.

——, 'Pen Drawings by Herrera the Younger', in *Hortus Imaginum: Essays in Western Art*, eds R.E. Enggass and M. Stokstad, Lawrence, KS 1974, pp. 128–38.

——, 'More drawings by Jusepe de Ribera', *Master Drawings*, XII, 1974a, pp. 367–72, 423–34.

——, 'Drawings by Herrera the Younger and a follower', *Master Drawings*, XIII, 1975, pp. 235–40, 299–313.

——, *Murillo and his Drawings*, exh. cat., Art Museum, Princeton, NJ 1976.

——, *Images and Ideas in Seventeenth-Century Spanish Painting*, Princeton, NJ 1978.

——, 'The Prints and Drawings of Ribera', in *Jusepe de Ribera lo Spagnoletto (1591–1652)*, eds C. Felton and W.B. Jordan, exh. cat., Kimbell Art Museum, Fort Worth, TX 1982, pp. 70–90.

——, 'Murillo: New drawings, old problems', *Master Drawings*, XXI, 1983, pp. 160–3, 208–22.

——, 'Drawings by Andalusian Masters', *Apotheca. Revista de Departamento de Historia del Arte, Universidad de Córdoba*, no. 3, 1983a, pp. 9–20.

——, *Velázquez: Painter and Courtier*, New Haven and London 1986.

——, 'Enemies of flattery: Velázquez' portraits of Philip IV', in *Art and History: Images and their Meaning*, eds T.K. Rabb and R.I. Rotberg, Cambridge 1988, pp. 137–54.

——, 'Academies of painting in seventeenth-century Spain', in *Academies of Art between Renaissance and Romanticism*, eds A.W.A. Boschloo, E.J. Hendrikse, L.C. Smit and G.J van der Sman, 'S-Gravenhage 1989, pp. 177–85.

——, *Jusepe de Ribera, Grabador (1591–1652)*, exh. cat., Sala de Exposiciones de la Fundación Caja de Pensiones, Valencia, and Calcografía Nacional Real Academia de Bellas Artes de San Fernando, Madrid 1989a.

——, *The Golden Age of Painting in Spain*, New Haven and London 1991.

——, 'Philip IV as patron and collector', in Úbeda de los Cobos 2005, pp. 45–62.

——, *The Spanish Manner: Drawings from Ribera to Goya*, exh. cat., The Frick Collection, New York 2010.

—— and J.H. Elliott, *A Palace for a King: The Buen Retiro and the Court of Philip IV*, New Haven and London 1980.

—— and S.G. Galassi, *Goya's Last Works*, exh. cat., The Frick Collection, New York 2006.

Buendía, J.R., and I. Gutiérrez Pastor, *Vida y obra del pintor Mateo Cerezo (1637–1666)*, Burgos 1986.

Burón Castro, T., 'Papel hispano-árabe en el Archivo de la Catedral de León', *Actas del V Congreso Nacional de Historia del Papel en España*, Girona 2003, pp. 93–101.

Bury, J.B., 'Juan de Herrera and the Escorial', *Art History*, IX, 1986, pp. 428–49.

Bury, J., review of Wilkinson Zerner and Brown 1990, *Print Quarterly*, VIII, 1991, pp. 77–82.

Bury, M., *The Print in Italy 1550–1620*, exh. cat., British Museum, London 2001.

Bustamente García, A., *La octava maravilla del mundo (estudio histórico sobre El Escorial de Felipe II)*, Madrid 1994.

Cabanes Pecourt, A., 'El comercio papelero de importación en el segundo cuarto del siglo XVII Valenciano', *Actas del II Congreso Nacional de Historia del Papel en España*, Cuenca 1997, pp. 123–8.

——, 'El papel en el arte efímero', *Actas del III Congreso Nacional de Historia del Papel en España*, Alicante 1999, pp. 321–4.

Cacho Casal, M., 'The "true likeness" in Francisco Pacheco's *Libro de retratos*, *Renaissance Studies*, XXIV, 2010, pp. 381–406.

——, *Francisco Pacheco y su Libro de Retratos*, Seville 2011.

Calvo Serraller, F., *La teoría de la pintura en el siglo de oro*, Madrid 1981.

——, *Luis Paret y Alcázar: 1746–1799 (Un retrato melancólico)*, Madrid 1996.

Camón Aznar, J., *Summa Artis. Historia general del arte*, XXIV: *La pintura española del siglo XVI*, Madrid 1970.

Canellas López, A., *Diplomatario. Francisco Goya*, Zaragoza 1981.

Cano de Gardoqui y García, J., *La construcción del Monasterio de El Escorial: historia de una empresa arquitectónica*, Valladolid 1994.

Cánovas del Castillo, C., and C. Lasarte Pérez-Arregui, 'La colección de estampas del Archivo y Biblioteca de la Real Academia de Bellas Artes de San Fernando y su papel en la enseñanza', *Academia (Boletín de la Real Academia de Bellas Artes de San Fernando)*, no. 78, 1994, pp. 181–223.

Capel Margarito, M., *Gaspar Becerra o el miguelangelismo español*, Jaén 1998.

Carducho, V., *Diálogos de la pintura, su defensa, origen, escencia, definición, modos y diferencias* (1633), ed. F. Calvo Serraller, Madrid 1979.

Carofano P., 'Francesco da Urbino y la decoración de la celda baja del prior', in *Los frescos italianos de El Escorial*, ed. M. di Giampaolo, Madrid 1993, pp. 99–104.

Carrete, J., and J.M. Matilla (eds), *Disparates. Francisco de Goya. Tres visions*, Madrid 1996.

Carrete Parrondo, J., 'Grabados de Manuel Salvador Carmona realizados en París' (1752–1762), *Academia (Boletín de la Real Academia de Bellas Artes de San Fernando)*, no. 50, 1980, pp. 127–57.

——, *La enseñanza del grabado calcográfico en Madrid*, Madrid 1980a.

——, 'El Libro de Retratos de Pacheco', *Goya*, nos 193–5, 1986, pp. 168–73.

——, 'El grabado y la estampa barroca', pp. 203–391, and 'El grabado en el siglo XVIII: Triunfo de la estampa ilustrada', pp. 395–644, in *El grabado en España (siglos XV al XVIII). Summa Artis. Historia General del Arte*, eds J. Carrete Parrondo, F. Checa Cremades and V. Bozal, Madrid 1987.

——, *El grabado a buril en la España ilustrada: Manuel Salvador Carmona*, exh. cat., Museo de la Casa de la Moneda, Madrid 1989.

——, 'Luis Paret. Ilustrador de libros', in Bilbao 1991, pp. 155–64.

——, *Colección de las principales suertes de una corrida de toros. Dibujada y grabada por Antonio Carnicero*, Madrid 1991a.

—— and A. Martínez-Novillo, *El siglo de oro de las tauromaquias: estampas taurinas 1750–1868*, Madrid 1989.

—— and E. Villena, *Joaquín José Fabregat: El grabado en el siglo XVIII: Valencia-Madrid-México*, exh. cat., Valencia 1990.

Casey, J., *The Kingdom of Valencia in the Seventeenth Century*, Cambridge 1979.

Castañeda Becerra, A.M., *Los Cieza, una familia de pintores del barroco Granadino: Juan, José y Vicente*, Granada 2000.

Castelló Mora, J., 'Historiadores del papel en la segunda mitad del siglo XVIII', *Actas del VII Congreso Nacional de Historia del Papel en España*, Madrid 2007, pp. 430–45.

Caturla, M.L., 'Documentos en torno a Vicencio Carducho', *Arte Español: Revista de la sociedad española de amigos del arte*, XXVI, 1968–9, pp. 145–221.

Ceán Bermúdez, J.A., *Diccionario histórico de los mas ilustres profesores de la bellas artes en España*, 6 vols, Madrid 1800.

Cerón, M., 'Defective perceptions: Vision as consumption in Spanish art, *c.*1766–1794', Ph.D. dissertation, University of London, London 2006.

Cervera Vera, L., 'Privilegio concedido por Gregorio XIII a Juan de Herrera para imprimir y vender sus estampas de El Escorial', *Academia (Boletín de la Real Academia de Bellas Artes de San Fernando)*, no. 58, 1984, pp. 79–99.

——, *Las estampas y el summario de El Escorial por Juan de Herrera*, 2nd edn, Madrid 1988.

Chapman, H., *Michelangelo Drawings: Closer to the Master*, exh. cat., British Museum, London 2005.

—— and M. Faietti, *Fra Angelico to Leonardo: Italian Renaissance Drawings*, exh. cat., British Museum, London 2010.

Checa, F., *Tiziano y la Monarquía Hispánica. Usos y funciones de la pintura veneciana en España (siglos XVI y XVII)*, Madrid 1994.

——, 'Arquitectura y decoracion en el Alcázar de Felipe II', in *El Real Alcázar de Madrid. Dos siglos de arquitectura y coleccionismo en la corte de los Reyes de España*, ed. F. Checa, Madrid 1994a, pp. 142–7.

Checa Cremades, F., 'La imagen impresa en el renacimiento y el manierismo', in *El grabado en España (siglos XV al XVIII): Summa Artis. Historia General del Arte*, eds J. Carrete Parrondo, F. Checa Cremades and V. Bozal, Madrid 1987, pp. 11–200.

——, *Felipe II mecenas de las artes*, Madrid 1992.

Chennevières, Ph. de, *Les dessins de maîtres anciens exposés a l'Ecole des Beaux-Arts en 1879*, Paris 1880.

Cherry, P., 'Artistic Training and the Painters' Guild in Seville', in *Velázquez in Seville*, exh. cat., National Galleries of Scotland, Edinburgh 1996, pp. 67–75.

——, 'La formación de los pintores en los talleres sevillanos', in *Zurbarán ante su centenario (1598–1998)*, Arte y arqueología, no. 17, Soria 1997, pp. 49–70.

——, *Arte y naturaleza. El bodegón español en el Siglo de Oro*, Madrid 1999.

——, *Luis Meléndez, Still-Life Painter*, Madrid 2006.

Churchill, W.A., *Watermarks in Paper in Holland, England, France, etc. in the XVII and XVIII Centuries and their Interconnection*, Amsterdam 1965.

Cioffi, I., 'Corrado Giaquinto's studies for the sculptural decorations planned for the staircases of the new royal palace in Madrid', *Master Drawings*, XXII, 1984, pp. 434–40, 497–507.

——, 'Corrado Giaquinto, the Academy and the New Royal Palace in Madrid', in *El arte en las cortes Europeas del siglo XVIII* (conference proceedings, April 1987), Madrid and Aranjuez 1989, pp. 184–90.

——, 'Corrado Giaquinto and the dissemination of the Italian style at the Bourbon court in Madrid', in Kasl and Stratton 1997, pp. 27–38.

Ciruelos Gonzalo, A., 'El dibujo en la Real Academia de San Fernando. Contribución al estudio de sus colecciones', *Academia (Boletín de la Real Academia de Bellas Artes de San Fernando)*, no. 78, 1994, pp. 133–78.

—— and M.P. García Sepúlveda, 'Inventario de Dibujos de la Real Academia de Bellas Artes de San Fernando (II)', *Academia (Boletín de la Real Academia de Bellas Artes de San Fernando)*, no. 65, 1989, pp. 255–406.

Claye, E., 'A group of portrait drawings by Jacopo Amigoni', *Master Drawings*, XII, 1974, pp. 41–8, 97–101.

Clifford, T., 'G.B. Castello's designs for the "Cupid and Psyche" tapestries', *The Burlington Magazine*, CXVII, 1975, pp. 234–9.

Collar de Cáceres, F., 'Más pinturas de Francisco Camilo en Segovia', *Archivo Español de Arte*, LIX, 1986, pp. 277–90.

Colomer, J.L., 'España, Nápoles y sus virreyes', in *España y Nápoles. Coleccionismo y mecenazgo virreinales en el siglo XVII*, ed. J.L. Colomer, Madrid 2009, pp. 13–37.

Cordellier, D., 'Les dessins de Fernando Yáñez de la Almedina', in *Hommage à Michel Laclotte. Etudes du la peinture du Moyen Age et de la Renaissance*, Milan 1994, pp. 415–29.

——, 'Los dibujos de Fernando Yáñez de la Almedina', in *Los Hernandos. Pintores hispanos del entorno de Leonardo*, exh. cat., Museo de Bellas Artes, Valencia 1998, pp. 222–34.

Corral, J. del, 'Teodoro Ardemans, maestro mayor de las obras de la villa Madrid y su fontanero mayor', *Anales del Instituto de Estudios Madrileños*, X, 1974, pp. 171–97.

Cotarelo y Mori, E., *Diccionario biográfico y bibliográfico de calígrafos españoles*, 2 vols, Madrid 1913.

Cumberland, R., *Memoirs of Richard Cumberland*, 2 vols, London 1806.

Dacos, N., 'Pedro Campaña dopo Siviglia: Arazzi e altri inediti', *Bollettino d'Arte*, LXV, 1980, pp. 1–44.

——, 'Pedro Machuca en Italie', in *Scritti di storia dell'arte in onore di Federico Zeri*, Milan 1984, I, pp. 332–61.

——, 'Peeter de Kempeneer / Pedro Campaña as a Draughtsman', *Master Drawings*, XXV, 1987, pp. 359–89, 422–43.

——, 'Aller apprendre à peindre à Rome en venant des anciens Pays-Bas ou de la Péninsule Ibérique. Un essai de périodisation, l'exemple de Luis de Vargas et un faux', in *El modelo Italiano en las artes plásticas de le península Ibérica durante el renacimiento*, ed. M.J. Redondo Cantera, Valladolid 2004, pp. 11–40.

Dalmases, N. de, *Orfebreria catalana medieval: Barcelona 1300–1500 (aproximació a l'estudi)*, I: *Consideracions generals i catalogació d'obra*; II: *Argenters i documents*, Barcelona 1992.

Davidson, B., 'Navarrete in Rome', *The Burlington Magazine*, CXXXV, 1993, pp. 93–6.

Davies, D. (ed.), *El Greco*, exh. cat., National Gallery, London 2003.

——, 'El Greco's scheme of decoration in Santo Domingo el Antiguo: the creative process', in *El Greco's Studio* (Proceedings of the International Symposium Rethymnon, Crete, 23–25 September 2005), ed. N. Hadjinicolaou, Iraklion 2007, pp. 83–134.

De Dominici, B., *Vite de' Pittori, Scultori, ed Architetti Napoletani* (1742), eds F. Sricchia Santoro and A. Zezza, 2 vols, Naples 2008.

DeGrazia Bohlin, D., *Prints and Related Drawings by the Carracci Family: A Catalogue Raisonné*, exh. cat., National Gallery of Art, Washington, DC 1979.

De la Mano, J., 'Nuevas aportaciones a la intervención de Maella en la decoración de la Colegiata de la Granja', *Archivo Español de Arte*, LXXI, 1998, pp. 375–90.

——, *Mariano Salvador Maella (1739–1819). Catálogo razonado*, 2 vols, Santander 2011.

De Lapuerta Montoya, M., *Los pintores de la Corte de Felipe III. La Casa Real de El Pardo*, Madrid 2002.

Defourneaux, M., *Daily Life in Spain in the Golden Age*, trans. N. Branch, Stanford 1979.

Degenhart, B., and A. Schmitt, *Corpus der italienischen Zeichnungen, 1300–1450*. I: *Süd-und Mittelitalien* (2 vols); II: *Venedig; Addenda zu Süd- und Mittelitalien* (4 vols), Berlin 1968–80.

Delenda, O., and B. Navarrete Prieto, 'El conjunto de San Buenaventura de Sevilla como exponente de naturalismo', in Pérez Sánchez and Navarrete Prieto 2006, pp. 99–122.

Delgado, O., *Luis Paret y Alcázar, pintor español*, Madrid 1957.

Deswarte-Rosa, S., '"Tudo o que se faz em este mundo é desenhar". Francisco de Holanda entre théorie et collection', in *El modelo Italiano en las artes plásticas de le península Ibérica durante el renacimiento*, ed. M.J. Redondo Cantera, Valladolid 2004, pp. 247–90.

Díaz García, A., 'Nuevos datos sobre Sebastián de Herrera Barnuevo en los Recoletos Agustinos y en el Colegio Imperial de Madrid', *Anuario del Departamento de Historia y Teoría de Arte (U.A.M)*, XVII, 2005, pp. 51–66.

Díez, J.L., *La pintura española del siglo XIX en el Museo Lázaro Galdiano*, Madrid 2005.

Díez García, J.L., *Vicente López (1772–1850). Vida y obra*, Madrid 1999.

Dizionario degli artisti italiani in Spagna (Documenti e ricerche IX), Madrid 1977.

Domínguez Ortiz, A., *Carlos III y la españa de la ilustración (1700–1833)*, 1st edn 1988, rev. edn Madrid 2005.

Dotseth, A., 'Maestro Bartolomé's use of prints in the altarpiece of Ciudad Rodigo', in Anderson, Dotseth and Roglán 2008, pp. 117–45.

Durán González-Meneses, R., *Catálogo de los dibujos de los siglos XVI y XVII de la colección del Museo de la Casa de la Moneda*, Madrid 1980.

Duran i Sanpere, A., *Populäre Druckgraphik Europas. Spanien (vom 15. bis zum 20 Jahrhundert)*, Munich 1971.

Elen, A.J., *Italian Late-Medieval and Renaissance Drawing-Books from Giovannino de' Grassi to Palma Giovane: A Codicological Approach*, Leiden 1995.

Elliott, J.H., *The Revolt of the Catalans: A Study in the Decline of Spain (1598–1640)*, Cambridge 1963.

—, *The Count-Duke of Olivares: The Statesman in an Age of Decline*, New Haven and London 1986.

—, *Spain, Europe and the Wider World 1500–1800*, New Haven and London 2009.

Escobar, J., *The Plaza Mayor and the Shaping of Baroque Madrid*, Cambridge 2004.

Espanyol Bertran, F., 'La transmisión del conocimiento artístico en la corona de Aragón (siglos XIV–XV)', *Saber y conocimiento en la Edad Media*, no. 5, 1997, pp. 73–113.

Espinós Díaz, A., 'Un dibujo de Roland de Mois en el Museo de Bellas Artes de San Carlos de Valencia', *Archivo Español de Arte*, XLVIII, 1975, pp. 411–12.

—, *Museo de Bellas Artes de Valencia: Catálogo de dibujos I (Siglos XVI–XVII)*, Madrid 1979.

—, 'Dibujos de José del Castillo preparatorios para los tapices de la Real Manufactura de Santa Bárbara', *Miscelánea de Arte*, 1982, pp. 188–92.

—, *Museo de Bellas Artes de Valencia: Catálogo de dibujos II (Siglo XVII)*, 3 vols, Madrid 1984.

—, *Dibujos Valencianos del Siglo XVII*, exh. cat., Fundación El Monte, Seville 1997.

—, *Ultimas adquisiciones 1996–1999. Museo de Bellas Artes, Valencia*, Valencia 1999.

—, *José Camarón Bonanat (1731–1803)*, exh. cat., Museo de Bellas Artes Gravina, Alicante 2006.

—, *Líneas maestras. Dibujos del Museo de Bellas Artes de Valencia*, exh. cat., Museo de Bellas Artes, Valencia 2010.

Falomir Faus, M., *La pintura y los pintores en la Valencia del renacimiento (1472–1620)*, Valencia 1994.

—, 'Imágenes de poder y evocaciones de la memoria. Usos y funciones del retrato en la corte de Felipe II', in Madrid 1998, pp. 203–27.

—, *Los Bassano en la españa del siglo de oro*, exh. cat., Museo Nacional del Prado, Madrid 2001.

Feinblatt, E., *Seventeenth-Century Bolognese Ceiling Decorators*, Santa Barbara 1992.

Fernández Agudo, M.P., and M.A. Sánchez de León Fernández, 'Índice de cargos académicos de la Real Academia de Bellas Artes de San Fernando en el siglo XVIII', *Academia (Boletín de la Real Academia de Bellas Artes de San Fernando)*, no. 67, 1988, pp. 374–458.

Fernández López, J., *Lucas Valdés (1661–1725)*, Seville 2003.

Fernández Martín, M.M., *Dibujos sevillanos de arquitectura de la primera mitad del siglo XVII* (Historia y Geografía, no. 64), Seville 2003.

Fernández Pardo, F., 'Dibujos perdidos, erróneamente atribuidos y conservados de Navarrete', in *Navarrete 'el mudo' pintor de Felipe II*, exh. cat., Centro de Exposiciones y Congresos y Museo 'Camón Aznar', Zaragoza 1995, pp. 219–31.

Fernández-Santos Ortiz-Iribas, J., 'Entre Agostino Carracci y Veronese: apuntes sobre el aprendizaje Italiano de Francisco de Herrera "El Mozo"', *Archivo Español de Arte*, LXXVIII, 2005, pp. 245–61.

Ferrari, O., and G. Scavizzi, *Luca Giordano*, 3 vols, Naples 1966.

Finaldi, G., 'Dibujos inéditos y otros poco conocidos de Jusepe de Ribera', *Boletín del Museo del Prado*, XXIII, 2005, pp. 24–44.

— and C. Garrido (eds), *El trazo oculto. Dibujos subyacentes en pinturas de los siglos XV y XVI*, exh. cat., Museo Nacional del Prado, Madrid 2006.

Fitz Darby, D., *Francisco Ribalta and his School*, Cambridge, MA 1938.

Fox, C.F., 'The PAU Visual Arts Section and the Hemispheric Circulation of Latin American art during the Cold War', *Getty Research Journal*, no. 2, 2010, pp. 83–106.

Fracchia, C., 'El retablo mayor de la Catedral de Astorga. Un concurso escultórico en la España del Renacimiento', *Archivo Español de Arte*, LXXI, 1998, pp. 157–65.

—, 'Gaspar Becerra: a Spaniard in the workshop of Daniele da Volterra', *The Sculpture Journal*, III, 1999, pp. 6–13.

Gallego Gallego, A., *Historia del grabado en España*, Madrid 1979.

García y Bellido, A., 'Avances para una monografía de los Churrigueras', *Archivo Español de Arte y Arqueología*, V, 1929, pp. 21–86.

García Cueto, D., *La estancia española de los pintores boloñeses Agostino Mitelli y Angelo Michele Colonna, 1658–1662*, Granada 2005.

García-Frías, C., 'Francesco da Urbino', in *Dibujos Italianos para El Escorial*, ed. M. di Giampaolo, Madrid 1995, pp. 61–83.

—, 'Romolo Cincinato', in *Dibujos Italianos para El Escorial*, ed. M. di Giampaolo, Madrid 1995a, pp. 47–60.

—, *Gaspar Becerra y las pinturas de la Torre de la Reina del Palacio de El Pardo. Una nueva lectura tras su restauración*, Madrid 2005.

García Hidalgo, J., *Principios para estudiar el nobilísmo y real arte de la pintura* (1693), ed. A. Rodriguez Moñino, Madrid 1965 (facsimile).

—, *Principios para estudiar el nobilísmo y real arte de la pintura por Don José García Hidalgo* (critical edn), ed. S.G. Mateo, 2 vols (I: essays, II: facsimile), Valencia 2006.

García-Toraño Martínez, I., 'El dibujo y su relación con el arte en la primera mitad del siglo XVIII', in *La real biblioteca pública 1711–1760. De Felipe V a Fernando VI*, ed. E. Santiago Páez, exh. cat., Biblioteca Nacional, Madrid 2004, pp. 359–79.

— (ed.), *Dibujos de arquitectura y ornamentación de la Biblioteca Nacional, Siglo XVIII*, Madrid 2009.

García de la Torre, F., *Dibujos del Museo de Bellas Artes de Córdoba*, exh. cat., Museo de Bellas Artes, Córdoba 1997.

—, *Dibujar al Mirada. Fondos del Museo de Bellas Artes de Córdoba*, exh. cat., Centro Cultural Casa del Cordón, Caja de Burgos, Burgos 2006.

Garcia Vega, B., *El grabado del libro español siglos XV–XVI–XVII*, 2 vols, Valladolid 1984.

Garín Llombart, F.V., *Joan de Joanes (+1579)*, exh. cat., Salas de Exposición, Madrid and Museo de Bellas Artes, Valencia 1979.

Garín Ortíz de Taranco, F.Mª, *La Academia Valenciana de Bellas Artes*, 2nd edn, Valencia 1993.

—, *Yáñez de la Almedina pintor español*, 2nd edn, Ciudad Real 1978.

Gassier, P., *The Drawings of Goya*, I: *The Complete Albums*, London 1973.

—, *The Drawings of Goya*, II: *The Sketches, Studies and Individual Drawings*, London 1975.

— and J. Wilson, *Goya: His Life and Work with a Catalogue Raisonné of the Paintings, Drawings and Engravings*, London 1971.

Gavara, J.J., and M. Gómez-Ferrer, 'Fernando Yáñez de la Almedina y el órgano renacentista de la catedral de Valencia', in *Los Hernandos. Pintores hispanos del entorno de Leonardo*, exh. cat., Museo de Bellas Artes, Valencia 1998, pp. 237–46.

Gaya Nuño, J.A., 'Luis Paret y Alcázar', *Boletín de la Sociedad Española de Excursiones*, LVI, 1952, pp. 87–153 (and plates).

Gaye, G., *Carteggio inedito d'artisti dei secoli XIV, XV, XVI*, 3 vols, Florence 1840.

Gayoso Carreira G., *Historia del Papel en España*, 3 vols, Lugo 2006.

Gere, J.A., and P. Pouncey, *Italian Drawings in the Department of Prints and Drawings in the British Museum: Artists Working in Rome c.1550–c.1640*, 2 vols, London 1983.

Gestoso y Pérez, J., *Biografía del pintor sevillano Juan de Valdés Leal*, Seville 1916.

di Giampaolo, M. (ed.), *Dibujos Italianos para el Escorial*, Madrid 1995.

Glendinning, N., *A Literary History of Spain: The Eighteenth Century*, London 1972.

—, *Goya and his Critics*, New Haven and London 1977.

—, 'The Spanishness of Spanish art in the Golden Age', *Oxford Art Journal*, XI, 1988, pp. 69–76.

—, 'La problemática historia de *Los Disparates* y su interpretación carnavalesca', in *Francisco de Goya, grabador. Instantáneas. Disparates*, Madrid 1992, pp. 19–32.

—, 'Motivos carnavalescos en la obra de Goya', in *Disparates, Francisco de Goya. Tres visiones*, eds J. Carrete and J.M. Matilla, Madrid 1996, pp. 57–73.

—, 'Goya y la guerra de la independencia', in *Miradas sobre la guerra de la independencia*, exh. cat., Biblioteca Nacional, Madrid 2008, pp. 39–60.

—, E. Harris and F. Russell, 'Lord Grantham and the taste for Velázquez: "The electrical eel of the day"', *The Burlington Magazine*, CXLI, 1999, pp. 598–605.

Gómez, J., 'Fuentes icónicas en los Hernandos', in *Los Hernandos. Pintores hispanos del entorno de Leonardo*, exh. cat., Museo de Bellas Artes, Valencia 1998, pp. 45–58.

Gómez Frechina, J., 'Ecos italianos en la pintura valenciana de los siglos XV y XVI', in *La impronta florentina y flamenca en Valencia. Pintura de los siglos XIV–XVI*, eds F. Benito Doménech and J. Gómez Frechina, exh. cat., Museo de Bellas Artes, Valencia, and Palazzo Medici Riccardi, Florence 2007, pp. 19–60.

Gómez Sicre, J., *Spanish Drawings XV–XIX Centuries*, New York, Paris and London 1949.

González García, J.L., '*Ut pictura rhetorica*: Juan de Juanes y el retablo de San Esteban de Valencia', *Boletín del Museo del Prado*, XVII, 1999, pp. 21–56.

González de Zárate, J.M., *Real colección de estampas de San Lorenzo de El Escorial*, 7 vols (incomplete), Madrid 1992–4.

Goris, J.-A., and G. Marlier (eds), *Albrecht Dürer: Diary of his Journey to the Netherlands, 1520–1521. Accompanied by the silverpoint sketchbook and paintings and drawings made during his journey*, London 1971.

Gradmann, E., *Drawings by Spanish Masters*, Basle 1946.

Greer, M.R., *The Play of Power: Mythological Court Dramas of Calderón de la Barca*, Princeton, NJ 1991.

Griffin, C., *The Crombergers of Seville: The History of a Printing and Merchant Dynasty*, Oxford 1988.

Griffiths, A., *Prints and Printmaking: An Introduction to the History and Techniques*, 2nd edn, London 1996.

Gutiérrez Pastor, I, 'Una pintura de fray Matías de Irala en Navarrete, y cuatro dibujos', *Berceo*, no. 102, 1982, pp. 39–53.

—, '"Sol que de vida y prudencia de todas las habilidades": Teoría y práctica del dibujo en la españa del barroco', in *Dibujo español del renacimiento a Goya: La colección de la Reina María Cristina de Borbón*, eds. A. Ansón Navarro and R. Centellas Salamero, exh. cat., Palacio de Sástago, Zaragoza 2008, pp. 37–51.

Hänsel, S., *Benito Arias Montano (1527–1598). Humanismo y arte en españa*, trans. D. Romero Álvarez and J. Espino Nuño, Huelva 1999.

Harris, E., 'Un dibujo de Francisco Camilo en el Museo Británico', *Archivo Español de Arte*, XXXIII, 1960, p. 88.

—, 'Angelo Michele Colonna y la decoración de San Antonio de Los Portugueses', *Archivo Español de Arte*, XXXIV, 1961, pp. 101–5.

—, *Velázquez*, Oxford 1982.

Harris, T., *Goya: Engravings and Lithographs*. I: *Text and Illustrations*; II: *Catalogue Raisonné*, Oxford 1964.

Heckes, F.I., 'Goya's *Tauromaquia*: A criticism of bullfighting?' *Print Quarterly*, XVIII, 2001, pp. 41–63.

Held, J., 'Michel-Ange Houasse in Spanien. Zum stil seiner gemälde und zeichnungen', *Münchner Jahrbuch der Bildenden Kunst*, XIX, 1968, pp. 185–206.

—, 'Drawings by Francisco and Ramón Bayeu', *Master Drawings*, VI, 1968a, pp. 31–6.

—, *Rubens: Selected Drawings*, Oxford 1986.

Hellwig, K., 'An unknown drawing by Juan Carreño de Miranda', *Master Drawings*, XLV, 2007, pp. 354–8.

— and K. Zeitler, *El Greco kommentiert den Wettstreit der Künste. Eine Ziechnung in der Staatlichen Graphishen Sammlung München* (Studio-Reihe der Staatlichen Graphischen Sammlung München. Band I), Munich and Berlin 2006.

Helman, E., *Trasmundo de Goya*, Madrid 1963.

Helston, M., *Painting in Spain during the Later Eighteenth Century*, exh. cat., National Gallery, London 1989.

Heredia Moreno, M. del C., 'Dibujos de Alonso Berruguete, Julio de Aquilis y Andrés de Melgar en la Fundación Lázaro Galdiano', *Goya*, no. 306, 2005, pp. 132–44.

Heriard Dubreuil, M., *Valencia y el Gótico Internacional*, trans. A.-P. Salas Martinelli, 2 vols, Valencia 1987.

Hermoso Cuesta, M., *Lucas Jordan y la corte de Madrid. Una decada prodigiosa 1692–1702*, Zaragoza 2008.

Hernández, C., Apéndice II: Filigranas', *Catálogo de las Estampas de Goya en la Biblioteca Nacional*, Madrid 1996, pp. 275–85.

Hernández Guardiola, L., *Pintura decorativa barroca en la provincia de Alicante*. II: *Antonio Villanueva (1714–1785)*, Alicante 1990.

—, *Nicolás Borrás (1530–1610). Un pintor Valenciano del renacimiento*, exh. cat., Museo de Bellas Artes, Valencia 2010.

Hidalgo Brinquis, M.C., 'Características del papel de las cartas de los Reyes Católicos: sus filigranas', *Archivo Secreto: Revista Cultural de Toledo*, no. 4, 2008, pp. 228–41.

Holcomb, M., *Pen and Parchment: Drawing the Middle Ages*, exh. cat., Metropolitan Museum of Art, New York 2009.

Hollstein, F.W.H., *Dutch and Flemish Etchings, Engravings and Woodcuts, c.1450–1700*, Amsterdam 1949–.

—, *German Engravings, Etchings and Woodcuts 1400–1700*, Amsterdam and Rotterdam 1954–.

—, *The New Hollstein: Dutch and Flemish Etchings, Engravings and Woodcuts, c.1450–1700*, Rotterdam 1993–.

Hunter, D., *Papermaking: The History and Technique of an Ancient Craft*, London 1957.

Ibáñez Martínez, P.M., 'El período valenciano maduro de Fernando Yáñez (H.1516–H.1521)', *Archivo Español de Arte*, LXVII, 1994, pp. 225–42.

—, 'Dibujos y grabados en el proceso creador de Fernando Yáñez', *Archivo Español de Arte*, LXX, 1997, pp. 127–42.

Idrisí, *Geografía de España* (Arabic/Spanish text), trans. E. Savaedra and A. Blázquez, Zaragoza 1988.

Jenni, U., *Das Skizzenbuch der Internationalen Gotik in den Uffizien. Der übergang vom musterbuch zum skizzenbuch*, Vienna 1976.

Jiménez, A., and A. Fernández Ávila, 'Aportaciones a las características morfológicas del papel hispano-árabe a través de las restauraciones realizadas en el Servicio de Libros y Documentos del IPHE', *Actas del VII Congreso Nacional de Historia del Papel en España*, Madrid 2007, pp. 98–129.

Jiménez Colmenar, A., 'Aportaciones a las características morfológicas del papel hispano-árabe desde el proceso de restauración de varios documentos intervenidos en el Instituto del Patrimonio Histórico Español', *Actas de la reunión de estudio sobre el papel hispanoárabe*, Valencia 2009, pp. 78–97.

Jordan, W.B., *Juan van der Hamen y León and the Court of Madrid*, New Haven and London 2005.

Jordán de Urríes y de la Colina, J., 'Un Goya exótico: *La osa hormiguera de Su Majestad*', *Goya*, no. 336, 2011, pp. 242–53.

Judson J.R., and C. Van de Velde, *Book Illustrations and Title-Pages*, Corpus Rubenianum Ludwig Burchard (pt XXI), 2 vols, Antwerp 1978.

Junquera, P., 'El obrador de bordados de El Escorial', in *El Escorial 1563–1963: IV Centenario de la Fundación del Monasterio de San Lorenzo El Real*, Madrid 1963, II, pp. 578–82.

Jurado, A., *Juan de la Cuesta, impresor de El Quijote por encargo del librero Francisco Robles y breves noticias de ambos y del autor de la obra de Miguel de Cervantes*, Madrid 2007.

Kamen, H., *Spain's Road to Empire: The Making of a World Power 1492–1763*, London and New York 2002.

—, *Spain 1469–1714: A Society in Conflict*, 3rd edn, London 2005.

—, *The Escorial: Art and Power in the Renaissance*, New Haven and London 2010.

Kasl, R., 'Painters, Polychromy and the Perfection of Images', in *Spanish Polychrome Sculpture 1500–1800 in United States Collections*, ed. S.L. Stratton, exh. cat., The Spanish Institute, New York, Meadows Museum, Southern Methodist University, Dallas and Los Angeles County Museum of Art, Los Angeles 1993, pp. 33–53.

— (ed.), *Sacred Spain: Art and Belief in the Spanish World*, exh. cat., Indianapolis Museum of Art, Indianapolis 2009.

— and S.L. Stratton (eds), *Painting in Spain in the Age of Enlightenment: Goya and his Contemporaries*, exh. cat., Indianapolis Museum of Art, Indianapolis and The Spanish Institute, New York 1997.

Kehrer, H., 'Un dibujo del Greco en el Gabinete de Estampas de Munich', *Archivo Español de Arte*, XI, 1935, pp. 283–6.

Kinkead, D.T., *Juan de Valdés Leal (1622–1690): His Life and Work*, New York and London 1978.

—, *Pintores y doradores en Sevila, 1650–1699*, 2nd edn, Bloomington, IN 2009.

Kitaura, Y., 'El Greco y Miguel Ángel: Problemas del dibujo en El Greco', *Archivo Español de Arte*, LXVIII, 1995, pp. 145–64.

Kowal, D.M., 'Unpublished drawings and a probable source for Franicisco Ribalta's "Vision of St Francis"', *The Burlington Magazine*, CXXVI, 1984, pp. 768–75.

—, *Ribalta y los ribaltescos. La evolución del estilo barroco en Valencia*, Valencia 1985.

Kraft, W.C., *Codices Vindobonenses Hispanici: A Catalog of the Spanish, Portuguese, and Catalan Manuscripts in the Austrian National Library in Vienna*, Corvallis, OR 1957.

Krill, J., *English Artists' Paper: Renaissance to Regency*, London 1987.

Kubler, G., 'Vicente Carducho's Allegories of Painting', *The Art Bulletin*, XLVII, 1965, pp. 439–45.

—, *Building the Escorial*, Princeton, NJ 1982.

Kunoth, G., 'Francisco Pacheco's *Apotheosis of Hercules*', *Journal of the Warburg and Courtauld Institutes*, XXVII, 1964, pp. 335–7.

Kusche, M., *Juan Pantoja de la Cruz y sus seguidores B. González, R. De Villandrando y A. López Polanco*, Madrid 2007.

Lacarra Ducay, M.C., 'Sobre dibujos preparatorios para retablos de pintores aragoneses del siglo XV', *Anuario de Estudios Medievales*, XIII, 1983, pp. 553–81.

Lafuente Ferrari, E., 'Velázquez y los retratos del conde-duque de Olivares', *Goya*, nos 37–8, 1960, pp. 64–91.

Landau, D., and P. Parshall, *The Renaissance Print 1470–1550*, New Haven and London 1994.

Laurentius, T., 'Paper in the Netherlands', *Fresh Woods and Pastures New: Seventeenth-Century Dutch Landscape Drawings from the Peck Collection*, eds F.W. Robinson and S. Peck, exh. cat., Ackland Art Museum, Chapel Hill 1999, pp. 29–33.

Lavalle-Cobo, T., 'Biografía artística de Isabel de Farnesio', in *El Real Sitio de La Granja de San Ildefonso. Retrato y escena del Rey*, ed. D. Rodríguez Ruiz, Madrid 2000, pp. 182–93.

Lenaghan, P., 'Los dibujos de Antonio Carnicero: proceso de trabajo e ilustración', in *De la palabra a la imagen: El 'Quijote' de la Academia de 1780*, ed. E. Santiago Páez, exh. cat., Biblioteca Nacional, Madrid 2006, pp. 59–84.

León, A., 'El grabado sevillano durante el lustro real: 1729–1733', in *El arte en las cortes europeas del siglo XVIII* (conference proceedings, 27–29 April 1987), Madrid and Aranjuez 1989, pp. 359–69.

—, *Iconografía y fiesta durante el lustro: 1729–1733*, Seville 1990.

León Tello, F. and M.V. Sanz Sanz, *La estética académica española en el siglo XVII: Real Academia de Bellas Artes de San Carlos de Valencia*, Valencia 1979.

—, *La teoría española de la pintura en el siglo XVIII: el tratado de Palomino*, Madrid 1979a.

Líter Mayayo, C., *La obra de Tomás López. Imagen cartográfica del siglo XVIII*, Madrid, 2002.

Lleó Cañal, V., 'The cultivated elite of Velázquez's Seville', in *Velázquez in Seville*, exh. cat., National Galleries of Scotland, Edinburgh 1996, pp. 23–7.

Llorca, J.A., 'Aspectos técnicos e históricos de la fabricación de papel en Xátiva', *Actas de la reunión de estudio sobre el papel hispanoárabe*, Valencia 2009, pp. 24–52.

Llordén, A., *Escultores y entalladores malagueños*, Avila 1960.

Llorens, M., and M.A. Catalá, 'Un monumento efímero exponente del idea de la monarquía del despotismo ilustrado: el de las fiestas de la proclamación de Carlos III en Valencia', *Traza y Baza*, no. 8, 1983, pp. 28–35.

Logan, A.-M., and M.C. Plomp, *Peter Paul Rubens: The Drawings*, exh. cat., Metropolitan Museum of Art, New York 2005.

Longhi, R., 'Comprimarj spagnoli della maniera italiana', *Paragone (Arte)*, no. 43, 1953, pp. 3–15.

López Azorín, M.A., B. Navarrete Prieto and S. Salort Pons, 'Vicente Salvador Gómez, Alonso Cano y la pintura valenciana de la segunda mitad del siglo XVII', *Archivo Español de Arte*, LXXIV, 2001, pp. 393–424.

López-Fanjul, M., 'The Spanish origins of the Marqués del Carpio's collection of drawings', *Master Drawings*, XLVIII, 2010, pp. 463–81.

López-Rey, J., *A Cycle of Goya's Drawings: The Expression of Truth and Liberty*, London 1956.

—, *Velázquez*. I: *Painter of Painters*; II: *Catalogue Raisonné*, Cologne 1996.

López Serrano, M., 'Reflejo Velázqueño en el arte del libro español de su tiempo', in *Varia Velázqueña*, Madrid 1960, vol. 1, pp. 499–513.

—, 'El Grabador Pedro Perret', in *El Escorial 1563–1963*, vol. 2, 1963, pp. 689–716.

—, 'El grabado en los incunables de las colecciónes palatina y escurialense', *Reales Sitios*, no. 35, 1973, pp. 25–32.

López Torrijos, R., 'Un dibujo de mitología para las pinturas del Palacio del Viso del Marqués', *Archivo Español de Arte*, LV, 1982, pp. 76–9.

—, 'Grabados y dibujos para la entrada en Madrid de María Luisa de Orleáns (1680)', *Archivo Español de Arte*, LVIII, 1985, pp. 239–50.

—, *La mitología en la pintura española del Siglo de Oro*, Madrid 1985a.

Lorenzo de Márquez, T., 'Carnival language in Goya's iconic language', in Pérez Sánchez and Sayre 1989, pp. LXXXV–XCIV.

Los Llanos, J. de, 'Les Tiepolo et Goya', in Paris 2008, pp. 47–53.

Loveday H., *Islamic Paper: A Study of an Ancient Craft*, London 2001.

Luna, J.J., 'Louis-Michel van Loo en España', *Goya*, no. 144, 1978, pp. 330–7.

—, 'El retrato de Fernando VI y Bárbara con su corte, por Amigoni', *Archivo Español de Arte*, LII, 1979, pp. 339–41.

—, *Miguel-Angel Houasse (1680–1730). Pintor de la corte de Felipe V*, Madrid 1981.

—, 'Apropos de M.-A. Houasse, J. Ranc et L.-M. Van Loo: œuvres inédites', in *Philippe V d'Espagne et l'Art de son temps* (conference proceedings, June 1993), ed. Y. Bottineau, Paris 1995, pp. 209–19.

Lunn, M.R., and V. Espinosa Carrión, 'Los dibujos de Juan Carreño de Miranda', *Archivo Español de Arte*, LII, 1979, pp. 281–306.

Luxenberg, A., 'Figardo and free agents: some perspectives on French painters in eighteenth-century Spain', in Kasl and Stratton 1997, pp. 39–64.

Lyell, J.P.R., *Early Book Illustration in Spain*, New York 1976 (1st edn 1926).

McDonald, M.P., 'The graphic context of Jusepe de Ribera's *The Poet*', *Art Bulletin of Victoria*, no. 32, 1991, pp. 51–8.

—, 'The print collection of Philip II at the Escorial', *Print Quarterly*, XV, 1998, pp. 15–35.

—, 'A drawing by Antonio del Castillo in the British Museum', *Melbourne Art Journal*, no. 2, 1998a, pp. 15–22.

—, 'Ribera's earliest drawing?', *Master Drawings*, XXXVII, 1999, pp. 368–72.

—, '"So as to avoid confusion": A contract drawing for a sculpture by Pedro de Mena y Medrano', *The Sculpture Journal*, IV, 2000, pp. 55–64.

—, 'Pedro Perret and Pedro de Villafranca: Printmakers to the Spanish Hapsburgs', *Melbourne Art Journal*, no. 4, 2000a, pp. 37–51.

—, *The Print Collection of Ferdinand Columbus (1488–1539): A Renaissance Collector in Seville*, 2 vols, London 2004.

—, 'A genealogy for the Count Duke of Olivares', *Print Quarterly*, XXIII, 2006, pp. 359–82.

—, 'A presentation drawing by Antonio Villanueva', *The Burlington Magazine*, CXLVIII, 2006a, pp. 192–4.

—, 'French woodcuts for a Spanish audience', *Print Quarterly*, XXIII, 2006b, pp. 288–94.

McKim Smith, G., *Spanish Baroque Drawings in North American Collections*, exh. cat., University of Kansas Museum of Art, Kansas City 1974.

—, 'The Problem of Velázquez's Drawings', *Master Drawings*, XVIII, 1980, pp. 3–24, 65–70.

Macías Rosendo, B., *La biblia políglota de Amberes en la correspondencia de Benito Arias Montano*, Huelva 1998.

Madrid 1994. *El cuaderno Italiano (1770–1786). Los orígenes del arte de Goya* (inc. facsimile), Museo Nacional del Prado, Madrid 1994.

Madrid 1996. *Estampas de la Guerra de la Independencia*, exh. cat., Calcografía Nacional, Madrid 1996.

Madrid 1996a. *Catálogo de la estampas de Goya en la Biblioteca Nacional*, exh. cat., Madrid 1996a.

Madrid 1996b. *'Ydioma Universal': Goya en la Biblioteca Nacional*, eds J. Wilson-Bareau and E. Santiago, exh. cat., Madrid 1996b.

Madrid 1998. *Felipe II. Un monarca y su época. Un príncipe del renacimiento*, ed. F. Checa Cremades, exh. cat., Museo Nacional del Prado, Madrid 1998.

Madrid 2001. *Del amor y la muerte. Dibujos y grabados de la Biblioteca Nacional*, exh. cat., Fundació Caixa Catalunya, Barcelona and Biblioteca Nacional, Madrid 2001.

Madrid 2008. *Goya en tiempos de Guerra*, ed. M.B. Mena Marqués, exh. cat., Museo Nacional del Prado, Madrid 2008.

Madrid 2008a. *Miradas sobre la guerra de la independencia*, exh. cat., Biblioteca Nacional, Madrid 2008a.

Maestre Maestre, J.M., E. Sánchez Salor, M.A. Díaz Gito, L. Charlo Brea and P.J. Galán Sánchez (eds), *Benito Arias Montano y los humanistas de su tiempo*, 2 vols, Mérida 2006.

Marías, F., *El Greco. Biografía de un pintor extravagante*, Madrid 1997.

—, 'El *Codex Escurialensis*: Problemas e incertidumbres de un libro de dibujos de antigüedades del último *quattrocento*', *Reales Sitios*, no. 163, 2005, pp. 14–35.

—, 'Estudiando dibujos; falsando atribuciones: un Joan de Joanes y un Greco', in *In sapientia libertas. Escritos en homenaje al Profesor Alfonso E. Pérez Sánchez*, Madrid and Seville 2007, pp. 216–22.

— and A. Bustamente García, *Las ideas artísticas de El Greco (Comentarios a un texto inédito)*, Madrid 1981.

— and A. Bustamente, 'Apuntes arquitectónicos madrileños de hacia 1660', *Archivo Español de Arte*, LVIII, 1985, pp. 34–43.

— and M. Cruz de Carlos Varona, 'El arte de las "acciones que las figuras mueven": Maíno, un pintor dominico entre Toledo y Madrid', in *Juan Bautista Maíno (1581–1649)*, exh. cat., Museo Nacional del Prado, Madrid 2009, pp. 57–75.

Martín González, J.J., *Juan de Juni, vida y obra*, Madrid 1974.

—, 'Nuevos dibujos de Alonso Berruguete', *Boletín del Seminario de estudios de Arte y Arqueología*, XLVII, 1981, pp. 444–6.

Martínez, J., *Discursos practicables del nobilísimo arte de la pintura* (c. 1673), ed. M.E. Manrique Ara, Madrid 2006.

Martínez de la Peña y González, D., 'Artistas españoles en la Academia de San Lucas (Documentos de los siglos XVI y XVII)', *Archivo Español de Arte*, XLI, 1968, pp. 293–313 (not paginated).

Martínez Iborra, A., 'Joseph del Castillo', *Boletín de la Sociedad Española de Excursiones*, XLI, 1933, pp. 62–70, 128–39 (and plates).

Martínez-Novillo, A., 'La Tauromaquia en su contexto histórico', in *Francisco de Goya grabador. Instantáneas. Tauromaquia*, Madrid 1992, pp. 19–40.

Martínez Ripoll, A., 'Francisco de Herrera "El Viejo", grabador', in *Actas del XXIII congreso internacional de historia del arte España entre el mediterraneo y el atlantico*, Granada 1973, pp. 145–54.

—, *Francisco de Herrera 'el Viejo'*, Seville 1978.

Matheron, L., *Goya* (1858), Madrid 1996.

Matilla, J.M., *La estampa en el libro barroco. Juan de Courbes*, Madrid 1991.

—, 'Approccio ai *Disparates* di Francisco de Goya', in *Goya*, exh. cat., Gallerie Nazionale d'Arte Antica, Rome 2000, pp. 107–57.

—, 'Alonso Cano y el grabado', in *Alonso Cano dibujos*, exh. cat., Museo Nacional del Prado, Madrid 2001, pp. 75–95.

Matilla, J.M., and J.M. Medrano, *El libro de La Tauromaquia. Francisco de Goya. La fortuna crítica. El proceso de creación gráfica: dibujos, pruebas de estado, láminas de cobre y estampas de edición*, Madrid 2001.

Matilla Rodríguez, J.M., 'Grabado y propaganda. La imagen de los palacios reales en la Europa moderna', in *El Real Alcázar de Madrid. Dos siglos de arquitectura y coleccionismo en la corte de los reyes de España*, ed. F. Checa, Madrid 1994, pp. 460–85.

Matilla Tascon, A., 'Estampas religiosas del siglo XVIII. Colección del Archivo Histórico de Protocolos de Madrid', *Goya*, no. 166, 1982, pp. 184–97.

Mayer, A.L., *Die Handzeichnungen spanischer Meister. 150 Skizzen und Entwürfen vom 16. bis 19. Jahrhundert*, 2 vols, Leipzig 1915 (Spanish edn *Dibujos originales de maestros Españoles: 150 apuntes y estudios de artistas del siglo XVI hasta el siglo XIX*, 2 vols, Leipzig and New York 1920).

Mellion, W.S., *The Meditative Art: Studies in the Northern Devotional Print 1550–1625* (Early Modern Catholicism and the Visual Arts Series, vol. 1), Philadelphia 2009.

Mena Marqués, M., 'Murillo as a draughtsman', in *Bartolomé Esteban Murillo (1617–1682)*, exh. cat., Royal Academy of Arts, London 1982, pp. 53–63, 198–221.

—, 'Goya "copista" de Velázquez', in *Goya und Velázquez: Das königliche Portrait / Goya y Velázquez: El retrato real*, exh. cat., Städtische Galerie im Städelschen Kunstinstitut, Frankfurt am Main, and Museo Nacional del Prado, Madrid 1991, pp. 44–9.

—, 'Drawing in the art of Ribera', in *Ribera*, eds A. E. Pérez Sánchez and N. Spinosa, exh. cat., Metropolitan Museum of Art, New York 1992, pp. 193–202.

—, 'El dibujo en Sevilla y Velázquez', in *Velázquez y Sevilla*, exh. cat., Monasterio de la Cartuja de Santa María de las Cuevas, Seville 1999, I, pp. 93–107.

— (ed.), *Goya: La familia de Carlos IV*, exh. cat., Museo Nacional del Prado, Madrid 2002.

— and G. Mühle-Maurer, *La duquesa de Alba 'musa' de Goya: el mito y la historia*, exh. cat., Museo Nacional del Prado, Madrid 2006.

Mendoza Díaz-Maroto, F., 'Gollerías para bibliófilos, 6: Las barajas antiguas', *Hibris: Revista de Bibliofilia*, nos 59–60, 2010, pp. 5–28.

Milicua, J., 'From Játiva to Naples', in Pérez Sánchez and Spinosa 1992, pp. 9–17.

Millard, J.W., *A History of Spanish Printing 1450 to 1600*, Thornton-Cleveleys 2007.

Mollinedo, D., 'Algunos dibujos de Mariano Savaldor Maella', *Archivo Español de Arte*, XLVI, 1973, pp. 145–57.

Moltedo, A., *La sistina riprodotta*, exh. cat., Istituto nazionale per la grafica, Calcografia, Rome 1991.

Montalbán Jiménez, J.A., 'Del zig-zag a la filigrana: aproximación a una tipología del papel hispano-árabe', *Actas del VII Congreso Nacional de Historia del Papel en España*, Madrid 2007, pp. 86–97.

Morales, A.J., 'Un dibujo del monumento de la Catedral de Sevilla por Lucas Valdés', *Laboratorio de Arte*, no. 6, 1993, pp. 157–67.

Morales, N., and F. Quiles García (eds), *Sevilla y corte. Las artes y el lustro real (1729–1733)*, Collection de la Casa de Velázquez, CXIV, Madrid 2010.

Morales y Marín, J.L., 'Los Bayeu', in *El arte de los Bayeu*, Seville 1992, pp. 25–101.

—, 'Un boceto de Antonio González Velázquez para la pintura del actual comedor de gala del Palacio Real de Madrid', *Archivo Español de Arte*, LXV, 1992a, pp. 239–40.

—, *Pintura en España, 1750–1808*, Madrid 1994.

—, *Francisco Bayeu, vida y obra*, Zaragoza 1995.

—, *Mariano Salvador Maella, vida y obra*, Zaragoza 1996.

—, 'José del Castillo. Aguafuertes y composiciones para ser grabadas', *Academia (Boletín de la Real Academia de Bellas Artes de San Fernando)*, no. 83, 1996a, pp. 85–122.

—, *Luis Paret: vida y obra*, Zaragoza 1997.

—, *La imagen de rey. Felipe V y el arte*, Madrid 1990.

Morán Turina, M. (ed.), *El arte en la corte de Felipe V*, Madrid 2003.

Mulcahy, R., *The Decoration of the Royal Basilica of El Escorial*, Cambridge 1994.

—, 'Juan Fernández de Navarrete "el Mudo", pintor de Feilpe II', in *Navarrete 'el mudo' pintor de Felipe II*, exh. cat., Centro de Exposiciones y Congresos y Museo 'Camón Aznar', Zaragoza 1995, pp. 141–78.

—, 'Federico Zuccaro', in *Dibujos Italianos para el Escorial*, ed. M. di Giampaolo, Madrid 1995a, pp. 101–19.

—, *Juan Fernández de Navarrete 'El Mudo', pintor de Felipe II*, Madrid 1999.

—, *Philip II of Spain: Patron of the Arts*, Dublin 2004.

—, 'Celebrating sainthood, government, and Seville: the *Fiestas* for the canonization of King Ferdinand III', *Hispanic Research Journal*, XI, 2010, pp. 393–414.

Muller, P., 'The drawings of Antonio del Castillo y Saavedra', Ph.D. thesis, New York University, New York 1963.

—, 'Juan de Juanes. Un dibujo problemático', *Archivo Español de Arte*, XLIX, 1976, pp. 176–80.

—, 'State of research: Contributions to the study of Spanish drawings', *The Art Bulletin*, LVIII, 1976a, pp. 604–11.

—, *Dibujos españoles en la Hispanic Society of America del siglo de oro a Goya*, ed. J. Manuel Matilla, exh. cat., Museo Nacional del Prado, Madrid 2006.

—, 'Sobre la supervivencia de los preciados dibujos de Antonio del Castillo y Saavedra', in Navarrete Prieto and García de la Torre 2008, pp. 15–27 (Spanish), 657–64 (English).

Muto, G., 'Capital y corte en la Nápoles española', in *España y Nápoles. Coleccionismo y mecenazgo virreinales en el siglo XVII*, ed. J.L. Colomer, Madrid 2009, pp. 63–76.

Nash, S., *Northern Renaissance Art (Oxford History of Art)*, Oxford 2008.

Natale, M. (ed.), *El renacimiento mediterráneo. Viajes de artistas e itinerarios de obras entre Italia, Francia y España en el siglo XV*, exh. cat., Thyssen-Bornemisza Museum, Madrid, and Museo de Bellas Artes, Valencia 2001.

Navarrete Prieto, B., 'Otras fuentes grabadas utilizadas por Francisco de Zurbarán', *Archivo Español de Arte*, LXVII, 1994, pp. 360–76.

—, 'Sobre Vicente Salvador Gómez y Alonso Cano: nuevos documentos y fuentes formales', *Ars Longa*, no. 6, 1995, pp. 135–40.

—, *La pintura andaluza del siglo XVII y sus fuentes grabadas*, Madrid 1998.

—, *El papel del dibujo en España*, Madrid 2006.

—, 'Salviati como modelo: su influencia en Luis de Vargas', *Boletín del Seminario de Estudios de Arte y Arquelogía*, LXXV, 2009, pp. 115–26.

—, 'A new preparatory drawing for Francisco Pacheco's *Last Judgement*: Creative process and theological approval', *Master Drawings*, XLVIII, 2010, pp. 435–46.

—, 'Dibujos de Antonio Palomino en el British Museum de Londres y la Biblioteca Nacional de España: El sagrario de la cartuja de Granada', *Archivo Español de Arte*, LXXXIII, 2011, pp. 59–88.

— and F. García de la Torre, *Antonio del Castillo (1616–1668). Dibujos. Catálogo razonado*, Santander 2008.

— and A.E. Pérez Sánchez, *Álbum Alcubierre (dibujos): De la Sevilla ilustrada del conde del Águila la colección Juan Abelló*, Madrid 2009.

—, T. Zapata Fernández de la Hoz and A. Martínez Ripoll, *Fuentes y modelos de la pintura barroca madrileña*, Madrid 2008.

Navascués Palacio, P., 'La obra como espectáculo: el dibujo Hatfield', in *Las Casas Reales: El Palacio (IV centenario del Monasterio de El Escorial)*, vol. 2, Madrid 1986, pp. 55–67.

Newcome Schleier, M., 'Artistas Genoveses', in *Dibujos Italianos para el escorial*, ed. M. di Giampaolo, Madrid 1995, pp. 17–45.

Nicholson, K., 'Making watermarks meaningful: Significant details in recording and identifying watermarks', in *Book and Paper Group Annual*, vol. 1, The American Institute for Conservation, Washington, DC 1982.

Nieves Rupérez Almajano, M., 'Tomás Francisco Prieto y la enseñanza del grabado en hueco en Salamanca durante la primera mitad del siglo XVIII', *Academia (Boletín de la Real Academia de Bellas Artes de San Fernando)*, no. 85, 1997, pp. 413–41.

Nuevo Ábalos, J.L., 'Proteccionismo y progreso papelero en España durante el siglo XVIII', *Actas del IV Congreso de Historia del Papel en España*, Córdoba 2001, pp. 351–8.

—, 'Legislación y progreso papelero en España y en Indias durante los siglos XVII y XVIII', *Actas del VI Congreso Nacional de Historia del Papel en España*, Valencia 2005, pp. 177–81.

Núñez de Arenas, M., 'Manojo de noticias. La suerte de Goya en Francia', *Bulletin Hispanique*, LII, 1950, pp. 229–73.

Ollero, J. (ed.), *Los Austrias. Grabados de la Biblioteca Nacional*, exh. cat., Madrid 1993.

Orellana, M.A. de, 'Biografía pictórica valentina, o vida de los pintores, arquitectos, escultores y grabadores valencianos', ed. X. de Salas, Valencia 1930.

Orozco Díaz, E., *Pedro Atanasio Bocanegra*, Granada, 1937.

Orso, S.N., *Philip IV and the Decoration of the Alcázar of Madrid*, Princeton, NJ 1986.

—, *Art and Death at the Spanish Habsburg Court: The Royal Exequies for Philip IV*, Columbia, MO 1989.

—, 'Praising the Queen: The decorations at the royal exequies for Isabella of Bourbon', *The Art Bulletin*, LXXII, 1990, pp. 51–73.

—, *Velázquez, Los Borrachos, and Painting at the Court of Philip IV*, Cambridge 1993.

Ostolaza Elizondo, I., 'El comercio de papel en Navarra en los siglos XVI–XVII: procedencia, rutas, costes y compradores', *Actas del II Congreso Nacional de Historia del Papel en España*, Cuenca 1997, pp. 129–37.

Pacheco, F., *Arte de la pintura* (1649), ed. B. Bassegoda i Hugas, Madrid 1990.

Páez Ríos, E., *Iconografía hispana. Catálogo de los retratos de personajes españoles de la Biblioteca Nacional*, 4 vols (plus index volume), Madrid 1966–7 (index 1970).

—, *Repertorio de grabados españoles en la Biblioteca Nacional*, 3 vols, Madrid 1981–3.

Palomino, A., *Lives of the Eminent Spanish Painters and Sculptors*, trans. N. Ayala Mallory, Cambridge 1987.

—, *El museo pictórico y escala óptica*, Madrid 1988.

Palomino de Castro y Velasco, A., *El museo pictorico y escala optica: tomo segundo practica de la pintura*, Madrid 1714.

Paris. *Goya graveur*, exh. cat., Petit Palais, Paris 2008.

Parrado del Olmo, J.M., *Talleres escultóricos del siglo XVI en Castilla y León*, (Arte, arquitectura y urbanismo, no. 2), Valladolid 2002.

Pemán, M., 'Murillo y Meneses Ossorio en Capuchinos de Cádiz', *Archivo hispalense: Revista histórica, literaria y artística*, LX, 1977, pp. 145–65.

Pérez Castro, F., and L. Voet, 'La Biblia políglota de Amberes y Benito Arias Montano. La historia de la mayor empresa escripturaria y tipográfica del siglo XVI', in *La Biblia políglota de Amberes*, Madrid 1973, pp. 54–74.

Pérez Pastor, C., *Bibliografía Madrileña de los siglos XVI y XVII (Descripción cronólogica de las obras impresas en Madrid desde el establecimiento de la imprenta en Madrid en el año 1566 al 1625, con anotaciones analíticas e históricas)*, 3 vols, Amsterdam 1970 (reprint of 1891 edn).

Pérez Samper, Mª Á., *Isabel de Farnesio*, Barcelona 2003.

Pérez Sánchez, A.E., 'Don Matías de Torres', *Archivo Español de Arte*, XXXVIII, 1965, pp. 31–42.

—, *Gli spagnoli da El Greco a Goya (I disegni dei maestri)*, ed. W. Vitzthum, Milan 1970.

—, *Museo del Prado: Catálogo de Dibujos. I: Dibujos Españoles siglos XV–XVII*, Madrid 1972.

—, *Mostra di disegni spagnoli* (Gabinetto disegni e stampe degli Uffizi, XXXVII), Florence 1972a.

—, 'Dibujos españoles en los Uffizi florentinos', *Goya*, no. 111, 1972b, pp. 146–57.

—, *Museo del Prado: Catálogo de Dibujos. III: Dibujos Españoles. Siglo XVIII, C–Z*, Madrid 1977.

—, 'Las colecciones de pintura del Conde de Monterrey (1653)', *Boletín de la Real Academia de Historia*, no. 174, 1977a, pp. 417–59.

—, *D. Antonio de Pereda (1611–1678) y la pintura Madrileña de su tiempo*, exh. cat., Salas de exposiciones del palacio de bibliotecas y museos, Madrid 1978.

—, 'Un "San Miguel" de escuela de Murillo y un dibujo de éste', *Archivo Español de Arte*, LV, 1982, pp. 303–5.

—, 'La academia madrileña de 1603 y sus fundadores', *Boletín del seminario de estudios de arte y arqueología (Universidad de Valladolid)*, XLVIII, 1982a, pp. 281–90.

—, *Juan Carreño de Miranda (1614–1685)*, exh. cat., Ayuntamiento de Avilés, Avilés and Oviedo 1985.

—, *Historia del dibujo en España: De la Edad Media a Goya*, Madrid 1986.

—, *Carreño, Rizi, Herrera y la pintura madrileña de su tiempo (1650–1700)*, exh. cat., Palacio de Villahermosa, Madrid 1986a.

—, 'Dibujos europeos contemporáneos de Velázquez', in *El dibujo europeo en tiempo de Velázquez. A propósito del retrato del Cardenal Borja de Velázquez de la Real Academia de Bellas Artes de San Fernando*, Madrid 1999, pp. 35–49.

—, *Jerónimo Jacinto de Espinosa (1600–1667)*, exh. cat., Museo de Bellas Artes, Valencia 2002.

—, 'Dibujos de Domingo Martínez', in *Domingo Martínez en la estela de Murillo*, exh. cat., Centro Cultural El Monte, Seville 2004, pp. 41–55.

— and B. Navarrete Prieto, *Tres siglos de dibujo sevillano*, exh. cat., Fundación Fondo de Cultura de Sevilla, Seville 1995.

— and B. Navarrete Prieto, 'Sobre Herrera "El Viejo"', *Archivo Español de Arte*, LXIX, 1996, pp. 365–87.

— and B. Navarrete Prieto, *De Herrera a Velázquez. El primer naturalismo en Sevilla*, exh. cat., Fundación Focus-Abengoa, Seville and Museo de Bellas Artes, Bilbao 2006.

— and E.A. Sayre (eds), *Goya and the Spirit of Enlightenment*, exh. cat., Museo Nacional del Prado, Madrid, Museum of Fine Art, Boston, and Metropolitan Museum of Art, New York, 1989.

— and N. Spinosa, *Jusepe de Ribera 1591–1652*, exh. cat., Metropolitan Museum of Art, New York 1992.

Pettas, W., *A History and Bibliography of the Giunti (Junta) Printing Family in Spain 1526–1628*, New Castle, DE 2005.

Pettegree, A., *The Book in the Renaissance*, New Haven and London 2010.

Piedra Adarves, A., 'Mateo Cerezo, dibujante', *Archivo Español de Arte*, LXXIII, 2000, pp. 97–115.

Ponz, A., *Viaje de españa* (1772–94), new edn, Madrid 1947.

Popham, A.E., and J. Wilde, *The Italian Drawings of the XV and XVI Centuries in the Collection of Her Majesty the Queen at Windsor Castle*, 2nd edn, New York and London 1984.

Portillo Muñoz, J.L., *La ilustración gráfica de los incunables sevillanos (1470–1500)*, Seville 1980.

Portús, J., and J. Vega, *La estampa religiosa en la españa del antiguo regimen*, Madrid 1998.

Quiles, F., *Alonso Miguel de Tovar (1678–1752)*, Colección Arte Hispalense, no. 77, Seville 2005.

—, 'Alonso Miguel de Tovar, entre Sevilla y la corte (1678–1752)', in *Alonso Miguel de Tovar (1678–1752)*, Seville 2006, pp. 13–34.

Quiles García, F., 'Cornelio Schut el Mozo, un retratista en la Sevilla del Barroco', *Goya*, no. 325, 2008, pp. 299–311.

Redín Michaus, G., *Pedro Rubiales, Gaspar Becerra y los pintores españoles en Roma, 1527–1600* (Biblioteca de Historia del arte 10), Madrid 2007.

Rekers, B., *Benito Arias Montano (1527–1598)*, Studies of the Warburg Institute, vol. 33, London and Leiden 1972.

Remie Constable, O., *Trade and Traders in Muslim Spain: The Commercial Realignment of the Iberian Peninsula, 900–1500*, Cambridge 1994.

Reuter, A., 'El *cuaderno italiano* de Goya', in Sureda 2008, pp. 87–97.

Robinson, A., *Paper in Prints*, Washington 1977.

Robinson, J.C., *Descriptive Catalogue of Drawings by the Old Masters, Forming the Collection of John Malcolm of Poltalloch, Esq.*, London 1869 (re-published 1876).

Roda Peña, J. (ed.), *Matías de Arteaga. Pinturas eucarísticas para la Hermandad Sacramental del Sagrario de la Catedral de Sevilla*, Seville 2003.

Rodríguez G. de Ceballos, A., *Los Churriguera* (*Artes y Artistas*), Madrid 1971.

—, 'Alonso Cano, arquitecto artista', *Archivo Español de Arte*, LXXIV, 2001, pp. 375–91.

Rodríguez Culebras, R., *José Camarón y Boronat (1731–1803), ein valencianischer maler zur zeit Goyas*, Munich 1968.

—, *José Camarón Bonanat, un pintor valenciano en tiempos de Goya*, Valencia 2006.

Rodríguez-Moñino, J.A., 'Sobre la supuesta inexistencia de dibujos antiguos españoles', *Boletín de la Sociedad Española de Excursiones*, LVIII, 1954, pp. 143–9.

Roettgen, S., *Anton Raphael Mengs 1728–1779, I: Das malerische und zeichnerische Werk*, Munich 1999.

—, *Anton Raphael Mengs 1728–1779, II: Leben und Wirken*, Munich 2003.

Rokiski Lázaro, M.L., 'Un dibujo de Diego de Tiedra', *Archivo Español de Arte*, XLI, 1968, pp. 278–80.

Rosand, D., and M. Muraro, *Titian and the Venetian Woocut*, exh. cat., National Gallery of Art, Washington, DC 1976.

Rose, I., 'Un proyecto dieciochesco malogrado: El plan de reproducir en grabados los cuadros principales existentes en las colecciones reales españolas', *Academia* (*Boletín de la Real Academia de Bellas Artes de San Fernando*), no. 53, 1981, pp. 171–81.

Roteta de la Maza, A.M., *La ilustración del libro en la España de la contrarreforma. Grabados de Pedro Angel y Diego de Astor 1588–1637*, Toledo 1985.

Rubió i Balaguer, J., *Imprenta i llibreria a Barcelona (1474–1553)*, Barcelona 1986.

Rubio Lapaz, J., 'El "Discuros de la comparación de la antigua y moderna pintura y escultura" de Pablo Céspedes', *Goya*, no. 217–18, 1990, pp. 15–27.

—, *Pablo de Céspedes y su círculo. Humanismo y contrarreforma en la cultura andaluza del renacimiento al barroco*, Granada 1993.

Rueda, M. de, *Instrucción para grabar en cobre, y perfeccionarse en el grabado a buril, al aguafuerte, y al humo, con el nuevo método de grabar las planchas para estampar en colores, a imitación de la pintura* Madrid, 1761 (facsimile edn 1990, Prologue by J. Carrete Parrondo).

Ruiz de Arcaute, A., *Juan de Herrera, arquitecto de Felipe II*, Madrid 1936.

Ruiz Manero, J.Mª *Pintura Italiana del siglo XVI en España. I: Leonardo y los Leonardescos. II: Rafael y su escuela*, Madrid 1996.

Rupprich, H. (ed.), *Dürer: Schriftlicher Nachlass*, 3 vols, Berlin 1956.

Sáenz de Miera, J., 'La magnificencia del rey prudente y la fama de El Escorial', in Madrid 1998, pp. 105–33.

Sáenz de Miera Santos, C., 'Entrada triunfal de la Reina Mariana de Austria en Madrid el día de noviembre de 1649', *Anales del Instituto de Estudios Madrileños*, XXIII, 1986, pp. 167–74.

Salort Pons, S., *Velázquez en Italia*, Madrid 2002.

—, 'Las relaciones artísticas entre Italia y Sevilla durante el primer tercio del siglo XVII', in Pérez Sánchez and Navarrete Prieto 2006, pp. 53–68.

Saltillo, M. del, 'Pinturas de Ribera', *Archivo Español de Arte*, XIV, 1940–1, pp. 246–7.

Sambrico, V. de, *José del Castillo* (*Artes y artistas*), Madrid 1958.

Sánchez Cantón, F.J., 'Los tiépolos de Aranjuez', *Archivo Español de Arte y Arqueología*, III, 1927, pp. 1–17 (and plates).

—, 'El dibujo de Juan Guas (Arquitecto español del siglo xv)', *Arquitectura*, no. 115, 1928, pp. 339–47.

—, *Dibujos Españoles*, 5 vols, Madrid 1930.

—, *Spanish Drawings from the 10th to the 19th Century*, London 1964.

Sánchez-Mesa Martín, D., 'Alonso Cano escultor', in *Alonso Cano (1601–1667) y la escultura andaluza hacia 1600*, Córdoba and Seville 2000, pp. 37–59.

Sancho, J.L., 'Mengs at the Palacio Real, Madrid', *The Burlington Magazine*, CXXXIX, 1997, pp. 515–28.

Santiago Páez, E., *El Escorial en la Biblioteca Nacional*, exh. cat., Biblioteca Nacional, Madrid 1985.

—, 'Miguel Jacinto Meléndez, un pintor de la transición', in *El arte en las cortes Europeas del siglo XVIII* (conference proceedings, 27–9 April 1987), Madrid and Aranjuez 1989, pp. 675–86.

—, *Miguel Jacinto Meléndez. Pintor de Felipe V*, exh. cat., Museo de Bellas Artes de Asturias, Oviedo 1989a.

—, *Miguel Jacinto Meléndez (1679–1734)*, exh. cat., Museo Municipal de Madrid, Madrid 1990.

— (ed.), *Dibujos de arquitectura y ornamentación de la Biblioteca Nacional: siglos XVI y XVII*, Madrid 1991.

—, 'Miguel Jacinto Meléndez (1679–1734), pintor de Felipe V', in *Philippe V d'Espagne et l'Art de son temps* (conference proceedings, June 1993), ed. Y. Bottineau, Paris 1995, pp.179–91.

—, 'El gabinete de Ceán Bermúdez. Un capítulo en la historia de las colecciones de la Biblioteca Nacional', in Madrid 1996b, pp. 53–67, 71–98.

— (ed.), *La real biblioteca pública 1711–1760: De Felipe V a Fernando VI*, exh. cat., Biblioteca Nacional, Madrid 2004.

—, 'Retratos de reyes en la real biblioteca pública', in *La real biblioteca pública 1711–1760. De Felipe V a Fernando VI*, exh. cat., Biblioteca Nacional, Madrid 2004a, pp. 155–63.

—, 'La biblioteca de Isabel de Farnesio', in *La real biblioteca pública 1711–1760. De Felipe V a Fernando VI*, exh. cat., Biblioteca Nacional, Madrid 2004b, pp. 269–84.

— (ed.), *De la palabra a la imagen: El 'Quijote' de la Academia de 1780*, exh. cat., Biblioteca Nacional, Madrid 2006.

—, 'El proceso de ilustración del 'Quijote' de la Academia', in *De la palabra a la imagen: El 'Quijote' de la Academia de 1780*, exh. cat., Biblioteca Nacional, Madrid 2006a, pp. 23–58.

— and P. Vinatea, 'El arte del grabado. De la tradición a la Academia', in *La real biblioteca pública 1711–1760. De Felipe V a Fernando VI*, exh. cat., Biblioteca Nacional, Madrid 2004, pp. 381–93.

Sanz Ayán, C., 'Felipe IV y el teatro', in *Felipe IV. El hombre y el reinado*, ed. J. Alcalá-Zamora y Queipo de Llano, Madrid 2005, pp. 269–89.

Sarrailh, J., *L'espange éclairée*, Paris 1954.

Sayre, E.A., *The Changing Image: Prints by Francisco Goya*, exh. cat., Museum of Fine Arts, Boston 1974.

—, 'Introduction to the prints and drawings series', in Pérez Sánchez and Sayre 1989, pp. XCV–CXXVII.

Scheller, R.W., *Exemplum. Model-Book Drawings and the Practice of Artistic Transmission in the Middle Ages (c.900–c.1470)*, Amsterdam 1995.

Schroth S., 'Más allá de la "identificación del modelo". Los estudio de Rubens para el retrato ecuestre del duque de Lerma', in *Rubens. Dibujos para el retrato ecuestre del duque de Lerma*, eds S. Schroth, A. Vergara and T. Vignau-Wilberg, exh. cat., Museo Nacional del Prado, Madrid 2001, pp. 31–46 (Spanish), 60–7 (English).

—, 'A new style of grandeur: politics and patronage the court of Philip III', in Schroth and R. Baer 2008, pp. 77–121.

— and R. Baer (eds), *El Greco to Velázquez: Art During the Reign of Philip III*, exh. cat., Museum of Fine Arts, Boston, and Nasher Museum of Art at Duke University, Durham, NC, Boston 2008.

Segorbe. *La luz de las imagines*, exh. cat., Segorbe 2001.

Serra Giráldez, S., *Francisco Meneses Osorio, discípulo de Murillo*, Seville 1990.

Serrano Marqués, M., 'Gaspar Becerra y la introducción del romanismo en España', *Boletín del Museo e Instituto 'Camón Aznar'*, LXXVIII–LXXIX, 1999, pp. 207–39.

Serrera, J.M., 'Pinturas y pintores del siglo XVI en la catedral de Sevilla', in *La catedral de Sevilla*, Seville 1984, pp. 353–404.

—, 'Pedro de Campaña: Obra dispersa', *Archivo Español de Arte*, LXII, 1989, pp. 1–14.

—, 'Velázquez and Sevillian painting of his time', in *Velázquez in Seville*, exh. cat., National Galleries of Scotland, Edinburgh 1996, pp. 37–44.

Sigüenza, J. de, *La fundación el Monasterio de El Escorial* (1605), Madrid 1988.

Silva Maroto, M., *Pintura hispanoflamenca castellana: Burgos y Palencia. Obras en tabla y sarga*, 3 vols, Valladolid 1990.

Silva Maroto, P., 'Flanders and the kingdom of Castile', in *The Age of Van Eyck 1430–1530: The Mediterranean World and Early Netherlandish Painting*, ed. T.H. Borchert, exh. cat., Groeningemuseum, Bruges 2002, pp. 143–55.

—, *Fernando Gallego*, Salamanca 2004.

Silvestre Visa, M. and A. Tomas Sanmartin, *Estampas y planchas de la Real Academia en el Museo de Bellas Artes de Valencia*, Valencia 1982.

Sistach, C., 'El papel árabe en la Corona de Aragón', *Actas del II Congreso Nacional de Historia del Papel en España*, Cuenca 1997, pp. 70–7.

—, 'Aportación al estudio del papel sin filigranas en la documentación de la Corona de Aragón' *Actas del IV Congreso Nacional de Historia del Papel en España*, Córdoba 2001, pp. 97–105.

—, 'Del papel árabe al papel con filigrana en el Archivo de la Corona de Aragón', *Actas del VI Congreso Nacional de Historia del Papel en España*, Valencia 2005, pp. 105–14.

— and V. Rabal, 'Ejemplos de Papel Hispano-Árabe (1325–1330): Resumen descriptivo y recreación experimental de su fabricación', *Actas del IX Congreso Nacional de Historia del Papel en España*, Madrid 2011, pp. 110–21.

Stein, P., 'Madame de Pompadour and the harem imagery at Bellevue', *Gazette des Beaux-Arts*, CXXIII, 1994, pp. 29–44.

—, 'Amédée Van Loo's *Costume Turc*: The French Sultana', *The Art Bulletin*, LXXVIII, 1996, pp. 417–38.

Stevenson, A.H., 'Watermarks are twins', *Studies in Bibliography*, IV, 1951–2, pp. 57–91.

Stubbe, W., *Spanische Zeichnungen von El Greco bis Goya*, Hamburg 1966.

Sueur-Hermel, V., 'Goya à la Bibliothèque nationale au XIXe siècle', in Paris 2008, pp. 141–9.

Sullivan, E.J., *Baroque Painting in Madrid: The Contribution of Claudio Coello with a Catalogue Raisonné of his Works*, Columbia, MO 1986.

—, and N.A. Mallory, *Painting in Spain 1650–1700 from North American Collections*, exh. cat., The Art Museum, Princeton, NJ and Detroit Institute of Art, Detroit, MI 1982.

Sureda, J. (ed.), *Goya e Italia*, II: *Estudios y ensayos*, exh. cat., Museo de Zaragoza, Zaragoza 2008.

Symmons, S., 'El galgo y la liebre: Francisco de Goya y Luis Paret', in *Goya, nuevas visiones. Homenaje a Enrique Lafuente Ferrari*, eds I. García de la Rasilla and F. Calvo Serraller, Madrid 1987, pp. 396–412.

—, *Goya: A Life in Letters*, trans. Philip Troutman, London 2004.

Tatsakis, S., and M.A. Roglán, *Spanish Master Drawings from Dutch Public Collections (1500–1900)*, exh. cat., Museum Boijmans Van Beuningen, Rotterdam, Meadows Museum, Dallas, and Appleton Museum of Art, Ocala 2004.

Taylor, R., 'Francisco Hurtado and his School', *The Art Bulletin*, XXXII, 1950, pp. 25–61.

Tokyo. *Goya: artista de su tiempo y artista único*, exh. cat., National Museum of Western Art, Tokyo 1999.

Tomlinson, J.A., *Francisco Goya: The Tapestry Cartoons and Early Career at the Court of Madrid*, Cambridge 1989.

—, *Graphic Evolutions: The Print Series of Francisco Goya (Columbia Studies on Art*, no. 2), exh. cat., Miriam and Ida D. Wallach Art Gallery, Columbia University, New York 1989a.

—, *Goya in the Twilight of Enlightenment*, New Haven and London 1992.

Tormo, E., 'Mateo Cerezo', *Archivo Español de Arte y Arqueología*, III, 1927, pp. 113–28, 245–74 (and plates).

Tovar Martín, V., *Arquitectos madrileños de la segunda mitad del siglo XVII*, Madrid 1975.

—, *Juan Gómez de Mora (1586–1648): Arquitecto y trazador del Rey y Maestro Mayor de obras de la Villa de Madrid*, exh. cat., Museo Municipal, Madrid 1986.

Tramoyeres Blanco, L., 'Un colegio de pintores en Valencia', *Archivo de investigaciones históricas, España, America Española, Filipinas*, I, 1911, pp. 277–314, 446–62, 514–36.

Trapier, E. du Gue, 'Notes on Spanish drawings', *Notes Hispanic*, no. 1, 1941, pp. 1–61.

Trusted, M., *The Arts of Spain: Iberia and Latin America 1450–1700*, London 2007.

Tufts, E., *Luis Meléndez: Eighteenth-Century Master of the Spanish Still Life, with a Catalogue Raisonné*, Columbia, MO 1985.

Turner, N., 'A proposal for El Greco as a draftsman', *Master Drawings*, XLV, 2007, pp. 291–324.

—, *From Michelangelo to Annibale Carracci: A Century of Italian Drawings from the Prado*, exh. cat., Museo Nacional del Prado, Madrid (2004), Frick Art and Historical Centre, Pittsburgh, PA, Mary and Leigh Block Museum of Art, Northwestern University, Evanston, IL, and Philbrook Museum of Art, Tulsa, OK 2008.

—, L. Hendrix and C. Plazzotta, *European Drawings*, III: *Catalogue of the Collections (J. Paul Getty Museum)*, Los Angeles 1997.

Ubeda de los Cobos, A., 'Propuestas de reformas y planes de estudio: La influencia de Mengs en la Real Academia de Bellas Artes de San Fernando', *Archivo Español de Arte*, LX, 1987, pp. 447–61.

—, 'El centralismo borbónico y la Escuela de Bellas Artes de Barcelona', in *El arte en tiempo de Carlos III* (IV Jornadas de Arte. C.S.I.C), Madrid 1989, pp. 467–74.

—, 'Consideración social del pintor y academicismo artístico en Madrid en el siglo XVII', *Archivo Español de Arte*, LXII, 1989a, pp. 61–74.

—, 'Felipe V y el retrato de Corte', in Morán Turina 2003, pp. 89–140.

— (ed.), *Paintings for the Planet King. Philip IV and the Buen Retiro Palace*, exh. cat., Museo Nacional del Prado, Madrid, and London 2005.

Urquízar Herrera, A., *El renacimiento en la periferia. La recepción de los modos italianos en la experiencia pictórica del Quinientos cordobés*, (Estudios de historia moderna. Colección maior no. 14), Córdoba 2001.

Urrea Fernández, J., 'El pintor José García Hidalgo', *Archivo Español de Arte*, XLVIII, 1975, pp. 97–117.

—, *La pintura italiana del siglo XVIII en España*, Valladolid 1977.

Valdivieso, E., 'The influence of Murillo on painting in Seville', in *Bartolomé Esteban Murillo (1617–1682)*, exh. cat., Royal Academy of Arts, London 1982, pp. 64–9.

—, *Valdes Leal*, exh. cat., Museo Nacional del Prado, Madrid, and Museo de Bellas Artes, Seville 1991.

—, *Pintura barroca sevillana*, Seville 2003.

—, 'Juan de Roelas en la Sevilla de 1600', in Pérez Sánchez and Navarrete Prieto 2006, pp. 69–82.

—, *Pedro de Campaña*, Seville 2008.

— and J.M. Serrera, *Historia de la pintura española. Escuela sevillana del primer tercio del siglo XVII*, Madrid 1985.

Valladolid. *Museo Nacional Colegio de San Gregorio* (collection cat.), Valladolid 2009.

Valls i Subirá, O., *La Historia del Papel en España*, 3 vols, Madrid 1978–82.

Van der Stock, J., *Printing Images in Antwerp. The Introduction of Printmaking in a City: Fifteenth Century to 1585*, Rotterdam 1998.

Varey, S., R. Chabrán and D.B. Weiner (eds), *Searching for the Secrets of Nature: The Life and Works of Dr Francisco Hernández*, Stanford 2000.

Vasari, G., *Le vite de' più eccellenti pittori, scultori e architettori nelle redazioni del 1550 e 1568*, ed. Rosanna Bettarini, commentary by Paola Barocchi, 6 vols, Florence 1966–87.

—, *Le vite de' più eccellenti architetti, pittori, et scultori italiani, da Cimabue insino a' tempi nostri*, eds L. Bellosi and A. Rossi, 1550 edn, Turin 1991.

Vega, J., 'El grabador: arte y técnica', in *La formación del artista. De Leonardo a Picasso*, exh. cat., Real Academia de Bellas Artes de San Fernando, Calcografía Nacional, Madrid 1989, pp. 83–109.

—, 'Los inicios del artista. El dibujo, base de las Artes', in *La formación del artista. De Leonardo a Picasso*, exh. cat., Real Academia de Bellas Artes de San Fernando, Calcografía Nacional, Madrid 1989a, pp. 1–29.

—, *Origen de la litografía en Espana: El real establecimiento litográfico*, exh. cat., Museo Casa de la Moneda, Madrid 1990.

—, *Museo del Prado: Catálogo de estampas*, Madrid 1992.

—, 'Fatales consecuencias de la guerra, Francisco de Goya pintor', in *Francisco de Goya grabador. Instantáneas. Desastres de la Guerra*, III, Madrid 1992a, pp. 17–48.

——, 'Impresores y libros en el origen del renacimiento en españa', in *Reyes y mecenas. Los reyes católicos – Maximiliano I y los inicios de la casa de Austria en españa*, exh. cat., Museo de Santa Cruz, Toledo 1992b, pp. 199–232.

——, 'Goya's etchings after Velázquez', *Print Quarterly*, XII, 1995, pp. 146–63.

——, 'El sueño dibujado', in *Realidad y Sueño en los viajes de Goya. Actas de la Jornadas de Arte en Fuendetodos*, Fuendetodos 1996, pp. 41–56 (and plates).

——, 'Los Disparates. Una colección de veintidos láminas grabadas', in *Disparates, Francisco de Goya. Tres visiones*, eds J. Carrete and J.M. Matilla, Madrid 1996a, pp. 75–95.

——, 'Goya y el dibujo', in *Goya 250 años despues*, Zaragoza 1996b, pp. 145–57.

——, *Ciencia, arte e ilusión en la españa ilustrada*, Madrid 2010.

Vélez de Guevara, J., *Los celos hacen estrellas*, eds J.E. Varey and N.D. Shergold, London 1970.

Véliz, Z., *Artists' Techniques in Golden Age Spain: Six Treatises in Translation*, Cambridge 1986.

——, 'Alonso Cano dibujante', in *Alonso Cano dibujos*, exh. cat., Museo Nacional del Prado, Madrid 2001, pp. 19–56.

——, 'Alonso Cano's drawings for the *Life of Saint Dominic* in Santa Cruz la Real, Granada', *Master Drawings*, XLV, 2007, pp. 325–44.

——, 'The authority of prints in early modern Spain', *Hispanic Research Journal*, IX, 2008, pp. 415–35.

——, *Alonso Cano (1601–1667). Catálogo razonado*, Santander 2011.

Vergara, A., *Rubens and his Spanish Patrons*, Cambridge 1999.

Vetter, E.M., *Die kupferstiche zur Psalmodia Eucaristica des Melchor Prieto von 1622*, Münster 1972.

Vignau-Wilberg, T., 'Los dibujos preparatorios de Rubens para el retrato ecuestre del duque de Lerma', in *Rubens. Dibujos para el retrato ecuestre del duque de Lerma*, eds S. Schroth, A. Vergara and T. Vignau-Wilberg, exh. cat., Museo Nacional del Prado, Madrid 2001, pp. 21–9 (Spanish), 54–9 (English).

Villalpando, J.B., *El tratado de la arquitectura perfecta en la ultima vision del profeta Ezequiel*, trans. L. Rubio, ed. J. Corral Jam, Madrid 1990.

——, *El Templo de Salomón*, trans. J.L.O. Domingo, ed. J.A. Ramírez, 2 vols, Madrid 1991.

Villena, E., 'Grabado en dulce y en hueco. Arte y técnica al servicio del Rey', in *Renovación. Crisis. Continuismo: La Real Academia de San Fernando en 1792*, exh. cat., Real Academia de Bellas Artes de San Fernando, Calcografía Nacional, Madrid 1992, pp. 83–97.

Volk, M.C., *Vicencio Carducho and Seventeenth-Century Castilian Painting*, New York 1977.

——, 'Addenda: The Madrid Academy', *The Art Bulletin*, LXVI, 1979, p. 627.

Vosters, S.A., *Rubens y españa. Estudio artístico-literario sobre la estética del Barroco*, Madrid 1990.

Van Waadenoijen, J., 'A proposal for Starnina: Exit the Maestro del Bambino Vispo?', *The Burlington Magazine*, CXVI, 1974, pp. 82–91.

Waldman, L.A., 'Two foreign artists in Renaissance Florence, Alsonso Berruguete and Gian Francesco Bembo', *Apollo*, CLV, 2002, pp. 22–9.

Wenger E., M.L. Ferrando Cusí, C. Hidalgo Brinquis and P. Rückert, *Cabeza de buey y sirena, la historia del papel y las filigranas desde el medievo hasta la modernidad*, Spanish text for EU Bernstein Project and exh. cat., *Bull's Head and Mermaid*, Stuttgart, Valencia and Vienna 2011.

Wethey, H.E., 'Anequín de Egas Cueman, a Fleming in Spain', *The Art Bulletin*, XIX, 1937, pp. 381–401.

——, 'Alonso Cano's drawings', *The Art Bulletin*, XXXIV, 1952, pp. 217–34.

——, *Alonso Cano: Painter, Sculptor, Architect*, Princeton, NJ 1955.

——, 'Sebastián de Herrera Barnuevo', *Anales del Instituto de Arte Americano e Investigaciones Estéticas*, II, 1958, pp. 13–41 and plates.

——, *El Greco and his School*, 2 vols, Princeton, NJ 1962.

—— and A.S. Wethey, 'Herrera Barnuevo and his chapel in the Descalzas Reales', *The Art Bulletin*, XLVIII, 1966, pp. 15–34.

Wilkinson-Zerner, C., *Juan de Herrera. Architect to Philip II of Spain*, New Haven and London 1993.

—— and C.P.M. Brown (eds), *Philip II and the Escorial: Technology and the Representation of Architecture*, exh. cat., Bell Gallery, Brown University, Providence, RI 1990.

Wilson-Bareau, J., *Goya. La década de los Caprichos, dibujos y aguafuertes*, exh. cat., Real Academia de Bellas Artes de San Fernando, Madrid 1992.

——, *Goya's Prints: The Tomás Harris Collection in the British Museum*, rev. edn, London 1996.

——, 'Goya pintor y grabador', in Madrid 1996a, pp. 33–52.

——, *Goya: Drawings from his Private Albums*, exh. cat., Hayward Gallery, London 2001.

——, 'Goya and France', in *Manet/Velázquez: The French Taste for Spanish Painting*, eds G. Tinterow and G. Lacambre, exh. cat., Metropolitan Museum of Art, New York 2003, pp. 139–59.

—— and M.B. Mena Marqués, *Goya: Truth and Fantasy, The Small Paintings*, exh. cat., Museo Nacional del Prado, Madrid, Royal Academy of Arts, London, and The Art Institute of Chicago 1994.

Witcombe, C.L.C.E., 'Herrera's Papal *Privilegio* for the Escorial Prints', *Print Quarterly*, IX, 1992, pp. 177–80.

Wolf, R., *Goya and the Satirical Print in England and on the Continent, 1730–1850*, Boston 1991.

Wunder, A., 'Murillo and the canonisation case of San Fernando, 1649–52', *The Burlington Magazine*, CLXIII, 2001, pp. 670–5.

Yarza Luaces, J., *Los reyes católicos. Paisaje artístico de un monarquía*, Madrid 1993.

——, 'Dibujos, esbozos, modelos', in *Bernat Martorell i la tardor del gòtic català: el context artístic del retaule de Púbol*, ed. J. Molina Figueras, exh. cat., Museu d'Art de Girona, Girona 2003, pp. 147–68, 294–301.

Zapata, T., *La entrada en la corte de María Luisa de Orleans. Arte y fiesta en el Madrid de Carlos II*, Madrid 2000.

Zapata Fernández de la Hoz, T., 'Dibujos festivos de José Jiménez Donoso', *Boletín del Museo del Prado*, XII, 1991, pp. 29–38.

——, 'Proyecto y participación de Teodoro Ardemans en la entrada pública en Madrid de Felipe V', *Archivo Español de Arte*, LXIV, 1991a, pp. 361–72.

——, 'Claudio Coello: Dibjuos Festivos', *Archivo Español de Arte*, LXVI, 1993, pp. 257–77.

—— and J. Carlos Gómez Aragüete, 'Nuevas aportaciones a la obra de Francisco Ignacio de la Iglesia (1649–1703), *Archivo Español de Arte*, LXXXV, 2012, pp. 17–36.

Websites

Arte Procomún: http://sites.google.com/site/arteprocomun/home
An important site for information about the history of prints in Spain, including portals to digitized texts, collections, documents etc.

British Museum collections online: britishmuseum.org/research

The following provide useful information on Western papermaking: Neil Harris 2010, 'Paper and Watermarks', http://ihl.enssib.fr/siteihl.php?page=272&aflng=fr

Timothy Barrett 2012, 'European Papermaking Techniques': http://paper.lib.uiowa.edu/european.php

List of exhibits

The following objects in this book feature in the exhibition *Renaissance to Goya: Prints and drawings from Spain*. Details correct at the time of going to press. Further information about objects in the collection of the British Museum can be found on the Museum's website at britishmuseum.org.

The list is organized alphabetically by artist within each exhibition section, and then each artist by date. Figure numbers and page references for where illustrations appear in this publication are given in bold at the end of each entry.

1. MADRID AND CASTILE 1500s

ANONYMOUS
Uncut Sheet of Twenty-four Playing Cards, 1587
Woodcut, hand coloured using stencils, additions in pen and ink, 235 x 353 mm
British Museum, London
1896,0501.1346
Bequeathed by Lady Charlotte Schreiber
Fig. 21, p. 39

MIGUEL BAROSSO / DIEGO LÓPEZ DE ESCURIAZ
Christ Distributing Bread to his Disciples after his Resurrection, 1587–9
Pen and brown ink, brown wash, white heightening over black chalk, pricked for transfer, 170 x 270 mm
British Museum, London
2011,7109.1
Purchase funded by the Ottley Group
Fig. 25, p. 74

ALONSO BERRUGUETE
Assumption of the Virgin, 1555–61
Brush drawing in brown ink and wash with pen and brown ink, heightened with white, over black chalk, 313 x 193 mm
British Museum, London
1895,0915.866
Fig. 14, p. 67

ATTRIBUTED TO ALONSO BERRUGUETE
The Entombment of Christ, c.1530–50
Engraving, 150 x 167 mm
British Museum, London
1860,0414.16
Fig. 15, p. 68

PEDRO PERRET
Section through Middle of the Basilica on North-South Axis Revealing the Interior, 1583–9
Engraving, 870 x 720 mm
British Library, London
Maps 3.tab.34 (fol. 83)
Fig. 29, p. 77

PEDRO PERRET
The Tabernacle of the Holy Sacrament in the Church of San Lorenzo el Real de El Escorial, 1583
Engraving, 480 x 344 mm
British Museum, London
1937,0915.240
Donated by Campbell Dodgson
Fig. 28, p. 76

PELLEGRINO TIBALDI
Christ Presented to the People, 1587–90
Pen and brown ink and brown wash over black chalk, heightened with white, squared for transfer, 548 x 293 mm
British Museum, London
1946,0713.608
Donated by Count Antoine Seilern
Fig. 8, p. 62

PELLEGRINO TIBALDI
Study for the Decoration of the Escorial Library, 1588–92
Pen and brown ink with brown wash over black chalk, 332 x 485 mm
British Museum, London
1846,0509.176
Fig. 9, p. 63

FEDERICO ZUCCARO
The Pentecost, 1586–8
Pen and brown ink with grey wash and white highlights on blue paper, squared for transfer, 355 x 260 mm
Royal Library, Winsor Castle
RL 06015
Fig. 10, p. 64

2. MADRID 1600s

EUGENIO CAJÉS
The Circumcision of Christ, c.1600–15
Pen and brown ink and brown wash over black chalk, squared for transfer, 251 x 172 mm
British Museum, London
1938,1210.4
Fig. 4, p. 24

EUGENIO CAJÉS
Saint Ildephonsus at the Tomb of Saint Leocardia, c.1615
Black chalk and brown wash, squared for transfer, 228 x 160 mm
British Museum, London
1973,0721.1
Fig. 7, p. 86

FRANCISCO CAMILO
The Rest of the Holy Family on the Flight into Egypt, c.1650–70
Brush with red-brown ink and red wash over red chalk, 266 x 206 mm
British Museum, London
1875,0710.2620
Fig. 33, p. 103

VICENTE CARDUCHO
Adoration of the Magi, c.1616–22
Red and black chalk, with brown wash, heightened with white, squared for transfer, 195 x 166 mm
British Museum, London
1946,0713.1024
Donated by Count Antoine Seilern
Fig. 8, p. 87

VINCENTE CARDUCHO
Saint Bruno Praying in La Torre-Calabria, 1626–32
Pen and black ink, chalk and brown wash, heightened with white, squared for transfer, 326 x 285 mm
British Museum, London
1875,0710.2621
Fig. 12, p. 88

VINCENTE CARDUCHO
The Duke of Feria at the Siege of Rheinfelden, 1634
Pen and brown ink, blue and brown wash over black chalk, squared for transfer, 318 x 415 mm
British Museum, London
1850,0713.9
Fig. 15, p. 91

JOSÉ DE CIEZA
Saint Francis de Paul before the King of Naples, c.1691
Pen and brown ink and brown wash, over black chalk, 210 x 207 mm
British Museum, London
1846,0509.169
Fig. 54, p. 114

LUCA GIORDANO
Miracle of Saint Anthony of Padua, 1698–1700
Black chalk, grey-brown wash, 300 x 382 mm
British Museum, London
1950,1111.6
Purchase funded by the H.L. Florence Fund
Fig. 55, p. 115

HENDRICK GOLTZIUS
The Circumcision of Christ, 1594
Engraving, 475 x 355 mm
British Museum, London
F,3.129
Bequeathed by Clayton Mordaunt Cracherode
Fig. 5, p. 25

SEBASTIÁN DE HERRERA BARNUEVO
The Assumption of the Virgin, c.1650–8
Pen and brown ink and brown wash over black chalk, squared for transfer, 250 x 198 mm
British Museum, London
1895,0915.876
Fig. 37, p. 105

SEBASTIÁN DE HERRERA BARNUEVO
Design for an Altarpiece in a Chapel, c.1650–60
Pen and brush, brown and black ink over black chalk, brown, grey, red and green wash, 517 x 345 mm
British Museum, London
1993,0724.2
Fig. 38, p. 106

FRANCISCO DE HERRERA THE YOUNGER
Angels in the Clouds Playing Musical Instruments, c.1650–6
Pen and brown ink and brown wash, touched with watercolour, 296 x 189 mm
British Museum, London
1846,0509.184
Fig. 43, p. 108

FRANCISCO DE HERRERA THE YOUNGER
Design for an Overmantel, c.1670–80
Watercolour, with pen, brown and black ink over black chalk, on several conjoined sheets, 136 x 479 mm
British Museum, London
1914,0901.2
Fig. 45, p. 110

Antonio Palomino
Abimelec Giving to David the Sword of Goliath, *c.*1711
Pen and brown ink and grey wash, 135 x 154 mm
British Museum, London
1846,0509.170
Fig. 49, p. 112

Antonio Pereda y Salgado
Saint Jerome in the Desert, *c.*1640–5
Red, black and white chalk with brown and grey wash, 255 x 215 mm
British Museum, London
1895,0915.883
Fig. 21, p. 94

Antonio Pereda y Salgado
Saint Ildephonsus Receiving the Chasuble from the Virgin Mary, *c.*1640–60
Red chalk with red wash and white heightening, 320 x 210 mm
British Museum, London
1846,0509.181
Fig. 22, p. 95

Francisco Rizi
The Virgin Appearing to a Trinitarian Monk, *c.*1650
Pen and brown ink, brown and grey wash over black chalk partly incised, 196 x 125 mm
British Museum, London
1895,0915.878
Fig. 26, p. 98

Francisco Rizi
The Dwarf 'Lusillo', *c.*1680–3
Black chalk with touches of red chalk, 268 x 161 mm
British Museum, London
1850,0713.6
Fig. 29, p. 100

Attributed to Francisco Ignacio Ruiz de la Iglesia
The Virgin Bestowing the Rosary on Saint Dominic Guzmán, *c.*1690
Pen and grey ink and brown wash over black chalk, 267 x 203 mm
British Museum, London
1850,0713.1
Fig. 46, p. 110

Matías de Torres
Saint Isidore Praying, *c.*1680
Pen and brown ink, grey-brown wash, squared for transfer, 217 x 257 mm
British Museum, London
1846,0509.166
Fig. 51, p. 113

Diego Velázquez
Studies of Rearing Horse and Horseman, *c.*1625–35
Black chalk, 247 x 164 mm
British Museum, London
1850,1014.101
Fig. 14, p. 90

Attributed to Diego Velázquez
The 1632 Auto da Fé in the Plaza Mayor, Madrid, 1632
Pen and brown ink with brown wash over black chalk, partly incised, 297 x 542 mm
British Museum, London
1850,0713.5
Fig. 13, p. 31

Pedro de Villafranca
Philip IV in the *Descripción breve del monasterio de S. Lorenzo el Real del Escorial ...*, 1657
Engraving, 277 x 185 mm
British Library, London
787.1.2
Fig. 58, p. 117

Pedro de Villafranca after Francisco Rizi
Portrait of Cardinal Baltasar Moscoso y Sandoval in Andrés Passano de Haro, *Exemplar eterno de prelados impresso en el corazón executado en la vida y acciones del ... Don Baltasar de Moscoso y Sandoval*, Toledo 1670
Engraving, 286 x 205 mm
British Library, London
BL 4683.f.29
Not illustrated

3. GRANADA 1600s

Pedro Atanasio Bocanegra
The Virgin and Child Appearing to Saint Francis of Assisi and Saint Teresa of Avila, *c.*1660–8
Pen and brown ink and brown wash over black chalk, 195 x 286 mm
British Museum, London
1846,0509.183
Fig. 30, p. 144

Alonso Cano
Saint Ildephonsus Adoring the Virgin and Christ Child and the Miraculous Chasuble Carried by Three Putti, *c.*1645–52
Pen and brown ink and brown wash over black chalk, squared for transfer, 183 x 311 mm
British Museum, London
1895,0915.877
Fig. 23, p. 140

Alonso Cano
Design for an Altarpiece, *c.*1660–5
Pen and brown ink, brown wash over black chalk, 309 x 232 mm
British Museum, London
1950,0211.16
Purchase funded by the H.L. Florence Fund
Fig. 26, p. 142

Alonso Cano
The Assumption of the Virgin, 1661–2
Pen and brown ink and brown wash over black chalk, 234 x 130 mm
British Museum, London
1910,0212.43
Bequeathed by George Salting
Fig. 27, p. 143

4. SEVILLE AND CÓRDOBA 1500s–1600s

Matías de Arteaga y Alfaro
View of the Tower of the Giralda in Seville, 1672
Etching, 450 x 280 mm
British Museum, London
1868,1114.393
Not illustrated

Frederick Bloemaert after Abraham Blomaert
Study of Seven Heads from *'Het Tekenboek'*, 1650–6
Engraving, 212 x 171 mm
British Museum, London
L,83.16
Bequeathed by Sir Hans Sloane
Fig. 33, p. 146

Antonio del Castillo y Saavedra
Study of Seven Heads, *c.*1650–68
Brush and brown ink over black chalk, 286 x 204 mm
British Museum, London
1946,0713.1308
Donated by Count Antoine Seilern
Fig. 32, p. 146

Circle of Francisco de Herrera the Elder
Study of a Seated Male Nude, *c.*1640–50
Pen and brown ink over black chalk, 418 x 263 mm
British Museum, London
Pp,4.54
Bequeathed by Richard Payne Knight
Fig. 19, p. 136

Francisco de Herrera the Elder
Saint Bartholomew, 1642
Pen and brown ink, 304 x 189 mm
British Museum, London
1895,0915.872
Fig. 17, p. 135

Francisco de Herrera the Elder
Saint Thomas, 1642
Pen and brown ink, 298 x 184 mm
British Museum, London
1895,0915.871
Fig. 16, p. 135

Attributed to Francisco Meneses Osorio
Saint Joseph Kneeling before the Virgin and the Christ Child, *c.*1665–1700
Black chalk, 403 x 282 mm
British Museum, London
1895,0915.884
Fig. 45, p. 155

Bartolomé Esteban Murillo
Saint Anthony of Padua and the Miracle of the Irascible Son, 1645–6
Pen and brown ink and brown wash over black chalk, 345 x 265 mm
British Museum, London
1920,1116.20
Fig. 35, p. 148

Bartolomé Esteban Murillo
Studies for Saint John the Baptist (verso), *c.*1650–5
Pen and brown ink over black chalk, 220 x 338 mm
British Museum, London
1873,0614.212
Donated by James Hughes Anderdon
Fig. 42, p. 152

Bartolomé Esteban Murillo
Saint Isidore of Seville, 1655
Pen and brown ink, brown and grey wash over black chalk, 260 x 208 mm
British Museum, London
1873,0614.214
Donated by James Hughes Anderdon
Fig. 39, p. 151

Bartolomé Esteban Murillo
The Archangel Michael, *c.*1655–60
Pen and brown ink over black chalk, 268 x 189 mm
British Museum, London
1873,0614.216
Donated by James Hughes Anderdon
Fig. 36, p. 149

Bartolomé Esteban Murillo
Saint Francis of Paola, *c.*1665–75
Black and red chalk, 332 x 232 mm
British Museum, London
1850,0713.2
Fig. 43, p. 153

Bartolomé Esteban Murillo
The Penitent Saint Peter, *c.*1670–80
Pen and brown ink, 190 x 153 mm
British Museum, London
1946,0713.1155
Donated by Count Antoine Seilern
Fig. 44, p. 154

Bartolomé Esteban Murillo
The Holy Family and Angels, *c.*1670–82
Red chalk, brown and grey wash over black chalk, heightened with white, 165 x 159 mm
British Museum, London
1895,0915.891
Not illustrated

Francisco Pacheco
Saint John the Evangelist, 1632
Pen and dark brown ink, brown wash, heightened with white, over black chalk, squared on prepared paper, 330 x 223 mm
British Museum, London
1928,0714.1
Fig. 12, p. 132

Francisco Pacheco
Saint Matthew and the Angel, 1632
Pen and dark brown ink, brown wash, heightened with white over black chalk on prepared paper, 342 x 236 mm
British Museum, London
1977,0507.11
Fig. 11, p. 132

Antonio García Reinoso
Sheet of Figure Studies, 1647
Red and black chalk, 214 x 303 mm
The Courtauld Institute of Art, London
D.1952.RW.4204
Fig. 34, p. 147

Attributed to Juan de Roelas
The Infant Christ, 1600–25
Pen and brown ink and blue wash, 155 x 106 mm
British Museum, London
1920,1116.22
Fig. 13, p. 133

Cornelio Schut
A Seated Ecclesiastic, *c.*1660–80
Pen and brown ink and brown wash over black chalk, 273 x 196 mm
British Museum, London
1946,0713.825
Donated by Count Antoine Seilern
Fig. 49, p. 157

Pedro Tortolero
View of Seville from Triana, 1738
Etching and engraving, 352 x 485 mm
British Museum, London
1917,1208.4276
Donated by Nan Ino Cooper, Baroness Lucas of Crudwell and Lady Dingwall in Memory of Auberon Thomas Herbert, 9th Baron Lucas of Crudwell and 5th Lord Dingwall
Fig. 59, p. 232

Juan de Valdés Leal
An Ephemeral Structure in Seville Cathedral, from two plates, 1671
Etching, 542 x 340 mm
British Museum, London
1868,1114.399
Fig. 15, p. 33

Luis de Vargas
The Execution of Jephthah's Daughter, 1550–68
Pen and brown ink, brown wash over black chalk, squared for transfer, 280 x 382 mm
British Museum, London
Nn,7.52.2
Fig. 2, p. 125

Francisco de Zurbarán
Head of a Monk, *c.*1635–55
Black chalk, grey wash with traces of pen and ink, 277 x 196 mm
British Museum, London
1895,0915.873
Fig. 15, p. 134

5. VALENCIA AND NAPLES 1500s–1700s

José Camarón y Bonanat
Saint Vincent Ferrer Preaching, *c.*1752–60
Brush drawing in grey and brown wash over black chalk, 205 x 151 mm
British Museum, London
1973,0120.5
Fig. 50, p. 225

José Camarón y Bonanat
Saint Mary Magdalene in the Desert, *c.*1760–90
Pen with grey and brown ink and wash, 204 x 150 mm
British Museum, London
1973,0120.9
Fig. 54, p. 228

José Camarón y Bonanat
An Algerian Woman Seated Beneath a Canopy, *c.*1771–80
Brush drawing in grey ink and wash, 214 x 149 mm
British Museum, London
1973,0120.4
Fig. 52, p. 226

Juan Antonio Conchillos y Falcó
Study of a Partly Kneeling Male Nude, 1690–1705
Black charcoal and white chalk on blue prepared paper, 393 x 251 mm
British Museum, London
2011,7065.1
Purchase funded by the Ottley Group
Fig. 20, p. 178

José García Hidalgo
Kneeling Female Nude, 1693
Etching, 159 x 115 mm
British Museum, London
1854,1020.9
Not illustrated

José García Hidalgo
Studies of the Female Nude, 1693
Etching, 159 x 115 mm
British Museum, London
1854,1020.8
Fig. 20, p. 38

Juan de Juanes
Saint Stephen Being Led to his Execution, late 1550s
Pen and brown ink, grey wash and traces of red chalk, 217 x 315 mm
Courtauld Institute of Art, London
D.1963.WF.4730
Fig. 4, p. 166

Luis Planes
The Last Supper, *c.*1802–4
Pen and brown ink and brown wash, over black chalk, scaled for transfer, 356 x 247 mm
British Museum, London
1946,0713.1507
Donated by Count Antoine Seilern
Fig. 55, p. 229

Juan Ribalta
A Miraculous Healing by a Saint, *c.*1610–28
Pen and brown ink and brush with brown wash over black chalk, heightened with white on red-prepared paper, 307 x 230 mm
British Museum, London
1846,0509.174
Fig. 9, p. 169

José de Ribera
The Martyrdom of Saint Bartholomew, *c.*1620–4
Pen and brown ink, 133 x 100 mm
British Museum, London
T,13.111
Bequeathed by William Fawkener
Fig. 30, p. 185

José de Ribera
Tityus or Prometheus, *c.*1620–5
Pen and brown ink and wash, 227 x 165 mm
British Museum, London
1937,1008.29
Fig. 31, p. 185

José de Ribera
Saint Jerome hearing the Trumpet of the Last Judgement, *c.*1621
Etching with engraving, 313 x 231 mm
British Museum, London
1862,0712.533
Not illustrated

José de Ribera
Large Grotesque Head, *c.*1622
Etching with engraving, 215 x 140 mm
British Museum, London
W,6.111
Fig. 23, p. 180

José de Ribera
The Martyrdom of Saint Bartholomew, 1624
Etching with engraving, 314 x 241 mm
British Museum, London
1874,0808.746
Bequeathed by Sir Hans Sloane
Fig. 25, p. 182

José de Ribera
Christ Beaten by a Tormentor, *c.*1625–30
Red chalk, 184 x 215 mm
British Museum, London
1946,0713.1411
Donated by Count Antoine Seilern
Fig. 33, p. 186

José de Ribera
A Saint (Albert?) Tied to a Tree, 1626
Red chalk, 232 x 170 mm
British Museum, London
1850,0713.4
Bequeathed by William Fawkener
Fig. 32, p. 186

José de Ribera
The Drunken Silenus, 1628
Etching with engraving, 274 x 349 mm
British Museum, London
1862,0712.534
Fig. 26, p. 183

José de Ribera
Equestrian Portrait of Don Juan of Austria, 1648
Etching, 350 x 270 mm
British Museum, London
W,6.92
Bequeathed by Clayton Mordaunt Cracherode
Fig. 28, p. 184

Vicente Salvadór Gomez
Saint Joseph Receiving the Christ Child from God the Father, 1674
Pen and brown ink and grey wash, 262 x 170 mm
British Museum, London
1846,0509.186
Not illustrated

Mosén Domingo Saura
Queen Esther Fainting, *c.*1660–80
Pen and brown ink and brown wash over black chalk, 176 x 266 mm
British Museum, London
1846,0509.202
Fig. 17, p. 176

Mosén Domingo Saura
Solomon and the Queen of Sheba, *c.*1660–80
Pen and brown ink and brown wash over black chalk, 171 x 257 mm
British Museum, London
1846,0509.203
Not illustrated

Francisco la Vega
Design for a Fan showing the Triumphal Procession of Charles VII entering Naples, after 1734
Pen and brown ink, with pink, brown and grey washes over black chalk, 275 x 533 mm
British Museum, London
1891,0713.606
Donated by Lady Charlotte Schreiber
Fig. 22, p. 40

Francisco la Vega
Pedimental Vase Design with Mythological Figures and Grotesques, 1736–60
Pen and brown ink over black chalk, 204 x 137 mm
British Museum, London
Ff,3.213
Bequeathed by Clayton Mordaunt Cracherode
Not illustrated

Antonio Villanueva
Design for an Altar Wall Dedicated to Saint John the Baptist, *c.*1780
Pen and grey ink and grey wash, 524 x 356 mm
British Museum, London
1946,0713.1519
Donated by Count Antoine Seilern
Fig. 57, p. 230

6. MADRID 1700s: GOYA AND HIS CONTEMPORARIES

Anonymous
Man from La Granja Holding Game, *c.*1770–90
Pen and brown ink with grey wash over black chalk, approx. 139 x 91 mm
British Museum, London
1985,0608.46
Donated by Christopher Mendez in Memory of Fernando Zóbel de Ayala
Fig. 46, p. 222

ANONYMOUS
A Satire on Napoleon's Political Ambitions, 1810
Etching, 246 x 150 mm
British Museum, London
1878,0112.38
Not illustrated

ANONYMOUS
A Satire on Napoleon's 'Ultimate Triumph', c.1810
Etching with yellow hand-colouring, 151 x 224 mm
British Museum, London
1878,0112.28
Fig. 34, p. 255

ANONYMOUS
View of the Bridge of Alcántara, Toledo, c.1750–60
Black chalk and grey wash, 270 x 430 mm
British Museum, London
1846,0509.178
Not illustrated

ANONYMOUS
View of Toledo from across the Tagus River, c.1750–60
Black chalk and grey wash, 273 x 420 mm
British Museum, London
1846,0509.177
Fig. 4, p. 194

ANONYMOUS AFTER FRANCISCO DE GOYA
The True Portait of a She Ant-bear (anteater), 1776
Etching and letterpress, 214 x 276 mm
British Museum, London
1917,1208.455
Donated by Nan Ino Cooper, Baroness Lucas of Crudwell and Lady Dingwall in Memory of Auberon Thomas Herbert, 9th Baron Lucas of Crudwell and 5th Lord Dingwall
Fig. 43, p. 220

TEODORO ARDEMANS
Design for the Exaltation of Saint Francis of Assisi, c.1700–26
Pen and brown ink and grey wash over black chalk, incised, 477 x 324 mm
British Museum, London
1846,0509.175
Fig. 2, p. 192

RAMÓN BAYEU Y SUBÍAS
The Attributes of the Virgin, after 1780
Etching, 289 x 95 mm
British Museum, London
1929,1021.2
Fig. 35, p. 214

RAMÓN BAYEU Y SUBÍAS
The Attributes of the Virgin, after 1780
Etching, 289 x 98 mm
British Museum, London
1929,1021.3
Fig. 36, p. 214

FERNANDO BRAMBILA AND JUAN GÁLVEZ
Agustina of Aragon, 1808–14
Etching and aquatint, 355 x 235 mm
British Museum, London
1899,0713.177
Fig. 31, p. 253

FERNANDO BRAMBILA AND JUAN GÁLVEZ
Ruins of the Church of the General Hospital, 1808–14
Etching and aquatint, 434 x 551 mm
British Museum, London
1899,0713.165
Fig. 30, p. 252

MANUEL SALVADOR CARMONA AFTER DIEGO VELÁZQUEZ
The Drunkards or *The Triumph of Bacchus*, 1793
Engraving and etching, 470 x 610 mm
British Museum, London
1845,1223.7
Fig. 39, p. 217

ANTONIO CARNICERO
A Picador Leaves the bullring after Stabbing the Bull, c.1789
Hand-coloured etching, 177 x 280 mm
British Museum, London
1871,0812.4514
Fig. 48, p. 223

ANTONIO CARNICERO
A Picador on Horseback Stabbing a Bull, c.1789
Hand-coloured etching, 177 x 267 mm
British Museum, London
1871,0812.4515
Fig. 49, p. 223

JOSÉ DEL CASTILLO AFTER MATEO CEREZO
The Supper at Emmaus, 1778
Etching, 268 x 319 mm
British Museum, London
1848,1125.237
Fig. 33, p. 213

JUAN DE LA CRUZ CANO Y OLMEDILLA AFTER MANUEL DE LA CRUZ
The Blind Guitarist, 1777
Etching and engraving, 304 x 224 mm
British Museum, London
1896,0511.131
Fig. 44, p. 221

JOSÉ JOAQUÍN FABREGAT AFTER ANTONIO CARNICERO
Don Quijote Defeated by the Knight of the White Moon, 1780
Etching and engraving, 207 x 142 mm
British Museum, London
1849,1208.85
Fig. 42, p. 219

ANTONIO GONZÁLEZ VELÁZQUEZ
A Standing Woman, 1781
Pen and brown ink, brown and grey wash over black chalk, 230 x 158 mm
British Museum, London
1998,0214.4
Donated by Adolphe Stein
Fig. 15, p. 202

FRANCISCO DE GOYA
Saint Francis of Paola, c.1776–8
Etching and drypoint, 132 x 95 mm
British Museum, London
1975,1025.12
Fig. 2, p. 236

FRANCISCO DE GOYA
The Blind Guitarist, 1778
Etching, 355 x 535 mm
British Museum, London
1854,1020.17
Fig. 4, p. 237

FRANCISCO DE GOYA AFTER DIEGO VELÁZQUEZ
The Drunkards or *The Triumph of Bacchus*, 1778
Etching, 320 x 434 mm
British Museum, London
1862,0712.178
Fig. 8, p. 239

FRANCISCO DE GOYA
The Garroted Man, c.1778
Pen and brown ink, incised, 264 x 200 mm
British Museum, London
1850,0713.11
Fig. 5, p. 238

FRANCISCO DE GOYA
The Garroted Man, c.1778
Etching, 327 x 211 mm
British Museum, London
1875,0612.95
Fig. 6, p. 238

FRANCISCO DE GOYA AFTER DIEGO VELÁZQUEZ
The Infante Don Fernando, 1778
Etching, aquatint and drypoint, 282 x 170 mm
British Museum, London
1848,1125.236
Fig. 7, p. 239

FRANCISCO DE GOYA
These Specks of Dust (*Los Caprichos*), 1796–8
Etching, burnished aquatint and drypoint, 218 x 150 mm
British Museum, London
1975,1025.91
Not illustrated

FRANCISCO DE GOYA
They Say Yes and Give their Hand to the First Comer (*Los Caprichos*), c.1797–8
Etching and burnished aquatint, 216 x 153 mm
British Museum, London
1975,1025.61
Fig. 13, p. 243

FRANCISCO DE GOYA
Pretty Teacher! (*Los Caprichos*), c.1797–8
Etching, burnished aquatint and drypoint, 210 x 148 mm
British Museum, London
1975,1025.170
Fig. 15, p. 243

FRANCISCO DE GOYA
The Sleep of Reason (*Los Caprichos*), c.1797–8
Etching and aquatint, 215 x 150 mm
British Museum, London
1975,1025.124
Fig. 12, p. 242

FRANCISCO DE GOYA
Pedro Roldán, 1798–9
Red chalk over black chalk, 173 x 126 mm
British Museum, London
2007,7077.4
Bequeathed by Enriqueta Frankfort
Accepted by H.M. Government in lieu of Inheritance Tax and allocated to the British Museum, 2007
Fig. 18, p. 245

FRANCISCO DE GOYA
For Having Jewish Ancestry, c.1808–14
Brush drawing in brown ink and wash, 205 x 142 mm
British Museum, London
1862,0712.187
Fig. 35, p. 255

FRANCISCO DE GOYA
Rocky Outcrop and Leaning Trees, before 1810
Etching and burnished aquatint, 168 x 278 mm
British Museum, London
1975,1025.32
Fig. 19, p. 245

FRANCISCO DE GOYA
An Heroic Feat! With Dead Men (*Disasters of War*), 1810–12
Etching, wash and drypoint, 155 x 207 mm
British Museum, London
1975,1025.251
Not illustrated

FRANCISCO DE GOYA
What Bravery! (*Disasters of War*), 1810–12
Etching, drypoint, burin and burnisher, 155 x 205 mm
British Museum, London
1975,1025.203
Fig. 32, p. 253

FRANCISCO DE GOYA
I Saw It (*Disasters of War*), c.1810–15
Etching, drypoint and burin, 157 x 235 mm
British Museum, London
1975,1025.421.46
Fig. 23, p. 248

FRANCISCO DE GOYA
Unhappy Mother! (*Disasters of War*), c.1811–15
Etching, burnished aquatint and drypoint, 155 x 205 mm
British Museum, London
1975,1025.421.52
Fig. 24, p. 249

Francisco de Goya
Arthur Wellesley, 1st Duke of Wellington, 1812
Red chalk over black chalk and graphite, 235 x 177 mm
British Museum, London
1862,0712.185
Fig. 28, p. 251

Francisco de Goya
Don Quijote Beset by Monsters, *c.*1812–20
Brush drawing in grey-brown ink and wash, 207 x 145 mm
British Museum, London
1862,0712.188
Fig. 36, p. 256

Francisco de Goya
Against the Common Good (*Disasters of War*), *c.*1814–15
Etching and burnisher, 174 x 218 mm
British Museum, London
1975,1025.421.73
Fig. 26, p. 250

Francisco de Goya
Dreadful Events in the Front Rows of the Ring in Madrid and the Death of the Mayor of Torrejón (*La Tauromaquia*), 1816
Etching, burnished aquatint, wash, drypoint and burin, 245 x 355 mm
British Museum, London
1862,0712.161
Fig. 38, p. 258

Francisco de Goya
The Moors Made a Different Play in the Ring Calling the Bull with the Burnous (*La Tauromaquia*), 1816
Etching, burnished aquatint and drypoint, 224 x 324 mm
British Museum, London
1975,1025.311
Fig. 37, p. 258

Francisco de Goya
An Elephant Intimidating Moors (*Disparates*), 1816–24
Etching, aquatint and drypoint, 250 x 355 mm
British Museum, London
1931,1012.6
Not illustrated

Francisco de Goya
Figures Dancing in a Circle (*Disparates*), *c.*1816–24
Etching, burnished aquatint and drypoint, 245 x 355 mm
British Museum, London
1975,1025.363
Fig. 43, p. 264

Francisco de Goya
Soldiers Fleeing a Phantom (*Disparates*), *c.*1816–24
Etching, burnished aquatint and drypoint, 245 x 353 mm
British Museum, London
1975,1025.325
Fig. 41, p. 262

Francisco de Goya
Inferno, *c.*1818–19
Lithographic ink-wash, 154 x 234 mm
British Museum, London
1876,0510.374
Fig. 46, p. 266

Francisco de Goya
Woman Reading to Two Children, *c.*1819
Lithograph, 123 x 125 mm
British Museum, London
1876,0510.356
Fig. 49, p. 269

Francisco de Goya
Bullfight in the Divided Ring (*The Bulls of Bordeaux*), 1825
Lithograph, 310 x 415 mm
British Museum, London
1975,1025.430
Not illustrated

Francisco de Goya
Picador being Gored on the Horns of a Bull (*The Bulls of Bordeaux*), 1825
Lithograph, 310 x 415 mm
British Museum, London
1975,1025.428
Not illustrated

Francisco de Goya
Spanish Entertainment (*The Bulls of Bordeaux*), 1825
Lithograph, 300 x 410 mm
British Museum, London
1975,1025.425
Fig. 50, p. 270

Francisco de Goya
Lunatics, *c.*1825–8
Black chalk and crayon, 191 x 147 mm
British Museum, London
1980,0628.56
Fig. 51, p. 271

Francisco Goya
Old Man on a Swing, *c.*1827–8
Etching and aquatint, 185 x 122 mm
British Museum, London
1975,1025.48
Fig. 53, p. 273

Francisco de Goya
Standing Woman Wearing a Mantilla, *c.*1827–8 (posthumous pre-1859 impression)
Etching and aquatint, 192 x 125 mm
British Museum, London
1975,1025.46
Not illustrated

Matías Antonio de Irala Yuso
A Design with Musical Putti, *c.*1730–9
Pen and brown ink and grey wash over black chalk pricked for transfer, 286 x 189 mm
British Museum, London
1846,0509.167
Fig. 7, p. 196

Mariano Salvador Maella
The Rest of the Holy Family on the Flight into Egypt, *c.*1780–90
Etching, 205 x 149 mm
British Museum, London
1860,0414.33
Fig. 34, p. 213

Miguel Jacinto Meléndez
Isabel de Farnesio, *c.*1714–20
Black chalk and brown wash, 195 x 128 mm
British Museum, London
1890,1209.48
Fig. 5, p. 195

Luis Paret y Alcázar
The Masked Ball in the Teatro del Príncipe, *c.*1766
Pen and grey ink and wash over black chalk, 305 x 493 mm
British Museum, London
1890,1209.50
Fig, 26, p. 209

Luis Paret y Alcázar
María Luisa de Borbón, *c.*1766–8
Pen and grey ink and grey wash over black chalk, 350 x 244 mm
British Museum, London
1890,1209.49
Fig. 29, p. 210

Fernando Selma after Bartolomé Esteban Murillo
Saint Ildephonsus Receiving the Chasuble from the Virgin, 1789–1800
Engraving and etching, 662 x 522 mm
British Museum, London
1845,1223.5
Fig. 41, p. 218

Domingo María de Servidori
Self-portrait, 1775
Pen and black ink on parchment, 192 x 170 mm
British Museum, London
1846,0509.198
Fig. 19, p. 205

Domenico Tiepolo
The Flight into Egypt, 1750–2
Etching, 186 x 240 mm
British Museum, London
1869,0410.2399
Fig. 30, p. 211

Domenico Tiepolo
The Flight into Egypt, 1750–2
Etching, 186 x 240 mm
British Museum, London
1865,1014.346
Not illustrated

Lorenzo Tiepolo after Giovanni Battista Tiepolo
A Miracle of Saint Anthony of Padua, 1750–80
Etching, 347 x 210 mm
British Museum, London
1865,1014.363
Not illustrated

Acknowledgements

The research for this book and the exhibition it accompanies was carried out mainly during a nine-month sabbatical generously funded by the Art and Humanities Research Board (AHRB). I am grateful to the readers of my application who gave it the fullest support and to the Board for providing the means to free me from my daily duties. I also benefited from a period as a Guest Scholar at the Getty Research Institute in Los Angeles. The Scholar Program provides a unique opportunity to work in a supportive environment and my time there was made all the more pleasurable by an exceptional group of Fall scholars in 2010. My greatest debt in LA goes to Lee Hendrix, whose enthusiasm for the subject of this study has never wavered. I must also record my debt to the Warburg Institute in London, a vital resource for this project.

At the British Museum, Antony Griffiths, the former Keeper of Prints and Drawings, supported my request for study leave and JD Hill was of great assistance in preparing the grant application. Our Director, Neil MacGregor, has supported the project from the outset. My other colleagues across the Museum have expertly assisted in preparing the objects and other exhibition related work. They are Andrew Basham, Jenny Bescoby, Rosemary Bradley, Barbara Canepa, Christopher Coles, David Giles, Coralie Hepburn, Philip Jell, Ivor Kerslake and his photographic team, Melanie Morris, Cat Oxley, Jennifer Ramkalawon, Judith Rayner, Janice Reading, Angela Roche, Helen Sharp, Emma Webb and Alison Wright. Daniel Godfrey conscientiously secured illustrations in this book. I am very grateful to Johanna Stephenson for her sensitive and expert editing and to Andrew Shoolbred for the elegant design. Claudia Bloch very efficiently managed the publication project. For reading sections of the text, offering invaluable suggestions and saving me from error, I am greatly indebted to Carmen C. Bambach, Xavier Bray, Dawson Carr, Mercedes Cerón, Hugo Chapman, Peter Cherry, Rosemarie Mulcahy and Juliet Wilson-Bareau.

Most of the research for this book was carried out in Spain. At the Biblioteca Nacional in Madrid I am very grateful to Isabel García-Toraño and Isabel Ortega, who did everything they could to facilitate my work, and the staff there in the Sala Goya, who brought materials for me to study. I would like to thank other colleagues throughout Spain: the staff at the Real Monasterio y Biblioteca de El Escorial; at the Museo del Prado, José Manuel Matilla and Manuela B. Mena Marques; at the Museo de Bellas Artes, Córdoba, Fuensanta García de la Torre and José Maria Palencia Cerezo; at the Museo de Bellas Artes, Valencia, Adela Espinos; at the Real Casa de la Moneda, Madrid, Mercedes López de Arriba and Fernando Seco; at the Museo del Catedral de Segorbe, David Montolío Torán; and at the Patrimonio Nacional José Luis Sancho. Outside Spain, Lizzie Boubli and Carel van Tuyll facilitated the study of works at the Musée du Louvre.

I would like to thank friends and other colleagues who have helped to bring this project to completion. Stijn Alsteens, Maite Alvarez, Lisa Banner, Peter Barber, Claire Barry, Lisa Beaven, Julian Brooks, Krista Brugnara, Stephanie Buck, Michael Bury, Frances Carey, Imma Casas, Martin Clayton, Elizabeth Cowling, Fred Croton, María Cruz de Carlos, Angie Donougher, Caroline Elam, Sir John Elliott, Jesús Escobar, Luly Feliciano, Jay Gam, Nigel Glendinning, George Goldner, Conchita Goméz, Ketty Gottardo, Tom Harper, Mark Hennessey, Selma Holo, Alison Inglis, Javier Irribaren, Catherine Jenkins, Susan Jenkins, Kirsten Kennedy, Luis Lafuente Batanero, Leanne Lee, Patrick Lenaghan, Stacy Lieberman, Aimee Lind, Maria Loh, Rachel Longaker, Sally McKay, Sheila McTighe, Susie Nash, Benito Navarrete Prieto, Angela Ndalianis, Nadine Orenstein, Roberto Palermo, Clara de la Peña, François Quiviger, Craig Reeves, Jonathan Ritter, Jane Roberts, Martin Royalton Kisch, Pat Rubin, Susan Russell, Rose Marie San Juan, Stephanie Schraeder, Jan Stuart, Naoko Takahatake, Helen Thomas, Marjorie Trusted, Jesusa Vega, Zahira Veliz Bomford, Amanda Wunder and the participants of the British Museum-Courtauld Institute Graphic Arts Group (GAG).

This publication has been generously sponsored by the Centro de Estudios Europa Hispánica (CEEH) under the direction of José Luis Colmer. I would like to thank their continued commitment to publishing on prints and drawings in Spain.

This book is dedicated to Noah and Harper.

Illustration acknowledgements

The publisher would like to thank the copyright holders for granting permission to reproduce the images illustrated. All objects are reproduced with the permission of the institutions to which they belong as stated in the captions. Below is a list of further acknowledgements and copyright details. Every attempt has been made to trace accurate ownership of copyrighted images in this book. Errors and omissions will be corrected in subsequent editions provided notification is sent to the publisher.

All photographs of British Museum objects are © The Trustees of the British Museum, courtesy of the Department of Photography and Imaging. Registration numbers for British Museum objects are included in the image captions. Further donor information for works included in the exhibition *Renaissance to Goya: Prints and drawings from Spain* can be found in the List of Exhibits on pages 307–11. Donor information for British Museum works not included in the exhibition can be found below.

CHAPTER 1

Fig. 9, p. 28
© Biblioteca Nacional de España

Fig. 10, p. 29
© Biblioteca Nacional de España

Fig. 12, p. 30
Reproduced courtesy of the Marquis of Salisbury

Fig. 17, p. 35
© Biblioteca Nacional de España

Fig. 18, p. 36
© Biblioteca Nacional de España

Fig. 23, p. 41
© 2011. Wadsworth Atheneum Museum of Art /Art Resource, NY/Scala, Florence

Fig. 24, p. 42
© Patrimonio Nacional, Madrid

CHAPTER 2

Fig. 3, p. 48
The Metropolitan Museum of Art, Rogers Fund, 2004 (2004.137). Image © The Metropolitan Museum of Art

Fig. 6, p. 50
Collection of the University of Arizona Museum of Art and Archive of Visual Arts, Tucson

Fig. 8, p. 51
© Kimbell Conservation Department

Fig. 9, p. 52
© British Library Board

Fig. 10, p. 52
© Biblioteca Nacional de España

Fig. 11, p. 53
© Biblioteca Nacional de España

Fig. 12, p. 54
© Biblioteca Nacional de España

CHAPTER 3

Fig. 2, p. 60
© Patrimonio Nacional, Madrid

Fig. 3, p. 60
© Patrimonio Nacional, Madrid

Fig. 4, p. 61
© Patrimonio Nacional, Madrid

Fig. 5, p. 61
© Patrimonio Nacional, Madrid

Fig. 6, p. 62
© Biblioteca Nacional de España

Fig. 10, p. 64
The Royal Collection © 2011 Her Majesty Queen Elizabeth II

Fig. 12, p. 66
© Staatliche Graphische Sammlung München

Fig. 13, p. 67
© Biblioteca Nacional de España

Fig. 19, p. 70
© Patrimonio Nacional, Madrid

Fig. 21, p. 71
© RMN / Jean-Gilles Berizzi

Fig. 22, p. 72
© Patrimonio Nacional, Madrid

Fig. 23, p. 73
© Biblioteca Nacional de España

Fig. 27, p. 75
Bequeathed by Clayton Mordaunt Cracherode

Fig. 29, p. 77
© British Library Board

Fig. 32, p. 79
© Biblioteca Nacional de España

CHAPTER 4

Fig. 1, p. 82
© Staatliche Graphische Sammlung München

Fig. 3, p. 83
© Biblioteca Nacional de España

Fig. 4, p. 84
© Biblioteca Nacional de España

Fig. 5, p. 85
© Biblioteca Nacional de España

Fig. 6, p. 86
Supplied courtesy Dpto. Patrimonio Santa Iglesia Catedral Primada de Toledo © Cabildo Primado, Toledo

Fig. 9, p. 87
Kindly supplied by the Dirección General de Patrimonio Histórico, Comunidad de Madrid. Photograph: Juan Carlos Martin Lera

Fig. 10, p. 88
© Biblioteca Nacional de España

Fig. 13, p. 89
© Bayonne, Musée Bonnat-Helleu. Photograph: A. Vaquero

Fig. 19, p. 93
© Biblioteca Nacional de España

Fig. 23, p. 96
© Biblioteca Nacional de España

Fig. 24, p. 97
The Metropolitan Museum of Art, Bequest of Harry G. Sperling, 1971 (1975.131.226) Image © The Metropolitan Museum of Art

Fig. 25, p. 97
© Biblioteca Nacional de España

Fig. 27, p. 98
Kindly supplied by the Dirección General de Patrimonio Histórico, Comunidad de Madrid Photograph: Juan Carlos Martin Lera.

Fig. 28, p. 99
Museo de Bellas Artes de Valencia

Fig. 31, p. 101
© Biblioteca Nacional de España

Fig. 34, p. 103
© Biblioteca Nacional de España

Fig. 35, p. 104
© Biblioteca Nacional de España

Fig. 39, p. 106
Kindly supplied by the Dirección General de Patrimonio Histórico, Comunidad de Madrid Photograph: Juan Carlos Martin Lera

Fig. 41, p. 107
© Biblioteca Nacional de España

Fig. 47, p. 111
© RMN / Michèle Bellot

Fig. 48, p. 111
Antonio Palomino
© Biblioteca Nacional de España

Fig. 52, p. 113
© Biblioteca Nacional de España

Fig. 56, p. 116
© Biblioteca Nacional de España

Fig. 57, p. 116
© Biblioteca Nacional de España

Fig. 58, p. 117
© British Library Board

Fig. 59, p. 117
© The National Gallery, London

Fig. 60, p. 118
© Biblioteca Nacional de España

Fig. 61, p. 119
© British Library Board

Fig. 62, p. 119
© British Library Board

Fig. 63, p. 120
© Biblioteca Nacional de España

Fig. 64, p. 120
© Biblioteca Nacional de España

CHAPTER 5

Fig. 4, p. 126
© Museo Casa de la Moneda, Madrid, Spain

Fig. 5, p. 127
© RMN / Michèle Bellot

Fig. 8, p. 129
© Biblioteca Nacional de España

Fig. 9, p. 130
© Museo de la Real Academia de Bellas Artes de San Fernando

Fig. 14, p. 133
Donated by Anonymous

Fig. 18, p. 136
© bpk Berlin. Photograph: Christoph Irrgang

Fig. 20, p. 137
© Biblioteca Nacional de España

Fig. 21, p. 138
© Biblioteca Nacional de España

Fig. 24, p. 140
© Museo de la Real Academia de Bellas Artes de San Fernando

Fig. 25, p. 141
The Pierpont Morgan Library, New York. Purchased as the gift of Mrs Charles Wrightsman, 1986.46. Photography: Schecter Lee, 2009

Fig. 29, p. 144
© Biblioteca Nacional de España

Fig. 38, p. 150
© Biblioteca Nacional de España

Fig. 41, p. 151
© RMN / Michèle Bellot

Fig. 46, p. 155
Bequeathed by George Salting

Fig. 50, p. 158
© bpk Berlin. Photograph: Christoph Irrgang

Fig. 52, p. 160
© Biblioteca Nacional de España

CHAPTER 6

Fig. 1, p. 164
Bequeathed by Richard Payne Knight

Fig. 2, p. 164
© RMN / Michèle Bellot

Fig. 6, p. 167
© Museo de Bellas Artes de Valencia

Fig. 7, p. 168
© Biblioteca Nacional de España

Fig. 8, p. 169
© Museo de Bellas Artes de Valencia

Fig. 10, p. 170
© Museo de Bellas Artes de Valencia

Fig. 11, p. 171
© Biblioteca Nacional de España

Fig. 12, p. 171
© Museo de Bellas Artes de Valencia

Fig. 19, p. 177
© Biblioteca Nacional de España

Fig. 21, p. 179
© Museo de Bellas Artes de Valencia

Fig. 24, p. 181
Bequeathed by Sir Hans Sloane

Fig. 27, p. 183
Alinari Archives, Florence; reproduced with the permission of Ministero per i Beni e le Attività Culturali

CHAPTER 7

Fig. 3, p. 193
© Biblioteca Nacional de España

Fig. 6, p. 195
© Biblioteca Nacional de España

Fig. 8, p. 197
© Biblioteca Nacional de España

Fig. 9, p. 198
© Biblioteca Nacional de España

Fig. 10, p. 199
© Museo de la Real Academia de Bellas Artes de San Fernando

Fig. 11, p. 200
© Patrimonio Nacional, Madrid

Fig. 12, p. 201
© RMN / Jean-Gilles Berizzi

Fig. 14, p. 202
© Biblioteca Nacional de España

Fig. 18, p. 204
© Patrimonio Nacional, Madrid

Fig. 21, p. 206
© Biblioteca Nacional de España

Fig. 25, p. 208
© Museo de la Real Academia de Bellas Artes de San Fernando

Fig. 28, p. 209
© Biblioteca Nacional de España

Fig. 38, p. 216
© Biblioteca Nacional de España

Fig. 47, p. 222
© Biblioteca Nacional de España

Fig. 53, p. 227
Donated by Nan Ino Cooper, Baroness Lucas of Crudwell and Lady Dingwall in Memory of Auberon Thomas Herbert, 9th Baron Lucas of Crudwell and 5th Lord Dingwall

CHAPTER 8

Fig. 29, p. 251
© English Heritage Photo Library

Fig. 33, p. 254
Bequeathed by William Meriton Eaton, 2nd Baron Cheylesmore

Fig. 40, p. 261
The Metropolitan Museum of Art, Harris Brisbane Dick Fund, 1935 (35.103.26). Image © The Metropolitan Museum of Art

Fig. 44, p. 264
© Museo de la Real Academia de Bellas Artes de San Fernando

Fig. 47, p. 267
© Biblioteca Nacional de España

Index

Academy of Fine Arts, Valencia 22, 224, 228
Academy of San Fernando, Madrid 22, 22–3, 193, 197, 198–207, 215, 220, 224, 233, 236, 240, 249, 262
Academy of Santa Barbara, Valencia 22, 128, 131, 149–50, 152, 155, 157, 224
Acosta, Pedro de, *Trompe l'oeil of Prints pinned to a Wall* (1741) 41–3, *43*
Agustina of Aragon *253*, 254
Al-Andalus 12
al-Idrisi 274
Alba, Duchess of 240, 244
Alberti, Cherubino, *Cross-section of the Reconstructed Temple of Solomon* (1604) 77–8, *77*
Alcalá, Duke of 180
Alcalá de Henares 51, 278
Alcázar, Madrid 28, 72, 89–90, 96, 98, 108, 195
Alfaro y Gámez, Juan 145–6
Alhambra, Granada 126
Ametller Rotlan, Blas 233
Amigoni, Jacopo 201, 211
Angel, Pedro 79
Aniello da Amalfi, Tomasso 184
Anjou, Duke of 11
Anthony Abbot, Saint 53
Antolínez, José 104
Antwerp 19, 76
aquatint technique 260
Arabesques, Serpents and Putti (*c.*1550–1600) (anonymous) 29, *30*
Arce, José de 152
Ardemans, Teodoro 191, 195
Design for the Exaltation of Saint Francis of Assisi (*c.*1700–26) 191, *192*
Arias Montano, Benito 23, 76
Armenini, Giovan Battista 72
Arteaga y Alfaro, Matías de, *Ferdinand III* (1672) 161, *161*
ascendance of the Spanish artists (eighteenth century) 205–211
Astor, Diego de 35, 79
Saint Francis and Brother Leo Meditating on Death (1606) 35, 79, *79*

Baldinucci, Filippo 187
Barcelón, Juan 217
Barcelona 12, 18, 50, 51, 52, 233
Barcelona Cathedral 47, 48, 50
Barco, Manuel 239
baroque style 189–91, 278, 281
Barrosso, Miguel 63, 72–4
Christ Distributing Bread... (1587–9) 27, 63, *74*, 275, *276*
Barsanti, Nicolo 217
Bartolomé, Master, *The Transfiguration* (*c.*1480–88) 49, *50*, *51*
Bassano, Francesco 170
Bassano, Jacopo 170
Bassano, Leandro 170
Bausá, Gregorio 171, 173
Bayeu y Subías, Francisco 202, 205–7, 214, 235, 236
Head of a Woman (after 1765) 32, *188*, 206–7, *206*
Studies of Two Men (*c.*1785) 206, *206*
Study of a Giant (*c.*1763) *205*, 206
Bayeu y Subías, Ramón 206, 214, 235
The Attributes of the Virgin (*c.*1788) 214, *214*, 280
The Attributes of the Virgin (after 1780) 214, *214*, 280
The Liberation of Saint Peter (*c.*1770–93) *32*, 35
Beauvarlet Firmin, Jacques, *The Sultana Taking Coffee* (*c.*1771) 227, *227*
Becerra, Gaspar 27, 71–2, 74, 75, 87, 125
Half Male Figure and a Female Profile (*c.*1562–8) 72, *72*
Mercury and Minerva (*c.*1562–3) *71*, 72
The High Altar in the Church of Descalzas Reales, Madrid (1563) 72, *73*
Beer, Cornelio de 120
Berenson, Bernard 20
Berlinghieri, Francesco 55
Bernini, Giovanni Lorenzo 191
Berruguete, Alonso 67–9, 71, 211
Assumption of the Virgin (1555–61) *56*, 67–8, *67*, 276
Fragment of an Architectural Drawing Showing Seven Figures (*c.*1540–50) 69, *69*
The Entombment of Christ (*c.*1530–40) *68*, 69
The Entombment of Christ (*c.*1530–50) *68*, 69
Bertelli, Cristofano 19
Bloemaert, Abraham 145
Bloemaert, Frederick, *Study of Seven Heads from 'Het Tekenboek'* (1650–6) 145, *146*
Blosius, Ludovico (Louis de Blois) 119
Bobadilla, Jerónimo 23
Bocanegra, Pedro Atanasio, *The Virgin and Child appearing to Saint Francis of Assisi and Saint Teresa of Avila* (*c.*1660–8) 143–4, *144*
Boel, Cornelio 116
Bonaparte, Joseph 11, 251
Bonasone, Giulio 139
book production 51–3, 76, 219–20, 227–8
see also Don Quijote
Borcht, Pieter van der 79
Bordone, Benedetto 55
Borrás, Nicolas 167
Bosse, Abraham 215
Boucher, François 233
Bourbon, House of 11, 12, 189, 191, 279
Braganza, Bárbara de 211
Brambila, Fernando 251–4
Agustina of Aragon (1808–14) *253*, 254
Ruins of the Church of the General Hospital (1808–14) 252, *252*
Brancacci Chapel, Florence 67
Brandi, Mariano 41
British Library, London 276
British Museum, London 15, 74, 150, 174, 175, 280, 281
Brugada, Antonio 268–9
bubonic plague 146–7
Buen Retiro palace, Madrid 19, 90–2, 94, 97, 114, 221
Burgos 12
Bustamente, Francisco de 111

Cajés, Eugenio 21, 22, 75, 81–90, 93
Saint Ildephonsus at the Tomb of Saint Leocardia (*c.*1615) 26–7, 86–7, *86*, 93, 278
Study of Christ for the Flagellation (*c.*1600–20) 87, *88*
The Circumcision of Christ (*c.*1600–15) 22–3, *24*, 89
Cajés, Patricio 75, 79
The Sons of Jacob Presenting Him with Joseph's Tunic (*c.*1607–12) 84, *84*
Calle, Cornelis 119
Callot, Jacques 23, 236, 247
Camarón y Bonanat, José 222, 224–8
An Algerian Woman Seated Beneath a Canopy (*c.*1771–80) *226*, 227, 280
Saint Mary Magdalene in the Desert (*c.*1760–90) 228, *228*, 280
Saint Vincent Ferrer Preaching (*c.*1752–60) *225*, 226
Cambiaso, Luca 58, 60, 75, 79, 168
Saint John the Baptist Preaching (1583–4) 60, *62*
Camilo, Francisco 94, 101–2, 121
Saint Charles Borromeo Interceding for the Pestilent (*c.*1660) 101, *103*
Saint Felix of Cantalice (before 1657) 101–2, *104*
The Rest of the Holy Family on the Flight into Egypt (*c.*1650–70) 101, *103*
Campaña, Pedro de *see* Kempeneer, Peter
Campi, Vicenzo 79
Campolargo, Pedro 158
Cano, Alonso 103, 120, 123, 128, 133, 137, 139–44, 147–8, 150, 172, 278
Christ in Limbo (*c.*1652) 139, *140*
Design for an Altarpiece (*c.*1660–5) 140, *142*, 278, *279*
Design for the Chapel of San Diego de Alcalá... (1657–8) 140, *141*
Saint Ildephonsus Adoring the Virgin and Christ Child... (*c.*1645–52) 139, *140*
Saint Matthew and the Angel (*c.*1625–35) 139, *139*
The Assumption of the Virgin (1661–2) 140–2, *143*
Caravaggio, Michelangelo da 90
Caravaggio, Polidoro da 125
Cardano, José María 266
Carderera, Valentín 249, 259
Carducho, Bartolomé 63, 72, 75, 83, 278
Saint Lawrence Baptizing the Prisoners (*c.*1598) 63, *65*, 276
Carducho, Vicente 22, 23, 63, 75, 81–90, 97, 120, 128, 211, 236, 278
A Group of Angels (*c.*1607–9) *83*, 84
Adoration of the Magi (*c.*1616–22) 86–7, *87*
Adoration of the Magi (1619) 86–7, *87*
Christ Appearing to Father Juan Fort (1626–32) 26, *27*
Diálogos de la pintura 89, 120, 128
Saint Bruno Praying in la Torre-Calabria (1626–32) 87, *88*, 170
The Duke of Feria at the Siege of Rheinfelden (1634) 90, *91*, 93
The Virgin Appearing to Father Juan Fort (1626–32) 26, *27*
Triumph of the Eucharist (*c.*1607–9) *83*, 84
Carlí, Maestro 47
Carnicero, Antonio 280
A Picador on Horseback Stabbing a Bull (*c.*1789) 223, *223*
A Picador Leaves the Bullring after Stabbing the Bull (*c.*1789) 223, *223*
Collection of the Principal Manoeuvres of Bullfighting (1787–90) 39–40, 222–3, *223*, 260
Don Quijote Defeated by the Knight of the White Moon (1780) 220
Carracci, Agostino, *The Temptation of Saint Anthony* (1582) *173*, 174
Carracci, Annibale 23, 186
Carracci family, the 187
Carreño de Miranda, Juan 94, 96, 98–101, 109, 114–15, 121, 278
Christ Baptized (*c.*1682) 99, *102*
Two Apostles (*c.*1660) 99, *101*
Casa de Pilatos, Seville 131–2
Castello, Fabrizio, *The Escorial under Construction* (*c.*1576) 30–2, *31*
Castello, Giovanni Battista 58–9
Mars and Apollo (*c.*1566/7–9) 58, *59*
Castelo, Félix 90
Recapture of the Island of San Cristobal by Don Fadrique de Toledo (*c.*1634–5) *92*, 93

Castile 10, 22, 168
Castillo, José del 203, 212–14, 217, 236
Saint Cecilia in Glory (1754) 203, *203*
The Supper at Emmaus (1778) 212, *213*
Castillo, Juan del 147
Castillo y Saavedra, Antonio del 123, 145–6
Study of Seven Heads (*c*.1650–68) 145, *146*
Castro, Giacomo de 182
Ceán Bermudéz, Juan Augustín 16, 25, 79, 114, 116–17, 119, 121, 125, 138, 142, 145, 149–50, 158–60, 184, 193, 196, 203–5, 210–11, 214, 236, 238, 244, 247, 249, 259, 262
Ceballos, Mariano 260
Cennini, Cennino 49
censorship 20
Cerezo, Mateo 114, 212
Cerquozzi, Michelangelo 174
Céspedes, Pablo de 120, 123, 125–6, 128
chalk drawings 128, 186–7, 193, 200
Chapel of San Diego de Alcalá 140, *141*
charcoal, underdrawings using 49
Charles II of Spain 11, 12, 110, 121, 191
Charles III of Spain 11, 40–1, 203–4, 215, 221, 224, 233
Charles IV of Spain 11, 210, 217, 223, 240, 244, *244*
Charles V of Spain 10–11, 12, 55, 57–8, 67, 126, 259, 275
Charles VII of Spain 40–1, *40*
Chennevières, Philippe de 15
Churriguera, José Benito de 111, 119, 191, 195
Elevation and Plan for the Retable of Saint Francis Xavier... (*c*.1709–13) *190*, 191
Cieza, José de 114
Saint Francis de Paul before the King of Naples (*c*.1691) 114, *114*
Cincinnato, Romulo 75, 79
Clement X, Pope 160
Cochin, Charles Nicolás 233
Coci, Jorge 51
Codazzi, Viviano 174
Coello, Claudio 97, 109–12, 114, 121, 189, 191, 200
An Hieronymite Monk (*c*.1685) 110, *111*
Colonna, Angelo Michele 96, 105
Columbus, Christopher 54
Columbus, Ferdinand 23, 54, 55
Columbus Archive and Library, Seville 54
Conchillos y Falcó, Juan Antonio 171, 175–9, 224, 278
Study of a Partly Kneeling Male Nude (1690–1705) 32, 178, *178*, 278, *279*
The Lamentation of Christ (1672) 176, *177*
View of Paterna (1690) 179, *179*
contractual drawings 29–30
copper-plate prints 53, 75–9
Cordier, Roberto 116
Córdoba 123, 145–6, 155–7
Cort, Cornelis 18
The Martyrdom of Saint Lawrence (1571) 75, *75*
Coscollà, Bartomeu, *The Veronica of the Virgin* (*c*.1398) 47, *47*
Cosin, Pierre 51
Costillares, Joaquín 223
Courbes, Juan de 116, 119
Cranach, Lucas 54
Crescenzio, Bartolommeo 21
Cromberger Dynasty 51
Cruz Cano y Olmedilla, Juan de la 198, 211, 221–2
A Slave from Puerto Rico (1777) 221, *221*, *222*
Collection of Spanish Costume (*Colección de trajes de España*) (1777–88) 39–40, 221–2, *221*
The Blind Guitarist (1777) *221*
Cruz, Diego de la 30
Cruzado, Alfonso 198
Cueman, Egas 48
Cuevas, Pedro de las 93, 94, 99
Cumberland, Richard 215

Dancart, Pieter 13
Datini, Francesco 274
De Dominici, Bernardo 184
Death Shooting Down the Human Race (*c*.1454) (anonymous) 52, *52*, 275
Delli, Dello, *Christ at the Column* (*c*.1440–60) 47–8, *48*, 49–50
Delli, Sansone, *Christ at the Column* (*c*.1440–60) 47–8, *48*, 49–50
Descalzas Reales church, Madrid 72, *73*
Design for a Ceiling Decoration (*c*.1660–70) (anonymous) 96, *96*
Deventer, Jacob van 75
disegno (*diseño*) 45, 58, 89
Doménech, Francisco, *The Virgin of the Rosary* (1488) 52–3, *54*
Dominic, Saint 142
Don Quijote 228, *256*, 257, 278
(Royal Academy of Spain) 37, 214, 219–20, 233
drawings 15–17
at the Escorial 58–67
contractual drawings 29–30
during the reign of Philip IV 89–94
early collecting 54–5
eighteenth-century 189–97, 199–200, 224–33
Madrid, 1650 94–115
Madrid, 1600–1700 81–115
pre-1500 45–50, 54–5
significance 21–5
sixteenth-century Andalusia 123–8
types of 25–32
Drevet, Pierre 194
Duflos, Augustin 207
Dupuis, Nicolás Gabriel 233
Dürer, Albrecht 23, 54, 55, 58, 169, 175, 236
Dutch papermakers 280

Edelinck, Gerard 191
El Greco 13, 17, 23, 35, 64–7, 79, 81
Saint John the Evangelist (*c*.1577) 65–7, *67*
Variation on Michelangelo's Sculpture of Day (*c*.1570) 65, *66*
'El Mudo' *see* Fernández de Navarrete, Juan
El Pardo, Madrid 72, 79, 83–4, 97
El Paular monastery 87, 278
El Pilar 203
engraving 198, 211, 215–20
Enlightenment, the 235, 238
Ephemeral Structure for a Royal Entry, An (*c*.1700–30) (anonymous) 29, *29*
Escorial monastery-palace 19, 22, 23, 27, 57–67, 76–9, 81–3, 87, 94, 97, 110, 114, 168, 170, 275, 276
drawing at the 58–67
library 61, 76
Espinel, Juan de 150
Espinosa, Francisco de 198
Espinosa, Jerónimo Jacinto 171
Esteve, José 227–8
etchings 120, 180, 238–9, 241–55, 257–60
Ezekiel 77

Fabregat, José Joaquín 224
Don Quijote Defeated by the Knight of the White Moon (1780) *219*, 220
fabrics, printed 41
fans 40–1
Federigui, Juan de 150
Felipe V 233
Ferdinand I 10, 11, 30, 48, 144
Ferdinand III 37, 160, 161, *161*
Ferdinand VI 11, 195, 201, 203, 205, 223
Ferdinand VII 11, 232, 246, 247, 249, 250, 267
Fernández de Moratín, Leandro 241–2, 268
Fernández de Moratín, Nicolás 257
Fernández de Navarrete, Juan ('El Mudo') 69–71
A Lion Drinking (*c*.1569) 70, 71
A Seated Male Nude (*c*.1560–79) 70, 71
Saint Jerome in the Desert (1569) 70, 71
Fernández, Francisco 120
Fernando Enríquez de Ribera, 3rd Duke of Alcalá 131–2
Fernando VI 211
Ferrer, Joaquin 269, 270
Ferrer, Saint Vincent 226–7
Flipart, Charles-Joseph 211
Floridablanca, Count of 215–17
Flos Sanctorum (Lives of the Saints) 51
Fosman, Gregorio, *Allegory of the Death of María Luisa de Orleans* (1690) 119–20, *119*
Francia, Carlos 224
Franco era 15
French art 191–3, 200–1
French papermakers 275, 276, 277–8, 280
Frías y Escalante, Juan Antonio de 114

Gaeta, Gerónimo 77
Gallardo, Bartolomé José 257
Galle, Philip 76
Gallego, Fernando 49
Gálvez, Juan 251–4
Agustina of Aragon (1808–14) *253*, 254
Ruins of the Church of the General Hospital (1808–14) 252, 252
García Hidalgo, José 114, 121, 176
Anamorphosis of a Face (1693) 121, *121*
Studies of the Female Nude (1693) *38*, 40
García Reinoso, Antonio 146
Sheet of Figure Studies (1647) 146, *147*
Gaspar de Haro y Guzmán, 7th Marqués del Carpiio 23–5
Gasull, Agustín 175
The Adoration of the Magi (1689) 175, *177*
Gaulon, Charles 268
Genoese paper monopoly 276–9
Ghirlandaio, Domenico 76
Giambologna 82
Giaquinto, Corrado 195, 201, 202–4, 206, 207, 231–2
Giordano, Luca 10, 114–15, 217
Miracle of Saint Anthony of Padua (1698–1700) 115, *115*
Giovanni Battista Crescenzi, Marques de la Torre 94
Giunti, Giovanni 79
Giunti, Julio 79
Godoy, Manuel 217, 241, 251
Goltzius, Hendrick, *The Circumcision of Christ* (1594) 23, *25*, 89
Gómez, Alonso 51
Gómez de Mora, Juan, *The High Altar of the Church of the Monastery of Guadalupe* (1614) 28, 84–6, *85*, 105
Gómez Sicre, José 16, 17
González Azaola, Gregorio 244
González de Rosende, Antonio 121
González Ruiz, Antonio 197, 200
Study of a Male Nude (*c*.1740–55) 200, *201*
González Velázquez, Antonio 202–3, 206–7
A Standing Woman (1781) 202, 203, 280, *281*
Design for a Ceiling Devoted to Mercury (*c*.1760) *202*, 203
Goya, Javier 236, 262
Goya y Lucientes, Francisco de 8, 13, 189, 202, 206–7, 217, 220–2, 232–3, 235–72
A Phantom Dancing with Castanets (*c*.1825–8) 272, *272*
Against the Common Good (*c*.1814–15) 250, *250*
appointed Painter to the King 240
Arthur Wellesley, 1st Duke of Wellington (1812) 251, *251*
on artistic liberty 240
'Black Paintings' 261, 263
Blind Guitarist (1778) 214, *237*, 238
Bordeaux Albums I and II 269–72, *271–3*
Bulls of Bordeaux prints 265, 268–9
Burial of the Sardine (*c*.1814–16) *264*, 265
caprichos enfáticos prints 250, 257
Charles IV and María Luisa (1799–1801) 244, *244*
deafness 16
death 235
Disasters of War prints 40, 245, 245–55, *245–50*, *254*, 260, 262, 263, 280
Don Quijote Beset by Monsters (*c*.1812–20) *256*, 257
drawings 30, 235–6, 240–1, 255–7, 260–1, 269–72
Dreadful Events in the Front Row of the Ring (1816) 258, 260
earliest graphic work–mid-1790s 235–41
Enlightenment ideology 235, 238
Equestrian Portrait of the Duke of Wellington (1812) 251, *251*, 281
etchings 238–9, 241–55, 257–60
exile in Bordeaux 241, 267–72
Figures Dancing in a Circle (*c*.1816–24) *264*, 265
Fools' Folly (*c*.1816–24) 265, *265*
For Having Jewish Ancestry (*c*.1808–14) *234*, 255, *255*
He Wakes Up Kicking (*c*.1819–23) 261, *261*
I Saw It (*c*.1810–15) *248*, 249
Images of Spain Album 255–7, *256*, 267
Inferno (*c*.1818–19) 30, 266, *266–7*
and the Inquisition 235, 241, 255–6
Inquisition Album 255–6, *255*
Large Carnivorous Vulture (*c*.1814–15) 250, *250*

and lithography 260, 266–9
Los Caprichos prints (1799) 40, 241–5, *242–3*, 257, 260, 263, 269, 270, 280
love of Rembrandt 236
Lunatics (*c.*1825–8) 270, *271*
Madrid Album 241
notebook 236
Of What Ill Will He Die? (*c.*1797–8) *243*, 244
Old Man on a Swing (*c.*1827–8) 272, *273*
Old Style Duel (*c.*1819) 267, *268*
painting 239–40
Pedro Roldán (1798–9) 244, *245*
poor health 240, 241
portraits 244
Pretty Teacher! (*c.*1797–8) *243*, 244
prints 235–9, 241–55, 257–60, 262–5
Rocky Outcrop and Leaning Trees (before 1810) 245, *245*
Sad Presentations of What is to Come (*c.*1810–15) *248*, 249
Saint Francis of Paola (*c.*1776–8) 236, *236*
Sanlúcar Album 240–1
Soldiers Fleeing a Phantom (*c.*1816–24) *262–3*, 263
Spanish Entertainment (1825) 269, *270*
The Black Border Album (1816–20) 260–1, 272
The Chinchillas (*c.*1797–8) *243*, 244
The Daring Martincho in the Ring at Zaragova (1816) *259*, 260
The Disparates (*Los Proverbios*) (*c.*1816–24) 262–5, *262–5*, 272
The Drunkards (1778) 239, *239*
The Garrotted Man (*c.*1778) 238, *238*, 280, *281*
The Infante Don Fernando (1778) 239, *239*
The Moors Made a Different Play in the Ring... (1816) *258*, 259
The Sleep of Reason (*c.*1797–8) 242, *242*
The *Tauromaquia* prints (1816) 257–60, *258–9*, 262, 265, 267, 280
The Third of May 1808 (1814) 246, *246*
They are Cutting the Old Woman in Two (*c.*1794–7) 241, *241*
They Say Yes and Give their Hand to the First Comer (*c.*1797–8) *243*, 244
Unhappy Mother! (*c.*1811–15) *249*, 250
Universal Language (1797) 242, *242*
use of paper 280–1
What Bravery! (1810–12) *253*, 254
Will She Rise Again? (*c.*1814–15) 250, *250*
Witches and Old Women Album (1819–23) 260–1
Woman Reading to Two Children (*c.*1819) 267, *269*
Young Woman in a Maja Costume (*c.*1794) 240, *240*
Goyeneche, Juan de 191
Graf, Urs 54
Granada 10, 12, 139, 140–4
Granada Cathedral 30, 140–2, 144
Grantham, Lord 239
Guadalupe monastery 28
Guas, Juan, *The Main Chapel of San Juan de los Reyes, Toledo* (*c.*1477) 28, *44*, *48*, *49*, 50
Guercino (Giovanni Francesco Barbieri) 187, *214*
Guerço brothers 275
Guillén de Brocar, Arnao 51
Gutiérrez, Juan Simón 148–9
Guzmán de Silva, Diego 170

Hamen y León, Juan van der 23
Hapsburgs, Spanish 11, 57, 90
Harris, Tomás 263
Hendrik III of Nassau 55
Hernández, Carmen 280
Hernández, Francisco 76
Herrera Barnuevo, Sebastían de 28, 103–6, 143, 191
An Apostle (*c.*1620–40) *136*, 137
Design for an Altarpiece in a Chapel (*c.*1650–60) 104–5, *106*
Design for a Cupola Decoration (*c.*1660–70) 105–6, *107*
The Assumption of the Virgin (*c.*1650–8) 103–4, *105*
The High Altar of the Church of San Isidro, Madrid (1650–5) 105, *106*
Herrera the Elder, Francisco de 106, 135–9, 147–8
Saint Bartholomew (1642) *135*, 136–7
Saint Thomas (1642) *135*, 136–7
The Holy Trinity... (1627) 137, *137*
Herrera the Elder, Circle of Francisco de, *Study of a Seated Male Nude* (*c.*1640–50) *136*, 137
Herrera, Juan de 57, 61, 76–9, 276
Herrera the Younger, Francisco de 22, 94, 106–9, 123, 149, 161
Angels in the Clouds Playing Musical Instruments (*c.*1650–6) 108, *108*
Design for an Overmantel (*c.*1670–80) 29, 109, *110*
The Baptism of Christ (before 1654) 106, *107*, 108
The Triumph of Saint Hermenegild (1654) 108, *108*
The Vision of Elisha (*c.*1665–80) 108, *109*
Hillo, Pepe 260, 223
Holanda, Francisco de 22
Hollander beater 280
Houasse, Michel-Ange 191, 193–4, 200, 226
A Seated Man Holding a Jar (1722–30) *193*
An Academy of Drawing (*c.*1725) 199, *200*
Saint Francis Regis Preaching (before 1722) *225*, 226–7

Iberian Peninsular 10, 17, 21, 45, 50–1, 274, *275*
Ignatio, Francisco, *Catafalque Raised for the Exequies of María Luisa de Orleans* (1690) 119–20, *119*, 191
Imprenta Real 79
incunabula 51
Infante Luis Antonio, Count of Chinchón 207
infrared reflectography 49, *51*
Inquisition 20, 172–3, 235, 241, 255–6
'International Gothic' 163
Irala Yuso, Matías Antonio 195–6
A Design with Musical Putti (*c.*1730–9) 195, *196*
Método... (1730–9) 195, *197*
Iriarte, Bernardo de 240
Isabel of Castile 10, 11, 12, 30, 48, 50, 144
Isabel de Borbón *116*, 118
Isabel de Farnesio 189, 194–5, 210, 233
Islamic papermaking 274–5, *275*
Italian art 20–2, 45, 81, 114–15, 123
Italian papermakers 274–9

James I of Aragon 274
James the Apostle 37
Joanes, Vicente 167
Joanna the Mad (Joanna of Castile) 10
John the Baptist 41, 60, *62*, 150, *152*, 157, *158*, *230*, 231–2
Juan II, King, on Horseback (1517) (anonymous) 51, *52*
Juan of Austria 182–4, *184*
Juanes, Juan de 165–7
Saint Stephen Being Led to his Execution (late 1550s) *166*, 167
The Virgin Seated (*c.*1555) 165, *165*
Juni, Juan de 135
Junti, Tomás de 79
Juvarra, Filippo 195

Kempeneer, Peter (Pedro de Campaña) 126–8
Saint George and the Dragon (*c.*1550–6) *12*, 126–8

La Rioja 275
La Vega, Francisco, *Design for a fan showing the Triumphal Procession of Charles VII entering Naples* (after 1734) 40–1, *40*
Labacco, Antonio 23
Lalande, Joseph de 280
landscape drawings 32, 179, 193–4
Lanfranco, Giovanni 19, 23
Triumph of a Roman Emperor (*c.*1640) 19, *20*
Lasne, Michel 168
Lavaña, Juan Bautista 116
Lawrence, Saint 57
Leonardo da Vinci 163
Leonardo, José 90–3
The Surrender of Jülich (*c.*1634–5) *92*, 93
Lerma, Duke of 81, 82–3, *82*
Leyden, Lucas van 23, 54, 175
Lippi, Filippino 163
Lippi, Circle of Filippino, *A Standing Man Seen from Behind* (1472–1504) 163, *164*
lithography 260, 266–9
Llanos, Fernando 163
Llorente, Juan Antonio 256
López, Diego 137
López, Francisco 120
López de Ayala, Adelardo 244
López de Escuriaz, Diego 74
Christ Distributing Bread... (1587–9) 27, 63, *74*, *275*, *276*
López y Portaña, Vicente 232–3
Logroño 51
Louis I 11
Louis XIV 189, 191
Luzán Martínez, José 235

Machén Casalins, Jaime 262
Machuca, Pedro 126–8
The Descent from the Cross (*c.*1520) 126, *127*
The Descent from the Cross (1547) 126, *127*
Macip, Vicente 163, 164–5
Madrazo family 15
Madrid 8, 12–13, 15, 18, 21–2, 35, 51, 57, 72, 74, 76–9, 123, 139–44, 154, 168, 171, 176, 236, 239–40, 244–52, 262, 265–7, 276–8
as artistic capital 1600–1700 81–121
eighteenth-century art 189–93, 195, 197–207, 211–21, 223–7, 231–3
famine 246, 249–50
Maella, Mariano Salvador 41, 205, 207, *224*, 232
Study of Flying Putti (1798) 207, *207*
The 'Disputa' from the School of Athens (1764) 207, *207*
The Rest of the Holy Family on the Flight into Egypt (*c.*1780–90) *213*, 214
Maino, Juan Bautista 82, 90
Mal Lara, Juan de 128
Man from La Granja Holding Game (*c.*1770–90) (anonymous) 222, *222*
Mantua, Duke of 82
Manuel de Acevedo y Zuñiga, 6th Conde de Monterrey 23–5
Maratta, Carlo 175, 206
March, Esteban 171, 176
Doge Francesco Donato before the Virgin and Other Saints (1651) 171, *171*
María Luisa de Borbón 210, *210*, 240, 241, 280
María Luisa de Orleans 29, 110, 111, 112, 119, 191
María Luisa of Parma 11, 244, *244*
María Luisa of Savoy 189, 194
Mariana of Austria 30, 97, *97*, 103, 108
Mariana of Neuburg 191
Martincho (Francisco Antonio Basson) *259*, 260
Martínez, Domingo 149–50, 158
Martínez, Jusepe 21–2
Martínez Montañes, Juan 139
Martínez Pérez, Sebastián 240, 247
Martorell, Bernat 48
Mary of Hungary 58
Masaccio 67
Master IAM of Zwolle 49
Master of the Retable of San Jorge del Centenar, *Archangel Michael* (*c.*1390–1400) 45–6, *46*
Mathonière, Denis de 18
The Crowning of Esther (*c.*1580) 18, *18*
Melchor de Jovellanos, Gaspar 244, 245
Meléndez, Luis 199–200
Self-portrait (1746) 200, *201*
Meléndez, Miguel Jacinto 194
Isabel de Farnesio (*c.*1714–20) 194, *195*
Isabel de Farnesio (1727) 194, *195*
Mena y Medrano, Pedro de, *Study for a Statue of Queen Isabel* (*c.*1673–4) 30, 144, *145*
Mencía de Mendoza, Marquesa de Zenete 55
Méndez, Juan, *Print commemorating the Foundation of the Cartuja de la Cuevas, Seville* (1629) 138–9, *138*
Meneses Osorio, Francisco 152
Saint Joseph Kneeling before the Virgin and the Christ Child (1665–1700) 152, *155*
Mengs, Anton Raphael 203–5, 206, 211, 215, 221, 236
A Naked Male Youth Seated (*c.*1774–6) *204*, 205
Fame, Putti with the Symbols... (1774–6) *204*, 205
metalcut printing 51–2
Meyer, Henry, *Manuela Sancho* (1811) *254*, 255
Michelangelo 22, 23, 64–5, 67, 71, 125, 128, 132
Mingot, Teodosio 74–5

Minguet, Juan 199
Mitelli, Agostino 96, 105
Mois, Roland de 167
Assumption of the Virgin (*c.*1571) 167, *167*
Mola, Pier Francesco 187
Moles, Pedro Pascual 220, 233
The Crocodile Hunt (1773) *231*, 233
Monells, Rafael 46
Monserrat, Virgin of 54, 55
Montalbergo, Pietro Paolo de 18
Moors 10, 12, 81, 167–8
Mor, Antonis 12, 58
Mora, Francisco de 280
Morales, Luisa 160
Motte, Charles 269
Moya, Pedro de 144
Muñoz, Evaristo 224
Murgía, José 199
Murillo, Bartolomé Esteban 8, 13, 16, 22, 35, 147–58, 161, 189, 219, 277
Penitent Saint Peter (*c.*1670–80) 152, *154*
Saint Anthony of Padua... (1645–6) 148, *148*
Saint Francis of Paola (*c.*1665–75) 152, *153*, 278
Saint Isidore of Seville (1655) 150, *151*
Studies for Saint John the Baptist (*c.*1650–5) 150, *152*
The Archangel Michael *122*, 148–9, *149*, 150
The Christ Child Sleeping on the Cross (*c.*1665–80) 150, *150*
Murillo, Circle of Bartolomé Esteban
The Virgin of the Immaculate Conception (*c.*1665–85) 152, *155*, 158
Museo del Prado 29

Naples 11, 12, 19, 179, 180, 182–4, 186–7
Napoleon Bonaparte 11, 255
Napoleonic invasions of Spain 245–7, 251–5
Nardi, Angelo 90
Nelli, Nicolò 18–19
Ages of Man (1560–80) 18–19, *19*
Noort, Juan de 116
Noviciado (Madrid), Capilla del 226
nudes 22
Nuevo Baztán 191

Obregón, Diego de 120, 142–3
Saint Catherine of Alexandria (*c.*1658–68) 143, *144*
Obregón, Pedro de 120, 142–3
Olivares, Count-Duke of 87, 90, 118, *118*, 137–8, 139
Oliveri, Giovanni Domenico 198, 201
Orellana, Marcos Antonio de 16, 175, 232
Orlandi, Giovanni 182
ornament drawings 29
Orrente, Pedro 169–71, 175
Abraham Departing for Caanan (1627) 170, *170*
Saint Bruno and the Duke of Calabria (*c.*1625–45) 170, *171*
Ortega et Cotes, Ignatius Joseph de 39
Ortelius, Abraham 75
Osuna, Duke and Duchess of 241, 244
Ovid 89

Pacheco, Francisco 22–3, 72, 89–90, 120, 123–5, 128–39, 139, 147–8
Arte de la pintura 128–33
Pedro de Campaña (*c.*1585–98) 128, *128*
Saint John the Evangelist (1632) *132*, 133
Saint Matthew and the Angel (1632) *132*, 133, 139
The Apotheosis of Hercules (1604) *130*, 131–2
The Last Judgement (*c.*1610–14) *131*, 132, 140
Torso (1595) 129–31, *129*
Palafox y Melci, General José 246–7
Palafox y Mendoza, Juan de *120*, 121
Palomino, Juan Bernabé 195, 196–7, 198, 215
Allegory of the Creation of the Royal Academy of Fine Arts of San Fernando (1753) 197, *198*
Palomino y Velasco, Acisclo Antonio 16, 23, 74–5, 90, 93–4, 97, 99, 105–6, 110–11, 114, 137, 142, 145–6, 155, 157, 168, 176–9, 196, 211, 278
Abimelec Giving to David the Sword of Goliath (*c.*1711) 111, *112*, 278, *279*
Design for the Catafalque for the Exequies of María Louisa de Orleans (*c.*1689) 111, *111*, 191
Palumba, Giovanni Battista 54
Panneels, Herman 116, 119
Pantoja de la Cruz, Juan 12, 82
paper/papermaking 274–81
blue paper 275–6
brown paper 278, *279*
Dutch papermakers 280
French papermakers 275, 276, 277–8, 280
Genoese paper monopoly 276–9
Hollander beater 280
Islamic papermaking 274–5, *275*
Italian papermakers 274–9
papel blanco 276
papel de Bula 275
papel de estranza 275
papel sellado 277
senyal (watermarks) 275, 276–8, *277*, 279–80, 281
taxation of paper 277
parchment 47–8
Paret y Alcázar, Luis 13, 205, 207–11, 222
A Family Saying the Rosary (*c.*1784) 41, *42*
A Masked Ball in the Teatro del Príncipe (*c.*1767) 207, *209*
Hannibal Visiting the Temple of Hercules in Cadiz (1766) 207, *208*
María Luisa de Borbón (*c.*1766–8) 210, *210*, 280
The Masked Ball in the Teatro del Príncipe (*c.*1766) 207, *209*
Parmigianino 236
Patinir, Joachim 58
Pavona, Francesco 195
pen-and-ink drawings 45, 47, 60, 63
Pencz, Georg 55
Peninsular War 246
Pereda y Salgado, Antonio de 90, 93–4, 191
Saint Ildephonsus Receiving the Chasuble from the Virgin Mary (*c.*1640–60) 94, *95*
Saint Jerome (*c.*1634–4) 94, *94*
Saint Jerome in the Desert (*c.*1640–5) 94, *94*
Pérez de Guzmán, Fernán 51
Perret, Pedro 23, 77–9, 116–17, 276
Allegory of Philip II (*c.*1594) 78, *78*
Section through the Middle of the Basilica... (1583–9) 77, *77*
The Tabernacle of the Holy Sacrament... (1583) 76, *77*
Philibert Emmanuel, Prince of Savoy 181
Philip the Handsome (Philip I of Castile) 10
Philip II 10–12, 23, 28, 57–8, 61, 64, 71–2, 75–6, 78–9, 81, 89, *116*, 170
Philip III 11, 12, 81–2, 90, 115–16, 181
Philip IV 11–12, 30, 35, 81–2, 87, 89–94, *89*, 96–7, 103, 116–17, *118*, 137, 155, 184
Philip V 11, 29, 154, 189, 191, 194–5, 198
Piombo, Sebastiano del 58, 164
Planes, Luis Antonio 228–31
The Last Supper (1802–4) 228–31, *229*
The Last Supper (1804) *229*, 231
Plantin, Christopher 75, 76
playing cards *14*, *39*, 40, 275
Pontius, Paulus, *The Count Duke of Olivares* (1626) 118, *118*
Pontóns, Pablo 171
Ponz, Antonio 205, 215
Popma, Alardo de 116
Recapture of the City of Salvador da Bahia (Brazil) (1625) *36*, 39
Pozzo, Cassiano dal 276
Prado, Blas de 74
Prieto, Melchor 116
Prieto, Tomás Francisco 198
prints 17–20
Andalusia, 1500–1700 158–61
Castile, 1550–1600 75–9
context 41–3
early collecting 54–5
eighteenth-century 189–97, 199, 211–33
Madrid, 1600–1700 81, 115–21
and papermaking 275
popular eighteenth-century 220–3
pre-1500 50–5
significance 21–5
types of 25–6, 35–41
Valencia 1500–1700 179–84
Procaccini, Andrea 195, 206
Ptolemy 55

Raimondi, Marcantonio 54
Ramírez de Prado, Lorenzo 97, 120
Ranc, Jean 191–3
Raphael 22, 23, 58, 79, 125, 126, 128, 207
Real Fábrica de Papel (Madrid) 280
Rembrandt, Harmensz van Rijn 236
Renaissance model 20–1
Ribalta, Francisco 168–71, 175, 179
Saint Bruno (*c.*1625–7) 168, *169*
The Entombment of Christ (*c.*1582–1600) 168, *168*
The Musical Appearing to Saint Francis (*c.*1620) 41, *41*
Ribalta, Juan 168–9, 175
A Miraculous Healing by a Saint (*c.*1610–28) 169, *169*
Ribera, José (Jusepe) de 8, 22, 94, 173, 179–87, 236, 278
A Saint (Albert?) Tied to a Tree (1626) 32, *162*, 186, *186*, 187
An Oriental Potentate Accompanied by his Halberd Bearer (*c.*1625–30) 187, *187*
Christ Beaten by a Tormentor (*c.*1625–30) 186–7, *186*
Drunken Silenus (1626) 182, *183*
Drunken Silenus (1628) 181–2, *183*
Equestrian Portrait of Don Juan of Austria (1648) 182–4, *184*
Large Grotesque Head (*c.*1622) 180, *180*
Saint Sebastian (*c.*1613–16) 180, *180*
Studies of Ears (1622) *37*, 40, 180
The Adoration of the Magi (*c.*1613–18) *185*, 186
The Martyrdom of Saint Bartholomew (*c.*1620–4) *185*, 186
The Martyrdom of Saint Bartholomew (1624) 181, *182*
The Poet (*c.*1620–1) 180, *181*
Tityus or Prometheus (*c.*1620–5) *185*, 186
Ricarte, Hipólito 198
Ricci, Antonio 97
Riguad, Hyacinthe 194, 200
Rizi, Francisco 93, 94, 96–9, 108, 109, 114, 191
Jupiter Delivering the Vase to Pandora (*c.*1659) 98, *99*
Saint Anthony of Padua in Glory (*c.*1668) 26, *26*, 98
The 1680 Auto de Fé in the Plaza Mayor, Madrid (1683) 98–9, *100*
The Dwarf 'Lusillo' (*c.*1680–3) 98–9, *100*
The Virgin and Child Adored by Saints Philip and Francis (1650) 97, *98*
Title-page Design for the Book Commemorating the Entry into Madrid of Mariana of Austria (1649) 30, 97, *97*
Virgin Appearing to a Trinitarian Monk (*c.*1650) 97, *98*
Robinson, John Charles 15
Rodríguez, Pedro 120, 158
View of a Harbour with Boats (*c.*1642) 120, *120*
Rodríguez, Ventura, *Interior Section of a New Temple Devoted to San Bernardo in Madrid* (1753) 28–9, *28*
Roelas, Juan de 133–5, 211
The Infant Christ (1600–25) 133, *133*
Roldán, Pedro 160, 244
Román, Bartolomé 99
Rome 18, 19, 21, 61, 125–6, 202–3
Romero, Pedro 223, 260
Romulo, Diego de 75
Romulo, Francisco de 75
Rosenbach, Juan 51
Rossi, Giovanni 182
Royal Academy of Spain, Madrid 37, 214, 219–20, 233
Royal Chalcography, Madrid 217, 241
Rubens, Peter Paul 81, 82–3, 89, 95, 99, 118–19, 120, 150
Philip IV in Outdoor Dress (*c.*1628–9) 89, *89*
The Count-Duke of Olivares (1626) 118, *118*
The Duke of Lerma on Horseback (1603) 82–3, *82*
Rueda, Manuel 215
Ruiz de la Iglesia, Francisco Ignacio, *The Virgin Bestowing the Rosary on Saint Dominic Guzmán* (*c.*1690) 110, *110*

Sacchetti, Giovanni Battista 195, 201
Salamanca 49, 51, 79
Salamanca Cathedral 101
Salanoba, Pedro 223
Salazar, Cristóbal de 276

Salset, Bartomeu 46
Salvador Carmona, Juan Antonio 207, 217, 233
A Masked Ball in Teatro del Princípe (1778) 207, *209*
Salvador Carmona, Manuel 198, 215, 217, 236
Allegory of Charles III (1761–3) *216*, 217
The Drunkards (1793) 217, *217*, 239
Salvador Gómez, Vicente 171–5, 178, 181
Saint Francis of Assisi Embracing the Crucified Christ (1675) 174–5, *174*
Saint Joseph and the Christ Child (1674) 172, *172*, 174
Salviati, Francesco 123
San Antonio de los Portugeses church, Madrid 26, 98
San Bernardo church, Madrid 28–9, *28*
San Francis Xavier church, Nuevo Baztán *190*, 191
San Isidro church, Madrid 105–6, *106*
San Pedro, Diego de 51
San Pedro church, Púbol 48
Sancha, Antonio de 239
Sánchez Coello, Alonso 58
Sánchez Reciente, Eugenio 233
Santos, Francisco de los 110
Sarmiento, Martín 280
Satire of Napoleon's 'Ultimate Triumph', A (*c*.1810) (anonymous) 255, *255*, 279–80
Saura, Mosén Domingo 175
Queen Esther Fainting (*c*.1660–80) 175, *176*
Schön, Erhard 55
Schongauer, Martin, *Saint John the Evangelist on Patmos* (1469–74) 49, *50*
Schorquens, Juan 116
Philip II Disembarking in Lisbon (1622) 37, 81, 116, *116*
Schut, Cornelio 155, 158–60
A Melancholic Pope (1614–84) 276, *277*
Seated Ecclesiastic (*c*.1660–80) 155, *157*
The Virgin and Child (1680) 160, *160*
Schut, Pedro 155
Segovia aqueduct 199, *199*
Selma, Fernando 217–19, 224
Saint Ildephonsus Receiving the Chasuble from the Virgin (1789–1800) 35, *218*, 219
Senefelder, Aloys 266
senyal (watermarks) 275, 276–8, *277*, 279–80, 281
Servidori, Domingo María de 205
Self-portrait (1775) 205, *205*
Sessia, Duke of 82
Seville 12–13, 15, 18, 23, 51, 106, 108, 123–39, 144, 146–61, 233, 240, 277
academy of 22, 128, 131, 149–50, 152, 155, 157
Seville Cathedral 13, 150, 158, 160
Sigüenza, Fray José de 57, 69–71
Siloé, Gil de 30
Simó, Francisco 168
Sistine Chapel 67, 71, 132
Solimena, Francesco 215
Solís, Antonio de 191
Solís, Francisco de 23
South America 10, 11
Spanish mannerism 123
Spanish national character 16
Spanish naturalism 123
Spanish Succession, War of 11
'Spanishness' 13
Spinola, Ambrosio 93
Starnina, Gherardo, *Various Figures* 46, *46*

Téllez Villar, Marcos, *Spanish Dances* (*c*.1780–90) 222, *222*
Tempesta, Antonio 93
Temple of Solomon 77–8, *77*
Testa, Francesco 18, 77
theatre design 97, 108–9, 114
Tibaldi, Pellegrino 58, 60–1, 75, 79
Christ Presented to the People (1587–90) 60–1, *62*
Study for the Decoration of the Escorial Library (1588–92) 61, *63*
Tiepolo, Giovanni Battista (Giambattista) 10, 204, 207, 212
Tiepolo, Domenico 204, 211–12, 214
Head of an Old Man (*c*.1757–70) 236, *236*
Saint Paschal Bailón Adoring the Eucharist (1770–3) 212, *213*
The Flight into Egypt (1750–2) 211–12, *211*
Tiepolo, Lorenzo 204
Monument to the Priestess Hero (1750–80) 212, *212*
Tiepolo family 236
Tintoretto 58, 64, 65, 174
Titian 12, 58, 64, 71, 75, 89, 171
Toledo 12, 13, 64, 65, 74, 79, 170
Toledo, Fardrique de *92*, 93
Toledo, Juan Bautista de 57
Toledo Cathedral 69, 86–7, 98
Torre Farfán, Fernando de la 160
Torres, Matías de 112
Saint Isodore Praying (*c*.1680) 29, 112, *113*
Triumphal Arch on the Puerta del Sol, Madrid (1680) 112, *113*, 119
Torri, Pedro Antonio 21–2
Tortolero, Pedro 233
View of Seville from Triana (1738) 232, 233
Tovar, Alonso Miguel de 154, 158
Putti beneath the Virgin of the Immaculate Conception (*c*.1690–1720) 154, *156*
Saint Joseph and the Christ Child (*c*.1700–10) 154, *156*
Trábaga, Manuel Ezquerra 280
Trapier, Elizabeth de Gué 20
Traverse, Charles François-Pierre de la 207
Trinitarians 137–9
Tristán, Luis 82
True Portrait of a She Ant-bear, The (1776) (anonymous) *220*, 221, 236

Ugarte, Hermenegildo Víctor 199
View of the Segovia Aqueduct (1757) 199, *199*
Uncut Sheet of Twenty-four Playing Cards (1587) (anonymous) *14*, *39*, 40, 275
underdrawing 48–9
Urbino, Francesco da 58–60, 72, 87
Study of a Prophet (*c*.1581) 60, *62*
The Executioners with the Living Child (*c*.1581) 59, *60*
The Judgement of Solomon (*c*.1581) 59, *60*
Urbino, After Francesco da *The Executioners with the Living Child* (*c*.1581) 59–60, *61*
Vaga, Perino del 58, 123
Valdés Leal, Juan de 150, 155–8, 160, 211
An Ephemeral Structure in Seville Cathedral (1671) *33*, 37, 160, *161*
Head of Saint John the Baptist (1658–60) 157, *158*
Vision of Saint Francis in the Porziuncola (*c*.1672) 157, *159*
Valdés, Lucas 158, 160
Valencia 12, 45–6, 50, 52, 224, 231–3
1500–1700 163–79
academy in 22, 224, 228
Valencia, Pedro de 126
Valladolid 51, 72, 81–3, 115, 224
Valsaín 79
Valverde, Juan de 71
Van Dyck 23, 99, 144
Van Loo, Carle 227
Van Loo, Louis-Michel 191–3
Vargas, Luis de 123–4, 126
Allegory of the Immaculate Conception (1561) 124–5, *125*
The Execution of Jephthah's Daughter (1550–68) 124, *125*, 126
The Virgin and Child (*c*.1530–4) 123, *124*
Vargas Ponce, José de 260
Vasari, Giorgio 67, 71, 124–5
Veen, Otto van 78
Vega, Lope de 82
Vega, Preciado de la 203
Velasco, Alonso de 48
Velázquez, Diego 12, 13, 17, 35, 89–90, 95–6, 98, 117–18, 123, 128, 139, 145–6, 215, 217, 238–9, 280
Philip IV (*c*.1655) *117*, 118
Studies of Rearing Horse and Horseman (*c*.1625–35) *80*, 90, *90*
Studies for the 'Surrender of Breda' (*c*.1634–5) 93, *93*
The 1632 Auto de Fé in the Playa Mayor, Madrid (1632) *31*, 32, 278
The Drunkards (1628–9) 217, *217*, 239
Velázquez, Paula 72
Vélez de Guevara, Juan 108
Vera Tassis y Villarroel, Juan de 119, 191
Vergara, José 228
Veronese, Paolo 58
Viana, Prince Carlos (*c*.1461) (anonymous) 51, *52*
Vicent, Joan 46
Vidal, Dionisio 179
Vieira, Domingo de 116
View of Toledo from across the Tagus River (*c*.1750–60) (anonymous) 32, 193–4, *194*
Vignola, Giacomo Barozzi da 79, 136
Villafranca y Malagón, Pedro de 35, 103, 116–20, 181
Isabel de Borbón (1645) *116*, 118
Juan de Palafox y Mendoza (1665) *120*, 121
Philip IV in the *Descripción breve del monasterio de S. Lorenzo el Real del Escorial* (1657) *117*, 118
Title-page for the Book Commemorating the Entry into Madrid of Mariana of Austria (1650) 30, 97, *97*
Virgin of the Immaculate Conception (1670s) *35*, 37–9
Villahermosa, Duke of 167
Villalpando, Juan Bautista 77–9
Villanueva, Antonio, *Design for an Altar Wall Dedicated to Saint John the Baptist* (*c*.1780) *230*, 231–2
Virgin of the Pillar (anonymous) (*c*.1550–1600) *34*, 37
Vitruvius 64
Volterra, Daniele da 71

watercolour 108–9
Watteau, Antoine 193, 200
Weiss, Leocardia 268
Wellesley, Arthur, Duke of Wellington 247, 251, *251*
Wierix workshop, *Saint Francis of Assisi Embracing the Crucified Christ* (before 1585) *174*, 175
woodcuts 51

Xátiva (Játiva) 179, 274, 275

Yáñez de la Almedina, Fernando 13, 163–4
Standing Woman in Profile Facing Left (*c*.1518–19) 163, *164*

Zapater, Martín 239, 244
Zaragoza 50, 51, 203, 206, 224, 246–7, 249, 251–2, 254
Zuccaro, Federico 10, 58, 61–3, 75, 79, 97
The Pentecost (1586–8) 61–3, *64*
Zuccaro brothers 126
Zurbarán, Francisco de 13, 90, 147
Head of a Monk (*c*.1635–55) *134*, 135
Saint Agatha (*c*.1640–60) *133*, 135